SOCIOLOGY

Focus on Society

Critical Readers

Robert Anderson, *Trenton State College*
Robert Bierstedt, *University of Virginia*
Lynne R. Davidson, *State University of New York College at Purchase*
Don C. Gibbons, *Portland State University*
Andrew J. Greeley, *University of Arizona*
Floyd Hammack, *New York University*
George Hesslink, *Pomona College*
Richard D. Knudten, *Marquette University*
Roger Libby, *University of Massachusetts, Amherst*
James R. Long, *Golden West College*
Peter Manning, *Michigan State University, East Lansing*
Hy Mariampolski, *Kansas State University*
Edward McDonagh, *Ohio State University*
Howard Robboy, *Trenton State College*
Lawrence Rosen, *Temple University*
Neil J. Smelser, *University of California, Berkeley*
Edward G. Stockwell, *Bowling Green State University*
John H. Strength, Jr., *San Antonio College*
Maria Volpe, *Rutgers University, Newark*
L. Alice Wallace, *Georgia State University*
Robin M. Williams, Jr., *Cornell University*
Irving Witt, *College of San Mateo*

SOCIOLOGY
Focus on Society

Lucile Duberman

Rutgers University, Newark

Clayton A. Hartjen

Rutgers University, Newark

Scott, Foresman and Company   Glenview, Illinois
Dallas, Texas   Oakland, New Jersey   Palo Alto, California   Tucker, Georgia   London, England

ISBN 0-673-15287-1

Library of Congress Card Number 78-68634

To my beloved brother, Martin Duberman, with admiration and respect.
  Lucile Duberman

To my brothers Gary, Wesley, and Glen
  Clayton A. Hartjen

Preface

"The whole of science is nothing more than a refinement of everyday thinking."

—Albert Einstein in *Physics and Reality*, 1936

Your first reaction to this quote might be, "that's easy for Einstein to say." But think about it for a minute. When you study a subject, especially for the first time, don't you try to relate new topics and theories to your own personal experiences and situations? Isn't it easier to understand something that you've never encountered before if you can relate it to something with which you're familiar?

This is exactly the strategy that we, the authors of SOCIOLOGY: FOCUS ON SOCIETY, have used to develop this new introductory text. Throughout the text, we have used many examples from everyday life. In this way, we hope you will be encouraged to learn general sociological terms and concepts. We hope you will feel as though you're sitting down to discuss the field of sociology with a friend rather than being lectured to by an instructor.

ORGANIZATION

SOCIOLOGY: FOCUS ON SOCIETY is divided into four parts, each concentrating on a particular aspect of our social world. Taken together, the four parts present a solid foundation of the study of human social life.

Part One: Human Society

The three chapters in this section deal with *culture, society,* and *change*—three concepts that are fundamental if we want to understand our social environment. In this section we examine how culture, society, and change allow human beings to create their social world.

Part Two: Becoming and Being Human

Chapters 4 and 5 deal with socialization, the process by which we learn certain behaviors that enable us to become useful members of society. This section treats socialization as a lifelong process, beginning at birth and ending with death.

Part Three: Social Institutions

All societies must satisfy certain universal needs and consequently have devised social institutions to meet these needs. The five social institutions found in every society and examined in this section are the family, education, religion, economy, and government. This section concentrates on the functions of these institutions and the changes that have affected or might affect them in the future.

Part Four: Sociology in Everyday Life

The chapters in this section focus on aspects of our daily lives. Here we deal with groups into which we are born and that influence the types of people we become—gender groups, racial and ethnic groups, and social classes. We also cover work and leisure, two spheres within which we spend much of our lives, and deviance, which is also a part of our daily lives since most of us tend to break rules at one time or another. Finally, we examine world population growth and the ecological consequences that ensue, a situation that affects us all.

PEDAGOGICAL AIDS

In addition to containing numerous illustrations, photographs, cartoons, tables, and graphs intended to make learning sociology both easier and enjoyable, *SOCIOLOGY: FOCUS ON SOCIETY* contains several other learning aids.

Boxed Material

Applying Sociology boxes, strategically positioned throughout each chapter, will aid you in relating the subject matter of the text to your everday lives. Questions posed within these boxes will enable you to see how sociology affects you personally.*Focus On* boxes, also found within each chapter, introduce you to both popular and sociological writings on a variety of contemporary topics. Subjects included in these boxes are body language, death and dying, leisure activities, female criminality, and the environmental crisis. *Features* boxes contain theoretical portraits of the most prominent sociologists who have influenced sociology. These boxes—for example on Charles Horton Cooley, Émile Durkheim, and Talcott Parsons—will help you to understand how theoreticians, theory, and concept work together.

End-of-Chapter Material

A *summary* at the end of each chapter will assist you in reviewing quickly and easily important concepts that were covered. If you have missed a point, they will alert you to the fact that you should go back to the chapter and review this material. A *glossary* also is included at the end of each chapter, containing definitions of key concepts from the text. In addition, the end of each chapter contains chapter *references* and *suggestions for additional reading* so you can add to your knowledge of any subject you find particularly interesting.

End-of-Text-Material

An *appendix* at the end of the book details the methods by which sociologists go about their work and is readily available for you to consult. Research methods are covered in clear, easy-to-understand terms, enabling you to grasp this often difficult subject. An all-inclusive *glossary*, also located at the back of the book, reviews all important terms covered in the text. Also, a *name index* and a *subject index* will assist you in referring to any person or topic included in the book.

ACKNOWLEDGMENTS

No book of this scope can be written without the aid and dedication of numerous people. We have been unusually fortunate in this regard.

We are extremely grateful to the critical readers who contributed their advice, counsel, suggestions, and criticisms. Their names are listed on the page facing the title page. They are all responsible, in some measure, for the success of this text, but none should be held responsible for any of its mistakes.

We would like to thank Lynne R. Davidson for writing the Appendix. We would also like to thank S. Priyadarsini for her contributions to the methodology material and for her invaluable assistance to us throughout the project. Joseph Curran, William Kaiser, and Dennis Miller helped us develop the "Features" and the "Focus On" sections. Stanford Lyman was extremely helpful with his comments on both these elements of the text.

We also had the help of the fine staff at General Learning Press. To Janet Barrett and Merydith Mark, we owe our appreciation for their skillful handling of secretarial and production details. To our designer, Howard Leiderman, our photo researcher, Margaret S. Koeniger, and our caption writer, Anita Samen, we are eternally grateful for their creativity and artful taste. Our special thanks, though, go to the editors with whom we may have disagreed at times, but with whom because of their understanding and congeniality we still remain close friends. To Judy Green, who guided us so amiably with her incredible publishing know-how; to Walter Kossmann, who helped us in the conception of this book initially and occasionally infuriated us with his questions and exclamations but was invariably right; and to Janet McHugh, who made us laugh as we obeyed her insightful additions and corrections, we owe a world of gratitude.

But special appreciation goes to our editor, Janice Lemmo, who gave so much of her time, thought, energy, and marvelous skills to this book. Although she apologized profusely for being "picky," Janice made us simplify, clarify, define, and explain. Without her persistence, intelligence, knowledge, and patience, this book would have lacked the clarity we think it now has. Janice Lemmo is a remarkably clever and brilliant young editor and our debt to her can never be fully paid.

Lucile Duberman
Clayton A. Hartjen

Contents

Introduction   1
What Is Sociology?   2
Why Study Sociology?   4
Sociological Assumptions   5
Sociological Perspectives   7   Structural-Functionalism   7
Conflict Theory   8   Symbolic Interaction   9   Comparing
the Three Perspectives   10
Glossary   11

ONE
Human Society   12

1   Culture   15
The Components of Culture   16   Ideas   16   Norms   17
Folkways   18   Mores   18   Laws   19   Materiel   21
The Individual and Culture   22   Culture as a Survival
Kit   22   Culture and Individual Freedom   22
The Transmission of Culture   23   Signs and Symbols   23
Language   25
Ethnocentrism   27
Cultural Relativism   29
Cultural Determinants   30   Environment   30
Biology   32   Culture as a Determinant of Culture   33
Subcultures   34   Language as a Subculture Sign   35
Why Subcultures Develop   37
Cultural Universals   39
Summary   40   Glossary   41   References   42
Suggested Readings   43

Applying Sociology   21, 29, 36, 38
Focus On: Body Language   26

2   Society   45
What Is Society?   46
Social Structure   48   Statuses   48   Roles   50

What Is a Social Group? 51 The Importance of the Group 54 Factors that Influence Groups 54 Size 55 *Types of Group Goals 55 Bases of Group Membership 56 Duration of Membership 57 Duration of the Group 57 Degree of Internal Differentiation 58 Degree of Group Cohesion 58 Patterns of Interaction Within the Group 58* Kinds of Groups 59 Primary and Secondary *Relationships 60 Primary Groups 60 Secondary Groups 62 In-Groups and Out-Groups 62 In-Groups 62 Out-Groups 63 Formal and Informal Organizations 63 Formal Organizations 63 Informal Organizations 64* Group Interaction Patterns 65 Exchange and Cooperation 65 Competition and Conflict 65 Accommodation and Assimilation 67 Summary 68 Glossary 69 References 70 Suggested Readings 71

Applying Sociology 49, 55, 59, 62
Feature: Charles Horton Cooley 60
Focus On: Role Playing 50/The Amish 52

3 **Social and Cultural Change 73**
Forms and Characteristics of Change 74 Social Versus *Cultural Change 75 Cultural Lag 76 Stability Versus Change 77* Processes of Change 78 Diffusion 78 Innovation 79 Factors Affecting the Rate of Change 80 Population 80 Contact and Isolation 81 The Cultural Base 83 Social Structure 84 Ideology 84 Patterns of Change 84 Theories of Social Change 85 *Evolutionary Theories 85 Cyclical Theories 87 Functional Theories 89 Conflict Theories 90 Social Movements and Directed Change 91 The Social Origins of Social Movements 91 Types of Social Movements 94* What the Future Holds 96 Specialization 96 Bureaucratization 96 Modernization 97 Industrialization 98

Applying Sociology 80, 83, 95
Features: Auguste Comte 86/Herbert Spencer 87
Focus On: The Preindustrial City 82/Postindustrial Society 99

TWO
Becoming and Being Human   106

4   Socialization in Childhood   109
The Process of Socialization   110   Studies by Harry
Harlow   111   Studies by Kingsley Davis   112
Nature and Nurture   114
The Functions of Socialization   116   Learning the Ways of
the Society   116   Social Control   119   Fitting Into
Society   119   The Development of Personality   120
Theories of Socialization   121   The Looking-Glass
Self   122   The Significant Other and the Generalized
Other   123   The Psychoanalytic Approach   126
The Eight Stages of Development   129   Cognitive Development
Approach   133   *Jean Piaget*   134   *Lawrence
Kohlberg*   135
Summary   136   Glossary   138   References   139
Suggested Readings   140

Applying Sociology   123, 125, 128
Features: George Herbert Mead   124/Sigmund Freud   126
Focus On: Child Rearing in the U.S. and the U.S.S.R.   114/
Masculine Socialization   117

5   Socialization from Adolescence Through
Old Age   141
Adolescent Socialization   142   Eight Properties of
Adolescence   143   The Status and Roles of Adolescence   144
Parents and Adolescents   146   Adolescent Society   146
Socialization in Adult Life   149   Socialization for
Work   150   *Work Choice*   154   *Socialization into an
Occupational Role*   155   Marital and Parental
Socialization   157   Socialization for Old Age   162

THREE
Social Institutions   170

6   The Family   173
Defining the Family   174   The Kinship Group   174
The Structure of Marriage   175   Restrictions in Marriage   177

Family Organization   179   Residence   180
Authority   180   Descent   181
Functions of the Family   182   Traditional Functions of the
American Family   182   The Economic Function   183
The Protective Function   183   The Religious Function   184
The Recreational Function   184   The Educational
Function   186   The Status Placement Function   186
Murdock's Theory of Universal Family Functions   187
Reproduction   187   Sexual Regulation   187   Economic
Cooperation   188   Socialization   188   Testing Murdock's
Theory   188
Patterns in American Family Life   190   Attitudes Toward
Sex   191   Premarital Sexual Behavior   191   Romantic
Love   194   Choosing a Mate   194   Marriage   196
Why People Marry   196   Marriage Work   197   Marital
Success and Failure   198   Remarriage   201
Marriage and the Family in the Future   202   Androgynous
Marriage   202   Cohabitation   203   Singlehood   203
Open Marriage   204   Mate-Swapping   204
Summary   205   Glossary   207   References   208
Suggested Readings   209

Applying Sociology   179, 195, 197
Feature: Talcott Parsons   189
Focus On: Female Sexuality   193

7   **Education   211**
Development of American Education   212   Functions of
Education   214   Transmission of Values, Attitudes, and
Behaviors   214   Transmission of Skills and Knowledge   215
Status Placement   218   The Role of Evaluation   219
Intelligence Testing   220   Tracking   222   Secondary
Functions of Education   226   Custodial Function   226
Social Function   227   Innovative Function   229
Higher Education   230
Credentialism   233
Education and Income   236
Summary   237   Glossary   238   References   238
Suggested Readings   240

Applying Sociology   218, 224, 233
Focus On: An Educational Failure   216/Meritocracy   223

8   **Religion   241**
What Is Religion?   242   The Characteristics of
Religion   242   Durkheim's Definition of Religion   243

The Sacred and the Profane 244 *Religious Beliefs and Practices* 245 *The Moral Community* 249
The Functions of Religion 250
Religious Organization 254
Religion in the United States 256 *Religious Groups* 256
Civil Religion 258
Changes in the Religious Institution 259
Religion and Science 263
Summary 267 Glossary 268 References 269
Suggested Readings 270

Applying Sociology 245, 250, 264,
Feature: Émile Durkheim 248
Focus On: The Unification Church 260/The Survival of
Religion 266

9 Economy 271
What Is the Economic Institution? 272
Functions of the Economic Institution 272 *Primary Function: Production and Distribution* 273 *Three Problems* 274 *Supply, Demand, and Price* 274
Secondary Functions 275 *Social Ranking* 275
Distribution of Power 276
Types of Economic Organization 276 *The Guild System* 276 *The Factory System* 277 *The Corporation* 278 *Rise of the Multinationals* 279
Social Forces and the Economy 281 *Forms of Exchange* 282 *Reciprocative Exchange* 282
Redistributive Exchange 282 *Exchange* 282
Marketing 282 *Advertising* 283 *The Sale* 285
Consumer Credit 287 *Consumer Behavior* 290
Culture 290 *Class* 291 *Group* 292 *The "Throw-Away" Society* 292
Economic Growth 294
Summary 295 Glossary 297 References 298
Suggested Readings 299

Applying Sociology 284, 286, 294
Focus On: Credit 288

10 Government 301
Development of Political Units 302
Forms of Government 304 Oligarchy 304
Monarchy 304 Dictatorship 306 Democracy 308
Functions of the Political Institution 310 Maintaining

Social Order   311   Coordinating Necessary Activities   312
Protecting Citizens   313
Political Parties   314   Political Party Membership   315
Voting Behavior   316
Power   318   Defining Political Power   319
Prestige   319   Influence   320   Dominance   321
Rights   321   Force and Authority   321   Sources of
Power   323   Types of Authority: Legitimate Power   323
Traditional Authority   324   Charismatic Authority   324
Legal-Rational Authority   325
Theories of Political Power   326   C. Wright Mills on
Elitism   327   David Riesman on Pluralism   328   Elitism
or Pluralism?   329   *Studies of Power   329*
Conclusion   330
Summary   331   Glossary   332   References   333
Suggested Readings   334

Applying Sociology   310, 317, 325, 330
Feature: C. Wright Mills   326
Focus On: Watergate   320/Obedience to Authority   322

FOUR
Sociology in Everyday Life   336

II   The Sexes   339
Differences Between the Sexes—Inborn or
Learned?   340   Viewpoints from Biology   341   *Biological*
Determinism   341   Neutrality Theory   341   Viewpoints
from Psychology   342   A Viewpoint from Anthropology   345
The Sociological Viewpoint   346
Testing the Sociological Viewpoint   347
Socialization for Gender Roles   351   Reasons for Gender-Role
Socialization   352   *Structural-Functionalism   352   Conflict*
Theory   353   The Ideal Female and the Ideal Male   353
The Consequences of Gender-Role Socialization   356
Interpersonal Relationships   356   *The Wife and Mother   356*
The Husband and Father   359   Who Has the Better
Deal?   360   The World of Work   360   *Stereotyped*
Occupations   361   Income   363
Changing Gender Roles   364
Summary   366   Glossary   367   References   368
Suggested Readings   369

xvi

Applying Sociology   342, 351, 356, 365
Feature: Jessie Bernard   357
Focus On: Baby X   348/The Total Woman   354

12   Racial and Ethnic Groups   371
Racial and Ethnic Groups   372   Racial Groups   372
Ethnic Groups   373   Minority Groups   374   Race,
Ethnicity, and Behavior   375
Ethnicity and Human Differences   375   Race and
Intelligence   375   Cultural and Technical Achievements   377
Prejudice and Discrimination   378   Prejudice   379
Discrimination   380   The Relationship Between Prejudice and
Discrimination   381   Sources of Prejudice and
Discrimination   383   *Psychological Theories   383*
Economic Theories   384   Social Theories   385   Reactions
to Discrimination   386   Behavioral Adjustment   386
Psychological Adjustment   388
Changing Ethnic Relationships   389   Changing
Attitudes   390   Changing Behavior: The Civil Rights
Movement   391   *From Emancipation to*
Segregation   391   Protests, Sit-ins, and Riots   392
Racial and Ethnic Minorities   393   Native Americans   394
Hispanic-Americans   394   Oriental-Americans   395
Jews   395   White Ethnics   396
Summary   397   Glossary   398   References   399
Suggested Readings   400

Applying Sociology   373, 386, 390
Focus On: An Experiment in Prejudice   380

13   Social Stratification   403
What Is Social Stratification?   404   Small-Scale
Societies   405   Agrarian Societies   406   Industrial
Societies   408   Postindustrial Societies   408
Why Is There Social Inequality?   409   Karl Marx   409
Max Weber   412   Structural-Functionalism and Conflict
Theory   413
The Social Class System in the United States   415
Number of Classes   418   *The Upper Class   419   The*
Upper-Middle Class   421   The Lower-Middle Class   422
The Working Class   424   The Lower Class   425   Social
Class Life-Styles   427   Marriage and Family Life   427
Language and Speech   428   Food and Drink   430
Sexual Behavior   431   Consumption Patterns and

Recreation 432   Social Mobility 433   *Vertical and Horizontal Mobility* 434   *Intergenerational and Intragenerational Mobility* 434   *Female Social Mobility* 435   Is America Really the Land of Opportunity? 436
Summary 438   Glossary 439   References 440
Suggested Readings 442

Applying Sociology 413, 432, 434
Feature: Karl Marx 410
Focus On: The Culture of Poverty 426/Christmas Cards 429

14 Work and Leisure 443
The Meaning of Work 444   A Necessary Evil 445   A Sign of Grace 445   Feeling Useful 447
The Labor Force 448   Age and Sex Composition 448   Occupational Groupings 450   A Nation of Employees 451   Specialization 452   Wages and Hours 453
Work: Problems and Prospects 453   Alienation 455   *Measuring Job Dissatisfaction* 457   *Causes of Job Dissatisfaction* 457   *Alleviating Alienation* 459   *Unemployment* 459   *Retirement* 462
Leisure as Fun and Fulfillment 464   Spending Leisure Time 465   Mass Leisure 457   Leisure and Self-Image 467
Summary 470   Glossary 471   References 471
Suggested Readings 472

Applying Sociology 452, 459, 469
Feature: Max Weber 446
Focus On: "Working" 456/Leisure Activities 466

15 Deviance 475
What Is Deviance? 476
Explanations of Deviant Behavior 478   Biological Explanations 478   Psychological Explanations 480   Sociological Explanations 481   *Durkheim's Theory* 481   *Merton's Theory* 482   *Sutherland's Theory* 484
Types of Deviant Behavior 485   Criminal Deviance 485   *White-Collar Crime* 487   *Juvenile Delinquency* 490   *Crimes Without Victims* 491   *Organized Crime* 491   Noncriminal Deviance 492   *Mental Illness* 492   *Alcoholism* 493   *Drug Addiction* 494   *Homosexuality* 495

The Functions and Dysfunctions of Deviance 496
Dysfunctions of Deviance 496 Functions of Deviance 498
Social Control 499 Informal and Formal Control 499
The Paradox of Social Control 501
Summary 502 Glossary 503 References 504
Suggested Readings 506

Applying Sociology 478, 489, 497
Feature: Robert K. Merton 483
Focus On: Female Criminality 486/White-Collar Crime 488

16 Population, Urbanization, and Ecology 509
Demography: The Study of Population 511 Determinants
of Population Size 511 *Birth Rate 512* *Death
Rate 515* *Migration Rate 517* Determinants of
Population Composition 518 *Sex Ratio 519* *Age
Composition 519* Determinants of Population
Distribution 523 *Geography 523* *Urbanization and
Industrialization 524*
Population Growth 525 Causes of Growth 526
Solutions to the Growth Problem 527 Ecological
Consequences of Growth 529 *The Problem of Food 529*
The Problem of Energy 531 *The Problem of Pollution 535*
Population in the United States 536 Size 536
Composition 536 Distribution 537 Implications 538
Summary 538 Glossary 539 References 540
Suggested Readings 541

Applying Sociology 522, 529, 533, 537
Feature: Thomas R. Malthus 530
**Focus On: World Population Growth 528/The
Environmental Crisis 532**

Epilogue 543
Problems in Sociology 544
Careers in Sociology 547

Appendix 549

Glossary 571

Name Index 587

Subject Index 591

Credits 600

Introduction

Imagine being reared in near isolation, with only your very basic needs met. You would not hear people talk, see people walk, or feel the warmth of another's touch. You also would be unable to perform these activities yourself. For although we take walking, talking, and embracing for granted, such actions are learned as we interact with other human beings.

Fortunately, most of us are not reared in near isolation—we interact with others from birth to death even when we are unaware of such interaction. We are frequently caressed by our parents soon after we are born. We are then often visited by doctors, friends, and relatives, all concerned with or fascinated by the new life that has been created. In childhood we come into contact with many more people. We form friendships with other individuals, we attend school with other children, and we recognize that we must behave differently when we are with certain persons. For example, we must address our teachers by their last names but may call our friends by their first names.

This process of interaction continues throughout the rest of our lives, although our relationships may vary in duration and importance. In adolescence we frequently become more concerned with our friends or peers than with other people. As adults, our working and personal relationships become the focus of our lives. Quite likely we may find ourselves so attracted to another person that we decide to marry. But no matter what the type of relationship, we continually interact with others as we go through life. And that is what sociology deals with— our interaction with others.

What Is Sociology?

Sociology is one of the *social sciences*—those disciplines concerned with the behavior of human beings. Unlike the other social sciences, which we will examine below, sociology encompasses all aspects of human life within a social setting. Sociologists study how societies are structured and the ways in which members of societies behave within these social structures. They try to understand why and how groups stay together or disintegrate. In addition, sociologists are interested in why and how societies change or resist change. We can define *sociology*, then, as *the scientific study of the patterns of human social life in groups.* To get a clearer picture of sociology, let us compare it with some of the other social sciences. It is important to note, however, that the descriptions of the other social sciences are in their purest form. There is currently much overlap among the disciplines, and the distinctions made in the following paragraphs are frequently blurred.

History and Sociology: While history is concerned with specific events, sociology looks at many events of the same nature and tries to find out what they have in common. For example, an historian may study World War I and examine its causes, its battles, its famous leaders, and the results of the conflict. On the other hand, a sociologist may study *several* wars to uncover similarities among their causes, leaders, battles, and results. While the historian usually looks for special unusual events, the sociologist seeks recurrent or typical events.

Political Science and Sociology: Political science is the study of the formal power relations between governments and within governments. It focuses on only the political institution. In contrast, sociology studies the interactions among many institutions—such as the family and education—and examines the ways in which they affect each other.

Economics and Sociology: Economics deals with the production and distribution of material goods and services among the members of a society. As is the case with political science, economics deals with only one institution. Sociologists are interested in the economic system of a society—after all, society could not function without it—but their interest is more interpersonal and intergroup. Sociologists who study economics might concentrate on the topic of motivation, the role of values, and the meaning of prestige rather than on such things as the Gross National Product.

Psychology and Sociology: Psychologists, like sociologists, are concerned with people. However, the emphasis of psychologists is on the individual person. In contrast, sociologists are interested in behavioral trends among groups of people. For example, whereas a psychologist may be concerned with individual test scores on a standardized test, a sociologist may be concerned with comparing scores of children from different economic backgrounds.

Psychology and sociology merge in a small, but important, subarea called *social psychology.* This subject deals with the study of individual behavior in terms of social factors and with the study of social structure in terms of individuals who are members of it. One of the topics that might be covered in social psychology is whether or not people will help an individual in distress.

Anthropology and Sociology: Of all the social sciences, anthropology, especially cultural anthropology, is most closely related to sociology. However, there are two major differences between the two disciplines. First, whereas anthropologists deal mostly with small, preliterate, self-contained societies, sociologists deal primarily with large-scale modern societies. Second, because anthropologists tend to focus on small societies, they can more easily study an entire group and all its structures and functions. Sociologists, on the other hand, must focus on parts of societies, since the societies they study are usually very large and complex.

3

The boys in the canoe *(left),* members of a tribe in Africa's Ivory Coast, would be likely subjects for an anthropologist to study—they belong to a small, primitive, self-contained social group that can be studied in its entirety. The big-city crowd *(right)* would be of interest to a sociologist, who might do an indepth study of several, but not all, aspects of the large-scale modern society the crowd represents.

From these comparisons of the disciplines comprising the social sciences we can get a good idea of what sociology is—and is not. But students also often wonder why they should study sociology. Let us now attempt to answer this question.

Why Study Sociology?

Although human behavior is fascinating and deserves to be studied for that reason alone, there are several other reasons for studying sociology. One such reason is to discover the different meanings that sociology has put on familiar taken-for-granted events. For example, until recently most of us assumed (and many of us still assume) that men must work and women must stay home and rear children. When we examine child-rearing practices in other societies, however, we often find that this does not hold true. In some societies children are reared by both parents; in others the father assumes this task. Thus, *sociology enables us to examine commonsense notions about the social world and find out if they are supported by evidence.*

Understanding the familiar in a new way is not always a pleasant experience. Very often we are startled to learn that the beliefs we have held onto for so long are not really true. Many people, for example, are shocked when they learn that crime is prevalent in all social classes, not just the lower class. But although such information may be surprising to some of us, at the same time we are expanding our knowledge of the world around us.

A second reason for studying sociology is related to the first. As we delve into ordinary events of everyday life, uncovering areas within our own experiences that have led us to false conclusions, we become more understanding and tolerant of people who are unlike ourselves.

4

We come to learn that our own ways of behavior and our attitudes are not necessarily the *only* ways or even the *best* ways. Let us return to our example of child-rearing practices. Can we say that our child-rearing practices are superior when other societies seem to be functioning smoothly while following different patterns? Of course we can argue either way, but in the process we gain an insight into the ways of other societies. And by doing so we may gain an insight into our own ways. This understanding increases our flexibility, enables us to adapt to new situations, and discourages us from taking the seemingly obvious for granted. In short, sociology can help free us of those prejudices that so many of us possess. We can learn to accept other people's points of view, their life-styles, their problems, their values, and their ways of dealing with life. Therefore, *sociology enables us to liberate ourselves from superstitions, biases, and myths.*

There are, of course, several other reasons for studying sociology. We may be interested in learning how our society is organized and what keeps it going. Or we may want to understand our own values, how these values developed, and how they can change. Many students may be concerned with some of our pressing social problems, such as drug abuse, political dishonesty, high illegitimacy rates, high divorce rates, the deterioration of our cities, pollution, or the problems of women and other minority groups. And they may want to study sociology in order to help resolve some of these problems.

Thus by studying sociology we can discover the underlying, unknown aspects of ordinary everyday social life. In so doing we can become more open and understanding, learning to accept the variety of behaviors, customs, values, and attitudes of people who are different from us. But before we can study sociology we must be aware of certain general assumptions sociologists make about society and its members.

Sociological Assumptions

Sociologists assume that there are patterns and order in social life. In our daily actions and interactions we often behave in expected ways. For example, most of us sleep during the night and are awake during the day. We wake up at a certain hour, eat our meals at designated times, and travel the same routes to and from work, school, or home. Many of us watch certain television programs every week and adjust our schedules accordingly. How many times have you heard someone say, "I can't talk to you now or I'll miss my program"? Thus our patterns enable people who know us well to quite accurately predict where we are and what we are doing at any given time during the course of any ordinary day. But our patterns extend even further; they allow others who do not know us well to predict our behavior. For instance, most of us would not telephone someone at 3 A.M. for fear of waking up that person.

A second assumption sociologists make is that people cannot become human unless they interact with human beings. As we mentioned at the beginning of this chapter, if we do not come in contact with other people, we would be unable to perform those basic activities we take for granted. Unlike other animals we are helpless at birth, unable to feed ourselves, keep ourselves warm, or keep ourselves clean. We need other people in order to survive. But our relationships with other people teach us more than basic survival. Through interaction we become human—we learn those qualities that make us different from other animals. And this enables us to create society; without human interaction society could not exist.

A third sociological assumption also concerns the way in which human beings differ from other animals: we are the only species that possesses culture—the rules, ideas, beliefs, and possessions shared by members of a society. To illustrate, as part of American culture most of us use clocks to tell time, send our children to school, and do not eat human flesh. Yet other societies that do not follow these same patterns also possess culture, for they too share among their members certain rules, ideas, beliefs, and possessions. Furthermore, not only do we pos-

Sociologists make certain assumptions about human social behavior. One such assumption is that there are patterns and order in our daily lives. Even a clown may follow a predictable schedule, eating, putting on make-up, or removing make-up at certain times.

 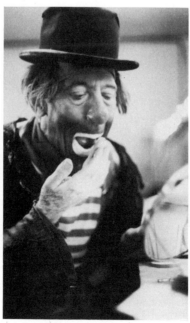 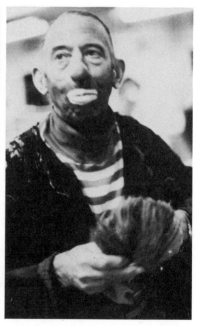

According to structural-functionalists, each member of a social system has a specific function, whether it's protecting people from danger, like these firefighters *(left),* or providing recreation, like this casino dealer *(right).* Structural-functionalists emphasize that each member and function is essential to the well-being of the social system as a whole.

sess culture, but we also transmit it to future generations. In addition, we also can change our cultural patterns. In this manner we ensure the continuation of society.

There are, then, at least three basic assumptions on which sociology is based. Using these assumptions sociologists can study the structure of societies and the behavior of the people who live within them. They do this by studying *social order* and *social change* and how and why these two phenomena occur. By focusing on what keeps society orderly or on what disrupts that order, on what occurs among the members of society, and on how change is brought about, sociologists try to understand the social world.

Sociological Perspectives

In sociology, as in other disciplines, there are different ways of interpreting events. Most sociology is based on three perspectives: structural-functionalism, conflict theory, and symbolic interaction. We will now examine each of these perspectives more closely.

STRUCTURAL-FUNCTIONALISM

Structural-functionalists tend to view society as a self-regulating and self-maintaining social system with certain basic needs, such as preserving social order, providing for the supply of goods and services, and protecting the younger generation. If these and other needs are met, the society will remain in balance or equilibrium. According to this view, each part (or each member) of the social system—in cooperation with the other parts—plays its own unique role in maintaining the social system.

7

Conflict theorists maintain that conflict is both unavoidable and potentially beneficial. For example, public demonstrations by groups such as these handicapped people call attention to social problems and injustices that otherwise might be ignored.

This process can be compared to the operation of the human body. Each part of the body has its own unique job to do and the parts are not interchangeable. In other words, our eyes have the job of seeing and cannot take the place of our legs, which have the job of propelling us around. When all the parts of the body are healthy and functioning properly, the whole body is functioning properly. If any one part is functioning poorly, the whole body is affected. Furthermore, no part of the body is useless; each has a function to perform that is indispensable to the whole body.

Structural-functionalists hold similar views, when examining a social system. Each part or member has its specific and special task, and there is no part that is unnecessary to the proper functioning of the whole. When all the parts are cooperating and in good working order, the society is healthy. What is good for the whole system is good for each part and vice versa. The parts work together because they share common values, goals, and interests.

CONFLICT THEORY

Not all sociologists view society as "one big, happy family" with each part contributing to the good of the whole. On the contrary, conflict theorists see society as a system made up of individuals and groups with competing interests.

According to conflict theorists, conflict cannot be avoided. Because there are not enough goods and resources to go around, each group must constantly fight to make its presence known and to survive.

8

Conflict usually takes the form of tension or competition, often resulting in disorder and destruction. Thus conflict theorists view society as an arena in which warring interest groups struggle to outdo each other. Such groups as the rich and the poor, the young and the old, and farmers and industrialists all must fight for their share of wealth and power.

Yet in the view of conflict theorists, conflict has positive results. Certain groups who otherwise might not have gained recognition are brought into the spotlight. For example, the civil rights movement and the women's movement might not have gained national attention had their members not engaged in social conflict. This brings us to a second benefit of social conflict, an extension of the first. If social conflict did not occur, many social problems and injustices, which we now recognize, might otherwise have been ignored. Although we may still be fighting for civil rights and equal opportunities for many people, we have made some progress in these struggles.

Thus social conflict breeds social change. And this allows the social system to survive in spite of the struggles among the members. Conflict theorists recognize the presence and effects of conflict and examine society accordingly.

SYMBOLIC INTERACTION

The two perspectives just described—structural-functionalism and conflict theory—are concerned with large social structures. However, such structures are created by members of society as they interact with each other.* Thus the basis of society lies in the interaction among individuals in everyday life.

Some sociologists, known as symbolic interactionists, concentrate their attention on this interaction and recognize that such interaction occurs in one of two ways: nonverbally and verbally. For this reason a teacher recognizes that a student raises a hand—a nonverbal communication—because that student wishes to speak. A nod, a smile, a shrug are all nonverbal communications, the meanings of which are shared by the communicators.

Symbolic interactionists point out that we can interact with each other because we all share the meanings of symbols—both nonverbal and verbal. Symbols consist of the gestures, body positions, and rules that we all use. Hence, in one of the above examples, students will raise their hands because they know that the teacher will recognize their wish to speak. Conversely, the teacher, when asking for volunteers, will

---

*It should be understood that while people create society, society is at the same time creating personalities. Thus we create society and society creates us.

call on students whose hands are raised. Both teacher and students share the meaning of a raised hand. Similarly, all Americans understand the meaning of a frown or a wink. These are all meaningful and useful symbols.

However, the most useful kind of symbol most of us use is verbal—language. While two people can exchange meanings using gestures, unless they have a common spoken language their communication must remain limited. To illustrate, all Americans understand the meaning of the word *study*. Yet if an American were to tell a Tibetan in English that it is important to study, no matter how eloquent the gestures, chances are that the Tibetan would not understand what was being said. Thus symbolic interactionists recognize the importance of symbols whose meanings are all shared and try to interpret our social behavior through our interaction with others.

COMPARING THE THREE PERSPECTIVES

In order to get a clearer picture of these perspectives, imagine for a moment that you are a sociologist observing a cocktail party. What aspects of the party would you find relevant, interesting, or important? Your theoretical perspective will influence your answer.

Since structural-functionalists are concerned with how groups preserve order, if you hold this viewpoint you might examine the mechanisms that keep the party harmonious. For example, you might note the rules of politeness. Or you might note the soft background music that serves to encourage an intimate atmosphere.

On the other hand, if you are a conflict theorist, you might analyze the factors that separate people into cliques or groups. You may observe that men are in one group and women are in another. You also might note the composition of the group by age and might ask why young people seem to be in the minority. Why do most of the people seem to be in the upper-income brackets? Why are there no blacks or Hispanics present? These are just a few of the questions and concerns a conflict theorist might have.

A symbolic interactionist would be interested in the interaction of people through symbols. The meaning of a gesture, the way refreshments are served, or the conversational topics may be among the concerns of a sociologist holding this viewpoint.

Thus we see that although you may be studying the same event as other sociologists, what you see and how you interpret it may vary greatly depending on your sociological viewpoint. While no perspective is more correct than another, each causes us to ask different questions and to analyze events differently. Each contributes to our interpretation of social phenomena. With these perspectives in mind we will now proceed to the study at hand—the study of sociology.

GLOSSARY

conflict theory   a sociological perspective based on the premise that the competing interests of individuals and groups in a society cause or result in social change.

social change   a modification in the social order of a society, such as in its social institutions or its behavioral patterns.

social order   a condition of a society characterized by harmonious social relations and a lack of conflict among individuals and/or subgroups.

social sciences   areas of study—such as anthropology or sociology—concerned with the behavior of human beings.

sociology   the scientific study of the patterns of human social life in groups.

structural-functionalism   a sociological perspective that regards society as a social system dependent upon each part or member for complete and proper functioning.

symbolic interaction   a sociological perspective that bases its interpretations of social behavior on the verbal and nonverbal symbols shared by members of a society.

one

Human Society

Before beginning this section, pause for a moment and look around at your immediate environment. Undoubtedly your observations will differ from those of others, but they will probably also have certain similarities. Chances are you will note the presence of some things and other people will notice other things. Furthermore, the things you will notice—a book on the shelf, a poster on the wall, or a cigarette in an ashtray—all serve to remind us that we do not go through life alone. As we mentioned in the introduction to this book, we constantly interact with others from birth to death. And the subject matter of sociology deals with this interaction—the *social* features of human life.

Sociologists studying our social behavior concentrate primarily on three areas that are essential to an understanding of such behavior. These consist of *culture, society,* and *change.* This section will introduce and discuss these three key sociological concepts.

Chapter 1 is concerned with culture. Briefly stated, culture consists of all the things, ideas, and actions people teach and learn from each other. Every human society or group of persons possesses a culture. And if the society is large and diverse enough, it is likely to have at least several subcultures as well.

From this description of culture, we note that culture does not and cannot exist in a vacuum. Culture is created by a group of people who live together and interact with each other. In turn culture shapes people, so that they can live together in a society. In Chapter 2 we will discuss society, a relatively independent and self-contained group of people who live in a particular territory and share a culture.

For purposes of discussion, we are talking here about culture and society as if they were static or unchanging. But the human social world is constantly changing. The patterns of behavior people exhibit, the ideas and beliefs they hold, the rules they live by, the people with whom they interact, are all constantly undergoing alteration. Chapter 3 focuses on this social and cultural change.

These three chapters attempt to introduce the basic concepts necessary for understanding human social behavior. Culture, society, and change, then, permit human beings to construct their social world.

Culture

The Zulu soccer team of South Africa was losing by a score of four to two. In hopes of reversing this trend, the team called on its sorcerer to work a miracle. But his efforts failed and the Zulus went down to defeat. The team then proceeded to fire the sorcerer.

As Westerners, we may find this firing difficult to understand. We may accept the fact that a sorcerer was called in initially—after all, we also are sometimes superstitious before important events. But why fire the sorcerer instead of the coach or manager, as we may have done?

The behavior of other cultural groups, such as the Eskimos, the headhunters of the South Pacific, or the Zulus of South Africa, often amazes, bewilders, or puzzles us. Even the behavior of certain groups within our own country can be surprising.

What accounts for the great diversity of human behavior? Why do different social groups behave differently under similar circumstances? Although many factors are involved, these differences in the practices, beliefs, and life-styles of human beings reflect differences in the cultures that are created by human groups. What is culture?

The Components of Culture

In lay terms, we tend to think of people as "cultured" or "uncultured." "Cultured" people understand how to behave properly in social situations and appreciate the refinements available within society—the arts, the literature, the theater, the music. On the other hand, "uncultured" people tend to close their eyes to these refinements. But sociologists use the word *culture* very differently. Sociologically, anyone living in a social group possesses culture—the rules, ideas, beliefs, and possessions shared by members of a society. Sociologist Robert Bierstedt defined culture more formally when he wrote that "culture is the complex whole that consists of all the ways we *think* and *do* and everything we *have* as members of society (italics added)."[1]

Each of these components of culture exists before we are born. Each is transmitted from one generation to the next during social interaction or as people meet and communicate with one another. We inherit our society's culture and learn its contents as we grow up. What are these thoughts, behaviors, and possessions we have inherited? Let us examine each of these components of culture in more detail. We will refer to the ways we think as our *ideas*, the ways we do as our *norms*, and our possessions as *materiel*.

IDEAS

Our ideas include, among many other things, all our values, myths, superstitions, scientific facts, arts, and religious beliefs. Most of us, for example, value education. We send all our children to school—both boys and girls—and encourage them to learn as much as they can. Similarly, most of us believe there is only one God—although we each may worship God differently. In addition, many of us knock on wood and revise our plans on Friday the thirteenth. Many skyscrapers do not even have a thirteenth floor. Furthermore, many of us follow the advice of medical doctors when we are ill.

All these ideas, and many more, are part of our culture. The values of education, religious beliefs, superstitions, and medical practices represent Western ideas. Other cultures, in contrast, may have different ideas about such things. In some Arab societies, for example, the education of women is not encouraged and is, in fact, frowned upon. The Trobriand Islanders of the South Pacific worship many gods instead of just one. In Nepal, even numbers are considered safe and odd numbers are avoided. Whereas Western medical practices are now available in much of the world, in some areas the witch doctor is also called in "just in case." Thus, although ideas are a component of all cultures, we see that the specific ideas found in each culture differ.

NORMS

The second component of culture is standards of behavior, or *norms*. Norms are defined as standards of behavior that are socially binding—or which people are expected by others to follow. They are based on the shared expectations of the group members. In our society, norms include washing one's hands before eating, obeying the government, and not killing another human being. As we will see later in this section, norms, like ideas, vary among societies.

In other animal "societies" instincts dictate how individual members will behave. In human societies the same job is filled by norms. One of the main tasks of every social group is to teach its norms to the young members of the group and to ensure that each accepts and follows them. Obviously this does not always happen successfully as people always violate some group norms. But most of the time most people conform for a number of reasons.

In part people obey the norms because they do not know any better, they have no particular reason to act in ways that are contrary to the norms, or they take the norms so for granted that they do not question them. For example, men in our society wear trousers, not skirts, because such an alternative does not enter their minds. In other cases, we obey norms because we believe they are correct. It makes sense to follow traffic regulations, for they are meant to speed the flow of traffic and at the same time protect people from accidents. And in some cases, norms are obeyed out of a fear of the consequences for violating them. Many of us know all too well that a police car lurking in a turn-off can

17

One of the reasons we obey norms is out of a fear of the consequences for violating them. For example, most drivers obey traffic regulations because of the likelihood of fines or arrest if they are caught violating the rules.

put a substantial dent in our wallets. Traffic police, therefore, are a very effective deterrent to violators, and the sight of radar equipment along the highway has a remarkable impact on slowing the pace at which people drive. Norms, in short, guide and constrain our behavior.

In 1906 sociologist William Graham Sumner classified norms into three types depending on how important or vital the members of a society feel they are to the welfare of the group.[2] He called these three types of norms *folkways, mores,* and *laws.*

Folkways

Sumner called the least important norms *folkways;* literally, the term means "the ways of the folk." These are the customs that the members of a group follow but that do not call forth strong reactions if violated. In American society, for example, it is considered proper for people to shake hands when being introduced. Similarly, the rules of table etiquette require one to remain seated at the table until others have finished eating, to refrain from smoking until the meal is completed, and the like. But if people violate these folkways, they probably will not lose their jobs or be arrested by the police. They may be laughed at, gossiped about, or thought to be rude if they do not follow the customs, but that will probably be the extent of society's reactions. In short, the behavior governed by folkways is considered proper behavior but is usually not obligatory.

Folkways vary considerably from society to society. In some cultures people eat together in groups, in others they eat privately, and in still others the men eat together, served by the women. In many American offices it is not unusual for people to work in informal clothing, but in other cultures this may be considered improper. In some societies it is considered correct for a man to "tip" his hat to a woman; in others, it is improper for a man to remove his headgear in the presence of a woman. Differences in the folkways of peoples throughout the world reflect and support the rich varieties of customs that are followed by the members of human societies.

Mores

Mores (pronounced mor-ays) are the social norms that provide the moral standards of the society. Rules governing mores are taken very seriously and compliance with them is severely enforced. They may or may not be written down, but all the members of a society are expected to know and adhere to them. While folkways tell us what is proper conduct, mores define what is right and wrong, moral and immoral. They tell the members of a society what they *must* or *must not* do. Compared to folkways, mores might be thought of as "mustways." In American society, for example, the mores require that we be honest, work hard, be morally upright, and care for our children. They demand that we do not steal, commit bigamy, or walk the streets unclothed. In some societies, mores dictate that a man never speak to his mother-in-law. While most Hindus consider it morally wrong to kill or eat any animal, whatever the reason, in other societies the practice of cannibalism is considered morally correct.

Some of the same mores are observed in all societies, but the ways in which they are interpreted vary considerably from society to society. For example, even though incest is morally prohibited in all known societies, what is considered incest in one culture is not so regarded in another. An American cannot marry a brother or a sister. In other cultures, however, such as the ancient Hawaiian, Incan, and Egyptian, members of royal families were expected to marry their siblings. In the same way, cultures differ in the ways in which they enforce mores. The Nuer of East Africa usually employ violence as a means of settling disputes. In contrast, most Americans rely on the court system, although violence might be used as an alternative. The Trobriand Islanders of the South Pacific would not openly punish someone for adultery, even though this is one of the most serious offenses a person can commit. Instead the offender is expected to commit suicide (and usually does) once the infraction becomes publicly known.

However it is accomplished, the enforcement of mores serves to remind us of their importance and the need to obey them. It is also possible that we feel a sense of retribution when someone is punished for doing something we refrain from doing ourselves.

As varied as they may be, rules of behavior exist in every known society. This fact has led sociologists to feel that some norms that are agreed upon and shared by the members of a society are essential for group life and, as a result, the survival of human beings and civilization. What the specific rules are is not as important as the fact that they exist and are shared by the members of a group.

Laws

The enforcement of folkways and mores is often informal. But in order to facilitate social control in large-scale societies, it is often necessary to formalize some folkways and mores by writing them down. In this manner, large-scale societies create laws. Conversely, a society that has no written language cannot have laws.

Laws are deliberately formulated rules of conduct that are enforced by a special authorized agency of the state. Compared to mores and folkways, laws are formal pronouncements of what is right and proper. The sanctions or punishments used to enforce laws are similarly formalized; they are specific and predetermined, and are supposed to deter people from violating the laws. For example, if we kill

Societies that have laws also have sanctions and punishments—such as imprisonment—to enforce the laws and to discourage would-be violators.

another human being, laws state that we can go to jail for a predetermined amount of time.

Generally, laws are designed to support the mores of a society, but sometimes they contradict these mores. In these cases they are more difficult to enforce. For example, the Eighteenth Amendment to the United States Constitution, which prohibited the sale of alcoholic beverages, was a failure because it had insufficient public support and conflicted with the folkways and mores of many Americans. Similarly, because laws prohibiting the sale and possession of marijuana have conflicted with the mores of many people, efforts have been made to abolish such laws and legalize the use of the substance. Often, however, legislators and courts impose laws on the public that are strongly opposed but that help to change the pattern of behavior supported by other norms. Opening public places to blacks as well as whites, for example, has probably helped improve relationships between the races.

From these examples we note that there is not always a harmonious relationship between laws and mores. Criminologist Edwin Sutherland once noted that there is a paradox regarding laws and mores. He suggested that "If the mores of a group are adequate, laws are unnecessary and if the mores are inadequate, laws are useless."[3] Whether or not this is true is difficult to prove. It does, nevertheless, appear that satisfactory laws are based on the society's mores and folkways. It may not be necessary to have a law requiring people to stop at red lights, or one allowing them to turn right at an intersection after stopping at a red light, but these regulations certainly make good sense to most people and do not conflict with other norms.

In summary, norms are essential to human group life. However, there is not always a clear or consistent relationship among the norms of a society, and sometimes conflicts can occur because of the incompatability of a society's norms. For example, we have a norm that divorce is to be avoided, especially when there are small children in a family. On the other hand, we have a norm that the most important relationship between human beings is that between a husband and wife. The result, for many people who are unhappily married, is that they must choose between their parental responsibility and personal happiness. In this case, two norms of equal weight vie for obedience.

Norms, along with ideas, comprise what we refer to as *nonmaterial culture*—those abstract concepts that we cannot measure physically. But no culture would be complete without its *material culture* or physical objects. We will now examine this third component of culture.

MATERIEL

Materiel refers to the material part of what we fall heir to at birth—all the physical things in our lives. The list of things, like ideas, is endless—cars, toothbrushes, shoes, tools, buildings, pianos, guns, and on and on. No one could ever compile a complete list of all the things in any society. What is important about this part of our culture is that individuals must learn to use many of these things and must adjust their lives to them. In our society, for example, many of us have

---

APPLYING SOCIOLOGY

List three folkways, three mores, and three laws in American society. Discuss the similarities and differences among these three groups of norms in terms of what would result if the norms are disobeyed. Take any folkway and violate it (for example, leave the table before everyone else has finished eating). How do you feel about violating the norm? Do you feel uncomfortable? Why? If not, why not? Note also how people reacted to you.

structured our lives around the automobile, although we may take this adaptation for granted. We use our cars for school, business, personal errands, and pleasure. In fact, frequently we live in places where alternative methods of transportation are not available and we are not within walking distance of necessary services. In contrast, the Yoruk of Turkey, a nomadic group, rely on camels to transport their household possessions during migration. From this example we see how differently we would live if automobiles were not part of our culture. Similarly, our lives would be much different if we lived in tents instead of houses. Wouldn't we behave differently if we had no clocks or calendars? So the material part of culture affects everything else in our lives.

The Individual and Culture

From what we have seen so far, culture plays an important role in our lives. It shapes all that we think, believe, do, and have. But culture plays an even greater role in the life of our species—it allows our species to survive.

CULTURE AS A SURVIVAL KIT

The newborn infant enters the world physically naked and culturally a *tabula rasa* (a clean slate, a blank). But the infant is born with some biological drives that must be met for survival. And these drives motivate actions. The hunger drive, for example, compels a person to search for food. No infant, however, can satisfy this drive unless others supply the food. And this is where culture comes in.

The ways in which the infant learns to fulfill biological needs are a product of what is gradually taught by means of culture. The infant therefore does not have to work out an individual survival kit; the parents are already prepared when the child enters the world. Because of this preparation, the infant learns more than how to fulfill biological needs. Children learn how to keep warm, how to get love, how to be clean, and so forth *all in ways that are considered appropriate by those who are doing the teaching.* In this way culture liberates individuals from most of the limitations of biology while at the same time shaping and directing their patterns of behavior.

CULTURE AND INDIVIDUAL FREEDOM

When we regard culture in this manner, we can see that culture acts to limit individual freedom. In the process of fulfilling our biologi-

22

cal needs we are also given certain restrictions. We are not only taught how to obtain food; we are also taught which foods are edible or proper, how to eat, and even when to eat. Children could very well satisfy their hunger without eating vegetables, but how many times is the American youngster told, "Eat your carrots and peas!"

These restrictions are necessary, though, if we value relative security. If each member of society had complete freedom, if there were no norms shaping our behavior, society would be chaotic. Thus, we face a dilemma. We can have complete individual freedom but that also means individual insecurity; or we can agree to curtail individual freedom and have civilization with relative security. Clearly, we have chosen to give up some of our freedom and accept the culture of the group into which we are born. The limitations placed by culture, however, are not very rigid. To return to the above example, while we are taught vegetables are good for us, we can, of course, choose from a variety of vegetables that are considered permissible.

Cultures vary greatly in the amount of "free choice" they offer the members. A person may choose to violate completely the dictates of the culture, but only under threat of punishment. Although we sometimes feel oppressed by the restrictions culture places on us, we conform to most of our culture's patterns without questioning them. In part this is because in the process of learning the aspects of culture, people also learn to perceive and define the world in terms of the ways their culture teaches them to perceive and define it.

The Transmission of Culture

We have shown that culture precedes the birth of any individual into a society. This fact is both positive and negative—it provides us with behavioral guidelines at the same time that it limits individual freedom. Now we must examine the question of how the culture is transmitted to each new generation.

SIGNS AND SYMBOLS

All societies use signs and symbols to transmit culture. How can we differentiate between these two terms that play such an important role in our lives?

One way to distinguish between a sign and a symbol is to compare a carrot (the *object*) with c a r r o t (the *word*). A real carrot is a *sign*. The letters that spell out the word representing the real object together are a *symbol*. Other languages have other symbols for the sign carrot.

Most social scientists agree that both animals and human beings

Only human beings (and perhaps the higher apes) can create and respond to abstract symbols that represent objects. Most people, for example, can interpret the meaning of each of the above symbols.

behave in response to signs. But only human beings (with the possible exception of the higher apes[4]) interact in terms of symbols. For example, both the rabbit and the human being know that the carrot is an item of food. But only the human being (again with the possible exception of the higher apes) is capable of creating abstract symbols to *represent* the object. A rabbit may be taught to respond to this representation, but the rabbit is responding to the meaning a human being has given to c a r r o t, not to any intrinsic meaning this combination of letters has, or to any meaning that has been bestowed upon it by the rabbit.

A sign, then, is a real object—book, piano, knife. B o o k, p i a n o, and k n i f e are symbols of the signs. Human beings attach artificial meanings to these symbols. For instance, we agree that t e a c h e r is a person who instructs. The letters and their arrangement, then, are arbitrary. It is only shared meaning that makes them a symbol for the sign.

Thus, human beings have a unique communication system which other animals lack—they can use signs and symbols. But their most effective network of symbols, and one without which civilization would probably be impossible, is language.

LANGUAGE

Although it is clear that other animals do respond to some symbols (dogs, for example, "understand" such commands as "sit" or "stay"), only human beings can create, recreate, and give meaning to language. Through their use of symbols they can communicate symbolically and thereby develop civilization.

With language, an infinity of accumulated wisdom is provided to each of us. We can learn from each other and build upon what we learn. With language we can organize elaborate activities. We can give directions, share our feelings, express our ideas, and communicate our discoveries. We can learn not only from one another but from those who came before us, and we can pass this knowledge on to those who will come after us. In short, language makes possible the development of human culture and allows us to build large, complex societies (see Chapter 3). The human ability to create and use language, in other words, makes human social life possible. Without it we might just as well return to the trees and caves of our prehuman ancestors.

After studying several cultures, anthropologists Edward Sapir and Benjamin Lee Whorf concluded that language was more than a part of culture in the sense that it is the storehouse of culture and also the major mechanism for transmitting culture to individual members. Even more important for understanding human behavior, they argued, was that when human beings think, they think in terms of language. Since language is a part of culture, it is human culture that actually shapes our thoughts.[5] But how does this influence our behavior?

According to the available research, the connection between language and behavior is by no means clear and is often very complicated. Generally, language provides people with the codes they use to define the various situations they encounter. As Sapir and Whorf noted, language, in effect, codifies reality for us since it provides us with the tools for interpreting the world around us. Hence, as individuals come to learn the language of their culture, they come to perceive situations, actions, and feelings in socially acceptable ways. Language tells us what to notice, what things to group together, and which ones to separate. It also provides us with the words we use to interpret the world and evaluate or judge it. For example, would ghosts exist for us if our language did not have a word that defines a "thing" called ghost?

Anthropologists have demonstrated that people codify reality considerably differently from culture to culture. The Hopi Indians, for instance, classify things quite differently from English-speaking people. The Hopi have one word that refers to all things that fly, except for birds. Thus, the Hopi would use the same word for *insect, airplane,* and *aviator.* We, of course, would find this cumbersome. However, our

25

FOCUS ON: BODY LANGUAGE

Some people argue that nonverbal forms of communication are a major key to a complete understanding of another's behavior. In his book *The Silent Language,* Edward T. Hall takes such a view. Hall identifies ten kinds of nonverbal forms of human communication that are available in each culture. He calls these forms of "the silent language" Primary Message Systems and they include: interaction, association, subsistence, bisexuality, territoriality, temporality, learning, play, defense, and exploitation of materials.

While interaction is based on language, the remaining activities are not, and together they form the overall pattern of a culture. Many people refer to some of these message systems as body language.

The term *body language* was popularized in a best-selling book of the same title by Julius Fast. The argument advanced by Fast is that our body language communicates a great deal of unintended meaning. For example, when we are embarrassed it is difficult to keep from "turning red" or becoming flushed because such a reaction is involuntary. Or, when we are nervous it is difficult to prevent ourselves from perspiring.

Have you ever noticed someone who was speaking in a manner contradictory to his or her body language? Have you ever been embarrassed because you misunderstood someone's body language?

Two factors that are especially important in the communication process are time and space. Time, or temporality, enters into much of our behavior as a form of communication. For example, it is generally unacceptable to telephone someone after 11 P.M. The other factor, space, or territoriality, has become a subject of interest only recently but it is of vital importance to human activity. What kind of response do people have when crowded into an elevator or a bus? How do you feel when a person you are conversing with repeatedly touches your arm? Clearly, the social distance we try to maintain plays an important part in our daily existence.

Societies vary dramatically in their approach to both time and space. Japanese culture accepts physical proximity as a normal part of life. Indeed, in Tokyo, hired professionals push additional travelers into a subway car. In some societies, developing a business contract includes a meeting during which pleasantries and etiquette completely dominate the evening. During the second meeting the more practical aspects of a contract are discussed. And, in some societies, the culture encourages men to embrace and women to keep physically distant.

How do these approaches to time and space differ from our approach to these forms of activity? How do our approaches to time and space affect other aspects of our lives?

Source: Edward T. Hall, *The Silent Language,* New York: Doubleday, 1973. Julius Fast, *Body Language,* Philadelphia: M. Evans & Co., 1970.

one word for snow does not make sense to some Eskimos. They use different words for different kinds of snow—falling snow, snow on the ground, wet snow, and so forth. As all immigrants know, when they interact with the members of a new group, half the battle is learning the thought patterns and the norms of the members of that group. This requires first that they learn the language of the group. They can then learn other aspects of their new culture, although they may retain much of their old culture.

Many people contend that our body language communicates a great deal of unintended meaning. What do the body positions of these people suggest to you?

Ethnocentrism

As people learn to think and behave according to the expectations of their culture, they often come to believe that their culture is the best in all respects. People may believe this even in the face of contradictory evidence. Anthropologist E. E. Evans-Pritchard observed this phenomenon while studying the Nuer of Africa:

> From a European's point of view Nuerland has no favorable qualities, unless its severity be counted as such, for its endless marshes and wide savannah plains have an austere, monotonous charm. It is throughout hard on man and beast, being for most of the year either parched or a swamp. But Nuer think that they live in the finest country on earth and, it must be admitted, for herdsmen their country has many admirable features. I soon gave up trying to convince Nuer that there is any country more suited for cattle husbandry than their own, an attempt rendered more useless since a few of them have been taken to Khartoum, which they consider to be the home of all white men, and, having seen the desert scrub of that latitude, have been confirmed in their opinion that their land is superior to ours.[6]

Similarly, it is common to hear New Yorkers, while complaining about their city, say "If you leave New York, you ain't goin' nowhere!" People living in other areas tend to hold similar beliefs about their cities. Recall, for example, the reaction an entertainer receives when he or she asks, "How many of you are from Des Moines?" Members of religious and ethnic groups also tend to think of themselves as superior to others. It was for this very reason that blacks and various "white ethnics" began to display pride in being part of their respective groups.

27

These attitudes are expressions of *ethnocentrism*—the tendency to view everything in relationship to the norms and values of one's own group. Because of ethnocentrism, people tend to view their own culture as the best, to think of others as "foreign," "odd," or "different," and to regard others as inferior to themselves. Many American citizens thus tend to wave American flags at rallies while the citizens of Communist China may carry pictures of Chairman Mao. Similarly, ethnocentrism leads students to judge their school as better than another and to take pride in a winning basketball team. It is ethnocentrism that leads people to call others "savages" and themselves "progressive," or the "superior race." In short, ethnocentrism leads the members of one group to view themselves and their way of life as superior—more moral, better, and more worthy than that of any other people.

Every group is ethnocentric to some extent. All people draw a distinction between "we" and "they," and in doing so, it is inevitable that "they" are rated somewhat less worthy than "we." Indeed, even when people imitate one another, they usually evaluate themselves as being "better at it" than the people they imitate. In part, ethnocentrism is a matter of habit. We rarely know much, if anything, about groups other than the ones in which we were reared and live. Hence, the ways of our own group seem to us to be the only ways—and naturally the right ways—simply because they are the only bases we have for judging others.

In part, also, the cultures of various people operate to encourage ethnocentrism. From early childhood the members of every culture are taught the group myths and are provided with cultural heroes to emulate. In Western nations, organizations are formed specifically to promote and protect the purity of each nation. In France, for example, an institute exists for codifying the French language, and this sometimes involves taking measures to prevent the invasion of non-French words. Thus, this organization recently banned from the French language much American slang (like *hotdog*). (Needless to say this effort has been far from successful. Pick up any French magazine or newspaper and you will see an abundance of English or American words.) The United States also attempts to protect its purity; in the 1950s an "un-American" activities committee in Congress sought to guard the country against people who did not seem to uphold American principles.

At the same time, a number of studies were conducted by sociologists about the kind of people who were most likely to be strongly ethnocentric. In one study, T. W. Adorno found that people who were ethnocentric in one area tended to be hostile and suspicious of other groups as well.[7] Similarly, Samuel A. Stouffer found that people who were highly ethnocentric were also intolerant of nonconformists.[8] Although it is not likely that ethnocentrism is peculiar to any

Cultures and societies often encourage ethnocentrism and guard their national purity. In America in the 1950s, for example, Senator Joseph McCarthy *(right)* led a congressional crusade against people whom he believed threatened American society and beliefs.

particular personality type, it does appear that those people who hold the most lofty opinions of their own group tend also to be more critical and negative toward others and toward those who do not share their values, attitudes, and behavior. Intolerance and a feeling of superiority tend to go together.

Cultural Relativism

Granted that we are all ethnocentric to some degree, could sociologists, who try to understand and explain the behavior of human beings, be successful if they viewed all other groups in terms of their own (the sociologists') culture? What kind of scientific understanding could they achieve, for example, if they considered the behavior of everyone but themselves to be "immoral," "stupid," "illogical," or "sinful"?

The answer, of course, is that they could not understand very much at all. Indeed, for sociologists to comprehend the behavior of a particular group, they must "step outside" their own culture and view

APPLYING SOCIOLOGY

Considering that ethnocentrism is universal, it probably has a number of advantages both for the group and for its individual members. At the same time, it also could have disadvantages. Make a list of both and debate with the other members of your class the advantages and disadvantages of ethnocentrism. Do the advantages outweigh the disadvantages or vice versa?

that group objectively. In other words, they must act like foreigners who know nothing about the conduct of the people being studied. One of the most difficult things for people, including social scientists, to do is to take an attitude that is just the opposite of ethnocentrism, that of *cultural relativism.* Cultural relativism refers to an attitude of respect toward cultural differences. Sociologists who have this attitude may agree with their culture that a certain kind of activity—let us say head-hunting—is bad and immoral. But when trying to understand such an activity, they view it, not in terms of their own culture, but in terms of the culture of the people they are studying. In this way they see that although headhunting may be a senseless and cruel activity from the perspective of Western culture, among the Marindese of New Guinea it was a moral obligation for a man; he had to have several heads around in case his wife presented him with a child. The Marindese believed that the only way for a child to get a name, and thus an identity, was to take it from another person in the form of that person's head. The head was given to the child when it was named and, like the name, the head was something the child carried around for the rest of its life.

Cultural Determinants

Where does culture come from? Why does one group have certain elements in its culture and another group entirely different elements? Several answers have been proposed to these questions. One argument places a high value on the role of the environment as a determinant of culture. Since human beings can exist in a variety of environments and are able to adapt to environmental change, perhaps the type of culture a people creates depends on the geography or ecological habitat they encounter. In other words, the process of adaptation to the environment causes people to form a certain type of culture. But why might two different groups of people living in the same environment form different cultures? Perhaps, then, culture depends on the make-up of the people—their race or other biological characteristics, for example. Let us consider these two arguments.

ENVIRONMENT

On the surface it would seem logical that the kind of culture a group develops is determined primarily by the environment in which it lives. For example, people in cold climates build sturdy homes capable of withstanding the rigors of winter. Those in warm, humid climates build light, airy houses, designed to shed the rain and maximize the

The type of culture that a group develops is determined by the people as well as by the setting. The same environment may produce two very different cultures. The Hopi and the Navaho both live in the desert, but the Hopi are farmers, whereas the Navaho are shepherds.

circulation of air. It is logical, then, that other aspects of culture are also subject to environmental forces.

Although plausible, this explanation is not totally accurate. The ecological habitat of a people may *influence* the kind of culture they produce, but it does not *determine* the culture. As a matter of fact, anthropologists, who have identified over one thousand different cultures throughout the world, report that similar cultures are found in quite different environments; and different cultures are found in similar settings. *It is not the setting alone but also the people who determine culture.*

Although the Cheyenne and the Comanche lived in the same environment and had similar cultural traits, many aspects of their cultures were still quite different from one another. For example, whereas the Comanche stressed complete freedom of expression of all sorts, the Cheyenne repressed or moderated any overt emotional expression. The Hopi and the Navaho shared the same desert environment, but the Hopi were cultivators and the Navaho herded sheep. The people that resided in the islands of the Pacific had similar Polynesian cultures even though they lived in extremely diverse environments. And the geography and climate of the United States vary considerably, yet the people of the United States have developed a general culture that is distinctly "American" in character.

This does not deny that the environment places limitations on the kinds of cultures people might create in some locales. The Eskimos, for example, could not develop an agricultural way of life in the harsh Arctic setting. Desert peoples probably would not be expert sailors. And the Pygmies of the African rain forest certainly have little need for horses. Obviously, a people are not apt to become sophisticated potters if their environment does not provide clay from which to make pots. But people surrounded by usable clay are not predetermined to become potters either. The ancient peoples of central Africa did not build elaborate stones walls around their frontiers as the Chinese did because there were not adequate deposits of usable stone in central Africa with which to build walls. But, archeologists have found in Central Africa the remains of mud and wood walls that rival the Great Wall of China. The Eskimos became superior hunters and fishers because their environment left them little choice and provided the resources necessary for hunting. But the hard, sparse environment of the Arctic made it impractical for the Eskimos to live in large settled towns. Instead, Eskimos developed a culture organized in terms of small, nomadic families or hunting units.

In all these cases, human beings overcame the restrictions of their environment and used what it provided to develop styles of life that protected them from the forces of nature. If the environment has some influence on the kinds of cultures societies develop, then perhaps the physical or biological characteristics of the people are also important.

BIOLOGY

When the European explorers first came into contact with the peoples of Africa, Asia, the Pacific Islands, and the Americas, they were shocked at the customs and styles of life they encountered. Being no less ethnocentric than anyone else, they saw the people they encountered as savage, barbarian, and inferior. Following the dominant ideology of their own cultures, they sought to attribute the behavior of these peoples to biological characteristics. This idea certainly seemed logical at the time. If racial characteristics are transmitted biologically, why not cultural ones as well? But the research of sociologists and anthropologists, as well as that of many other scientists, suggests that culture and race are not related in any way. The following facts about culture and race clearly demonstrate that culture is a social and not a biological phenomenon.

Fact #1: Anthropologists have distinguished over a thousand different cultures, but there are fewer than a dozen different races throughout the world.

Fact #2: There is virtually no evidence to show that people of different biological types differ as to their drives or physical or mental capacities.

Fact #3: A person of any racial or biological origin can learn the culture of any group.

Fact #4: There are more biological differences *among* the people of any one racial group than there are *between* the people of different races.

Fact #5: Only a small proportion of any biological group resembles exactly the ideal physical type of that group. Therefore a race or biological type is simply a characterization that includes members, whether or not they conform to that type.

Fact #6: Genetic or biological change occurs very slowly, while culture changes constantly and often very rapidly.

From this assortment of facts, and from the preceding discussion of environment, we see that neither environment nor biology is the cultural determinant—although environment does influence culture to a certain degree. To what, then, may we attribute the development of culture?

CULTURE AS A DETERMINANT OF CULTURE

Anthropologist Robert H. Lowie once stated that "culture is a thing *sui generis* [in itself] which can be explained only in terms of itself."[9] He meant that while human beings might be genetically "programmed" to develop culture, neither their physical make-up nor their environmental setting suffices to explain either culture itself or the type of culture a people creates. A combination of historical accident, contacts with different people, and the choices people make in the development of their culture seem instead to be the underlying forces behind culture.

The people of the United States, for example, have a culture that is based on individualism, political democracy, hard work, success, and freedom. They have also produced one of the richest and most advanced material and technological cultures in the world. United States culture, however, was not shaped overnight or because the people who possess it are somehow biologically unique or superior. Historical accident, more than anything else, may be responsible for the peculiar features of our present-day culture.

The diverse people who immigrated here from around the world were fortunate to find a land rich in natural resources. But more important, the diverse cultural backgrounds and common goals of these individuals allowed them to master their new environment and build a way of life unprecedented in the world's history. Moreover, the elements of contemporary United States culture were heavily influenced by the historical circumstances of its founders. The industrial revolution was just getting underway in Europe, the land was undeveloped and largely unsettled, the ideology of individualism was just taking hold, and people were fleeing religious and political oppression. As a result, they built an industrial culture, were required to work hard in order to transform the virgin land into a livable place, and had room enough in which to practice the principles of freedom and democracy they brought with them to the new land.

Thus we can see that a combination of factors—accident, contact, and deliberate choice—acts to determine cultural development. And because human beings are not slaves to biological factors and environment, they can transform their environment to some extent to suit their needs and desires. The ways that human beings have done so are as diverse as the unique events they each encounter. It is mostly the culture of human beings that determines how and to what extent people adapt to the world around them, and it is in the process of transforming their surroundings that they generate, and consequently alter, their cultures.

Subcultures can emerge along many lines, among them, age, occupation, region, and religion. Large, diverse societies such as America tend to have many subcultures.

Subcultures

The members of any society tend to share a common culture and, as a result, they usually behave in similar ways. Some societies, however, like the United States, are large, heterogeneous, and consist of many very diverse people. Because of these factors, it is likely that the members do not all share the same culture to an equal extent. As a result, we can expect to find a number of distinct *subcultures* existing in larger societies. Sociologists use the term *subculture,* to denote a segment of a larger society that possesses a perspective and a life-style that is significantly different from that of other people in the society. In this respect, the members of a subculture share a set of norms, attitudes, and values that differ to some degree from those of the dominant or majority group and that, therefore, set the subgroup apart from the other members of the society.

Given the diversity of the people who live in American society, some sociologists have suggested that we cannot speak of an "American culture." Rather, America is a conglomeration of different subcultures. These subcultures can emerge along regional, ethnic, occupational, religious, economic, or age lines. For example, "hard hats" are considered different from "intellectuals," young people are thought to be different from adults, southerners are distinguished from northerners, and the rich are unlike the poor. We can note these differences in such areas as recreational patterns, educational beliefs, and world views. What are the elements by which we might recognize a particular subculture? Style of dress is one obvious element. The Amish people in their tailored black clothes and students in their jeans and t-shirts are readily identifiable. Style of life is another such element—the casual manner in which many students live, for example, serves to distinguish them as different from their parents. A most important differentiating element is language.

LANGUAGE AS A SUBCULTURE SIGN

Frequently the members of a subculture share a distinct language. This language may even be completely foreign to the major culture. Immigrant groups often live together in enclaves and retain the language of their former country along with many of their original culture's beliefs, customs, and values. To a lesser extreme, subgroups often develop their own unique slang. Young people, for example, often use expressions not common to older people. As a result, many adults complain about the language of teenagers and often have difficulty understanding their own children. Many black Americans speak a separate kind of English—"Black English"—and some educators believe it should be considered a distinct language in its own right.

Occupational groups frequently develop distinct jargons, too. Indeed, part of the process of entering an occupation, especially a profession, is to acquire the special language. Physicists, sociologists, mathematicians, electricians, geographers, economists, carpenters, athletes, and members of many other occupational groups share the unique languages of their professions.

35

Language, then, is one of the clearest signs that people are members of different subgroups. Just as language plays an important role in culture itself, it has important functions for subcultures as well. Perhaps the most significant of these is to establish the group's separateness from the dominant culture. This serves to enhance the solidarity of the subculture's members and to give them a greater sense of "we-ness" or cohesion than they otherwise would experience. It also serves effectively to exclude outsiders, to make them feel unwanted or ignorant.

An example of how language can serve to bring members of a subculture closer can be seen in the work of criminologist David Maurer, who investigated the culture and behavior of professional pickpockets in American society. In this study Maurer found that professional pickpockets share a distinct *argot*, or slang, that can be analyzed and thereby reveals much about the way of life and profession of pickpockets. The quotation below, taken from Maurer's study, demonstrates quite clearly just how specialized a subculture's language can become.

> Yeah . . . I was forcing it up, high up under his chin, like this. That insider was tight, very tight . . . After I unsloughed his vest I could tell . . . his leather, Doc, I'm not lying, it was that thick. But I couldn't come with it. This bates, he was tall, lots taller than I am and that is bad when you're taking it from the front. And I felt him try to go for his kick, as far as he could . . . Them broads had him right in the frame, but there was no doubt in my mind I rumbled him. And when I rumble one like that, a pit score or an insider, I let him go. There is too many okuses in too many other pockets. Well, I must've fooled around just a second too long, so he felt to me like he tried to make a grab for my mitt, like I said. The broads split me clean, or we'd've been in for it. He just thought he felt something, but he couldn't get ahold of nothing.[10]

Most people would have difficulty understanding exactly what was being said in this interview, because they have had no contact with the subcultural world of pickpockets, except, perhaps, as victims. The speaker is saying that he was having trouble taking the vic-

---

APPLYING SOCIOLOGY

Why do you suppose professional pickpockets would describe their activities in a different language? Are there similarities between criminal subcultures, such as pickpockets, and other subcultures, such as youth groups or medical doctors? What might these be?

In a large-scale society, subcultures can develop when people are isolated by choice or by exclusion from the rest of the society. Immigrant subcultures can develop for both reasons—the newcomers may choose to band together out of fear or reluctance to change, or they may be excluded by the rest of society because of their different culture, customs, and appearance.

tim's (bates') wallet (leather) from his inside jacket pocket because the victim was taller than the thief and had felt the thief attempting to rob him, even though his two female partners (broads) had managed to squeeze (frame) the victim between them. Since the pickpocket knew there were many easier victims (okuses) available, he felt that it was better not to try this one. Realizing this, his partners helped him to escape (split clean).

WHY SUBCULTURES DEVELOP

Subcultures develop in a large-scale society when the members of that society are isolated from one another either by their own choice or because the main society excludes them. Some groups, like professional thieves, various immigrant groups, and the aristocracy have imposed social distance between themselves and the rest of society. Professional thieves have done so for their own protection from the law and also because it is easier to rationalize stealing from other people if the victims are not identified as being like themselves. Some immigrant groups isolate themselves in distinct communities out of a need for mutual help, or a fear of outsiders, or because it is often easier to retain the old ways than to change their life-style and habits to conform with the customs and norms of the new country. The aristocracy feels it is superior to others and therefore prefers to remain unpolluted by the "lower" classes by avoiding any contact beyond what is necessary.

In most cases, however, subcultures emerge because certain segments of the society are, through custom, law, or both, excluded from participating with other groups in the society. The course of the cultural development of both groups—the subculture and the mainstream of society—thus grows wider apart the longer the wall of discrimination remains. For example, because many blacks have been excluded from the mainstream of American economic and social life, they have developed a subcultural way of life somewhat different from whites. This, in turn, has also been used by many whites as a reason for continued exclusion.

Sociologists disagree over whether or not young people as a group constitute a true subculture, but a good deal of evidence shows that young people in modern America have developed separate worlds because of their unique social position—no longer children but not yet adults. It is possible that they have come to see themselves and are seen by adults as being different because their entrance into the adult world of work has been delayed for an extensive period of their lives. Rather than being allowed to work when they are physically and mentally mature enough to do so, young people are expected to continue in school and to pursue their education for increasingly longer periods of time (see Chapter 7).

As a society grows in size and complexity, it appears that the number of subcultures it produces tends to increase. This phenomenon can have certain advantages and disadvantages for the society (and for the members of each cultural group). Sociologist Émile Durkheim[11] (see pages 248–249) recognized one such advantage when he noted that diversity prevents a society from stagnating. Diversity allows the society to change in the face of new demands. But Durkheim also noted a disadvantage of such diversity. Any group needs similarity (communality) so that it can operate smoothly. Diversity often brings some confusion and disruption. Ideally, then, a society should have groups that are similar to each other and groups that are different from each other.

Given these two requirements, subcultures can be both beneficial

---

APPLYING SOCIOLOGY

Taking black Americans as an example of a subgroup, list the positive and negative effects of subcultures for the society as a whole and for individual subculture members. Give reasons why American culture in general has benefited or been hurt by the diversity of its members. Relate the benefits or detriments to your own experience.

Despite the disparity of the many human cultures, all societies share certain universal needs. One such need is caring for and socializing children.

and harmful for a society as well as for their individual members. And as the world becomes more populated and complex, the advantages and disadvantages of cultural diversity will become increasingly significant for the future well-being of the human species.

Cultural Universals

One of the most striking things about human beings is the apparently infinite number of cultures they have developed throughout history. No other animal species comes even close to the diversity of behaviors and styles of life created by human beings. But at the same time, for all their differences, human cultures also show some remarkable similarities. As we will see later on in this book (Part Three) all societies must satisfy five universal needs: providing a means of social control, educating the young, providing goods and services, caring for and socializing children, and explaining the unknown. All must satisfy these requirements to maintain the well-being and survival of the human family as a species.

Yet the ways in which societies meet these requirements differ. What works for one group of human beings may not work for another. But if any group of human beings is to survive as a group, its members must devise and use ways that they find workable for meeting their physical and social needs. To the extent that all human beings have similar needs and drives, the cultures of every human group will be similar. But to the extent that human groups encounter different experiences and have the capacity to shape their own responses to these experiences, the cultures of human groups will differ. The existence of any group depends, therefore, on how adequately its culture fulfills its needs and drives.

SUMMARY

Although all human beings are members of the same biological species, their ways of life, behaviors, and beliefs differ. Sociologists use the concept of culture to describe the wide variations among human groups. Culture consists of everything we think, do, and have as members of a society.

Culture can be described as consisting of three major components. One component, which we call *ideas*, includes all our myths, superstitions, scientific facts, arts, and religious beliefs. The second component is the *norms* that guide the behavior of a culture's members. Norms can be classified in terms of their importance to the group as *folkways*, *mores*, or *laws*. The third component of culture, *materiel*, consists of all the material items a society possesses, from a toothpick to an apartment complex.

In addition to influencing all our thoughts, beliefs, behaviors, and possessions, culture allows our species to survive. It provides the knowledge, rules for organizing, and tools necessary to survive in a hostile world. By doing so, however, culture acts to limit individual freedom.

Culture is transmitted from one generation to the next by means of signs and symbols. All animals use signs, but only human animals (with the possible exception of the higher apes) are capable of creating symbols—the most important of which is language. Language allows human culture to develop and allows us to build large, complex societies.

The members of any group tend to evaluate others from the culturally determined perspective of their own group. This tendency, called *ethnocentrism*, is to judge behaviors and life-styles of others as inferior or strange. *Cultural relativism* is just the opposite of ethnocentrism and is the attitude social scientists attempt to adopt when studying the behavior of other groups.

Many efforts have been made to explain the origins of culture. One approach suggests that culture is determined by the environment. A second approach suggests that biological factors determine culture. Yet neither has been shown to be the cultural determinant. Instead culture is determined by culture. That is, culture is the product of human interaction and human interaction is possible because we possess culture. Cultures emerge, develop, and change as the result of historical accident, contact with other societies, and choice. Cultures will differ and change over time, regardless of environment or biology.

In almost every society it is likely that *subcultures* will develop. Subcultures are similar to the dominant culture but differ from it in specific ways so as to be recognizably different. Dress, language, style of life, and ideology all may serve to identify subcultures.

Subcultures are beneficial and harmful for both the larger society and the subculture. Subcultures provide people with a sense of identity and belonging. Subcultures may also enrich the society by providing diversity. At the same time their existence poses problems of unity and organization for the larger group.

Although cultures differ considerably throughout the world, all cultures share certain universal needs. These are providing a means of social control, educating the young, providing goods and services, caring for and socializing children, and explaining the unknown.

GLOSSARY

cultural relativism   an attitude in which one evaluates cultural differences in relation to the culture of the people being studied.

cultural universals   the behavior patterns and other cultural items that are found in every known society.

culture   everything that the members of a society teach one another; the rules, ideas, beliefs, and possessions shared by members of a society; a group's social heritage.

ethnocentrism   the tendency of a group to take for granted the superiority of its own culture, and to see its values, beliefs, and customs as being the only "right" ones.

folkways   the customs that the members of a group follow but that do not call forth strong reactions if violated.

ideas   all the values, myths, superstitions, scientific facts, arts, and religious beliefs shared by members of a society.

language   a form of communication which provides people with the codes needed to define the world around them.

laws   deliberately formulated rules of conduct that are enforced by a special authorized agency of the state; folkways and mores that are written down.

material culture   all the physical objects in our lives.

materiel   our material culture.

mores   the norms that provide the moral standards of the society. Violation of mores often results in severe punishment.

nonmaterial culture   the abstract concepts in our lives, consisting of our norms and ideas.

norms   the standards of behavior that are socially binding, or which people are expected by others to follow.

signs   real objects to which both human beings and animals respond.

subculture   a group of people whose behavior, beliefs, values, and/or life-style is somewhat different from those of the dominant culture; a group who perceives itself and is perceived by others as being distinct from the larger group.

symbols   socially understood arbitrary words assigned to represent tangible and intangible objects.

values   conceptions of what is desirable, precious, attractive, good, or preferable. Values influence how we evaluate or judge people, thereby shaping our attitudes and behaviors.

REFERENCES

1. Robert Bierstedt, *The Social Order*. 4th ed. New York: McGraw-Hill, 1974, p. 128.

2. William Graham Sumner, *Folkways*. Boston: Ginn, 1906.

3. Quoted in Isador Chein, "Behavior Theory and the Behavior of Attitudes: Some Critical Comments." In Martin Fishbein, ed., *Readings in Attitude Theory and Measurement*. New York: John Wiley & Sons, Inc., 1967, p. 52.

4. Several studies have been done to show that chimpanzees can create and interact in terms of symbols. See, for example, Allen Gardner and Beatrice Gardner, "Teaching Sign Language to a Chimpanzee." *Science* 165 (1969): 664–672.

5. John B. Carroll, ed., *Language, Thought and Reality: Selected Writings of Benjamin Lee Whorf*. Cambridge, Mass.: The M.I.T. Press, 1956.

6. E. E. Evans-Pritchard, *The Nuer*. New York: Oxford University Press, 1968, p. 51.

7. T. W. Adorno et al., *The Authoritarian Personality*. New York: Harper & Row, 1950.

8. Samuel A. Stouffer, *Communism, Conformity, and Civil Liberties*. Garden City, N. Y.: Doubleday, 1955.

9. Robert H. Lowie, *Culture and Ethnology.* New York: Basic Books, 1966, p. 66.

10. David Maurer, *Whiz Mob.* New Haven, Conn.: College and University Press, 1964, p. 55.

11. Émile Durkheim, *The Division of Labor in Society.* Trans. by George Simpson. New York: The Free Press, 1964.

SUGGESTED READINGS

Bain, Read. "Our Schizoid Culture." *Sociology and Social Research* 19 (January 1935): 266–276.

An insightful and classic description of American cultural contradictions.

Hall, Edward T. *The Silent Language.* New York: Doubleday, 1973.

A highly readable and diverse analysis of cultural differences and the misunderstandings that can occur among people from different cultures who do not understand the clues of interaction transmitted by nonverbal means.

LaFarge, Oliver. *Laughing Boy.* New York: New American Library, 1971.

A sociological novel about a native American boy caught between two cultural worlds.

Lewis, Oscar. *Five Families: Mexican Case Studies in the Culture of Poverty.* New York: Basic Books, 1975.

A study based on the author's participant observation of five Mexican families. A dramatic and touching study of poor people and their culture.

Maurer, David. *Whiz Mob.* New Haven, Conn.: College and University Press, 1964.

An indepth description of the subculture of professional pickpockets that primarily focuses on their argot and behavior patterns. Interesting and revealing in its depth of analysis.

Montagu, Ashley (ed.). *Culture: Man's Adaptive Dimension.* New York: Oxford University Press, 1968.

A book of readings on a variety of aspects concerning culture, including biology and culture, culture and personality, culture and evolution, and the ways that culture shapes human society.

Turnbull, Colin. *The Mountain People.* New York: Simon & Schuster, 1972.

A dramatic portrayal of cultural disintegration.

Wallace, Anthony. *Culture and Personality.* New York: Random House, 1963.

Presents theories of culture and personality and the relationship between culture and personality. Technical in content, but a concise and readable analysis of culture and personality.

Whyte, William H. *The Organization Man.* New York: Simon & Schuster, 1956.

A description of the work and family life of American men who work for bureaucratic organizations and industries. Demonstrates how modernization has affected contemporary American life and offers an indepth description of many aspects of American culture.

2

Society

everal years ago a fifteen-year-old singer gained almost overnight success when she recorded a song about interracial relationships. In "Society's Child," Janis Ian, a white singer, tells of society's extreme hostility toward the black man she is dating. Because of this reaction she decides that she can no longer maintain the relationship.

Many males have experienced similar negative reactions from society. Although they may want to openly express feelings of loss or sorrow, they believe they must be strong and keep a "stiff upper lip." They fear that any reaction resulting in tears would endanger their masculine image.

These two examples suggest the tremendous impact that society has on our lives. It influences many of our beliefs, attitudes, and behaviors. What is society? In this chapter we will examine what is meant by society, our positions within it, and the groups that comprise any society.

What Is Society?

Very often we confuse the terms *society* and *culture*. When we use the term society we are referring to a particular group of people. On the other hand, when we speak of culture we are referring to the rules, ideas, beliefs, and possessions shared by those people. In the last chapter we discussed culture; we will now focus on society.

According to sociologist Marvin Olsen, societies are the most inclusive, complex, and dominant type of social organization. He defines a society as *"a broadly inclusive social organization* that possesses both functional and cultural autonomy and *that dominates all other types of organization."[1]* We can state more simply that a *society* is a *relatively independent and self-contained group of people that interact with each other within a particular territory and share a distinct culture.*

The main feature of a society that differentiates it from all other forms of social organization is its self-sufficient character. Olsen notes four characteristics of societies that seem to be related to their self-sufficiency. First, almost all social relationships among the society's members occur within the boundaries of the society. Outside relationships, as with persons in foreign countries, are more difficult to maintain and are subject to strict control through passports, immigration laws, visas, and the like. Second, compared to any group, a society is relatively independent. This does not mean that the society satisfies all the needs of its members or provides all the resources required to satisfy these needs. Rather, independence refers to the idea that the society establishes the ways and means for satisfying its members' needs.

46

For example, a society regulates commerce among its regions. Third, the society makes the final decisions for its members, possessing authority over all decisions. Although groups within the society can make decisions, the society may then either support or override these decisions. Hence, the Supreme Court often overrides decisions by lower courts. Fourth, the society is the highest organization to which its members give loyalty. This often involves defending the society against disruptive forces, either external or internal. Thus citizens serve in the Army to protect the society.

As we stated earlier in our definition of society, each society possesses its own distinct and unique culture that is shared by its members. Specific aspects of a society's culture, however, may also be shared with other societies. For example, "American" clothing styles have become popular in much of the world, and vice versa. Yet despite such borrowing, the culture of each society remains unique in its totality. As Olsen states, "the common culture of the total society—and especially its dominant social values and norms—forms a distinctive and unified set of values that is unique to that society."[2]

Even though each society possesses its own unique culture, not all members of the society share this culture equally. As we discussed in Chapter 1, subcultures can flourish, especially in large complex societies. Such subcultures substitute aspects of their own culture for aspects of that of the larger society. For example, although American Indians are American citizens, their style of life can clearly distinguish them from the mainstream of American society.

The Pueblo Indian community of Taos, New Mexico, is a subculture of American society. The Pueblos, although they are citizens of the United States, have retained many aspects of their own culture—aspects such as customs, ceremonies, religious beliefs, style of attire, and language.

Olsen has further defined the concept of society by distinguishing society from *community*. Because of our inability to see beyond our immediate surroundings, many of us mistake our community for the larger social organization we call society. Our communities, however, are smaller than our society, are "closer to home," and are contained within our society. Olsen defines a community as *"a social organization that is territorially localized and through which its members satisfy most of their daily needs and deal with most of their common problems."*[3] Essentially, this definition suggests that a community has two distinctive characteristics. First, most of the experiences individuals have and most of the activities conducted by them take place in the community. Second, the members of the community are bound together by a shared sense of identification. Consequently, we not only live in places called Chicago, Georgia, or the "West Side"; we also identify ourselves as Chicagoans, Georgians, or West Siders. We are not merely part of a community; the community is also a part of us.

Although the term society is somewhat abstract, we note that societies are composed of people. And these people interact in a somewhat predictable manner within what sociologists call the *social structure* or *social organization*.

Social Structure

We can think of society as a structure composed of people who have various statuses with recognized rights and obligations to each other. For example, doctors take care of us when we are ill; butchers supply us with meat; and shoemakers repair our shoes. In this section we will examine the statuses and roles that form the social structure of a society.

STATUSES

A *status* is a position in society. Statuses may be either sequential or concomitant. *Sequential statuses* are those that follow each other. For example, we are first infants, then children, then adolescents, and finally adults. *Concomitant statuses* are those that we occupy at the same time. A teenager, for instance, can be a daughter, a sister, a friend, and a student, all during the same period of her life.

There are two distinctly different kinds of statuses that we all occupy—ascribed statuses and achieved statuses. An *ascribed status* is one into which a person is born and which can rarely be changed throughout life. In every society each member has at least three ascribed statuses: sex, race, and age. In some societies one is also born

One's ascribed status probably has a strong effect on one's achieved status. Until recently, for example, it was difficult for women or blacks to enter certain occupations such as medicine and law enforcement.

into a social class. In fact, there are some sociologists who argue that even in the United States, which is supposed to be the most open society in the world, social class is ascribed (see Chapter 13).

An *achieved status* is one that is chosen or earned. A human being can choose to become a married person, a parent, or a friend. He or she can earn the right to be a doctor or a lawyer. Achieved statuses are those over which people have some control, as opposed to ascribed statuses over which they have little or no control. Nevertheless, some will argue that much of what an individual achieves depends on the ascribed statuses into which that person was born. Most likely, those born into high ascribed statuses will reach high achieved statuses and those born into lower ranking ascribed statuses will reach lower ranking achieved statuses. For example, in our society the female is in a lower ascribed status then the male. Only recently have women been able to consider the possibility of becoming doctors or lawyers. And they may still have difficulty because of their ascribed sex status.

APPLYING SOCIOLOGY

Below are ten statuses. Determine whether each is an ascribed status or an achieved status.

1. Twenty-three-year-old
2. Athlete
3. Computer programmer
4. Boy
5. Elderly person
6. Woman
7. Black person
8. Nurse
9. Club president
10. Priest

ROLES

A *role* is the expected behavioral pattern attached to a status; it has certain specific rights and obligations. For example, the status of college professor requires one to prepare lectures, to attend classes, and to grade students on what they have learned. A professor may deviate slightly from this role—he or she may miss a few classes—but severe deviation will not be tolerated. A professor who cancels classes every day is sure to be disciplined by higher authorities.

The rights and obligations of roles depend on another's acceptance of them. A teacher cannot teach if the students do not exercise their duty (or right) to learn. A person cannot engage in the act of buying if no one fills the role of seller. One cannot fill the role attached to the status of employer without another person filling the role attached to the status of employee. Such corresponding relationships are known as *role reciprocity*.

FOCUS ON: ROLE-PLAYING

Each of us plays many social roles. The performances we give, and how well we manage other people's impressions of ourselves in these roles, are the subject of much conversation and social comparison. In his book *The Presentation of Self in Everday Life*, Erving Goffman discusses the factors that affect a person's performance in a role.

Goffman argues that several distinct elements contribute to a successful performance. Using the comparison between the social role and the theatrical role, he suggests that one element is the creation of a "front." The front consists of "props," "stage," and "scenery." For example, if you imagine a doctor, Goffman suggests that you see such "props" as the white lab coat. You also may envision a large office—"the stage"—with a medical library and medical degrees—"the scenery."

An individual playing a role must also engage in a dramatic presentation of the role. Thus, if a college professor followed up every question you asked with the statement, "I'll look it up," he or she would be damaging the dramatic impact of the role. Similarly, if two referees in a professional basketball game made opposite calls on the same play, they too would lessen the dramatic impact of the role.

Performers in a given role also try to control anything physically expressive about themselves. Any inappropriate gesture, word, or movement could damage one's credibility. Consider, for example, the public speaker who takes a step and disappears from the speaker's platform. This is difficult to handle gracefully and it is very hard to recover from such mistakes.

What do you think makes a person convincing in a role? What are some of the things that might flaw or disrupt a person's performance? Have you ever seen an audience challenge a performer's presentation and make the person forget part of the role? Are there any people who make a living teaching others aspects of successful performances?

Source: Erving Goffman, *The Presentation of Self in Everyday Life*, New York: Doubleday, 1959.

Often we find ourselves filling several roles that are compatible. In our society, for example, the roles attached to the statuses of father and worker are generally compatible. Sometimes, however, we fill roles that conflict with each other. Sociologists use the term *role conflict* to describe the condition that develops when an individual is expected to fill two roles at the same time that are inconsistent or incompatible. Thus, women in our society often find it difficult to fill simultaneously the roles attached to the statuses of mother and worker.

Frequently we are criticized for not filling our roles appropriately. For instance, students can be flunked out of school (in effect, have the status of student taken away from them) for poor academic performance. A father can be imprisoned for failing to support his children. But since most people dislike social disapproval, they behave according to the ways society demands.

In the process of playing roles, individuals interact with other individuals in different ways. Sometimes this interaction is casual, such as when we pass people on the street. Sometimes, however, we interact with others and share a common purpose or goal. In these cases we form social groups. These groups shape and influence our lives to a large degree, affecting our values, attitudes, and behavior.

What Is a Social Group?

A *social group* is a set of people who have a common identity, a sense of unity, and at least some common goals and shared norms. Implied in this statement is that these people are aware of being part of their particular group. For example, the individuals who organized to ban the SST from landing at Kennedy Airport in New York were a group. They were consciously working together toward a common goal. This contrasts with those individuals who might have been waiting for a flight to land. Such individuals might have had a common goal—to meet their friends and families—but they were not organized and shared no sense of unity. These individuals formed an *aggregate*, which is simply a gathering of people in physical proximity who are unorganized and without a sense of "we-ness" toward a common goal.

It is sometimes possible for an aggregate to become a group. If those waiting for the flight in the above example were told that the plane had been hijacked, chances are they would then have become a group. They would have been conscious of their common predicament and would have all begun working toward a common goal—getting their loved ones back safely. In the process they might have comforted each other, looked out for the well-being of one another, and tried to make the waiting as painless as possible. In short, they would have

FOCUS ON: THE AMISH

Within American society we find many subcultures, one being the Old Order Amish. In his book *Extraordinary Groups*, William Kephart discusses these people.

In certain respects, the Amish, like other groups in our society, share in the beliefs and ideas of the larger society. For example, they attach a great value to work and have a very thorough concern for the system of free enterprise.

Yet, the Amish are distinct in almost every imaginable way regarding their life-style. Religion is organized only in the context of home and family so that there are no churches or professional clergy requiring financial support. The Amish have rejected all sophisticated forms of technology, such as cars, appliances, and farm equipment. Since they are an agricultural group, their use of animal power rather than machinery makes work much more difficult.

The Amish are referred to as the "Plain Folk" because they dress in conservative black or other simple colors and use no decorative ornamentation. For example, sunglasses and wedding rings are forbidden objects. The most astonishing fact about the Amish, however, is that their style of dress has not changed over the past 250 years.

While the Amish are geographically spread across large portions of the Eastern and Midwestern United States, they remain isolated in their agricultural communities. Their isolation, combined with their distinctive appearance, creates tremendous group cohesion. This enables them to develop a sense of commitment to the group. There are frequent opportunities to reinforce this commitment. One such way is through formal schooling, which the Amish have struggled to keep under their own control. Second, the Amish have a series of sanctions, which range from gossip and ridicule to banishment and shunning. The latter sanction, which is removal from the group, is used only in extreme cases, as when group members buy an automobile.

As in all groups, all major life activities and events, such as marriage and courtship, are governed by group norms. Among the Amish, however, behavior is watched extremely closely by the group. In fact, every young girl has an identical hair style. The Old Order Amish display the great durability as well as rigidity of a social group based on "primary group" principles of organization.

Why do you think the Amish try to keep "new" objects out of their group? How would the Amish deal with outsiders? Do you know of any groups as distinctive as the Amish? How do you think Americans regard such groups as the Amish? Do you think that the Amish can continue to resist assimilation into American society?

Source: William M. Kephart, *Extraordinary Groups,* New York: St. Martin's Press, 1977.

A group need not disband when its membership changes. For example, although its individual members are different today than they were a century ago, the Democratic Party continues to be a major political influence in the United States.

been transformed from a simple gathering of people in close proximity into a social group, conscious of their common goal. As soon as this goal was achieved, they would once again have become an aggregate.

Many groups, however, remain intact even when their membership shifts. For example, the Democratic and Republican parties were both formed over a century ago by a number of individuals who joined together to achieve a common goal. Although the founding members died long ago, these political parties still remain. Thus, even though groups are composed of individuals, the group does not necessarily cease simply because the composition of its membership changes over time.

Sociologist Emile Durkheim (see pages 248–249) recognized this independent quality of groups when he noted that the group is an abstraction greater than the sum of its parts. Durkheim said a group is *sui generis*, meaning it is a thing in and of itself. This "thing," in turn, becomes a force that shapes the lives of the individuals within it.[4]

53

THE IMPORTANCE OF THE GROUP

Frequently we are not aware of social groups or the influence they have on our individual lives. Yet they are important to us as human beings. Indeed, the essence of human life is that it is *social*—it is lived in the company of others. Sociologists use the word *social* in a special way—to describe two or more people engaged in action, reaction, and interaction.

Without the group no individual person could survive physically for very long. It takes many years for human beings to mature to the point where they are no longer physically dependent on others. But even though they may achieve physical independence, they can never achieve total emotional independence. Thus, the group is essential for both the physical and emotional well-being of the individual.

It is the group, too, that creates and transmits culture to the individual. (See Chapter 1 for a complete discussion of culture.) It is through the group and because of it, then, that the individual person becomes transformed into a human being. None of us could have become human had we not been born into and reared by a group of similar beings.

For these reasons alone, the groups in which we live have a profound influence on our lives. But this is not all that is significant about the fact that human life is a social form of life. Besides providing for the individual's physical and emotional well-being, acting as the source for the creation and transmission of culture and, thus, being the source for our humanness, groups also impart to the individual a sense of belonging and, therefore, of identity. In addition, it is the person's location in the structure of a particular group that in large part determines his or her pattern of interaction with other members. And it is the person's membership in various groups that provides that person with an identity as an individual. Without groups, in short, we not only could not exist physically, we could not become the kind of persons we are.

FACTORS THAT INFLUENCE GROUPS

Although all groups have certain common characteristics that allow them to be classified as groups, groups still differ in a number of ways. For example, we can easily note differences between two lovers holding hands in the moonlight, a political rally of three hundred people, and a family gathered around the dinner table. These differences have important consequences for a group's behavior and for the impact a group has on its membership. Of the rather large number of possible differences among groups, the ones listed below are generally thought by sociologists to be the most important.

**TABLE 2-1
Relationship Between
Group Size and
Number of Potential
Relationships of Its
Members**

Size of Group	Number of Relationships
2	1
3	6
4	25
5	90
6	301
7	966

Source: A. Paul Hare, *Handbook of Small Group Research*, Glencoe, Ill.: The Free Press, 1962, p. 229.

Size

From the above example we can see that groups can range in size from very small groups consisting of two persons to very large groups having hundreds of members. And the size of the group affects the interaction, both in number of relationships and in content, between group members. As the size of a group increases arithmetically, the number of possible channels of interaction and relationships among group members increases geometrically (see Table 2-1). However, increasing group size has an opposite effect on the demands any one person can place on any of the members of the group. As the group increases in size, the demands placed by any one member on the other members decrease. Thus, a two-person group or *dyad* differs substantially from a university. In the dyad there can be only one relationship, and all demands by one member are directed toward the other member and vice versa. In the university there can be thousands of relationships and demands are divided among various members.

Types of Group Goals

Almost all group goals may be defined as either task or effectual. A basketball team is oriented toward winning the game. This goal is a

---

APPLYING SOCIOLOGY

Cities are generally described as cold, hostile places where nobody cares about anybody else. In contrast, small towns and rural areas are thought of as warm, friendly places. Considering the differences in population size and the tendency for people to restrict their interactions with strangers, how can we explain the differences in the way people often perceive city life compared to rural life? Can size alone account for differences in the behavior of urban and rural people? If not, what other factors might be important?

This basketball team has a specific, easily defined group goal—winning the game. Such *task* goals are distinguished from less clearly defined *effectual* goals.

task goal since it is highly specific and easily definable. In order to win and accomplish this goal the team must score more points than its opponent. On the other hand, the Spring City Cultural Club is oriented toward an *effectual goal* of providing entertainment for its members. This can consist of providing music or contests. The goal itself is not clearly definable.

Groups differ considerably in their goals and how clearly these goals are perceived by each group's members. Sometimes a group may have several different goals, some of which may clash. If one is accomplished, another may be denied or violated. In families, for example, parents may want to protect their children from physical harm. But in order to accomplish this goal, they often find themselves in the position of inflicting physical harm. Similarly, the police have two major goals—law enforcement and maintaining public order.[5] According to the law, people have certain individual rights, and it is the job of the police to see that these rights are protected. But the police must also maintain public order. In doing so they may violate the very rights they are supposed to protect. For example, at a civil rights rally, in order to maintain public order, the police may be forced to violate the rights of the demonstrators. Thus, one goal may be enforced at the expense of the other.

Bases of Group Membership

Although all groups have some criteria for membership, these criteria differ among groups. Some groups are very exclusive and select their members carefully. For example, the Sun City Country Club chooses its members from among certain social strata. In contrast, some groups are open to just about anyone. If coffee prices become too high, then all consumers can join together as a group in boycotting it. Such was the case with the coffee boycott that took place in 1977.

The criteria a group uses to determine its membership indirectly influence our lives by regulating our social contacts. If all members of the Sun City Country Club belong to the upper class, their interrelationships at this club will be limited to people like themselves. Also, these criteria help to differentiate groups into various types. Some groups, like the country club, are homogenous. In other words, its members resemble each other racially, socially, economically, and often politically. Other groups, like those boycotting coffee, consist of people from various social and economic strata. Still other groups have members that resemble each other in some ways and differ from each other in other ways. Delegates to a political convention may vary considerably in their social and economic status, but all must be members of the same political party.

Duration of Membership

Individuals tend to be members of groups for various lengths of time. In some groups, membership is set and not expected to last for long. People are drafted into the Army for a designated period of time. Students join school clubs until they graduate. In other groups, membership is expected to last for life, or at least for a good portion of it. Once people are born into a family, for instance, they remain members of the family for life.

Duration of the Group

Groups differ considerably in the length of time they last as entities. Some groups are formed only to perform a specific task; they disperse once that task has been accomplished. A jury in a trial, for instance, ceases to exist as a group once it has been discharged from duty.

Groups that are formed to perform a specific task usually disperse once that task has been accomplished. Chances are that this group, which supports the passage of the Equal Rights Amendment to the Constitution, will disperse when the amendment is passed.

Other groups last throughout the life span of the members. The partners in a business may remain associated for many years. Friends sometimes retain close relationships throughout life. Still other groups are more or less permanent. Our two houses of Congress have lasted for almost two centuries.

A group's duration can have a good deal to do with its behavior. Long-term groups tend to be oriented toward the continued maintenance of the group as an ongoing entity, a political party being a good example. Short-term groups are generally more oriented to specific tasks or to an immediate goal. But often the life of a short-term group can be extended beyond the immediate task by changing the goals of the group to new ones. The March of Dimes, for example, no longer provides funds to fight polio. Following the development of the polio vaccine, it changed its activities and now supports research to cure birth defects.

Degree of Internal Differentiation

Patterns of interaction among people in groups can vary greatly from one group to another. In some groups everyone may be nearly equal in rank, power, or authority and may interact on an equal footing (although total equality is practically unknown for any group). Such an equal footing is typical of friendship groups, but it also exists to a considerable extent in other types of organizations. Groups in which people are equal tend to be small in size. Two business partners, for example, tend to see each other as relatively equal. In other groups, there is a clear hierarchy of members, each of whom has specific rights and duties and levels of authority. An army is one of the clearest examples of an unequal group.

Degree of Group Cohesion

How much solidarity or unity exists among members of a group? Although all groups must have some degree of solidarity, this amount differs among groups. Some groups, such as a coalition government that unites only to defeat a common enemy, might dissolve given the slightest provocation. Other groups, such as a couple who are deeply in love, are almost impossible to break up. The degree of group cohesion depends on the size of the group, the goals of the group, and the feasibility of attaining those goals.

Patterns of Interaction Within the Group

In one kind of group certain members interact in one way with some people and in a different way with others. Husbands and wives interact differently with each other than they do with their children.

APPLYING SOCIOLOGY

The following diagrams are called sociograms. Sociologists use sociograms to investigate the interaction patterns and relationships among members of a group. Which group appears to engage in the most interaction and maintain the greatest number of relationships— Group A or Group B? Based on material in this chapter thus far, what conclusions might you draw about each group?

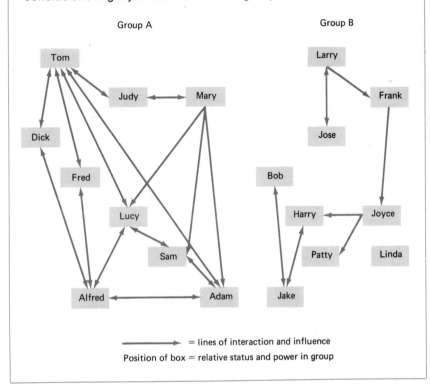

Group A   Group B

```
———————————▶  = lines of interaction and influence
Position of box = relative status and power in group
```

Workers on an assembly line must merely coordinate their actions, but their relationship with the supervisor takes on a different quality. What the interaction patterns are and what the quality of interaction might be among members of a group vary considerably from group to group and even within groups of a similar kind.

Kinds of Groups

On the bases of the factors listed above, sociologists have devised a number of ways in which to categorize groups. Let us now examine several of these categories.

Charles Horton Cooley (1864–1929)

Charles Horton Cooley made two major contributions to sociology. One is the concept of the *primary group;* the second is the concept of the *looking-glass self.*

Primary groups are small, intimate, sharing groups whose members interact very often and believe in a principle of open and complete concern for each other. Members of the primary group associate with each other as whole persons. Families, play groups, and very small communities are examples of primary groups. Cooley argued that membership in such groups was the essential link between the individual and society. It is these links that create the cooperation that characterizes society.

Although Cooley did not use the term *secondary group,* this term has been used to distinguish larger, less intimate groups from those that are primary. Secondary groups are usually formal groups where specific roles are required of members and where their total personalities may not be brought into play. In such groups, goals are more specific and organization more structured than in primary groups.

Cooley's second contribution—the looking-glass self—is related to how people develop their sense of "self." Cooley believed that people develop a sense of self through their impressions of others' attitudes about them. He likened this development to the experience of using a looking glass—the sense of self includes the reflection of others' opinions.

In addition to developing these ideas, Cooley emphasized that it is only in the context of sharing ideas of self and others within the primary group that the individual matures.

PRIMARY AND SECONDARY RELATIONSHIPS

One of the most basic differences between groups is the degree of intimacy members feel toward one another. In this regard, groups may be divided into two types: personal (primary) and impersonal (secondary) groups.

Primary Groups

The elemental form of social relationship is typically found in the family and *peer group*—the intimate, direct, immediate contact one has with a loved one or friend. This relationship is called a "primary" relationship and the groups in which it is found are called *primary groups.* The person who first formulated the primary group concept, noted American sociologist Charles Horton Cooley (see box above), described it as follows:

> By primary groups I mean those characterized by intimate face-to-face association and cooperation. They are primary in several senses, but chiefly in that they are fundamental in forming the social nature and

60

ideals of the individual. The result of intimate association, psychologically, is a certain fusion of individualities in a common whole, so that one's very self, for many purposes at least, is the common life and purpose of the group. Perhaps the simplest way of describing this wholeness is by saying that it is a "we"; it involves the sort of sympathy and mutual identification for which "we" is the natural expression.[6]

It would be hard indeed for us to live without at least one primary relationship. The degree of loneliness to which we would be subjected would be intolerable, for it is the primary group that gives us our intimate sense of self, affection, and human importance. Within the primary group, members recognize that all their actions are important to other members of the group. Each member cares about the others in all ways. If our primary relationships are unsatisfactory, we generally feel frustrated and sad. And if we should lose a member of a primary group, we would probably experience a sense of irreplaceable loss. Thus, it is in the primary group that we cease to be simply student A in row 1 seat 3, a plumber, an accountant for ABC Accounts, Inc., or a Republican candidate. We become Lynn, Sue, Emilio, or Jason. We become "my friend," "my brother," "my wife." We become, in short, someone who counts for his or her own sake.

Primary groups and secondary groups differ in the degree of intimacy and commitment found among their members.

APPLYING SOCIOLOGY

In terms of the characteristics of groups listed in the text, compare the features of one primary group with those of one secondary group of which you are a member. What similarities and differences do you note? What factors seem to be associated with personal and impersonal relationships?

Secondary Groups

In addition to being members of primary groups, people are also members of *secondary groups*.* These are groups in which there is less intimacy and personal interaction than in primary groups. Secondary groups may still involve face-to-face interaction on a daily basis, but they do not demand the same commitment of self that is characteristic of primary groups. We are concerned merely with that aspect of the other person with which we are involved. In a seminar, for example, students are only concerned about learning a particular subject. Hence, they interact with each other in a more formalized manner and commit only a very limited part of their lives to that interaction. In secondary groups people are more concerned with accomplishing a particular task than with any intimacy.

Within secondary groups it is also possible for primary groups to form. In the seminar we just mentioned, two students can develop an intimate friendship. The focus of their interaction would then be broadened to include their entire selves.

IN-GROUPS AND OUT-GROUPS

Sociologist William Graham Sumner devised another way in which groups might be categorized. He divided them into two types—in-groups and out-groups.[7]

In-Groups

An in-group can be defined as that circle of people to which the individual feels he or she belongs. In other words, an in-group can be described in terms of what sociologist Franklin H. Giddings called the "consciousness of kind" felt by the group's members. In-groups convey a notion of "we"—a sense of unity. Although in-group members most often know each other, an in-group feeling may also emerge between

*While Cooley used the term primary group, he never used the term secondary group.

persons who have never met. For example, people who went to the same school, even during different times, share some common characteristic or background experience yielding this sense of togetherness.

Out-Groups

By recognizing and labeling one group as "we," we also call attention to another group of "they" or "those others." This other group is called an *out-group* and can be defined as that circle of people to which the individual feels no sense of belonging. Persons not in our circle of in-group members are considered outsiders, strangers, and a variety of other "thems" to whom we feel little if any allegiance or sense of belonging. At times we even feel hostility toward these people. If we are rich, then "they" consist of the poor. The poor, in turn, regard the rich as an out-group. All persons whom we feel to be different from ourselves in various ways comprise our out-groups.

Whatever the reason for dividing ourselves into "camps" of *we* and *they,* it is likely that by so doing we restrict our relationships and interaction with other human beings. In this regard, the more inclusive our in-group definitions and the less numerous the number of out-groups we create, the more extensive our network of relationships and the broader our spectrum of contacts with others will be.

FORMAL AND INFORMAL ORGANIZATIONS

A third way of classifying groups is based on their structure and ranking of members. When examining groups with this in mind we note that groups can be very formal, very informal, or in between.

Formal Organizations

At one extreme we have a *formal organization* or *bureaucracy,*[8] which can be defined as a highly organized hierarchical group with explicit objectives, rules and regulations, and specifically defined roles with clear rights and obligations. Since the turn of the century one of the most striking features about the Western world has been the growth of such organizations. In fact, hardly anyone today can escape dealing with such groups, and most people will find themselves working for one at some point in their lives.

Bureaucracies are frequently categorized as being highly impersonal and requiring one to go through miles of red tape in order to get anything accomplished. Hence, being associated with or required to deal with a large-scale bureaucracy—the electric company, a government agency, a large corporation, the school system—can be trying at times. Many times we even give up in disgust, believing we will never see the light at the end of the tunnel. Nevertheless, we can appreciate the formal operations of these groups if we try to imagine what life in mass society would be like if all relationships were personal and everything was handled informally. It would be almost impossible to hire individual tutors for the millions of children who must be educated each year, nor could these tutors provide the wealth of information that each child now receives from several teachers. Simply getting the bread on the table for over 200 million people takes more than the baker and local store. Thus, bureaucracies are necessary, although we must sacrifice something when dealing with them. We may lose our sense of intimacy and self by being processed through a seemingly endless maze; we may lose our sense of importance by being restricted to performing certain specific tasks in the organization's division of labor; and we may expend much time and energy accomplishing our goals.

Informal Organizations

At the other extreme, we have informal organizations. It is doubtful if any large-scale organization could function were it not for the informal friendship cliques that seem somehow to emerge within them. Sometimes these cliques add to the efficiency of the organization and sometimes they impede its functioning. But it appears that within any formal group, informal relationships ultimately emerge. We will use a typical sociology department to illustrate this point.

According to our definition of bureaucracy, a typical department of sociology can be classified as such. It is a highly organized hierarchical group—full professors, associate professors, assistant professors, instructors, and teaching assistants—with the goal of discovering and disseminating sociological knowledge. Each member has a particular role to play and specific rules provide guidelines for playing that role. For example, a teaching assistant cannot issue orders to a full professor. Yet within such a department several members may become friends, independent of their positions within the bureaucracy. A teaching assistant and a full professor may eat lunch together or socialize after work. They will interact on a personal level rather than within their limited roles imposed by the bureaucracy.

Such an informal group can either contribute toward or work against the efficiency of the department. Teaching assistants, for example, might combine forces to protest their teaching schedules, thus undermining the department's routine. On the other hand, the teaching assistants as a group may offer suggestions that would improve the department's efficiency.

All groups, whatever their size or category, exhibit certain patterns of behavior as members interact with each other. Some of these patterns are described in the following section.

64

Group Interaction Patterns

There are several basic and universal interaction patterns that typically occur among and within groups of all types. The more important of these patterns are exchange and cooperation, competition and conflict, and accommodation and assimilation.[9]

EXCHANGE AND COOPERATION

Exchange is one of the most basic forms of social interaction. It occurs when one individual or group trades off one service or commodity for another of equal value. In the Trobriand Islands, for example, the hill people plant and gather fruit so that they can obtain fish from the sea people.[10] *Cooperation* occurs when individuals or groups band together and pool their resources, talents, and efforts to achieve some common goal. Team members band together to win a game.

Exchange is often accomplished through interrelated acts of cooperation. In essence, then, cooperation is the principal glue of society. Without some degree of cooperation, no group or individual could realize its goals or satisfy its wants. As isolated individuals we are singularly vulnerable, but through mutual dependence, unity, and cooperation we gain increased strength.

COMPETITION AND CONFLICT

The world would be a harmonious place if cooperation and exchange were the only forms of social interaction. However, other forms of interaction also occur, and they are just as essential to a group's existence and its successful interaction with other groups (although in a different way). One such form is *competition*, which can be defined as a form of social interaction in which two or more individuals or groups strive toward a goal that only one can attain.

Competition occurs just as frequently as exchange and cooperation and serves several functions for groups. For one thing, competition may actually be the basis for group interaction. In our society, for example, football games would not be much fun if there were no winners and losers. Competition also serves to heighten individual effort, something that is often necessary if either the group or the person is to achieve goals or satisfy needs.

Frequently competition and cooperation can exist alongside each other. In a football game, team members are cooperating with each other, but at the same time each team member wants to achieve recognition, high status, and prestige. In not all societies, however, do individuals value competition. Among the Hopi Indians, for example, the

Cooperation, a basic form of social interaction in which people band together to achieve a common goal, can help us satisfy such human needs as keeping warm.

In the presidential election of 1976, incumbent Gerald Ford *(right)* and challenger Jimmy Carter engaged in competition as they strove for a goal only one of them could attain —the presidency of the United States.

goal of a race was not to win, for winning might hurt the other's feelings. The sport was in the running of the race.

Competition, like exchange and cooperation, is governed by rules regulating the behavior of group members. Sometimes, however, these rules may be breached and the interaction may be transformed into open and often harmful *conflict*. The goal of the conflict becomes the destruction, elimination, or control of the opponent. This contrasts with competition, in which competitors try to win out over each other without destroying each other. Conflicts can range in scope from a lovers' quarrel to a nuclear war.

Typically, conflict is thought of as destructive and as something to be avoided. We can see that this view has some merit. It has taken years for people to forgive if not forget the antagonisms generated between the North and the South both before and after the American Civil War. Similarly, conflict has caused many marriages to end in divorce. And wars between nations are surely "unhealthy for children and other living things," as is a street brawl between delinquent gangs, which often leads to injury and sometimes to death.

But conflict can also be viewed positively.[11] As with competition, conflict among various groups may serve to unite the members of each of these groups into a stronger entity. By having an enemy "out there" threatening the group as a whole, the members of the group have a common cause for banding together. There is rarely more harmony within a group than when that group is at war with another group.

In addition, conflict can lead to innovation and change; it can heighten awareness of injustice and revitalize the norms of the group. For example, many advances in medicine and changes in the structure of government resulted from World War II. The conflict generated by the black civil rights movement led to many positive changes in universities and in business organizations.

ACCOMMODATION AND ASSIMILATION

Conflict is frequently resolved when opposing groups agree to *accommodation*, a process by which they agree to cease hostile activity and work toward peaceful coexistence. A variety of techniques, such as compromise, outside intervention, or mediation. may be used to achieve accommodation.

It must be noted, however, that accommodation is a temporary working agreement. It is based solely on each group's need to work with the other. Each group therefore retains its own views and goals but puts them aside during the accommodation process. In this manner, the Egyptians and Israelis began peace talks. Essentially, then, accommodation is a form of interaction based on mutual give-and-take that makes exchange possible.

Accommodation can produce *assimilation*, a process by which a minority group merges its identity with the majority. Throughout

The 1978 peace talks between Israel's Prime Minister Menachem Begin and Egypt's President Anwar Sadat were attempts at accommodation—a temporary cessation of hostilities to work toward peaceful coexistence.

American history there have been numerous instances of assimilation. One such instance involves the immigrant groups who came to the United States. Gradually these groups learned to speak English, wear American-style clothing, and adopt American habits and customs. In short, they became part of the larger society.

As conflict may destroy the unity of a group, the process of assimilation is a form of interaction wherein persons are absorbed into the group. This process not only applies to the interaction among groups, but it also occurs in the interaction between the individual and the group. Thus, assimilation occurs when an individual becomes a member of a team.

All of these patterns form the basis of group interaction. And without such interaction society would be unable to exist.

SUMMARY

A *society* is a relatively self-contained group of people that interact with each other within a particular territory and share a distinct culture. Societies are the most complex type of social organization and influence many of its members' beliefs, attitudes, and behaviors.

Within societies there are certain positions with recognized rights and obligations. A *status* is a position in society. Statuses can be *sequential*—following each other—or *concomitant*—occurring at the same time. Two distinctly different kinds of statuses are ascribed statuses and achieved statuses. An *ascribed status* is one into which we are born, whereas an *achieved status* is one that is earned or chosen.

A *role* is the expected behavioral pattern attached to a status. It has certain specific rights and obligations that depend on others' acceptance of them. A teacher, for example, cannot teach if students do not exercise their duty (or right) to learn. Such a relationship is known as *role reciprocity*. Often we fill several roles that are compatible. Sometimes, however, we fill roles that clash. In such cases *role conflict* occurs. .

In the process of filling our roles we interact with other individuals. Sometimes we form a *social group*, which is a set of people who have a common identity, a sense of unity, and at least some common goals and shared norms. This contrasts with an *aggregate*, which is simply a gathering of people in physical proximity who are unorganized and without a sense of "we-ness."

Groups are important for several reasons. No individual could survive for very long without the group. In addition, the group creates and transmits culture to the individual. The group also gives the individual a sense of identity. Finally, a person's location in the structure of the group determines his or her pattern of interaction with other members.

Although all groups have certain factors in common that allow them to be classified as groups, they differ in a number of ways. The factors that influence groups include size, types of group goals, bases of group membership, duration of membership, duration of the group, degree of internal differentiation, degree of group cohesion, and patterns of interaction within the group.

On the basis of these factors, sociologists have devised a number of ways in which to categorize groups. *Primary groups* and *secondary groups* are classified by the degree of intimacy members feel toward each other. *In-groups* and *out-groups* are categorized by the degree of belonging an individual feels toward the group. *Formal* and *informal organizations,* are determined by the structure of the group and the ranking of its members.

There are several different interactional patterns that typically occur among and within groups of all types. These are *exchange* and *cooperation, competition* and *conflict,* and *accommodation* and *assimilation.* No society can survive without such interactional patterns.

GLOSSARY

accommodation   a form of social interaction between two or more opposing individuals or groups who agree to cease hostility and engage in peaceful coexistence.

achieved status   a position in society that one chooses or earns.

aggregate   a gathering of people in close proximity who are unorganized and without a sense of "we-ness."

ascribed status   a position in society into which one is born and which can rarely be altered.

assimilation   a form of social interaction in which different individuals or groups are merged into one entity.

bureaucracy   a highly organized hierarchical group with explicit objectives, rules and regulations, and specifically defined roles with clear rights and obligations.

community   a localized social organization through which members satisfy most of their needs and deal with most of their common problems.

competition   a form of social interaction in which two or more individuals or groups strive toward a goal that only one can attain. The individuals or groups strive to outdo each other without destroying or eliminating each other.

concomitant statuses   positions in society that are held at the same time.

69

conflict a form of social interaction in which two or more individuals or groups strive toward a goal that only one can attain. The individuals or groups strive to destroy, eliminate, or gain control of the opponent.

cooperation a form of social interaction that occurs when individuals band together and pool their resources, talents, and efforts to achieve some common goal.

dyad a two-person group.

effectual goal a group goal that is vague and not easily definable.

exchange a form of social interaction that occurs when one group trades off one service or commodity for another of equal value.

formal organization a bureaucracy.

informal organization a social group formed within a bureaucracy which is not officially recognized but which may enhance or detract from the organization's functioning.

in-group that circle of people to which an individual feels he or she belongs.

out-group that circle of people to which an individual feels no sense of belonging.

peer group members of a group who are equals, usually in terms of age, education, and social class.

primary group a small group in which the members know and interact with each other as individuals in an intimate relationship.

role the expected behavioral pattern attached to a status, carrying specific rights and obligations.

role conflict a condition that develops when an individual is expected to perform two roles at the same time that are inconsistent or incompatible.

role reciprocity the mutual acceptance and communication by at least two individuals according to their expected behavioral patterns.

secondary group a group in which relationships and interaction are impersonal and geared toward accomplishing a particular task.

sequential statuses positions in society that follow each other.

social group a set of people who have a common identity, a sense of unity, and at least some common goals and shared norms.

social structure the social organization of a society consisting of people in various roles and statuses with recognized rights and obligations.

society a relatively independent and self-contained group of people that interact with each other within a particular territory and share a distinct culture.

status a position in society.

task goal a group goal that is highly specific and easily definable.

REFERENCES

1. Marvin E. Olsen, *The Process of Social Organization.* New York: Holt, Rinehart & Winston, 1968, p. 96.

2. Olsen, p. 96.

3. Olsen, p. 91.

4. Émile Durkheim, *The Rules of Sociological Method*. 8th ed. Trans. by Sarah A. Solovay and John H. Mueller and edited by George E. G. Catlin. New York: The Free Press, 1950.

5. Egon Bittner, "The Police on Skid Row: A Study of Peace Keeping." *American Sociological Review* 32 (October 1967): 699–715. Jerome Skolnick, *Justice Without Trial*. New York: John Wiley & Sons, 1966.

6. Charles Horton Cooley, *Social Organization*. New York: Charles Scribner's Sons, 1966.

7. William Graham Sumner, *Folkways*. Boston: Ginn, 1906.

8. The classic work on bureaucracy is Max Weber, *The Theory of Social and Economic Organization*. Trans. by A. M. Henderson and Talcott Parsons. New York: The Free Press, 1947.

9. Olsen, pp. 117–171.

10. Bronislaw Malinowski, "The Primitive Economics of the Trobriand Islanders." In Thomas G. Harding and Ben J. Wallace, eds., *Cultures of the Pacific*. New York: The Free Press, 1950, pp. 51–62.

11. Lewis A. Coser, *The Functions of Social Conflict*. Glencoe, Ill.: The Free Press, 1956.

SUGGESTED READINGS

Bales, Robert F. *Interaction Process Analysis: A Method for the Study of Small Groups*. Reading, Mass.: Addison-Wesley, 1950.

A description of a method for examining social interaction within small groups. It provides a scientific approach for analyzing small group dynamics.

Cartwright, Dorwin, and Alvin Zander, (eds.). *Group Dynamics: Research and Theory*. 2nd ed. New York: Harper & Row, 1960.

A book of readings dealing with research and theory on group behavior. It offers readings on a variety of group processes.

Coser, Lewis A. *The Functions of Social Conflict*. Glencoe, Ill.: The Free Press, 1956.

An in-depth analysis of conflict in groups and the various functions it provides for promoting change in groups.

Durkheim, Émile. *The Rules of Sociological Method*. 8th ed. Trans. by Sarah A. Solovay and John H. Mueller and edited by George E. G. Catlin. New York: The Free Press, 1950.

The classic sociological statement as to the "reality" of the group.

Etzioni, Amitai. *Modern Organizations*. Englewood Cliffs, N.J.: Prentice-Hall, 1964.

A brief study of modern organizations, both formal and informal, and the forces that shape behavior within them.

Goffman, Erving. *Relationships in Public.* New York: Basic Books, 1971.

A readable and integrated analysis of the relationship between the person and society, especially concerning private behavior in public places.

Greer, Scott. *Social Organization.* New York: Random House, 1955.

An early analysis that emphasizes the interrelationships between group structure and the dynamic processes of groups.

Kesey, Ken. *One Flew Over the Cuckoo's Nest.* New York: Viking Press, 1962.

A powerful illustration of group interaction and social control in a bureaucratic organization.

Lenski, Gerhard. *Human Societies.* New York: McGraw-Hill, 1970.

A highly readable analysis of various types of societies and the differences among them.

Linton, Ralph. *The Study of Man.* New York: Appleton-Century-Crofts, 1936.

A classic work that offers many still relevant insights into the basic character and features of groups and societies.

Olsen, Marvin E. *The Process of Social Organization.* New York: Holt, Rinehart & Winston, 1968.

A detailed analysis of the nature of social organization and the process of groups. It offers a concise distinction between forms of social organization.

3

Social and Cultural Change

With the words, "That's one small step for man, one giant leap for mankind," astronaut Neil A. Armstrong announced that the seemingly impossible had been accomplished. The United States had placed human beings on the moon.

Although this event was indeed "one giant leap for mankind," it was only one of many changes that has occurred since civilization began. If we trace our existence from the first band of human beings that crossed the land bridge between Asia and the Americas approximately 40,000 years ago, we can note the extent of these changes. America has evolved from a society of preliterate hunter-gatherers who neither cultivated the soil nor built permanent dwellings to one of the most economically and technologically advanced cultures in the world.

In this chapter we will explore how and why change occurs. In doing so, we will see the patterns of change over the millenia, and we will try to see what present trends suggest for the future of human society.

Forms and Characteristics of Change[1]

When we think of different changes that have occurred, we note that change can take several forms. Change can be so minute, or may occur so slowly, that we may not even notice any changes in the social structure or the culture of a group. For example, if we examine a document from colonial days, we may not be able to understand all of the language. Yet our language has not undergone any radical transformation; rather it has gradually evolved since that time. In contrast, change can totally transform a group's way of life. The invention of the automobile, for example, has had a tremendous impact on our society. Some changes are abrupt, such as President Lincoln's freeing of the slaves. Others are continuous, such as the steady increase in the average income earned by American families.

Change can have *manifest consequences*—that is, those that are intended and recognized—or it can have *latent consequences*—those that are unintended and unrecognized. For example, modern medical technology has deliberately extended our life expectancy by several years but unintentionally caused problems related to old age. Another example involves the attempt to eliminate the importation of marijuana over the Mexican border. This has the manifest intent of reducing drug use and the latent effect of damaging relationships with Mexico and increasing the price of marijuana so that it becomes more attractive to organized crime. No matter what the change, though, it has some effect on the group.

74

Change need not be abrupt; it can be a gradual process. For example, although women demonstrated over a half century ago to win the right to vote *(top)*, in the 1970s, women are still marching for equal rights *(bottom)*. Among the demonstrators shown in the bottom photo are Isola Dodic *(third from left),* who walked in a 1913 march, and former member of Congress Bella Abzug *(fourth from left).*

SOCIAL VERSUS CULTURAL CHANGE

Change in a group can occur in either its social structure or its culture. Sociologists use the term *social change* to describe those alterations that take place in the structure of a group or in the relationships among its members. Social change can include a variety of things, such

Cultural change can take place in any aspect of a culture. For example, note the differences between this small turn-of-the-century country store *(left)* and this modern supermarket in Mexico City *(right)*.

as a shift in the power distribution between workers and managers after a labor union has been formed, an increase in the educational level of the population, or a shift from an extended family form to a nuclear family form (see Chapter 6).

The term *cultural change* describes alterations in the culture of a group. This kind of change can take place in any aspect of a culture. The introduction of a new word into the vocabulary, the invention of the airplane, and the development of the supermarket are all instances of cultural change.

Theoretically, changes in the social sphere can occur independently of changes in the cultural sphere, and vice versa. In practice, however, any significant change in one has implications for the other. For example, when the assembly line was adapted for large-scale use in manufacturing, the social relationships between workers and employers, and even among the workers themselves, became quite different from what they had been in the old system of manufacturing.

CULTURAL LAG

Although change can occur in a group's social or cultural sphere, very often the change is not put into effect immediately. Sociologist William Ogburn coined the term *cultural lag* to denote that period between the time a change is introduced into a group and the time the group adapts to that change.[2] Ogburn also noted that there are two aspects of culture—the material and the nonmaterial—and these both relate to how readily change is accepted.

In general, when change involves material culture, the period of time between when the change appears and when it takes effect is very short. For example, many people purchased hula hoops as soon as they appeared on the market in the 1950s. But when change concerns nonmaterial culture—ideas, norms, or values—it often takes people a long time to accept it. In the 1960s, for instance, young men began to let their hair grow long, and adults were often violently upset by this. Yet within a decade, many older men were also wearing their hair long. Thus change was accepted, but it took some time for this to happen.

Yet change is only one side of the coin. In order to understand change we must also look at stability.

STABILITY VERSUS CHANGE

Auguste Comte, one of the founders of sociology in the nineteenth century, argued that the new science was to be concerned with *social statics,* the study of stable social forms, and *social dynamics,* or the study of social change.[3] Since that time two contrasting perspectives have emerged concerning the nature of change and stability and their sociological significance. One school of thought argues that stability is the normal condition of society and it is change that needs to be explained.[4] The other school contends that change is a universal, persistent, and continuous process and what has to be accounted for is stability. Most sociologists would probably agree that human society is characterized by both harmony and conflict and that both are essential to survival.

Both views have corresponding political, ideological, and theoretical implications. If, for example, we were to accept the notion that change needs explanation, we would probably advocate conservative political policies on the grounds that change is a disruptive force and should be avoided. In contrast, if we accept the notion that stability requires explaining, we would probably advocate liberal political policies on the grounds that change is good for society and should be encouraged.

Arguments over which of these views is correct sometimes become quite heated, but it is virtually impossible to test the validity of either view. Hence, whether or not social change or social stability is the "normal" state of human society is not a valid question. Actually, within societies change and stability coexist. What can be analyzed are the processes through which change takes place, the factors that operate to stimulate or suppress change, and the patterns of change that have occurred and are now taking place.

77

Diffusion often occurs when two societies come into contact. At left, African historian Adiko Assoi *(in white shirt)* uses an American tape recorder to preserve the legends told by an Ivory Coast chief. At right, McDonald's, the hallmark of American fast food, seems right at home in Tokyo, Japan.

Processes of Change

Research has demonstrated that two major processes underlie all of the social and cultural changes that take place.[5] These processes consist of *diffusion* (or adoption) and *innovation* (invention and discovery).

DIFFUSION

Most of the changes that take place in any society are not created by the people who experience them. Rather, items are adopted, either intact or in modified form, from others. This process of social and cultural adoption is called *diffusion*. It has been responsible for producing the vast similarities among human societies.

Diffusion is likely to take place whenever two societies come into contact. Just about any aspect of the cultures of the people in contact can be diffused from one to the other. In the 1920s, for instance, American jazz diffused from a small number of black performers to become a significant feature of American music. In the 1950s it spread throughout Western Europe and other parts of the world. Similarly, the ideology of democracy, the Christian religion, the laws of thermodynamics, the making of pottery, and the development of agriculture originated at some time in one or more places and, to varying degrees, have spread around the world.

In the process of diffusion, we do not necessarily adopt a particular social or cultural item itself, even though this is frequently the case. Instead we often adopt the idea or the technology behind the item. For example, American automobiles were exported to many countries. Some of these countries took the idea of the automobile or the technology required for its manufacture and made models of their own. They now sell their versions back to the United States.

Although diffusion may take place whenever two groups interact with each other, the process is not an automatic or a one-sided phenomenon. The interacting groups may reject certain items, accept items with their own modifications, or accept them as they are. Which will occur depends on a variety of factors—how much the adopting group feels it needs the item and how compatible the item is with the group's existing cultural base.

INNOVATION

Before a social or cultural item can diffuse from one group to another, it obviously must originate somewhere. The process for introducing something new is called *innovation*.

Innovation can take two basic forms—inventions or discoveries. An *invention* results when existing cultural items are recombined into new forms, creating something that did not exist before. The development of vaccines, the aqualung, and the decimal point are all inventions. A *discovery*, on the other hand, involves finding something that was already there. The findings of the DNA molecule, the North American continent, and the fossil remains of Cro-Magnon man are all discoveries. Both processes are forms of social and cultural innovation that have continually contributed to the transformation of human social life.

As with diffused items, some innovations are not accepted by the members of a group and, hence, may not have a significant impact on their lives. Many inventions and discoveries go unnoticed and unaccepted for many years, if not forever. The United States Patent Office has literally thousands of patents for devices that have never been put into production or used by the larger society.

Also, some inventions are lost and have to be "reinvented" later. For example, anthropologist Arthur Kroeber showed how the diffusion of one invention was lost for centuries when not all the aspects of it were diffused along with the physical object itself.[6] The Europeans, Kroeber writes, imported porcelain invented in China. But they were unable to reproduce it locally until centuries later because they lacked the necessary technological knowledge. Ultimately Europeans had to reinvent "china" by discovering the process by which it is made.

APPLYING SOCIOLOGY

Below is a list of discoveries and inventions. Identify which are which.

Fire	The English language
Atoms	Steam engines
Nuclear submarines	Wheels
Franklin stoves	The Mississippi River
Bacteria	Antibiotics

The above list contains several items that are logical pairs and are, in fact, dependent on each other. Identify these and then describe what relationships might pertain between discoveries and inventions.

Thus we see that some innovations are not accepted and others are lost. Yet innovation occurs in all societies, although societies differ considerably in the rate and extent of their innovative behavior. Such innovation, in turn, is important to the social and cultural changes that take place within the society.

Factors Affecting the Rate of Change

As we have hinted, societies react to change in different ways. Some readily accept change while others do not. If we look at American society, for example, we will note that in the past three hundred years America has gone from an agricultural society to one of the most industrial and technological societies in the world. In contrast, the Dobe !Kung Bushmen of Africa have changed very little over the years. Still other societies have changed in some respects but not in others. Despite the fact that several European nations have tried to influence Indian culture, basic elements such as religion have never changed, although many Indians wear Western clothing and speak English.

Social scientists have attempted to discover why societies react to change so differently. They have investigated several factors that have some bearing on this question.[7] Among these are population characteristics, the degree of contact a group has with others, the society's existing cultural base, the characteristics of the society's social structure, and the ideology of the members regarding change.

POPULATION

Any major increase or decrease in a population is likely to lead to dramatic changes in a society. When a population increases in size, the

80

interpersonal relationships of people become more extensive and less intimate. Interactional patterns tend to become more complex and the general pace of life seems to quicken. In addition, increases in population place additional demands on the economy and environment, and greater coordination of effort is needed just to keep the system running. All of this acts as a stimulus for change.

Change also occurs when a population decreases in size. For example, a town that is dominated by one industry may experience more than an economic loss if and when the industry moves out. Employable people may leave the town in droves, greatly altering the composition of the town's population. The town usually begins to decay physically and socially since it is left with those residents who most need the services and support of earners. The tax base for the town decreases, new construction becomes practically nonexistent, businesses move out, and needed repairs on municipal facilities are delayed or not even attempted. In effect, unless a new economic base is substituted, the town is likely to begin to decay because of economic reasons and the drastic alteration in its population's characteristics.

CONTACT AND ISOLATION

Since change occurs through diffusion, those societies having the greatest amount of contact with other peoples are the most likely to change and to be the impetus for changes in other cultures. Those regions that are centrally located tend to be the most apt to change. For example, the religion of Islam spread throughout the Arabic world in

Whereas those people that are centrally located are most apt to change, those that are isolated are likely to change very little. The Tasaday of the Philippines, for example, had been isolated from other societies for centuries. When discovered recently, the Tasaday seemed not to have changed very much since the Stone Age.

FOCUS ON: THE PREINDUSTRIAL CITY

How can we analyze phenomena as complex as social and cultural change? To many sociologists, cities provide a classic source of analysis since they are one of the largest forms of human groups. Thus, within cities, the connections between different types of change are magnified and are more easily visible.

Although all cities have some similarities that enable them to be classified as cities, they are remarkably distinct from each other in terms of size, shape, and geographical spread. For example, if we compare Houston, Texas, with Reading, Pennsylvania, we will note such distinctions. One of the essential questions being asked today in an attempt to explain such differences is how does industrialization affect city growth or urbanization? How does industrialization bring about different social and cultural changes for each city?

Gideon Sjoberg tried to answer these questions in a study dealing with industrialization entitled *The Preindustrial City.* In this study Sjoberg questioned the differences between cities with and without industry. After investigating cities from antiquity to modern times, he concluded that the preindustrial city had some combination of the following characteristics:

First, the population was small, often between 5,000 and 10,000 persons. In these cities the elite lived in the center of the city, while the poor were scattered outside the city.

Second, these cities had a very distinct upper class who, were socially isolated from the remainder of the population. This remainder consisted of the lower class. Most preindustrial cities had an "outcast group" whose members performed essential, but lowly, tasks. Thus, according to standards in such cities, the merchant, for example, was often regarded as an outcast.

Third, the family was very important in the organization of social, political, and economic life. Marriage was of important consequence to one's life and determined all aspects of one's future. Thus marriage did more than unite two people; it determined one's occupational status, economic status, and social status.

Fourth, all economic activity occupied low status because it required contact with "common" persons. In addition, the growth of economic activity was slow because of simple technology—the absence of factories and machines—and the lack of organization in the guilds and handicraft associations. The business world also lacked any standard forms of pricing, monetary systems, or weights and measures.

Fifth, political and religious life was "personal," although bureaucratic. That is, members of the upper class gained their political and religious positions because of their family and friendship ties. In addition, communication in the preindustrial city was limited to word-of-mouth and occasionally, among the upper class, to written forms.

How are modern cities different from those described by Sjoberg? Do you think there are any cities today that are large but resemble this model? Can you identify the social and cultural changes caused by modern city growth? What happens to a small town, for example, when a large company decides to build a factory there?

Source: Gideon Sjoberg, *The Preindustrial City*, New York: The Free Press, 1965.

part because the town in which its founder, Mohammed, lived was on a major caravan route. This provided Mohammed with a large audience to hear his philosophy and to carry it to other people. The conquest of other areas by those who accepted the Islamic religion helped to spread the teachings of Mohammed even further.

Conversely, isolation slows the rate and number of things that diffuse to or from a group, and thus acts to retard the course of change. People located in hard-to-reach regions of the world tend to have cultures that have changed very little over the millenia. The Tasaday of the Philippines, for example, are a small band of people who apparently had no contact with anyone else for generations until they were discovered recently. Their material culture is exceptionally sparse, and it is believed that these gentle people have changed very little since prehistoric times.

THE CULTURAL BASE

Another factor that influences change is the cultural base of a society. The *cultural base* consists of the amount of knowledge and techniques available to the inventor. The larger the cultural base, the more likely change will occur; if the cultural base is small, the reverse is true.

Innovation is affected by the existing number of items a people have developed. The greater the number of items, the more likely it is that new items will be added to the culture. This is because innovation involves the modification of some existing item or the combining of two or more to form a new one. Television would have been impossible if a way to harness electricity had not been invented, the vacuum tube created, and a host of laws regarding the activity of light and sound waves discovered. Indeed, the television set is a combination of two mutually independent things—the viewing screen and the radio. Similarly, the automobile is a combination of a large number of independent inventions including the wheel, the internal combustion engine, the axle, and the pump. Had one or more of these things been absent from nineteenth-century culture, the automobile might not yet exist.

APPLYING SOCIOLOGY

The rate of change in the world appears to be faster than ever before. This is especially true in the United States and other industrialized countries. Why might this be so? How can we explain why the pace of change is beginning to increase in many Third-World nations? What might be some of the consequences of the increased rate of change in those countries?

SOCIAL STRUCTURE

Just as the cultural bases of societies differ, the social structures of societies also differ. The differences in the characteristics of social structures influence the kinds and likelihood of changes in various societies. The degree of unity among the members of society, the structure of authority, the degree of individualism, and the bases for interpersonal relationships are all significant in determining a society's inclination to change.

Change is more likely to be promoted in societies where there is no despotic authority, where members have a wide range of individual choice, where the members are not highly integrated into one common group, and where personal goals are more important than communal ones. On the basis of these criteria, compared to most other countries, the United States is not only geared to change, but its social system is such that it actively promotes change, particularly in the realm of technology.

IDEOLOGY

In the United States change is defined as good. The people believe in change and strive for it. The nation's founders, for example, were convinced of their manifest destiny—to conquer the continent. They believed that progress could not be denied. And they felt that concerted action could transform the wilderness into a Garden of Eden.

Not all people throughout the world, however, feel the same way about change. For many people it is neither desired nor, in some cases, even conceived of as possible. For example, although many efforts have been made to introduce methods of birth control to the people of India, these efforts have met with resistance. The population is still rising at an alarming rate. In most societies change is considered good in some areas and bad in others. In Nepal, for example, there is great interest in technological innovations; but at the same time, the people are very resistant to change in male-female relationships.[8]

Thus, the way in which a society reacts to change is determined by many factors. Each determines how readily a society will accept a change and how quickly the change will take effect.

Patterns of Change

Another way to study social and cultural change is by examining the ways or patterns in which change occurs. There are three basic patterns of change. One pattern, known as *evolution*, refers to slow, gradual change that takes place with minimal human intervention or effort. Our

84

language, for example, has evolved over time. Another basic pattern is *revolution*, which is rapid, intentional change that can drastically alter a society's existing ways of doing things. Revolutions are purposive and caused by direct human action. Throughout history we have had many revolutions, such as the Russian Revolution and the French Revolution. A third pattern, *reform*, is similar to revolution in that it too is produced by direct action. But in contrast to revolutions, reform movements are less drastic and extensive. The women's movement is one example of a reform movement. Society and/or culture are *altered* by reforms, whereas they are *transformed* by revolutions.

Although all three forms of change have taken place in history, it is only in the past four hundred years that people have come to believe they can purposively and directly alter and guide the speed and direction of change. This belief has been expressed in the writings of several social scientists.

THEORIES OF SOCIAL CHANGE

A number of theories of social change have been proposed by sociologists and others concerned with the transformations in society. We can classify these into four categories: evolutionary theories, cyclical theories, functional theories, and conflict theories. We will now examine each of these and its proponents more closely.

Evolutionary Theories

Evolutionary theories were derived in part from the notions of Charles Darwin, whose book *On the Origin of Species* (1859) demonstrated that all forms of life evolve in a gradual, uninterrupted process from the most simple to the extremely complex. Borrowing from Darwin's theory, evolutionary theorists (sometimes referred to as Social Darwinists) assumed that if human beings had evolved from lower forms, then all societies also gradually develop from simple to complex forms. That is, societies evolve steadily and directly in a straight upward line. To these theorists, social change meant progress. Societies got better and better as they got larger, stronger, and more technologically complex.

Auguste Comte saw society as having evolved through several stages: the *theological*, where thought is dominated by religion, to the *metaphysical*, in which thought is philosophical, to the final *positive* or scientific stage, in which thought is based on empirical knowledge, or knowledge that can be verified through the senses rather than by intuition. According to Comte, the major problem of society during the first half of the nineteenth century was that all three modes of thought were operating at the same time, causing confusion. Ultimately, he ar-

85

Auguste Comte (1798–1857)

Auguste Comte coined the term "sociology" and is therefore called the "father" of the discipline. One of Comte's major arguments was that it was possible to study society scientifically. In other words, research on society should be subject to a set of strict guidelines to ensure that the research leads to valid generalizations. Since strict rules or guidelines were being applied to such sciences as biology, Comte believed they should also apply to the study of society. Second, Comte believed that there was a hierarchy of the sciences, with sociology at the peak. According to Comte, the development of the sciences was the basis for progress.

Comte was born in France after the French Revolution, which was a period riddled with social controversy. This instilled within him a concern for social order and inspired him to formulate the concepts of *social statics* and *social dynamics*. According to Comte, "statics" is concerned with order, while "dynamics" involves progress and evolution. Comte further believed that these two concepts are closely linked, since progress requires order. Thus, very early, Comte identified two basic concerns of modern sociology—order and change.

Unlike Spencer (see box on page 87), Comte believed in planned intervention in the social system. In other words, intervention by the state or other formal groups could serve to improve or reform society. Sociologists, Comte felt, could direct such intervention by applying sociological knowledge to specific social problems.

Another contribution of Comte is his development of an evolutionary scheme. This scheme consists of three stages, through which, Comte believed, all societies and individuals must pass. In the first stage, the "theological," the behavior of the members of the society is influenced by the ideas of God and supernatural elements. In the second stage, the "metaphysical," the behavior of individuals is guided by philosophy and law. In the final phase, the "positive" stage, the findings of scientific investigation determine the organization of society. Comte referred to these three stages as "The Law of Human Progress."

---

gued, the theological and metaphysical mentalities would have to give way to the scientific, at which point society would have reached the end of its social evolution.

Herbert Spencer carried this line of reasoning further. Spencer claimed that all societies move in a unilinear way from their simple beginnings as hunting and gathering societies to highly developed, technologically advanced societies. Applying Darwin's theory of "the survival of the fittest," Spencer even stated that white races had advanced more rapidly than nonwhite races because they could adapt more easily to the environment.

Throughout the nineteenth century and into the twentieth century evolutionary theories carried much weight with social scientists be-

Herbert Spencer (1820–1903)

Herbert Spencer is regarded as an *organic theorist* because he compared society to living organisms. He emphasized the basic principles of evolution, which he referred to as *natural law.* Unlike many other thinkers, Spencer believed that natural law was superior to social law.

Spencer reasoned that as societies grow in size and density, they distinguish among their various parts. The parts thus become more unlike each other and, in turn, more interdependent. As a result, these specialized parts must cooperate in order to function properly. Like living organisms, then, societies changed from being unicellular to being multicellular. And, also like living organisms, they became more complicated in size and structure as well as in behavior.

Spencer's ideas on the growth and development of society led to his larger view of evolution as progress. Societies, he believed, evolved naturally from one form to another and progressed—or became better—in the process.

For example, Spencer considered military societies to be less evolved than industrial societies. He viewed military societies as being based on "compulsive" cooperation while industrial societies are based on the "voluntary" cooperation of the members. And voluntary cooperation was more desirable.

Since societal evolution was, to him, a natural process, he further believed that the state should not interfere in social life. Consequently, he was against government planning and the regulation of activities in the social sphere. These ideas were compatible with the doctrine of *laissez-faire* or the "hands off" policy applied in the economic sphere during the late nineteenth century. Spencer believed that individuals naturally pursue freedom and act on the basis of self-interest; government intervention could neither stop this natural inclination of individuals nor affect the natural evolution of societies.

---

cause they explained why preliterate peoples did not achieve as much as literate peoples. They also provided Westerners with a rationalization for their dominance over and exploitation of what they considered to be "inferior" societies.

Today, however, it is no longer possible to believe in inevitable progress because we can see that societal change does not follow a universal, unilinear pattern. And we can also see that change is not necessarily a synonym for progress. It is clear to us now that industrialization can, in fact, mean social disorganization. Thus, cyclical theories gradually replaced the older notions of evolution to explain social change.

Cyclical Theories

Cyclical theorists do not assume that societies move in a steady upward trend, eventually leading to industrialized civilization. Instead, they assume that while societies frequently move toward higher civilization, they can also move downward and even become.extinct. The Greeks, Romans, and Incas were often offered as examples of societies that had reached high points in civilization, only to decay and disappear.

Oswald Spengler in *The Decline of the West* (1918) stated that civilizations, like living organisms, go through life cycles from birth to maturity to old age and finally to death. He advanced the notion that Western civilization had passed this peak period of productivity and creativity (maturity) and was now starting on a downward path toward decay (old age). Wars and social disorganization (such as high crime rates and high divorce rates) were among the evidence he used to show that such societies were approaching their end. Spengler's theory, however, is not regarded seriously by modern sociologists because it is too speculative.

Harvard sociologist Pitirim Sorokin, in his book *Social and Cultural Dynamics* (1937), tried to demonstrate that there are three types of cultures in Western societies—sensate, ideational, and idealistic. In a sensate culture stress is on the material aspects of life. Members of such societies are hedonistic and pleasure-seeking. In an ideational culture people are concerned with matters of the mind, such as religion and the search for truth. In the idealistic culture, which is the perfect one between the two extremes, people give equal attention to the joys of life and to the spiritual. According to Sorokin, no society ever completely achieves any of these cultures. This theory has also been disregarded by modern sociologists because Sorokin offered no data to support his theory, and he never explained why or how a society would have moved from one type of culture to another.

Perhaps the most acceptable of the cyclical theories was that proposed by the British historian Arnold Toynbee in *A Study of History* (1946). Toynbee examined twenty-one societies in an effort to explain patterns in the rise and fall of societies. He claimed that every society is faced with challenges from the environment and from internal and external pressures. The manner in which a society responds to such challenges determines whether or not the society will survive. If it can overcome the challenges successfully, it will live on; if not, it will die. Toynbee is more optimistic than most cyclical theorists because he believes that societies get "second chances" and one generation can profit from the errors of the past or can learn from other societies. In spite of this, Toynbee's views are not popular today. One reason is that he only gives examples of societies that support his theory and ignores those that contradict it. Second, he does not explain why some challenges are successfully overcome by some societies but not by others.

Cyclical theories are as unacceptable as evolutionary theories in modern sociology. Although it is an historical fact that societies rise and fall, there is no evidence that they do so in any cyclical fashion. The theories rely too little on hard data and too heavily on "mysterious destinies" to be logical.

Functional Theories

Functionalists have often been accused of stressing social statics over social dynamics. Émile Durkheim tried to explain social change from a functional perspective. He suggested that societies progress from a form of social organization he called *mechanical solidarity* to one of *organic solidarity*. In societies characterized by mechanical solidarity, people are able to be more independent because they all can perform the functions necessary for survival. Each family can grow its own food, make its own clothing, educate its children, and so forth. In societies characterized by organic solidarity, people become increasingly specialized so that each person is responsible for fewer and fewer types of activity and dependence on each other increases.

According to Durkheim, the shift from mechanical solidarity to organic solidarity is tied in with the *division of labor*. Because each person is responsible for a few types of activity, societal harmony requires the coordination of many people. People become dependent on each other. For example, in our society, the doctor can cure our ills, the butcher supplies us with meat, the electrician wires our houses. But neither the people nor the tasks are interchangeable. The doctor cannot butcher meat and the electrician cannot prescribe medicine. Thus, we become interdependent in order to have a smoothly running society.

Durkheim saw the change from a mechanical to an organic form of social solidarity as being the major social change of modern times. He predicted that a host of social ills, such as increased rates of suicide, crime, and mental illness, would result from it. On the other hand, organic solidarity offered opportunities for creativity and human freedom which might offset the security of traditional society.

Another prominent functionalist, sociologist Talcott Parsons (see page 189), believes that a society is made up of interdependent parts (people), each doing its share to preserve the society in an orderly and stable fashion. Thus each part works with the other parts to maintain the society's equilibrium. This means, of course, that social change would be resisted, especially by a stable society. And such a theory would not address the question of social change in any depth.

Parsons has been criticized for disregarding social change. To answer his critics, in the 1960s he finally confronted the problem and attempted to incorporate it into his basic theory. At first, Parsons regarded change as disruptive to equilibrium, but he presently acknowledges that innovation can lead to a new equilibrium. Change, he says, comes either from forces within the society itself or from contact with other societies.

Parsons' present stance is somewhat evolutionary. He claims that in simple societies one group may serve many functions. In many of the thirteen original colonies, for example, a family educated its children, taught religion, and provided its own food and clothing. But as societies become more complicated, these functions are delegated to many groups, so that in large-scale societies, each function is performed separately. Families no longer formally educate their children; schools have taken over that function. Religion is no longer taught solely in the home; churches and temples have that function. Food and clothing are often purchased from outside sources. Nevertheless, these groups are integrated, still working together to preserve social order.

Although many sociologists agree with Parsons, there is a large minority who feel he still focuses too much on stability. In addition, while he does speak of some change, he may underestimate the importance of strains in societies that can cause many other kinds of change. These are dealt with more thoroughly by the conflict theorists.

Conflict Theories

Conflict theorists see society as an arena for combat. They base their explanations of social change on the notion that there are always competing groups, with dissimilar interests and goals, in every society. Some groups are exploited; others exploit. And there is a constant struggle between the two.

Karl Marx, the most prominent of the conflict theorists, held that "All history is the history of class conflict," as stated in *The Communist Manifesto* (1848). He showed how, through different periods of history, the conflict between the two classes could always be seen. Ancient society was based on slavery, the master exploiting the slave. Feudalism was based on serfdom, with the lord exploiting the serf. Capitalism is based on wage labor, with the capitalist exploiting the worker. Another mode, Asiatic, was not discussed in detail by Marx. It is a mode whereby the government owns everything and thus exploits the citizen.

Marx argued that the nineteenth century was experiencing a stage of capitalism and it would inevitably move to the next and final stage of pure communism. According to Marx, capitalism would die as the other stages had died, and the perfect society—classless and stateless—would come into existence. (See Chapter 13 for a fuller discussion of Marx's theories.)

Modern conflict theorists still stress Marx's notions of class conflict as the basis for social change, but they have extended the notion to include other groups. Ralf Dahrendorf, for example, demonstrates that conflict also exists among religious groups, racial groups, political groups, and so forth. All such conflict, says Dahrendorf, may lead to social change.[9]

90

None of these theories fully accounts for social change and none can predict with accuracy its direction, it causes, or its time of occurrence. However, each has contributed in its own way to understanding this complex phenomenon. It is quite possible that someday these theories will be integrated in such a way as to provide an adequate explanation of social change.

SOCIAL MOVEMENTS AND DIRECTED CHANGE[10]

Does history shape the person or does the person shape history? This "chicken and egg" kind of question cannot, of course, be answered definitively. World War II might have happened whether or not Hitler ever lived. It is possible that events beyond the control of any single person gave rise to the war itself and also made it possible for someone like Hitler to come to power in Germany. On the other hand, some people believe that Hitler himself shaped the course of World War II.

Sociologists do not yet agree to what extent social change is caused by forces beyond human control or to what degree it can be directly influenced by human intervention. Innovations like the atom bomb, the automobile, democracy, and the printing press may have been inevitable developments that were based on prior knowledge. On the other hand, as some sociologists contend, the course and consequences of change can be foreseen and predicted. For example, with our recognition of the energy crisis, we can predict a trend toward more fuel-efficient cars. Moreover, changes considered desirable can be encouraged while those that have negative implications can be avoided or prevented or can have their impact lessened.

Rather than leaving things to fate, those sociologists who favor planned change would argue that human beings can control their own destiny. The most pronounced and dramatic of these efforts at control are generally called *social movements*, a classification that covers a wide range of phenomena from revolutions to reform efforts to programs designed to prevent the occurrence of change in one or more areas. Although specific instances of social movements differ considerably in detail, all rest on the proposition that human beings can control the events that influence their lives.

The Social Origins of Social Movements

If people believe they can act to promote or prevent change, they may act in certain ways to alter the course of their lives. What forces operate to generate actions geared to this end? Do people organize and mobilize their efforts for just any reason and under any circumstances, or are there factors that operate to stimulate the rise of a social move-

91

Does history shape the person or does the person shape history? Would conditions in Tsarist Russia have caused the Communist Revolution of 1917 without the leadership of V. I. Lenin *(left)*? Might World War II have occurred without Germany's Adolf Hitler *(right)*? Should Allied leaders such as American President Franklin D. Roosevelt and British Prime Minister Winston Churchill *(bottom)* have been able to predict and head off the conflict?

ment? So far sociologists have not been able to offer many satisfactory answers to these questions, but some common features of social movements have been discovered.

Change as a Cause   It appears that change itself promotes the emergence of a social movement. Some change must have occurred and been perceived to cause people to organize their efforts either to promote other changes or to prevent them from occurring.

In the case of movements to block change, those who prefer to keep things as they are are likely to mobilize actively when they perceive a threat to the *status quo*. Sometimes their efforts can be quite extensive and elaborate and continue for a considerable period of time. The extensive campaign to prohibit the use of alcohol in the United States is an example of such a movement. This social movement ac-

92

The black civil rights movement of the 1960s was encouraged, among other factors, by a sense of relative deprivation and an era of rising expectations. These demonstrators are advocating open housing in Gage Park, Illinois.

tually lasted from the end of the Revolutionary War to the beginning of World War II. It reached a high point with the passage of the Eighteenth Amendment in 1919.

In contrast, the black civil rights movement of the 1960s was oriented toward promoting change and toward increasing the speed at which it was occurring (see Chapter 12). Improvements in the status of black Americans in the early 1960s, an awakened recognition of the political and economic strength black people possessed, and the apparent willingness of the government to facilitate further improvements all acted to promote the civil rights movement. It was not simply because black people were deprived that they organized in protest, for they had been much more deprived in earlier times. Rather, the changes that had occurred caused blacks to experience a condition of *relative deprivation*, a realization that they were not as well off as those above them. At the same time, the era was one of *rising expectations*, an era in which people felt they were entitled to more of the society's resources and rewards. These two situations caused blacks to try to narrow the gap that existed between them and those in power.[11]

Social Disorganization   In most instances change must generate a particular condition before a social movement will arise. Primarily, the changes underlying social movements must be extensive enough to stimulate sufficient disorder so that a breakdown in the norms and social alignment will result. In the United States this happened following the Revolutionary War as well as the Civil War. During both these periods the old power structures that prevailed were destroyed or drastically altered, leading to numerous reform movements throughout the country.

This breakdown in the norms and structure of a society can stimulate consequences that appear to spark social movements. First a condition of *anomie* (normlessness) is likely to arise. Since most people are used to structure in their lives, this loss of basic rules leads to a feeling of frustration, insecurity, and confusion. This feeling, in turn, leads to the desire among people to restore things to their former (usually thought of as "natural") state or to find a more satisfactory alternative to the disorganized situation. For example, much of the opposition to the women's movement is a result of a fear that equality of women would undermine the existing power structure.

Belief in Change   Poverty, injustice, despair, and deprivation do not in themselves cause social movements. Rather, expectations that poverty or injustice can be eliminated or, at least, substantially reduced must emerge to override the fatalism that often blocks efforts to promote change. It is likely that people will organize for their own benefit when

93

changes take place revealing that improvement is possible or that unless something is done, the situation will worsen. If a leader can be found and a cause successfully defined, and if unity can be maintained, it is highly probable that a fully formed social movement will materialize.

Types of Social Movements

Every social movement is a unique phenomenon. But all have certain attributes in common so that it is possible to classify them into types. For our present purposes, we can categorize social movements into reform, revolutionary, and resistance movements.

In general, *reform movements* are oriented toward modifying some part of society or changing some condition without totally restructuring the culture or organization of the society. The labor movement of the 1930s is one example of a reform movement. It was geared to improving the lot of the worker, not to destroying industry or taking over the ownership of factories. *Revolutionary movements,* such as the communist takeover of China and the American War for Independence, are directed to overthrowing existing systems and replacing them with different forms. Revolutionary movements are more extensive than reform movements since they are geared to entire systems, not just one aspect of a system. *Resistance movements,* like the Ku Klux Klan, are

The communist takeover of China in the late 1940s is an example of a revolutionary movement. Revolutionary movements tend to involve all members and aspects of a society. Here very young revolutionaries guard their village gate against nationalist forces.

America's Ku Klux Klan is an example of a resistance movement— a movement that tries to prevent reform or revolution. The burning of crosses, as is shown here, is one method by which the Klan seeks to keep change from occurring.

geared to preventing any substantial reforms (and surely any revolutions) from taking place. Rather than regarding reform progressively, resistance movements try to return to "the good old days."

The conditions that give rise to social movements could spawn any or all of these types. Each type of social movement has occurred in our past. Let us now examine what the future holds in store for us.

APPLYING SOCIOLOGY

List several examples of each type of social movement. Describe the characteristics of each movement you selected. What differences as well as similarities do you find among them?

What the Future Holds[12]

Scientists in all disciplines strive to predict events. A chemist tries to predict what would result if various chemicals were mixed together under different conditions. The economist seeks to determine what would happen to the economy if government subsidized an industry or if a new tax program were instituted. An anthropologist is concerned with predicting what would happen to a village if its major food supply were suddenly to disappear. Similarly, the sociologist attempts to predict what short- and long-term social and cultural changes are likely to take place and what consequences these changes might have.

Among the more significant and widespread changes that sociologists expect to take place in the immediate future are increased specialization, bureaucratization, modernization, and industrialization. Each of these changes is briefly discussed below. Another major trend is secularization. This will be covered in Chapter 8.

SPECIALIZATION

In America, until the Industrial Revolution, families were largely self-sufficient and took care of many aspects of daily life. Before the advent of mass production and the assembly line, workers in many industries were involved in all operations of production. And before the expansion of mass education, children of all ages were taught together in one-room schoolhouses by one teacher.

Today, however, society is divided into a variety of social rankings. The family has relinquished many of its former tasks, workers on assembly lines typically have only a few simple operations to perform, and teachers increasingly teach only one subject to students of similar age. Almost all aspects of society and daily life have become (and are likely to continue to become) increasingly specialized. Behaviors, relationships, jobs, and interactions are divided into limited and constricted units or forms.

In addition, each individual person in modern Western society is already engaged in a limited number of highly specialized activities. It is quite likely that coming generations will perform even more specialized activities.

This is especially true in developing countries that are beginning to experience change. In many developing nations, for example, the central importance of the family is beginning to diminish. The tasks it once performed for its members are now being assigned elsewhere. Hence, rather than the family caring for sick or impoverished relatives, social security, nationalized medicine, and nursing homes have taken over these functions. The family may increasingly become limited merely to providing emotional support for its members.

96

BUREAUCRATIZATION

As a society and the activities of its members become more and more specialized, the problem of coordinating individual actions increases considerably. Where once Benjamin Franklin gathered the news, wrote the reports, printed the paper, and sold his product to the citizens of Philadelphia, now a large force of individuals is required to accomplish the same task. Just "putting the paper to bed" (going to press) each day requires a massive coordinated effort. Some mechanism had to evolve to accomplish that task, a mechanism we now know as *bureaucracy*. (See Chapter 2 for a more extensive discussion of bureaucracies.)

If the past is any indication of the future, there is little doubt that bureaucratization will become more widespread. As several sociologists have theorized, this growth may result in increased alienation of people from their bureaucratized activities and, consequently, a greater degree of frustration and anomie for those of us who have to deal with each other as bureaucrats.

MODERNIZATION

The general world movement toward modernization has sometimes been called a trend toward *Westernization* because the developing countries of the world have increasingly come to imitate Western styles, forms, and orientations. While this is surely true, in the course of diffusion many "Western" traits have been modified by the borrowers so that the word modernization, rather than Westernization, more accurately depicts the course of this trend.

Primarily, modernization signifies a general movement toward a centralized form of government, an increase in the rate of urbanization, an extension of literacy, a loosening of commitments to traditional economic and political structures, and an abandonment of traditional social roles. In effect, modernization means that a society has become unified into a nation state, where once it was comprised of communities or groups of people allied by ties of family or residence. As sociologist Daniel Lerner found in his study of modernization in the Middle East,[13] traditional alliances, life-styles, and patterns of behavior based on family ties tend to give way under modernization to more individualism.

According to Lerner, modernization also implies change from a belief that one cannot control one's life to a belief that one can. Such an outlook provides human beings with a sense of control over their destinies and stimulates them toward organizing and planning so that they can direct the course and the outcome of events. This, in turn, has the effect of planning change and hastening its occurrence.

Modernization has become increasingly prevalent and widespread. Saudi Arabia is one country that has become increasingly modernized.

97

INDUSTRIALIZATION

Perhaps the single most significant change to occur in the last two hundred years has been the transformation of societies from rural agrarian states into industrialized nations. The development of industry and the forces that it set into motion have been responsible for accelerating, if not actually causing, the three changes just discussed, as well as numerous other alterations in human life. This was especially true in Western Europe and the United States, which were the first to industrialize. But the impact of industrialization has spread throughout the world.

Technically, one can say that a society is industrialized when at least one-half of its work force is engaged in nonagricultural occupations. Most nations do not yet fit into this category, but almost every preindustrial country is actively striving to industrialize as rapidly as possible. Since specialization, bureaucratization, and modernization are all related to industrialization, what is likely to happen to formerly agrarian nations as they become increasingly industrialized?

Some sociologists feel that the major overall development likely to take place is that the cultures and social structures of nonindustrialized nations will more and more come to resemble those of advanced industrialized nations. This, they argue, will occur regardless of the unique characteristics of the individual societies, because industrialization requires a specific set of values and behaviors in order to exist in the first place.

It will be interesting to note whether these nonindustrialized nations will indeed carry out these predictions. In the meantime, we can only wait to evaluate the accuracy of sociologists in predicting events.

The trend in highly industrialized societies is toward postindustrialization. In such societies, of which America is a primary example, the majority of workers are engaged not in agricultural or manufacturing occupations, but in tertiary occupations. A tertiary occupation is one in which the worker provides services to the other members of the society. Entire cities, such as Las Vegas and Atlantic City, are service-oriented.

A second characteristic of a postindustrial society is highly sophisticated electronic engineering. For example, the accounting departments in many companies have computerized payrolls, whereas in the past an individual made out paychecks. Such automation is both beneficial and harmful to a society. It is beneficial as it makes work easier and more efficient. It is harmful inasmuch as machines can replace workers and raise unemployment rates. It will also be interesting to note how the trend toward postindustrialization will proceed in the future.

98

FOCUS ON: POSTINDUSTRIAL SOCIETY

What will our future be like? Sociologist Daniel Bell predicts the emergence of a postindustrial society in such areas as the United States, the Soviet Union, Japan, and Western Europe. In his book, *The Coming of Post-Industrial Society: A Venture in Social Forecasting,* Bell claims that such a society will emerge in these regions within thirty to fifty years.

Postindustrial society can be characterized by two basic features. First, we note a move away from a manufacturing economy toward one based on service activities, such as health, automobile maintenance, and financial services. Second, we find a growing importance placed on theoretical knowledge—for example, theoretical physics and mathematics—needed to meet increasingly complex human and technical needs. As a result, the economy of postindustrial society is based on services and on the storage, retrieval, and transmission of knowledge. This contrasts with the economy of preindustrial (or agrarian) society, which is based on extracting resources from nature, and that of industrial society, which is based on the manufacture of material goods. Of course, postindustrial society still contains agricultural and manufacturing elements, but these are not of primary importance.

It follows that the university, the place where knowledge is acquired and transmitted, will become very important in this new society.

In fact, universities (through government sponsored research) will play an increasingly greater role in determining the direction and growth of society. Also, claims Bell, technical and professional occupations ("the knowledge class") will grow faster than any other type of occupation.

The character of work will also be different in postindustrial society. Whereas in preindustrial society work is a game against the physical world, and in industrial society work is a game against machines, in the postindustrial world, states Bell, work is "primarily a game between persons." Consequently, people will have to know how to interact smoothly with each other. And this requirement, says Bell, "is a completely new and unparalleled state of affairs . . . in the history of human society."

Finally, Bell notes the new society's increasing reliance on information processing (computers) and electronic media and communications. Such apparatus is required to store, retrieve, and transmit technical knowledge.

How well do you believe such a society will work? Do you think people will treat each other with consideration in an impersonal "computerized" society? What dangers may result in a society with increasingly sophisticated electronic technology? How do you think the rights of individualism and personal privacy will fare?

Source: Daniel Bell, *The Coming of Post-Industrial Society: A Venture in Social Forecasting,* New York: Basic Books, 1973.

SUMMARY

Many changes have taken place since civilization began. These changes have taken several forms. They have been minute or drastic, abrupt or continuous, and have had manifest and/or latent consequences.

Change can take place in either the social structure or the culture of a group. Change in the structure is termed *social change* and change in the culture is called *cultural change*. Although changes in each sphere can occur independently of each other, changes occurring in one sphere have implications for the other.

Often a change is not put into effect immediately after it occurs. Sociologists use the term *cultural lag* to denote the period of time between when a change is introduced and when that change takes effect. In general, changes in a group's material culture take effect more quickly than changes in a group's nonmaterial culture.

Two major processes underlie all social and cultural change. The process by which societies adopt changes from other societies is called *diffusion*. The process by which societies introduce a change is called *innovation*. Innovation can take two basic forms—*invention* or *discovery*.

All societies do not change at the same rate. Some change rapidly, others hardly at all. Certain factors seem to stimulate or impede change. These are population characteristics, the degree of contact a group has with other groups, the society's existing cultural base, the characteristics of the society's social structure, and the ideology of the members regarding change.

There are three major patterns in which change occurs. One pattern, known as *evolution*, refers to slow, gradual change. *Revolution*, which is the second pattern, refers to rapid, intentional change that can drastically alter a society's earlier ways of doing things. The third pattern, *reform*, is similar to revolution, but is less drastic and extensive. Based on these three patterns, social scientists have formulated several theories of social change. These have been classified as *evolutionary theories, cyclical theories, functional theories,* and *conflict theories*.

When people view change in a positive way and/or when they feel that change can be influenced by direct human intervention, they are likely to organize to promote or block change. Sometimes these efforts take the form of social movements. Such movements may arise in a variety of ways, but they are typically preceded by change, a degree of disorder, and the existence of a change-oriented ideology. Social movements can be classified into three types: *reform movements*, which are oriented toward changing some condition without restructuring the culture or organization of a society; *revolutionary movements*, which are geared to overthrowing existing systems and replacing them with new ones; and *resistance movements*, which try to prevent any reforms and revolutions from taking place.

Just as sociologists can predict the course of a social movement, they also try to predict what the future holds for society. Among the more widespread changes that sociologists expect to take place in the immediate future are increased specialization, bureaucratization, modernization, industrialization, and postindustrialization.

GLOSSARY

anomie   a state of normlessness; the absence of group norms.

cultural base   the amount of knowledge and techniques available to an inventor.

cultural change   an alteration in the culture of a group.

cultural lag   that period between the time a change is introduced into a group and the time the group adapts to that change.

diffusion   a process of change involving the adoption of cultural items from another society, or from a subculture or group within the society.

discovery   a form of innovation that involves finding something that was already there.

evolution   a pattern of change referring to slow, gradual change that takes place with minimal human intervention.

innovation   a process of change based on the introduction of a new item into a society by that society.

invention   a form of innovation in which existing cultural items are recombined into new forms, creating something that did not exist before.

latent consequence   a consequence of change that is unintended and unrecognized.

manifest consequence   a consequence of change that is intended and recognized.

reform   a pattern of change that is similar to revolution, but is less drastic and extensive.

reform movement   a social movement that is oriented toward modifying some part of society or changing some condition without totally restructuring the culture or organization of the society.

relative deprivation   a realization by a group that it is disadvantaged as compared to another group.

resistance movement   a social movement that is oriented toward preventing any substantial reforms and revolutions.

revolution   a pattern of change referring to rapid, intentional change that can drastically alter a society's existing ways of doing things.

revolutionary movement   a social movement that is oriented toward overthrowing existing systems and replacing them with different forms.

rising expectations   a situation in which people feel they are entitled to more of the society's resources and rewards.

social change   an alteration in the structure of a group or in the relationships among its members.

social dynamics   the study of social change.

social movement   a concerted action by a group that is united and has definite aims and a program to change or block change in some aspect of society.

social statics   the study of stable social forms.

REFERENCES

1. The points discussed in this section are more thoroughly discussed in Amitai Etzioni and Eva Etzioni, eds., *Social Change: Sources, Patterns and Consequences.* New York: Basic Books, 1964.

2. William F. Ogburn, *Social Change.* New York: Viking Press, 1950.

3. Auguste Comte, *The Positive Philosophy.* Trans. and ed. by Harriet Mattineou. London: George Bell and Sons, 1915.

4. Ralf Dahrendorf, "Toward a Theory of Social Conflict." In Etzioni and Etzioni, p. 103.

5. George Peter Murdock, "How Culture Changes." In Harry L. Shapiro, ed., *Man, Culture and Society.* New York: Oxford University Press, 1960, pp. 247–260.

6. Arthur Kroeber, *Cultural Patterns and Processes.* Rev. ed., New York: Harcourt, Brace, World, 1948.

7. Barton M. Schwartz and Robert H. Ewald, eds. *Culture and Society.* New York: The Ronald Press, 1968, pp. 433–459. John P. Billin, *The Ways of Man.* New York: Appleton-Century-Crofts, 1948, esp. Chap. 25. Immanuel Wallerstein, ed., *Social Change: The Colonial Situation.* New York: John Wiley & Sons, 1966.

8. Lucile Duberman and Koya Azumi, "Sexism in Nepal." *Journal of Marriage and the Family.* 37:4 (November 1975): 1013–1021.

9. Dahrendorf, pp. 100–113.

10. Joseph R. Gusfield, ed., *Protest, Reform and Revolt: A Reader in Social Movements.* New York: John Wiley & Sons, 1970. C. Wendell King, *Social Movements in the United States.* New York: Random House, 1964. Joseph R. Gusfield, *Moral Crusade: Status Politics and the American Temperance Movement.* Urbana, Ill.: University of Illinois Press, 1963.

11. For example see Thomas F. Pettigrew, *Racially Separate or Together?* New York: McGraw-Hill, 1971.

12. A number of writers have discussed these trends in detail. For example, see Burnham Putnam Beckwirth, *The Next 500 Years: Scientific Predictions of Major Social Trends.* New York: Exposition Press, 1967; James L. Peacock and A. Thomas Kirsch, *The Human Direction.* New York: Appleton-Century-Crofts, 1970.

13. Daniel Lerner, *The Passing of Traditional Society: Modernizing the Middle East.* New York: The Free Press, 1958.

102

SUGGESTED READINGS

Aceves, Joseph. *Social Change in a Spanish Village.* Cambridge, Mass.: Schenkman, 1971.

Brief and easy to read, this book describes the changes that have recently taken place in a Spanish village and the impact these changes have had on the people of the village.

Bennis, Warren G., Kenneth D. Benne, and Robert Chin (eds.). *The Planning of Change.* 2nd ed. New York: Holt, Rinehart & Winston, 1969.

This book contains a number of readings regarding the process of, forces behind, impact of, problems involved in, and other aspects of planning and generating change.

Etzioni, Amitai and Eva Etzioni (eds.). *Social Change: Sources, Patterns, and Consequences.* New York: Basic Books, 1964.

This book presents the classic and modern theories of change and discusses the processes of change and some of the spheres and directions of change. This is a basic reader for anyone interested in the phenomenon of change.

Fuller, R. Buckminster. *Utopia or Oblivion: The Prospects of Humanity.* New York: Bantam, 1969.

This book explores the possibilities for the future —utopia or total destruction.

Gusfield, Joseph R. *Protest, Reform, and Revolt: A Reader in Social Movements.* New York: John Wiley & Sons, 1970.

A highly informative and interesting reader, this book discusses all aspects of social movements. An essential reference for anyone interested in the subject.

Hartjen, Clayton A. *Possible Trouble: An Analysis of Social Problems.* New York: Praeger, 1977.

Defining social problems as the result of efforts to bring about or produce change, this book offers a theory of social problems and a paradigm for their study.

Lerner, Daniel. *The Passing of Traditional Society: Modernizing the Middle East.* New York: The Free Press, 1958.

Based on an extensive study of change in the Middle East, this book presents an insightful and in-depth analysis of the phenomenon of modernization and its occurrence in several Middle Eastern countries.

Marx, Karl. *On Society and Social Change.* Edited by Neil J. Smelser. Chicago: University of Chicago Press, 1973.

This book presents Marx's theory of society and social change in a concise, readable manner. A classic work on the thoughts of a major classic writer.

103

Mau, James A. *Social Change and Images of the Future.* Cambridge, Mass.: Schenkman, 1968.

Based on research on several Caribbean Islands, this book relates social change and belief systems and the impact each has on the other.

Oppenheimer, Martin. *The Urban Guerrilla.* New York: Quadrangle, 1969.

This book develops three scenarios depicting what might happen in the near future.

Reich, Charles. *The Greening of America.* New York: Random House, 1970.

An optimistic view of the possibilities for cultural change.

Turnbull, Colin. *The Mountain People.* New York: Simon & Schuster, 1974.

This book dramatically illustrates the problem of enforced rapid social change and the consequent social disintegration of the culture.

Wallerstein, Immanuel (ed.). *Social Change: The Colonial Situation.* New York: John Wiley & Sons, 1966.

This book offers an extensive collection of readings dealing with various aspects of change in Third-World countries as a consequence of colonialism and recent independence. A good source book for anyone interested in social change in Third-World countries.

Zaltman, Gerald, Philip Kotler, and Ira Kaufman (eds.). *Creating Social Change.* New York: Holt, Rinehart & Winston, 1972.

As a general reader on the causes of change and strategies to produce, block, or direct change, this book offers a diverse body of information concerning how to produce (generally small-scale) change and what to expect as a consequence of such efforts.

TWO

Becoming and Being Human

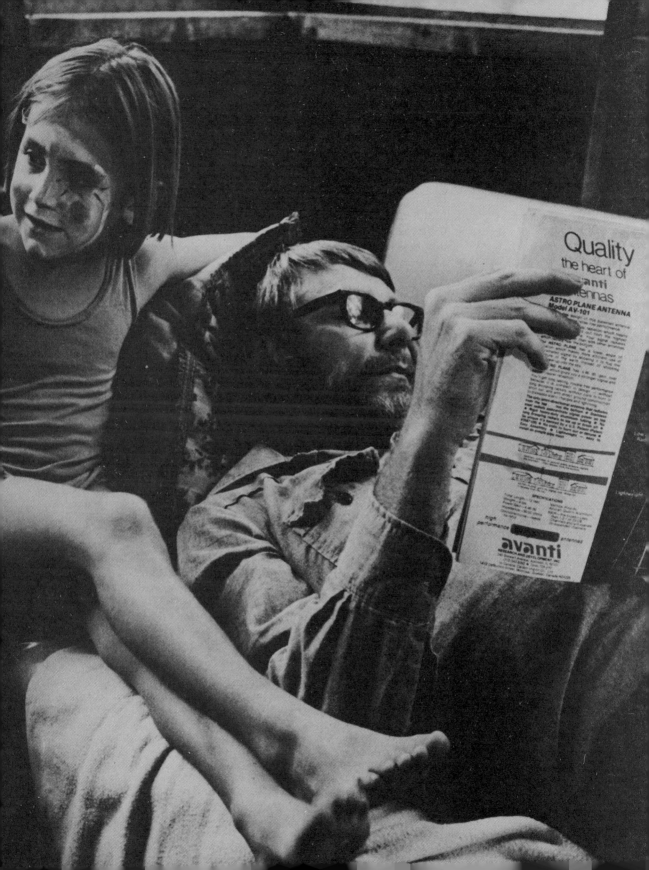

Most people plan ahead and look toward the future. For example, you may be thinking of marriage or planning a career. But how much do you really know about being a spouse, a doctor, a social worker, a carpenter, or a teacher?

Similarly, if you think back to your childhood, you also may realize that you knew very little about being a student, a brother or a sister, or a friend, until you were cast into those roles. Thus, although we take many of our behaviors for granted, in reality, each behavior must be learned. And the way we learn behavior is by interacting with other people. As we mentioned at the beginning of this book, if we did not interact with others, we would not be able to perform even such basic tasks as walking, talking, or feeding ourselves.

Socialization is the process by which we learn certain behaviors that enable us to become members of our society. Many sociologists would contend that socialization and membership in a social class are the two most influential aspects of our lives. Actually, socialization and social class are related since our social class determines to a certain extent how we will be socialized. An upper-class child would be taught many different values, attitudes, and behaviors than a lower-class child.

These sociologists believe we can never escape our socialization. For example, personnel managers in many corporations report that when they interview perspective job applicants, hints of childhood socialization, such as speech patterns, body movements, and facial expressions, escape regardless of education or adult life experiences. These clues are then part of the evaluation of the applicant.

On the other hand, some sociologists believe we can be resocialized and thus can rid ourselves of our early patterns. For example, they believe that an adult who was reared in a lower-class atmosphere and later placed in an upper-class environment could lose many lower-class traits.

No matter who is correct (if indeed either is), socialization plays an important part in our lives. This section will deal with socialization. Chapter 4 will focus on socialization in childhood, and in Chapter 5 we will discuss socialization from adolescence through old age. Just as interaction occurs throughout our lives, we are also socialized from birth to death.

4

Socialization
in Childhood

From the group of young, eager children, arms straining toward the ceiling, one was chosen. She was proud of being selected and performed the task flawlessly. With the words "I pledge allegiance to the flag. . ." the class was officially in session.

Many of us will remember this ritual quite well if we think about our childhoods. We also will remember other prescribed do's and don't's. We were always told to say "please" when we asked for something and "thank you" when we received what we requested. Similarly, we were always told never to come to the table with dirty hands.

Each of these patterns, along with uncountable others, represents part of our early socialization. In this chapter we will examine the process of socialization, the functions of socialization, and the theories of socialization.

The Process of Socialization

Socialization is a basic social process by which an individual becomes part of the society into which he or she was born. Through this process, which begins in infancy, young children learn and internalize (take into themselves) the values, skills, attitudes, and norms of their society. This acceptance or *internalization* soon becomes so thorough that it is hard to believe there are other ways to act. Internalization also leads members of society to form groups because the members share many common experiences and a common sense of belonging.

In a certain sense socialization begins even before a child is born because the infant's parents themselves were socialized as they grew up. Thus, they prepare for the birth of their child in socially acceptable ways. They usually get married before the mother becomes pregnant. They buy a crib, infant clothes, and a baby carriage, all of which they have learned are necessary to care for the baby. Today, most mothers go to a hospital for the birth of the child.

Once the baby is born, socialization goes into full swing. Soon after birth the baby is covered with a blue or a pink blanket (although some hospitals now use yellow), and everyone knows from that moment on the sex of the child. The parents and everyone else who comes in contact with the new infant will then behave differently toward the child, depending on the infant's sex. (Chapter 11 treats gender-role socialization.)

The mother is usually the first *socializing agent* because, in most families, she is the one who spends the most time with the baby. Bear in mind, however, that the mother is replaceable; "she" does not even have to be a female. Actually, the person doing the mothering, whether it is the father, a nurse, a grandparent, or any nurturing person, can be

Socialization, the process by which an individual becomes part of society, begins at birth. A baby's first socializing agent is usually his or her mother.

the "mother" and thus the first important socializing agent. But no matter who this first socializing agent is, the mother or the substitute mother very quickly develops a relationship with the baby that both of them understand. For instance, the mother rapidly learns that when the baby cries, the baby is uncomfortable for one or more reasons. She (or he) therefore tries to comfort the child accordingly. The baby, in turn, also learns that by crying he or she can get the attention that is needed.

As infants grow older, they become more aware of other people, besides their parents, in their environment. Brothers, sisters, grandparents, other relatives, and peer group members then become socializing agents also, all exerting influence on the young child as they interact together.

This sort of interaction between the child and other human beings is not only helpful to the child but is also biologically necessary. Human infants are helpless and therefore physically dependent on others for a long period of time. Such interaction, however, seems necessary for the emotional development of infants as well.

STUDIES BY HARRY HARLOW

In a study by psychologist Harry Harlow it was discovered that when baby monkeys are deprived of emotional contact with a real mother who has and reciprocates feelings, they do not develop into normal adult monkeys. Here a baby rhesus monkey that was part of the study clings to its terry-cloth-and-wire "mother."

Harry F. Harlow, a well-known psychologist, did several famous experiments with rhesus monkeys that illustrate the infant's need for emotional, as well as physical, contact.[1] Harlow raised some monkeys in total isolation except for a choice between two substitute "mothers." One consisted of a bare wire frame and the other of a wire frame covered with terry cloth. Half the monkeys were fed by each "mother" with a baby bottle attached to the frame. As infants, these monkeys (even those fed by the wire "mothers") preferred the terry-cloth "mothers" and appeared to be satisfied with them. All clung to the cloth-covered "mothers" and tried to cuddle up to them when frightened.

Yet when the monkeys grew up, they did not know how to get along with other monkeys. Some simply withdrew from any contact with their peers. Others showed extreme hostility and aggression. But not one of the monkeys that was raised without a living mother who offered warmth, security, and affection knew how to behave when it was placed in the company of normal adult monkeys.

Thus, Harlow's studies suggest that physical contact alone is not sufficient for baby monkeys to develop into normal adult monkeys. They need emotional contact as well. As Harlow states, the substitute mother cannot show emotion or reciprocate feelings:

The [substitute] cannot cradle the baby or communicate monkey sounds and gestures. It cannot punish for misbehavior or attempt to break the infant's bodily attachment before it becomes a fixation.[2]

111

Sociologist Kingsley Davis has shown that isolation from other human beings can have devastating effects on a child. In extreme cases isolation can make a child almost totally unresponsive.

STUDIES BY KINGSLEY DAVIS

Sociologist Kingsley Davis dramatically demonstrated the same sort of phenomenon in human children.[3] Davis observed two children who had been isolated from human contact since birth. The first child, Anna, who was born to an unwed mother, was kept alone in an attic room by her grandfather. She was given only enough attention to keep her alive, and thus when Anna was discovered at about age six, she appeared to be almost a vegetable. She was very thin, had a bloated stomach, and neither walked nor talked. She simply lay in a flat position without any expression at all on her face. At first, she was thought to be deaf and blind because she was so totally unresponsive. Later observation, however, proved this was not the case.

Unfortunately, Anna died when she was about ten and a half of hemorrhagic jaundice, but by that time she had improved considerably with the help of medical doctors and psychologists. She could walk; she showed love to a doll; she could follow directions; she could keep herself clean; and she could talk, although she could not carry on a complete conversation. She had even learned to run, although she was clumsy. After four and a half years of training, Anna was socialized to about the age of a child of two or three. Despite the fact that she had had

112

a very late start, she proved that progress can be made. Her early death, however, makes it hard to know if she would have ever caught up with children of her own age.

The second case Davis discussed in his study concerns Isabelle, and it helps us to understand Anna's problems better. Isabelle was found at about the same time and was approximately the same age as Anna. She had also been isolated from people for the same reason. The important difference between the two little girls was that Isabelle did have some contact with her mother as both were locked up together. The mother, however, was a deaf-mute and could not communicate with Isabelle verbally. Yet she could gesture and show her affection, and thus provided some socialization.

When Isabelle was found, she showed a great deal of hostility and fear, especially toward men. As with Anna, doctors who worked with Isabelle thought she was deaf since she did not respond to questions and her speech consisted only of grunting noises. At first, the people who worked with her decided that she was also retarded because of her infantile behavior; nevertheless, they tried to teach and train her. Progress was very slow but once she began to improve, her development was remarkable. She moved through all the normal stages of learning in the proper order, but much faster than the ordinary child. In two years, she learned what it takes the average child six years to learn. By the time she was about nine years old, she was in school and keeping up with the other children.

Isabelle and Anna both started out at about the same level. However, while Isabelle made remarkable progress, catching up to her peers within two years, Anna, although improved, was still far behind her age group after four and a half years. No one can be sure of the cause of the different rates of development. Could it be that Anna was innately inferior intellectually? Is it possible that Isabelle received better care from more highly trained people than Anna did? Kingsley Davis believes that because Isabelle had absorbed some socialization and human contact from her mother, her progress was faster. Davis also points out that delayed socialization does not mean that one can never be socialized, although he cannot be sure at what age socialization would become impossible. His guess is that age fifteen is probably too late, but age ten is still possible depending on the individual. Most important:

> Both cases, and others like them, reveal in a unique way the role of socialization in personality development. Most of the human behavior we regard as somehow given in the species does not occur apart from training and example by others. Most of the mental traits we think of as constituting the human mind are not present unless put there by communicative contact with others.[4]

FOCUS ON: CHILD REARING IN THE U.S. AND THE U.S.S.R.

The methods by which children are reared affect their later development. According to sociologist Urie Bronfenbrenner, the methods used in the United States and the Soviet Union differ radically. In *Two Worlds of Childhood,* Bronfenbrenner describes how a society's methods of rearing children are related to its expectations of those children as adults.

In the earliest years of life, Soviet children attend nurseries operated by the state and staffed by state-trained professionals. These nurseries are warm, supportive, yet disciplined environments. As children mature in this system they become aware of the large number of adults, in addition to their parents, who are responsible for their upbringing.

Activities and academic work in the school setting are group-oriented. Kindergarten children play games that involve group competition rather than individual competition. For example, one group of children will push a large ball in the opposite direction from another group until it passes over a goal line in the room. In their academic efforts, each row of students forms a "link." The work each row does is graded as a group and is compared to the work of other "links" in the class. Soviet students are also responsible to their "link" for their personal habits, punctuality, neatness, personal hygiene, and so forth.

Classroom chores as well as academic work are completed in groups. When someone misbehaves, students who are members of the Young Pioneers (an association comparable to the Boy Scouts and Girl Scouts of America) form a review board to publicly confront the offender and determine the appropriate punishment.

In contrast, American kindergartens stress competition and individuality. Here children are taught to recognize the importance of self-advancement, and are encouraged to develop a sense of personal advancement and achievement.

One of the major differences between the two societies is the way in which each interprets freedom. Because the child in the United States is taught to value individual freedom, there is less sense of "collective responsibility." Soviet children are taught to interpret freedom as a shared group experience.

Why does child rearing in the Soviet Union stress group competition and rewards? Why are Soviet children given such extensive responsibility for the conduct of their peers? How do the relationships among children in the Soviet Union differ from those among children in the United States? Do the methods each society uses to socialize children seem consistent with its goals? How might children in each society view their society after they are grown?

Source: Urie Bronfenbrenner, *Two Worlds of Childhood,* New York: Pocket Books, 1973.

Nature and Nurture

Neither scientists nor lay people have always realized the impact of socialization on human personality development. During the nineteenth century many people believed that nature influenced our personalities. These people felt that human beings were born with basic personalities, inheriting character traits and abilities from their

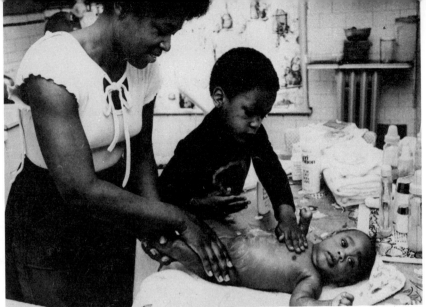

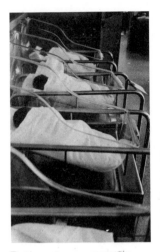

Both *nature*—genetic characteristics that are present at birth—*(left)* and *nurture*—the way we are reared—*(right)* interact to shape human personality development. Neither factor alone determines the kind of people we become.

parents in their genes. Those who favored this notion pointed out that "good" families frequently had members who were talented in many areas, while "bad" families frequently produced generation after generation of criminals, alcoholics, and so on. In other words, some families passed on "good" genes to their descendants and some passed on "bad" genes.

Other evidence for the importance of natural tendencies came from the physical resemblances children often had to their parents and to each other. The reasoning went that if we can inherit physical traits, why can we not inherit such things as intelligence, ability, talent, and emotional makeup?

Much of this kind of thinking came out of a theory put forth by naturalist Charles Darwin in the mid-nineteenth century. He believed that *homo sapiens* and apes have a common ancestor and that people therefore are simply one kind of animal. Like the other animals, then, they are born with innate qualities and instincts that cannot be altered. Instinct was an important concept during this era and up to the 1920s. The maternal instinct explained that all females desire to become mothers and care for children; the herding instinct explained why people tend to live in groups rather than separate from each other; an aggressive instinct explained that wars are inevitable. Instincts were used to explain all our behaviors.

A famous American psychologist, John B. Watson, was a leading proponent of an opposing theory in the 1920s. He believed that nurture influenced our personalities. According to Watson, a baby is born with a mind that is *tabula rasa* (a blank slate) and becomes a person because of the way he or she is reared. Watson wrote:

115

> Give me a dozen healthy infants, well-formed, and my own specified world to bring them up in, and I'll guarantee to take any one at random and train him to become any type of specialist I might select—doctor, lawyer, artist, merchant, chief, and, yes, even beggar-man and thief, regardless of his talents, penchants, tendencies, abilities, vocations, and race of his ancestors.[5]

Today both these extreme theories have been rejected. People no longer believe that all our characteristics are inherited at birth and cannot be changed. Nor do they accept the notion that everything in our personalities is learned. Neither nature nor nurture completely determines the kind of person a human being will become. Instead we know that biological and social factors each play a role in determining our personalities. Our biology determines *how much* and *how well* we can learn. If we are born with a limited intelligence, there is nothing the society can do to teach us beyond that inborn ability. On the other hand, we can learn only *what* the society has to teach us. American children do not learn to become headhunters because headhunting is not part of our culture. But they might learn how to become lawyers, plumbers, accountants, taxicab drivers, ice-skaters, thieves, or any other occupation the culture includes. The Nepali child does not learn to become a nuclear physicist or a sociologist because at the present time Nepal does not have the capacity and the technology to offer such training. Instead, Nepali children learn how to herd goats and grow rice. Thus, both nature and nurture interact to produce the human being. The former says whether or not we can learn; the latter says what we can learn.

The Functions of Socialization

Social scientists generally agree that socialization has four major functions. First, the values, attitudes, customs, behaviors, and skills of the society are transmitted to the next generation. Second, socialization serves as a means of social control by instilling a sense of morality in those growing up. Third, people learn what their unique places are in the society and how to interact within that framework. Fourth, during socialization, human beings develop their personalities or their sense of self. Let us look at each of these functions in more detail.

LEARNING THE WAYS OF THE SOCIETY

Each society has different ways of attaining the same goals and doing the same things. For example, all people must have a place in which to live, although housing preferences may differ among them.

116

FOCUS ON: MASCULINE SOCIALIZATION

Are children being socialized to their maximum potentials? Are boys and girls being properly prepared to face our changing society? Educators Dorothy and Jerome Singer think not. In an article entitled "Raising Boys Who Know How to Love," the Singers outline their plan for rearing children.

The Singers believe that children are currently being reared according to certain beliefs about each sex. For example, girls are thought to be nurturant and passive, while boys are believed to be dominant and aggressive. In fact, a study by psychologist Jeanne Humphrey Block has shown that by the age of two-and-a-half girls are encouraged in their play to be nurturant, protective, and providing, while boys are encouraged to be aggressive and adventurous.

While many believe that such sex differences are inborn, the Singers believe that they are acquired. They feel that children learn these attitudes from their parents. Thus, a boy who has been hit by another child and goes crying to his mother would hear the words, "Go back and stick up for yourself. Don't be a sissy." The boy, in turn, would learn that crying is not manly. On the other hand, if a girl displayed the same behavior, she would be comforted and would learn that crying was acceptable.

What is needed, according to the Singers, is a major revolution in our beliefs about masculinity and femininity. Women and men will have to be taught to recognize that true manliness involves the fullest development of a man's capacities, including the capacity to feel and express tenderness. True manliness involves commitment and responsibility for others, a sense of sharing, and a willingness to risk something for a full family relationship.

From an early age, boys will have to be allowed from time to time to run away from battle; they will have to be allowed to cry. They will have to be given a chance to play with dolls or to engage in make-believe play as nurses or teachers. Fathers will have to be willing to accept some softness in their sons and, indeed, to set examples in their own behavior. Women, too, will have to face up to some of their own myths about masculinity so they can allow their sons to develop more fully.

Do you believe that children are still being reared along masculine/feminine lines? What changes would have to occur in the rearing of girls to enable them to develop more fully? Do you think it is possible to have a society in which both sexes will be socialized equally?

Source: Dorothy Singer, Ed. D. and Jerome L. Singer, Ph.D., "Raising Boys Who Know to Love," *Parents Magazine*, December 1977, pp. 32+.

Many Eskimo children learn that proper housing is an igloo. Many American Indians once taught their children that people live in tepees. Those Americans who live in rural areas or in suburbs give their children the notion that single-unit homes are preferable, while people who live in cities are more likely to instill in their children a preference for apartment-house dwelling. Each group teaches its children which type of housing is desirable.

Food is another example, and societies differ in the kinds of things they eat. The Chinese consider dog a delicacy. Many Indian Hindus are prohibited from eating cattle. Other Indians—for example, the Jains, who are also settled in the Caribbean Islands—eat no meat at all. Orthodox Jews are forbidden to eat meat and milk at the same time or to eat any pork products. In addition, each society cooks food differently. Many Japanese like to eat raw fish. The French prefer to prepare many foods with wine sauces. Children from different societies, then, learn these preferences as they grow up and come to develop tastes for different kinds of foods and different ways of cooking this food.

We can see examples of differences in many other customs. Traditional Indian women wear saris; many Japanese women wear kimonos. Frequently French people kiss each other on both cheeks as a greeting, but most Americans shake hands. In Israel on the kibbutzim (collective farms) children are raised in children's houses, apart from their parents. In the United States, most children are brought up in their parents' homes. In Upper Volta in Africa, a man is expected to have many wives; in the United States, having more than one wife at a time is illegal.

In short, there are many variations in customs, habits, attitudes, beliefs, and norms cross-culturally and even in different regions of the same country. If children are to be able to function productively and happily within their societies, they must learn what these patterns are. If they do not, they may be laughed at, punished, even ostracized, depending on how severely they stray from these patterns. If an American girl were to go to school dressed in animal skins, she would be laughed at by her peers, just as her father would be considered strange if he were to greet his business associates by placing the palms of his hands to-

The type of home you choose to live in probably depends on that type of home your family and society taught you was preferable. This South Ugandan tribal hut *(left)* and this Eskimo igloo *(right)* are two housing preferences.

gether and bowing his head as the South Asians do. Thus, starting with infancy, we teach our children what we consider to be proper in our society.

SOCIAL CONTROL

Every society must have mechanisms for *social control*—means of ensuring that its members will behave in socially accepted ways. Some of the society's more serious norms are enforced by such government agencies as police departments. But in order to maintain general order, society must depend heavily on the discretion of its members. Even when no one is in sight, we seldom drive our cars through red lights. Even though we may hate another individual, we rarely kill that person. Even when we admire an article in a store that we cannot afford to buy, we rarely steal it. Our socialization therefore prevents us from committing serious violations against society and each other. If we had not internalized social control mechanisms during socialization, societies would need to have a police officer on every corner.

The process of socialization also operates to control our daily behavior. We normally stand quietly in lines and do not push to be "first." We are usually polite even to people we do not like. Most of us know the proper utensils to use at the table. Most of us know not to wear jeans to weddings or formal clothes to picnics.

Socialization, then, is a means of learning how to control our own behavior according to socially approved standards. Most of us conform without needing to think each act through individually. We follow norms without question because they become part of our knowledge during childhood and we come to believe that these ways of thinking and acting are right and proper. Thus, socialization helps society by imposing restraints on our behavior without our conscious realization and by helping us to develop moral judgment.

FITTING INTO SOCIETY

Every society has a social structure, and part of our socialization involves learning where we fit into that structure. As we discussed in Chapter 2, our *statuses* and *roles* help us determine our behavior in society.

A *status* is simply a position in society. It can either be assigned at birth, such as race, or earned during one's lifetime, such as occupation. The former is an *ascribed status* and the latter an *achieved status*. We also occupy several statuses at once. A woman can be a wife, a mother, and a doctor during the same period of her life.

119

A *role* is the expected behavioral pattern attached to a particular status. Each role has certain specific rights and obligations. For example, as a student you are expected to attend classes, to prepare assignments, and to study for examinations. Although you may deviate somewhat from your role—perhaps you may cut a few classes—severe deviation will not be tolerated.

Socialization points out our various statuses and teaches us the proper role behavior attached to each. In doing so it provides guidelines for social action. Hence, once we know the general expectations for a particular status, we can perform its associated roles with relatively little difficulty. Life would be troublesome indeed if in every situation we encountered we had to experiment with all possible behaviors to find the one best suited to the situation.

Similarly, by knowing what is expected of people who occupy various statuses, we can predict the likely behavior of those with whom we interact. We can tell how bus drivers will act while driving their buses, how teachers will act in a classroom, or how our teammates will act on the playing field. In this manner, we can provide regularity and stability in our lives. By knowing beforehand what will probably happen in specific situations, we are able to prepare for these situations and, as a result, carry out our interactions with a minimum of trouble.

Thus, the third function of socialization is to make us aware of the social statuses that people occupy and of how to behave in them. These social statuses, taken together, determine the social structure of the society. For the society to function smoothly, members must know the social statuses they occupy and the patterns of rights and obligations that accompany the statuses.

THE DEVELOPMENT OF PERSONALITY

Infants have no knowledge of anything beyond their immediate physical needs. Even this cannot correctly be called "knowledge," only simple reaction. Newborns feel a pain in their stomachs, but they do not connect that pain to hunger and they do not understand that it can be removed by ingesting food. They feel pain; they do not "know" they are hungry.

In the same way, infants do not know anything about themselves. They do not know if they are male or female, white- or brown-skinned, blue- or brown-eyed, kind or mean, smart or ignorant. No infant has a notion of its "self" or its *personality*, which sociologists define as an individual's typical patterns of attitudes and behaviors that are recognized by the individual and by others.

Personality is made up of three components, all of which are learned during socialization. The cognitive component includes what

120

we perceive, think, and remember. The behavioral component consists of our abilities, talents, and skills. The emotional component comprises our feelings, such as hate, love, sympathy, and anger. Children are born with varying potentials for developing each of these components. How fully these potentials are developed and what direction they take depends on what a child learns during socialization. Some children learn to think more clearly, some develop talents more quickly, and some feel emotions more strongly. Thus, such differences among children depend partly on biology and partly on socialization.

Much of our personality is a reflection of our culture. Different cultures admire and encourage different kinds of personalities in their members. For example, the Yanomamö Indians of Brazil encourage male children to strike their parents as a means of expressing anger.[6] Similarly, the Mundugumor of New Guinea were fierce and aggressive and always seemed to be fighting. In contrast, the Arapesh, also of New Guinea, encouraged passivity and cooperation among their members.[7]

Yet, although members of societies share certain personality traits because they have been similarly socialized, each member of a society is unique. Each interacts with different people. Each belongs to different subgroups within the larger society. Americans in the upper classes are socialized differently from those in the middle or lower classes. Catholics do not learn exactly the same values as Jews or Protestants. Southerners may be encouraged to develop different characteristics from Northerners. Rural people have different viewpoints from urbanites, and so on.

One of the most important functions of socialization, then, is the development of personality. But the personalities that emerge vary according to inborn dissimilarities, the values of the society or the subgroups, and the individuals with whom the person being socialized interacts. If this were not so—if all of us were exactly alike—what a monotonous world we would live in!

Theories of Socialization

Most of the scholars who have addressed themselves to the study of socialization have been advocates of a sociological perspective called *symbolic interaction* (see pp. 9 and 10). This perspective focuses on human beings interacting in everyday life. Its basic premise is that people interact by communicating with each other using symbols, most frequently language, whose meanings are shared by all those interacting. If we did not have shared symbols, we could not interact or communicate and socialization would be impossible. Without socialization, civilization would also be impossible and society could not exist.

121

Thus, symbolic interactionists try to understand the process of socialization, although they take various approaches to it and are interested in various aspects of it. How does it work? Why is it necessary for the development of the human being? Do all societies socialize their children? Let us look more closely at some of the theories sociologists use to answer these and other questions.

THE LOOKING-GLASS SELF

Charles Horton Cooley[8] (see page 60) explained how people develop a self-image. According to Cooley, our image of ourselves can come only from our interaction within society. There can be no "I" unless there is also a "they." "They" consists of all the people in the society in which we live. The first "they" is the parent. As we get older, more "theys" come into our worlds. We learn to see ourselves as the reflection of what we think others see, especially those others in the primary group (see Chapter 2). According to Cooley, then, we are not what we think we are. But neither are we what "they" think we are because we can never be absolutely sure that we are understanding and interpreting the attitudes of others toward us correctly. Nor can we be absolutely sure that, even if we ask people directly what they think of us, they will tell the truth. Therefore, we can only imagine how others see us. Our selves are always the result of how we believe we look to others. Gradually we build up an image of ourselves from notions of others' opinions of us—our *looking-glass self*.

For example, if a little girl is told from the very first years of her life that she is intelligent, she will eventually come to see herself as a smart girl. She will internalize the picture of herself that all the people with whom she interacts reflect. It does not matter whether or nor she is really intelligent; she will think that she is and this will cause her to attempt to act as if it were true. One's self-image, derived from the way one is treated by others, however, is not necessarily a true image. Objectively, the girl in this example may be of only average intelligence, but in her own mind she will be very intelligent. This is what sociologist W. I. Thomas meant by the statement: "If men define situations as real, they are real in their consequences."[9]

The same process may work to give us an undesirable picture of ourselves. A boy who is told repeatedly that his ears are too large and his hair is too stringy will develop a self-image of himself as physically unattractive. Whether or not these statements are actually true does not matter. What is important is that he believes they are true.

In short, children decide whether they are intelligent or stupid, handsome or ugly, talented or dull, lovable or unlovable through the way they understand others' attitudes toward them. This is the "self"

APPLYING SOCIOLOGY

Try an experiment to see how valid Cooley's notion of the looking-glass self is. Tell a friend or a relative that you think he or she is looking different today. Then treat that person somewhat differently from the way you usually treat him or her. Does the individual's self-image seem to change? How does the change manifest itself? Does the person act nervous? Unsure of himself or herself? Confused? You could extend this experiment by having several people inform your friend or relative of the same observation. Is the person even more disoriented? If so, does this confirm Cooley's notion that our personalities are merely reflections of what we think others think of us?

---

that Cooley called the "looking-glass self." Cooley maintained that the looking-glass self has three components: 1) our perceptions of how we appear to others; 2) our perceptions of how others judge us; and 3) our feelings about those judgments.[10]

THE SIGNIFICANT OTHER
AND THE GENERALIZED OTHER

All the childhood impressions we get of what people think of us are internalized; they become very real and almost unchangeable. Sociologist George Herbert Mead (see page 124) traced the process through which the "self" develops.[11]

Basing his work on Cooley's, Mead contended that the self has two parts: the "I" and the "me." The "I" is that part of one's "self" that is innate and that contains the spontaneous, natural, creative special aspects of one's self—the part that makes each one of us a unique person. The "me" is the side of one's "self" that is socialized, the part that has internalized the rules of society. The "me" is the conforming part of the self that makes each of us similar to the other members of our society. *"I" represents inner demands; "me" represents societal demands.*

According to Mead, the first individuals who impose restrictions on the "I" are called *significant others*. These are the people who are important in a person's life, people who are admired and whom we try to please. Significant others may be considered as *role models*, individuals we want to be like and to imitate. For example, most little girls choose their mothers and most little boys choose their fathers as role models.

Groups of people who are meaningful in the development of the self are called *reference groups* because we refer to them in our minds,

George Herbert Mead (1863–1931)

George Herbert Mead made his greatest contribution to a subspecialty called social psychology. This area of study bridges the gap between sociology and psychology (the study of the individual). In his theory of the social self, Mead agreed with Cooley that personality is the product of society. From infancy through old age, individuals interact with others and learn to put themselves in other people's positions. As they take on the "role of the other," they learn which behaviors will evoke approval or disapproval. Furthermore, during interaction and role-taking, individuals develop a sense of who they are in relation to others.

Mead called the people who influence our sense of self "significant others." These people consist of our parents, siblings, other relatives, peers, and teachers. Gradually people internalize the values and attitudes of these significant others and apply them to the whole moral community—the "generalized other." Thus significant others are real persons, but the generalized other is composed of societal values.

Human beings respond to the definitions of "good" and "bad" as set forth by the generalized other and behave accordingly, reflecting the expectations of others. Mead referred to this aspect of the self as the "me," the product of socialization. Mead was aware, however, that there is another part of the self—the "I." This part remains independent of the generalized other and socialization. The "I" is the spontaneous, unique, unconforming, creative part of each of us that makes us special.

Society needs its members to have both aspects. If our selves were all "I," society would be chaotic and disorganized. Group life would be impossible. If our selves were all "me," there would be no innovation, invention, or social change. We all would be robots.

consciously or unconsciously, as we make decisions about our behavior. A reference group, for a girl who wants to become an actress, would be all actresses. A role model would be some particular actress whom she especially admires.

This imitation of role models involves *role-taking*, a process during which we put ourselves in the place of the role model, essentially taking that role, so that we can understand his or her reactions to our self. When we imagine ourselves in the role of the significant other, we can anticipate the response we will get to our behavior, and in this way we can see how we appear to the other and modify our behavior accordingly. For example, a young child who is about to talk out of turn in class would stop and say to himself or herself, "No, you must raise your hand." Children role-take when they play house and imitate their own parents, neighbors, or teachers.

124

Drawing by Opie; © 1978 The New Yorker, Magazine, Inc.

As children grow older and their world enlarges, the significant others become more numerous; gradually Mead's *generalized other* becomes real to them. This means that they repeatedly role-take with significant others, and as they come to know many people, their notion of the values of the whole community becomes set in their minds. Significant others increase to become all of "them out there." Awareness widens to include all of society; in this way children learn to conform to societal mores and norms. In addition to seeking approval from the significant others, they realize they should conform to the whole society's expectations—the generalized other.

The acceptance of the values and norms of the generalized other by the "me" part of the self accounts for the *similarities* among people. The "I" accounts for the *differences* among people because we select different role models and different things about them to imitate.

APPLYING SOCIOLOGY

Try to remember some of the roles you took when you were a child. Do you remember the reactions of your friends or family to these roles? Can you think of people you have known during your life who have been or who still are your role models? Why do you suppose you chose them? Which of their characteristics do you think you have adopted as a part of yourself?

THE PSYCHOANALYTIC APPROACH

Cooley and Mead viewed socialization as a process that gradually brought society and the individual (or the self) into harmony with each other. On the other hand, psychoanalyst Sigmund Freud (see box on this page) believed that society and the individual were in constant conflict.[12] Part of the reason for the disagreement was that Cooley and Mead thought of the individual as a social product, while Freud was more concerned with the biological aspect of the individual and the constraints that society imposed on the natural impulses of people. Freud contended that socialization was forced on children and that all through life, even as adults, they tried to resist the rules of society. The major area in which these thinkers agreed, however, was that childhood and the experiences one has during the earliest years of life have a lasting effect on one's self.

Freud viewed the infant as a completely self-centered individual, who is always seeking personal pleasure without regard for others. According to Freud, the very young child is aggressive, amoral, and

Sigmund Freud (1856–1938)

Sigmund Freud's intellectual contributions to the contemporary world are numerous. His ideas have spread far beyond the scholarly community and into popular culture.

One of Freud's major contributions is that he left us a technique for analyzing individual personality structure and behavior. This technique, which is known as psychoanalysis, is used in clinical psychotherapy to help individuals discover and resolve personal problems. Freud wrote extensively about several specific psychoanalytic methods, including dream interpretation and free association.

Freud believed that human beings are in a constant state of conflict resulting from their biological drives. According to Freud, people must choose whether to allow their drives full expression or whether to control them. If we choose the first, we must live without the security of society; if we choose the second, we must accept the frustrations imposed by social restrictions. Clearly, as Freud points out in *Civilization and Its Discontents*, most of us have chosen the second possibility.

One of Freud's most revolutionary contributions is his doctrine of the unconscious. Essentially Freud argued that we are unaware of much of what is going on in our minds. This often becomes evident through our frequent "slips of the tongue" and in our dreams. Hence, according to Freud, we say or dream things that reflect our true feelings, even though we may not always be aware of such feelings.

Among the most original of Freud's many ideas are his theories on psychosexual development. One of these theories is that young children

egocentric—an animal who behaves according to its own selfish instincts and impulses. Freud used the term *id* to describe that part of us that contains all our innate biological drives, including our sexual and aggressive tendencies.

Parents gradually interfere with the baby's pleasure-seeking id. Instead of feeding the baby as soon as he or she demands food, parents follow feeding schedules and force the child to wait for food until the proper time. As children get a little older, they are taught how to use the bathroom. According to Freud, this is another control over the impulses of the id, which would prefer to let the child urinate and defecate whenever and wherever it wanted to. All the "do's" and "don't's" that parents impose on their children restrict the id's impulses and selfishness.

Because children need love and approval, they try to obey the demands of parents, who represent society. As they struggle to comply, they develop an *ego*. The ego is the rational part of the person. It attempts to satisfy the demands of the id in ways that will be acceptable to society. But this does not mean that the id's impulses disappear; they

---

feel sexually attracted toward the parent of the opposite sex. In young females, Freud termed this phenomenon the *Electra complex*, while in young males he labeled it the *Oedipus complex*. In each case, Freud was referring to the *castration complex*, the fear among boys that they will be castrated and the fear among girls that castration has already occurred. Freud's view was that children could mature only by resolving the complex. However, children could become "fixated," "delayed," or have their interests shift from one object to another which might impede sexual maturity. Freud also recognized that sexuality appears in very young children and that socially unacceptable sexual preferences are potential outcomes for anyone.

Freud's contributions to the definition and study of psychological problems are also important. Freud believed, as do many therapists today, that a psychological disturbance is related to the stage at which a person was exposed to stress or trauma as a child. During the "oral stage," for example, babies receive gratification by the stimulation of their gums and mouths. Adults who were frustrated in the oral stage as children are thought to go back to oral-type behaviors, such as excessive drinking or compulsive eating, when under stress. During the "anal stage," babies obtain pleasure through excretory activities. According to Freud, any frustration experienced during this stage can cause a person to become stingy, compulsive, or stubborn. During the "phallic stage," the area of pleasure shifts to the sex organs. In this stage children go through either the Electra or Oedipus complex. If the conflicts generated by these complexes are not resolved, Freud believed that serious problems in personality adjustment and interpersonal relationships can result.

APPLYING SOCIOLOGY

Try to think of times in your own life when you have turned your aggressive feelings toward a person in power and placed them on a powerless person or an inanimate object. For example, have you ever thrown a book against the wall when you felt anger at a teacher? Have you ever provoked an argument with one person when you were really furious with another? Discuss such episodes with other members of the class. It is unlikely that there is anyone in the class who has not experienced such feelings and acted in such ways.

are simply channeled to avoid punishment. A common example of this channeling can be seen in children who hit their dolls when they really are angry with a parent or sibling. They can get into trouble if they talk back to a parent or hit a brother or sister; no one will notice if they abuse a doll.

By about the age of five, children realize that their parents (and society) have enormous power over them. They become very fearful that they will be strongly punished for the id's aggressive and sexual impulses. During this period of life, the superego starts to develop. The superego is really the conscience. It is the part of the human personality that internalizes the parents' and society's notions of good and bad, right and wrong, moral and immoral. The superego suppresses the id's desires, unlike the ego, which tries to find acceptable ways to satisfy the id's desires.

Here is an example of how the three parts of the personality work. Suppose a child sees a cookie and wants to eat it. The id would tell the child to snatch the cookie and gobble it down quickly. The superego would tell the child that he or she really doesn't want the cookie at all. The ego would make the child ask the parent for permission to take the cookie.

Thus, according to Freud, the three aspects of personality are always in conflict with each other, each trying to gain control. None of them ever wins out completely. When the id is strongest in someone, that person is often in conflict with society. When the superego is strongest, the person is often overconforming and fearful of ever doing what he or she really wants to do. When the ego is the strongest, the person is most in balance between the desires of the id and the restrictions of society. But in Freud's view, no one can ever be completely at peace; as long as one lives in society, there is some discontent within the individual.

THE EIGHT STAGES OF DEVELOPMENT

One of Freud's most brilliant students, psychologist Erik H. Erikson,[13] expanded and integrated the theories of his teacher, as well as those of Cooley and Mead. He stressed the role of the ego as the mediator between the id and the superego in the battle between the self and society.

Erikson was one of the first social scientists to write about socialization as it occurs throughout life. He theorized that human beings pass through eight stages of development. In each stage there are physiological changes and new social situations. Each individual must adapt to these changes and therefore experience a crisis in each stage. Sometimes individuals react to these crises positively and other times negatively. If a person adapts well, if he or she is well oriented to each new situation, the individual will grow and the possibilities of new experiences and new relationships will be enhanced.

Stage one is infancy, spanning the first year of life. During stage one children are totally dependent on the adults who take care of them. If the needs of children are met during this stage with warmth and love, they will develop feelings of basic *trust* and a notion that there is security, reliability, and comfort in the world. If their needs are not met, or if the people who take care of them are not dependable and affectionate, children develop feelings of basic *mistrust*, a sense that the world is a frightening, suspicious, insecure place. Thus, during stage one, infants form their first impressions of the world. Either they can trust themselves and others or they cannot trust themselves and others.

Ages two and three compose stage two. During these years children learn many things: how to walk, talk, control their bodily functions, climb, open and close things, and so on. Usually they are proud of these new accomplishments and abilities, but a crisis can arise if the parents react to these skills incorrectly. It is during this period that

**FIGURE 4–1
Erikson's Eight Stages
of Life**

Stage	Age	Psychosocial Crisis
One	First year	Trust vs. Mistrust
Two	Two–Three	Autonomy vs. Shame and Doubt
Three	Four–Five	Initiative vs. Guilt
Four	Six–Eleven	Industry vs. Inferiority
Five	Adolescence	Identity vs. Role Confusion
Six	Young Adult-hood	Intimacy vs. Isolation
Seven	Middle Age	Generativity vs. Self-absorption
Eight	Old Age	Integrity vs. Despair

129

children can learn that they are able to take care of themselves or that they are weak and ineffectual, unsure of their own capabilities. If parents allow children freedom to try and even to fail, the children will gain confidence that they can control their lives. They will develop a sense of *autonomy,* or control over themselves. If the parents do not help the child during these years, showing impatience and being critical or overprotective, a sense of *doubt or shame* will be reinforced. In stage two, then, children learn whether or not they can stand on their own two feet.

Stage three occurs over the next two years of life and it is crucial for the growth of either *initiative* or *guilt.* Since children have learned how to control their own movements in the previous stage, they now try to extend their abilities—to explore, imitate, exploit opportunities, try new adventures. If parents praise children's efforts in these new behaviors and encourage them to keep on finding out about the world on their own, the children will develop feelings of self-worth and initiative. If they are punished or ridiculed for their failures in these attempts, or if they are made to feel inadequate or stupid, they will develop feelings of guilt. Stage three, therefore, is the time during which children learn either that they can successfully go out to seek and conquer new worlds or that they had better not try to be leaders because they will fail.

During infancy *(left),* the first stage of human development, infants develop either a sense of *trust* or a sense of *mistrust* toward others and the world. During the second stage of development—ages two to three—*(right)* children develop either a sense of *autonomy* or a sense of *doubt or shame.*

During the third stage of development, which includes ages four and five *(top)*, children develop either a sense of *initiative* or a sense of *guilt*. During the fourth stage—the elementary-school years of ages six to eleven—*(bottom)* children acquire either a sense of *industry* or a sense of *inferiority*.

The elementary school years (ages six through eleven) represent the fourth stage. The social setting of the school replaces the social setting of the home as the most important arena. Rewards for following the rules and learning skills are offered during this period. If children are praised and encouraged in their attempts to learn about the world and to develop the necessary talents to live in it successfully, they will acquire *a sense of industry*. If they do poorly in school and therefore are not encouraged, or if they face discrimination because of such things as race or religion, they will develop *a sense of inferiority*.

Adolescence occurs during the fifth stage between the ages of twelve and eighteen (adolescent socialization is treated in the following chapter). This is the time when children draw on all their past experiences in order to develop a sense of self. Mind and body both undergo extraordinarily rapid and often disturbing changes as the young people become sexually mature. The looking-glass self comes into full play as an understanding develops of the importance of how others regard oneself. If the adolescent can understand most of the aspects of his or her self, the ego will be strengthened and a sense of *identity* will develop. Such young people will know who they are, what they are capable of doing, where they are going, and what their goals are. On the other hand, if adolescents arrive at this point in life with feelings of mistrust, doubt, shame, guilt, or inferiority, they will be unable to integrate their personalities and *role confusion* will occur instead. The self will be hazy and unformed rather than clearly defined.

The sixth stage is the time of young adulthood. It is the time for learning to make close friends, to fall in love, and to start families. If young adults have acquired all the positive traits from the previous stages, they will be capable of forming close attachments and will have the ability to share and give of themselves without fear. This is *intimacy*. If, instead, young adults have acquired negative self-feelings from past stages, there will be *isolation*, an inability to allow the self closeness with friends and lovers.

Middle age marks the seventh stage. Most alternatives are no longer open to the individual. Life is moving on a path from which there is little possibility to change direction. At this point people begin to be concerned with those outside their immediate world, concerned with the future and the kind of society in which those who come after them will live. Erikson calls this interest in the welfare of younger people *generativity*. When individuals experience generativity, they feel they are helping to create a world that will be better for future generations. They feel their lives have been productive and that they have been useful members of society. Failure to establish a sense of generativity results in a sense of *self-absorption*. Such people find middle age a time of unhappiness. They are absorbed in what they feel is the failure of their lives. They are childishly selfish and unconcerned with the welfare of the generations that will follow them.

The eighth and final stage occurs in old age. In coming to terms with the inevitability of death, the elderly person reacts with either *integrity* or *despair*. Integrity gives a person the ability to look back on his or her life with satisfaction and self-acceptance, recognizing that there have been good times and bad times, joy and pain, happiness and sadness. And all of them have been meaningful and part of life. On the other hand, when one's old age is characterized by despair, that person reflects on his or her life and sees it as a series of failures and disappointments. Despair occurs because it is now much too late to change anything. Thus life ends in either integrity or despair, depending on the alternatives that have occurred and have been taken in all the previous stages.

Erikson agrees with the theorists we have discussed earlier when he stresses the significance of the earliest years of life for the future. However, he also believes that modifications can occur during any stage. We get many chances to alter the course of our lives. If we learn distrust during stage one, we can perhaps make up for it by choosing initiative over guilt in stage three. If guilt dominates the third stage, it is still possible to overcome feelings of inferiority during stage four. Of course no one goes through life always getting the best or the worst of each stage. There is always a little of each. Most important, there are almost always opportunities to reverse negative aspects and to enhance positive ones.

COGNITIVE DEVELOPMENT APPROACH

When we talked about the functions of socialization, we discussed social control and how important it is for society that people learn its moral values. But what are these moral values—these rules of conduct or established standards of behavior? How do theorists think people are socialized to accept them?

Moral values are beliefs about good and bad that are shared by the members of a group or a society. A moral person is someone who obeys the norms of the society. All societies have moral rules. Most societies have certain rules in common, such as rules against killing. But even the definition of killing is not shared by all groups at all times. For example, in the United States killing another human being under normal circumstances is forbidden, but killing during war time is not only legal, it is also rewarded with medals if someone kills the enemy in large enough numbers.

In addition, some societies have rules prohibiting a certain kind of behavior, while other societies have rules encouraging that very same behavior. In the United States, for example, stealing is generally considered immoral. But in some East African tribes it has been socially defined as morally right to steal cattle from another tribe. Among some American Plains Indians, stealing horses from the tribe's enemies was considered a mark of great courage, while among settlers in the Old West, horse thievery was an offense punishable by hanging.

Thus, there are some moral rules that are almost universal and some that only certain groups choose at certain times. The important point is that social order comes about because societies have systems of rules. When the rules are clear to the majority of the members and when most of the people obey them, society will be orderly.

During socialization young children usually learn the rules, understand them, internalize them, and obey them. Very young children have not yet internalized the rules and so they often experience conflict between what they want to do and what they should do. As children get older, training lessens the conflict. If the socialization process is completely successful (which it almost never is), the conflict will disappear because the individual will hold the same moral values as the society. Not only will such people conform to the rules, but they will also accept them as their own personal values.

Jean Piaget

The great Swiss child psychologist, Jean Piaget,[14] tried to explain how human beings learn and accept the morality of their societies. He did his research by systematically observing children at play, because in the games they play there are rules that must be obeyed. Piaget contended that how children handle the rules of their games could explain how they handle the rules of their societies.

Piaget wanted to learn how the rules of the children's games come about, how they are changed, the meanings children attach to them, and how the meanings change as the children grow older. He reasoned that there are stages in the moral development of children. This development begins before children even know there are rules in a game and it ends when the rules are internalized. The phases are difficult to separate because they flow into each other.

At first children's behavior is not rule-bound because they have no awareness of rules and morality. Infants do not understand the difference between "right" and "wrong" or "good" and "bad." This is the period of life when one is most *egocentric*. Children consider themselves the center of the world. At this stage children cannot take the role of the other and therefore cannot understand and do not care how others may feel. Infants, as we all know, demand parental attention without any consideration for the adults' rights and preoccupations.

Gradually children come to see the morality of their society as "out there" and unchangeable. According to Piaget, they regard it as imposed upon them from outside, something over which they have no control and which they must obey. At the same time, since the rules are imposed from "above," children do not feel that they must do any more than obey them. They do not have to believe in them or feel the rules are beneficial. Nevertheless, at this stage, rules are regarded as sacred and one must not deviate from them. The child believes that although he or she did not create the rules, they must be followed.

Finally, children come to recognize that the rules are good for all the members of the group. They are necessary for social order. All members agree, at this stage of development, that the society created the rules so that all people can benefit. They are created, Piaget tells us, by mutual consent and can be changed by mutual consent.

The game of hopscotch provides a good example of this development. During the first stage the child does not know the game exists, does not know the rules, and certainly does not play the game. As time passes, the rules are learned and the young child follows them blindly because "all the kids" play hopscotch exactly that way. During the next stage, it becomes apparent that the rules are really flexible and, if all the players agree, the game can be played in several different ways. Thus, slowly, children learn that rules are meant to be followed. If everyone thinks, however, that changes in them will make the game more interesting, exciting, or fair, then changes can be allowed without disrupting the game and making it unplayable.

These, then, are the steps by which, Piaget theorizes, people come to accept society's norms. In this way, people realize the importance of preserving social order and the part they can play in maintaining it.

Lawrence Kohlberg

Like Piaget, psychologist Lawrence Kohlberg is also concerned with the moral development of the child.[15] In order to trace this development, Kohlberg described situations to children that offered moral problems and examined the behavior they considered to be correct under the circumstances. For example, if a child notices that his or her best friend is cheating on a test, should the incident be reported to the teacher or should one's friend be protected? Kohlberg asked such questions of children from many nations and concluded that the development of moral judgment occurs on three levels, each containing two stages. Kohlberg does not put these levels into age groups because he claims that not all people reach each level at the same point in the life cycle.

The *preconventional level* includes stage one, during which children behave out of a fear of punishment, and stage two, during which children behave to get rewards. In neither of these stages is there a sense of "good" or "bad." Rather, children first behave so as to avoid unpleasantness and then to gain pleasure. At the preconventional level, then, the child might not report the cheating out of fear that the friend would be angry or in order to receive thanks from the friend.

The second level is called the *conventional level,* during which people develop a sense of caring what others think of them. In stage three, children behave well because they want approval. They want to be liked by others. Slowly, as they enter stage four, notions of "good" and "bad" become meaningful and children learn the rules of their particular society. Youngsters at the conventional level would probably report cheating because it is simply wrong—always—to cheat, regardless of circumstances.

The *postconventional level* occurs as people move into the wider world where they discover ideas that differ from those they learned in their home environments. At this point, stage five, moral judgment really begins because there is less rigidity about rules than at the conventional level. People recognize that morals can be in conflict and reasoning must be applied in specific situations. By the sixth stage, moral values become internalized and people behave in what they consider to be proper ways. On the postconventional level, the dilemma of the cheating friend could be resolved either way, in accordance with one's own conscience and notions of justice and loyalty.

Thus socialization teaches human beings how to live within their societies and become productive human beings. In many ways it creates conformity, yet each of us is a unique person. As anthropologists Clyde Kluckhohn and Henry A. Murray remind us: "Every man is in certain respects: like all other men, like some other men, like no other men."[16]

SUMMARY

Socialization is a learning process through which all members of a society must pass. The mother or the person who does the mothering is the infant's first *socializing agent.* As infants grow older they become aware of other people in their environment, many of whom become socializing agents as they interact with the child and the child interacts with them. Such interaction is both biologically and emotionally necessary to the child.

Many scientists and lay people did not realize the importance of socialization on human personality development. During the nineteenth century and into the twentieth century many social scientists debated the question of nature versus nurture. Today most social scientists believe that biological factors determine how much we can learn, while social factors determine what we can learn.

Socialization has four major functions. One is to transmit the values, attitudes, customs, behaviors, and skills of the society to the next generation. A second is to instill moral judgment that serves as a means of social control. A third function is to help people realize their place in the society and how to interact within that framework. As its fourth function, socialization is a means through which human beings develop their *personalities* and their sense of "self."

Several social scientists, primarily *symbolic interactionists,* have put forth theories to explain socialization. Charles Horton Cooley claimed that the self is based on imagined reflections of others in the society. The "self" is a *"looking-glass self."*

George Herbert Mead contended that the self has two parts. The "I" is the natural, spontaneous aspect; the "me" is the socialized aspect. During socialization, the individual learns societal rules and roles by interacting with *significant others.* Over time the significant others become *role models,* and individuals *role-take* with them in order to anticipate reactions to themselves and in order to learn how to play future roles. Gradually, the number of significant others in a child's life increases, and the *generalized other* also becomes internalized. The generalized other is really the whole society whose standards of behavior the well-socialized person observes and follows.

Cooley and Mead viewed the relationship between the individual and society as harmonious. Sigmund Freud saw the relationship as disharmonious. He noted three aspects of personality. The *id* contains the instinctive sexual and aggressive human tendencies. The *ego* attempts to channel these tendencies into socially acceptable behaviors. The *superego,* or conscience, tries to suppress the id's spontaneity. All are fighting for control over the individual.

Erik H. Erikson described eight stages of life. These are trust versus mistrust; autonomy versus doubt; initiative versus guilt; industry versus inferiority; identity versus role confusion; intimacy versus isolation; generativity versus self-absorption; and integrity versus despair.

Cognitive development theory is concerned with the development of morality. Jean Piaget observed children at play in order to understand how they learn rules, how they change the rules, and what meanings they attach to them. He concluded that at first children are unaware of rules. Gradually they view rules as external to themselves, sacred, and unchangeable. Eventually they realize that rules are necessary for an orderly society and they abide by them voluntarily.

Lawrence Kohlberg, also concerned with moral judgment, sees socialization as occurring on three levels. On the preconventional level, obedience is the result of fear of punishment or hope of reward. On the conventional level, behavior is oriented toward the approval of others and a rigid notion of rules. On the postconventional level, people seek self-approval and rules are seen as flexible, depending on individual circumstances.

GLOSSARY

achieved status   a position in society that one chooses or earns.

ascribed status   a position in society into which one is born and that usually cannot be altered.

ego   the term Freud used to describe the aspect of an individual's personality that attempts to satisfy the demands of the id in socially acceptable ways.

generalized other   an abstract concept referring to the whole society whose values and expectations individuals observe and follow.

id   the term Freud used to describe the aspect of an individual's personality that contains the innate sexual and aggressive tendencies.

internalization   the absorption by members of a society of the approved values, skills, attitudes, and norms of their society.

looking-glass self   Cooley's theory that the development of the self is the product of interpreting the reactions of others to oneself.

personality   an individual's typical patterns of attitudes and behaviors that are recognized by the individual and by others.

reference group   a social group to which individuals want to belong that serves as a model or standard by which they pattern their behavior.

role   the expected behavioral pattern attached to a status, carrying specific rights and obligations.

role model   a person whom one imitates in order to become like that person.

role-taking   a process by which individuals put themselves in the role of another person in order to understand that person's reactions to their selves.

significant other   a person who has great influence on the development of an individual's self-image.

social control   the means a society uses to ensure that its members will behave in socially acceptable ways.

socialization   a process through which a human being learns and internalizes the values, skills, attitudes, and norms of the society into which he or she was born, develops a sense of self, and learns his or her place in society.

socializing agent a person who teaches the individual the values, skills, attitudes, norms, and morality of the society, his or her place in the society, and a sense of self.

status a position in society.

superego the term Freud used to describe the aspect of an individual's personality that internalizes the social norms and imposes them on the id. "Conscience" is a suitable synonym.

REFERENCES

1. Harry F. Harlow, "Love in Infant Monkeys." *Scientific American* (June 1959): 68–74. Harry F. Harlow and Margaret K. Harlow, "The Effect of Rearing Conditions on Behavior." *Bulletin of the Menninger Clinic* 26 (September 1962): 213–224. Harry F. Harlow and Margaret K. Harlow, "Social Deprivation in Monkeys." *Scientific American* (November 1962): 137–146.

2. Harlow and Harlow, "Social Deprivation in Monkeys," p. 142.

3. Kingsley Davis, *Human Society*. New York: Macmillan, 1967, pp. 204–208.

4. Davis, p. 208.

5. John B. Watson, *Behaviorism*. Chicago: University of Chicago Press, 1924, p. 104.

6. Napoleon Chagnon, *The Yanomamö: The Fierce People*. New York: Holt, Rinehart & Winston, 1968, p. 84.

7. Margaret Mead, *Sex and Temperament in Three Primitive Societies*. New York: William Morrow, 1935.

8. Charles Horton Cooley, *Social Organization*. New York: Charles Scribner's Sons, 1909.

9. William I. Thomas and Dorothy Swaine Thomas, *The Child in America*. New York: Alfred A. Knopf, 1928, p. 572.

10. Charles Horton Cooley, *Human Nature and the Social Order*. New York: Schocken Books, 1964.

11. George Herbert Mead, *Mind, Self, and Society*. Chicago: University of Chicago Press, 1934.

12. Sigmund Freud, *Civilization and Its Discontents*. Trans. and ed. by James Strachey, New York: W. W. Norton, 1961.

13. Erik H. Erikson, *Childhood and Society*. New York: W. W. Norton, 1950.

14. Jean Piaget, *The Moral Judgment of the Child*. London: Kegan Paul, 1932.

15. Lawrence Kohlberg, "Stage and Sequence: The Cognitive Development Approach to Socialization." In David A. Goslin, ed., *Handbook of Socialization Theory and Research*. Chicago: Rand McNally, 1969, pp. 347–380.

16. Clyde Kluckhohn and Henry A. Murray, *Personality in Nature*. New York: Alfred A. Knopf, 1949, p. 35.

SUGGESTED READINGS

Baldwin, James. *The Fire Next Time*. New York: Dial Press, 1963.
  The story of the author's childhood in Harlem.

Benedict, Ruth. *Patterns of Culture*. Boston: Houghton Mifflin, 1961.
  An anthropological classic, showing how societies encourage in their members certain personalities that are useful for the society.

Elkin, Frederick, and Gerald Handel. *The Child and Society*. New York: Random House, 1972.
  A short overview of the socialization process, using both sociological and social psychological perspectives.

Erikson, Erik. *Childhood and Society*. New York: W. W. Norton, 1950.
  Classic psychoanalytic description of the development of self in society, including the eight stages of ego development.

Goffman, Erving. *Presentation of Self in Everyday Life*. Garden City, N.Y.: Doubleday, 1959.
  A careful description of how personality slowly develops as people go through everyday routines, stressing role expectation and performance.

Piaget, Jean. *The Moral Judgment of the Child*. London: Kegan Paul, 1932.
  Classic presentation of personality development, showing how children's moral characters are formed during socialization.

Skinner, B. F. *Walden Two*. New York: Macmillan, 1960.
  Fictionalized account of a utopian behavioristic community, emphasizing how community members socialize their children.

Spiro, Melford, with Audrey G. Spiro. *Children of the Kibbutz: A Study of Child Training and Personality*. Cambridge, Mass.: Harvard University Press, 1975.
  A panel study of child-rearing practices in the Israeli kibbutzim over a twenty-five year period.

5

Socialization
from Adolescence
through Old Age

Socialization does not end when childhood does. Instead it is a lifelong process—we are continuously being socialized and resocialized as long as we live. If we were not, we would act forever as children, not knowing how to deal with going on that first date, with taking on a job, with becoming a husband or a wife, with growing old.

As we leave childhood and pass into the later phases of the life cycle, we must learn to play the roles those phases call for. Just as no infant is born knowing how to use a knife and fork or what is considered "good" and "bad" behavior, none of us is born knowing how to behave as a teenager, a married person, or a parent. Nor do we know how to behave as sick people or as old people. We see others in these statuses all the time and so when we come to occupy them ourselves, we are partly socialized in an informal way to perform the roles. But our knowledge is incomplete because all the intricacies of these roles may not be visible to us as outsiders. In this chapter we shall discuss socialization—formal and informal—for several statuses: adolescence, occupation, marriage, parenthood, and old age.

Adolescent Socialization

Let us look first at *adolescence*, the stage of life after childhood. Adolescence is defined as a period of physical and emotional transition that begins at about age twelve and ends at approximately age eighteen.

Like infancy, childhood, or any other stage of the life cycle, adolescence is a category that society creates and defines. Such categories may change over time. For example, in medieval society the concept of childhood did not even exist. As soon as children were old enough to survive without the constant attention of a mother figure, they were considered adults.[1] In the sixteenth and seventeenth centuries children were regarded as toys to amuse adults because they were thought to be simple, sweet creatures. By the eighteenth century upper-class children were defined as delicate beings who needed to be safeguarded at all times. The majority of children, though, were in the lower classes and were regarded as workers.

It was not until almost the end of the eighteenth century that there was any recognition of a distinct life stage between childhood and adulthood. At that time persons between the ages of beginning puberty and the time when they took on marital and occupational responsibilities were coming to be seen as members of a separate group. They began wearing clothing different from that worn by adults and began developing different life-styles. Special labor and criminal laws were enacted that were meant to differentiate adolescents from adults. Certain kinds of activities were defined as being appropriate for adolescents only, while other activities came to be considered inappropriate for them.

Today in the United States, adolescence is a full-fledged stage in the life cycle, beginning at the end of childhood and ending at the onset of adulthood. It is a social status, having an attached social role with clearly defined rights and obligations. Certain behaviors are expected. Adolescents are not allowed to be as irresponsible as children nor are they expected to be as responsible as adults.

There is great variability among adolescents. Urban, suburban, and rural youth are all different from each other. Those from the upper classes behave differently from those in the lower classes. The behavior of young people from minority groups differs from the behavior of those in white Anglo-Saxon Protestant groups. But each of these groups cannot be covered separately in this chapter. Therefore the discussion here is general, applying mostly to urban (and perhaps suburban), middle-class adolescents, although some of it pertains to adolescents in all settings. As you read this section, you may find it interesting to see if what is said applies to the adolescent groups with which you are familiar.

Just what is the special status of adolescence? How are adolescents expected to behave? How do they learn these behaviors? How well do they perform them? What unique experiences do they have?

EIGHT PROPERTIES OF ADOLESCENCE

Sociologist Ernest Q. Campbell lists eight special properties of adolescence.[2] These properties distinguish adolescence from other stages in the life cycle.

First, this is the time that individuals initially become conscious of their "selves" and try to change their personalities. We have all watched young people pose in front of mirrors, for example, as they try to formulate pleasing images of themselves to present to the world.

Second, the adolescent, for the first time, is active in his or her own socialization. During childhood adults were the active agents, but during adolescence young people try to define their own rights and responsibilities.

Third, adolescents are pressured to define themselves, not only in terms of the present—Who am I now?—but also in terms of the future—What am I going to be when I grow up? When a six-year-old says, "I am going to be a doctor," the meaning is different from when a sixteen-year-old says the same thing. The intention is more serious in adolescence than it was at six.

Fourth, adolescence entails *resocialization*, the process by which human beings unlearn one set of rules of behavior and replace it with

143

During, adolescence, according to sociologist Ernest Q. Campbell, young people develop a sense of self and experiment with creating pleasing images of themselves to present to the rest of the world.

another. Adolescents have to learn to stop being dependent and to question values that they never questioned before. Little children, for instance, accept the notion that parents love them, but adolescents are prone to hold long and serious conversations during which they argue about the meaning of parental and other kinds of love.

Fifth, choices become concrete and meaningful at this age. What people decide during adolescence can have irreversible effects on the rest of their lives. When a person chooses to go to college, his or her whole life may well be different from what it would have been had this choice not been made. A decision to become a lawyer instead of a truck driver sets the stage for a vastly different future life. Some adolescents even select lifetime mates during this stage of life.

Sixth, one's self-identity becomes strongly fixed during adolescence. This identity is conditioned more firmly by one's peers, teachers, and admired adults than by members of one's family.

Seventh, during adolescence young people learn social skills. Society starts to put heavy demands on members of this age group. The behaviors that were tolerated at six are not tolerated at sixteen. That is why it is not uncommon to hear parents say in annoyance, "Stop acting like a five-year-old! Remember you are fifteen!"

Eighth, adolescents come to accept the fact that ideals and reality are not always the same thing and they must learn to compromise between the two. For example, although many adolescents may indeed want to become doctors, they often find they do not have the money or the abilities to fulfill this goal. Adolescents find the world less comfortable and more frustrating, a place where it is impossible to get everything they want or dream about.

THE STATUS AND ROLES OF ADOLESCENCE

As children enter the adolescent stage, they are likely to consider the members of their families less important than they did before. The members of their *peer groups* become more significant socializing agents. (Peer group can be defined as the members of a group who are equals, usually in terms of age, education, and social class.) During this stage young people are expected to seek new experiences in an effort to learn more about who they are, how they relate to other people— including members of the opposite sex—and who they hope to become. They are also supposed to be acquiring the social skills of adults, practicing self-control, and accepting standards of "right" and "wrong." In the opinion of many people, the period of adolescence constitutes the best years of life, although at the same time they realize that it can be a very frustrating and confusing period.

144

In today's society, adolescence tends to last for more years than it did in the past. Physiologically, our bodies are maturing earlier, primarily because of improved nutrition. Because of this earlier physical development and because of changes in societal attitudes, we are beginning to interact with members of the opposite sex at an earlier age than our parents and grandparents did and to have overt sexual interests earlier. So, on one end, adolescence is starting at a younger age than it formerly did. On the other end, our technology is such that advanced education is becoming more and more in demand (see Chapter 7). This often extends the period of adolescence into the twenties.

Such a situation means that young people remain in limbo for longer spans of time. They lose the right to the total dependency of childhood, but they are not accepted into the "real" world. The result is that peers become very important to young people in that they provide guides for behavior, companionship, feelings of being needed, and understanding of each other's fears and anxieties. In a sense, then, adolescents develop a subculture of their own, influenced by the mass media, that is separate from the world of their parents, teachers, and other adults. They develop a special language and slang, style of dress, music, value system, and heroes, and try to behave as much like their peer group as possible. Most of their time is spent with their friends, and the ties to the family are gradually replaced by ties and loyalties to peers outside the family. Parents and teachers still have some power

A major change during adolescence is that the peer group often replaces the family as the most significant agent of socialization.

over adolescents, but adolescents care more about what their peers —their significant others—think of them. They will confide more readily in each other, cooperate more fully, and share more willingly with peers who are their equals than with those who have power over their lives and therefore control over them.

PARENTS AND ADOLESCENTS

Although it is probably true that during adolescence children are more influenced by their peers than by their parents, and although most people claim there is a "generation gap," sociological research shows that parents continue to serve as role models during this stage. For example, the educational and occupational aspirations of adolescents are often based on parental educational levels and occupations. Adolescents frequently follow their parents' political preferences and vote (when they reach voting age) along the same party lines that their parents do. If parents reveal biases against certain groups, adolescents frequently hold the same biases. Thus, all the talk and worry about youth rebellion and alienation is probably exaggerated. While there is no doubt that the peer group is influential, that influence is in addition to, not in place of parental influence. Sociologist James S. Coleman showed that this is probably true when 53 percent of the adolescents he questioned said it would be more difficult to give up parental approval than it would be to break up with a friend.[3]

This is not to say that the notion of a "generation gap" is entirely wrong. Adults value many things that adolescents despise, and adolescents value many things that arouse adult contempt. For example, some high-school students openly admire those who successfully cheat on examinations, while adults usually do not express such values. It is true that the teenage value system is, in many ways, the opposite of the adult value system. Yet adolescents and adults do not differ as much as many believe. In fact, as adolescents mature into young adulthood, they eventually find that their own and their parents' values and attitudes have become very similar.

ADOLESCENT SOCIETY

The most extensive study ever done on adolescents was the one referred to above conducted by James S. Coleman.[4] After interviewing students at ten high schools in Chicago during the late 1950s, Coleman sought to describe the teenage subculture. His focus was on adolescence as a distinct social system, and he tried to learn about teenagers' heroes and values. He concentrated on factors that make some adolescents successful and others not, on school performance, and on the things that are important to students.

One of Coleman's most revealing findings was that although the high school is the center of the adolescent's world, scholastic achievement in school is valued less by students than athletic prowess, club membership, and personal appearance. Like any other social system, adolescent society offers rewards and punishments. And like members of any social system, teenagers direct their attention and energy to those activities that will bring them the highest rewards. Thus, students apply themselves most diligently to being popular, as opposed to being well educated. Coleman found that the leaders of teenage groups were much more likely to value excellence in extracurricular activities than scholarship.

Several sociologists disagree with Coleman when he states that adolescents have a separate social system, claiming that generational ties are stronger than friendship ties. Depending upon how we define a "separate society," we can take either side.

If we think of a separate society as a group whose members prefer each other's company and communicate more openly with each other than with members of another social system, then we can say teenagers have a separate society. But if we define a separate society as a group that is alienated from and hostile toward the other group, then we cannot say adolescents have a completely separate society from that of their parents and other adults. Why? Because the adolescents are still influenced by the adults and they still care to attain adult approval.

In some ways adolescents do live in a world of their own. They do have some values that are contrary to adult values. They do have different heroes, behaviors, and attitudes. But, as stated earlier, they still have much in common with adults, and as adolescents grow older, the consensus between the two groups grows greater.

Sociologist S. N. Eisenstadt[5] contends that problems arise during adolescence because the experiences of childhood are very different

---

APPLYING SOCIOLOGY

Thinking back over your own adolescence, do you believe you were closer to your family than you were to your peer group? In whom did you confide? To whom did you tell your secrets? Whom did you trust more? Whose company did you prefer? Compare your responses to such questions with those of other students in your class. Can you conclude that adolescents in your age group formed a separate society from that of their parents?

from the experiences of adulthood. The life of a child is protected and secure; the life of an adult is independent, competitive, and relatively insecure. The adolescent peer group fills the "space" between these two life-styles, allowing the emerging adult to experience new things gradually so that the "jump" is not sudden and overwhelming. The teenage years are shared with others undergoing the same kinds of changes and there is comfort in the sharing. One need not feel alone.

Therefore, adolescents work out a way of life that allows them to bridge the gap as easily as possible. This way of life has several apparent features. First, adolescents value "having fun," especially with young people of the opposite sex. Second, adolescents value physical appearance over achievement. They admire the athlete over the person who gets "A's" in every subject. Third, most adolescents believe in equality among themselves. To them power is a negative value because it is too reminiscent of their relationships with parents and teachers. This attitude toward equality is important for two reasons. Teenagers learn to reciprocate power and they learn to deal with the power adults have over them. (Being able to cope with power, whether it is the power we hold over others or the power others hold over us, is very necessary in group interaction at all stages of the life cycle.)

A fourth feature of adolescent society is the desire to "play" at deviance, or breaking the rules. Teenagers "flirt" with danger. How far can they go in defying their parents? How much aggression can they display to teachers? How much sexuality can they allow themselves to express? The stress is on challenges and adventure without getting caught. Sociologist David Matza[6] claims that this "playing" at deviance is good for society because it reduces real deviance. The adolescent can

Adolescents often "play" at deviance, or breaking the rules. Some sociologists maintain that this "playing" at deviance is good for society because there is enough satisfaction in the "game" to prevent adolescents from getting into real trouble.

experiment with misbehavior without getting into serious trouble. For most teenagers there is enough satisfaction in the "game" to prevent them from committing real crimes.

In summary, adolescence is an important stage in the life cycle because it bridges the gap between dependence and independence. It allows young people time to learn slowly how to be adults. They can do this because youth creates a subculture of its own where the members are free of adult authority, where relationships are relatively equal, where experimentation can occur, and where autonomy and a sense of self can develop. In short, it is a period that prepares children for the adult roles they will play for the rest of their lives.

Socialization in Adult Life

The process through which roles are learned after adolescence is usually called *adult socialization*. By the time we reach this stage in life, we have established a sense of identity. We have made a commitment to the norms of the society to which we belong. Most of us have acquired the basic skills needed to function properly within our society. Moral values, which are stressed during early childhood and adolescent socialization, have probably been internalized.

Nevertheless, we still have much learning to do, primarily in the special behaviors we need to perform correctly in the many statuses that we must occupy as adults. But adult socialization is easier than childhood socialization because by this time we have come to understand why socialization is necessary. Hence, we will help in the process. We will, in fact, socialize ourselves as much if not more than other socializing agents will. Furthermore, since we are being socialized into roles to which we usually aspire (except, of course, almost no one welcomes the roles of the aged, the ill, or the dying), we are motivated to cooperate in order to achieve our goals.

Thus, socialization in adulthood is partly a continuation of the values and attitudes learned during childhood and adolescence. It is also learning to modify the old habits so they will "fit" into each new status we come to occupy. In a sense, then, adult socialization could be called *resocialization*.

In a famous essay on socialization in later life, sociologist Orville Brim[7] notes that early socialization makes later socialization both easier and harder. In some ways we build on what we learned in childhood and in other ways we must give up the old ways and substitute new ways. For example, in order to become a leader in the community, we can build on our experiences as a leader in high school. On the other hand, being single does not help us to learn how to be married.

149

Brim also contends that there are three things an individual must acquire before being able to perform satisfactorily in a status. First, the person must know what values and behaviors are expected. Second, he or she must be capable of meeting these requirements. Third, there must be a desire to meet them and perform them well. In short, for adult socialization to be successful, there must be knowledge, ability, and motivation. We must find out what we need to know, we must have the talent to do what must be done, and we must want to do it. For example, in order to become a truck driver, we must first learn how to start the truck, stop it, slow it down, and skillfully maneuver it. Then we must be capable of doing these things. A blind woman, for instance, cannot be a truck driver. Finally, we must want to drive a truck—no one can be forced to do it.

SOCIALIZATION FOR WORK

Though adults occupy many statuses, none is so important, especially in the United States, as the occupational status. Our occupations are often the centers of our lives, and even if our jobs are not satisfying, most of us recognize that we are evaluated by society according to the work we do. * One of the first questions Americans ask each other when they are introduced is: "What do you do?" As soon as we have that information, we know—at least to some extent—how to interact with the individual. If the person is a doctor, we will direct the conversation toward medicine. If he or she is a lawyer, we will talk about law. Therefore, when we find out what a person does for a living, we discuss topics we think will be of interest.

Furthermore, we show different degrees of respect for people once we know what kind of work they do. Occupations, as we will discuss more fully in Chapters 13 and 14, are ranked by members of societies. We assign more prestige (and often higher income) to some occupations and to those in them than we do to others. A doctor, for example, ranks higher than a carpenter; a teacher has more prestige than a plumber. Therefore, we often feel and act differently toward certain people. The salesperson shows respect for the accountant; the laborer is deferential toward the doctor.

In short, what we do for a living is important not only because we must eat. It is also important because it gives us an identity and it determines the amount of respect other members of our personal social groups will give us. For these reasons, almost all American men and about 50 percent of all American women work. For some people, work

*Sometimes, however, occupational status becomes secondary to race, sex, or age. For example, people refer to Arthur Ashe as a black athlete, not just an athlete. Ella Grasso is known as the woman governor from Connecticut. Vladimir Horowitz is thought of as a seventy-four-year-old pianist.

FOCUS ON: "PASSAGES"

Socialization throughout the entire adult life cycle may create expectations of self that are inconsistent with one's potentialities or needs. Author Gail Sheehy makes this point in her book *Passages*.

Sheehy discusses relationships between women and men aged sixteen through sixty. She uses a model of a "Sexual Diamond" to illustrate the relationship between the sexes at different ages. According to this model, men and women are closest at age eighteen, farthest apart during their late thirties and forties, and close again during their fifties and sixties.

At the age of eighteen men and women share similar interests, are not yet attached to occupational roles, and have a similar potential for sexual arousal. Nevertheless, the socialization process emphasizes the sexual prowess and availability of men and the lack of sexual desires among women of this age. This image is partially responsible for the stereotype that "good girls" are not supposed to enjoy sex, at least not to the extent young men do. Although this stereotype is untrue, this idea has affected women. In fact, many of those Sheehy interviewed reported repressing sexual urges.

As men and women approach their twenties and early thirties, they begin to diverge in several important ways. Women reach their peak childbearing period during their twenties, which simultaneously reduces their sexual availability. Men begin their involvement with work at this time and begin to develop interests that revolve around their occupations.

If the age of eighteen marks convergence on the diamond, the late thirties and forties represent the furthest spread between the sexes. Although men have been socialized to accept an image of themselves as sexually aggressive, during this time period they become sexually more passive. They become less of the "teenagers" that they used to be—they are no longer multi-orgasmic. However, at the same time, women are experiencing their most active sexual interest. They are capable of achieving orgasm over and over again with their partners. This contrast in males between expectations and performance may lead to impotence.

As men and women move into their fifties and sixties, there is a convergence of social and sexual interest and experience. Yet once again there is a discrepancy between socialization and personal potential. Whereas the society assumes and teaches its members that aging implies "disengagement" from both social (particularly work) and sexual roles, there is little evidence that there is any need to retreat nor that older people actually do retreat. Assuming good health and practice with sexual activity, one could continue sexual intercourse through the very latest years of life.

Sheehy is suggesting that as we give up one role and take on others, we are going through *passages*. The crises that accompany the transition from one stage to the next are, in her estimation, predictable.

Do you think there are any ways to overcome the crises of adult life? Is there anything our society could do to ease the experiences adults have as they grow older? Do separation and divorce seem any more likely to occur at the "bulge point" in the diamond?

Source: Gail Sheehy, *Passages,* New York: E. P. Dutton, 1976.

is pleasurable; for others it is only necessary. In either event, a person must be socialized into being a worker in general and a certain kind of worker in particular. Sociologist Wilbert Moore states: "Thus socialization to the world of work may be for some a kind of conditioning, a re-

151

Drawing by Lorenz; © 1976 The New Yorker Magazine, Inc.

luctant preparation for harsh realities, and for others a kind of commitment to a calling."[8]

For everyone, there is some mixture of conditioning and commitment, but the amount of each differs, depending upon how people feel about their work. Work is social action and therefore it involves norms. The very least a worker in any occupation must learn are the occupational norms. In addition, these norms must be internalized so that workers can be productive. If the norms are not internalized, then workers would have to be watched and supervised much more than they usually are. For example, college professors are expected to meet their classes when scheduled. The chairperson assumes that professors in the department will miss a class only when circumstances make it absolutely impossible for them to meet their obligations. If the chairperson could not take this norm for granted, he or she would have to check on each class each hour to be sure the professor was there. Clearly, this would be close to impossible. Therefore, we depend upon people to internalize the norms of their occupations, and in most cases, they do.

How do workers learn occupational norms and how do they come to internalize them? In part they do this through a process that sociologists call *anticipatory socialization*—training for a status that a person will occupy sometime in the future. Such training begins during childhood. For example, children see parents and others go off to work regularly. As time goes on, these children learn that it is rare for

The learning and internalization of occupational norms begins in childhood, in part through the process of *anticipatory socialization.* When children play at being doctors or teachers or firefighters, they are learning about the world of work and its rules.

an adult to pretend to be ill in order to avoid work. They hear their parents discuss the problems of work. They realize that work is taken seriously and that most people try to do a good job of whatever work they do. They also learn that workers try to produce something useful or perform a service well in the hopes of getting higher salaries and promotions. They come to see that workers seem to care about their work and to act responsibly about it. So, early in life children begin to learn generalized occupational norms and to understand and internalize them.

Schools also provide opportunities for the internalization of these norms. Schools are places where young people can formally acquire knowledge and information about work. Schools, along with books, television, and movies, spell out the rules for children to learn. This is especially true if the teacher or the writer or the performer is a significant other to the child. Then what is taught will be taken much more seriously and the norms are much more likely to be internalized than if the message-giver is not important to the child. Furthermore, schools, especially such professional schools as medical or dental colleges, socialize students in attitude, dress, and even vocabulary. The doctor's stethoscope dangling from a white coat pocket enhances the medical student's self-image as a physician. Learning medical terms separates medical students from the lay people in the society and enhances their prestige in the eyes of both the students and the outsiders.

Work Choice

As we shall see in more detail in Chapter 7, many people are "sorted" into occupations by the schools. Guidance counselors and teachers tend to encourage certain children into more productive areas of learning and other children into less productive areas. In addition, some home environments are more likely to promote certain types of ambition than others. For example, when children are encouraged at home to read, we can expect that they will be attracted to occupations requiring a great deal of study. On the other hand, when children are encouraged by parents to participate in sports instead of reading, we can expect that they will choose occupations in which physical prowess is valued over mental ability. Therefore, for these reasons, some proportion of young people are always limited in their occupational choices. They are left with those jobs whose requirements they can meet after they leave school.

For other children, career choice is limited for another reason. These children follow their parents into occupations, especially if there is a family business or farm. Such children are often simply expected to enter the business when they complete school. Since there is still some status ascription (as opposed to status achievement) in our society,

154

APPLYING SOCIOLOGY

Consider the career you are thinking about at the moment. What factors in your own life have led you toward that career? Have you had role models you are trying to imitate? Is one of your parents in an occupation he or she has encouraged or discouraged you from entering? What factors have ruled out other occupations? Have your ambitions changed over time?

neither they nor their parents give much thought to alternative possibilities (see Chapter 14).

For most young people, though, luck or chance plays a major role in occupational choice. Although they enter an occupation after consciously and subconsciously narrowing down possibilities, they actually get a job by luck or chance. However, the whole topic of occupational choice has not been researched very much by sociologists. It is known that schools provide a good deal of misinformation or out-of-date information. It is also known that young people often overrate their abilities or have unrealistic fantasies about work possibilities. But other than this, not much is actually known about how choices are made.

In short, for some young people occupational choice is limited early in life by poor preparation or by lack of encouragement by families and teachers. For other young people, choice is limited because of expectations beyond their control. For the majority, there is more chance than choice. Occupations, then, are often not chosen—they "happen."

Socialization into an Occupational Role

Once a person has chosen, been forced into, or falls into an occupation, the first thing needed is specific training. No matter how well educated or how well trained a person may be for an occupation, each individual job demands individual learning. When do people go to lunch? May I use the telephone to make personal calls? Should I call my secretary by his or her first name? What exactly am I required to do? To whom do I report? In any job, the neophyte must be socialized into the specific work setting.

In most large bureaucracies in our modern, technological society, many of the rules and norms are formal and elaborate. New employees may even be given a pamphlet which explains almost anything they need to know about the company that has just hired them. Such companies often leave little room for individuals to make major decisions

Whatever occupation one ends up in, whether it is by choice, coercion, or chance, one needs specific training for each individual job. Every new worker must be socialized into the specific work setting.

on their own. The norms are spelled out. There may even be specific training programs. The new employee, therefore, has only minimal difficulty becoming oriented.

What are some of the things that workers must learn and internalize? Wilbert Moore lists four important occupational norms. First, people must develop a sense of identification with a specific occupation. That is, they must feel part of a group consisting of workers doing similar work. Plumbers must consider themselves members of a group called "plumbers"; teachers must feel they belong with other teachers. Second, workers must feel identification with an occupational status. An apprentice carpenter must be at home with other apprentices. A manager must sense a kinship with other managers and not with secretaries. Third, there must be loyalty to an employer. Workers have to believe they are part of the company or organization for which they work so that they develop pride in the product they produce or the service they offer. Finally, there must be an identification with the whole industry. The social worker must be concerned with public welfare; the teacher with education; the steel worker with the steel business.[9]

Moore discusses a very interesting mechanism used in occupational socialization that he calls a punishment-centered theory of socialization.[10] Moore claims that in some occupations, particularly in the professions, beginners are subject to punishment in the form of "hazing" or isolation. For example, in military academies, cadets are required to perform arbitrary tasks that are difficult and unpleasant. The medical student who expects to enter psychiatry is still required to learn all the bones in the human body. Many Ph.D. candidates are burdened with so much work that they are forced into isolation because they have no time for social activities.

Moore believes this type of socialization is important and useful. The difficulties that the graduate student, for instance, experiences are challenging, and since they are shared with others in the some position, a feeling of camaraderie builds up. In addition, such students use their professors as role models and often feel great closeness and affection for them. Finally, professionals must learn a technical language, which shuts out those not in the profession and draws those within it closer to each other because only "one of our own can communicate with us." These three factors, shared suffering with peers, attachment to those above, and a shared language, lead to occupational identity and commitment. Moore concludes:

> The person who successfully learns the language and skills of a trade and survives the ordeals that punished him and his fellows will emerge, we are arguing, not only with an internalized occupational commitment but also with an identification with the collectivity, the brotherhood.[11]

MARITAL AND PARENTAL SOCIALIZATION

Just as we must be socialized into occupational statuses, we must also be socialized into two other adult statuses—marriage and parenthood, both of which are almost as important as occupations in American social life. How do we move from being a single person to being a married person? How do we go from childless person to parent? How do we learn to interact with a spouse, with in-laws, and with a child? Certainly we are not born with the knowledge we need to perform these roles. Therefore we must acquire it in some way.

Marriage involves two people. It is a very intricate relationship, and socialization into married life is complicated by many obstacles. One problem is that marriage involves two people of different sexes. Females and males are not brought up to view the world in the same way. The more the woman has been socialized into the female status (the more "feminine" she is) and the more the man has been socialized into the male status (the more "masculine" he is), the more difficult it will be for each member of the pair to understand the other (see Chapter 11).

Furthermore, each partner in a marriage has been trained differently for marriage by his or her own family. For example, a young wife may have had a mother who had a career and a young husband may have had a mother whose only job was to be a homemaker. This pair might have a difficult time agreeing on what the wife's obligations are in a marriage.

Then too, marriage is very intimate and there is supposed to be great closeness. This tends to complicate the relationship because as single people we are not expected to share all our thoughts and possessions. We have much privacy and independence when we are unmarried, and at least some of it must be given up in marriage.

Finally, most American husbands and wives must learn to accept the changes that occur in each other over time. In sum, then, marriage has peculiarities that make socialization into it complicated. It is a small group of two people of different sexes, brought up to view marriage differently, lacking privacy, and requiring acceptance of change. How do we become socialized for such an arrangement?

As is the case with our occupations, we are partially socialized for marriage ahead of time. Unlike occupational socialization, how-

---

APPLYING SOCIOLOGY

Suppose that the two young people described below became romantically involved and were considering marriage:

John comes from a tightly knit ethnic family. His parents were born in Eastern Europe and came here as children with their parents. John grew up in a home that housed his parents, four brothers and sisters, his grandmother, and an unmarried uncle. His father and uncle both worked at factory jobs, while his mother and grandmother worked only at home, tending the house and the children.

Mary is an only child from a "Yankee" family that prides itself on being descended from the original colonists. Highly independent people, her parents moved to another section of the country when they married, leaving their families 2,000 miles behind. Both have built professional careers there, and they have achieved a high social position in their community. Religious membership has been important to them socially, but they could not be called devoted believers.

List briefly the areas of life in which the upbringing of these two people differed. How might these differences affect their expectations about the role of each partner in marriage, about the kind of family life they would have, and about where they might live? In what specific ways would these people have to resocialize themselves if they were to have a good marriage? Is it likely that they would get married at all?

ever, socialization for marriage is informal. Parents subconsciously serve as role models, while children, also subconsciously, observe their parents playing the roles of husband and wife. Neither parents nor children realize the influence parental behavior can have on children in later life.

Such informal socialization, however, is often limited. Children usually have only one couple they know well with whom to role-play and role-take—their fathers and mothers. Even this example is distorted by the meaning and interpretations they place on it. In addition, when children role-play and role-take with their parents, they are interacting with people of an older generation, but their spouses will be part of their own generation. Furthermore, much of married life cannot be observed by outsiders, even by the children in the family. Thus the anticipatory socialization by parents for marriage is informal, uncertain, limited, and even may be potentially detrimental.

Fortunately, many children have other opportunities inside their immediate families for marital socialization, but these opportunities also are limited. One important source of socialization for marriage is through one's own siblings. In many ways a brother-sister relationship can resemble a marital relationship. The interaction is between two human beings of the same age group, but of different sexes. It is usually

Siblings can be an important source of anticipatory socialization into marriage. The relationship between a brother and sister can resemble a marital relationship.

a sharing relationship and a supportive one. How often have you heard a parent say, "Give half to your sister" or "Help your brother"? In addition, most brothers and sisters love each other even if they quarrel occasionally, in much the same way husbands and wives love each other in spite of arguments. Thus, siblings are significant role models within the nuclear family in the process of socialization for marriage. They frequently are more significant than parents. Yet even this socialization is not totally effective, because it cannot prepare children for the sexual aspect of marriage.

Children's sources for marital socialization extend outside the family as well. Young people have their own friends to watch and imitate. They have their friends' parents, as well as their own aunts, uncles, cousins, and grandparents, who also serve as role models. They have thousands of chances to observe marriage in books and in the mass media, especially in the endless family situation shows on television. But, as in the sibling relationship, this socialization is indirect and incomplete.

All the stages of courtship are also socialization for marriage. Even little children as young as eight and nine talk about their "boyfriends" and "girlfriends." When they interact with these friends, we can see the beginnings of adult male and female interaction. As the children get older and begin real dating in high school (or even in junior high school), the situation offers even greater opportunity for marital socialization. Young people begin to role-take with members of the opposite sex in a serious manner. They can "practice" relating to each other in ways that will be helpful when they do marry. By the time a couple become engaged, their role-playing and role-taking are intensified. Two sociologists, Reuben Hill and Joan Aldous, point out the functions of the engagement:

1. Couples have an opportunity to see if the differences in their family backgrounds can be compatible.
2. Once the courtship period is over and the two people feel secure about each other, the relationship has a chance to stabilize. The couple can really get to know each other as people because they no longer have to be on their best behavior when together.
3. Sharing and planning increases because the two people now view each other as a "couple" and topics that they could not discuss before are now permitted. They may begin buying things together, opening joint bank accounts, more freely discussing their attitudes toward sex, religion, having children, their occupations, their own families, and so forth.[12]

Like all socialization, marital socialization is a continuing process—it does not stop at the wedding ceremony. In fact, some sociologists view the wedding as the actual beginning of the socializa-

160

High-school dating is another source of marital socialization. It is an opportunity for young people to "practice" role-taking and relating to members of the opposite sex. Such "practice" can be helpful when young people marry.

tion process. Now the couple must put into practice what they have only been hearing and watching all their lives. This is not always easy. It is one thing to watch a tennis game and quite another to play. What appears simple and straightforward to the observer is usually more difficult for the participant. After the wedding most couples learn how to be a couple by trial-and-error and by mutual socialization. They must learn how to communicate with each other and how to keep the lines of communication open even when they are quarreling with each other or one is frustrated or angry.

Learning to be a parent is also continuous, beginning in childhood and lasting through parenthood. Unlike marital socialization, however, children more actively participate in this training just because they occupy the status of child. They actually take part in this socialization process, although they are playing the role opposite from the one they may play some day. In effect, they are role-taking with their own, as yet unborn, children. Thus, the socialization for parenthood is more effective than the socialization for marriage. Children can readily tell which characteristics belong to "good" fathers and which characteristics define "bad" mothers. They cannot as easily respond to the question: What makes a good husband or wife? It follows, then, that individuals are more likely to be the kind of parents their own parents were than to be the kind of spouses their own parents were.

In addition, as in marital socialization, persons can turn to outside sources for parental role models. Friends, friends' parents, relatives, books, movies, and television all serve to prepare people for that new status they may occupy in the future.

To summarize, socialization for marriage in the United States is limited. One reason is that young people are primarily socialized by one couple, their parents, which restricts their view of the many possibilities of male-female relationships and interactions. A second reason

161

APPLYING SOCIOLOGY

Watch the children of parents you know as they play "house." Can you detect behaviors in their interaction that are similar to those of their parents? If the parents speak gently to one another, do the children, acting as husband and wife, copy that behavior? If the children are used to hearing harsh tones, do they speak harshly to their dolls? Do you notice that children seem to imitate the parent of the same sex more than the parent of the opposite sex? Why do you think this occurs?

is that most socialization is implicit and indirect; that is, no one explains openly what marriage is all about. Youngsters must make their own observations and interpretations. Much of the more useful and anticipatory marital socialization occurs between siblings and peers. On the other hand, parental socialization is more effective because the children participate in it directly. When it is time to be parents people can fall back on their experiences as children to help them role-play as parents.

SOCIALIZATION FOR OLD AGE

Two important events occur for men and women in their late middle years. For most people there comes a time when they must retire from their occupations, either voluntarily or because many organizations require retirement at a given age. Women, especially if they have not been engaged in employment outside the home during their married lives, face an additional adjustment. There comes a time when the last child leaves home to go away to school, to set up a separate home, to marry, or for some other reason. People need preparation for these significant events because major changes in attitudes and behavior are required.

When people retire, they no longer have an identity in their occupations. They can no longer say, "I am a bus driver" or "I am an advertising executive." They must now identify themselves as "retired." They no longer have an office or factory to go to every day. There is no place for them to spend seven or eight hours a day working. They must give up the interaction with co-workers that they have had for many years.

As parents grow older, they also lose the structured activities that caring for children imposes on them. There is no one coming home for lunch. Cooking is easier. The house does not seem to get as messy. There is less laundry. There is no one to mow the lawn. There is no one

FOCUS ON: DEATH AND DYING

A new area in sociology is becoming popular; it is called the sociology of thanatology, the study of death and dying. Research in this area is still in its infancy, but it deals with such questions as: How do different societies handle the death of members? How are dying patients treated in hospitals by medical personnel? How do dying patients' families react to the loss of a loved one? What are the rituals surrounding death? How do people behave after the death of someone they love?

One of the most important questions is: How is the dying person socialized to accept death? Elizabeth Kübler-Ross addresses this question in her book, *On Death and Dying.* Kübler-Ross studied dying patients and found that they socialized themselves through five stages from the time they were told they were going to die until the moment of actual death.

The first stage is called *denial.* During this stage people refuse to believe death is actually happening to them. At this stage patients have been known to insist that the doctors have misdiagnosed their illnesses, or that the hospitals have mixed up their records with someone else's, or that the labs have confused their reports with those of really ill people.

The second stage is *anger.* The patient no longer denies that death is approaching, but is enraged that he or she is the victim and not someone else. Anger may be directed at God, the physician, family members, hospital personnel, or even friends.

In the third stage, patients make *bargains* with God. If they can just be allowed to live long enough to see a child married or a grandchild born or the Christmas holidays, they will die quietly without bothering anyone.

Eventually patients cannot deny that they are terminally ill; they cannot justify anger; and they realize that God cannot be bargained with. Then the fourth stage—*depression*—begins. During this stage some patients try to control the lives of others. They attempt this through such means as promising to leave money in return for compliance with some condition. In this way they think that they can remain in control, even after death.

The fifth and final stage is *acceptance.* Patients feel at peace, ready to die. They often can rationally and calmly say goodby to people they love. Sometimes they show remarkable strength, becoming the comforters instead of the other way around.

Why do you think young people are interested in studying death and dying? How do the attitudes of our society toward death and dying affect our personal feelings on the subject? How will studying death help people to face their own fears about death?

Socialization for death is largely self-socialization. No dying patients can be socialized, however, unless they agree to accept the help of others. Do you think outsiders can really help in this process or must each of us come to terms with death alone? Who do you think would be best equipped to help the dying person? How would you go about trying to help someone accept this final status in life?

Source: Elizabeth Kübler-Ross, *On Death and Dying,* New York: Macmillan, 1969.

with whom to play "catch." There are more quiet hours in the home without the children and their friends constantly underfoot.

Both men and women, then, must make major structural changes in their lives. How well prepared are most people for these changes?

While some people "disengage" as they grow old as Cumming and Henry suggest *(top)*, others find new roles and new interests *(bottom)*.

How do they gain knowledge about the ways to fill these now-empty days? It is unfortunately true that in most Western societies people are not properly socialized for old age. They are given little incentive or motivation to enter old age the way they have been given incentive to become workers or married people or parents. After all, Western society clearly favors youth and beauty. Why would anyone ever want to become old? Therefore, socialization for old age should be stronger than socialization for anything else because people need to have reasons for wanting, or at least accepting, the new status.

The fact is, however, that the norms and roles of old age are not clear. Parents who have devoted most of their lives to caring for other people often do not know how to be independent. They feel unneeded. They have little to do. Workers who have given most of their time, thought, and energy to their occupations are no better off than parents when they retire. How can they fill their days? What can they talk about? There is little for these people to fall back on and they have been poorly prepared to deal with the problems.

Two sociologists, Elaine Cumming and William Henry, developed a theory of old-age behavior called the *theory of disengagement*.[13] The theory states that as people age, they give up their major life roles: for men it is generally the occupational role and for women it is generally the parental role. For workers the transition is abrupt; for parents it is gradual. In addition, people reduce the number of individuals with whom they interact, and there are even changes in the kind of interaction in which they involve themselves. For example, older people are less interested in the lives of other people. They tend to turn inward and become preoccupied with themselves. At the same time, other people turn away from the aged. According to this theory, then, old people and society mutually disengage from each other.

Cumming and Henry claim that this preoccupation with oneself deepens over time. Individuals, from any type of society, come to accept their loss of roles and statuses; they withdraw more and more from others; and eventually they come to accept the inevitability of death. They thus undergo a process of self-socialization. They teach themselves to accept what must be accepted.

Most sociologists have found fault with the theory of disengagement, claiming that instead of turning inward, old people often find new roles and new interests because they now have more time and freedom. Another criticism states that the theory does not apply to all societies. In some Eastern societies, for example, old people are accorded great respect and deference and maintain a well-defined position in society.

However, in some Western societies and in the United States especially, old people are often treated as unnecessary and shunted

164

*"As the days dwindle down to a precious few,
I say to hell with everybody!"*

Drawing by J. Mirachi; © 1975 The New Yorker Magazine, Inc.

aside. They are poorly prepared to accept old age and death as normal stages of the life cycle. In fact, there are no roles that are clearly attached to the status of old age, unless we include "getting out of the way" as a role. Some old people may respond by disengaging, but more likely they respond by finding new roles and new things to do. In either event, it appears that they prepare themselves for the old-age status with little help from society. Just as in the adolescent stage, the norms are unclear and the prescriptions for behavior are largely unstated. Both groups, the young and the old, tend to be treated as "in the way." They are tolerated as long as they do not bother anyone. The result is that both live in a subculture, outside the mainstream of society.

SUMMARY

Adolescence is the stage of life that follows childhood. It serves to bridge the gap between dependence (childhood) and independence (adulthood) and, in effect, allows young people time to prepare for the statuses they will occupy later in their lives. During adolescence, members of one's *peer group* become more important than members of one's family. Adolescents seek to spend most of their time with peer group members and thus develop a subculture of their own. Yet parents continue to serve as role models during this stage. Peer group influence is in addition to, not in place of, parental influence.

The process through which roles are learned after adolescence is called *adult socialization*. It can also be called *resocialization* or *so-*

cialization modification because we must modify our old habits to fit each new status we will occupy as adults. Orville Brim claims that there are three essential ingredients for successful adult socialization: 1) people must know what is expected of them; 2) they must have the ability to do what must be done; and 3) there must be motivation to succeed.

There are four important statuses in adult life for which people must be socialized. The first is our occupational status, and socialization for it is partially accomplished through a process sociologists call *anticipatory socialization*. Within the families in which they grow up, children learn and internalize certain occupational norms. Schools also provide socialization for work, and there is always on-the-job training once a position has been secured. Wilbert Moore lists four important work norms that are part of occupational socialization: 1) People must identify with their occupation; 2) they must identify with a specific status within that occupation's hierarchy; 3) they must be loyal to their employer; and 4) they must identify with the whole industry. These norms, and others, must be learned and internalized if occupational socialization is to be considered successful.

The second and third statuses into which most people must be socialized are marriage and parenthood. Marital socialization is accomplished primarily by watching the interactions between parents and between friends' parents. The mass media are also primary agents in socialization. Brother-and-sister relationships and courtship interaction provide useful opportunities for practice as married people. Marital socialization is always less than desirable because many aspects of the marital relationship cannot be observed by children. On the other hand, training to become a parent is more readily available within the family because, as children, we are actively participating in the process although we take the opposite role from the one we will later take as parents. The result is that socialization for parenthood is more effective than socialization for marriage. Consequently, we are more likely to be the kind of parents our parents were than to be the kind of spouses they were.

There is very little socialization provided for the fourth and last status of life—old age. For the most part, old people must socialize themselves because most Western societies generally do not pay much attention to the elderly and their needs.

GLOSSARY

adolescence   that stage in the life cycle roughly between the onset of puberty and the reaching of maturity, usually beginning at about age twelve and ending at approximately age eighteen.

166

adult socialization the process through which postadolescent roles are learned.

anticipatory socialization a process that involves training for a social status a person will occupy in the future; socialization in advance of attaining a social position.

peer group members of a group who are equals, usually in terms of age, education, and social class.

resocialization a process that involves unlearning one set of rules of behavior and replacing it with another.

REFERENCES

1. P. Ariès, *Centuries of Childhood*. Trans. by Robert Baldick, New York: Vintage Edition, 1965.
2. Ernest Q. Campbell, "Adolescent Socialization." In David A. Goslin, ed., *Handbook of Socialization Theory and Research*. Chicago: Rand McNally, 1971, pp. 825–826.
3. James S. Coleman, *The Adolescent Society*. New York: The Free Press, 1961, p. 5.
4. Coleman, p. 5.
5. S. N. Eisenstadt, *From Generation to Generation*. Glencoe, Ill.: The Free Press, 1956.
6. David Matza, "Subterranean Traditions of Youth." In *The Annals of the American Academy of Political and Social Sciences* 338 (1961): 102–118.
7. Orville G. Brim, Jr., "Socialization Through the Life Cycle." In Orville G. Brim, Jr., and Stanton Wheeler, *Socialization After Childhood: Two Essays*. New York: John Wiley & Sons, 1966.
8. Wilbert Moore, "Occupational Socialization." In Goslin, p. 862.
9. Moore, p. 877.
10. Moore, pp. 878–880.
11. Moore, p. 880.
12. Reuben Hill and Joan Aldous, "Socialization for Marriage and Parenthood." In Goslin, pp. 911–912.
13. Elaine Cumming and William Henry, *Growing Old: The Process of Disengagement*. New York: Basic Books, 1961.

SUGGESTED READINGS

Becker, Howard S., et al. *Boys in White*. Chicago: University of Chicago Press, 1961.

Deals with medical students, demonstrating how people are slowly socialized into their professions.

Brim, Orville G., Jr., and Stanton Wheeler. *Socialization After Childhood: Two Essays*. New York: John Wiley & Sons, 1966.

One of the first books to explore the area of adult socialization.

Coleman, James. *The Adolescent Society*. New York: The Free Press, 1961.

A study of students in ten high schools, showing the social life of teenagers, their values, and the social status systems that emerge in high schools.

de Beauvoir, Simone. *The Coming of Age*. New York: Putnam, 1972.

Famous French feminist discusses the joys and sorrows of growing old in Western societies.

Kart, Cary S., and Barbara B. Manard, (eds.). *Aging in America*. Sherman Oaks, Calif.: Alfred Publishers, 1976.

An anthology introducing social gerontology.

Kübler-Ross, Elizabeth. *On Death and Dying*. New York: Macmillan, 1969.

A pioneering treatment of the attitude that should be taken toward dying people and death.

Levinson, Daniel J., et al. *The Seasons of a Man's Life*. New York: Alfred A. Knopf, 1978.

A study based on interviews with forty men describing specific developmental periods of their lives.

THREE

Social Institutions

Every society must have social institutions to survive. To understand what a social institution is and how it works, it is necessary to define and understand two concepts—*association* and *institution.*

An association is (1) a *formal group* that (2) is *organized for some special purpose.* An association always has (3) a *name* and a *location,* (4) *written rules and regulations,* and (5) a *hierarchy,* or ranking, of statuses so that everyone in it knows his or her place in the association. Associations also have (6) rules for deciding how to select *members* and how members will be replaced. A parent-teachers association is an example of an association. It is a real group of people that meets each of these criteria.

An institution, in contrast, is not a real group. It is a *procedure.* An institution is an organized, formal, recognized, stabilized way of doing something, of performing an activity in society. An activity is institutionalized when a regular set of statuses is developed (when people know their positions in the structure) and when this system of statuses has been accepted by the society. A way of doing something is institutionalized when the members of the group agree on the proper procedures involved. For example, when the members of a society establish ways to formally educate their young, we have the institution of education.

Institutions need associations to carry out their activities. In fact, there can never be an institution without at least one association attached to it. How could we worship together if we did not have the necessary associations called churches and temples attached to the institution of religion? How could we go from Alabama to New Mexico without such associations as airlines and railroads attached to the institution of transportation? Institutions are worthless without associations to do the work. In short, institutions are ways of doing things; associations are groups that do them.

There are many institutions in every society, but all societies in every period of history have needed five basic institutions to satisfy certain fundamental needs or the societies would have ceased to operate for the benefit of their members. These needs are caring for and socializing children, explaining the unknown, educating the young, providing goods and services, and providing a means of social control. The five institutions that meet these needs are the family, religion, education, economy, and government. In the following chapters we will explore these five universal institutions in detail. We will also note the extensive interplay among them.

6

The Family

In America today, most families consist of the mother, the father, and the children. When the first group of settlers came to our land, the family included grandparents, aunts, and uncles as well. Among the Yoruba of Nigeria, the family is composed of a husband, many wives, and their offspring. In Tibet, several women can be married to one man at the same time. Clearly, the family seems to be an institution found in all societies, but the structure of families appears to differ from society to society.

Families seem to differ in other ways as well. In many American families, the father goes off to work while the mother cares for the children. Among the Alorese of Indonesia, the children are left soon after birth with a father, grandfather, or an older sibling while the women tend the family gardens. In some societies both parents work at jobs and share the housekeeping and child-rearing chores.

Can we define an institution that seems to vary so greatly? In this chapter we will examine the family and its formation, the functions of the family, American marriage and family patterns, and the future of the family.

Defining the Family

All known societies have an institution known as *the family*, with thousands of attached associations. In this book we will formally define *the family* as a *universal institution whose most important functions are socializing and nurturing the younger generation.* The institution of the family differs from its attached associations, which consist of small groups of people, found in various forms, who are related by blood or law or both, who care for each other, and who live together in an economic unit. One way in which people note such relationships is through kinship.

THE KINSHIP GROUP

Kinship is a social relationship based on family ties. Each society decides which relationships are important. In America several kinds of ties can make us kin. We call people our kin if we are descended from them or they from us. My mother and father are my kin and I am theirs. We also call people kin if we share an ancestor. My brother and I have the same parents so we are kin to each other. My cousins and I are kin because we have, at least on one side, the same grandparents. My half sister and I are kin because we may have the same father, though not the same mother.

But what about my stepsister? She and I have two different sets of

Kinship groups can be determined by social as well as biological ties. Therefore a kinship group may include spouses, in-laws, step-parents, and stepsiblings as well as "blood relatives" such as parents, siblings, aunts, uncles, and cousins.

parents, although one of her parents is married to one of mine. What about my wife or my sister-in-law who also have no blood relatives in common with me? Are they my kin? Sociologists would say that my stepsister, my wife, and my sister-in-law are all my kin because we have *social ties* between us that are just as important, sometimes even more important, than biological ties.

In America, then, kinship can be more of a social relationship than a biological one. We have very few laws in this country that compel us to take care of our biological kin or even to see them. Americans are very permissive about kin; we *choose* our kin and they are the people with whom we share a sense of warmth, companionship, obligation, interest, and love. So in this country a kinship group is composed of all those people who are emotionally involved with each other, whether the ties are biological, legal, or social, or any combination of the three.

Legal ties often occur through marriage. We will now examine the relationship between marriage and the family.

THE STRUCTURE OF MARRIAGE

In all societies most families are formed through marriage. Just as families differ, the types of marriage structure also differ. The type of marriage structure found in a society depends on the way in which the family institution in that society wants to create new families. The type of marriage structure we in the United States are most familiar with is called *monogamy*. "Mono" means "one" and "gamy" means "marriage," so we can define monogamy as the marriage of one man to one woman.* Other societies favor a marriage form known as *polygamy*.

---

*It has been mentioned in jest that Americans practice "serial monogamy"; that is, although they are married to only one person at a time, they go through life with a series of partners, remaining faithful to each.

175

Some societies, such as the Yoruba tribe of West Nigeria, practice *polygyny*—the marriage of several women to one man. In this photo the King of Akure is being shown respect by some of his 156 wives.

"Poly" means "many," so polygamy means marriage of one person to two or more people at the same time. There are two kinds of polygamy: *polygyny* and *polyandry*. "Gyny" means "female," so polygyny refers to the marriage of two or more women to one man; "andry" means "male," so polyandry describes the marriage of two or more men to one woman.

Polygyny is often found in Africa, Asia, and parts of the Arab world. It is sometimes practiced in societies that have more women than men because it is a way of providing many women with husbands, which would be impossible if the society were monogamous.

Often in polygynous societies a man gains prestige from having several wives. In fact, the first wife will sometimes encourage her husband to marry other women because then the whole family gains more prestige. Furthermore, the first wife almost always has higher status than those who come after her, and in agricultural countries especially, this means the first wife will have less farm work to do.

Usually in polygynous societies each of the wives has a separate hut in her husband's compound or a separate room in his house. The husband is not supposed to show favoritism among his wives, so he usually lives with each wife for one day at a time, rotating around the compound or house.

176

To most Americans, in their ethnocentrism, this kind of marriage seems unnatural. We tend to think that these women are just being used by their husbands and are really no better than slaves. We suspect they must be jealous of each other. But anthropologists have shown that this is apparently not the case. For one thing, even in societies that approve of polygyny, only the wealthiest men can afford more than one wife, and usually there are not enough extra women for more than a few men to have second or third wives. Then too, no one has been able to prove that women in monogamous societies are any happier, have any more prestige, or are better treated than women in polygynous societies.

Many Americans take a similar kind of attitude toward polyandry —one wife having two or more husbands. This is a rare marriage form, usually found in societies with a surplus of males. The Kandyans of Ceylon are one example. Among these people, when a woman marries a man, she is allowed to marry his brothers as well.

A fourth marriage form is *cenogamy,* or group marriage, which is also rarely found. Cenogamy is a form in which several men and several women are all married to each other. Some early utopian American communities practiced group marriage—for example, the group who settled in Oneida, New York, in the mid-nineteenth century. Some modern communes also claim to have group marriages, but cenogamy is not a legal practice in the United States.

RESTRICTIONS IN MARRIAGE

Every society has rules concerning whom people may or may not marry. The requirement that people marry outside of certain groups is known as *exogamy* ("exo" = "without" or "outside of"). In our society we must marry outside of our immediate families and must not marry close blood relatives. In some states first cousins are forbidden to marry. In some tribal societies people are required to marry outside of their clan or village.

Exogamy is related to the *incest taboo,* which forbids sexual relations between people who have close blood ties. Of course, every society defines close blood ties in its own way. Most agree that parents and children and brothers and sisters may not cohabit (the best known exceptions to this rule are the ancient Egyptian and Hawaiian royal families and the early Peruvians), but some modern societies extend the taboo to include cousins, in-laws, step-relatives, and so on.

The requirement that people marry within the same group is known as *endogamy* ("endo" = "within"). Again, each society has different groups that are considered important to stay within when members marry. In India, for example, most people marry others within their own caste. In the United States, most people marry within the same religious and racial groups and within the same social class.

According to the 1957 report from the Bureau of the Census[1] (the latest information on religion we have because the Census Bureau no longer collects such data), approximately 7 percent of all Jews, 9 percent of all Protestants, and 22 percent of all Catholics marry outside of their religions. A study conducted in 1970 confirms these percentages, reporting that 91.4 percent of Protestants, 78.4 percent of Catholics, and 92.8 percent of all Jews marry partners of the same faith.[2]

Interreligious marriage is probably related somewhat to population distribution. When people live where there are few other members of their religious group—and therefore few people to choose from—they are more likely to marry outside of their religious group. When people live in large cities, where people from all religious groups are likely to live, they are more likely to meet and marry others of the same religion.[3]

Religious exogamy is more common than racial exogamy. Again, it is difficult to know exactly how many people marry into different racial groups because very few states request such information on marriage license applications. According to a 1973 report, the total number of interracial marriages, including white-black, white-Oriental, and white-American Indian, was only 0.7 percent of the 2,277,000 American marriages that occurred that year.[4] Of all racially mixed marriages, black and white interracial marriage is the most common.

When intermarriage occurs between blacks and whites, it is usually the man who is black and the woman who is white. Sociologist Thomas B. Monahan's study of interracial marriage in Indiana revealed that in 72 percent of the mixed marriages, the black male was in a high social status and the white female was in a lower social status.[5] Robert Merton theorizes that such marriages represent an exchange. The male offers his high economic position in exchange for the female's higher racial rating.[6]

There seem to be many reasons why Americans usually marry those in the same racial group. One is simply prejudice; we see members of other races in a negative light and we do not think of them as possible wives and husbands. Another reason is that people in different racial groups do not get to meet each other as often as members of the same race. Even when they do meet, the relationships are often formal and not conducive to getting to know each other in a personal way. As a final reason, people are afraid to marry a member of another race because they think they will be rejected by their families and friends.

Most of us marry people who are also in a similar social class. The reason for this is that when people are in the same class, they tend to

APPLYING SOCIOLOGY

Americans think that among their many freedoms, they have the freedom to marry anyone they choose. Yet as you have seen, there are several restrictions placed on who can marry whom in American society.

Think about married couples you know. Have most of them followed these restrictions in choosing a marriage partner? Do you think they are aware that they have followed (or not followed) the societal norms?

Imagine yourself selecting a mate who had characteristics the society thinks are wrong for you. Do you think it would be difficult for you to marry such an individual? Why? Do you think you would be happy or unhappy in a marriage of which society did not approve? Why?

have similar attitudes toward life, similar goals and beliefs, and similar life-styles. When two people agree on many things, marriage is easier. When social class exogamy does occur, it is usually the woman who marries "up." This is called *hypergamy* ("hyper" = "above"). When a woman marries a man from a class lower than her own, it is called *hypogamy* ("hypo" = "down").

FAMILY ORGANIZATION

The nuclear or conjugal family is the most common form of family organization in the United States.

There are two main kinds of family organization. In the United States the most common form is called the *nuclear* or *conjugal family* ("con" = "with" and "jugal" = "to unite in marriage"). This family consists only of the husband and wife and their dependent children. The core of the family is based on marriage, and the members are expected to care for and help the other members before they help any other kin. For example, on gift-giving occasions, we buy nicer presents for our mothers than for our aunts. In modern society, the nuclear family provides children with a legitimate position in society and with the nurturance that will enable them to function in their society.

The second type of family organization is called the *extended* or *consanguine family* ("sanguine" = "blood"). This family consists of several generations of blood relatives all living either with or near each other. In this family the relationships are based on blood, not marriage. The key alliances may be to one's blood relatives, not to one's spouse. In this family, for example, a man might buy his brother a more expensive present than he would buy his wife. This type of family organization is rarely found in the United States. It was common in ancient China and Japan and can still be found in some African and Asian na-

179

An extended or consanguine family in Rome, Italy. This form of family organization is rare in the United States.

tions. Figure 6–1 shows the difference between these two types of family organization.

Membership in a nuclear family and membership in an extended family entail several additional differences besides where loyalty is placed. There are also differences in residential, authority, and descent patterns.

Residence

The nuclear family lives apart from both the husband's and the wife's relatives in a *neolocal* setting ("neo" = "new" and "local" = "location"). Newly married couples set up their own home; they try not to live with relatives. Extended families, on the other hand, stay among their kin. Such families may be *patrilocal* ("patri" = "father") or *matrilocal* ("matri" = "mother"). If the system is a patrilocal one, the husband brings his wife and children to live in or near his father's house. If it is matrilocal, the couple resides with or near the wife's family.

Authority

We usually like to believe that power and authority are equally divided between the wife and the husband in the nuclear family. When both actually share the power and authority, we have an *egalitarian* family. That is the ideal, but in most families one of the partners usually makes more decisions than the other.

180

FIGURE 6–1
A Nuclear and an
Extended Family

Extended or Consanguine Family

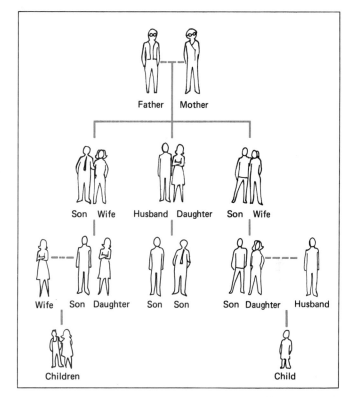

Nuclear or Conjugal Family

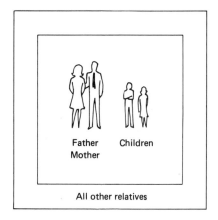

While the nuclear family consists of the husband and wife and their dependent children, the extended family consists of several generations of blood relatives all living with or near each other.

An extended family may be either a *patriarchy* or a *matriarchy* ("arch" = "rule"). When a family is strictly patriarchal, as ancient Greek, Hebrew, Chinese, and Japanese families were, the women have no authority at all. When a family is matriarchal, as some African families are, the power passes to a male in a woman's kinship group, generally to her oldest brother or oldest male relative. It is the rare society indeed where the female actually controls the family.

Descent

Every society must be able to identify the relationship of children to families. We must be able to say that Mary is the daughter of John or James is the son of Helen because it is necessary to establish who is responsible for a child and who should inherit the family's wealth and

181

FIGURE 6–2
A Comparison of
Nuclear and Extended
Families

Nuclear or Conjugal Families	Extended or Consanguine Families
Based on marriage ties	Based on blood ties
Allegiance to one's spouse	Allegiance to one's blood kin
Neolocal residence	Patrilocal or matrilocal residence
Egalitarian power	Patriarchal or matriarchal power
Bilateral descent	Patrilineal or matrilineal descent

social position. Therefore, every society has a system of deciding authority, inheritance, and responsibility. In a nuclear family system both parents have equal authority over the children and equal responsibility for them. In such a system the descent is *bilateral* ("bi" = "two" and "lateral" = "side"); children inherit from the two sides of their family. They can inherit money or the family business from either parent. They can learn the occupation of either parent. There is only one thing that almost all American children inherit from their fathers only—the father's last name. Although there is no law requiring that children be called by their father's name, tradition and our societal norms have made it seem legal. In contrast, most Spanish and Portuguese children carry the names of both parents.

In some other societies, descent is *unilateral* ("uni" = "one"). The child inherits from either the mother's side of the family or from the father's side. If the important ancestors are thought to be on the father's side, it is a *patrilineal* society; if they are on the mother's side, it is a *matrilineal* society ("lineal" = "line").

All of these types of family organization are rarely found in perfect form because human beings rarely follow their own rules exactly. In general, though, we can say that nuclear and extended families are each characterized by certain features. Figure 6–2 illustrates this point.

Functions of the Family

We observed in the opening to Part Three that all societies have important needs that must be met if the society is to survive. We also indicated that needs are satisfied by institutions, which are accepted, established ways of doing things. The family is one such institution.

TRADITIONAL FUNCTIONS OF THE AMERICAN FAMILY

Before America became as industrialized as it is now, most Americans lived in small towns or on isolated farms. At that time the family had several functions that it has little responsibility for now or that it no longer performs at all. What were some of these functions? How were they carried out in the past? How are they carried out today? In order to understand how the functions of the family have changed, we shall compare family life a hundred and fifty years ago with family life today.

The Economic Function

A hundred and fifty years ago, an American family was likely to be engaged in farming or perhaps running a small shop. Every member had his or her own job to do. The mother took care of the house, reared the children, cooked all the food, and made all the clothing (sometimes even weaving the cloth). The father tended the farm or the shop, often doing a lot of the farm work by hand because there were few mechanical tools. Each child had a share of the work. One might help the mother to do the food canning; another might help the father plant the seeds and harvest the crops. At this time children were economic assets because they were actively involved in earning the family living.

Today families are much more likely to live in cities, and adults are more likely to go outside the household to work rather than staying within it. Most fathers and many mothers go to offices and factories to earn money to support the family. Present-day children usually do not contribute significantly to the family income. In fact, it costs a great deal of money to rear children in modern society. Therefore, children are more apt to be economic liabilities than assets.

The Protective Function

When Americans lived far away from neighbors or in very small towns that did not have real police forces, the parents actually had to guard the family from robbers and wild animals. Most families had guns in their houses and even the children learned how to use them.

There were other kinds of protection, too. The family provided economic protection to children and old people. There were no welfare agencies, Social Security, or orphanages, so the family guaranteed that old people and children would always be taken care of.

There was also health protection. Even if there were doctors or hospitals, they were often far away, and since there were no cars, doctors could not go to visit patients very easily. The family learned how to perform many medical services that we would not think of doing ourselves today. For example, most babies were born at home, with the grandmother, aunts, and older female children helping the mother give birth.

In the modern family almost all kinds of protection are offered by agencies outside the family. We have police forces and armies. Old

In the eighteenth and nineteenth centuries, the family served a vital protective function in the absence of neighbors and police forces.

people and orphaned children often go to state-supported homes. The ill are often cared for in modern hospitals.

The Religious Function

Once there was a time when America had very few churches, and those that did exist were often far from the family's home. Consequently, the family had a religious function. Family members read prayers together and conducted services in their homes. Within the family circle grace was said before meals, hymns were sung, sermons were given, and the Bible was read.

Today when people pray, they usually do so in a formal church or temple. Ministers, priests, and rabbis, not parents, read the prayers and conduct the services. Most parents no longer give much religious training to their children at home, although they do provide them with a religious identity.

The Recreational Function

On farms and in small towns a hundred and fifty years ago, family members learned to depend on each other for recreation and fun. There were no radios, television sets, bowling alleys, movie houses, sports stadiums, museums, and so forth. Parents and children had to invent their own pleasures. In the evenings after the work was done, some members of the family read aloud to others. Maybe they popped corn, played games, or pulled taffy. Sometimes the whole family sang together.

Modern families do few things together as a group. Parents often go out together as a couple, apart from their children. Each child has his or her friends. Some families have more than one television set, so that all the members do not even watch television together. Instead of families making their own fun together, individual members tend to go to recreational facilities for entertainment.

A century and a half ago, family members depended upon one another for recreation *(top)*. In modern times, however, few families do things together as a group *(bottom)*.

185

The Educational Function

One hundred and fifty years ago, few people went to high schools and only a very special few went to college. Most learning was acquired at home. Parents taught children just enough reading, writing, and arithmetic to enable them to run the farm or the small store when they grew up. Girls were taught to take care of a home and children. Education beyond these basic skills was considered unnecessary.

Now, of course, virtually all of our young people go to formal schools. In 1977, 61.3 million Americans, about three out of every ten persons in the United States, were students in formal schools.[7] Many parents in modern society cannot even help their children with their homework because schools use methods and give students information that is beyond their parents' knowledge.

The Status Placement Function

Later on in this book we will see that people in societies are members of social classes (see Chapter 13). How do they get that class membership? When children are born they are given the social status of their family. If the family has high status, the child will automatically be in a high status group. If the family has low status, he or she will be a member of a low status group. If the parents are wealthy, the children will be born into a higher class. If the parents are poor, the children will be in a lower class.

In the past, once a child was born into a family, his or her status rarely changed, and the rest of that person's life often depended on who his or her parents were. John Smith's son knew quite well how far he would probably go in school, what work he would do (usually the same as his father), whom he would marry, where he would live (usually in the same town as his parents), and so forth. A person's *family of orientation*—the family into which one is born and in which one is socialized—determined much of his or her future life.

To some extent, this is still true. It is more advantageous to be born into a rich family than into a poor one. But the modern family has less influence over a child's future place in the social hierarchy. One reason why young people have more control over their own destinies is that educational opportunities are more available to them today than ever before. It is no longer only rich children who go to college; poor children also get a chance to learn something that will help them to move higher up on the social ladder than their parents. For another reason, most businesses have grown so large that a rich parent cannot leave the management of a business to a child (unless that child is trained to run it properly). In our technical society, then, more children of all classes get a chance to compete for important positions. Now talent and training are more important than the accident of birth.

186

MURDOCK'S THEORY OF UNIVERSAL FAMILY FUNCTIONS

We have just seen that many of the traditional functions of the family have been taken over by other institutions. What is left for the family to do? If families serve no purpose, why should we have them at all? We have already noted that an institution must have at least one function or there would be no reason for it to continue to exist. What does the institution of the family still do for society?

Anthropologist George P. Murdock argues that the family institution in any society, regardless of its structure, has a nuclear family embedded within it and that the nuclear family always performs four functions: *reproduction, sexual regulation, economic cooperation,* and *socialization of the children.*[8]

Reproduction

All societies must find a way to replace members who die or leave the group. They are able to replace some members by immigration—by allowing people from other countries to become citizens. But this is a very inefficient method because no society can be sure foreigners will migrate in sufficient numbers. Therefore, one universal function of the nuclear family has been to have children. Societies have ways of discouraging or encouraging large families. When the members of a society feel the population is growing too large, they can distribute free birth control information and devices. If they wish to increase the birth rate, they can offer bonuses for each child born or permit tax exemptions for children. In any event, in the United States it is the nuclear family that is responsible for producing the children that will maintain a population of the desired size.

Sexual Regulation

The function of reproduction is related to the function of sexual regulation. If we had a society in which everyone was permitted to have sexual relations with everyone else, we would have chaos. Therefore, the norms of a society establish who may have sexual relations with whom and under what conditions.

All known societies approve of sexual contact between married couples. In fact, most demand that husbands and wives maintain sexual relationships. In most of the United States, if one spouse deprives the other of sexual gratification, a divorce can be granted. Some societies permit sexual activity between certain members other than legally married people. For example, in ancient China concubinage (cohabitation between persons not legally married) was a legal status. American sexual rules will be discussed later in the section on courtship. But the point here is that, according to Murdock, the family institution must regulate sexual behavior as well as it can. Of course, no society can ever get all of its members to conform completely to its norms. There are always some who deviate from sex norms.

Economic Cooperation

Economic cooperation really means a *division of labor*. Murdock claims that in each nuclear family there is cooperation in the way the tasks are divided. Most societies assign the physically strenuous work to the males and the lighter tasks to the females. Thus, in preliterate societies men usually do the hunting and fishing; women gather the roots and berries, prepare the food, and tend to the children. In industrialized societies, men generally earn most of the family money and women usually care for the home and children.

Murdock observes that there are sexual relationships between men and women, such as those between lovers, that are not marked by economic cooperation. Similarly, there are economic relations between males and females without a sexual relationship, for example, between brothers and sisters or between employer and employee. "But marriage exists only when the economic and the sexual are united into one relationship, and this combination occurs only in marriage,"[9] says Murdock.

Socialization

Socialization is said to be the fourth universal function of the family. It is of such vast importance that it has been discussed separately in earlier chapters. Here it is enough to recall that socialization is the process that converts the human animal into the human being. The nuclear family is charged with the greater part of the responsibility for seeing to it that the children learn the society's norms, beliefs, rules, values, and attitudes.

TESTING MURDOCK'S THEORY

Murdock is very emphatic about his theory of the nuclear family. He argues that the nuclear family exists everywhere at all times and performs these four functions, even in the extended families that seem to overlay the nuclear families they contain. Murdock writes:

> In the nuclear family. . . we thus see assembled four functions fundamental to human social life—the sexual, the economic, the reproductive, and the educational [or socialization]. Without provision for the first and third, society would become extinct; for the second, life itself would cease; for the fourth, culture would come to an end.[10]

There is no doubt that Murdock is correct when he points out that these functions must be performed so that a society can survive. But is he correct when he claims that only the nuclear family can perform

Socialization—the process that converts the human animal into a human being—is a primary function and responsibility of the family.

Talcott Parsons (1902–   )

Talcott Parsons is a structural-functionalist who has theorized about almost every aspect of the individual and society. During forty years as a writer and lecturer, he has constructed an elaborate theory of modern society.

Functionalists assume that there are orderly patterns of behavior exhibited by members of a society and found in such institutions as the family. When these patterns are common to most individuals within a society, they become normative. Functionalists evaluate behavior as to whether or not it is normative. Thus behavior is either "normal" or "abnormal."

Functionalists look at society as being stable within the midst of change. And in order to maintain the survival and stability of society, institutions must satisfy four basic needs. These needs, according to Parsons, are adaptation, goal attainment, integration, and latency. *Adaptation* is the need to effectively use and distribute the available resources of the society. *Goal attainment* is the need to define goals and to order them or set priorities. *Integration* is the need to maintain relationships and harmony among the units of the system. *Latency* is the need to provide individuals with the skills necessary to play their roles and to deal with psychological strain and tension. If these needs are satisfied, then the institutions, and hence the society, will function properly.

The modern society, however, is faced with a number of obstacles to stability. Some of these are the geographical and social mobility of its members, the occupational complexity and specialization of individuals, and the lack of consensus on values. How does the modern society overcome these obstacles? Let us look at the Parsonian view of the family as an example.

According to Parsons, the structure of the nuclear family provides the solution to a number of problems facing the urban industrial society. For one thing, the nuclear family is small (as compared with the extended family). Thus, if a job change requires a family to move, relatively few individuals are affected. In addition, the nuclear family provides emotional support, which is necessary for individuals to pursue specialized occupations within the larger society. Hence, Parsons believes the nuclear family serves an important function in our modern economic system.

Parsons has also analyzed the functions of the members of a nuclear family, presumably using a 1950s middle-class family as a model. He identified occupations and financial success as goals for the male in the family structure, and labeled the male role the *instrumental role.* The female within the family structure performs domestic duties and provides emotional support for her husband and children. Parsons calls her role the *expressive role.* According to Parsons, these role assignments promote harmony within the family. Parsons believes that through such roles and the emotional support provided by the family, individuals are better equipped to function in modern society. Most sociologists no longer accept this view of the modern American family.

them? Is he correct when he says that the nuclear family always exists even when it is so deeply embedded in other family forms that we can hardly see it? Sociologists and anthropologists have challenged Murdock's theory by describing societies in which the nuclear family does not exist and therefore cannot possibly perform these functions.

One such society is the Nayar military caste in India. In this society there is no nuclear family. Instead the Nayar have a system of polyandry and polygyny. There is no important central group based on marital ties within the family containing one husband, one wife, and their children. The husband does very little interacting with any of his wives and children.

In addition, reproduction and sexual relations are not regulated by a nuclear family. Reproduction can result from the union of a woman with any of her husbands, and sexual relations are not confined to one woman with one man.

Furthermore, the biological father and mother do not cooperate on an economic basis. The mother and the children live with the mother's *taravad* (clan or tribe), and her father or oldest brother is responsible for his own sister's children instead of his wife's.

Finally, socialization is not the responsibility of the nuclear family because of the residence pattern. The biological father has almost nothing to do with educating his own children. He educates and socializes his nieces and nephews.

Nayar society is only one example of societies having family institutions that do not fit Murdock's theory. Therefore, while we must conclude that some societies contain the nuclear family form that carries out the functions of reproduction, sexual regulation, economic cooperation, and socialization, not all societies have such nuclear family forms. Thus, while these functions are universally performed by some group within every society, they are not necessarily carried out by nuclear families.

Patterns In American Family Life

As we saw earlier in this chapter, many of the functions of the American family have changed considerably over the past century and a half. As the functions have changed, so too has the very nature of marriage and family life. In truth, if a person who had been dead a hundred and fifty years were miraculously to come back to life today, he or she would probably be astonished by modern attitudes toward sex and marriage and by the structure of modern family life. What are these changed attitudes and structures? Where are they likely to lead marriage and family life in the future? These are questions with which we will deal in the remainder of this chapter.

ATTITUDES TOWARD SEX

Among the norms that American parents pass on to their children are regulations concerning premarital sexual conduct. What are American sex norms? How permissive are American parents toward their children when it comes to sexual activity? How closely are the norms followed?

All societies have sex norms, which define what is "right" and what is "wrong." But there is a great deal of variety among different groups in the behavior considered proper and in the way the rules are enforced. In almost all societies where there are restrictions against premarital sex, there are institutionalized ways of enforcing the restrictions. Some groups, like the people of Jamaica in the Caribbean, try to keep their young people, especially their daughters, ignorant of sexual matters. In other groups, like those in some countries of South America, teenage boys and girls are kept apart from each other as much as possible. Other societies permit their young people to intermingle, but adults are present at all times to serve as chaperons. In short, in most parts of the world where premarital sexual relations are not permitted, the society either deprives the young generation of knowledge about sex or the opportunity for sexual encounters.

In the United States we have a curious situation. Parental attitudes toward premarital sex are almost always negative. Many parents place a high value on virginity, and many Americans believe that people should not have sexual relations unless they are married to each other. Unlike most other societies, however, we do not provide institutionalized ways to reinforce our norms. We do not prevent young people from being alone together. We allow them to learn about sex and even to have access to birth control information and devices. So the American creed is contradictory and confusing to many young men and women. On one hand, we stress that they must have no sexual activity; on the other, we provide enormous opportunity for sexual relations to occur.

Premarital Sexual Behavior

Although Americans have never totally accepted premarital sexual relations, they have become more tolerant under certain conditions. Before noting these conditions, we will examine different patterns of premarital sex.

Ira Reiss has identified four types of premarital sexual patterns:[11]

Abstinence. Sexual intercourse is not permitted for either sex under any conditions.

Double standard. Unmarried males may have sexual relations, but unmarried females may not.

191

MOMMA, DID YOUR MOTHER EXPLAIN ABOUT LIFE TO YOU?

YES, MARYLOU, SHE DID.

SO HOW COME YOU NEVER EXPLAINED ABOUT LIFE TO ME?

BECAUSE IN THOSE DAYS, IT WAS A LECTURE. THESE DAYS, IT WOULD BE A DEBATE...

Sex with affection. Intercourse is permitted when a couple feels it is in love.

Sex without affection. Sexual relations are allowed, even when the two people are not in love, if they feel a strong physical attraction for each other.

In our society, studies show that the double standard and abstinence are still the traditional patterns. Sex without affection is definitely the last acceptable form of behavior. Sex with affection, however, is gaining approval. So there has been a change in our attitudes, although it is not a great change. We are beginning to accept sexual relations as an expression of love between two people who care for each other even if they are not married. Yet our sexual norms still discourage premarital sex.

How obedient to our sex norms are young Americans? Even in the most restrictive societies, some people always break the sexual taboos. How often do young Americans break them?

Until the famous "Kinsey Reports" in 1948 and in 1953,[12] we really did not know very much about the private sex lives of Americans. Zoologist Alfred C. Kinsey and his associates were followed in 1966 and 1970 by sexologists Masters and Johnson and their equally famous research on sexual behavior.[13] Because of these four important studies, we have learned a great deal about American attitudes toward sex and sexual behavior.

Kinsey found that 81 percent of the females and 84 percent of the males reached orgasm at least once by the age of eighteen by means of masturbating a sexual partner. He also found that approximately 50 percent of his female subjects were not virgins when they married, although almost all had had sexual relations only with the men who eventually became their husbands. What was very interesting about Kinsey's findings was that of the women who were nonvirgins at marriage, 69 percent said they did not feel guilty and had no regrets. The

Kinsey Reports shocked the American public especially at learning how many young women were not virgin brides and how many were not sorry about it.

Since the 1960s, research suggests that there has been an increase in premarital sexual activity. Most studies report higher rates of female premarital sex, but almost no change for males. A survey of 100,000 women conducted by journalists Robert J. Levin and Amy Levin in 1975 reported that 90 percent of the respondents under the age of twenty-five had engaged in premarital sex.[14] This finding indicates that men and women are becoming more alike in their sexual behavior, and that the double standard may eventually disappear.

There are several reasons for this change in female premarital sexual behavior. One has been the development of extremely effective birth control methods that have decreased the probability and the fear of pregnancy. A second reason is the changed attitude about male and female sexuality. We have now learned that one's gender has nothing to do with one's need for sexual expression, so we are slightly more permissive toward females today than we have been in the past. A third reason is a change in our moral code. Sex is no longer considered sinful and evil. Many people are beginning to believe that if two people have

---

FOCUS ON: FEMALE SEXUALITY

Although our norms attempt to regulate sexual behavior, many people violate these norms. In her book *The Hite Report,* Shere Hite studied female sexuality. The 3,000 responses to a detailed questionnaire that she received from women across the United States were compiled and used as the basis for her book.

In discussing their feelings and responses toward sex and sexuality, women challenged the common belief that they are less interested than men in sex. The study indicates, however, that many men have not been able to completely satisfy their partners sexually.

Despite their interest in sex, women expressed ambivalent feelings about the "sexual revolution." While many felt that it allowed more openness, very few totally accepted it for their daughters. Many also felt that there was no revolution at all, and others felt that it removed women's right *not* to have sex. In addition, many women who tried to experience their newly found sexual freedom realized that the double standard was still in operation. As a result, they felt disrespected and consequently were often hurt.

Do you believe that there really has been a "sexual revolution"? How different do you think your attitudes toward sex are from those of your parents, your friends, and others you know? Do you think that the findings of *The Hite Report* reflect the sexual behavior of the entire female population?

Source: Shere Hite, *The Hite Report,* New York: Macmillan, 1976.

sexual relations without hurting anyone, there is nothing wrong with such behavior. In short, our attitudes are becoming more permissive, and because the majority of people in a society follow the society's rules even when these rules change, more unmarried people are engaging in sexual activities.

Romantic Love

Of all the societies in the world, none puts such a high value on romantic love as does the United States. Most Americans believe that love is the chief reason to marry.

Not only do we marry for love, but we also continue to believe there is one ideal mate for everyone. We pursue this dream person, and when we fall in love, we think the miracle has occurred—we have found the one and only! As soon as we find that person, we tend to put him or her on a pedestal and believe that together we can do anything, overcome any obstacle (because love conquers all), and live happily ever after.

This notion of romantic love as a basis for marriage is really both dangerous and misleading. Married life is not mysterious and glamorous and the romantic part generally fades away over time. Then people who are unprepared for the routine of everyday life often become disenchanted with each other and marriage.

Choosing a Mate

Let us suppose now that you are ready to select your husband or wife. You have reached an approved age, you have finished your education, you have a job. As we noted earlier, your choice of a husband or wife is already somewhat limited by your religion, race, social class, age, even your region of the country. Out of the remaining possible choices, whom do you select?

There are two totally opposite theories about this. One, *the theory of homogamy* ("homo" = "the same") holds that we marry people who have personality traits similar to our own. Like attracts like. That is, generous people marry other generous people. Men who like sports marry women who are athletic, conservatives marry conservatives, and liberals marry liberals. The other theory, called *the theory of complementary needs,* claims that we look for opposite traits in our mates. Opposites attract. That is, if we are shy, we look for an outgoing personality to help us overcome the shyness. If we like to be taken care of, we select a person who likes to be protective. If we have domineering personalities, we select people who like to be told what to do. Neither theory claims that people make these selections consciously.

Robert Winch was the first sociologist to test the theory of complementary needs,[15] and his research showed that the theory was only

"Sometimes, Eric, I wish the computer dating hadn't been so accurate."

> **APPLYING SOCIOLOGY**
>
> Which of these theories of mate selection do you think is correct? Consider the married couples you know. Are they similar to each other? Do they like the same things and the same people? Do they enjoy the same movies? Do they have the same ideas about rearing their children? Or do their tastes differ on most things? Does one like to go to the seashore for vacations while the other likes to go to the mountains? Is one permissive with the children and the other strict? Is one aggressive and the other timid? What can you conclude from your observations? Which theory describes more of the couples you know?

partly true. Other sociologists tested it and were also unable to prove that opposites attract. When the theory of homogamy was tested, however, the researchers found strong evidence that supported it. Not only do married people have similar personality traits, they are amazingly similar in many ways. For example, tall people tend to marry tall people; good-looking people tend to marry other good-looking people; smart men tend to marry smart women; healthy women tend to marry healthy men. Human beings are likely to marry other human beings who have the same values, attitudes, goals, and interests.

In short, although many Americans believe they marry for love and that they may marry anyone they wish, it has been shown that the rules of exogamy and endogamy are very firmly followed. We tend to marry people who are like ourselves even in physical and psychological ways. So the group we live in sets up norms and influences our thinking much more than we realize or are likely to admit even to ourselves.

It is true, of course, that Americans have more freedom in mate selection than the people of many other societies who have their marriages arranged by their parents. In India, Nepal, and many African nations, individuals traditionally expect their parents to choose their mates because they believe the older people are wiser and more experienced and will make a better choice than they can make themselves. They also claim that love comes after marriage—the husband and wife will grow to love each other as they live together and share their lives.

Most American young people probably would be horrified at the notion of their families choosing their spouses. They probably think they could not be happy with someone they had not fallen in love with before marriage. Yet studies of marital success and happiness show that there is very little difference between parent-arranged marriage and participant-arranged marriage. Romantic love tends to change over time and eventually a quiet kind of affection develops between two people in any successful marriage, whether they chose their own partners or their parents did it for them.

MARRIAGE

Marriage has always been popular in the United States. Recently, however, there has been a decrease in the number of marriages and an increase in the age of people marrying for the first time. In 1973, 2,277,000 marriages took place in this country. In 1974, there was a 2 percent decrease for a total of 2,223,000 marriages. And in 1975, there was an additional decrease of 4 percent with only 1,960,000 marriages occurring.[16] In 1960, the average age at time of first marriage was 22.8 for males and 20.3 for females. In 1975, the average age for males had risen to 23.5 and for females to 21.1[17] It is too soon yet to say whether or not these changes signal trends, but we should keep an eye on these statistics in the future.

Societies exercise control over all aspects of people's lives, and marriage is no exception. The state is always an interested third party in a marriage. People can draw up other kinds of contracts among themselves that may be broken at any time with mutual consent, but the state is always part of the marriage contract. Even when you are married by a minister, a priest, or a rabbi, he or she is acting not only as a representative of the religious group but also as a representative of the state. Notice next time you go to a wedding that the person who performs the ceremony will probably say, "By the power vested in me *by the state,* I now pronounce you husband and wife."

Marriage in the United States, then, is a legal contract among three parties: the bride, the bridegroom, and the state. The state is the only one of the three parties that can dissolve the contract. Why is the state concerned with marriage? The answer is that the state has an interest in preserving the family because the family performs several functions that are necessary for its survival. The institution of the family must exert control to help the state survive.

Why People Marry

Since our society is becoming more permissive about premarital sex, Americans do not have to marry in order to live with each other. Yet most Americans still marry. Why do most people choose to enter marriage?

Most Americans marry for love. Once they have found a suitable mate, they believe that love and marriage go together.

Another reason people marry is to be considered adults. Young people are neither children nor grown-ups in our society, but if they marry, they are generally considered adults, no matter what their age may be. So one way young people in our society escape the awkward "in between" age is to marry.

We also marry to fulfill our gender roles (see Chapter 11). This is especially true for females. Although males are accepted as "men" if they discharge their occupational obligations, they are still not completely accepted as adults until they marry. This is even more true for females, who are not considered fully to be "women" (no matter how successful they may be in their occupations) unless they marry and have a child.

An additional reason to marry is that ours is a "two-by-two" society and single people often find themselves in uncomfortable situations. Even though a husband and a wife lead different lives—he satisfying his identity needs through his occupation, she satisfying hers through her occupation outside the home or as a homemaker—society regards them as a "couple," as one unit in social situations.

Furthermore, some Americans marry for social approval. Although societal attitudes toward living together are more liberal than in the past, not all of society accepts such informal living arrangements. People believe that only by marrying can they legitimate their relationship in society's eyes.

Marriage Work

Sociologist Leonard Benson[18] claims there are six basic marital obligations, and he calls them "marriage work" because he says it takes a certain amount of effort to perform them. First, married couples are expected to be reliable, truthful, and dependable. Second, couples are expected to divide the work of the marriage between them and each partner is expected to carry his or her share of the work load. Traditionally, men have earned the family living, and women have kept house and reared children, but this division of labor is changing now (see Chapter 11). Third, husbands and wives are expected to be sympathetic to each other and to understand one another. Fourth, married couples should be able to talk to each other, to express their deepest secrets and be sure they will not be revealed, and to take an interest in the things that in-

---

APPLYING SOCIOLOGY

There are probably other marital obligations that could be added to Benson's list. Think about your own views of marriage, your experience with it, direct or indirect, and your expectations of it. What obligations would you add to Benson's list? Why? Are there any that you might delete? Why?

terest each other. Fifth, wives and husbands should give sexual satisfaction to, and receive it from, each other. Sixth, couples should do more than just what is expected of them. They should be willing to go out of their way to please each other.

Marital Success and Failure

When sociologists try to measure marital success, they always encounter a great deal of difficulty. One problem is getting honest answers from married people when they are asked if they consider their marriages happy. People sometimes lie because they want to appear to obey the norm that we *should* be happily married. Sometimes couples even deceive themselves because there is still some stigma attached to getting divorced in our society. In addition, it is hard to know what the answers mean. What one person would call a happy marriage may be very different from what another person calls a happy marriage. So sociologists are not sure, when they ask their questions, if their subjects agree on what having a happy marriage means.

Also, it is hard to say what marital success really means. Can we freely substitute "happiness" or "adjustment" or "stability" for "success"? Can we ask people if they believe their marriage is "successful"? Is a marriage a success if both spouses are happy? Is it a success if only one partner is happy? Can we say a marriage is successful if two people have adjusted to each other's habits?

When we try to substitute "stability" for "success," we also run into difficulty. Stability means firmness, steadiness, and endurance. Marital stability, then, means that the marriage has lasted—there has

THE LOCKHORNS

"I'M SUCH A DUMMY! I THOUGHT 'LOVE, CHERISH, HONOR AND OBEY' WAS A MULTIPLE-CHOICE QUESTION."

198

been no separation or divorce. Can we claim a marriage is successful because the two people involved have stayed married to each other? Is that sufficient evidence of success?

It seems apparent that it is difficult to measure marital success, but we have one way of finding out without doubt which marriages are unsuccessful. All we have to do is look at marriages that break up. We *cannot* be sure that people who stay together are successfully married, but *we can* be sure that those who part were unsuccessfully married.

There are four common ways people can voluntarily end a marriage: annulment, desertion, legal separation, and divorce. There is a fifth way that ends a marriage—the death of one of the partners—but that is not from choice.

Annulment   Annulment means that legally the marriage never existed. Usually the ground for annulment is fraud, meaning there was some legal reason why the ceremony should never have been performed in the first place. One partner may have lied about his or her age, or about how much money he or she earned, or about whether he or she wanted to have children. One partner may still be married to someone else. Perhaps one spouse was legally insane or perhaps one forced the other into marriage in some unfair way. Annulment, then, is granted when one partner can prove that the other seriously lied before the ceremony. Annulments constitute about 3.5 percent of all marital terminations, and the people involved return to a single status as if they had never been married at all.

Desertion   An informal way of ending a marriage is desertion. It means that one partner moves out of the family home, often without leaving any address and without any legal procedures. Because there are no reliable records of desertion, we can only guess at the number that occur each year in the United States. Estimates range from 100,000 per year to four times that number. In the past the husband was more likely to desert than the wife, probably because women felt a stronger sense of parenthood than men did and were more hesitant to leave their children. Recently, sociologists have noted that the rates for female desertion have risen considerably. Some now estimate that female desertion rates are as high as, if not higher than, male desertion rates.[19]

Legal Separation   Legal separation accounts for between 2 and 3 percent of all marital terminations. Legal separation means that the husband and wife agree to live apart, but they may not remarry. It is a partial divorce. Legal separation is a useful procedure because it allows a couple time to reconsider before they get a permanent divorce. It is also a way to end a marriage when religion forbids divorce.

199

Desertion—the abandonment of the family by either spouse—is one way in which people can end a marriage.

Divorce Divorce is defined as the legal termination of a marriage, allowing each partner to remarry. The United States has the highest divorce rate in the world with the exception of Egypt, and its rate is climbing. In 1900, about one in every eight American marriages ended in divorce; today more than one in every three (actually 43 percent) ends in divorce.[20] Approximately 40 percent of all divorcing couples have one or two children and 20 percent have three or more.[21]

When people worry about the high American divorce rate, they are most concerned about the children. Most people believe that children from divorced homes do not do as well in school as children from intact homes. It is also believed that there is more juvenile delinquency and more mental illness among children of divorced parents.

A great deal of research in this area, however, reveals that divorce does not hurt children as much as is commonly believed. As a group, children of divorced parents do just as well in school, they are no more apt to be delinquents or mentally ill, and they are just as happy as children in families where there has been no divorce. Of course, children of divorced parents must make some adjustments in their relationships with both parents, especially the absent one, who is usually the father.[22]

200

REMARRIAGE

Today one in about every five marriages contains at least one partner who has been married before. And just like first marriages, remarriages are often homogamous. Divorced people tend to remarry other divorced people; widowed people remarry widowed people.

If we take all marital statuses (single, widowed, and divorced), we find that, for people within the same age group, divorced individuals marry more than any other group. For example, in any given year for every 1,000 single women between the ages of 25 and 29, 140 will marry. On the other hand, 319 of every 1,000 divorced women in the same age range will remarry. Samuel Johnson, the famous eighteenth-century journalist and critic, once remarked, "Remarriage is the triumph of hope over experience." Most divorced people must be very hopeful because their remarriage rate is very high. About 25 percent of divorced people get married again within one year; at the end of nine years, 75 percent have remarried.

This high rate of remarriage means that divorced people are not against marriage; they are only rejecting one particular mate. Remarried people believe marriage is a rewarding way of life and they try to recapture that life-style as soon after a divorce as possible. Furthermore, divorced people have a shorter "mourning" period than widowed people because they were probably emotionally "divorced" long before they were legally divorced. Then too, because divorced people tend to be younger than the widowed, they are more likely to have young children and would like to provide a "normal" home for them. Finally, remarriage offers divorced men and women a chance to erase the stigma of divorce. Remarried people have a new opportunity to "prove" that they can be successful in marriage, even if they "failed" before.

Not much is known about the step-family relationships that remarriage often creates. A recent study[23] shows that the most "typical" remarried family contains a husband, a wife, and *her* children. A divorced father's children are likely to be weekend or summer visitors rather than permanent members of the household. It is still rare in America for a divorced father to get custody of his children.

The same study also reveals that the remarriage of widowed people is more likely to be successful than the remarriage of previously divorced people. In addition, stepfathers seem to be more successful in their roles than stepmothers. Perhaps this is partly because stepmothers have a bad reputation (remember Cinderella and Snow White?) and the children *expect* her to be cruel and to hate her. Also, the stepmother is the more active parent, which means she often will have to discipline her stepchildren. This is not likely to make for good relations.

201

The study also found that step-siblings (children who are not blood relatives but who are in a position of brother and sister because the parent of one is married to the parent of the other) do not often get along well with each other. They are frequently jealous of each other and jealous of their own parent's attention to the step-sibling.

However, there is not enough information about remarriage as yet to make many definite statements. Most step-relationships seem to work out better than might be expected, although there are surely problems because the new relationships are complicated. One thing does seem clear: Children whose parents are remarried to people they like even moderately well are happier than children who live with their biological parents when the parents do not get along.

Marriage and the Family in the Future

The increased divorce and remarriage rates are only two examples of the way American family life is changing, but they indicate that we are beginning to think about the family in a different way. Not many years ago marriage was thought of as permanent. Divorce was rare and scandalous. Also not too many years ago, marriage was thought of as an exclusive arrangement and husbands and wives were not supposed to have sexual relations with anyone except each other.

But today permanence and exclusivity are more difficult to maintain in marriage. For one thing, people live longer now. Since 1920 males have increased their life expectancy from fifty-five years to sixty-seven years. Couples who marry in their early twenties can expect to live together for forty to fifty years. That is a very long time for two people to stay together and to remain faithful to each other. In addition, families were larger in the past and mothers were busier with their children for many more years. Finally improved transportation has made it easier for people to be in contact with strangers, and therefore married people have more opportunity to meet potential sexual partners.

All these changes, and more, have led to a great deal of talk over the last decade about alternatives to traditional marriage. We will examine a few of them.

ANDROGYNOUS MARRIAGE

One proposal for an alternative to traditional marriage is androgyny, defined as "a society in which there are no stereotyped behavioral differences between the roles of males and females on the basis of their sex alone."[24] In an androgynous marriage the wife and the husband are considered completely equal. The husband does not automatically earn the family living and the wife does not necessarily care for the home and children. Each partner does the chores that are most congenial to his or her personality, interests, and needs. Or the couple may rotate jobs so that neither partner is always left with the dullest ones.

The incidence of androgynous marriage may be on the upswing in this country because of the changing nature of the work force. At the present time there are more women in the labor force than ever before in American history. In 1950, one-fourth of all married women were in the work force, compared to 46.6 percent in 1977. For women with children under the age of six, the rate has more than tripled from 1950 to 1977, from 12 percent to 39.3 percent.[25] With so many women working outside the home, especially those with small children, it may be that androgyny will become a necessity.

COHABITATION

Some people no longer see any reason to get married at all. They believe that the state has no right to be a party to individuals' private lives and so they live together as if they were married (and sometimes, though rarely, they have children together). Most people believe that the young college students in our society are those most attracted to this life-style, but it is also rather widespread among older people who have been married before and have raised children, especially when the woman has a personal income. One reason for living together among older people is that both can collect Social Security checks, whereas if they marry, they would receive only one payment.

SINGLEHOOD

The social pressures to marry that have always been applied to single people in the United States seem to be lessening. Being single is no longer as stigmatizing as it once was. According to sociologist Peter

"It's my Donald. We have an open marriage."

Stein, the number of people who are choosing to stay single is increasing.[26] Stein estimates that of the 47 million unmarried people over the age of eighteen, about 15 percent are in some kind of custodial institution; another 5 percent are members of religious sects which forbid marriage; and about 20 percent will eventually marry. It is, then, possible that as more women become financially independent and as our mores about sexual behavior become more permissive, a sizable proportion of our population will choose never to marry.

OPEN MARRIAGE

This concept of marriage was expounded by Nena and George O'Neill[27] and it is based on the notion that jealousy and possessiveness are destructive to marriage. Therefore, husbands and wives should be free to have relationships, including sexual ones, with other people, although the marital relationship should always take priority over others. The O'Neills claim that such an arrangement, instead of hurting the marital relationship, actually makes it stronger because people do not feel tied down—they can have variety, independence, and freedom that will result in greater individual happiness.

MATE-SWAPPING

Mate-swapping is also called "swinging" or "co-marital adultery." It is a marital arrangement in which the two spouses agree to have sexual relations with outsiders, generally while both are in the same house or apartment. Sometimes a couple exchanges partners with another couple for a night. Sometimes a group meets at one couple's house and members have sexual relations with any other member of the group. Participants in co-marital adultery are typically middle-class, white, conforming suburbanites who believe that sexual variety· will revitalize their marriages.

All of these alternative forms of the family seem to be seeking to unite two things that have been difficult to achieve in marriage before: security and freedom. Some people seem to want safety, intimacy, and closeness with one person in a traditional relationship; at the same time, they want at least some freedom to form outside attachments. Such a combination certainly sounds desirable, but it is almost impossible to achieve.

The 1970 United States Census showed that only about 8 percent of the population actively experiment with any of the alternatives just described. Of these 8 percent most have been unsuccessful. But there does seem to be a continuing attempt to find new ways for men and women to live together more peacefully than they have done in the past. Gradually we will have to redefine the meaning of marriage, the roles of males and females, and the utility of sexual exclusivity. There is no doubt that there are pressures to change the structure and functions of marriage. We do not know yet in which direction these changes will eventually lead us or how far they will go. Undoubtedly the women's movement, which stresses sexual equality, will be a great influence. But more of that in Chapter 11.

SUMMARY

All societies have an institution known as *the family*. In this book we define the family as a universal institution whose most important functions are socializing and nurturing the younger generation.

All families note relationship through kinship. *Kinship* is a social relationship based on family ties. In our country a kinship group is composed of people who are emotionally involved with each other, whether the ties are biological, legal, or social, or any combination of the three.

In all societies most families are formed through marriage. There are two major types of marriage structure—monogamy and polygamy. *Monogamy* can be defined as the marriage of one man to one woman, whereas *polygamy* is the marriage of one person to two or more persons. There are two types of polygamy—polygyny and polyandry. *Polygyny* refers to the marriage of two or more women to one man; *polyandry* describes the marriage of two or more men to one woman.

Each of these marriage structures has rules of exogamy and rules of endogamy. *Exogamy,* which is related to the *incest taboo,* is the requirement that people marry outside of certain groups. *Endogamy* is the requirement that people marry within certain groups.

There are two major kinds of family organization. The *nuclear* or *conjugal* family is based on the marriage tie and is characterized by *neolocal* residence, *egalitarian* authority, and a *bilateral* descent system with two primary functions: legitimation and nurturance of the children. The *extended* or *consanguine* family is based on blood ties and is characterized by *patrilocal* or *matrilocal* residence, *patriarchal* or *matriarchal* authority, and a *unilateral* descent system.

The institution of the family serves a society in different ways. Before America became industrialized, the family served several functions that it has little responsibility for now or no longer performs at all. These functions are the economic, protective, religious, recreational, educational, and status placement ones.

Today the functions of the family differ. Anthropologist George P. Murdock believes that a family institution in any society has a nuclear family embedded within it. This nuclear family, he argues, always performs four functions: *reproduction, sexual regulation, economic cooperation,* and *socialization* of the children. Although these four functions are universally performed, sociologists do not agree that the nuclear family must perform them.

American marital patterns are different today than they were a hundred and fifty years ago. Even though we still are restrictive about premarital sex, our attitudes seem to be more permissive than in the past.

Americans place a high value on romantic love, and most believe that they marry a particular person because of love. However, they actually marry for many other reasons.

Sociologists have proposed two opposite theories as to why we choose a particular mate: the *theory of homogamy* (like attracts like) and the *theory of complementary needs* (opposites attract). Research supports the theory of homogamy.

Although marriage has always been popular in the United States, approximately 43 percent of all marriages end in divorce. Yet this does not seem to sour people on marriage as 75 percent of all divorced people eventually remarry.

The increased marriage and divorce rates are only two ways in which American family life is changing. Some people are seeking alternatives to traditional marriage. A few of these alternatives are androgynous marriage, cohabitation, singlehood, open marriage, and mate-swapping. We do not know yet in which direction these changes will eventually lead or how far they will go.

GLOSSARY

androgyny   a term describing attitudes and behaviors that are neither strongly masculine nor strongly feminine, but that are *both* masculine and feminine.

association   a formal group that is organized for some specific purpose, has a name, a location, written rules and regulations, a hierarchy of statuses, and rules for selecting members.

bilateral descent   a system in which descent is traced through both parents.

cenogamy   a form of marriage in which several men are married to several women at the same time.

egalitarian family   a type of family in which the husband and wife equally share authority and responsibility.

endogamy   a marriage restriction that requires people to marry within certain groups, usually racial and religious groups and social class.

exogamy   a marriage restriction that requires people to marry outside of certain groups; the forbidden groups vary from one society to another, but the immediate family is excluded in all known present-day societies.

extended family   (also called *consanguine family*) a type of family organization, rarely found in Western societies, in which several generations of blood relatives live together.

family   a universal institution whose most important functions are socializing and nurturing the younger generation.

family of orientation   the family into which one is born and in which one is socialized.

hypergamy   the marriage of a woman to a man who is a member of a higher social class.

hypogamy   the marriage of a woman to a man who is a member of a lower social class.

incest taboo   a universal social norm forbidding sexual relations between persons defined by the society as too closely related.

institution   an organized, formal, recognized, stabilized way of performing an activity in society.

kinship   a social relationship, defined differently by different societies, based on family ties.

matriarchy   a type of family in which power is traced through the female's side of the family to her closest male relative.

matrilineal system   a kind of unilineal descent pattern in which the descent is traced through the mother's family.

matrilocal residence   a type of family residence pattern in which a newly married couple lives with or near the wife's family.

monogamy   the marriage of one man to one woman at a time.

neolocal residence   a type of family residence pattern in which a newly married couple lives apart from both the husband's and wife's relatives.

nuclear family (also called *conjugal family*) a type of family organization, most common in Western societies, in which the family consists of the husband and wife and their dependent children.

patriarchy a type of family over which the eldest male has the authority.

patrilineal system a kind of unilineal descent pattern in which the descent is traced through the father's family.

patrilocal residence a type of family residence pattern in which a newly married couple lives with or near the husband's family.

polyandry a form of polygamy in which one woman is married to two or more men at the same time.

polygamy the marriage of one person to two or more people at a time.

polygyny a form of polygamy in which one man is married to two or more women at the same time.

theory of complementary needs theory holding that "opposites attract" and that most people marry people whose needs and characteristics are the opposite of their own.

theory of homogamy theory holding that "like attracts like" and that most people marry people who are socially, psychologically, and even physically similar to themselves.

unilateral descent a system in which descent is traced through either parent, but not both.

REFERENCES

1. U.S. Bureau of the Census, *Current Population Reports*, Series P-20, no. 79. Washington, D.C.: U.S. Government Printing Office, February 2, 1958, p. 2.

2. H. Carter and P. Glick, *Marriage and Divorce: A Social and Economic Study*. Cambridge, Mass.: Harvard University Press, 1970.

3. H. T. Christensen and K. Barber, "Interfaith Versus Intrafaith Marriage in Indiana." *Journal of Marriage and the Family* 29 (August 1967): 462.

4. *The New York Times*, February 18, 1973.

5. Thomas P. Monahan, "Marriage Across Racial Lines in Indiana." *Journal of Marriage and the Family* 35 (November 1973): 632–642; see also Larry D. Barnett, "Interracial Marriage in California." *Marriage and Family Living* (November 1963); David M. Heer, "Negro-White Marriage in the United States." *Journal of Marriage and the Family* 28 (August 1966); and Ernest Porterfield, *Black and White Mixed Marriages*. Chicago: Nelson-Hall, 1978.

6. Robert K. Merton, "Intermarriage and the Social Structure: Fact and Theory." *Psychiatry* 4 (August 1941): 361–374.

7. U.S. Bureau of the Census, *Current Population Reports*, series P-20, no. 324. Washington, D.C.: U.S. Government Printing Office, April 1978, p. 11.

8. George P. Murdock, *Social Structure*. New York: The Free Press, 1949, p. 1.

9. Murdock, p. 8.

10. Murdock, p. 10.

11. Ira Reiss, *The Family System in America.* New York: Holt, Rinehart & Winston, 1971, p. 156.

12. Alfred C. Kinsey, Wardell B. Pomeroy, and Clyde E. Martin, *Sexual Behavior in the Human Male.* Philadelphia: W. B. Saunders, 1948; Alfred C. Kinsey, Wardell B. Pomeroy, Clyde E. Martin, and Paul H. Gebhard, *Sexual Behavior in the Human Female.* Philadelphia: W. B. Saunders, 1953.

13. William H. Masters and Virginia E. Johnson, *Human Sexual Response.* Boston: Little, Brown, 1966; William H. Masters and Virginia E. Johnson, *Human Sexual Inadequacy.* Boston: Little, Brown, 1970.

14. Robert J. Levin and Amy Levin, "The Redbook Report on Premarital and Extramarital Sex." New York: Redbook, 1975.

15. Robert Winch, *Mate Selection.* New York: Harper, 1958.

16. *The World Almanac.* New York: Newspaper Enterprise Associates, 1976, p. 960.

17. U.S. Bureau of the Census, "A Statistical Portrait of Women in the U.S." *Current Population Reports,* Series P-23, no. 58. Washington, D.C.: U.S. Government Printing Office, April 1976, p. 15.

18. Leonard Benson, *The Family Bond.* New York: Random House, 1971.

19. M. Bralowe, "Runaway Wives." *Wall Street Journal,* October 1, 1975, p. 5.

20. *The New York Times,* April 3, 1976, p. 7.

21. U.S. Department of HEW, *Monthly Vital Statistics Report,* 18:12. March 1970, p. 3.

22. F. Ivan Nye, "Child Adjustment in Broken and in Unhappy Unbroken Homes." *Marriage and Family Living* 19 (1957): 356–361; Joseph B. Parry and Erdwin H. Pfuhl, "Adjustment of Children in 'Sole' and 'Remarriage' Homes." *Marriage and Family Living* 25 (1963): 221–223; Alan J. Crain and Caroline S. Stamn, "Intermittent Absence of Fathers and Children's Perceptions of Parents." *Journal of Marriage and the Family* 27 (August 1965): 344–347.

23. Lucile Duberman, *The Reconstituted Family.* Chicago: Nelson-Hall, 1975.

24. Joy D. Osofsky and Howard J. Osofsky, "Androgyny as a Life Style." *Family Coordinator* 21:4 (1972): 411–418.

25. Bureau of Labor Statistics, "Special Labor Force Reports," Washington, D.C.: U.S. Government Printing Office, March 1977.

26. Peter Stein, *Single.* Englewood Cliffs, N.J.: Prentice-Hall, 1976.

27. Nena O'Neill and George O'Neill, *Open Marriage: A New Lifestyle for Couples.* New York: Avon Books, 1973.

SUGGESTED READINGS

Clear, Val, Patricia Warrick, Martin Harry Greenberg, and Joseph D. Olander (eds.). *Marriage and the Family through Science Fiction.* New York: St. Martin's Press, 1976.

A collection of fantasies about marriage and the family in the future where technology and science have had their full impact.

Cuber, John F. and Peggy B. Harroff. *Sex and the Significant Americans.* Baltimore: Penguin Books, 1966.

A study of upper-class American marriages, in which the authors offer a typology of five styles of marriage: conflict-habituated, passive-congenial, devitalized, vital, and total.

Delora, Joann S. and Jack R. Delora (eds.). *Intimate Life Styles: Marriage and Its Alternatives.* Pacific Palisades, Calif.: Goodyear, 1972.

A collection of exciting and challenging articles on change now occurring in all aspects of marital and sexual life in America.

Duberman, Lucile. *Marriage and Other Alternatives,* 2nd ed. New York: Praeger, 1977.

A short textbook, summarizing existing knowledge about most aspects of marriage and the family and predicting what personal life in these areas will be like in the year 2000.

Duberman, Lucile. *The Reconstituted Family.* Chicago: Nelson-Hall, 1975.

An empirical study of eighty-eight families in which at least one adult has been married before and has at least one child from a previous marriage.

Lewis, Oscar. *The Children of Sanchez: Autobiography of a Mexican Family.* New York: Random House, 1961.

A classic case study of a poor Mexican family and their warm interpersonal relationships.

Rimmer, Robert. *The Harrad Experiment.* New York: Bantam, 1973; *Proposition Thirty-One.* New York: New American Library, 1971.

All of Rimmer's novels deal with possible alternative family forms of the future, incorporating the best of the human potentials movement.

Rogers, Carl. *Becoming Partners, Marriage and Its Alternatives.* New York: Dell, 1972.

An interesting examination of different marital partnerships.

Toffler, Alvin. *Future Shock.* New York: Random House, 1970. Chapter XI.

A view of the family of the future. Many predictions are familiar, such as a rise in the number of group marriages and serial marriages. But many are surprising, such as new "birth technology," which will permit people to preselect the sex of their children or to purchase embryos.

Wernick, Robert. *The Family.* Boston: Little, Brown, 1974.

Easy to read book from Time-Life Books. Stress is cross-cultural, focusing on the eternal, yet changing character of the family. Although the tone is romantic, family life and marriage are treated realistically. The book is heavily illustrated with many beautiful pictures.

Willie, Charles V. (ed.). *The Family Life of Black People.* Columbus, Ohio: Merrill, 1970.

A book of readings giving differing points of view about family life among black Americans.

7

Education

society cannot continue to exist if new members do not learn its social norms, values, and goals. Some institution must fulfill this function. In the past, the American family educated the children to a great extent, but times have changed. Today the educational institution has taken over much of this task.

What is the *educational institution?* It can be defined as a *system of interrelated statuses and roles that ensures the transmission of the values, attitudes, behaviors, skills, and knowledge of a culture from one generation to the next.* Educational associations include schools on all levels that carry out this cultural transmission.

Sociological interest in the educational institution is sharp and varied. One area of interest, especially since the Supreme Court handed down its order to desegregate public schools, concerns educational reform. Another deals with the relationship between the economic institution and the educational institution. Some sociologists focus on federal interference in our public school systems; others study the problem of bilingualism; still others concentrate on teaching methods, goals, and results. Many sociologists, along with educators and psychologists, are involved with the problems of intelligence tests and what they mean. In this chapter we will address some of these issues and see how sociologists and other social scientists are working to resolve some of these often troublesome concerns.

Development of American Education

The first schools in colonial America were run by the churches to educate male children to become clergymen. Actually, only the wealthier boys went to school because the poorer boys were needed on the farms. Also, it was not considered necessary for girls in any social class to have a formal education. They needed to know only how to be good wives and mothers, and this could be taught to them by their own mothers at home.

Such an educational system was not based solely on the notion that only the sons of the wealthy deserved an education. It also had its roots in the fact that societies were not industrialized during this era and education was usually considered more of a liability than an asset. During this time period a strong back was much more in demand than a strong mind. Educated people in an agricultural society were regarded as nonproductive because they did not work with their hands. Only in industrial societies, where there is a greater need for people who work with *ideas* rather than *things,* are educated people viewed as productive.

In colonial America, only sons of the wealthy were sent to school. At that time, education was viewed negatively by most of the population.

Public schools began in Massachusetts in 1647. The colonial fathers wanted to be sure that people could read the Bible, so they passed a law requiring all towns with more than fifty families to set up tuition-free schools. Soon people in other states began to do the same. By the middle of the nineteenth century, almost all northern cities had elementary schools supported by taxes.

As the system of tuition-free education became widespread, laws were passed requiring youngsters to attend school. Today all but three states have compulsory education, usually from the age of five or six until between the ages of sixteen and eighteen.

At the present time almost one-third (31 percent) of our population are students. As of the fall of 1977, 61.3 million people were enrolled in some type of school.[1] About 85 percent of us who are between the ages of twenty-five and twenty-nine are high-school graduates and about 15 percent of all Americans have completed college. However, the picture of American education is changing primarily because the birth rate has declined over the past few years, meaning that fewer chil-

213

dren are entering schools. There is also a decline in school enrollment throughout the first twelve grades, particularly the elementary grades. Nearly 5 million fewer children were enrolled in elementary school in 1977 than in 1970.

College and graduate enrollments, however, are still rising, despite the increasing costs of higher education. This results partly from open enrollment programs that attract students who otherwise would not go to college, partly from the increase in older people who are returning to school, and partly from the fact that fewer jobs are available to high-school graduates. Students reason that since they cannot get good jobs after high school, they may as well go to college in the hope that a college degree will increase their chances of getting well-paid, high-status positions.

Functions of Education

As we have seen in Chapter 6, all social institutions must serve at least one social need in order to exist. One of the major social needs served by education is the transmission of the values, attitudes, and behaviors of our culture from one generation to the next. A second function is the transmission of skills and knowledge; a third function is status placement.

TRANSMISSION OF VALUES, ATTITUDES, AND BEHAVIORS

Education shares the function of transmitting values, attitudes, and behaviors with the family institution and in part with the religious institution. Young people must be integrated into the societies of which they are members and in which they are likely to spend all of their lives. Thus, American schools teach students what it means to be American, what the dominant American values are, what is considered proper behavior, what are thought to be correct attitudes, and so forth. Chinese, British, Indian, or Russian schools offer similar training reflecting their own cultures to students in their societies. Some of this training is direct. Almost all American students are required to study American history, for example, just as children in other nations learn their own national histories. Some of the training is indirect. Teachers and other students give spoken and unspoken messages that indicate what "nice" children are expected to do, think, wear, and so on. Children soon learn that they will not receive their teachers' approval (usually good grades) and they will not be invited to join other students in social activities unless they conform to these expectations. Thus one

Schools serve to encourage students to conform to standards of acceptable behavior and performance. If students misbehave—as this student has—then schools will resort to such punishments as making students stay late.

very important function of education is to help to indoctrinate young people into the society by teaching them the approved values, attitudes, and behaviors.

TRANSMISSION OF SKILLS AND KNOWLEDGE

In addition to learning the values, attitudes, and behaviors appropriate to a given society, young people must also acquire the knowledge and skills needed to become useful members of the society. In many earlier societies boys followed in their fathers' occupations and girls learned to be wives and mothers. Often there was a period of apprenticeship for an occupation. Young men, for example, who wanted to become lawyers "read" the law in an attorney's office until the older man decided that the apprentice was ready to begin a practice of his own. Young women who wanted to become dressmakers went to work for established dressmakers to learn the trade.

In our modern industrial society, though, a great deal has changed. For one thing, many young people no longer are satisfied to follow in their parents' footsteps. For another, knowledge is so vast that rarely can one person teach another all the necessary skills and pass along all the information that is available in most occupations. There-

215

Such innovations as the use of computers in the classroom assist schools in transmitting the skills and knowledge necessary for students to become useful members of their society.

FOCUS ON: AN EDUCATIONAL FAILURE

Are schools always successful in transmitting knowledge? Do the grades a student receives really reflect the amount of knowledge he or she acquires?

In the case of Stephen Jackson (and probably thousands like him) the answer to both questions is "no." For although he graduated as valedictorian from Western High School in Washington, D.C., Stephen's Scholastic Aptitude test scores showed that he could not read or compute well enough to get through college. (Stephen scored 320 in verbal ability and 280 in math.) Despite the A's he received in school, the amount of knowledge he acquired was probably minimal.

How can this discrepancy be explained? On the one hand, some feel that high-school grades have become so inflated that they are now virtually meaningless. On the other hand, some feel that college admissions officials are placing too much emphasis on standardized test scores. At any rate, Stephen was still short-changed.

Nevertheless, Stephen's dreams of becoming an accountant may eventually come true. He was accepted by several colleges and chose to attend Howard University. But several questions regarding the ability of schools to educate students still remain.

Do you believe that schools are adequately preparing students for college or for later life? Who do you think can be held responsible for this situation?

Source: "The Valedictorian," *Newsweek,* September 6, 1976, p. 52.

FIGURE 7–1
Reasons Parents Give When Asked Why They Want Their Children To Get an Education*

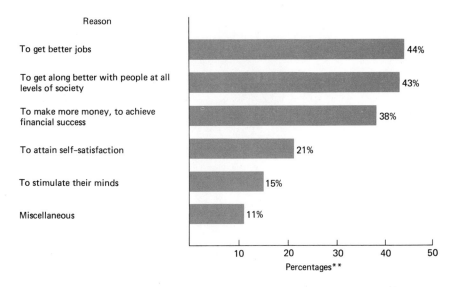

Reason

To get better jobs — 44%

To get along better with people at all levels of society — 43%

To make more money, to achieve financial success — 38%

To attain self-satisfaction — 21%

To stimulate their minds — 15%

Miscellaneous — 11%

Percentages**

*Adapted from Gallup Opinion Index, September 1972, Report No. 87.

**Percentages do not total 100 because parents were permitted to give more than one reason.

fore, we store knowledge in books, in data banks, and on film. Students now must learn the techniques of their future work in formal settings where this knowledge is available.

The curious thing, however, about the educational institution in Western societies is that while the importance of practical education is recognized, intellectual subjects are still stressed. Students are often required to study such subjects as history and the classics. Our problem is that we are unsure whether to "train" our students, to prepare them for practical careers, or whether to "educate" our children, so they will be well-informed on matters that are not practical, such as art, music, or literature. In other words, how do we decide what skills and knowledge to transmit?

The Gallup Poll findings shown in Figure 7–1 indicate that most parents want their children trained for jobs that will provide high income and prestige and that fewer are concerned with their children's acquisition of knowledge for its own sake. When asked why they wanted their children to get an education, approximately 40 percent of the responding parents gave such reasons as better jobs and more money. while only 21 percent wanted their children to attain self-satisfaction, and only 15 percent wanted their children's minds to be stimulated. Clearly, the education Americans want for their children and the education provided are not the same things.

217

The debate continues over whether the goal of schools should be to provide a well-rounded education that includes less practical subjects, such as art, music, and literature *(left),* or to give students vocational training for practical careers *(right).*

Although we have not resolved the question of "education" versus "training," both are available to students in our society. Perhaps no resolution is really necessary and the educational institution is serving the needs of both factions.

STATUS PLACEMENT

A third function of education is related to the second one, although the relationship is implicit rather than explicit. This function is to recruit people into specific occupational statuses. In order to understand how schools screen children so that some are evaluated as probable candidates for the high occupational statuses and some for the low ones, let us follow "typical" American children as they progress through the educational system.

APPLYING SOCIOLOGY

In our society we are unsure as to whether to stress "education" or "training." Do you think your own education is preparing you for what you hope to do when you graduate? What courses would you offer in your school that are not available to students now? Why? What courses do you have available that you think are unnecessary? Why?

The Role of Evaluation

As soon as five-year-old children enter kindergarten, initiation into the system begins. Children learn how to behave in the status of student. They learn that they must sit quietly and must not speak unless the teacher acknowledges a raised hand. They are required to exhibit their ability to learn what is being taught. Well-socialized students learn what to do to please the teacher, how to get along with other students, how to be patient while standing in lines, how to behave as if interested, even when bored, and how to accept the fact that the group (or class) has become more important than the individual.

This type of training accelerates as children move through the system. And as academic subjects become increasingly more varied and intensified, students learn that they are constantly being evaluated. A good deal of this evaluation is done by teachers privately, through grades, but much of it is done publicly, through teachers' comments to individuals in front of the class and through the attitudes teachers display toward individual students.

Eventually, students gain reputations that are close to irreversible, because teachers' official evaluations are recorded and are available to other teachers and because the peer group accepts such evaluations. Therefore, one child will become known as a "trouble-maker," another as "slow," still another as "poorly-motivated." Similarly, Jane is considered "cooperative"; Susie is "bright"; and John is "well-behaved."

These evaluations and the reputations they produce are based on several factors. One of the most significant is the teacher's subjective or personal reaction to the child. One study revealed how teachers' assumptions influence their evaluations of their pupils.[2] In order to test the idea that teachers' beliefs and expectations about students can strongly influence school performance, elementary school children in one neighborhood were given a standardized intelligence test. Each teacher was told which of these children had scored high on the test and were considered "late bloomers." Actually, the children were selected randomly and the selection had nothing to do with real scores. At the end of the school year, all the children were retested. On the second test, 47 percent of the "late bloomers" scored higher than they had on the first test, compared to only 20 percent of the other students. The study, then, supports the notion that teachers have preconceptions about students that affect the way the teachers behave toward them—how much support and encouragement they offer—and this, in turn, affects the students' work.

By the time a student reaches high school, a degree of conflict develops between the norms of the school and the norms of the peer group. In the elementary grades, school authorities clearly and rigidly define the expected behavior for students, but in high school, students are given some latitude in determining their responsibilities. Students begin to choose norms for themselves and these are sometimes contradictory to official norms.

Enthusiasm for school is considered acceptable for elementary school students, but high-school students are expected by peers to be more casual and "cool" about schoolwork and to be more concerned with social activities. High-school students must draw a fine line between interest in school and a disdain for school if they want approval from both adults and other students. Assignments must be completed, but not at the cost of sacrificing social life or popularity. For most students, neither scholastic achievement nor peer group relationships can be ignored in favor of the other. This situation, common among the approximately 17 million high-school students in the United States, can produce *role conflict*, which means that an individual is expected to perform two roles at the same time that are inconsistent or incompatible.

Such role conflict is not the only problem high-school students face. At the same time that they are making these personal adjustments, they are also being subjected to an evaluation system that can be very destructive.

Prior to World War II, American high schools were largely preparatory schools for those students who planned to attend college. Other young people discontinued their education after junior high school or went to vocational or trade schools. Until that time, the majority of all high-school graduates went to college; today only about one-third do so. Thus, high schools today must have two courses of study available to students: academic courses for those who are college-bound, and commercial or vocational courses for those who will complete their formal education with high-school graduation.

Several questions are involved here: How is it decided which students will go on to college and which ones will not? Is college a privilege or is it a right? Should only those who can afford the fees be allowed to go to college or should higher education be available to all? Is college only for the smartest young people in our society or should mediocre and poor students also be encouraged to try?

These are difficult questions for societies to resolve. In the United States today, higher education is supposed to be available to everyone. But is it really?

Intelligence Testing

One criterion for determining whether or not a student will be able to cope with college requirements is level of intelligence. Measuring intelligence, however, is difficult to do. For one thing, intelligence itself has never been properly defined. Second, although standardized

"WE REALIZE YOU DO BETTER ON YOUR IQ TESTS THAN YOU DO IN ANYTHING ELSE, BUT YOU JUST CANNOT MAJOR IN IQ."

intelligence and aptitude tests (IQ tests, for example) have been designed for this purpose, it has never been proved that these tests really measure intelligence at all. Rather, what has been shown is that these tests measure what children have learned in a limited number of fields. The "knowledge" children acquire is often determined by the subculture in which they have been raised. Thus, poorer children, who are less exposed to the things in our culture that are part of the test, often score lower than children from middle- and upper-income backgrounds. Even the region of the country a child comes from can influence test scores. For the child from a farm in Iowa, the definition of "litter" might be "baby pigs." In contrast, an urban child might define the term as "trash on the street."

Social scientists also believe that poorer children obtain lower test scores because they are not as well motivated as the children in the social classes above them. Many poor children simply do not have the same opportunities to learn that children from middle-income backgrounds have. They may not have creative toys or crayons or children's books. Poor parents may spend less time interacting with their children than wealthier parents do. They are often too tired from working at their jobs to talk to their children or to stimulate their imaginations with stories. When poor parents do communicate with their children, they are more likely to use fewer nouns and adjectives than do parents in higher social classes. Children from lower-income backgrounds are told, "Bring that thing to me." Children from middle-income backgrounds are told, "Please bring the red book that is lying on the big round coffee table to me." In these ways, children whose parents earn more money tend to acquire greater familiarity with words and ideas, so the tests are naturally easier for them.

Furthermore, when parents have failed in the work world, they often feel that they are inferior, rejected, and stupid. Such parents pass these notions of themselves on to their children so that even at a very young age, poor children may already feel "dumb." They also cannot believe that education will change their "luck," since their families have been "unlucky" all of their lives. Thus, poorer children, although they may obtain lower scores on standardized intelligence, aptitude, and achievement tests than other children, are not *biologically* inferior. Instead, they are often exposed to a different culture that does not pass on the values and knowledge or give them the opportunity and encouragement necessary to pass these tests.

Unfortunately, though, these test scores influence a student's later education. They are accepted by schools all over the United States and are used to place young people from all classes into categories, supposedly based on intelligence. Because of poor test scores, then, children from lower-income backgrounds are more likely to be "tracked" into noncollege-bound courses in high school.

Tracking

Tracking or *ability grouping* is a system commonly used in schools to channel students according to their talents as defined by the standardized tests. It was begun originally to keep children who did not like (and did not do well in) academic subjects in school by offering them a choice of courses that would maintain their interest. In other words, students who were bored by math, biology, social science, and the like could enroll in such classes as shop or typing, which might be more interesting to them and which might have more practical value.

Tracking is widespread in the United States. According to Warren Finley and Miriam Brian, in 1970, 77 percent of the school systems in a national sample used tracking in some way.[3] Generally, classification of students starts in kindergarten and does not change significantly thereafter.[4]

> On the basis of teachers' evaluations and tests, students are allocated to reading groups and special classes or advanced sections for differentiated types of elementary school programs. By junior high school, they are classified into different groups according to some

222

FOCUS ON: MERITOCRACY

Imagine a society where IQ ratings were the basis for admission to all advanced education programs and no other criteria were used. All decisions, positions, advancement, and so forth would be based on these test scores.

In his book *The Rise of the Meritocracy*, Michael Young considered the impact of such a society on individuals. The fictional setting is Britain in 2033, where people are selected for positions and advanced strictly on merit.

Young focuses on some of the major problems that develop as a result of such a system. First, in spite of efforts to distribute the educational resources equally, inequalities persist. As a result, there is a sharp class distinction based on merit, and not heredity. Second, because all those with leadership qualities are members of the elite class, the lower class (as defined by IQ ratings) lacks leadership. Finally, the realization that it has limited academic and social prospects creates discontent within the lower class.

With tongue in cheek, Young describes how the meritocracy deals with these shortcomings. First, gymnastics, sports, and handicrafts are stressed in the lower class, although it receives some basic instruction in reading, writing, and mathematics. The objective of lower-class education is to cultivate physical strength.

Second, everyone can attend "adult education" courses and periodically take IQ tests to see if their scores have improved. This allows for social mobility throughout all classes.

Third, even though their IQ scores may be low, parents are persuaded that their children have an opportunity to succeed in the meritocracy. This enables parents to enjoy success through that of their children.

Fourth, although the lower class plods along without perceiving the implications of its lot, there is a chance that some members may realize their plight and rebel. To compensate for this, the meritocracy removes from the lower class (promotes to a higher class) all those who might promote discontent within the group.

Finally, promotion by merit is extended to industry and replaces the seniority system. Ultimately the merit system is incorporated into the military and government.

How does this society differ from contemporary America? Is the United States moving toward a time when education, knowledge, and IQ will be the primary factors in determining an individual's place in society? If so, how will this affect our society?

Source: Michael Young, *The Rise of the Meritocracy 1870–2033*, Baltimore: Penguin, 1958.

measures of ability and assigned to differentiated subject matter programs. . . . By this time, the flexibility is quite low and life decisions have largely been determined.[5]

Several sociologists have conducted studies in order to discover if the tracking system has been successful in its basic efforts. They have found that tracking failed to keep students in school, that it failed to improve student performance, that it was of no administrative value, and that it continued to keep the children from different social classes separated. In short, tracking has not achieved its stated purposes, and therefore probably has little merit for poorer children. On the other

Although tracking enables students to learn practical, vocationally oriented skills, some social scientists argue that tracking limits opportunity for poorer children, who frequently are channeled into non-college-bound tracks.

hand, ability grouping has merit for teachers and for children from middle- and upper-income backgrounds. Certainly teaching is easier and children benefit when a class is composed of students of equivalent ability.

The problem is that poorer children generally end up in the tracks that are not college-bound. As a result, poorer children have less opportunity to go to college regardless of their innate intelligence or ability.[6] In addition, according to sociologists Paul Lauter and Florence Howe, "tracking harms some children, depriving those we call 'deprived,' making them less competent, less able to reach, let alone to use, the instruments of power in American society. In the light of tracking, schools become for such children not the means of democratization and liberation, but of oppression."[7]

These researchers and others conclude that the *real* function of tracking is to control the supply of workers entering the labor force. It is a means of limiting, not expanding, opportunity. Our economic system has less need for medical doctors, lawyers, engineers, and other profes-

---

APPLYING SOCIOLOGY

Think back over your own school history, starting with the elementary grades and going through high school. How do you know you were "tracked"? What effect do you think tracking had on you? Do you think you were a better or worse student as a result of it? Why? What social implication did tracking have for you? Did you look down on others in lower tracks or did you feel looked down upon by those in higher ones? Given your own experience and what you have learned about tracking, do you favor it or not? Why?

sionals than it has for salespeople, technicians, sanitation workers, factory workers, and other blue- and white-collar workers. Tracking is one way to direct young men and women into those jobs that are less prestigious, but in which people are more in demand.[8]

If this is the real purpose of tracking, it might be called successful. We indeed do channel a majority of students—especially those from the lower classes—into the less prominent but more numerous jobs. At the same time schools place children from the middle- and upper-income brackets in college-bound tracks, and they are the people who eventually enter college, complete it, and occupy the high-status occupations. While many schools now have "open admission" policies, many bright young people from the lower classes still do not go to college, while many youngsters from the higher classes with below average intelligence do go.

Most researchers find that a child's early school performance is not affected by his or her social class. However, by the fourth grade a pattern becomes clear and by junior high school that pattern is almost unchangeable. This happens because as children get older, behavior is influenced more by environment than by intelligence. In short, the lower-class academic environment composed of teachers and peers discourages higher education and that of the upper class encourages it. Membership in a social class seems to be the most important influence on the decision of whether or not to continue education beyond high school.[9] Table 7–1 and Figure 7–2 show the role that social class plays in this decision. Table 7–1 shows the relationship between social class

TABLE 7–1
Level of Education in Relation to Social Class of Youth in the Upper Quarter of Intellectual Ability (IQ = 110+), 1965 (by percent)

| | Social Class | | |
	Upper and Upper-Middle	*Lower-Middle*	*Working*
Do not finish high school.	0	2	10
Graduate from high school but do not enter college.	10	10	24
Enter college but do not finish.	10	26	37
Complete a four-year college program.	80	62	29

Source: Robert J. Havighurst and Bernice Neugarten, *Society and Education*, Third Edition, Boston: Allyn & Bacon, 1967, Tables IV-1 and III-5.

225

**FIGURE 7–2
High School Seniors'
Plans To Attend
College, by Family
Income, October 1975***

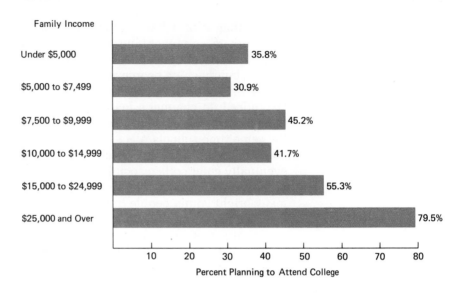

*Adapted from *College Plans of High School Seniors: October 1975*, U.S. Department of Commerce, Bureau of the Census, Series P-20, No. 299, Washington, D.C.: United States Government Printing Office, November 1976, p. 9.

and college attendance even when intelligence is the same. Figure 7–2 shows the relationship between family income (which is the best indicator of social class) and high-school seniors' plans to attend college.

In summary, the educational institution fulfills the function of status placement very well. Our schools in their efforts to satisfy societal needs, however, have failed to provide the same opportunity to students of all social classes to obtain higher education.

SECONDARY FUNCTIONS OF EDUCATION

We have examined the three most important functions of the educational institution: the transmission of values, attitudes, and behaviors; the transmission of knowledge and skills; and status placement. Now let us look at some secondary functions that may not be intentional, but that are often unanticipated consequences of any educational system.

Custodial Function

Compulsory attendance at school for young people under a specified age has the effect of keeping them off the streets and out of the labor market. Schools take responsibility for youngsters for a good part of the day, permitting their parents the freedom to work, shop, or simply have time to themselves. Being in school also means that young

226

people cannot spend their time riding around in cars or just "hanging out." If it does nothing else, then, the school keeps children occupied and out of mischief.

More important for the society, however, is the fact that compulsory education keeps young men and women from competing with adults for jobs. When young people attend college, their entry into the job market is postponed for an even longer period of time. Therefore, the society requires people to be unproductive for many years of their lives (at both the beginning and the end) and employs instead those who are in their middle years. Hence, schools act as custodians, often keeping students beyond the time that is really necessary.

Social Function

Schools provide opportunities for young people to interact with teachers and with other young people. This is an important function because it can have lifelong effects on personality, aspirations, and achievement.

Interaction with teachers is meaningful for students in many ways. Teachers often serve as role models or "significant others" (see Chapter 4), and youngsters sometimes pattern their entire lives on one teacher, even choosing an occupation because of a particular teacher's influence.

As mentioned earlier, interaction with teachers can also have negative effects, because some teachers have a tendency to favor children from more privileged families.[10] Furthermore, many teachers evaluate students by middle-class standards—for example, neatness, promptness, ambition, responsibility, and cooperation. Teachers believe the disadvantaged student is less likely to exhibit these characteristics because they are not stressed in such homes. Thus such a student may often be belittled by the teacher and may develop a poor self-image. In addition, teachers may perpetuate sexual stereotyping (see Chapter 11) by treating boys and girls in traditional sexist ways and by using examples that depict males and females in traditional sex statuses.

Association with peers is equally important. Students exert great influence on one another in terms of behavior, values, and ambitions. Furthermore, interaction among students frequently results in lifetime friendships, marriages, and contacts for jobs. A great deal of research has been carried out in this area, generated primarily by the work of sociologist James S. Coleman, which revealed, among other things, that social relations among adolescents are extensive and consequential for later life.[11]

One consequence of these peer relations is that young people influence each other's values. For example, if a group considers high scholastic standing important, the students within that group will

Interactions with teachers *(top)* and with peers *(bottom)* in the school setting greatly influence students' personality development, aspirations, and achievements.

strive for high academic grades. If a group values athletics, students will turn their attention toward achieving in that area.

Another Coleman finding showed that young people's educational and occupational aspirations are influenced more by their friends than by their parents. This finding held true regardless of students' social class or academic record. Finally, Coleman reported that neighborhood schools, which are preferred by most American parents, are actually detrimental to social development because students tend to associate only with other children who are very much like themselves. When students from different neighborhoods get an opportunity to mix with one another and to learn how other kinds of people live and think, virtually everyone benefits.

Regarding school composition, Coleman showed that when black

228

students from poor academic environments attend schools containing a majority of white students from high academic backgrounds their performance improves. At the same time, if the majority of whites are good students, they will continue their high performance. In many American communities one way to achieve integrated schools has been to bus children out of their own neighborhoods and into schools in other neighborhoods. Most parents, however, reject the notion of busing their children away from their own neighborhood schools. Quite possibly these people are using the issue of busing to camouflage, either from themselves or from others, their real fears about school integration. Middle-class white parents may wonder: Will lower-class or black students corrupt their children? Might a white girl want to date a black boy? Would class standards have to be lowered to accommodate children from poor academic backgrounds? Similarly, black parents may fear that integrated schools would be controlled completely by whites, so that the needs of their children would not be met. Many black parents also sincerely doubt whether their children would really get a better education in an integrated school. In short school integration has become a serious and unresolved social problem in the United States.

Innovative Function

As we have seen, schools transmit the existing culture to the younger generation, thus preserving that culture. At the same time technological societies experience social change constantly, much of it thought of as "progress." Schools—colleges and universities more than elementary and high schools—are supposed to contribute to change by gathering new knowledge, storing it, and transmitting it. They are expected to be innovative and committed to seeking new ways of making social life more practical, comfortable, and enjoyable.

It is important to realize, however, that the dedication to improvement is centered much more on technological or material improvement than on change in our social order, social mores, or social institutions. University grants for research are more likely to be forthcoming when the request is for funds to discover new techniques, new weaponry, or new medical procedures or products than for more social purposes, for example, improving interpersonal relationships.

The educational institution, then, serves two competing functions. It maintains the status quo and acts as a conservative agent when it instills the sense of the past in students. At the same time it encourages innovation and change when it provides opportunities for research and when it exposes students to new ideas. This is a delicate balance that schools sometimes have difficulty in maintaining. Let us now examine higher education in more detail.

Higher Education

American colleges and universities have become huge, powerful bureaucracies. They are now centers of research and criticism, as well as protectors of the status quo. They have produced most of the nation's leaders in the worlds of business, science, government, and finance. Nevertheless, controversy runs through the university system.

For one thing, there is confusion about what the goals of American higher education should be. Some social scientists suggest the goals should be oriented toward maintaining the existing social order.[12] Others hold that undergraduate education is merely a watered-down version of graduate education as it attempts to create professionals.[13] Sociologist Clark Kerr believes that college is a vehicle used by industrial society to produce the needed trained workers.[14] And still other researchers contend that Boards of Trustees and administrators shift educational goals to suit their own interests at different points in time.[15] All such viewpoints imply that faculties have no goals of their own as they go about their daily task of teaching college students.

A recent study, however, revealed that such an implication is untrue. From a national sample of faculty at 301 institutions of higher learning, 92.2 percent claimed to have very precise teaching goals. Table 7–2 shows these faculty goals.

In spite of the controversy over goals, higher education in the United States is valued for a number of reasons. For one thing, Americans believe that it is within the university that young people will acquire the knowledge to develop better technology, which is believed capable of resolving our national and international problems. Furthermore, on the individual level, many people have come to accept the idea that without a college education, it is close to impossible to move up the social and economic ladders. For a long time, until as late as the early 1960s, education was seen as a means of reducing poverty and redistributing income so that most of the population would be in the middle class. Americans were confident that college would soon be readily available to most citizens and that the atmosphere created there would go a long way toward blurring social-class lines.

At this time, however, it seems fair to say that there is a discrepancy between these beliefs and reality. Although it is true that more young people from the lower socioeconomic classes are entering colleges than ever before, a very high percentage of them never graduate. Another disheartening fact is that higher education is becoming less available for blacks in comparison to whites—over the past decade and a half, the gap between the percentage of blacks and whites graduating from college has been increasing. According to the 1960 census, 4.1 percent of blacks between the ages of sixteen and thirty-four had com-

TABLE 7-2
Ranked Order of Undergraduate Teaching Goals, 1973

Goals	Percent of Faculty Who Hold Goal
To develop the ability to think clearly	95.4
To master knowledge in a discipline	91.4
To increase the desire and ability to undertake self-directed learning	89.4
To develop creative capacities	78.0
To prepare students for employment after college	60.7
To develop responsible citizens	57.4
To provide tools for the critical evaluation of society	57.3
To convey a basic appreciation of the liberal arts	55.1
To achieve deeper levels of students' self-understanding	54.9
To prepare students for graduate or advanced education	53.8
To provide the local community with skilled human resources	46.0
To develop moral character	44.6
To develop the ability to pursue research	43.4
To provide for students' emotional development	38.2
To prepare students for family living	20.1
To develop religious beliefs or convictions	9.3

Source: Gerald M. Platt, Talcott Parsons, and Rita Kirshstein, "Faculty Teaching Goals, 1968–1973," *Social Problems* 24:2, 1976, 303. Reprinted by permission of the Society for the Study of Social Problems.

"*First of all, I'd like to say I really feel I got my thirty-two thousand dollars' worth.*"

Drawing by Lorenz; © 1978 The New Yorker Magazine, Inc.

231

pleted college, compared to 11.9 percent of whites in the same age group. By 1974, the figures were 8.1 percent for blacks and 21 percent for whites. Although the proportion of blacks completing college had doubled, the gap between blacks and whites had actually increased from 8 to 13 percentage points.[16]

Then, too, although low-income families can receive financial aid for college tuition and expenses, in reality the benefits are often questionable. For example, a study of the subsidy system in California reveals how the system can work to classify students and keep them locked into their social class.[17] California has the highest percentage of high-school students entering the state higher education system (which charges no tuition, only fees) than any other state. However, the amount of subsidy the state grants per student depends on the type of school. In the 1960s, the University of California was receiving $5,000 per student in subsidy; the state colleges received $3,000 for each enrolled student; junior or community colleges were getting $1,000 per student. Since students from the higher social classes were more likely to attend the university and those from the lower classes were more likely to go to state or community colleges, those who needed subsidy money the most were getting the least and vice versa. The effect is to create three separate educational systems, educating three classes of students.

In short, the study of the California subsidy system, which is similar to systems in other states, reveals discrimination against students from low-income families. For one thing, poorer students more frequently drop out of high school than middle-class students and therefore receive no college subsidy at all. Furthermore, since they go to the colleges offering the lowest subsidies, they often cannot afford to stay in college. In short, the lower socioeconomic classes end up with a smaller slice of the subsidy pie, thus reducing their educational attainment chances.

The researchers who conducted this study conclude their report:

> The claim that the American system of higher education contributes to equality of educational opportunity is largely fiction. . . . In practice, a perverse redistribution of higher education subsidies from low income to high income families takes place. Those with the most need for higher education are getting the least in terms of public benefits. . . . the mythology of equal educational opportunity for all is just that: mythology.

In summary, most researchers have found that although the United States has an official policy of equality of higher educational opportunity, the reality is that such opportunity is frequently denied to youths from the lower socioeconomic classes. This discrepancy can

232

APPLYING SOCIOLOGY

The fact that you are taking this course means that you have opted to continue into higher education. Were you motivated by parental pressure, peer pressure, your own goals, or your desire for a particular career? How necessary do you think higher education is in helping you reach your goals?

---

be seen in the widening gap between the percentage of blacks and whites graduating from colleges. Furthermore, students from lower-income backgrounds, who need subsidies in order to continue their education, are frequently given a smaller slice of the subsidy pie. This often forces them to drop out of school, thus limiting their chances of obtaining a higher education.

Credentialism

An important unanswered question about the American educational system concerns the stress placed on the degree. Employers are demanding more and more education, but the question remains: How much education is really needed to do the job? America is a "credential society," which means that in order to obtain desirable jobs, people must have the necessary "passport"—a B.A., Ph.D., or whatever. Those who have such credentials are more likely to be hired than those who do not. But how meaningful in the long run are these "passports"? Is the degree necessary for *doing* the job or only for *getting* the job?

There are two different sociological explanations to account for the ever-increasing demand for education. Some sociologists claim that such requirements reflect the needs of a highly technical society for skilled technicians. Such theorists argue that the increasing demand for education is based on the fact that constant technological changes require the continuous acquisition of new skills. This training can come only through formal education. The result is that educational requirements must rise and more and more people must spend longer periods of time in school to master these new skills. On the other hand, some sociologists argue that the expanding educational requirements are simply a means of keeping the power in the hands of the elite because the elite can more easily afford to stay in college.

Sociologist Randall Collins, in his comparison of these two notions, supports the latter argument.[18] He disputes the claim that in industrial societies the number of low-skill jobs decreases and the

As increasing numbers of Americans obtain advanced degrees, many people are beginning to wonder whether the degrees are necessary to actually *do* most high-status jobs—or merely to *get* them.

number of high-skill jobs increases. Collins believes that this is true only during early industrialization. He also disputes the argument that in today's world it takes more skill to do a job than it took to do the same job fifty years ago—that it requires more knowledge to be an electrician now than it did then. Consequently, Collins claims that most people are actually overeducated for their jobs.

The first theory also asserts that the only way to acquire the necessary skills to do a job is through formal education. However, Collins offers evidence showing that better-educated people are often less productive at both manual and nonmanual work than those with less education. In fact, the most skilled workers usually acquire their abilities in a casual way or on the job. Even in professional occupations, a great deal of learning is done after graduation from school.

Why, then, have educational requirements spiraled in the United States? Because, says Collins, as educational opportunities become more available to lower-status groups, upper-status groups seek to maintain their monopoly on higher-status positions by maintaining the educational "gap" between themselves and those below them. Collins states:

> Educational requirements for employment can serve . . . to select new members for elite positions who share the elite culture. . . . Employers use education to select persons who have been socialized into the dominant status culture . . . [and] as a means of selection for cultural attributes.[19]

Another sociologist who has strongly attacked the stress placed on credentials is Ivar Berg. Berg conducted an empirical study (a study based on observation or experiment) showing that higher education does not guarantee better job performance.[20] He interviewed personnel managers in several public and private companies. All of them claimed that workers' attitudes toward work, their trainability, their adaptation and adjustment to their jobs, and their probabilities for promotion were all related to their level of education. All believed that the more education a worker had, the more likely it was he or she would perform better on the job.

Berg then went on to see if the statements made by the personnel managers were indeed true. For example, by examining the records of 4,000 life insurance salespersons, he found that their level of education had nothing to do with the number of policies they sold. When he looked at the work records of 200 clerks, he found no difference that could be related to education. In a large chemical company, Berg discovered that the technicians with the most education did not perform as well as others and indeed were more likely to resign from their jobs. Among a group of blue-collar workers in the South, Berg found the same pattern: Better-educated workers produced less and changed jobs more often. He concluded that regardless of the occupational level, from the professional to the blue-collar worker, employers overestimated the value of education, favoring those with more education when hiring, but actually getting better work performance from less educated people.

The stress on credentialism has had still another adverse effect. So many people have come to believe that there is no other way to obtain a prestigious job in this country that there has been an ever burgeoning supply of educated workers. So many, indeed, that the labor market can no longer absorb them. Increasingly, highly trained workers are being forced to accept jobs for which they are overqualified. For example, many individuals holding Ph.D.s are driving taxi cabs. Many with M.A.s are working as secretaries while many holding B.A.s are selling shoes. Obviously, because attaining high educational levels and getting specialized training have been taken very seriously over recent years, many people are underemployed.

Overeducation has led to high expectations, but the inability to find the kind of employment that young people have come to think they deserve has led, in turn, to job dissatisfaction, frustration, and status conflict. Many recent college graduates, working at what they feel are jobs beneath their qualifications, are becoming extremely disturbed. This disturbance manifests itself in ways that are detrimental to society—for example, low production levels, absenteeism, high turnover rates, mental illness, and accidents in the work place.

235

We are, then, on the horns of a dilemma. Is it more advantageous for the society and its individual members to continue to extol the virtues of higher education even though the need for highly trained personnel is diminishing? Or is it more realistic to curtail our national enthusiasm for higher education and recognize that the time when education and economic security were correlated has passed?

We can probably conclude that educational requirements for hiring are overstressed. Nevertheless, it is likely that the demand for credentials will not only continue, but will probably accelerate. This means that occupational opportunities will remain unequal until educational opportunities become more equal. And many highly educated people will become frustrated because they will be unable to obtain jobs for which they qualify.

Education and Income

The relationship between level of education and the opportunity to obtain high-status jobs has been demonstrated in the preceding section. However, education is related not only to occupation but also to income. Those who are using their education often have higher incomes. This fact illustrates once again the importance of having that "piece of paper." Many of those who have it not only get into higher prestige occupations, but they also earn more money. Table 7–3 shows the relationship between education and income.

Americans have assumed for a long time that the road to equality is through education. Table 7–3 suggests that they are correct since the person who completes college has about a ten times greater chance of earning over $25,000 a year than the person who does not complete high school. But some sociologists, such as Christopher Jencks[21], claim that schooling hardly affects economic inequality. The environments people grow up in, the life experiences they have, their personalities,

TABLE 7-3
Percent Distribution of Families by Income Level and Years of School Completed by Head of Household, 1974

Income Level of Head of Household	Years of Schooling Completed			
	Elementary	High School	1–3 Years College	4 or More Years College
Under $10,000	60.1	27.9	21.5	12.8
$10,000–$14,999	21.1	28.2	25.2	17.8
$15,000–$24,999	15.6	33.7	37.3	37.9
$25,000 and Over	3.2	10.2	16.0	31.5
Mean Income	$9,867	$15,063	$17,187	$22,084

Source: United States Department of Labor, Bureau of Labor Statistics, *Handbook of Labor Statistics, 1976,* Washington, D.C.: United States Government Printing Office, 1976, 350.

and chance and luck all profoundly affect people's attitudes toward work, and consequently their income. Jencks recommends, then, that attention should be directed toward changing the social environment rather than toward educational and school reform.

In short, there may be other factors associated with income levels besides education. No doubt education is very important. Throughout the years the American educational system has given millions of immigrants and native-born children the knowledge and skills they needed to enter into the American mainstream and rise up the occupational ladder. But willingness to work hard, intelligence, personality, and social class are also very meaningful in determining the amount of money a person will earn.

SUMMARY

All societies have some sort of institution through which younger members must learn the social norms, values, attitudes, and goals of the society. The educational institution has developed to handle much of that task.

The major social needs served by education are the transmission of the values, attitudes, and behaviors of our culture from one generation to the next; the transmission of skills and knowledge; and status placement. Each of these is an important function of any educational system. In carrying out the first function, education enables young people to learn the attitudes, values, and behaviors that are considered proper in their society. The second function equips children to do a job in the society. Status placement serves to put people into societal positions and teach them how to play the roles attached to those positions. This last major function is complicated by the fact that our educational institution does not truly grant all children the same opportunities to learn and get into the higher positions. Evaluations by teachers and peers and standardized testing favor children from middle- and upper-income backgrounds because their family environments are more conducive to helping them do well in school and on tests.

Education also has three secondary functions—custodial, social, and innovative. The custodial function enables schools to keep young people under supervision and out of the labor market longer than is probably necessary. The social function helps children select role models among teachers and peers and allows them to form social relationships that may endure for a lifetime. The innovative function serves to encourage students to help improve social life by creating new ideas and inventions. This function, however, sometimes conflicts with the transmission of values, attitudes, and behaviors because innovation *promotes* social change while transmission *preserves* things the way they are and helps maintain the status quo.

Higher education is greatly valued in our country because it is seen as a means of resolving social problems, such as poverty and pollution, and as a way of helping people to get ahead in the world. However, some of the ways we have used in trying to achieve this purpose, for example, tracking and subsidies, have actually had the opposite effect. Lower-class children, for a variety of reasons, have not had the same opportunity to go to college as have children from higher social strata.

Ours is a society that places a great deal of stress on credentials. Therefore, there is a tendency to hire people who have the proper "passport" for prestigious positions. Researchers have revealed, however, that we may be overemphasizing credentials, and the person who has a high level of education may actually not perform as well as someone who has a lower level of education.

Finally, although there is clearly a close relationship between educational level and income, there are other factors that influence how much money people will earn during their lifetimes. Some sociologists believe that the environments people grow up in, the life experiences they have, their personalities, and chance and luck all contribute to a person's earning capacity.

GLOSSARY

credentialism a system of granting official status to an individual by awarding a degree or certificate that attests to expertise in a given area.

educational institution a system of interrelated statuses and roles that ensures the transmission of several kinds of values, attitudes, behaviors, skills, and knowledge from one generation to the next.

role conflict a condition that develops when an individual is expected to perform two roles at the same time that are inconsistent or incompatible.

status placement the process of putting people into positions in society by using either their innate characteristics or their achievements as criteria.

tracking the grouping of school children according to their scores on aptitude, intelligence, and achievement tests.

REFERENCES

1. U.S. Bureau of the Census, *Current Population Reports*, Series P-20, no. 324. Washington, D.C.: U.S. Government Printing Office, April 1978, p. 11.

2. Robert Rosenthal and Lenore Jacobson, *Pygmalion in the Classroom.* New York: Holt, Rinehart & Winston, 1968.

REFERENCES

3. Warren G. Finley and Miriam M. Brian, *Ability Grouping 1970—Status Impact and Alternatives*. Athens, Ga.: University of Georgia, Center for Educational Improvement, 1971, p. 7.

4. Ray C. Rist, "Student Social Class and Teacher Expectations: The Self-Fulfilling Prophecy in Ghetto Education." *Harvard Educational Review* 40 (1970): 411–451.

5. Wilbur B. Brookover, Richard J. Gigliotti, Ronald D. Henderson, Bradley E. Niles, and Jeffrey M. Schneider, "Quality of Educational Attainment, Standardized Testing, Assessment, and Accountability." In C. Wayne Gordon, ed., *Uses of the Sociology of Education, Part II*. Chicago: University of Chicago Press, 1974, p. 174.

6. Brookover, et al., p. 175.

7. Paul Lauter and Florence Howe, "How the School System Is Rigged for Failure." In Robert Lejeune, ed., *Class and Conflict in American Society*. Chicago: Rand McNally, 1972, p. 206.

8. Kathleen Wilcox and Pia Moriarty, "Schooling and Work: Social Constraints on Equal Educational Opportunity." *Social Problems* 24:2 (1976): 204–213.

9. Rist, p. 413; *Julius W. Hobson v. Carl Hansen*, Superintendent of Schools, and the Board of Education of the District of Columbia, U.S. District Court for D.C., Civil Action No. 82-66, 1967, from *Congressional Record, House*, June 21, 1967, p. 16740; Wilcox and Moriarity, pp. 204–213; Walter E. Schaffer, Carol Olexa, and Kenneth Polk, "Program for Social Class: Tracking in High School." *Transaction* 7 (October 1970): 40; Brookover, et al., p. 174.

10. Robert L. Green, "Northern School Desegregation: Educational, Legal, and Political Issues." In Gordon, pp. 213–273.

11. James S. Coleman, *The Adolescent Society*. New York: The Free Press, 1961; and James S. Coleman, et al., *Equality of Educational Opportunity*. Washington, D.C.: U.S. Department of HEW, 1966.

12. Samuel Bowles and Herbert Gintis, *Schooling in Capitalist America*. New York: The Free Press, 1976.

13. Christopher Jencks and David Riesman, *The Academic Revolution*. New York: Doubleday, 1968.

14. Clark Kerr, *The Uses of the University*. Cambridge, Mass.: Harvard University Press, 1963.

15. Rodney T. Hartnett, *College and University Trustees: Their Backgrounds, Roles, and Educational Attitudes*. Princeton, N.J.: Educational Testing Service, 1968.

16. Judith Cummings, *The New York Times*, May 5, 1976, p. 51.

17. Lee W. Hansen and Burton A. Weisbrod, "Inequalities in Higher Education." In Lee Rainwater, ed., *Social Problems and Public Policy*. Chicago: Aldine Publishing Co., 1974, pp. 116–118.

18. Randall Collins, "Functional and Conflict Theories of Educational Stratification." *American Sociological Review* 36:6, 1971(1):1002–1019.

239

19. Collins, p. 1011.
20. Ivar Berg, *The Great Training Robbery*. New York: Praeger, 1970.
21. Christopher Jencks, *Inequality: A Reassessment of the Effects of Family and Schooling in America*. New York: Basic Books, 1972.

SUGGESTED READINGS

Becker, Howard S., Blanche Greer, and Everett C. Hughes. *Making the Grade.* New York: John Wiley & Sons, 1968.

A case study of undergraduates and life on a college campus.

Jones, Anne. *Uncle Tom's Campus.* New York: Praeger, 1973.

An account of a white professor's experience on a poor black college campus in the South.

Kozol, Jonathan. *Death at an Early Age.* Boston: Houghton Mifflin, 1967.

This book shows the dehumanized way in which black children in public schools are discouraged from improving their lives.

Leonard, George B. *Education and Ecstasy.* New York: Dell, 1969.

An interesting attempt to merge aspects of the human potentials movement with education.

Neill, A. S. *Summerhill.* New York: Hart, 1960.

A radical approach to child rearing and schooling that spawned the "free school movement" of the 1960s and early 1970s.

Robertson, Don, and Marion Steel. *The Halls of Yearning.* New York: Canfield, 1969.

A scathing indictment of formal higher education.

Social Problems 24:2, December 1976.

The first section deals with educational reform; the second considers the relationship between school and home; the third focuses on the problems and stigmatization of bilingual children in school; the fourth stresses the role of the federal government in education; and the final section examines the resistance of college professors to changing their teaching goals.

Young, Michael. *The Rise of the Meritocracy, 1870–2033: An Essay on Education Equality.* Baltimore: Penguin, 1958.

A science-fiction novel of a society in which people are evaluated very early in life for talent and motivation and then rewarded accordingly.

8

Religion

he religious institution can be called universal because it has existed in some form in every known society since the beginning of recorded time and probably long before that. Even the Neanderthals, who lived as far back as 100,000 years ago, seem to have practiced *religion*; artifacts found in Neanderthal graves suggest a belief in an afterlife. Thus, according to sociologist Glenn M. Vernon, "For all practical scientific purposes it is safe to assume that the origins of religion are lost in antiquity. We merely accept the fact that religion exists."[1]

But sociologists do not merely accept the fact that religion exists, nor do they rank religions by their merits. Rather, sociologists study and analyze religion in order to see how it affects human behavior and human interaction. They examine religion objectively in an attempt to discover the social consequences that flow from membership in any religion. The sociology of religion concentrates on the practices and beliefs of different religions, on how these beliefs affect human life and social relationships, and on how different societies generate different beliefs.

In this chapter we will focus on the various aspects of the religious institution. We will discuss what religion is and the functions it serves. We will also look at religious organizations and religion in the United States and see how the religious institution is changing. Finally, we will examine the relationship between religion and science.

What Is Religion?

Sociologists as far back as Émile Durkheim have groped with this question and have come up with a variety of definitions. A few of these are described in the sections that follow.

THE CHARACTERISTICS OF RELIGION

All religions include a concept of the supernatural. That is, there is always a belief that something exists that human senses cannot detect. It cannot be known through taste, smell, touch, sight, or hearing. This "something" may include a being that resembles in some ways the physical and/or social characteristics of human beings, as the concept of God in the Judeo-Christian religion. Or the supernatural may be seen as a force or a power having no human properties, such as *totems* in American Indian religions. In either case, the supernatural is almost always regarded as taking an interest in human beings. One characteristic of religion, then, is that it deals with that which is scientifically unknowable.

A second characteristic of religion is that the supernatural being or power is sacred. The supernatural is believed to transcend concrete social reality and is therefore to be worshipped and obeyed. In Greek mythology, for example, gods were given special powers and were obeyed.

Religions are also always characterized by a body of practices and beliefs that provide followers with the ways and means of "knowing" the supernatural, accepting its holiness, learning its wishes and orders, and complying with them. Practitioners of religion, then, follow a moral code or value system and demonstrate their beliefs through accepted rituals. Moslems, for example, follow the Koran, and various religions use the Bible as a guideline for religious behavior.

This moral code or value system is the fourth characteristic of religion. Not only does the believer relate to the supernatural or to the unknown, but also to the known and to the real world. Religion provides rules of moral behavior that are assumed to be approved by the supernatural. The Ten Commandments are examples of some of the "Thou shalts" and "Thou shalt nots" that religions define as "good" or "bad" practices. Members of any given religion share such common values and common notions of what is moral and what is immoral. The widespread acceptance of such codes illustrates the active role religion plays in the lives of most people.

Incorporating all these characteristics, Vernon provided a definition of religion:

> Religion is that part of culture composed of shared beliefs and practices which not only identify or define the supernatural and the sacred and man's relationships thereto, but which also relate them to the known world in such a way that the group is provided with moral definitions as to what is good (in harmony with or approved by the supernatural) and what is bad (contrary to or out of harmony with the supernatural).[2]

As stated earlier, though, this is only one of several definitions of religion. We will now examine another.

DURKHEIM'S DEFINITION OF RELIGION

One of the first sociologists to become interested in the study of religion was Émile Durkheim. He believed that religion plays a key role in maintaining society. According to Durkheim, religion has three elements. It consists of "sacred things" that are related to a system of "beliefs and practices." These beliefs and practices unite all who adhere to them into one "moral community."[3] What did Durkheim mean by these three elements?

Ordinary (profane) objects can become sacred if members of a society agree that the objects symbolize religious beliefs. Here, an Orthodox Jew selects an *ethrog* (a kind of citrus fruit), a sacred symbol used on the Jewish holiday of Succoth, a nine-day festival celebrating the end of the harvest season.

The Sacred and the Profane

Durkheim divided all things into two categories: the sacred and the profane. *Sacred things* are considered by the members of the society to be beyond everyday life and experience. They are rare, extraordinary, even dangerous, and inspire both fear and awe. *Profane things* are the exact opposite. They are ordinary and commonplace. What happens in society, according to Durkheim, is that we can make any profane thing sacred. A cross is sacred to a Christian because Jesus Christ died on a cross. A six-pointed star is sacred to a Jew because it was the symbol on King David's shield when he unified the Jews into one nation. Anything can be changed from the profane to the sacred if the members of a society agree that it is a symbol of religious belief.

Most religions in the world have sacred objects and most of them have sacred beings or gods. Christians, Jews, and Moslems believe in one God and are thus called *monotheists*. Others, who believe in several gods, like the ancient Greeks and modern Hindus*, are called *polytheists*. Most religions worship gods who are considered divine creatures, but some religions worship ordinary people who once lived. For example, modern Japanese Shintoists worship their own ancestors whose spirits they believe return to exist in living objects or in particular temples.

Even a moral principle or an ideal can be sacred. For example, Confucianism stresses human relationships over relations with a god or the unknown. In fact, this religion is centered around the Standards for the Five Relationships: husband and wife, parent and child, older and younger, ruler and subject, and friend and friend.

Almost all religions have a variation on what we call the "Golden Rule." Hindus order: "Do not unto others that which if done to thee would cause thee pain." Buddhists are told: "Administer to your friends and familiars by treating them as you treat yourself." Confucianism refers to the "silver rule" as: "What you do not want done to yourself, do not do unto others." Jews are admonished: "What thou thyself hatest, do to no man." Taoists are taught: "To those who are good to me I am good, and to those who are not good to me I am also good." When a religion focuses on a principle thought to have been passed to the people by the god or gods, that principle becomes as important as the deity itself.

Also in the realm of sacred things, especially among many preliterate societies, are *totems*. A totem may be a plant, an animal, or a piece of sculptured wood or stone (sometimes imbued with human charac-

*Contrary to popular Western belief, Hindus do not consider the cow sacred for religious reasons. In the same way that Americans do not slaughter and eat cats or dogs, Hindus do not slaughter and eat cows merely because of social custom.

Many American and Canadian tribes crafted sacred totem poles. This totem pole now stands in Saxman Park in Ketchikan, Alaska. The opening in the bottom section indicates that it may once have served as the entrance to a building.

teristics) that the group believes to have supernatural powers. These powers enable the totem to bestow blessings on human beings or to bring harm or destruction to them if it is not treated according to the rules. Many of us have seen pictures of the sacred totem poles made by various American and Canadian tribes.

Thus, all things that we designate as sacred—crosses, stars, gods, ancestors, moral principles, plants, animals, and carvings—are among Durkheim's sacred things. People construct beliefs and rituals around these things that unite them into a moral community.

Religious Beliefs and Practices

Durkheim's second element was religious beliefs and practices. What are religious beliefs? And what kind of rituals do people practice when they are participating in religious ceremonies? *Religious beliefs* are convictions people hold concerning the things they consider sacred. The beliefs explain the nature and meaning of the sacred things on two levels—the intellectual and the emotional. For example, intellectually we can admire Christ as a moral teacher and emotionally Christians worship him as a supernatural being. However, not all religious groups or members of a given religious group actually hold the same beliefs. To illustrate, in the United States 94 percent of the population claim to believe in God.[4] But when sociologists Charles Y. Glock and Rodney Stark asked members of different Protestant groups whether or not they believed in God, the answers they received varied.[5] They found that 99 percent of the Southern Baptists replied they had no doubt that God exists, but only 63 percent of the Episcopalians were sure of God's existence, and only 41 percent of the Congregationalists agreed that there is undoubtedly a God.

About 3 percent of the Protestants who responded to Glock and Stark thought that the existence of God is debatable, or that God does not exist but some power higher than human beings does, or that there is no way to find out if God really exists or not. These people are called *agnostics* because they have not made up their minds about God's existence. Only 1 percent of all Protestants questioned denied completely that God existed. These people are called *atheists*.

Religious practices can range from receiving a blessing from a member of the clergy *(left)* to gathering at a body of water to experience baptism by total immersion *(right).*

Religious practices are the expressions people give to their religious beliefs. They can be very simple, like kneeling in a Catholic church or wearing a yarmulke or skullcap in a Jewish temple. Or they can be very elaborate ceremonies. In Nepal, for example, every year each village celebrates the deaths of those who have died during that period by holding an all-day parade and party during which the families of the deceased carry totem poles decorated with the dead person's favorite personal belongings.

Throughout the world, religious practices can be infinitely varied. They can include praying, drum-beating, singing, dancing, parading, drinking, offering sacrifices (sometimes the sacrifice is food, animals, or even human beings), feasting or fasting, and taking drugs. The list of practices that express religious beliefs is very long.

Frequently people ignore all or some of the practices characteristic of their religion. Many Jews eat taboo foods, such as pork; many Catholics practice certain kinds of birth control forbidden by the Church. Many people in all religions do not attend religious services, although most religions teach that such attendance is important. A Gallup Poll conducted in 1976 showed that only 40 percent of all Americans go to their houses of worship regularly, but the percentages vary by religion. In this study 54 percent of all Catholics said they attend church services on a regular schedule, followed by 38 percent of all Protestants. Jews comprise the lowest percentage with only 20 percent attending temples or synagogues on a regular basis.[6] (See Table 8–1 for a more detailed analysis of the church-going population.)

APPLYING SOCIOLOGY

Using Table 8–1, describe the person who attends church with the most regularity and then describe the person who attends least often. What other factors might influence how often a person attends church?

TABLE 8–1
Attended Church During
Average Week, 1975

	National	Protestants	Roman Catholics	Jews	No religious preference
NATIONAL	40%	38%	54%	20%	5%
SEX					
Male	35	34	49	19	5
Female	45	42	57	21	5
RACE					
White	40	37	54	20	4
Nonwhite	39	42	40	*	9
EDUCATION					
College	40	40	62	15	3
High School	39	36	50	29	6
Grade School	43	40	54	16	7
AGE					
Under 30	30	31	39	24	5
18–24 years	29	30	39	19	4
25–29 years	32	33	38	34	6
30–49 years	41	38	56	18	5
50 & older	46	42	64	20	4
INCOME					
$20,000 & over	38	33	58	16	7
$15,000–$19,999	44	40	62	32	5
$10,000–$14,999	38	36	50	19	3
$ 7,000–$ 9,999	37	37	47	38	5
$ 5,000–$ 6,999	41	40	52	25	5
$ 3,000–$ 4,999	40	40	47	24	5
Under $3,000	41	41	52	9	6
POLITICS					
Republican	45	43	60	13	10
Democrat	41	37	56	24	7
Independent	34	35	48	13	3
OCCUPATION					
Professional & Business	41	40	63	18	3
Clerical & Sales	40	39	53	29	3
Manual Workers	37	35	47	23	6
Nonlabor Force	44	41	60	20	5
MARITAL STATUS					
Married	41	39	54	19	5
Single	31	31	47	18	6
Divorced/Separated	40	39	56	26	2
Widowed	49	44	68	21	*

*Insufficient cases on which to base percentages.
Source: Adapted from The Gallup Opinion Index, *Religion in America 1976,* Report #130, 26.

247

Émile Durkheim (1858–1917)

Émile Durkheim is noted for his contributions to the development of sociology and the social sciences. His writing covered a variety of subjects.

Durkheim's first publication was in 1893 and is entitled *The Division of Labor in Society*. In this book, he proposed that every society has a division of labor, which is the way tasks are divided among its members. This division of labor, and the specialization resulting from it, is the critical element influencing all of social life. According to Durkheim, it is responsible for holding the society together. Durkheim noted two types of social cohesion—mechanical solidarity and organic solidarity.

In societies characterized by *mechanical solidarity,* individuals perform essentially the same tasks and thus develop similar beliefs and value systems. Members are independent of each other because everyone can perform whatever is needed for survival, but the society is held together because all members share the same values. In societies characterized by *organic solidarity,* individuals become specialized and are held together because they are dependent on each other. (The farmer, for example, relies on the work of the doctor, and vice versa.) But in this process people develop competing interests and social values. Formal authority is then required to constrain behavior because informal negative sanctions are no longer sufficient.

Durkheim's second book, which was published two years later in 1895, is a series of essays entitled *The Rules of Sociological Method.* This book contains a discussion of his critical concept—a social fact.

A social fact is something to be understood and located outside of the individual. For Durkheim (and for much of sociology since), a social fact is created by one's culture and cannot be reduced to the experiences of an individual. Rules, customs, and beliefs are examples of social facts.

Sociologists make a distinction between the religious person and religiosity. The religious person is one who is committed or dedicated to the principles of a given religion. In contrast, *religiosity* is defined by sociologists in terms of the amount of participation in and adherence to religious ritual and church rules. A religious person may display any degree of religiosity and someone who displays a high degree of religiosity may or may not be religious. Let us see how this works.

Just because people go to religious services (thereby showing a degree of religiosity), it does not necessarily follow that they are religious. Some may go to conform to their group's norms; some to please parents; some to set an example for their children; some out of habit; and some because churchgoing is a social occasion.

On the other hand, not going to church or to temple does not necessarily mean a person is irreligious. One might dislike the rigidity of formal services. Another might stay away because of illness or

This concept is illustrated in his third major publication, *Suicide,* published in 1897.

The most important contribution Durkheim made in this penetrating analysis is his conclusion that suicide rates must be understood as social facts rather than as individual acts without pattern. Essentially, Durkheim's argument is that societies have different kinds of suicide rates depending upon their amount of integration. When societies are very fragmented and individuals can count only on themselves, there is likely to be an increase in the *egoistic* suicide rate. When societies are so tightly knit that individuals count only on others, there is likely to be an increase in the *altruistic* suicide rate. Finally, when group norms are insufficient to guide personal conduct, the *anomic* suicide rate will increase. Thus, society shapes the individual, rather than the other way around. Durkheim argued that suicide rates must be understood in a broad social context and that social circumstances are the *only* way that suicide patterns can be explained.

Durkheim's final major work, published in 1912, is entitled *The Elementary Forms of the Religious Life.* In this work, Durkheim analyzed the role of religion in society. He believed that religion bound together a society's members. It did this by persuading the members to obey the rules of the society, instead of bowing to their own egos. In the process, certain social elements are designated as "sacred." In the United States, for example, democracy has a sacred as well as a political meaning for many people. Because of such sacred designation, it is easier for a society to get people to follow its rules—people are less likely to question fear-invoking or awe-inspiring symbols. Thus, according to Durkheim, religion aids society in promoting social cohesiveness.

fatigue. The point is that sociologists do not measure how religious a person is only by the number of times he or she actually enters a house of worship. There are many other ways to be religious without performing the traditional practices and rituals.

The Moral Community

The last element in Durkheim's definition of religion is also important. What did he mean by a *"moral community"*? Durkheim meant that religion is a means of cementing and holding a group of people together because they share the same beliefs and the same collective values and ideas. Through religion, people gain a sense of identity, a feeling that they are bona fide members of a group. They are part of a cohesive collectivity, with loyalty and strong bonds of belonging. This is the moral community. All the members of one faith, regardless of how widely they are scattered about the earth, sense a kinship and integration with each other. But providing people with a sense of identity and belonging is only one of the functions of religion. Sociologists have identified many more.

The Functions of Religion

According to Durkheim, two functions of religion are tied to the concept of moral community. One is rooted in the idea of *community*, and the other in the word *moral*. The first function of religion is to bind the members of the group together in a feeling of "one-ness." Each religious group usually believes that it is the "true" religion and so the members develop a sense of superiority. This leads to a sense of group cohesion and group solidarity that few other beliefs can generate. In other words, Jews probably feel closer to each other than do all the red-headed people in the world or all the residents of Nevada.

The second function of religion, according to Durkheim, is related to social control. Durkheim used the word *moral* to indicate that religion is a means of social control. Most religions explicitly state what is right and what is wrong, what is good and what is bad, although church leaders continually reevaluate these edicts. Since these moral judgments are thought to have been passed down from a divine Being (for example, Moses is thought to have received the Ten Commandments from God through the burning bush), many men and women do not question them. To deviate from the laws of God can mean that one loses one's membership in the religious group and one's place in the hereafter, and most people hesitate to risk that. Religion thus helps to establish and preserve a moral order by exercising social control over the members.

Related to this function of social control is religion's tendency to maintain the status quo. Sometimes, however, religion can bring about social change. One instance where this has occurred can be seen in the rise of modern capitalism. In his book *The Protestant Ethic and the Spirit of Capitalism*, sociologist Max Weber discusses the relationship between religion and capitalism.[7] Weber notes that early Protestants

---

APPLYING SOCIOLOGY

Think about religion in your own community. How important do you think religion is in the lives of most of the people there? How important do you think religion is to the community? In what ways? On what factors do you base your opinion?

Religion offers us formal observations of and rites for such important life events as marriage.

(primarily Calvinists) believed that only through hard work could one discover that one was destined to go to heaven. Thus people worked hard to accumulate signs that they were among the elect or chosen. In the process they amassed money. But, according to their religion, the use of money for material comforts was regarded as a disgrace. Money was not to be spent on worldly goods. Instead they reinvested their money in their businesses, thus giving rise to capitalism. (Weber and his theories on religion and capitalism will be discussed more fully in Chapter 14.)

Another function of religion, with its ceremonies and rituals, is to help people feel that their existence is meaningful. Religion offers its adherents formal observations of the important events in their lives. Many religions, for example, have special rites for birth and death. Some take notice of the passage from childhood to adulthood, such as the Catholic and Protestant confirmation or the Jewish Bar Mitzvah. In many cases, engagements, marriages, the birth of a child, and serious illnesses are noted by some form of religious ceremony. Most of the major transitions people pass through during the life cycle can be marked by their religion, so that they feel the divinity is approving of human endeavors and human achievement. The fact that every known society has some form of such rites indicates that there is a universal need for this sort of approval.

Still another important function of religion is to explain incomprehensible events. Such questions as: How did the world come into existence?; Where do we come from?; Why are we born?; Why is there suffering in the world?; Why is there evil in the world?; and Why do we die? have troubled the human race throughout its existence. If people did not have the solace of religion in times of stress—death, war, famine, illness—they might not have the strength to continue to fight and live. If they did not have the assurance many religions offer that the soul, at least, survives death, many human beings might not be able to bear the deaths of those they love or contemplate their own deaths.

Besides explaining the unknown, religion functions to fill the gap between the time when people wonder about what causes a phenomenon and the time when they learn of a scientific explanation for it. For example, there was a god of thunder before we understood what really caused thunder. There was a god of fertility until we discovered a biological explanation of how babies are conceived. Some people believe in a God who created the world in seven days. Others accept an evolutionary theory and no longer believe in the former explanation.

Organized religions also serve many practical purposes for social groups. They often set up and maintain humanitarian services for those in need—hospitals, orphanages, homes for the aged, schools. Religious

Religion can offer solace in times of grief and mourning. The assurance offered by many religions that the soul survives death can help us to bear the loss of loved ones.

Throughout history religion has led, on occasion, to conflict. For example, hostility has raged for centuries between Protestants and Catholics in Ireland. Here, Catholic students in Belfast, Northern Ireland, taunt British troops representing Protestant forces.

groups even provide emergency care in cases of such natural disasters as earthquakes, floods, tornadoes, and fires. So religion has a practical aspect as well as a social, emotional, and moral aspect.

In addition to identifying the functions of religion, sociologists have identified two dysfunctions created by religion—two ways religion has produced adverse effects on society. One is that religion often creates conflict between groups because members of each group believe that theirs is the best and only true religion. Many wars throughout history have been fought between opposing religious groups. During the Middle Ages, Christians fought Moslems. There is continuing conflict between Indian Hindus and Pakastani Moslems. The hostility between Catholics and Protestants in Ireland has been raging for centuries and has led to many deaths. Furthermore, religion has been used to camouflage other reasons for dispute. The Crusades, for example, were really attempts to gain control of desirable trade routes. Although the dispute is not directly religious, the Arabs and the Israelis have been struggling on and off for decades. So, while religion unites the in-group, it sometimes creates hatred toward out-groups.

The second dysfunction of religion is personal. A religion can serve as a psychological crutch, assuring believers that a divinity, and not they themselves, is responsible for their fate. Religion thus can offer a way out of responsibility for oneself, taking feelings of self-doubt away from human beings and allowing them to "blame" the supernatural for personal failure and personal behavior. In short, religion may provide some of us with a ready-made instrument of denying responsibility for our own actions and our own destiny. It permits some of us to say, "What happens to me is not my fault. God did this to me."

253

Religious Organizations

Like all institutions, religion has many associations attached to it, and we can divide them into different types. In premodern societies, religion required little formality because it was part of everyday life. Natural phenomena and daily events were explained in terms of the supernatural, and religion was not clearly differentiated from everyday life. As societies became more industrialized, however, people began to make distinctions between the supernatural and the natural. Religion, instead of being part of daily life, became a separate aspect of life, and special religious associations developed that carried out the beliefs and practices of religion. Christian churches and temples are such religious associations.

Churches and temples are composed of groups of people who are organized to practice religious beliefs and carry out religious functions. They are formal organizations with stated goals and values, hierarchies of leaders, and rules and regulations that make clear the qualifications for membership and the rights and obligations associated with membership. These associations have systems of interrelated roles (ministers and congregants) and social norms (rituals and rites).

Within religions there are three different types of organizations —the denomination, the sect, and the cult. A *denomination* is a formal, organized religious group within a church, which also has stated goals and values, hierarchies, trained clergy, rules, and rights and obligations. Episcopalians, Baptists, and Congregationalists, for example, are separate denominations within the Protestant Church.

A *sect* is a small group that separates itself from the denomination. The separation usually occurs because certain members feel that the denomination is no longer doing what it is supposed to do and they want to reform it. Sects are less formalized than denominations but are still highly organized. Sometimes sects become new denominations as they become more formalized and attract new members. An outstanding example of a sect becoming a denomination is the Society of Friends, better known as Quakers. The Quakers broke away from the Church of England in the middle of the seventeenth century and are now an established denomination.

A *cult* is a type of religious organization whose members respond to experience on an emotional rather than a rational level. According to sociologist David O. Moberg, "cult members seek satisfactions through some sort of personal religious thrills."[8] Cults are poorly organized, unstable groups, often composed of people who feel themselves outside the mainstream of society. They are unlikely to challenge the social order on an institutional level, although they may do so on a personal level. Furthermore, because there is a general lack of objectivity about

The Snake Handlers are an example of a religious cult in the United States. Here the Rev. Lester Ball of Newport, Tennessee, handles a poisonous snake during a religious service.

the external world and the society, cults are frequently ultraconservative and sometimes even reactionary groups.

Cults are usually very small groups founded and led by charismatic leaders—leaders who engender an incredible loyalty and enthusiasm among their followers. Since members of cults are often so emotionally attached to their leaders, they may frequently obey directions and behave in ways that are contrary to the norms of the larger society because their leaders direct them to do so. For example, the followers of Charles Manson killed many people and one of them even attempted to kill the President of the United States. On the other hand, a leader can also influence members to behave in ways that are beneficial to the group. As the leader of the Black Muslims, Elijah Muhammad helped many black people to establish their own businesses and to stabilize their family lives. Thus, charismatic leaders can guide their followers in either destructive or constructive ways. Cults often die when the charismatic leader dies because charisma cannot be passed on from one person to another.

Of the types of religious organizations described in this section, the two that dominate the American scene are the sect and the denomination. Figure 8−1 offers a comparison between these two kinds of religious organizations.

FIGURE 8–1
Comparison of Sect and Denomination

Characteristic	Sect	Denomination
Size	Small	Large
Relationship with other religious groups	Rejection—feeling that only it has "the truth"	Acceptance—able to work in harmony with others
Wealth (church property, buildings, salary of clergy, income of members)	Limited	Extensive
Religious services	Emotional—attempts to recapture conversion thrill; informal; congregational participation	Intellectual—concerned with teaching; formal; little congregational participation
Clergy	Unspecialized—little or no professional training; often part-time	Specialized—professional training; full-time
Doctrines	Literal interpretation of Bible; stress on other-worldly rewards	Liberal interpretation of Bible; stress on rewards in this world
Membership requirements	Conversion experience; emotional commitment	Born into group or ritualistic requirements; intellectual commitment
Relationship with secular world	"At war" with the secular world which is defined as "evil"	Endorses prevailing culture and social organization
Social class of members	Predominantly lower class	Predominantly middle class

Source: Glenn M. Vernon, *Sociology of Religion,* New York: McGraw-Hill, 1962, 174.

Religion in the United States

In 1975, out of a total population of 212.8 million Americans, about 60 percent were members of a church. Of these church members, 72 million were Protestants, 49 million were Catholics, 6 million were Jews, and 2 million were members of smaller churches, such as Buddhist and B'Hai Churches.[9]

RELIGIOUS GROUPS

Research shows that membership in a religious group, whether by birth or by choice, is related to other aspects of life (see Table 8–2). For example, the same percentage of Protestants and Catholics attend college, but the percentage of Jews who go to college is more than twice that of the other groups.

Career patterns also differ according to religion. The same percentage of Protestants and Catholics are in the upper echelon of the occupational structure, but a much greater percentage of Jews are in the top

256

TABLE 8–2
Profiles of Major Religious Faiths in the United States (Based on total national sample)

	Population distribution (%)	Protestants (%)	Roman Catholics (%)	Jews (%)	No religious preference (%)
SEX					
Male	48	46	45	52	68
Female	52	54	55	48	32
RACE					
White	89	86	96	99	86
Nonwhite	11	14	4	1	14
EDUCATION					
College	26	24	24	54	42
High School	55	56	58	35	49
Grade School	19	20	18	11	9
AGE					
Under 30	28	23	31	20	54
18–24 years	17	14	20	13	36
25–29 years	11	9	11	7	18
30–49 years	34	34	35	33	26
50 & older	38	43	34	47	20
INCOME					
$20,000 & over	15	14	16	34	16
$15,000–$19,999	14	13	17	13	13
$10,000–$14,999	22	22	25	17	20
$ 7,000–$ 9,999	11	11	10	8	13
$ 5,000–$ 6,999	11	11	10	7	11
$ 3,000–$ 4,999	9	10	7	6	9
Under $3,000	18	19	15	15	18
POLITICS					
Republican	21	26	14	8	9
Democrat	44	40	52	59	36
Independent	33	31	31	32	49
OCCUPATION					
Professional & Business	21	20	20	46	27
Clerical & Sales	11	10	13	15	13
Manual Workers	40	40	44	13	36
Nonlabor Force	20	23	17	20	13
Farmers	3	4	2	*	2
MARITAL STATUS					
Married	68	73	71	67	49
Single	17	11	18	16	40
Divorced/Separated	7	14	9	14	10
Widowed	8	2	2	3	1

*Less than 1 percent.

Source: Adapted from The Gallup Opinion Index, *Religion in America 1976*, Report #130, 39.

257

ranks. The fact that Jews are concentrated in the higher level occupations accounts for the fact that they also are in the higher income brackets, compared to Protestants and Catholics. One reason for both the high occupational statuses and the high incomes found among Jews is the high level of education that they have attained.

Political affiliation also bears some relation to religious membership. Jews have the greatest affiliation with the Democratic party of the three religious groups. But perhaps this is because they tend to live in urban centers to a far greater extent than any other group, and, in general, large cities are more likely to have populations that vote Democratic. Political affiliation for Protestants can be predicted on the basis of denomination. Most Episcopalians, for example, tend to be Republicans while most Southern Baptists are likely to be Democrats. However, race also acts as an important intervening variable. White Protestants tend to vote Republican while black Protestants are more likely to vote Democratic.

Besides political affiliation, educational, economic, and many other aspects of life are all related to religious affiliation. In fact, sociologist Gerhard Lenski claims that religion is as strong a factor and has as great an influence on behavior and attitudes as social class. Lenski goes so far as to say that when it comes to such things as education and occupation, as well as a personal value system, one's religion is not only correlated with them, but in fact causes them.[10]

Clearly, religion seems to be an important factor in American life. One sociologist has added a somewhat different twist, though, by saying that America is characterized by a "civil religion."

CIVIL RELIGION

In 1967, a well-respected sociologist, Robert N. Bellah,[11] proposed that in America there is something he called *civil religion,* which is quite apart from recognized religious groups, like Catholics, Protestants, or Jews. Civil religion, according to Bellah, transcends all specific religions and is a combination of a belief in a deity (although not any special God belonging to any special church) and patriotism. Civil religion permeates our lives.

Bellah claims that America's civil life has a religious quality. In Bellah's view the Declaration of Independence and the Gettysburg Address are sacred scriptures and Memorial Day and Veterans Day are religious holidays. It is easy to note other examples of how religion enters our everyday lives: "In God We Trust" is on all our coins; the Boy Scouts award a "God and Country" prize; our national anthem includes references to God.

258

But despite the prevalence of civil religion, our recognized religions are still important in our lives. These organized religions, however, have undergone—and are still undergoing—change and revision.

Changes in the Religious Institution

We saw earlier that according to a Gallup Poll, 60 percent of all Americans are members of a church. Yet only about 40 percent attend services regularly. This is a much lower percentage than in 1955 when 49 percent were regular churchgoers. Figure 8-2 shows that in 1957, 14 percent of the people questioned believed that religion was losing its influence. Ten years later, in 1967, 58 percent felt the same way. The percentage continued to rise until it peaked in 1970 when 75 percent agreed that religion was losing its hold. After that, the figures dropped to 58 percent in 1974 and 50 percent in 1975.[12] It is interesting to compare the Gallup Poll figures above, which are taken from a national sample, with a study conducted on college campuses. The study of col-

FIGURE 8–2
Percentage Saying Religion Is Losing Influence

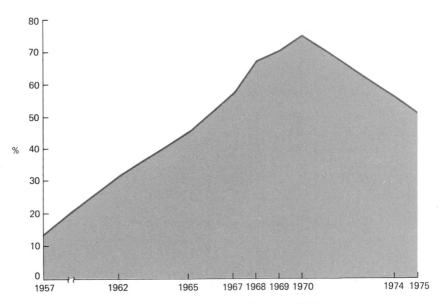

Source: The Gallup Opinion Index, *Religion in America 1976*, Report # 130, 56.

The percentage of Americans who believe that religion is losing its influence has varied over time. Whereas in 1957, 14 percent felt this way, the figure peaked in 1970 with 75 percent holding this opinion. In 1975, the figure dropped to 50 percent.

FOCUS ON: THE UNIFICATION CHURCH

One of the more controversial cults to emerge recently has been the Unification Church, founded and led by the Rev. Sun Myung Moon. The Rev. Richard A. Walsh discusses this group in an article entitled " 'Moonies'—Religious Converts or Psychic Victims?"

A major point of controversy stems from the church's religious indoctrination program. On the one hand, the church contends that these young adults have been converted after living in a communal center and attending long hours of lectures, prayers, and group discussions. On the other hand, adversaries contend that these people—physically exhausted by lack of sleep, mentally overwhelmed by the incessant indoctrination, and emotionally seduced by the friendly atmosphere of the commune—have been "brainwashed."

Several parents have initiated court hearings against such alleged "brainwashing." These parents have asked the courts to return their offspring to their custody so that they can be "deprogrammed" from their faith in Mr. Moon and his church.

Clearly an issue in these hearings is the religious liberty of these adult members of the Unification Church. Also, Walsh claims, the religious liberty of the church itself is at stake. Far more important, however, is the fact that these hearings involve every church in America, since all churches conduct religious indoctrination programs, irritate the parents of some adult converts, and are open to the charge of "brainwashing."

Does indoctrination constitute brainwashing? Do churches have the right to encourage adult members to live in communes, to work long hours, to break family ties? Is religious liberty an unlimited right?

Walsh argues that the Unification Church does not violate the rights of citizens, nor does it threaten public morality or public peace. The church and its members have every right to hold and to manifest their religious beliefs. According to Walsh, the continuing harassment of the church and its members by civil authorities, by parents of members, by misguided churchgoers, and by deprogramming experts must be seen as a violation of the right of the church and its members to full religious liberty.

How do you feel about the "Moonies"? Should adults be free to join any religion, even one alien to their national culture and to family traditions?

Source: Richard A. Walsh, " 'Moonies'—Religious Converts or Psychic Victims?" *America*, May 14, 1977, pp. 438-440.

lege students revealed that in 1974, 75 percent felt that religion currently has little influence.[13]

The term *secularization* is used to describe this decline of religion. Secular means "worldly." Therefore, secularization is a process during which religion becomes less influential and people are less likely to turn to religion for identity or for answers to troubling questions.

Not only does religion seem to be losing its appeal to the people, but there have been upheavals within the formal religious organizations themselves. The three major religious groups in the United States have been undergoing self-examination and self-criticism in their efforts to understand why their membership is decreasing and how they can bring people back to the religious life. The Catholic Church has been struggling with questions of birth control rules, marriage for members of the clergy, the role of women in the Church, and the Church's relations with Protestants and Jews. Jewish leaders are concerned with the loss of membership and the decline in attendance as more and more Jews, especially young Jews, move away from orthodoxy toward secularization, reformed Judaism, assimilation, and agnosticism. Protestant denominations also have problems similar to those of Catholicism and Judaism—decreasing church attendance, skepticism among members, doctrinal disputes, and so forth.

Nevertheless, religion can hardly be said to be absent from life in modern society. It is still a force in economic and political life because it involves itself in such matters as abortion, divorce reform laws, the rights of homosexuals, and public funding of private schools. It was an issue in the 1976 presidential election. It is, also, still part of family life insofar as parents sometimes carry out religious observances in the home and send their children to religious schools. And advocates of religion are very visible on city streets and on radio and television as they strive to bring religion back into daily life. But the amount of influence that religion has varies among different segments of society. Table 8–3 shows that, among other things, women are more likely than men to consider religion important. Similarly, religion is more important to nonwhites than to whites, to the less educated than to the well-educated, and to older people more than to other age groups.

While the established religions seem to be losing members and influence, fundamentalist churches, such as Seventh Day Adventists, Mormons, Assemblies of God, and Jehovah's Witnesses, and "new" cults, such as the Children of God, Hare Krishna, and the Jesus Movement, are experiencing growth. The latter groups in particular have been clearly increasing since the late 1960s, with most of their membership comprised of white, upper- and upper-middle-class youth, frequently former drug addicts. These are essentially evangelical cults that interpret the Bible literally and demand strict conformity from their members.

The Jesus Movement is perhaps the best example of the new type of religious group in America. Its adherents are called "Jesus People" or sometimes "Jesus Freaks." The cult seems to have begun during the 1960s among the "street people" and the "trippers" in California. The rock music of that period—a blend of blues, country, gospel, and western—carried a message of alienation, and gospel themes and lyrics stressed "meaning" and "experience" in religion rather than ritual and dogma.[14]

Although religion may have become less influential in recent years, it has not by any means disappeared from modern life. Elements of religious life are often found on city streets, as shown by this record store in a Hispanic section of New York City.

Members of the Jesus Movement demonstrating at the Republican Convention in Kansas City, Missouri, in August 1976. Such "new" religious cults (other examples are the Hare Krishnas, the Unification Church, and the Children of God) have become increasingly influential among young people since the 1960s.

TABLE 8-3
Importance of Religious
Beliefs in the
United States

	Very important	Fairly important	Not too important	Not at all important	Don't know
NATIONAL	56%	30%	8%	5%	1%
SEX					
Male	47	36	11	5	1
Female	66	25	5	4	*
RACE					
White	54	32	8	5	1
Nonwhite	72	20	6	1	1
EDUCATION					
College	49	33	11	6	1
High School	58	31	7	4	*
Grade School	70	21	3	5	1
AGE					
Under 30 years	45	35	15	5	*
30–49 years	58	30	7	5	*
50 & older	63	27	5	4	1
OCCUPATION					
White-collar	54	29	9	8	*
Blue-collar	47	36	13	4	*
Housewives	68	25	4	3	*
All others	56	31	6	5	2
RELIGION					
Protestant	68	27	4	1	*
Catholic	60	35	5	*	*
MARITAL STATUS					
Married	57	32	8	3	*
Single	43	35	13	8	1
Divorced/Separated	52	29	12	7	*
Widowed	76	16	4	4	*
Church members	65	30	5	*	*
Nonmembers	28	32	21	19	*

Source: Gallup Opinion Index, *Religion in America 1976, Report # 130,* 9.

Many Jesus People live communally, obeying strict ascetic moral codes. The basic principle of the religion is to return to "pure" Christianity by finding personal salvation through the teachings of Jesus Christ. The stress is on experiencing religion collectively and directly, not independently or intellectually. Jesus People get "high" on Jesus, not on drugs, alcohol, violence, or sex.

Religion and Science

For many centuries, in our search for an understanding of the natural phenomena of the earth and the universe around it, we turned to reli-

APPLYING SOCIOLOGY

In what way does this cartoon reflect a worldliness in religious matters? Do you agree that people are less influenced by religion now than they have been in the past? To answer this question, you might compare your own feelings about religion with those of your parents and, if possible, even your grandparents when they were your age.

gion for explanations. But over time, as our scientific and technological methods and theories became more sophisticated, science challenged many religious explanations.

A study by anthropologist Bronislaw Malinowski demonstrates how scientific knowledge can replace a belief in magic or religion.[15] In the Southwest Pacific, the Trobriand Islanders are expert fishermen. Fish are the main staple of their diet and are plentiful in the quiet, safe lagoon and in the open seas. The Trobrianders developed an excellent technique for harvesting the fish in the lagoon and Malinowski observed that they practice no religious rituals to help them when fishing in this area. However, fishing in the dangerous open sea is a different story. There the fishermen have little knowledge of tides and winds, so they conduct elaborate rites to protect them from the dangers and to ensure a good catch before they go out in their canoes. Malinowski reasoned that because the Trobrianders feel they control the lagoon and possess a technology for exploiting it, they have no need to turn to magic or religious practices to deal with it. On the other hand, when they need to venture into unknown territory without technological skills to support them, they need superstition, rituals, and magical rites to guarantee security and protection. We can infer from Malinowski's observations, then, that when people deal with phenomena about which they have scientific knowledge (however primitive), they feel no need to rely on religion. When they deal with phenomena for which they have little or no technology, they turn to the supernatural.

Carried to its logical conclusion, the argument would be that the growth of scientific knowledge presents a serious threat to the religious institution. If human beings achieve the ability to control all of their environment scientifically and technologically, how would religion be affected? Would it still play an important role in human life?

Religion deals in areas and answers questions that are unanswerable by science. It seeks answers to such questions as: What is God's relationship to human beings? Is there a heaven and a hell? Is there a soul? What happens after death? These questions are outside the realm of scientific study and may always be. The scientific method at this point does not lend itself to dealing with questions about phenomena that cannot be observed by the senses. Thus our scientific advances may never enable us to control everything in the universe and every aspect of human life.

Science and religion coexist and will continue to do so because they each serve human beings in different ways. Science concerns itself with natural phenomena; religion with the supernatural. Neither science nor religion can supply all the answers to all the questions.

Therefore, regardless of the fact that scientific thinking seems to be replacing religious thinking in some areas, religion in America is

FOCUS ON: THE SURVIVAL OF RELIGION

Will religion become useless and eventually perish in contemporary society? Andrew Greeley thinks not. In *Unsecular Man,* Greeley provides some insights into why religious involvement persists and will continue to do so. He describes five functions that religion still serves in present-day America.

First, Greeley points out that religion still gives meaning to social life and creates some communal integration among individuals. Religion still serves such traditional functions despite the fact that it has been challenged by the large corporate structures created to house government, the military, business, labor, and education.

Second, although many phenomena that were previously understood through religious interpretation are now explained by science, Greeley argues that science is still unable to deal with the basic questions people ask about life. As a result, religion still serves to answer these questions.

Third, Greeley argues that even though religious and other types of myths have been in-terpreted by science, human beings still need to rely on such myths. Thus, the development of sophisticated rational thought processes has not put an end to religion's usefulness.

Fourth, today religion has changed and become more flexible, allowing for individual interpretation and decision-making. The religious community still exerts great pressure on the individual, but considerably less so than in the past.

Finally, Greeley argues that the greater decision-making and choice actually increase the meaning of religion. Individuals can now actually "shop around" for a religion that fits their outlook on life, rather than inheriting one from their parents.

Do you practice the same religion as the other members of your family? Do you believe that religion will survive in a period where so much can be explained by science? Do you think there are some things, such as how and why intelligent life started on our planet, that science can never answer?

Source: Andrew M. Greeley, *Unsecular Man,* New York: Dell, 1974.

still alive and well, although it has become more secularized and new forms of religion have emerged. It has retained most of the functions discussed earlier, although perhaps to a lesser degree. People still need to feel a sense of identity with an "in-group." They still enjoy the ceremonies that commemorate milestones in life. They still require explanations about human existence and death. As a result, both science and religion are necessary in society and they need not be competitive because their functions differ. Society is richer for having both of them.

SUMMARY

Religion is a universal social institution inasmuch as it has been found in every known society. Sociologists are not concerned with evaluating one religion over another. They only study religion in an attempt to see how it affects human behavior and human interaction.

All religions contain a concept of the supernatural, a belief in the sacred quality of the supernatural, a set of rituals, and a moral code. Through these qualities religion enables people to relate both to the supernatural and to the real world.

Émile Durkheim was one of the first sociologists to become interested in the study of religion. According to Durkheim, religion had three elements: sacred things, beliefs and practices, and a moral community.

Durkheim separated all phenomena into "sacred things" and "profane things." *Sacred things* are rare and awe-inspiring; *profane things* are ordinary and commonplace. Things are either sacred or profane, not because of any intrinsic qualities, but because people define them as such.

Religious beliefs are the convictions people hold concerning the things they consider sacred. They explain the nature and meaning of sacred things on both intellectual and emotional levels. *Religious practices* are the means by which people express their religious beliefs. These forms of expression can be very simple or very elaborate. Both beliefs and practices vary greatly among people. People rarely accept all the beliefs of their particular religion and rarely follow all of its religious practices.

By *"moral community"* Durkheim meant that all the members of one faith share a sense of kinship and integration with each other. They share the same beliefs and the same values and ideas, thus feeling part of a collectivity.

Like all universal social institutions, religion has several functions. First, it binds people together into a cohesive group. Second, religion is a means of social control because it establishes a moral code. Third, religion gives meaning to life by providing rituals that mark the passages through the life cycle. Fourth, religion explains incomprehensible phenomena, such as death, evil, or catastrophe. Finally, religions serve the society in practical ways by establishing and maintaining humanitarian services. Unfortunately, religion has two serious dysfunctions. It serves to divide people into hostile camps because members of a religion tend to believe their religion is the one "true" religion. And it can be used as a psychological crutch, allowing people to deny responsibility for their actions.

Like all institutions, religion has many associations attached to it. Churches and temples are the most formal and most highly organized of these associations.

Within the religious institution there are different types of organization—the denomination, the sect, and the cult. *Denomina-*

tions are formal organized religious groups within a church. *Sects* are small groups that separate themselves from denominations, but over time they often become denominations themselves. *Cults* are unstable fringe groups, based on emotionality rather than on objectivity or rationality.

Religious affiliation influences many aspects of life—level of education, political orientation, occupational level, income level, and so forth. Some sociologists believe that religion is the decisive factor in life.

Many changes have occurred in the American religious institution. Most significant is the decrease in religiosity. There is also a decrease in the number of people who believe that organized religion is an influence on social life, especially among college students. *Secularization* is the term used to describe this turning away from religion. In addition, over the past two decades all three of the major American religions have experienced significant upheavals and have had to make serious adjustments. On the other hand, fundamentalist and "new" religions have grown in the United States.

The most serious challenge to religion today is science because it offers alternative explanations to many universal questions. However, it is improbable that science will ever be able to address certain types of questions because they are not susceptible to the scientific method. Therefore, science and religion serve human beings in different ways and need not be in competition. Both institutions are necessary for society's well-being.

GLOSSARY

agnostic   a person who is undecided about the existence of God.

atheist   a person who denies the existence of God.

civil religion   a type of religion, peculiar to America, which blends a belief in a nondenominational deity and patriotism.

cult   a loosely organized group whose members respond to experience on an emotional rather than on a rational level.

denomination   a formal organized religious group within a church.

monotheist   a person who believes in one God.

moral community   according to Durkheim, a group of people of one faith who share a sense of kinship and integration with each other.

polytheist   a person who believes in two or more gods.

profane things   according to Durkheim, the everyday, ordinary, commonplace items in the world.

religion   a social institution characterized by a belief in the sacred quality of the supernatural, a set of rituals, and a moral code.

religiosity   interest and participation in religious activities.

religious beliefs   the convictions people hold concerning the things they consider sacred.

religious practices   the expression people give to their religious beliefs.

sacred things   according to Durkheim, those elements that are considered by members of a religious group to be rare and awe-inspiring.

sect   a small group that separates itself from a denomination and which may eventually evolve into a denomination itself.

secularization   the process by which religion becomes less influential in a society.

totem   a plant, animal, or piece of sculptured wood or stone believed to have supernatural powers.

REFERENCES

1. Glenn M. Vernon, *Sociology of Religion.* New York: McGraw-Hill, 1962, p. 43.
2. Vernon, pp. 55–56.
3. Émile Durkheim, *The Elementary Forms of Religious Life.* Trans. by Joseph Ward Swain. New York: The Free Press, 1965, p. 62.
4. *The Gallup Opinion Index—Religion in America,* Report no. 130, 1976, p. 14.
5. Charles Y. Glock and Rodney Stark, *American Piety: The Nature of Religious Commitment.* Berkeley: University of California Press, 1968.
6. *Gallup Poll,* p. 26.
7. Max Weber, *The Protestant Ethic and the Spirit of Capitalism.* New York: Charles Scribner's Sons, 1958.
8. David O. Moberg, *The Church as a Social Institution.* Englewood Cliffs, N.J.: Prentice-Hall, 1962, p. 88.
9. *Yearbook of American Churches,* 1975.
10. Gerhard Lenski, *The Religious Factor.* Garden City, N.Y.: Doubleday, 1961.
11. Robert N. Bellah, "Civil Religion in America." *Daedalus.* Winter 1967.
12. *Gallup Poll,* p. 56.
13. Dean R. Hoge, *Commitment on Campus: Changes in Religion and Values over Five Decades.* Philadelphia: Westminister Press, 1974.
14. Winthrop S. Hudson, *Religion in America.* 2nd ed. New York: Charles Scribner's Sons, 1973, p. 432.
15. Bronislaw Malinowski, *Science, Magic, and Religion.* Garden City, N.Y.: Anchor Books, 1954.

269

SUGGESTED READINGS

Berger, Peter L. *A Rumor of Angels: Modern Society and the Rediscovery of the Supernatural.* Garden City, N.Y.: Doubleday, 1970.

   Amusing short essay on the role of religion in modern society, claiming that experience cannot be understood without a belief in the supernatural.

Cox, Harvey. *The Secular City.* New York: Macmillan, 1965.

   An examination of the rise of urbanization, the collapse of traditional religion, and new possibilities.

Demerath, N. J., III. *Social Class in American Protestantism.* Chicago: Rand McNally, 1965.

   An analysis of the relationship between social class and religiosity, using the sect typology.

Lenski, Gerhard. *The Religious Factor.* Garden City, N.Y.: Doubleday, 1961.

   An empirical study, showing differences between white Protestants, black Protestants, Catholics, and Jews in economic and political attitudes and behaviors.

Plowman, Edward E. *The Jesus Movement in America.* Moonachie, N.J.: Pyramid Publications, 1971.

   A good descriptive account of this recent movement.

9

Economy

Since the beginning of history, human beings have had certain basic physical *needs*. For example, members of all societies have had a need for food and shelter. Similarly, the members of every society have had certain material *wants*. These wants can vary from a new mask for ceremonial dances to a new sports car. The mechanism designed to satisfy such needs and wants is known as the *economic institution*. In this chapter we will focus on the functions of the economic institution, the types of economic organization, and the social forces that affect the economy. We will also take a look at economic growth.

What Is the Economic Institution?

The *economic institution* can be defined as the ways people in a society produce, distribute, and consume goods and services. Although the economic institution is universal, societies differ as to the kinds of economic institutions they have created. For example, the !Kung Bushmen of the Kalahari Desert have a hunting and gathering economy—they depend on naturally occurring plant and animal food sources for survival. In contrast, Americans and Canadians possess an industrial economy since they rely on machines and technology to provide them with most essentials.

Although economic life and social life may seem to be far apart, these two spheres overlap considerably. During an economic depression, for instance, crime and suicide rates and the incidence of mental illness tend to rise. On a more personal level, when individuals acquire a large amount of money, they may tend to purchase such items as yachts, which are traditionally reserved for members of the upper social classes. An entire area of research called *economic sociology* deals with the interrelationships between the economic institution and the social world.

As with any other institution, the economic institution serves a variety of purposes or functions. Let us take a look at what these functions are.

Functions of the Economic Institution

The functions of the economic institution can be classified as *primary* or *secondary*. The primary function concerns the production and distribution of goods and services. Secondary functions pertain to social ranking and the distribution of power. Each of these sociologically significant functions will be discussed in this section.

"The only thing I believe in is my Volvo."

PRIMARY FUNCTION: PRODUCTION AND DISTRIBUTION

In the broadest sense, the primary function of the economic institution is to provide the goods and services the members of a society feel they need or want. In order to fulfill this function, two tasks are involved. First, the members of a society must devise ways in which to produce these goods and services. Second, they must distribute these products among themselves. How people accomplish these two tasks—production and distribution—differs considerably from one society to another.

For example, in one society, cosmetics might be manufactured in a large factory and sold by a department store. In another society, aprons might be handmade at home and sold directly to the consumer. Both systems operate to satisfy the economic needs or wants of people. But they do so in different ways and with different implications as far as human interaction is concerned. In the first society, chances are the producer and consumer will never meet. In the second society, the producer and consumer will come in close contact with each other.

Three Problems

In carrying out the production and distribution functions, the economic institution must solve three specific problems. These are: the decision of *what to produce*, the decision of *how and by whom goods and services are to be produced*, and the decision of *how goods and services will be distributed*.

In every society the decision of *what to produce* must be made. In some societies, such as tribal societies, this may not present a serious problem, since the range of things to produce is limited and unchanging over long periods of time. In technologically advanced societies, on the other hand, the range of possibilities is very great. Since everything cannot be produced all at once, societies must decide what to produce and when.

The second decision that must be made in carrying out the production and distribution function concerns *how and by whom goods and services are to be produced*. For example, should individual farm families handle production or should this task be reserved for large corporate agricultural firms? Should coal miners handle steel production or should they be concerned solely with mining coal? Questions such as these must be answered if the production and distribution functions are to be carried out effectively.

In addition to deciding what to produce and how to produce it, the economic institution of a society must make a third decision—*how the goods and services will be distributed* among the members. Should people be allowed to buy and sell whatever they wish to anyone who can afford to pay the price? Or should controls be imposed so that goods and services are distributed to members of society according to their needs? Of central interest to sociologists is the extent to which goods and services are shared among the members of a society. In other words, societies vary greatly in terms of economic equality, and where one is located on the scale of rich-poor has immense consequences for a person's life. (See Chapter 13 for a more detailed discussion of economic inequality in the United States.)

Supply, Demand, and Price

In our society, each of these three basic questions can be answered partly by the mechanism of *supply and demand*. The supply and demand of goods and services together determine the *price* at which they will sell. Stated simply, if the supply of goods and services increases and the demand decreases, the price will fall; if the supply decreases and the demand increases, the price will rise.

Thus, in solving the problem of what to produce, people try to manufacture what other people want most and are willing to pay for. Similarly, in deciding how goods and services are to be produced, people seek the least costly means of production. For example, if the cost of machinery is high, producers might replace the machine with human labor to maximize their profits. Finally, the distribution of goods and services is also affected by supply and demand. In our society, those who want certain goods and services and are able to pay the price are given a larger slice of the economic "pie."

At one time it was believed that the laws of supply and demand totally regulated the economy. We will see later on in this chapter, however, that various social forces also play an important role in the production and distribution of goods and services.

SECONDARY FUNCTIONS

While the primary function of the economic institution is the production and distribution of goods and services, the manner in which this function is carried out has a variety of consequences for the members of any society. Of major sociological significance are the social ranking and the distribution of power that result.

Social Ranking

As we saw in Chapter 3, early sociologists realized that as a society becomes more technologically advanced, it tends to become more complex in a variety of ways. The sociologically most important way is in the increase of what Émile Durkheim called the *division of labor.*

As the economic structure of a society becomes more complicated, the variety of economic roles and relationships among people increases. In a society that subsists primarily by hunting and gathering, few economic roles are likely to exist. Everyone is involved in the production of the necessities of life, and the goods produced are usually shared equally among all the members of that society. With the development of agriculture and the production of a food surplus, however, some individuals are freed from full-time food production. This allows them to pursue other activities, such as making clothing, building houses, or forging tools. Thus, as societies become complex, there is an increase in the number of economic roles and a further division of labor.

The advent of industrialization causes this economic role specialization to increase tremendously. Consequently, various social classes and status groups come into being. Whereas in a hunting and gathering society few distinctions are likely to exist among members, in an industrial society we have owners, managers, and workers. We also have a widening division between rich and poor with people falling into a variety of other income categories in between. Furthermore, occupational titles become more specialized and specific. People are no longer "doctors"; they are dermatologists, gynecologists, pediatricians, and internists. To a considerable extent, the distinctions among people come to be based on their ability to control or command the rewards of the economic institution. In short, the economic institution within an industrial society serves as a major mechanism for social ranking.

Distribution of Power

Just as one's position in the economic structure affects one's social standing relative to others, it also plays a part in the distribution of power among people. Sources of power include one's influence in making decisions regarding production, distribution, or consumption, as well as wealth. Thus, the chairperson of the board of a large corporation has power both because he or she has wealth and because he or she can greatly influence what and how much will be produced, what price it will be sold for, where it will be distributed, who will be employed to make the product, and what they will be paid. In comparison, the worker in the company's assembly plant can command relatively little wealth and, alone, has almost no power. That is why workers often join together in organized labor unions. There they can gain the power they lack as individuals to influence the course of production.

In summary, different societies have devised different ways of fulfilling the primary economic function of producing and distributing goods and services. Similarly, the secondary functions of social ranking and distribution of power also vary among different societies. We will now take a look at several types of economic organization to see how they have carried out these functions.

Types of Economic Organization

The forms of economic organization that have existed throughout the world have ranged in scope from individual efforts, as in the extended family, to complex organizations of diverse people, as in the modern corporation. In this section we will trace the development and note some of the features of these various forms of economic organization.[1]

THE GUILD SYSTEM

One could, of course, trace modern systems of economic organization back to primitive society. But, the system that is perhaps most responsible for our current economic structure existed from the tenth to thirteenth centuries in Western Europe. This was an era of major economic development and growth. To regulate trade and commerce,

Labor unions enable workers to gain the power that they lack as individuals. Here, striking members of the San Francisco police force demonstrate their demands to the city.

as well as to shut out competition, merchants and workers in the various crafts joined together to form *guilds*. These organizations served to recruit and regulate the manufacture and sale of different products.

In addition, they established a well-defined system of ranks among the merchants and craftspeople. A young member would be an "apprentice" for many years before being allowed to become a "journeyman." And, even then, the guild member worked under a "master craftsman" for years before being promoted to that rank. The public rationale behind this was to guarantee equality. But, in fact, the system operated to restrict innovation and to maintain the authority of the senior members of the guilds. In part, this contributed to the downfall of the guilds because an economic organization needs flexibility in order to survive. The guild system curbed flexibility, thus making it unable to meet the challenge of changing economic conditions.

Originally, the craft (producer) and merchant (seller) guilds were independent of each other. However, over time the craft guilds became dependent on the merchants for marketing and, in the process, lost their own independence.

Ultimately, a variation of the guild system emerged known as the *"putting out" system.* In this arrangement, independent workers manufactured goods for particular merchants who paid the worker a price for each piece produced. The goods were usually of poorer quality than those produced by the guilds, but they also tended to be cheaper. The English textile industry, for example, got its start as independent producers spun wool at home for merchants in their spare time.

In spite of efforts to regulate and suppress the "putting out" system, the power of the guilds was eventually undermined and they ceased to exist. The demise of the guilds marked the transition to a totally new form of economic activity in which both production and the role of the producer became impersonalized and regimented. The factory system had come into being.

THE FACTORY SYSTEM

In the eighteenth century, when factories were starting to appear in England, society was still dominated by a landed aristocracy. The possession of land was wealth, and one's status was determined by lineage or ancestry and the ownership of land. Manufacturing was thus considered an unusual and less respectable way to make money. The reinvestment of profits into expanding businesses was a unique development of the originators of the factory system.

The concept of reinvesting profits may have been an essential aspect of the development of the factory system, but just as important was a second factor—the existence of a pool of excess cheap labor. Such a surplus was caused in part by a plunging death rate and a booming birth rate. Equally significant, though, were several other factors. Prior to this time, there was a relatively clear personal relationship between the employer and employee, almost that of teacher and student. Such a relationship, however, was largely destroyed by factory employment.

The factory system provided the manufacturer with much greater direct control over the speed and amount of production and allowed a sharper watch over quality than had been possible under the "putting out" system. And because of the extension of their productive capacity, the factory owners were able to expand markets and profits.

It was no accident that factories originated in clusters at certain locales in England. Manchester and Sheffield, for example, had the natural water, transportation, and raw material resources essential for enterprises designed to produce items under one roof. In addition, there was an abundance of children who could be put to work as factory operatives. (It was not until the early twentieth century that child labor laws were enacted to forbid such practices.) As these regions developed, large numbers of people migrated to these cities, so that in a brief span of time the population distribution of the country changed dramatically.

The use of steam power and the development of iron and steel machinery greatly increased the factory's capacity to produce and furthered the standardization of goods and the specialization of tasks. A much greater number and variety of goods became available to many more people than before. But much was lost in the process. For, as the factory brought an increased ability to produce more and more, it also led to a decrease in worker control over labor activities, destroying the intimacy among employer, worker, and consumer, and lowering pride in the product of one's labor (see Chapter 14).

THE CORPORATION

The dominant mode of economic organization in the twentieth century is the corporation, a form of organization that grew with industrialization at about an equal pace. A *corporation* can be defined as a socioeconomic organization consisting of a group of people joined by legal bonds to pursue economic interests for the benefit of those who compose it. A corporation is a legal entity having many of the rights and duties of individuals. That is, a corporation can sue and be sued, hold property, and enter into contracts. But corporations cannot be totally regulated in the way an individual can. For example, a corporation cannot be imprisoned for committing an offense (although individual members can). Thus, a corporation exists independently of the lives of any or all of its members.

278

In the United States a handful of corporations employs most of our working population. In fact, 5 percent of American corporations employ over three-fourths of all workers.[2] These giant corporations have achieved such tremendous economic power that their individual assets are greater than the assets of some states in the United States. The Exxon corporation, for example, has a fleet of ships that is larger in number than the navies of many countries. The eight major oil companies in our nation control almost 65 percent of our oil reserves, 50 percent of production, and between 50 and 60 percent of refining and marketing.[3] Therefore, a relatively small number of organizations has considerable economic power.

Perhaps the major feature of modern corporations, other than their immense influence and power, is the separation between ownership and control. In the past, under the factory system, the owner controlled the plant directly. Now a new stratum has been created—corporate managers—who are neither the producers of the goods nor the owners of the firm engaged in production. While the stockholders technically "own" the corporation, it is the salaried managers who run it. Increasingly, the owners of corporations are not individuals, but other organizations including large corporations, religious groups, universities, insurance companies, and labor unions.

This ownership of one corporation by another has greatly altered the relationship between the producer and the product. Just as the worker has become alienated from the products of his or her labor, the owners of corporations may have little relationship with the goods and services the firm produces. Indeed, in some instances, the stockholders may not even know what the company they own makes or sells. This has greatly reduced the accountability of owners for the quality of their products and the conduct of the corporation. Even though the corporate managers can be held criminally responsible for misconduct (as occurred in the 1961 electrical conspiracy where several officials of General Electric were punished for price-fixing),[4] it is difficult to blame the "corporation" itself because of its structure.

RISE OF THE MULTINATIONALS

According to sociologist Irving Louis Horowitz, "the emergence of the multinational corporation is the paramount economic fact of the present epoch."[5] As Horowitz defines *multinational corporations,* they tend to have the following characteristics:[6]

1. They operate in at least six foreign nations.
2. Their foreign subsidiaries account for at least 10 to 20 percent of total assets, sales, or the labor force.

3. They have annual sales or income of more than $100 million.
4. They have an above-average rate of growth and profit margins.
5. They are most often found in high technology industries that devote a high proportion of assets to research, advertising, and marketing.

Horowitz speculates that we may very well be entering an era in which corporate giants may be exercising more international political power than governments. He theorizes that although formal borders

Globe-trotting Americans can enjoy a taste of home in many countries throughout the world now that McDonald's has become a multinational corporation. Amsterdam, the Netherlands, is one foreign city in which you can find a Big Mac or a Filet O'Fish.

may be retained between nations, an international one-world society will eventually emerge, which will be dominated by relatively few corporate enterprises. These corporations will have great impact on the economic well-being of people throughout the world.

As these firms grow in size and number, several profound changes are likely to take place in international economic and political relations. Among those discussed by Horowitz is a growth in militant unionism. Workers throughout the world are competing with one another on a broader scope than ever before. High-paid workers in one nation find themselves competing with low-paid workers in another country who are making essentially identical products. The result of this, Horowitz claims, will be that, as Marx predicted, the working class will develop greater class solidarity than loyalty to a nation or a government. Indeed, a study by sociologist Koya Azumi, et al. suggests that there are more differences in attitudes between managers and workers within the countries he studied than between workers in different countries.[7]

A second change, according to Horowitz, is that the rise of multinationals has operated to reduce the likelihood of international confrontations between countries. When major economic interests require cooperation across national boundaries, the countries pursuing these interests are not likely to want to upset the balance by engaging in dispute.

On the other hand, a major power and a less powerful country may sometimes engage in hostilities when the interests of the corporation are threatened. The involvement of the United States in the Vietnam struggle, for instance, may have been sparked by ideological and world political motives, but the interests of several oil companies operating in the area were also involved. Similarly, the desires of multinational firms can influence governmental relations with other countries. Sometimes a powerful government might even become directly involved in the internal affairs of another country for the benefit of the multinational corporation.[8] (This happened in 1974 when International Telephone and Telegraph approached the CIA about overthrowing a government in Chile that the corporation considered unfriendly to it.) But just what the ultimate influence of these organizations will be in the future is presently difficult to determine accurately. It seems clear, however, that their influence will be considerable.

Social Forces and the Economy

In an earlier section we discussed how the mechanism of supply and demand affects the production and distribution of goods and services. We also mentioned that various social forces have an effect on the economy. In this section we will focus on some of these social factors and note how they influence the economic institution.

FORMS OF EXCHANGE

According to sociologist Neil Smelser, there are at least three forms of exchange that are not governed by economic factors.[9] The three forms of exchange described by Smelser include *reciprocative exchange, redistributive exchange,* and *exchange.*

Reciprocative Exchange

The gifts people give to a bridal couple or to a baby, the services of a friend who helps fix the car, or the "good turn" offered by someone in times of need all involve the exchange of goods and services, but it would be inappropriate and insulting to offer to pay for them. Rather, we expect that the receiver of the gift may someday offer a gift or a service in return. Such reciprocative exchanges, of course, may be based on considerations of social relationships or status, but they hardly can be thought of as oriented toward economic gain. For example, although we may want to increase our social prestige by giving a bridal couple a very expensive or unique gift, we do not expect to gain economically from it.

Redistributive Exchange

The redistribution of wealth by means of charity may also affect the operation of the economy, but such redistribution is not governed by economic factors. People may, of course, give away some portion of their income in order to take advantage of a tax deduction and, in this respect, charity can be seen as an economic-oriented activity. But frequently people donate to charity out of humanitarian motives, not economic ones.

Exchange

Mobilizing economic resources to achieve public goals is another from of exchange that is not governed solely by economic forces. This could consist of such things as taxation, drafting people into military service, or the direct appropriation of income or possessions. Such cultural or social motives as threats to national security, cultural values of equality, or an orientation to "progress" are used to explain this form of exchange.

MARKETING

The methods by which products are marketed also affect the economy. Yet, like the forms of exchange described by Smelser, the effect of these methods cannot be explained solely in terms of economic factors. Two marketing methods with which we will be concerned here are advertising and the sale.

Advertising

Advertising plays a major role in our lives, affecting both important and ordinary everyday decisions. In his book *The Selling of the President, 1968,*[10] journalist Joe McGinnis has contended that advertising even influenced the outcome of a presidential election. Had it not been for the carefully planned advertising campaign by Richard Nixon's staff, history might have been different.

In 1976, over $33 billion was spent in the United States on advertising, the same amount spent by the federal government on health.[11] If we turn on the radio or television, or flip through any newspaper or magazine, we can see abundant evidence of how this money was spent. In fact, when reading a magazine or watching a television program, we often complain that there seems to be more advertising than anything else.

Advertising creates a demand for products in several ways. First, it makes the product and the results of its use seem desirable. We really want our teeth to look their "whitest white" and believe Brand X toothpaste will help us to achieve that goal. We even want our dog's teeth to look their cleanest and buy a certain product that we hope will perform that task.

Second, advertising leads us to believe favorable social consequences will ensue from using a product. Thus, we should not buy a particular soft drink because it tastes better than another (often it tastes the same), or is healthy (which it almost never is); rather, we should buy it to gain popularity. After all, the men and women in the commercial are surrounded by attractive people and seem to be enjoying themselves. Author Jerry Della Femina makes this point in his book *From Those Wonderful Folks Who Gave You Pearl Harbor.*[12] Here he shows how the advertising for a particular product may not concentrate on the benefits of the product at all. For example, advertisements for various airlines sometimes concentrate on flight destinations rather than on benefits, which often do not differ from those offered by the competition. Similarly, advertisements for Virginia Slims cigarettes ("You've come a long way, baby!") stress the "liberated" woman and not the cigarette's tar and nicotine content.

Third, advertising creates the image of an affluent society and leads us to believe that by purchasing advertised products we will become part of that society. We rarely see a lower-class housewife making a pitch for a floor cleaner, although her floors get as dirty as anyone else's. Rather, we usually see a middle-class housewife inside a modern home complete with the latest appliances.

283

Many companies use "psychological probing" of consumers to help sell their products. By discovering what consumers *really* want (this may differ from what they say they want) they can boost their sales substantially. In *The Hidden Persuaders*,[13] Vance Packard shows how this can be done. When cake mixes first appeared on the market, they required the housewife to add only water. Consequently, many women felt the mixes were "a sign of poor housekeeping and threatened to deprive them of a traditional source of praise."[14] Thus, although the product saved time, it was not readily accepted. Manufacturers then recognized that we all have a need to feel creative and altered the mixes accordingly. Instead of adding just water, housewives now have to add milk and fresh eggs. As a result, women were "persuaded" to buy the product and sales boomed.

Although advertising usually increases the wants of people, in some cases it can have a negative effect on consumer demand. Rather than spurring sales, it can cause a product's popularity to dwindle. Della Femina gives several instances where this has occurred. In one instance, a beer company used a series of ethnically oriented commercials to sell its product. Members of many of New York's ethnic groups were shown at such events as a party, a wedding, or a family gathering. Theoretically, New York's beer drinkers were supposed to be able to identify with the product. Instead of selling beer, however, the commercials generated antagonism. Since all of the groups really disliked each other, members of one group refused to buy a product consumed by members of another.

Another case involved advertisements for a painless antiseptic for cuts and scratches. Although the company thought it had a good product, consumer demand decreased. Why? Because people felt they had to experience a burning sensation before they could believe that such a product was working. When research scientists added alcohol to the product, sales once again started to rise.

APPLYING SOCIOLOGY

The woman who uses a particular perfume and is surrounded by attractive men, the man who drives around in a certain car and is the envy of all, and the fun-loving crowd sipping a popular soft drink are only three of the images companies create to sell their products. How influential do you think such images are in boosting a company's sales? How often do you buy an item just because you saw it advertised on television or in a magazine? To what extent do you believe the mass media influence your spending habits?

The sale is more than an economic exchange— it is an interaction between buyer and seller that involves role-playing and is affected by compatability and social status.

The Sale

The sale, which is an important aspect of our economy, is also governed to some extent by social and cultural considerations. The sale is a form of interaction that can be understood as a form of role-playing by the participants. The seller in the interaction might play any of a number of roles. He or she might act as an ''aggressive'' salesperson. Everyone has encountered the ''pushy'' salesperson who can be very irritating. Sometimes it seems as if such a person is able to sell in spite of him or herself. Then, too, the buyer might play a variety of roles, for example, the tough negotiator in a car sale, the ''I know what I want!'' appliance buyer, or the ''I can't make up my mind!'' purchaser of a pair of shoes. Many of us patronize certain stores merely because we like the salespeople, or avoid others (which may even be superior) because we are not compatible with the salespeople. The interaction between buyer and seller, then, consists of a social exchange, not merely an economic one. And, the character of this social exchange varies by such factors as social class as well as group membership.

For example, W. T. Tucker has analyzed the typical sales techniques that can be found in three different classes of furniture stores.[15] One class sells largely to lower- and lower-middle-class customers. Another caters to middle-class customers and handles better quality merchandise, although of standard manufacture. The third sells high-fashion merchandise and draws a high status, affluent clientele. As Tucker notes, the social role of the salesperson in each of these types of stores must vary in terms of the merchandise and the status of the customers.

In the low-status store, the salesperson is usually of higher status than the customer and operates on the assumption that the customer knows less than he or she does about the merchandise. As a result, the salesperson is apt to act in an abrupt forceful manner.

285

In the second-level store, the customer and salesperson may be of equal status. Rather than "selling" the customer, he or she is more likely to treat the potential buyer as an equal. Thus, the salesperson will tend to act friendly and deferential to the customer, relying on establishing a relationship of trust, and will try to emphasize the "nice guy" or helper role.

The seller in a high-fashion store probably is very knowledgeable about products it carries, but is of lower status than the customer. As a result, he or she must rely on expertise in the buyer-seller relationship, often deferring outwardly to the customer's wishes. Sometimes the seller even refuses to sell a product to the customer because it would not "be right" for the person.

In Tucker's terms, the underlying social relationship between buyer and seller in these three different stores can be described in terms of the salesperson's private feelings as follows:[16]

> [Lower and lower-middle class]—"Look, I'm a busy man. Make up your mind and let's get it over with."
>
> Middle Class—"Look, I'm a nice guy, and I've tried hard. Won't one of the things I've shown you do at all?"
>
> High Fashion—"This is an absolutely perfect combination. If you don't buy it, I'll know that you either can't afford to purchase in this store or are completely lacking in taste."

While this illustration may be a bit exaggerated, considerations of status, as well as the norms of social congeniality are often involved in economic relations. Anyone, for example, who has been snubbed by a waiter in a "high-class" restaurant realizes that it sometimes takes more than money to engage in an economic exchange. Economic exchanges that take place between businesses, governments, or any other buyers and sellers are also affected by social factors.

Just as marketing forces cannot be understood solely in economic terms, consumer credit also can be viewed as a social factor affecting the economy. In the next section we will examine this influential force.

APPLYING SOCIOLOGY

Business enterprises do not always purchase what they need from suppliers that can give them the best price, delivery schedule, or credit terms. Sometimes they will buy only from firms with which they have been dealing for years. Why might this be the case? What factors, other than economic ones, might be involved in the relationships between businesses? How might these factors affect the production and distribution of some goods or services?

Many Americans have at least one credit card, and more than half of all American families incur debts on installment credit.

CONSUMER CREDIT

At the turn of the century, economist Thorstein Veblen used the term "conspicuous consumption" to describe the spending patterns of Americans. According to Veblen, wealthy Americans wanted others to know that they had a surplus of wealth. Consequently, they spent all their time, money, and efforts to demonstrate this fact. As Veblen noted, "In order to stand well in the eyes of the community, it [was] necessary to come up to a certain, somewhat indefinite conventional standard of wealth."[17] This philosophy encouraged citizens to purchase all that they could as a means of impressing others. If we look around us, we will note that such a philosophy still prevails in our society. Today, however, much of our purchasing is done with credit.

Consumer credit includes both *installment credit* and *noninstallment credit*. With installment credit, a person can purchase an item by paying for it over a period of time, usually paying substantial interest charges. Many expensive items such as automobiles are purchased "on time." People who use noninstallment credit can pay for their purchases at a later date (usually within thirty days) in one lump sum without having to pay any interest or carrying charges. Department store charge accounts generally involve the use of noninstallment credit.

As a result of such credit, more than half of the families in the United States today owe installment debt.[18] At the end of 1976, Americans owed $217.8 billion,[19] which averages out to over $1,000 for every man, woman, and child. Clearly, such slogans as "Buy now, pay later!" and "No money down—up to 24 months to pay!" have had an impact on our population. Why do we purchase items on credit? Which segments of society are most likely to use credit?

Installment buying affects all segments of the population. The belief that the rich pay in cash while the poor rely on credit is a myth that is reflected in the preceding paragraph. Clearly, over one-half of our population is not poor. In fact, in 1973, the average person who borrowed from a finance company was a semi-skilled or skilled worker, had an income of between $6,000 and $12,000, and frequently owned a home.[20]

The willingness with which people go into debt can be explained by several factors, some of which we will now examine. For one thing, many people would have to go without items they feel are necessary if it were not for installment credit. There would be considerably fewer cars on the roads, a greater percentage of unfurnished living rooms, and a sharp decrease in the number of appliances sold. Through the use of installment credit, people can buy and begin using such items immediately.

287

FOCUS ON: CREDIT

Although consumer credit is used by all classes of people, the poor are particularly vulnerable to its negative effects. In *The Poor Pay More,* sociologist David Caplovitz discusses the relationship between credit and the ghetto poor.

Caplovitz notes that for the most part the poor cannot improve their status through their jobs. Consequently, they turn to consumption as a means of achieving the American dream. Such articles as expensive television sets, appliances, and automobiles become substitutes for their blocked aspirations. But the poor do not have the necessary cash to pay for their purchases. As a result, they resort to credit. And the institution of credit has been adapted to meet the needs of the ghetto poor. For example, some forms of credit are extended to those that might be considered bad credit risks. In addition, rather than having to make large monthly payments, the poor can pay for their purchases in very small amounts over an extended period of time.

Despite such advantages, however, the adaptation of credit for the poor also has negative consequences. Frequently they are victimized by unscrupulous credit practices. For example, they are often convinced to sign contracts without understanding the conditions. High-pressure door-to-door salespeople often persuade them to buy unnecessary items for much higher prices than those charged by stores. Many times they are lured to stores by misleading advertising and the easy availability of credit and wind up purchasing expensive items.

In addition, when the poor sign installment contracts with ghetto merchants, they are often not subject to the same guarantees as are other consumers. Whereas other customers usually can exchange merchandise if they are not satisfied with it, the poor who pay on credit often do not have this option. They must continue to meet the payments regardless of whether the merchandise is defective, unsatisfactory, or not what they thought they were getting initially. Also, if a merchant does not live up to a guarantee, the customer can very rarely do anything

Source: David Caplovitz, *The Poor Pay More,* New York: The Free Press, 1967.

A second reason is related to the first. Many people believe that by going into debt they will be saving money in the long run. For example, if they buy a washing machine their laundry bills will be considerably lower. Or, perhaps the washing machine is on sale. Then despite the interest they will have to pay, the washing machine will still be a good buy.

Third, many people equate installment credit with mortgages. Since it is all right to purchase a house without paying for it all at once, why not purchase other items as well? Such reasoning demonstrates the change in attitude that has accompanied the easy availability of installment credit. Whereas in the past, people borrowed only in desperation—to meet such emergencies as long-term sicknesses or unemployment—today borrowing is a sign of prosperity and a contribution to such prosperity.[21] In fact, many people who rely on installment credit can afford to pay for their purchases in cash. The con-

about it. The customer is often ignorant of the law or cannot afford to miss time at work in order to take legal action.

The penalties for not meeting credit terms are also very severe, and the poor, who often have difficulty meeting their payment deadlines, must pay them. The merchandise in question can be repossessed, salaries can be withheld, or other goods not involved in the credit transaction can be confiscated. In one instance, a New York City housewife lost a television set, a radio, and a bicycle over a relatively minor purchase. Because she was unable to pay $52 (which in itself was questionable), a marshal took all those items as compensation. And such confiscation is legal. Any item not essential for living can be seized and sold at a public auction in order to pay off the debt.

As a result of credit practices in the ghetto, Caplovitz concludes that the poor pay more for their purchases. Why do you think the poor have not acted to curb unscrupulous credit practices? Do you believe the merchants are totally at fault? What valid excuses might they have for their credit policies? What do you think can be done to improve the situation?

venience of credit just makes substantial purchases more accessible, so people use it.

At any rate, installment credit is definitely a social force affecting the economy. People are purchasing more and more items that they would not or could not buy otherwise. When examining consumer credit, however, we also have to look at noninstallment credit, another important social force.

Whereas installment credit is used by all segments of the population, the use of noninstallment credit is often related to income. To illustrate, in 1972, 81 percent of families making at least $25,000 per year used a credit card, while only 17 percent of families making less than $3,000 a year did so.[22] One of the major reasons for this is that those in the low-income brackets are considered poor credit risks and usually are not issued such credit privileges.

Because those using noninstallment credit are more likely to be in

289

the higher income brackets, their reasons for using credit often differ from those using installment credit. For the most part, people using noninstallment credit do so for convenience. It is easy to walk into a store and say, "Charge it" when one is on a vacation and does not have extra cash on hand. Credit cards also enable consumers to order goods over the telephone, treat themselves to expensive meals, and travel around the world virtually penniless. An article in *The New York Times* reported the story of a man who was arrested after fraudulently using a Diner's Club card to finance a $27,278 tour of Europe that included accommodations at some of the finest hotels in Rome, Paris, Vienna, and Zurich.[23]

Although circumstances surrounding the use of noninstallment credit differ from those surrounding installment credit, both have virtually the same effect on the economy. As we mentioned, installment credit leads people to purchase items they ordinarily would not buy. Similarly, noninstallment credit often leads consumers to buy articles that are not really needed or that are more expensive than usual. With the opportunity to use credit a distinct possibility, many often find it hard to resist temptation. In short, both types of credit have spurred the economy and have contributed to increasing prosperity.

CONSUMER BEHAVIOR

Although advertising can create a "demand" for many things, and credit makes it easier for people to satisfy their wants, not all people want the same types of things. For example, while some people relish owning a farm in the country, others prefer city living. Similarly, some people favor contemporary-style furniture over colonial furniture, while in other cases the reverse is true. Sociologically, wants vary in terms of culture, class, and group (see also Chapter 13).[24]

Culture

Many Americans would probably not eat raw fish unless they were starving (and maybe not even then), although the Japanese consider it a delicacy. Few Americans savor the hot and spicy food of India, while many Indians would not eat meat. In short, what people want and how they choose to satisfy their needs are influenced by their culture (or subculture).

The more diverse the culture of a society, the more ways people have to satisfy their wants and needs. In turn, the demands placed on the productive sector increase. The diverse population of a city like San Francisco, for instance, offers an immense variety of restaurants and shops so that in San Francisco one can buy just about anything. A homogeneous community, on the other hand, may be able to offer little to the traveler who has varied tastes.

A small, homogeneous community may have all its consumer needs met by one general store, like this country store in Maine *(top)*. However, a large, diverse population of a city like Philadelphia may need several shopping districts to satisfy consumer demands *(bottom)*.

Class

The bright red, tasseled, velvet couch and purple, gold-trimmed, matching chairs one finds marketed in some stores would be repugnant to some buyers but considered beautiful by others. The antique clock with the cracked wood cover would be considered a piece of junk by one person, but another would spend a good deal of money to own it. These differences in taste and corresponding consumer demand are strongly influenced by social class.

In part, differences in taste are the result of the very limited communication that occurs among social classes. People tend to "stick to their own kind," and relatively little personal interaction occurs among people of different classes. Hence, one's tastes are usually derived from one's family and associates and are constantly reinforced by patterns of interaction.

Furthermore, what we buy serves as symbols of status. So strong is the tie between social class and possessions that people who attempt to imitate members of another class by purchasing goods characteristic of that class are often scorned by their friends. For example, a working-class man who purchases a ticket to the opera might be laughed at by his peers. Our economic behavior is also used as a measure of our moral attributes. Words like "spendthrift," "miser," "tightwad," and the like are all used to describe a person in negative or positive terms according to his or her economic behavior. And, as with what one buys, how much one spends and how that spending is evaluated is affected by one's social-class standing.

Group

What we buy is also conditioned by the groups with whom we associate. These include age, ethnic, regional, and occupational groups. Teenagers and young adults, for example, share a style of dress that is different from that of older persons. Similarly, dried fish, rice noodles, and Chinese cabbage may not sell very well in Mountain Home, Idaho. But riding boots, saddles, and camping gear are not common items of trade in New York's Chinatown either.

As with culture and class, if the groups that comprise a society are separated by sharp boundaries, their consuming patterns will probably differ substantially. If, on the other hand, they are separated by boundaries that are less distinct and are easier to cross, there is more of a chance that they will resemble each other as far as tastes and purchases are concerned.

THE "THROW-AWAY" SOCIETY

Our attitude toward our possessions is another social factor affecting the economy. If we drive along any highway and note the array of soda bottles, beer cans, and assorted rubbish that lines the road, we can conclude that we do not feel a sense of permanence toward many products. As soon as they have finished serving our needs, we simply discard them. Clearly, we live in what Alvin Toffler in his book *Future Shock* called a "throw-away" society.[25]

One major factor contributing to the throw-away spirit is the limited uses products are designed to have. Such products as paper plates, disposable cigarette lighters, and nonrefillable pens are all virtually useless after they have served their purpose. These products, in turn, cause us to develop what Toffler calls a "throw-away mentality." We learn that it is all right to buy new products to replace the old ones since the latter are no longer functional.

Another major factor contributing to our wastefulness is *planned obsolescence*. This can be defined as the deliberate attempt by a manufacturer to cause a product to become outmoded. According to Vance Packard in his book *The Waste Makers*,[26] such obsolescence can take three forms: *obsolescence of function, obsolescence of quality,* and *obsolescence of desirability.*

Such factors as planned obsolescence and the rapidly changing needs of people in a rapidly changing world have contributed to a "throw-away" society in the United States.

In the first instance, a product becomes outmoded when an improved product comes on the market. For example, the old-fashioned egg beater was replaced by the electric mixer. Similarly, the washing machine replaced the scrub board.

In the second case, a product is designed to wear out after a certain period of time. Electric light bulbs and women's hosiery are only two examples of products that have a deliberately planned life span.

In the third type of obsolescence, products become outmoded in the consumer's mind. They are still structurally sound and capable of performing their functions adequately, but a change in style or design makes them less desirable. We do not have to look far for examples of obsolescence of desirability. A quick glance at the automobile industry or the clothing industry will provide us with all the examples we need. Probably many of us have closets full of clothes that are in perfect condition but are no longer in style. As a result, we claim that we have nothing to wear despite appearances to the contrary.

293

> **APPLYING SOCIOLOGY**
>
> Toffler and Packard present two different arguments regarding planned obsolescence. Which view seems more correct to you? Does each argument seem to have some merit? Can you think of any other forces that might account for the rate of product turnover in our lives?

Although we tend to regard obsolescence of function favorably— we applaud such improvements as the refrigerator and the washing machine—we often consider the other two types of obsolescence to be dishonest. Yet all three types have the same effect on the economy. All cause us to throw away the old in favor of the new, whether or not the new really represents an improvement.

Toffler argues that planned obsolescence only partially accounts for the rate of product turnover in our lives. He believes that in a society that is changing as rapidly as ours is, the needs of people also change. And as their needs change, people try to satisfy them, thus causing products to become outmoded without deliberate planning. At any rate, whether our attitudes stem from planned obsolescence or rapid social change, we are clearly a throw-away society.

Economic Growth

In the previous section we have mentioned that advertising, consumer credit, and the "throw-away spirit" all promote the growth of the economy. It seems, then, that growth is good since it accompanies prosperity. In actuality, though, economic growth also has such negative effects as overpopulation, an increase in pollution, and a depletion of natural resources. Consequently, the merits of economic growth have been and continue to be debated by many social scientists. A look at the growth/no growth controversy will point out the arguments of each side.

Fifty years ago our concern with material well-being was overwhelming. A chicken in every pot and two cars in every garage was the ideal toward which Americans strove. At that time, few people questioned whether or not economic growth was a good thing. It was assumed that growth automatically meant progress.

In recent years, however, there have been numerous attacks on economic growth. Opponents have shown that growth leads to overpopulation, contamination of our air and water, exploitation of our environment, and dehumanization in the work world as machines replace human labor. In addition, they argue that we will run out of natural re-

Whereas opponents of economic growth cite such negative consequences as environmental pollution *(left)*, proponents of economic growth cite increased employment opportunity as one of its benefits *(right)*.

sources and sources of energy if economic growth continues. Such antigrowth proponents paint a dismal picture of the future. How can anyone counter such arguments?

Those favoring economic growth view its effects differently. They note benefits rather than negative consequences. For one thing, the proponents say that economic growth will enable us to develop new technologies so that we can locate new resources and fuels to combat the energy shortage. Second, economic growth will help alleviate unemployment by providing job opportunities. Third, such growth will help to combat social inequality by financing such programs as food allotments, welfare payments, medical care to the poor, and so on.

At this point it is difficult to say which of these views is correct, if indeed either is. Events usually can be evaluated only in retrospect—that is, after they happen. But whichever policy toward economic growth we pursue, it is certain to have a profound influence on our society. Economic growth is one of the key issues in the present as well as the future.

SUMMARY

The *economic institution*, which is universal, can be defined as the ways people in a society produce, distribute, and consume goods and services. This institution serves several functions. The primary function is to produce and distribute the goods and services members need or want. In carrying out this function, societies must make three decisions. These are: what to produce, how and by whom goods and services are to be produced, and how they are to be distributed. These decisions are usually based on the laws of supply and demand. However, other social forces also play a role.

Secondary functions include social ranking and the distribution of power. As societies become more complex, the division of labor increases and distinctions among people arise. This, in turn, leads to an unequal distribution of power depending upon one's position in the decision-making hierarchy.

Types of economic organization have varied throughout the world and throughout history. An early form of organization, on which our modern economic system is based, is the *guild system*. Because of its inflexibility, it eventually gave way to the *factory system*. Such a system was characterized by a decrease in worker, owner, consumer, and product interaction. The twentieth century is dominated by the *corporation*, which is a socioeconomic organization consisting of a group of people joined by legal bonds to pursue economic interests. Corporations have considerable economic and political power. In addition, unlike the old factory system, they are controlled by corporate managers rather than owners. The *multinational corporation* is becoming the dominant form of economic organization in the world.

In addition to the laws of supply and demand, several social forces affect the economy of a society. One such social force is marketing, which takes the form of advertising and selling. The availability of consumer credit—both installment and noninstallment credit—also affects the economy. *Installment credit* allows a consumer to pay for an item over a period of time usually with substantial interest. *Noninstallment credit* allows the consumer to pay for purchases in one lump sum without any interest or finance charges. People in all social classes use consumer credit.

Consumer behavior is influenced by the culture in which people live, the class to which they belong, and the group with whom they are associated. There can be marked differences among such groups.

Another social force in our society is *planned obsolescence*, which is the deliberate attempt to cause a product to become outmoded. There are three types of obsolescence—obsolescence of function, quality, and desirability.

One of the major controversies facing modern societies is the question of whether or not we should pursue a policy of economic growth. Those who oppose growth claim it will lead to environmental destruction. Those favoring growth believe it will enable us to develop new technologies. Although the debate cannot be resolved, economic growth is a key issue in our society.

GLOSSARY

conspicuous consumption   a term coined by Thorstein Veblen to describe how wealthy Americans were concerned with impressing others with their wealth.

corporation   a socioeconomic organization that has certain rights such as owning property, signing contracts, and pursuing economic interests for its own benefit.

division of labor   the distribution of tasks and services in a society by its members.

economic institution   the ways people in a society produce, distribute, and consume goods and services.

economic sociology   an area of sociology that deals with the interrelationships between the economic institution and the social world.

exchange   according to sociologist Neil Smelser, a form of exchange, not governed by economic factors, in which economic resources are mobilized to achieve public goals.

factory system   a form of economic organization that revolved around manufacturing.

guild system   a form of economic organization in which persons in the same trade joined together to regulate trade and commerce.

installment credit   a form of credit that enables a person to purchase an item by paying for it over a period of time with substantial interest.

multinational corporation   multimillion dollar business establishment that operates and has extensive investment in production and distribution in at least six foreign countries, wielding enough power to affect governmental relationships with these countries.

noninstallment credit   a form of credit that enables a person to pay for an item in one lump sum without having to pay any interest or carrying charges.

planned obsolescence   the deliberate attempt by a manufacturer to cause a product to become outmoded.

"putting out" system   a variation of the guild system in which independent workers manufactured goods for particular merchants who paid the workers a price for each piece produced.

reciprocative exchange   according to sociologist Neil Smelser, a form of exchange, not governed by economic factors, in which gifts and services are given and received reciprocally.

redistributive exchange   according to sociologist Neil Smelser, a form of exchange, not governed by economic factors, in which wealth is redistributed.

REFERENCES

1. This discussion relies heavily on Wilbert E. Moore, *Industrial Relations and the Social Order*. New York: Macmillan, 1951.

2. U.S. Department of Commerce. *1972 Census of Manufacturers, Vol. I, Subject and Special Statistics*. Washington, D.C.: U.S. Government Printing Office.

3. Richard Parker, "The Energy Crisis is Coming." *Ramparts* (March 1974): 30.

4. Richard A. Smith, "The Incredible Electrical Conspiracy—Part I." *Fortune* 63 (April 1961): 132–218; Smith, "Part II." *Fortune* 63 (May 1961): 161–224.

5. Irving Louis Horowitz, "Capitalism, Communism, and Multinationalism." *Society* (January/February 1974): 32.

6. Horowitz, p. 32.

7. Koya Azumi, David J. Hickson, Dezso Horvath, and Charles J. McMillan, "Trust and Organizational Structure: A Cross-National Comparison." Paper presented at *Cross-Cultural Studies in Organizational Structure*, Hawaii, September 1977.

8. P. G. Bosk, "The Transnational Corporation and Private Foreign Policy." *Society* (January/February 1974): 44–49.

9. Neil J. Smelser, *The Sociology of Economic Life*. Englewood Cliffs, N.J.: Prentice-Hall, 1963, pp. 86–87.

10. Joe McGinnis, *The Selling of the President, 1968*. New York: Pocket Books, 1968.

11. U.S. Bureau of the Census, *Statistical Abstracts of the United States 1977*, Tables 409 and 1445, pp. 250 and 844.

12. Jerry Della Femina, *From Those Wonderful Folks Who Gave You Pearl Harbor*. New York: Simon & Schuster, 1970.

13. Vance Packard, *The Hidden Persuaders*. New York: David McKay, 1957.

14. Packard, p. 77.

15. W. T. Tucker, *The Social Context of Economic Behavior*. New York: Holt, Rinehart & Winston, 1964, pp. 73-81.

16. Tucker, p. 76.

17. Thorstein Veblen, in Robert L. Heilbroner, *The Worldly Philosophers*. New York: Simon & Schuster, 1961, p. 199.

18. Sylvia Porter, *Sylvia Porter's Money Book*. Vol 1, Garden City, N.Y.: Doubleday, 1975, p. 88.

19. *Statistical Abstracts* 1977, Table 859, p. 534.

20. 1975 Financial Facts Yearbook, *National Consumer Finance Yearbook*, p. 65.

21. George Katona, *The Mass Consumption Society*. New York: McGraw-Hill, 1964, p. 235.

22. Lewis Mandell, *Credit Card Use in the United States*. Ann Arbor, Mich.: Institute for Social Research, The University of Michigan, 1972, p. 10.

23. "Big Spender Held on Charge of Using Nonexistent Funds." *The New York Times*, March 12, 1966, p. 11.

24. Tucker, pp. 28–49.

25. Alvin Toffler, *Future Shock*. New York: Bantam, 1970.

26. Vance Packard, *The Waste Makers*. New York: David McKay, 1960.

SUGGESTED READINGS

Bell, Daniel. *The Cultural Contradictions of Capitalism*. New York: Basic Books, 1976.

A major statement by a leading sociologist regarding the problems of managing a complex society under the conditions of unrestrained appetite as dictated by the values of capitalism.

Caplovitz, David. *The Poor Pay More*. New York: The Free Press, 1967.

This book details the economic realities encountered by a group of low-income families in a housing project in New York City. As the title says, the poor do pay more.

Forbe, C. Daryll. *Habitat, Economy, and Society*. New York: Dutton, 1963.

A classic and detailed analysis of the economic and social life of a number of groups at diverse levels of cultural achievement throughout different parts of the world. It provides a clear and stimulating understanding of the interdependence of cultural and economic forces.

Horowitz, Irving Louis. "Capitalism, Communism, and Multinationalism." *Society* (January/February 1974): 32–43.

This entire issue should be consulted for several lively articles on various aspects of the American economy in the mid-1970s.

Jacobs, Jane. *The Economy of Cities*. New York: Random House, 1969.

A controversial look at the economic base of cities. The author argues that rural development occurred after cities appeared.

Moore, Wilbert E. *The Impact of Industry*. Englewood Cliffs, N.J.: Prentice-Hall, 1965.

A brief and pointed analysis of the economic changes that are taking place throughout many nonindustrialized nations, the forces behind these changes, and the consequences they are having on society and culture.

Tucker, W. T. *The Social Context of Economic Behavior*. New York: Holt, Rinehart & Winston, 1964.

A lively and stimulating introduction to economic sociology that ranges from the study of broad cultural patterns to an in-depth analysis of sales techniques and advertising.

10

Government

philosopher Thomas Hobbes suggested that one reason people form governments is to prevent "the war of every man against every man." Although there is no final answer as to why governments exist, Hobbes' answer seems to be commonly accepted by many sociologists. Clearly, if a society does not protect itself against those who would disrupt it, it would probably become chaotic and would eventually die. Thus, some form of government must exist in every society, even though the form of government varies a great deal from one society to another.

The institution that has the power to make and to enforce rules and laws, thereby protecting society, is known as the *political institution*. It serves to maintain social order and to compel obedience to some system of authority.

In this chapter we will examine the political institution from the point of view of political sociologists. To do this, we will address the relationship between the political system and the larger social system, focusing on societal conditions that affect the political scene and the government. We will study the development of political units, the major focus of government, and the functions of the political institution. We will also examine political parties, concentrating on party membership and the voting behavior of the American population. Finally, we will investigate various aspects of power, especially its role in government.

Development of Political Units

The first known political association was the kinship group or the clan. In ancient China, for example, there was no strong central government. Families got together and formed large clans. Each clan undertook the functions we would consider belonging to the government today. The clan, for instance, protected the family against hostile groups. It served as a welfare agency, giving or lending money to poor branches of the family. It also provided the children with education, regulated marriage, and enacted and enforced laws. The clan rulership, then, was a forerunner of modern government.

But as populations grew, the family institution could no longer continue to perform all political functions. As towns developed and geographic mobility increased, government became less personal and more formal. The ties of kinship lost much of their ability to regulate behavior. Political specialization became necessary, because neighbors were no longer related and people had to interact with strangers. The forces of love and relationship could no longer be depended upon to bind people together and to maintain order.

Over the years political entities known as cities began to develop. Once human beings learned how to cultivate crops and domesticate animals, they no longer needed to wander about seeking food. They could settle down in one place where the land was fertile, water plentiful, and climate comfortable. Archeologists estimate that the first such settlements appeared approximately 10,000 years ago. But these early villages were not truly cities. Many factors, such as population growth, trade, transportation, architecture, and public administration, had to develop and interact in order to gradually bring about the transformation of these villages into cities.

The first real cities grew up around the Tigris and Euphrates rivers about 6,000 years ago in the area that is now Iraq. Most of them were city-states usually including the city itself and the villages and farms surrounding it, but independent of any larger political unit. Many such cities had populations numbering in the thousands. Ordinarily they were protected by high stone walls. Government was controlled by kings or priests. In the West, such city-states reached a high point of development in Greece and Rome.

By the end of the fourteenth century, many of these European city-states gradually began to form into nations. In order to accomplish this, they had to meet each of the following conditions. One, there had to be geographic proximity—people had to live close to each other. Two, the people had to be able to communicate—that is, they had to have a common language and had to share at least some common values and attitudes. Three, there had to be a sense of unity among the citizens. Four, there had to be some means of protecting the nation's borders. All these developments were dependent, to some extent, on technology; the greater the technological advance, the more likely it is that nations will emerge.

By the beginning of the sixteenth century all of the above conditions were met and France, England, Russia, Portugal, and Spain could all be described as true nations. They traded among themselves and set out to find new parts of the world that they could conquer. Spanish explorers, for example, went to Cuba, Florida, Mexico, and parts of South America. The French occupied Canada and Madagascar. The Portuguese went to Brazil and around Africa, and the English occupied the East coast of the United States. Colonies were established to increase a nation's trade and its wealth. Such colonies were governed by the mother country, either directly or indirectly. If the colonies were ruled directly, their institutions were shaped after the conquering nation. If they were ruled indirectly, the native people were allowed to retain their own customs and to be freer of the governing country's influence.

Forms of Government

As these nations developed, so did their governments. Each society established a political structure by which it would be governed. Because there is no one way to organize political power, these political structures varied. Societies established different ways of deciding who would get political power, when power was legitimate or rightful, how laws would be made and enforced, and how responsive a government would be to the wishes and needs of the governed.

Of the forms of government that emerged, four major types will be discussed in this section. They are *oligarchy, monarchy, dictatorship,* and *democracy.*

OLIGARCHY

An *oligarchy* is a form of government in which a few people rule ("olig" = "few" and "archy" = "rule"). Sociologist Robert Michels did the most famous study of oligarchies in his book *Political Parties.*[1] In that book Michels coined the term "the iron law of oligarchy," by which he meant that power in any social organization is inevitably concentrated in the hands of a few people at the top. Those who are lower in the hierarchy tend to be very submissive because the leaders hold a great deal of power. (Even in organizations that profess to be democratic, control tends to become concentrated in the hands of a powerful few.) Michels explained that the tendency toward oligarchy is the result of the way ordinary members behave in organizations. Most people participate irregularly. They are often not well informed. They are frequently indifferent. Those few who are willing to give time and attention to the organization are usually able to gain control of it.

Oligarchy is an old form of political structure—it flourished in ancient Athens and ancient Egypt. But there are many oligarchies in the modern world. (In fact, Michels would claim that all modern political entities are oligarchies.) Among the more prominent examples are some of the developing countries in Africa, where military elites sometimes seize power when they are dissatisfied with the government's indecisiveness or inability to act quickly. In such countries, then, the elite group at the top is composed of military leaders or people at the head of the largest businesses.

MONARCHY

A *monarchy* is a form of government in which one person rules ("mono" = "one"). There are two types of monarchies. In both types the king or the queen comes to power through inheritance, usually from a

Monarchies can be either absolute or constitutional. Queen Elizabeth of Great Britain is a constitutional monarch.

parent. In the first type, an *absolute monarchy,* the monarch's power is considered divine—it is bestowed directly on the monarch by a Supreme Being or God. Therefore it is absolute in the sense that no mere human being can defy or disobey a divinity or a deity's representative on earth. Since the absolute monarch derives power from God, his or her word is the same as God's word. Japanese emperors, for example, ruled by divine right until shortly after World War II, when the Emperor of Japan declared that he was not divine. At the present time, there are only a few countries, such as Nepal, that still have "divine" kings.

The second type of monarchy, often called a *constitutional monarchy,* is more common in the modern world. In this type of government, the king or queen is the head of the state in title only. The power to rule lies in the hands of a governing group. Great Britain is a good example of this type of monarchy. There the monarch holds the title of "Queen" or "King," but the real power to rule lies with the Parliament and the prime minister.

DICTATORSHIP

In a country that is a *dictatorship,* one person (usually with advisors) controls all the power to make and enforce laws. Dictators frequently acquire power by seizing it. They seldom are freely elected to office nor do they inherit their positions the way a monarch does. Once dictators get power, however, they usually try to legitimate it—they try to persuade the people that the dictators really should have the power. Adolf Hitler is the best example of a dictator who convinced the people to accept his iron rule. (It should be noted, though, that Hitler was freely elected.) Millions of Germans before and during World War II believed Hitler was going to save Germany from ruin and make it the greatest and most powerful country in the world. Hitler was able to gain his large following because he was a persuasive leader and orator who knew how to use propaganda in very effective ways.

Dictatorships are *totalitarian states.* Totalitarian means that the government *totally* controls almost all aspects of life. A *state* is an organization that monopolizes the legitimate use of physical force within a given territory.[2] The government in such states is almost completely centralized, and there is no limit to the amounts or kinds of power that the government has. Similarly, there is no limit to the methods such a government can use to wield that power. Understandably, attaining this kind of total control and keeping it are not easy tasks, and most totalitarian states use a variety of methods to achieve these ends.

Although Idi Amin's official title is "president," the government of Uganda is a contemporary example of a dictatorship.

One such method is to forbid all political parties except the official one. This is a very useful tactic because it makes elections meaningless. There is no contest between candidates for office, and therefore only people that the official party approves can get elected. Allowing only a single party is useful in other ways as well. Since people do not have the option of joining other parties, the one party becomes special to them. Along the same line of reasoning, parties do not compete for members; therefore becoming a party member is more difficult. Thus, a one-party system can turn party membership into a reward. For example, in the Soviet Union, it is an honor to be allowed to join the Communist party, and so people strive to be good citizens in order to get into this prestigious group. At the present time only about 4 percent of the Soviet population are party members, but they are people who devote themselves to the state. They work toward its objectives, they follow its rules, and they learn how to be Communist leaders.

In short, then, the official party in a dictatorship ensures that only people who are loyal to the government can get elected. The party also serves as a reward system to encourage people to conform. Finally, it can serve to strengthen the system because it is a training ground for future leaders who can be counted on to maintain the same type of government.

A second way that totalitarian states preserve their power is by devising and circulating an official *ideology* or system of beliefs. People are expected to be absolute conformists, and they are told whom they must hate, what they must sacrifice, and what and whom they must support. Attitudes and behaviors in almost every area of life—from the political to the personal—are defined for them. But most important of all, they are taught that everyone is subordinate to the state. The good of the state is more important than any individual. Such official doctrines are rarely challenged because no effective competing doctrines are allowed to exist.

One of the most efficient means of spreading the official ideology and preventing opposing ones from developing is to control all public communication. For this reason, totalitarian countries own and operate virtually all newspapers, radio and television stations, movie companies, and publishing houses. They use all these avenues of communication to spread the official word. Such a system of government ownership works very well because if anyone or any group disagrees with public policy, there is no way of sending out a competing message. So, there can be no open debate on issues because the people can receive only the opinions the government wants them to receive.

A third method by which totalitarian governments can maintain complete control is by taking over the leadership of all social groups. When a dictatorship first emerges, the leaders either destroy existing social organizations or take control of them. Associations, such as trade unions, youth groups, business associations, athletic teams, and private social clubs, lose their independence and autonomy. This method ensures that dissident individuals cannot get together in groups and plan to change or overthrow the existing system.

Taking control of all sectors of the economy, especially large business corporations and banking establishments, is a fourth tactic totalitarian governments use to gain and maintain power over a society. This means that all important business transactions, both domestic and foreign, are controlled by the government. In this way the government not only has enormous financial control over businesses and banks, but it also gains further control over the country. It comes to manage the economy, which means that it has the power to decide what things get produced, how they are produced, who produces them, who gets them, and how much they will cost. Obviously, such economic control strengthens the hold of the totalitarian government over the people.

Finally, most totalitarian governments are police states. In addition to having an ordinary police force, dictatorships may also have special secret police agencies that are under the control of, and act for, the state alone. The primary responsibility of such a police force is to spy on citizens and to try to uncover any secret, antigovernment conspiracies or political opposition. Such agencies focus on political crime, and they are given a great deal of unrestricted power to deal with it. They are not required to allow people fair, public, and legal trials with legal representation. They usually have the power to execute, exile, or imprison those suspected of disloyalty to the state, and such suspects have little or no power to resist or protect themselves.

A dictatorship, then, is a complete fusion of state and society. Its aim is total control over all aspects of human life. Often such societies cannot continue to exist because they either lose the leaders that made them possible or because the people find the restraints placed upon their lives too constricting.

DEMOCRACY

A *democracy* is a form of government based on rule by the consent of the majority of the governed ("demos" is the Greek word for "the people"). It is the form of government considered to be ideal in the United States. There are basically two types of democracies—participatory democracy and representative democracy. *Participatory democracy* occurs when societies are small and *all* eligible voters can gather together at a town hall or in a town square to decide issues. Such was the case in the towns of New England two hundred years ago. Even today there are some tribal societies in which the population is still

The United States is a representative democracy since American voters elect people to represent them in government. Here we see the Arizona House of Representatives in session.

small enough so that every qualified adult in them can have a direct voice in the government.

When societies grow larger and more complex, however, every citizen cannot possibly participate directly in the government. As a result, some societies have adopted a system of government called *representative democracy,* in which adult citizens decide who shall represent them by voting for those people they believe will best serve their interests. In other words, the citizens choose representatives who they think will vote on legislation the way they want them to vote.

Yet once we have elected our representatives, we cannot be sure that they will always vote on issues the way we might like. Though we may write letters to our representatives in Congress expressing our opinions on policies, our representatives still vote according to their own personal judgment. They do so because not everyone in their *constituency* (the voters in their district, city, state, or country) wants the same thing. Some constituents want their representatives to vote "Yes" on an issue and some want them to vote "No." But usually such representatives try to be reasonably responsive to the majority because if they are not, they run the risk of not being re-elected.

APPLYING SOCIOLOGY

In our society all democracies are traditionally portrayed favorably while all dictatorships are usually thought of in a bad light. Do you think all dictatorships are necessarily bad? Under what conditions might a dictatorship be preferred to a democracy? What do you think are some of the advantages and disadvantages of a democratic form of government? In what ways are democracies and dictatorships similar? Do you believe that a democracy is really possible in a large, complex society?

In the mid-1960s Herbert Marcuse, a political philosopher, predicted that there would be a trend toward participatory democracy.[3] This means that the population would get more involved in government and its processes. In our own country we can see how certain groups of people have demanded more participation in controlling their own lives. For example, there has been pressure to have neighborhood control over schools in some large cities. In the late 1960s, many students in universities and even in high schools began insisting on permission to be on faculty committees so they could share in the decisions that concerned their own lives. Many neighborhood "mayor's offices" have opened in some large cities so that mayors would become more available and responsive to citizens' wants. In some respects, then, Americans have attempted to gain more control over their government.

Yet Marcuse's prediction has not come true entirely. With the occurrence of "Watergate" in the early 1970s, many Americans have been "turned off" to the workings of government. They no longer feel that government is responsive to their needs or that participation in government will actually be to their advantage. Instead of becoming involved in government, they have become apathetic to the political process.

It will be interesting to note if this trend of apathy will continue or if Marcuse's prediction will become reality. At any rate, the political institution will continue to exist—both in our society and in others—because it serves several functions. We now will take a closer look at each of these functions.

Functions of the Political Institution

Three major functions served by the political institution are maintaining social order, coordinating necessary activities, and protecting citizens. Each function is necessary to the successful running of a society.

MAINTAINING SOCIAL ORDER

One function of the political institution is to maintain social order. If government did not perform this function, society would be chaotic and citizens would not feel safe as they went about their daily lives. To some extent, social order is maintained because most people have been socialized early in their lives to behave in nondestructive ways. But not all people learn and accept norms against destructiveness to the same degree. Some individuals are very conforming; others are very nonconforming. When internal checks do not control behavior, the political institution enacts and enforces societal laws that are considered necessary to the welfare of the people.

These laws can be divided into three categories. In the first category we have *constitutional laws*—norms that are written into the constitutions of national or local governments. They might include such rules as "due process" (for example, in the United States, we are entitled to a trial by jury), which serve to protect citizens from unjust persecution by government. Such laws are usually broad definitions of the obligations and rights that the state and citizen owe each other.

Statutory laws make up the second category. These are norms enacted by a legislative body like the United States Senate. They tend to be more specific than constitutional laws. Laws controlling air and water pollution are examples of statutory laws.

Finally, there is *common law*, a term borrowed from the early English legal system. It originally referred to laws that regulated the behavior of all people "in common." Everyone came under the protection of common law, while other laws, such as Church and canon laws, did not apply to everyone. Today the term is usually used to refer to unwritten laws—those that have come about through custom and precedent.* Common laws are part of the traditions of a people and are subject to change as the values and life-styles of a society change. Some forms of marriage are regulated by common law.

In America, once laws are enacted, the judicial and executive branches have the obligation to enforce them. We have police agencies and a court system to carry out this function. In our civil courts, individuals can sue each other for any harm committed against them. For example, if the dry cleaner loses a customer's clothing, the customer can sue to get money to replace it. People can sue each other to determine who is at fault in an automobile accident. Tenants can sue landlords if buildings are not maintained properly. Judges, who are elected

---

*The term "common law" is actually a misnomer. In Chapter 1 we noted that laws, by definition, are norms that are written down. According to sociologists, a common law is really a norm.

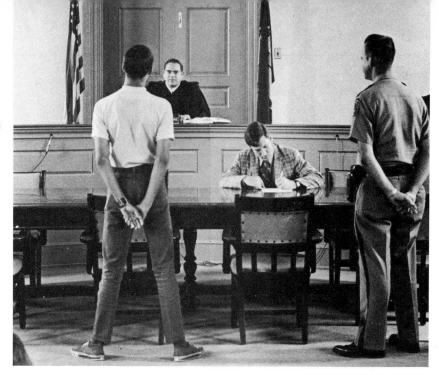

In the United States the court system, in conjunction with police agencies, is charged with law enforcement.

or appointed, can act as arbitrators between such people and can decide who is right.

We also have criminal courts that try people who are accused of committing crimes. Even though crimes involve individuals, legally a crime is an offense against the state (or "the people"). Judges and juries act in the interest of society to punish the guilty, protect the innocent, and prevent criminal activity from recurring. They do this by imposing penalties, such as fines or prison terms, on those convicted of committing criminal acts.

Thus we note a difference between a civil offense and a criminal offense. In civil cases, one individual or group accuses another individual or group of some offense. In the case of the dry cleaner, John Jones sues the Acme Cleaning Corporation for losing his clothes. In criminal cases, the state is the accuser and the one who is injured. Therefore, if John Jones steals a car from Mary Smith, the State of California will prosecute because John Jones has violated the state's law. Briefly, then, the political institution arbitrates disputes and protects people from injustices committed against each other.

COORDINATING NECESSARY ACTIVITIES

A second task assigned to the political institution is to coordinate the activities necessary for the smooth functioning of a society. Some governments, such as in the Soviet Union, may do this by regulating the production of consumer goods. Others, like the French government, may do this by controlling public utilities such as the airlines and the railroads. Most governments try to ensure that products meet certain standards and that the health and welfare of people are protected. In addition, since some items cannot be produced by private industry, it is the responsibility of government to see that citizens are provided with such necessities as highways, harbors, and dams.

PROTECTING CITIZENS

A third function of the political institution is to protect citizens from enemies, whether from other countries or from those people who would destroy society from within. To preserve order against intrusion from foreign enemies, armies, navies, and air forces are maintained. Similarly, a country will have laws to keep undesirable persons out of the country.

Laws are also passed to protect a country from enemies within, from people who may seek to overthrow the existing system by violent or subversive means. A government cannot tolerate such activities. Of course, this does not mean that citizens cannot express their desire for change; countries frequently allow their citizens to express such opinions. For example, Americans and Canadians can demonstrate, distribute literature, and assemble to discuss change. But no one is allowed to advocate overthrowing the government by violence. Thus governments protect themselves and the people who support them from internal enemies as well as from foreign enemies.

In the preceding sections of this chapter, we have traced the development of political units and analyzed four forms of government— oligarchy, monarchy, dictatorship, and democracy. We have also seen that in every society, regardless of its form of government, the political institution performs several functions.

At this point it is important to note that these functions are not performed in a vacuum. Many factors—tangible and abstract, political and nonpolitical—influence the political process. The mass media, for example, may play an important role in the passage or defeat of a congressional bill. Economic factors may cause cutbacks in police or fire personnel, thus affecting the protection of citizens. The personality or attitude of a government official may influence how well, or how poorly, some laws are enforced. A political party's stand on a particular issue may play a major role in the outcome of a national election. In the following sections we will analyze two factors that have a profound effect on the political institution—political parties and the concept of power.

Political Parties

A *political party* is an organization of people who are interested in controlling the political structure of a society. Parties are a primary link between the government and the people because they keep the government informed of the public's opinion on a variety of issues. At the same time, parties work to get their members to support governmental decisions. Thus parties serve to unify the governed and those governing.

In order to attain their goal of controlling the political structure of a society, political parties select candidates to run for political office who they believe will be able to persuade the majority of the voters to support and elect them. The parties then go to work to "sell" their candidates to the voters.

Political parties are a link between the government and the people. Here delegates to the Republican Convention of 1976 demonstrate support for their presidential nominee, Gerald R. Ford.

Unlike totalitarian states, democracies and other forms of government have at least two political parties. In the United States the two major political parties are the Democratic and the Republican parties. There have been and still are other political parties, but their memberships usually are small and their power usually is slight. Third parties, or minor parties, however, can be influential in local elections and even

in national elections. For example, in 1912, Theodore Roosevelt, running on the Bull Moose Party ticket, took enough votes from the Republican candidate to enable the Democrat, Woodrow Wilson, to win the election. In addition, because third parties are often formed on the basis of ideology and issues, they sometimes are responsible for the introduction of new programs. For example, the Socialist Party's push for a minimum wage law may have been responsible for its enactment in the 1930s. Some of the third parties in the United States have been the Populist party, the American Independent party, the Socialist party, and the Communist party.

POLITICAL PARTY MEMBERSHIP

Sociologists have discovered that membership in a political party is frequently related to other social factors. Members of the Republican party tend to be Protestant, white, suburban, business-oriented members of the upper classes. Democrats, on the other hand, are likely to be southern Protestants and Catholics from the Northeast, working-class nonwhites, and ethnic minority group members.

The Republican party is traditionally thought to favor big business and the status quo; the Democratic party is traditionally thought to favor the workers and social reform. When examined more closely, though, the two parties do not stand for very different ideologies. Over the years they have both tended toward a middle-of-the-road position on most issues in order to avoid offending any groups and to attract as many voters as possible.[4] Nevertheless, many Americans regard the Republicans as conservative and the Democrats as liberal. The fact is that some difference does exist and voters express their preference. The differences may be small, but they are real to the voters.

In general, compared to other social classes, lower-class people are less likely to join organizations of any kind. This holds true even for membership in political parties because poor people do not see political organizations as the best means of resolving their problems. Voting turnout among lower-paid workers is approximately one-half the rate of participation among professional people and upper-echelon executives. Furthermore, lower-class people are not encouraged to join parties. Indeed, according to political scientist Walter Dean Burnham, there are still mechanisms, such as the requirement for personal registration, that operate to prevent lower-class participation.[5]

Other sociologists, like Maurice Pinard, have found that poverty actually works to stop people from joining political parties because of feelings of hopelessness and helplessness.[6] Poor people have many worries and these tend to make them self-centered and fatalistic. They do not expect relief from their situations and so working for a political party appears to them to be meaningless and worthless. On the other hand, worry often leads middle-class people to activism. Such people tend to believe they have some control over their own destinies and are therefore willing to put forth effort in order to achieve their goals. Pinard also found that poor people are less exposed to propaganda because they read fewer newspapers, watch less television, and interact less with people outside of their own groups. Because of this social isolation, poorer people are less sophisticated and have less political knowledge and so they avoid joining political organizations.

VOTING BEHAVIOR

As is the case with joining political parties, not as many Americans vote as we could expect. Table 10-1 shows that even in a national election only 44.7 percent of the eligible voters actually went to the polls. Of those who did vote, the table reveals that the same social variables affecting party membership also affect voting behavior. Whites

TABLE 10–1
Participation in the 1974 Election, by Selected Population Characteristics

Characteristics	Persons of voting age (millions)	Percent reporting they voted
TOTAL	141.3	44.7
Race:		
White	125.1	46.3
Black	14.2	33.8
Age:		
18–20 years	11.6	20.8
21–24 years	14.1	26.4
25–34 years	29.3	37.0
35–44 years	22.4	49.1
45–64 years	43.0	56.9
65 years and over	21.0	51.4
Education:		
8 years or less	24.4	34.4
9–11 years	21.7	35.9
12 years	51.7	44.7
More than 12 years	43.4	54.9
Employment Status:		
Employed	83.1	46.8
Unemployed	5.0	28.8
Not in labor market	53.2	43.0

Source: Abridged from United States Bureau of the Census, *Statistical Abstracts of the United States: 1976* (97th ed.) Washington, D.C., 1976, 467.

APPLYING SOCIOLOGY

Although we consider the United States to be a democracy, not all groups participate equally in the electoral process. What do you think government policy in the United States would be like if more poor people, women, and blacks were to actively take part in our government? How do you think party membership would be affected?

---

vote more often than blacks, the well educated more often than the poorly educated, and the employed more often than the unemployed or those not in the labor market.

In addition to this pattern, we note another pattern regarding voting behavior among American youth. Of those who are between eighteen and twenty years old, voting turnout is lower than for any other age group. Clearly, although the voting age is now eighteen, American youth do not participate as fully in our government as they are permitted.

Also, a new pattern regarding voting behavior and political parties is developing. There is currently a steady increase in the number of voters who claim to be "independent." These voters express little allegiance to either party and declare that they vote "on the issues," not for the party or for the candidate. Yet such voters, regardless of what they say, continue to vote for the party for which they voted in the past and for which their parents voted. These voters have also been found to have two other characteristics. One, they are less likely than committed voters to be informed about politics in general, any election in particular, and the candidates. Two, they are more apathetic than committed voters, usually because they feel themselves to be under cross-pressures. For example, they may be married to someone who holds different political convictions from those they hold themselves. Or they may be blue-collar workers whose parents were Republicans. A great number of such voters never vote at all because both candidates and both political platforms seem inadequate to them.

You may be wondering how sociologists find out about voting behavior. How do they learn the process through which people make their choices among candidates? How do they find out if political campaigns really change people's opinions? One method is through survey questions (see Appendix). Figure 10-1 shows only a few of the questions asked by sociologists who studied the voting patterns of people in Elmira, New York, in 1948. These questions will give you an idea of how sociologists learn about political preferences in a democratic society.

FIGURE 10–1
Selected Questions Asked of Voters in Elmira, 1948

1. Where do you get most of your news about things like the coming presidential election?

Radio _____

Newspapers _____

Magazines _____

Talking to people _____

Other _____

Don't know _____

2. As you read or listen to the news these days, do you find you are paying a great deal of attention to things about the election, only a little attention, or no attention at all?

Great deal _____

Only a little _____

None at all _____

Don't know _____

3. Well, how much *interest* would you say you have in this year's Presidential election?

A great deal _____

Quite a lot _____

Not very much _____

None at all _____

Don't know _____

4. Do you ever get as worked up about something that happens in politics or public affairs as you do about something that happens in your personal life?

Yes _____   No _____   Don't know _____

5. How about keeping living costs from rising further—will whoever is elected President affect this, or won't it make any difference?

Affect _____   No difference _____   Don't know _____

6. On the whole, would you say it is more important this year to elect a president who can handle domestic affairs here at home or one who can handle international affairs and foreign relations?

Domestic _____

International _____

Both _____

Don't know _____

7. Do you think that people like you have a lot of influence on how the government runs things?

Lots of influence _____

Some _____

Not much _____

Don't know _____

8. Do any of your closest friends disagree with your political opinions?

Yes _____   No _____   Don't know _____

Source: Bernard R. Berelson, Paul F. Lazarsfeld, and William N. McPhee, *Voting,* Chicago: University of Chicago Press, 1954, Appendix B.

Power

Throughout this chapter the word power has been used frequently. It is a word that most of us are familiar with and one that we use a great deal, but also one that we cannot define very readily. Yet power is universal in all social relationships and it is of central interest to sociologists.

There are, for example, power relationships between institutions and associations. The medical institution may set itself against pharmaceutical companies on questions of drug manufacture and standards. Similarly, there are power relationships between institutions. The religious institution may be in conflict with the political institution over such issues as abortion. The economic institution and the military institution may oppose each other when the question of military spending arises. We also may have power relationships between individuals and institutions. Farmers may be in conflict with the government over the issue of price controls.

Power also exists in one-to-one relationships. In some situations, the holder of power is clear. Bosses have power over employees. Teachers have power over students. Corporals have power over privates. Wardens have power over prisoners. But power contests are also found in very personal relationships, and the power-holder is often less clear. Courting couples, husbands and wives, parents and teenage children all contend with each other for power. The German sociologist Georg Simmel claimed that, except for the most casual of acquaintances, all individuals engage in power contests with each other.[7]

DEFINING POLITICAL POWER[8]

When we talk about government, we are often talking about political power. What is political power? Who has it? How do they get it? How do they keep it? How do they use it? How do they lose it? Before we can begin to answer such questions, it is necessary to define power. Because power is often used interchangeably with other concepts that really have different meanings, it seems best to define these concepts first to see what power is *not* in order to define what it *is*. The well-known sociologist Robert Bierstedt distinguished clearly between power and prestige, influence, dominance, rights, force, and authority.

Prestige

Prestige can be defined as a social standing that carries recognition, admiration, deference, and respect. It is the honor given to groups or individuals by others. All societies have prestige systems, but the basis of prestige varies considerably from society to society. Frequently we confuse prestige and power, since the two often go together. The President of the United States, for instance, has both prestige and power. However, Bierstedt claims that power can occur without prestige and vice versa. For example, Dr. Jonas Salk, who discovered a cure for polio, has prestige but little power. A successful criminal may have a great deal of power but little prestige. In general, we can say that prestige can come from power but it is not necessarily part of it.

Dr. Jonas Salk, discoverer of the vaccine that prevents polio, is an example of a person who has great prestige. He has little political power, however.

319

FOCUS ON: WATERGATE

On June 17, 1972, five men were arrested for burglarizing the Watergate apartment complex, which housed the Democratic Party headquarters in Washington, D.C. What appeared to be a simple, routine burglary, however, turned out to be an extremely complex event, implicating over a score of people, including the President of the United States.

Bob Woodward and Carl Bernstein, two investigative reporters from *The Washington Post,* were the first outsiders to decipher the mystery surrounding the incident. In their books, *All the President's Men* and *The Final Days,* Woodward and Bernstein discuss the effects of the burglary and its climactic conclusion—the resignation of President Richard M. Nixon.

Prior to his landslide victory and reelection over the Democratic candidate, Senator George McGovern, on November 7, 1972, President Nixon had begun to use his authority, as well as the enormous resources of his office, to impede further investigation of the Watergate burglary. In fact, he and his White House Chief of Staff, H. R. Haldeman, used their influence to stop any possible in-depth FBI investigation of the incident, suggesting that the FBI inquiry be limited to only the five burglars.

A series of later disclosures implicated the President in several illegal activities, including the actual Watergate event. It was reported that in 1970, the President approved a plan for burglary, wiretapping, and the secret opening of first-class mail of all persons suspected of threatening national security and presidential power. However, the President claimed that he withdrew such a plan five days after its approval.

In addition, members of the burglary team and their lawyers received large sums of "hush money" to prevent them from leaking details of their involvement. Also, a member of the President's staff ordered sabotage activities in 1972 against Democratic presidential candidates.

Probably the most damaging part of the revelations, though, was that President Nixon was covertly taping all meetings and conversations held in his presence. These tapes provided tangible proof that the President's knowledge of Watergate was more extensive than he later admitted.

As Woodward and Bernstein's investigation continued, President Nixon attempted to protect himself by appointing a special prosecutor, Archibald Cox, to examine the Watergate incident. As Mr. Cox approached the truth of the matter, however, he was fired. This led to a series of resignations of top officials in the Department of Justice. At this point, President Nixon's credibility was seriously damaged.

On August 9, 1974, President Nixon resigned—the first American president ever to do so. The office of the presidency was then turned over to Gerald Ford, the Vice-President. President Ford subsequently granted Mr. Nixon immunity from criminal prosecution.

What does the Watergate incident teach us about political power? Do you believe that President Nixon was corrupt and misguided regarding the burglary of the Democratic headquarters or that he was a victim of political power? Do you think the President should be given less power than he now has? Why or why not?

Source: Bob Woodward and Carl Bernstein, *All The President's Men,* New York: Simon and Schuster, 1974. Bob Woodward and Carl Bernstein, *The Final Days,* New York: Simon and Schuster, 1976.

Influence

Most people can be influenced if they admire or respect the person who has influence. Yet, they can only be influenced if they allow themselves to be. On the other hand, when someone has power over someone else, there is no choice. Thus, power is coercive; influence is persuasive. We submit to influence voluntarily, even if subconsciously; we submit to power because we must. Teachers have power over their students because teachers assign lessons and give and grade tests. Students must do the lessons, take the tests, and accept the grades. But this does not mean that all teachers have influence. They can influence students only if they have characteristics that students admire or want to imitate.

Like power and prestige, power and influence can go together, but do not necessarily. One's position (for example, teacher) can automatically carry power; but one must earn the ability to be influential by having qualities or ideas that others value. Karl Marx influenced many people, but he did not have the power to force anyone to accept his ideas. Influential people may be powerless, but usually powerful people have influence. As Bierstedt noted, "Influence attaches to an idea, a doctrine, or a creed, and has its locus in the ideological sphere. Power attaches to a person, a group, or an association and has its locus in the sociological sphere."[9]

Dominance

Dominance is an individual trait, affecting the psychological relationship between two or more people. It is a personal characteristic and a part of one's personality. In most interpersonal relationships, there is a dominant and a submissive person. Sometimes it is easy to see which person has each characteristic. Other times outsiders find it hard to tell who is dominant. However, being dominant does not necessarily mean one is powerful. There are defenses against dominance, but there are few defenses against power. The submissive person can lie to avoid being dominated or can pretend to obey the other. Therefore, dominance is not true power because it can be circumvented, which power cannot.

Rights

Rights are attached to social statuses, just as are privileges, obligations, and responsibilities. Usually a right has social support if people see it as legitimate. For example, children have the right to expect their parents to support them and parents have the right to expect their children to obey them. However, a person may have rights, but may not have the power to claim them. For example, lower-class people may have the right to vote, as we noted earlier, but may not have the power to exercise that right.

Force and Authority

It is fairly easy to see how power differs from prestige, influence, dominance, and rights. But it is more difficult to see the difference

321

FOCUS ON: OBEDIENCE TO AUTHORITY

Not many people realize how treacherous authority can be. When the Nazi trials at Nuremberg took place after World War II, many wondered how these "criminals" could justify their participation in the genocide of Jews and other minority groups on the simple grounds that they were only following orders.

The puzzle surrounding obedience is still an important topic among social scientists. Stanley Milgram, a social psychologist, has shown in a series of experiments that individuals will willingly inflict pain on others if instructed to do so by someone in authority. Milgram's book *Obedience to Authority: An Experimental View* discusses his experiments.

In one experiment, Milgram told his subjects that they were taking part in a learning test—testing the effect of punishment on learning. Each subject was to play the role of "teacher." The role of "learner" was to be played by another researcher, although the subject did not know that. The "learner" supposedly was to memorize a series of words. If the "learner" gave an incorrect answer or failed to respond to a question, the "teacher" was commanded to administer an electric shock as punishment.

The shock generator contained thirty switches ranging from 15 to 450 volts. Their intensity varied from "Slight Shock" to "Danger—Severe Shock." With each successive wrong answer, the "teacher" was instructed to give the "learner" increasingly strong shocks. And with each shock the "learner" painfully reacted.

Actually, the experiment was rigged and the "learner" did not experience any pain. What the "teacher" heard were tape-recorded protests piped through an intercom. At 75 volts he heard the "learner" moan and grunt; at 125 volts the "learner" shouted "I can't stand the pain"; at 150 volts the "learner" demanded to be released from the experiment; and, at 180 volts the "learner" complained of heart trouble. When the "teacher" administered the 330-volt shock, the "learner" did not answer at all.

Yet, unexpectedly, 62 percent of the subjects went to the limit and administered the 450-volt shock. The remainder refused to complete the experiment, but only after they had administered at least the 300-volt shock. In no instance did the "teacher" disobey the experimenter.

In all fairness to the "teachers," it must be stated that most of them experienced conflict during the experiment. But, in spite of their feelings, they continued the experiment because an authority figure instructed them to do so.

What does this experiment tell us about blind obedience? Do you believe there are any instances in which blind obedience is justified? Why might such a study generate controversy?

Source: Stanley Milgram, *Obedience to Authority: An Experimental View*, New York: Harper & Row, 1974.

between power and force and between power and authority. Using Bierstedt's comparison between power, force, and authority we can now define power. Bierstedt contends that *power is latent or hidden force. Force is manifest or open power. Authority is institutionalized or legitimized power.*

Force is the actual exercise of power; it is action that overcomes resistance. It can be synonymous with coercion insofar as it imposes the will of one individual or group on the will of another individual or group. For example, the thief who says "Your money or your life," gives the victim no choice. The soldier who says "Surrender or die," gives the enemy no choice. Thus force is power in the most open sense. There can be no refusal. If someone holds a gun to your head, that is *power*. But if he or she shoots the gun, that is *force*.

From this explanation we can see that power is potential. Power is the ability to use force and because of that ability, power is always successful, according to Bierstedt. When it is not successful, it is simply not power. If the gun should jam, power can no longer turn into force and so it is no longer power.

In formal organizations or associations, power becomes authority because it is legitimate. When we elect political officers or hire people in executive positions, we are giving them legitimate power, or authority, to impose whatever they believe should be imposed. We give them the legal authority to use power if necessary.

In short, power is related to both force and authority. It makes both possible. Power becomes manifest when it is challenged and turned into force or when it is legalized and turned into authority. Power itself is only a prelude, an introduction to something else. As soon as it is used, it turns into either force or authority. According to Bierstedt, then, "Without power there would be no force and without power there would be no authority."[10]

SOURCES OF POWER

Bierstedt also pointed out that there are three sources of power: number of individuals, social organization, and resources. According to Bierstedt, the number of individuals is the least important of the three. A minority of people can always exercise power over a majority if it has at least some of the other two sources—organization and resources. That is why a small police force can control a huge mob. The police are organized and have resources—guns and clubs. And the majority is aware that the minority has these resources and thus it obeys the minority's orders.

None of these sources by itself can enable a group to exercise power. A group is most powerful when it has all three. It must be reasonably large, although it can still be a minority. It must be organized so that it can behave effectively without members going off in different, unrelated directions. And finally, it must have the resources (weapons, wealth, ability, and so on) to enforce its will on others.

TYPES OF AUTHORITY: LEGITIMATE POWER

Max Weber gave us another definition of power. He said that power is "the chance of a man or of a number of men to realize their own will in a communal action even against the resistance of others who are participating in the action."[11] And like Bierstedt, Weber felt

323

The *Deji* (king) of the Akure people of Nigeria has traditional authority. He is both the religious and the secular leader of his subjects. Here he conducts a Moslem prayer service.

there was a difference between power and authority. To him, power always rests on force, while authority rests on the consent of the governed. Authority is power used in a way the people consider legitimate. Weber wrote about three kinds of authority: traditional, charismatic, and legal-rational.

Traditional Authority

Traditional authority derives from custom and is accepted by people because it is regarded as close to sacred. People who live under traditional authority think that this is the way things always have been and always will be. Traditional authority is usually found in societies that have kings, chiefs, or councils of elders. It usually is hereditary, meaning that one acquires authority because one is born to inherit it. Thus, sons inherit the authority from their fathers. A prince will become king when the king dies. People accept the ruler as the authority because it is "meant" to be that way.

Charismatic Authority

Charisma comes from the Greek word meaning "gift" or "favor." Those who hold *charismatic authority* are people who are seen by their followers as having special personal qualities. They may be thought to have healing power or the gift of prophecy or the ability to perform miracles. Such leaders get and keep their authority because people are devotedly loyal to them and believe they are saviors. Martin Luther King, Jr., Malcolm X, Mahatma Gandhi, Joan of Arc, and Jesus Christ

Former President John F. Kennedy was endowed by the Constitution with legal-rational authority, but he had great charisma as well.

are all examples of charismatic leaders. In one sense, however, charismatic authority and traditional authority are very different. In a society where leadership is acquired through inheritance, there is no question about the successor's right to rule. But when the leader is a charismatic one, the personal qualities that brought him or her to power die when he or she dies. There is rarely a reason to pass the power to the next generation or even to the leader's close associates because they may not—probably do not—have the unique personal qualities necessary for charismatic leadership.

Legal-Rational Authority

Legal-rational authority is characteristic of modern, industrial societies. Power lies in the office or the position, not in the person. The individual elected or appointed to a position derives power and authority from the explicit rules that clearly define the limits of the office. The police, for example, have the authority to stop a person who is driving too fast and give out a speeding ticket, but they do not have the authority to decide on the amount of the fine. Such authority belongs to the judge or the jury who, on the other hand, do not have the authority to give out the ticket. Legal-rational authority, then, is based on the consent of the governed, using legitimate means, such as elections, to confer limited power on those they place in legal positions of authority.

The three types of authority are described here as independent of each other. But in reality they very often overlap, even though one type may be dominant over the other two. Former President John F. Kennedy had legal-rational authority, but he also had charisma. Kings may be traditional leaders, but they may be especially loved by their people because they seem to have unusual personal qualities. Popes—John XXIII, for example—may have charisma in addition to having legal-rational authority as the elected heads of the Roman Catholic Church and traditional authority as priests. The most successful leaders, then, whether in government, religion, industry, or universities, are those who combine as many of these types of authority as possible.

APPLYING SOCIOLOGY

Below is a list of people who have had political power. Can you classify them according to the dominant type of authority they held? Which of these people have held more than one type of political power and which types did they hold?

Attila the Hun	Mahatma Gandhi	Richard M. Nixon
Cleopatra	Winston Churchill	Robert E. Lee
Adolf Hitler	George Washington	Robert F. Kennedy

C. Wright Mills (1916–1962)

C. Wright Mills was a noted and controversial sociologist. One of Mills' major ideas was that the important decisions in American society are made by a relatively small group of leaders. In other words, he claimed that decisions concerning policies regarding, for example, whether or not to wage war, levels of production and employment, income tax laws, and international trade agreements, were not made by ordinary people through the democratic process; rather, they were made by a small group of powerful individuals.

Mills recognized that American society is so complex that power tends to become centralized. According to Mills, in modern society power is concentrated in the military, big business, and the executive branch of government. The leaders of these three spheres are the most powerful individuals in America. Mills called this group of individuals the "power elite."

In his book *The Power Elite* (1956), one of the most influential sociological works of the post-World War II era, Mills examined some of the common characteristics and interrelationships among these elite leaders. He claimed that the members of this power elite usually know one another, socialize together, have family members who intermarry, and share a similar social background. For example, most of the military, governmental, and corporate leaders come from the East, have received their educations from Ivy League colleges, are likely to be Protestant, and generally share the same attitudes and values. However, although they

Theories of Political Power

In totalitarian states or in countries with absolute monarchies, it is usually not difficult to determine who holds political power. But in democracies, especially when the societies are very large and contain many different types of people, it is more difficult to see who is in control.

In the United States, sociologists have generally agreed that there is a distinct upper class (see Chapter 13), but they have not been able to agree as to whether or not that upper class is also a *governing elite*. Is the upper class merely the richest and most prestigious group in America or does it also have enough political power to control the society?

Some social scientists claim that the upper class does indeed hold sufficient political power to centralize it in the hands of this elite group. Other social scientists dispute this view. They contend that no

share such social characteristics, Mills explicitly rejected the notion that this power elite consciously conspires to plot the direction of American society.

Rather, the interests of the military, big business, and the federal government coincide. For example, the military is the single biggest consumer and spender in America. As a result, it is certainly going to be of interest to business. And until recently, when Congress passed laws placing restrictions on campaign contributions, politicians relied heavily upon campaign contributions from big business.

Mills also argued against the common notion that those with the power to run society will make decisions that reflect the will of the majority of people. Instead, Mills argued that the power elite makes decisions according to its own vested interests. Hence, these decisions may or may not reflect the interests and desires of the working and middle classes. Furthermore, Mills claimed, the people who comprise these classes are not very interested in the workings of government anyway, and thus seldom understand the real source of power.

In addition to the powerful elite group and the powerless masses, Mills also recognized a middle group which has some power. This middle-level group is made up of local opinion leaders, lobbying groups, and the legislative branch of government. Many of Mills' critics, most notably David Riesman, claim that such middle-level groups are the real purveyors of power. Mills claimed, however, that the power elite holds the bulk of power in society and that the power that middle-level groups hold is at best of secondary importance.

---

single group wields the bulk of political power. Instead, these social scientists contend that power is divided among a number of different groups, each one organized around or held together by a separate interest.

One of the most important advocates of the first theory—called *elitism*—was the late sociologist C. Wright Mills.[12] One of the leading supporters of the second theory—called *pluralism*—is sociologist David Riesman.[13] Let us take a longer look at each of these theories.

C. WRIGHT MILLS ON ELITISM

Mills' theory states that there is an elite group at the top of the American social hierarchy consisting of those who are the heads of the largest business corporations, the top of the military services, and the leaders of government. He refers to these individuals collectively as the "power elite." They constitute a governing elite and they actually control the country, make the important decisions, and wield the power.

**FIGURE 10-2
Elitist View of the
American Power
Structure**

According to Mills' theory, members of the power elite are likely to know each other personally, or at least know of each other. They live in the same neighborhoods, socialize with each other, belong to the same clubs, vacation together, and cooperate with each other to retain their power.

Mills contends that below the power elite is a group of people who have middle-level power, but members of this group are much less personally acquainted with each other and much less well organized. Therefore, they have much less power. The majority of people, according to Mills' theory, are members of a powerless mass, which is always manipulated by the two groups above them, especially the power elite. The result is that, although most Americans think they share in the decision-making of their government because they have voting rights, only a few very powerful individuals are really in command. Figure 10-2 illustrates Mills' notion of how power is distributed in the United States.

DAVID RIESMAN ON PLURALISM

Riesman's theory is quite different from that of Mills. Riesman claims that power in this country is divided among veto groups. *Veto groups* are diversified power groups, each representing special interests and concerned with protecting its own rights. These special interest groups are called veto groups because, while guarding their interests, they often block, or veto, the efforts of opposition groups. An interest group of corporate managers may veto the efforts of an interest group of organized labor, for example. The American Medical Association may engage in conflict with a national health care interest group.

On the other hand, such groups often tolerate each other and cooperate with each other. If the veto group interested in women's rights wants the help of the veto group interested in the tobacco industry and vice versa, they will help each other out by voting in each other's interests, provided these interests do not conflict. Even when two groups are in competition over an issue, they may compromise in some way so that neither would actually "win" or "lose." For example, a group interested in ecology and a group of paper manufacturers interested in cutting down trees may reach a compromise through which only some of the trees would be cut down and would then be replaced immediately with a new planting.

The pluralists' view of power, then, is that power is divided among groups that are interested in getting power only within the area of their own concerns. No one group tries to get control of all the power. It is impossible, according to Riesman, for a few people to control all the power in the United States because it is such a large country

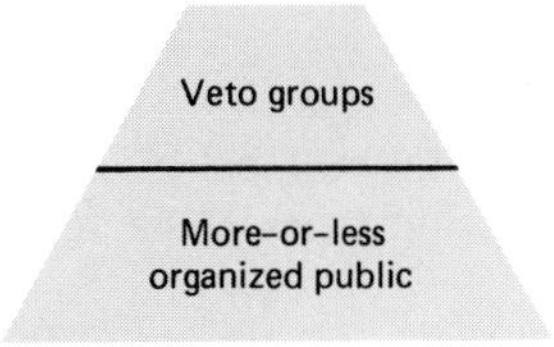

Veto groups

More-or-less
organized public

**FIGURE 10-3
Pluralist View of the
American Power
Structure**

with so many diversified interests. No small group could possibly control everything. Therefore, each group concentrates on its own special interests and makes "deals" with other groups. In this way, there is no national power group, no power elite. Riesman's power structure is shown in Figure 10-3.

ELITISM OR PLURALISM?

If we are to be able to interpret the American political structure, it makes a big difference which one of these theorists is correct. If Mills is right, the power elite dominates the country without really considering the rights of the masses. Furthermore, when power is concentrated in a few hands and the powerful do not have to account to the public, *democracy is weakened.* If Riesman is correct, the veto groups share the power. They cooperate and compromise in ways that usually, but not always, protect the general public. However, since each veto group is primarily concerned with defending its own sphere without consideration for the whole country, *leadership is weakened.*

In order to test theories of political power, many sociologists have conducted empirical studies in small communities, hoping to understand their power structures. We can look at these studies to see what light they may cast upon whether our national power structure is elitist or pluralist. We must be cautious, however, in generalizing from the community level to the national level, since such generalizations are clearly limited.

Studies of Power

In 1937, sociologists Robert S. and Helen M. Lynd conducted a study of a small city they called "Middletown." There they found that political power was held by five brothers who owned a large manufacturing company. These brothers were powerful because they wanted to be politically active. An equally wealthy family in the town was politically powerless because it was not interested in politics.[14]

In 1949, sociologist August B. Hollingshead conducted another study and came to similar conclusions. The wealthy farmers, professionals, and businesspeople he found in "Elmtown" owned most of the real estate, and public office was held only by those who would protect these important families by keeping taxes and town expenses low. Once more it seemed as if the wealthy controlled the town and its power structure.[15]

Sociologist Floyd Hunter asked known leaders in "Regional City" to identify those who made important decisions or who were powerful in the community. A power elite emerged composed of the city's top industrial and business leaders. These people saw to it that the mem-

329

APPLYING SOCIOLOGY

Given your knowledge of the workings of our national political structure, where would you place it on this scale running from elitist to pluralist? Why?

ELITIST   PLURALIST

---

bers of government were sympathetic to their economic interests. While there was no formal tie between the government and the community's economic interests, the members of the policy-making committees were people who could be trusted to protect the businesspeople. In this way, the government was made subservient to the wishes of the power elite.[16]

A fourth study by sociologists Arthur J. Vidich and Joseph Bensman revealed that an "invisible government," dominated by two lawyers, the editor of the local newspaper, and one businessman, made all the politically important decisions in a small upstate New York town. Elected government officials had no genuine ruling power at all.[17]

In short, these four studies of the power structures in four towns all appear to support Mills' theory that political power is concentrated in the hands of an elite. Each town had such an elite. The people in control were all wealthy, were all willing to enter political life, and were all close friends. These elites held the decision-making power of each community. The elected officials were without independent power and abided by the decisions of the elites.

Other studies of city governments, however, have lent support to the pluralistic theory. Sociologist Robert A. Dahl, for example, examined community power in New Haven, Connecticut, and was able to identify several veto groups with interests in different issues. There, political power was held by many groups and not by a ruling elite.[18]

Conclusion

All in all, there were fifty-four studies conducted between 1953 and 1965 of community power in small cities and towns in the United States. Eighteen of the communities had a clear ruling elite. Seventeen had veto groups that were relatively permanent in terms of membership and issues. Fourteen had veto groups that continually changed. The remaining five communities were difficult to categorize because they seemed to have combinations of both types. The question, then, of who has the political power remains unresolved. Most sociologists agree that *probably* communities have informal ruling elites that are comprised of the wealthier members of the community.

Nevertheless, we cannot say the same is true for national power. We cannot be sure that what is true on a local government level would be true on a national level. Sociologist Suzanne Keller comes closest to resolving the problem by stating that there are national "strategic elites."[19] These are collectivities of people (really interest groups) each having power in different areas. In addition to an economic elite, a military elite, and a political elite, Keller identifies such others as a cultural elite, a scientific elite, a religious elite, and a moral elite. These groups share power, according to Keller; there is no one single group that has it all.

We can see, then, that no one really knows who holds political power in the United States. The only point on which all researchers are in agreement is that, contrary to myth, the masses of people, the ordinary American citizens, do not possess as much political power as we would like to think they do.

SUMMARY

All societies have some kind of political institution that primarily serves to maintain social order and social control. The political institution developed and became more complex as societies grew from kinship groups to nations.

As nations appeared, four major types of government emerged. These are oligarchies, monarchies, dictatorships, and democracies. An *oligarchy* is a government ruled by a few people. A *monarchy* is a government ruled by a king or queen who inherits the right to rule. Monarchies can be either absolute, where the monarch's power is considered divine, or constitutional, where the monarch is a figurehead. A *dictatorship* or a *totalitarian state* is a nation whose ruler takes complete control without limitations and often without the consent of the people. A *democracy* is a political system based on rule by the consent of the majority of the governed. There are basically two kinds of democracies. A *participatory democracy* is one in which all the adults have a direct say in the government. A *representative democracy*, such as we have in the United States, is one in which people elect representatives to take care of their interests in the government.

The most important function of the political institution is to maintain social order. It does this by enacting and enforcing laws. Another function is to coordinate activities necessary for the smooth running of society and to provide citizens with those things which private industry cannot provide. A third function is to protect the members of a society from enemies, both foreign and domestic.

Participation in the political system, such as joining political parties and voting, is strongly related to a variety of social factors. Among them are age, educational level, race, ethnicity, religion, and social class.

According to Robert Bierstedt, *power* is different from many other concepts (such as prestige, influence, dominance, and rights) that are commonly confused with it. He suggests that force is manifest or open power and authority is institutionalized power. Power derives from three sources: number of individuals, social organization, and resources. A group is most powerful when it has all three sources.

Max Weber identified three kinds of authority. *Traditional authority* derives from custom and usually is hereditary. The ruler has the power because he or she inherited it. *Charismatic authority* is given to a leader who is believed by the followers to have magical qualities or special personal gifts. *Legal-rational authority* comes from the societal position, not the individual, and it is based on the consent of the governed. These three kinds of authority can overlap.

A controversy exists in sociology over who holds political power in the United States. Elitists, like C. Wright Mills, believe there is a "power elite," composed of heads of large corporations, military leaders, and top government officials, which controls the nation. Pluralists, like David Riesman, believe political power is divided among many veto groups. Studies of the power structures in towns and small cities have not been able to resolve this question, although there is some indication that most communities have at least an informal power elite that works behind the scenes.

GLOSSARY

authority   institutionalized or legitimized power.

charismatic authority   authority based on mystical personal qualities attributed to a popular leader.

common law   unwritten laws that have developed through custom and precedence.

constitutional laws   norms that are written into the constitutions of the national and local governments.

democracy   a form of government based on rule by the consent of the majority.

dictatorship   a form of government in which one person (usually with advisors) controls all the power to make and enforce laws. This form of government is often acquired by usurping the power of the former government.

elitism   a sociological theory which holds that national power is controlled by the leaders of business, government, and the military.

ideology   a system of beliefs held by a group that reflects, rationalizes, and defends the group's own interests, justifying that group's behavior, goals, attitudes, and values.

legal-rational authority   authority legitimated by a system of formal, written laws, invested in the office rather than in the individual.

monarchy   a form of government in which one person rules by inheritance. The government can either be absolute, in which the monarch is considered to be divine, or constitutional, in which the monarch is the head of state in title only.

oligarchy   a form of government in which a few people rule.

participatory democracy   a type of democracy in which the adult population is directly involved with the decision-making processes of government.

pluralism   a sociological theory which holds that power is diffused among interest or veto groups.

political institution   the social institution that serves to maintain social order and obedience through the creation and enforcement of rules and laws.

political party   an organization of people who are interested in controlling the political structure of a society.

power   the ability of one person to control the behavior of others; power is based on force and cannot be circumvented.

representative democracy   a type of democracy in which adult citizens elect representatives who they feel will best serve their interests.

statutory laws   specific norms enacted by a legislative body such as the Senate.

totalitarian state   government which is almost completely centralized and controls most aspects of a citizen's life.

traditional authority   authority derived from custom and accepted by people as being close to sacred.

veto groups   diversified power groups, each representing special interests and protecting its own rights.

REFERENCES

1. Robert Michels, *Political Parties*. New York: The Free Press, 1966.

2. Max Weber, *From Max Weber: Essays in Sociology*. Trans. by Hans H. Gerth and C. Wright Mills. New York: Oxford University Press, 1946, p. 78.

3. Herbert Marcuse, *One Dimensional Man: Studies in the Ideology of Advanced Industrial Society*. Boston: Beacon Press, 1964.

4. Theodore L. Becker, *American Government: Past*, Present*, and Future*. Boston: Allyn & Bacon, 1976. See especially Chapter VI.

5. Walter Dean Burnham, "Equality of Voting." In Lee Rainwater, ed., *Social Problems and Public Policy*. Chicago: Aldine, 1974, pp. 288–298.

6. Maurice Pinard, "Poverty and Political Movements." *Social Problems* 15:2 (1967): 250–263.

7. Kurt H. Wolff, trans. and ed., *The Sociology of Georg Simmel.* Glencoe, Ill.: The Free Press, 1950.

8. This section is based on the work of Robert Bierstedt, "An Analysis of Social Power." *American Sociological Review* 15:6 (1950): 730–738.

9. Bierstedt, p. 735.

10. Bierstedt, p. 736.

11. Weber, p. 180.

12. C. Wright Mills, *The Power Elite.* New York: Oxford University Press, 1959.

13. David Riesman, *The Lonely Crowd.* New Haven, Conn.: Yale University Press, 1961.

14. Robert S. Lynd and Helen M. Lynd, *Middletown in Transition.* New York: Harcourt, Brace, 1937.

15. August B. Hollingshead, *Elmtown's Youth.* New York: John Wiley & Sons, 1949.

16. Floyd Hunter, *Community Power Structure.* Chapel Hill, N.C.: University of North Carolina Press, 1953.

17. Arthur J. Vidich and Joseph Bensman, *Small Town in Mass Society.* Garden City, N.Y.: Doubleday, 1958.

18. Robert A. Dahl, *Who Governs?* New Haven, Conn.: Yale University Press, 1961.

19. Suzanne Keller, *Beyond the Ruling Class.* New York: Random House, 1963.

SUGGESTED READINGS

Aiken, Michael, and Paul Mott (eds.). *The Structure of Community Power.* New York: Random House, 1970.

A collection of articles that evaluate all sociological knowledge of community power.

Bottomore, T. B. *Elites and Society.* Baltimore: Penguin, 1967.

A short review of political theory from Pareto to Mills.

Dahl, Robert A. *Who Governs? Democracy and Power in an American City.* New Haven, Conn.: Yale University Press, 1961.

The strongest argument against Floyd Hunter, insisting that community power is diffused among interest groups and not concentrated in a power elite.

Domhoff, G. William. *The Higher Circles: Governing Class in America.* New York: Random House, 1970.

Empirical evidence supporting C. Wright Mills' notion of a national ruling class.

Hunter, Floyd. *Community Power Structure*. Chapel Hill, N.C.: University of North Carolina Press, 1953.

  The first study of community power, which asserts that there is a governing elite.

MacIver, Robert. *The Web of Government*. New York: The Free Press, 1947.

  A classic analysis of the interrelationships among political institutions.

Milgram, Stanley, *Obedience to Authority: An Experimental View*. New York: Harper & Row, 1974.

  In some startling experiments where subjects are directed to administer electrical shocks to a protesting victim, Milgram probes the strong tendency people seem to have to obey an authority figure.

Mills, C. Wright. *The Power Elite*. New York: Oxford University Press, 1959.

  The first sociological description of a national ruling elite, composed of the people at the top of government, industry, and the military.

Rose, Arnold M. *The Power Structure: Political Processes in American Society*. New York: Oxford University Press, 1967.

  The major challenge to Mills' concept of a power elite.

Tretick, Stanley and William V. Shannon. *They Could Not Trust the King*. New York: Macmillan, 1974.

  An account of the recent Watergate episode in the United States.

FOUR

Sociology in Everyday Life

We have seen that sociology affects our society, our development, and our social institutions. But sociology also plays a major role in other aspects of our existence. In this section we will examine how sociology influences our everyday lives.

From the moment of birth we are cast into certain groups. And it is within these groups that we spend our lives. Consequently, these groups help determine the types of people we become. Of major concern to us here are gender groups, racial and ethnic groups, and social classes. These topics will be covered in Chapters 11, 12, and 13.

The worlds of work and leisure play a major role in our daily lives, too. Although we usually do not enter the work world until we are adults, we are constantly surrounded by people who are a part of it. In addition, all of us engage in the pursuit of leisure activities. The topics of work and leisure will be the focus of Chapter 14.

Throughout our lives we encounter rules. As we discussed in Chapters 1 and 4, most of us obey most rules most of the time. Yet most of us deviate from some rules at one time or another. In Chapter 15 we will discuss deviance, a phenomenon that occurs when people are believed to have violated a group rule.

In Chapter 16 we will discuss the physical world we inhabit and the consequences of the population explosion. Such consequences affect us all, regardless of where we live.

In this section, then, we will see how sociology affects our everyday lives. We will discover that everything we are, have, own, think, do, or believe is in some way related to sociology.

The Sexes

Outside the nursery window at General Hospital, a man and a little boy admire the newborn baby wrapped in a blanket being held up by a nurse for them to see. The little boy asks a lot of excited questions. "Why doesn't it open its eyes, Daddy?" "Why is its face so red?" "Can it hear me talking?" "When can we take it home?"

The father smiles at his son. "Why do you call your new sister 'it,' Jeffrey? Can't you tell we have a little girl?"

"How am I supposed to tell?"

"Because," answers the father patiently, "The baby is wrapped in a pink blanket. Everyone knows that pink is for girls and blue is for boys."

Such a scene happens every day in the United States. Whenever we encounter a new person, whether it is a newborn sibling, a new classmate, a person at a party, or a stranger at our door, the first thing we do is identify that person's sex. Why should sex be so important?

The reason is that society places much emphasis on *sex status*—whether a person is born male or female. This status determines *gender role*—how a person will be socialized, what position he or she will hold in society, and what behavior will be expected from him or her. Along with the male sex status goes the masculine gender role; along with the female sex status, the feminine gender role. It is these statuses and roles that we will examine in this chapter.

Differences Between the Sexes—Inborn or Learned?

Much of what happens to men and women during their lives is symbolized by the different color blankets first placed on them as newborn

babies. From that very first hour of life, they are treated according to their sex. Hence, men and women come to think of themselves differently, have different experiences, and go through life as if they are almost different species.

But are the sexes really all that different from each other? Or do we just think of them as being so different? Are the differences we perceive biological in origin? Are they cultural? Or are they a little of both? In short, are the different gender roles that men and women develop inborn or are they learned?

These are some of the questions we will deal with in this chapter. In an attempt to answer these questions, we will look at viewpoints offered by scientists from several disciplines.

VIEWPOINTS FROM BIOLOGY

Among modern biologists there are two schools of thought concerning sexuality. One group argues that how a person develops psychosexually is determined biologically at birth; the other group argues that babies are psychosexually neuter at birth, neither masculine nor feminine.

Biological Determinism

The first group claims that there are inherent physical differences between the sexes that are apparent almost at conception. For example, more male fetuses than female fetuses die before birth. More boys than girls are stillborn, and more boys than girls die during the first year of life. Males are more likely to have congenital defects, circulatory diseases, pneumonia, diarrhea, and influenza. Males have poorer vision and more color blindness, and they are more prone to deafness. These biologists reason that if such innate physical differences exist, then innate psychological differences exist as well. That is, females are born passive, dependent, sensitive, intuitive, and emotional; while males are born aggressive, rational, self-controlled, independent, and active.[1] Biologist Corinne Hutt's study is typical of those claiming that psychosexual differentiation is present at birth. Hutt believes that differences in terms of growth, maturation, abilities, attitudes, and interests are all present at the time an infant is born.[2]

Neutrality Theory

Biologists who subscribe to the neutrality theory take an opposing view. They postulate that while there are some small differences between newborn infants of different sexes, it is the training they receive that determines their gender roles. One such biologist wrote:

Psychologic sex or gender role appears to be learned—that is to say, it is differentiated through learning during the course of the many experiences of growing up. . . .We [postulate] a concept of psychosexual neutrality in humans at birth. Such neutrality permits the development and perpetuation of many patterns of psychosexual orientation and functioning in accordance with the life experiences each individual may encounter and transact.[3]

Such scientists, led by John Money, claim that from the moment an infant is identified in the hospital delivery room as male or female, society does everything possible to reinforce the gender role it considers appropriate.[4] Money refutes the biological determinists' claim that gender roles are present at birth by showing that children can be socialized into the "wrong" gender roles. As one example, Money studied *hermaphrodites*, those individuals who exhibit a contradiction between their external genital appearance and their chromosomes or their internal reproductive systems. His research showed that the gender role into which a person is reared has a greater influence than one's chromosomal patterns. Thus, hermaphrodites who were male chromosomally thought of themselves as female if they were reared as females.[5]

As a second example, Money cites one case involving boy twins. In this instance, the penis of one was mutilated at birth. Doctors and parents decided that the best solution was a sex reassignment. Surgery was performed and the boy was then reared as a normal girl.[6]

Biologists, then, are divided in their conceptualization of masculinity and femininity. Some claim sexual characteristics, like physical characteristics, are innate; others claim that nature does not do its job without help from nurture.

VIEWPOINTS FROM PSYCHOLOGY

Comparative psychologists use animals as subjects because experiments can be conducted on animals that cannot be conducted on human beings. Many of these studies seem to indicate that there are

---

APPLYING SOCIOLOGY

Sometimes we hear about individuals who undergo long and complicated sex-change operations, often because of hormonal imbalances that cause them unhappiness in their assigned gender role. How would biological determinists and neutrality theorists react to news of such operations? Which do you believe has a greater influence on our behavior, our sex at birth or the gender-role training we are taught? Why?

sex-linked differences in the hypothalamus—a part of the central nervous system and fhat part of the brain which influences the endocrine system. In one such study, psychologist R. W. Goy injected pregnant rhesus monkeys with androgen, a male sex hormone. The female monkeys born of these androgen-injected mothers showed what are considered typical "masculine" traits—aggressiveness, toughness, and roughness.[7] When another psychologist, S. N. Levine, injected newborn female rats with testosterone, another male hormone, he found that the rats did not display normal female physiology.[8]

Many other comparative psychologists have conducted similar experiments on several species of animals. They all have come to similar conclusions. Sex hormones strongly influence the behavior of animals. When young males receive extra male hormones, they become more "masculine"; when young females receive male hormones, they become "masculinized." (The reverse, however, is not true. When young males received doses of estrogen, a female hormone, they did not necessarily become more "feminine.")

But just how much can these animal studies tell us about how human beings behave? Is what is true for animals necessarily true for people? Comparative psychologists may say, "Probably so," but most social scientists do not agree that such leaps from animal to human being are acceptable. Therefore, they usually reject these conclusions. As Naomi Weisstein says, "It would be reasonable to conclude [from animal studies] that it is quite useless to teach human infants to speak since it has been tried with chimpanzees and it does not work."[9]

Other psychologists[10] work with young human infants in their attempts to explain why males and females display different personality patterns. Infants are preferable to adults as subjects because they have had less time to learn the society's norms about masculine and feminine personalities. These psychologists reason that if sex-linked differences are discovered in such young babies, the probability is greater that they are inborn rather than learned.

Studies by these scientists reveal that many sex-linked differences exist in very young infants. For example, boy babies are more active than girl babies, and girl babies are more responsive to touch than boy babies.[11] However, many of these findings are still inconclusive because no matter how young the child, it is still possible that the society has had an effect on it. After all, from the moment of birth, males and females are handled in different ways.

Other psychologists who work with infants believe that gender roles are learned. Such psychologists, known as *social learning theorists*, postulate that young children learn to behave in ways that invite rewards and avoid behavior that incurs punishment. Behavior that corresponds with one's sex status is looked upon favorably by others

343

Social learning theorists postulate that gender roles are learned at an early age. Little girls generally are encouraged to exhibit "feminine" behavior, whereas little boys are urged to act "masculine."

and hence rewarded. In this manner, girls learn to be "feminine" and boys learn to be "masculine."

One study by Albert Bandura[12] offers evidence supporting the social learning theory. Bandura showed a film on aggression to groups of boys and girls. One segment of the film portrayed the actor being rewarded for aggression; in another, the actor was punished; and in the third segment, aggression was neither rewarded nor punished. The children were then asked to imitate the actor's behaviors. Both boys and girls were much more likely to imitate the behavior that had been rewarded in the film. The implication here is that females can be taught to be aggressive if they are shown that aggression is rewarded.

Still other psychologists, known as *cognitive development theorists*, believe that both nature and nurture play a part in the acquisition of gender roles. Lawrence Kohlberg,[13] for example, believes that children learn gender roles in two ways—through their recognition of themselves as males or females and through their identification as such by others. Once sexual identity is established, children identify with members of the same sex group and learn to prefer stereotypical behaviors and objects. In other words, Kohlberg believes that children construct their own gender roles in a process that interweaves biology and culture. As support for his theory, Kohlberg conducted a study in which he asked children to identify males and females. They were able

344

to do this very accurately and when asked on what they based their answers, the children replied that they had looked at the people's shoes.

In the same study, Kohlberg further shows that children are uncertain of gender identity until about the age of six. A group of four-year-olds were asked if a girl in a picture could be a boy if she wanted to or if she wore boys' clothing or played boys' games. The four-year-olds agreed that such change was possible. Another group of six- to eight-year-olds, asked the same question, believed that such change was impossible.

Thus, like biologists, psychologists hold different views explaining how gender roles are acquired. Some stress the role of nature, some place an emphasis on nurture, and some feel that both nature and nurture share the responsibility.

A VIEWPOINT FROM ANTHROPOLOGY

The famous anthropologist Margaret Mead visited three tribes in New Guinea in the early 1930s.[14] One group, the Arapesh, did not think there were any temperamental differences between the sexes. All the people in this society were brought up to be noncompetitive and nonaggressive. Both men and women were gentle, kind to each other, home-loving, and generous. Both took care of the children and both gathered food. In short, both sexes displayed what most societies would consider "feminine" qualities.

The second group, the Mundugumor, was just the opposite. Relationships among all members of this group were aggressive, competitive, and hostile. Violence was a common occurrence. Both parents were indifferent to their children and gave them little love or attention. Like the Arapesh, then, the Mundugumor did not differentiate between females and males and most people of this tribe displayed what most Americans would think of as "masculine" qualities.

The Tchambuli, the third group, did distinguish between the sexes, but the characteristics that were admired for each sex were exactly the opposite of those Americans admire. Men were passive and were allowed to display their emotions. Males spent their time gossiping, adorning themselves, caring for the children, and just lounging around. Tchambuli women, on the other hand, were in charge of the society's economic life, doing the hunting and fishing, and even trading. The women did little to make themselves attractive and were practical and businesslike in their dealings with other groups. Even in courtship, the women were the aggressors. For the Tchambuli, then, women displayed American "masculine" traits and men displayed American "feminine" traits.

345

Mead's study offers solid evidence for the viewpoint that gender roles are determined by what the society considers appropriate. According to this study, there is little that is innate in our gender-role behavior. Societies provide the guidelines and members of societies adhere to them in establishing their sexual identity.

THE SOCIOLOGICAL VIEWPOINT

Most sociologists take a position that includes social learning theory, biological neutrality theory, and anthropology, resulting in an interdisciplinary explanation. Yet for the most part sociologists focus on the socialization process and on the relationship between the child and the culture. According to most sociologists, sexual identity is developed as children interact with the members of their families, who are agents of the society.

For example, one study showed that children tend to imitate the role models who are most able to reward behavior. Little girls, there-

Most sociologists agree that sexual identity develops as young children interact with parents and other family members.

fore, interact with their mothers and have the opportunity to learn to be more verbal and more sensitive to others—a feminine trait. In the process they copy their mothers' behavior and are likely to be rewarded.[15] Another study demonstrated how differential handling begins at birth and helps to determine masculinity and femininity.[16] This research shows that our society sets up such characteristics as activity-passivity and independence-dependence as valid indexes of masculine-feminine development. A third study showed the influence of reinforcement on appropriate gender-role behavior, even in very young children.[17] Preschool children were found to respond to praise for proper gender-role behavior from teachers and peer group members. But when teachers tried to reinforce feminine behavior in little boys, the boys continued to show a preference for masculine behavior.

Most sociologists, then, take a position similar to the biological neutrality theory and incorporate parts of social learning theory and socialization theory. Although they realize that there are obvious physiological differences between the sexes beginning at birth, they do not believe that these differences affect the acquisition of gender roles. Rather, they believe that gender roles are learned according to the prescriptions and the needs of the society. In other words, children are born with almost no psychosexual differences. Psychosexual differences are learned during the socialization process as we interact with members of our groups. To what extent does research support this viewpoint?

Testing the Sociological Viewpoint

One question that has plagued scientists for a long time is who is more intelligent, females or males? The answer has always been inconclusive because there is no accurate way of measuring intelligence (see Chapter 7). For a long time tests that tried to measure intelligence seemed to indicate that whites were more intelligent than blacks, upper-class people were more intelligent than lower-class people, and urban people were more intelligent than rural people. Then the designers of the standardized intelligence tests discovered that the tests themselves were biased, favoring whites over blacks, rich over poor, and urban over rural. The designers found that the groups that appeared more intelligent were really just more *familiar* with the items used in the tests.

The same kind of test bias existed for the sexes. Intelligence tests in the past included items favoring males over females and consequently males *appeared* to be more intelligent. Today, however, standardized intelligence tests have come a long way toward removing

347

FOCUS ON: BABY "X"

What would happen if we did not label our children "boys" or "girls"? Author Lois Gould wrote a story called "X: A Fabulous Child's Story" in which she shows what might happen if a baby were not given a sexual identity.

When "X" was born relatives, neighbors, and friends thought the parents were joking when they refused to tell the child's sex. Later, though, most of the people became very angry. They couldn't decide what gifts to buy for "X." They couldn't admire "her" cute dimples or "his" husky biceps. Some relatives were even embarrassed because they were afraid people would think something was wrong with the child.

Of course the parents' resolution to treat their child as if its sex didn't matter caused them a number of problems. They couldn't toss it up in the air too often—that would be treating it like a boy. They couldn't cuddle it gently too often—that would be treating it like a girl. Buying clothes and toys was also difficult because most such items were clearly marked for one sex or the other.

When the child entered school new problems developed. There were boys' lines and girls' lines; boys' books and girls' books; boys' bathrooms and girls' bathrooms. But gradually teachers and school administrators worked out ways to resolve these and other problems.

At first the children tried to trick the new student into telling its sex, but that didn't work. Later when X still refused to reveal its sex, the other pupils finally gave up and discovered that X enjoyed doing all kinds of things that it would not have been able to do if it had to obey the rules for either sex. X liked dolls *and* electric trains. X could play house *and* baseball.

Slowly, the other children imitated their new classmate. Girls began to refuse to wear "feminine" clothes and became interested in getting newspaper routes and mowing lawns. Boys began to play with their sisters' dolls and wanted to help their mothers in the kitchen. Both sexes had realized they were missing out on a lot of fun that X was having.

Of course the parents were upset and angry by the new behaviors of their children and they refused to let them play with X. They even went to see the school principal to complain that the new pupil was a "disruptive influence" and to insist that the parents of X should be forced to reveal the child's sexual identity. At a PTA meeting it was decided to have X tested by the school psychiatrist in order to discover its sex and if it were confused about itself.

Everyone waited expectantly outside the psychiatrist's office for the report. At last the door opened. X didn't look any different; in fact, X was smiling. But the psychiatrist looked terrible. He looked as if he were crying! Wiping his eyes and clearing his throat, the psychiatrist said, "In my opinion, young X here is just about the least mixed-up child I've ever examined!"

And so it turned out that X wasn't mixed up at all because it had not been labeled "girl" or "boy." X knew exactly what it was and by the time it mattered—when it came time to choose a mate—everyone else would know too.

Gould's story shows what life might be like if individuals were reared without any emphasis on sex status or gender role. Do you think it would be a good idea to rear children that way? Why or why not? What kind of attitudes would such children have when it came time to choose a mate? Do you think any society could ignore the fact that some of its members are males and some are females? Why or why not?

Source: Lois Gould, "X: A Fabulous Child's Story," *Ms. Magazine,* Vol. 1, December 1972, pp. 74–77.

sex biases, and the result is that no meaningful or consistent differences seem to exist between the sexes. Neither group tests out to be smarter on general intelligence.[18] Yet there are consistent differences in specific subareas. According to research, girls score higher on tests of verbal ability and memory tests involving verbal skills. Boys score higher on tests of mechanical ability, mathematical skills, spatial orientation, scientific ability, and motor ability. In addition, boys do better on memory tests involving numerical skills. Although males excel on some tests involving problem-solving, there is little difference between the sexes in other types of problem-solving. Let us look at each of these subareas and try to explain why these differences exist.

Girls are superior on all tests involving the use of verbal skills. They speak and read earlier and faster than boys, they better understand what they read, their vocabularies are larger, and they have fewer speech defects. Researchers believe the reason for female verbal superiority has to do with the way females are socialized. Girls are encouraged to stay indoors more than boys, and so they spend more time during early childhood interacting with the people who are raising them. Thus they engage in more conversations at an earlier age than boys and are more comfortable using words. In short, girls learn to talk more, while boys learn to use their bodies more. Apparently, girls do not really have greater innate verbal skills, just more practice with words.

Males score higher on all tests of mechanical ability for precisely the same reasons that females score higher on tests of verbal skills—as boys are growing up, they are encouraged to develop these skills. One proof that this difference is probably a psychological one lies in the fact that the differences in mechanical skills do not show up until children are of school age. There are no differences among preschool children. If the cause were biological, the superiority of boys would be evident from the beginning of life. Since it takes time for boys to outperform girls mechanically, it means the culture has had time to work.

We usually think that boys are better with numbers than girls. Girls supposedly do not like arithmetic or mathematics nor are they expected to do well in these subjects in school. The test results, however, are similar to those on mechanical skills. There is little or no difference in numerical ability between the sexes until about fourth grade, when boys begin to score higher than girls. Most social scientists claim that this occurs because at about this age girls begin to "get the message" that it is not "feminine" to be good at arithmetic. Therefore, we may probably conclude that social expectations are dominant over biological factors in this area.

The differences in test scores on memory between males and females depend on what is being memorized. Girls score higher when

Although school-age males score higher than females on tests of mechanical and mathematical skills, there is no difference in performance between the sexes during the early childhood years. This leads us to believe that social factors rather than biological factors account for the difference.

the test involves verbal skills; boys score higher when the test involves numerical skills. It seems clear that neither sex is superior to the other in terms of memory itself. Rather the differences have to do with whether or not children are interested in or familiar with the topics they are being asked to memorize.

It is a cultural belief in American society that women have no sense of direction, and research appears to uphold this belief. When people are placed in distorted situations, males are better than females at orienting themselves. Males can determine the position of their own bodies much better than females can without dependence on the external visual field. Psychologists explain this by saying that females are taught from childhood to be more dependent, and therefore they rely on external validation of their physical (and probably social) positions. Once again, the explanation is probably social rather than biological.

Although there is a much greater proportion of males who take science courses in school and there are many more male than female scientists, tests show no significant differences between the sexes in scientific ability. Most researchers explain the higher percentage of males in these fields on the basis of encouragement and interest. Males apparently are not better scientists; they are just more likely to be supported in such endeavors because science is thought of as a "masculine" field.

In tests of problem-solving, males are superior in some types and there is little or no difference between the sexes in others; but in no type are females superior. Why? Partly because women tend to think that solving problems is not "feminine" and partly because women, on the basis of their socialization, cannot make independent decisions as easily as men can.

Finally, males do much better than females in most motor ability tests, starting at preschool age and continuing through life. Once again, the researchers attribute these findings to differences in culturally induced motivation rather than in real innate physical ability.

In summary, it appears that when researchers compare males and females on many skills and abilities, they frequently find differences, but they find little proof that the differences are biological or innate. Rather, these differences seem to be related to cultural influences. Females and males are encouraged to like different activities and their interests diverge at an early age because of this encouragement. Thus, they are socialized to develop different gender roles.

Socialization for Gender Roles

Just how are people socialized into their gender roles? They are socialized by going through the same process that they go through to learn any other social role. Once a society decides the appropriate gender role attached to a sex status, each generation passes this knowledge down to the next generation. Try to recall how many times in your life someone has said to you, "Little boys don't do that"; or "Little girls don't behave that way." Children hear these phrases and others like them over and over again. They are being socialized to be masculine or feminine according to their sex status. They are acquiring and internalizing the values, attitudes, goals, and behaviors associated with that

APPLYING SOCIOLOGY

Think back over your childhood to see how you were socialized into your gender role. What kinds of toys did you play with? Do you remember being rewarded for "appropriate" masculine or feminine behavior while being punished for behavior that was not considered proper for your sex? If you have children, do you think you will socialize them into their gender roles as you were socialized into yours?

sex status. Eventually these attributes of masculinity and femininity come to seem like the only possible ways for males or females to behave.

In most Western societies male children are traditionally taught to be brave and strong, never to show weakness or fear, never to cry, always to be cool, independent, aggressive, and active. Female children are taught to be dainty, sweet, soft, gentle, polite, and neat. But these characteristics are not natural. People are not born with them. They are learned. *To be born male, then, does not guarantee one will be masculine. To be born female does not guarantee one will be feminine.* People must be carefully taught their gender roles in order to fit their sex statuses.

If gender roles are not natural, then why do they exist? Why do we not eliminate such roles and allow each sex to develop to its fullest potential?

REASONS FOR GENDER-ROLE SOCIALIZATION

As we mentioned in the Introduction (p. 7), sociologists view society through different sociological perspectives. To answer the above questions let us turn to two of these perspectives—structural-functionalism and conflict theory.

Structural-Functionalism

Structural-functionalists view the distinctions between men and women as useful for a society's well-being. Societies function more efficiently if there is a clear division of labor and if the members are socialized to perform their assigned tasks willingly and well. Of course, a division of labor can be along several dimensions—age, level of education, race, and so forth. And in each society the division of labor is structured somewhat differently. Yet in almost all societies there is a division of labor along sex lines. Men have their tasks to perform; women, theirs; and this division of labor is usually viewed as "natural." Men are expected to provide the family income, to protect the family, and to be the dominant adult members. Women are expected to care for the home and to raise the children.

Two functionalists, Talcott Parsons and Robert F. Bales, argue that families in modern industrial societies need males and females in these specialized roles just as much as families did in preliterate societies.[19] The *instrumental role* is the male role, meaning that the father serves as a bridge between the family and the rest of the society because he earns the family's living. The mother plays the *expressive role*, focusing on internal family relations and providing the love and affection that cements the family members into a united group. This sharp division of labor, according to the functionalists, demands that the male be dominant, aggressive, and protective and the female be nurturant, passive, and dependent.

Conflict Theory

Conflict theorists take issue with structural-functionalism on gender-role socialization as they do on almost every social issue. They claim that such tightly structured gender roles were appropriate in traditional societies, but are unnecessary in the modern family. Males' brute strength and females' constant child rearing are no longer needed.[20] Muscles have been replaced by machines and, although women still must give birth to the children, they no longer need to spend their entire adult lives rearing them. Conflict theorists accuse functionalists of trying to maintain the status quo and in so doing they deprive men of the pleasures of being gentle and nurturing and women of the satisfactions of being successful in the world outside the home.

Sociologist Randall Collins argues that gender-role inequality is based on a conflict of interests between the sexes. In order to enhance their own power, men try to keep women in a subordinate position and prevent them from operating in the political and economic areas of social life. If women remain in their inferior positions, men stand to gain because they have less competition to deal with. Conflict theorists do not claim that men consciously keep women down. Rather, since men derive benefits from the present arrangement, they take that arrangement for granted and are not motivated to alter it. Furthermore, as the dominant group, men are able to control the continuation of the traditional gender-role patterns.[21]

At any rate, both structural-functionalists and conflict theorists agree that gender roles exist. And based on our ideas about these roles and our socialization into them, we can paint a picture of what men and women are supposed to be like.

THE IDEAL FEMALE AND THE IDEAL MALE

If you were asked to describe the traditional American middle-class stereotype of a perfectly feminine woman, you would probably not have any trouble doing so. You might say that a feminine woman is gentle and kind and likes to help people. You might also say that she does not feel "normal" unless she is married and has children because women have a natural "maternal instinct."

Your description might also include the belief that a woman without a man is unnatural. For this reason, you would look at an unattached woman with pity, thinking no man ever wanted her. Your view would be based on society's assumption that women need to depend on

FOCUS ON: THE TOTAL WOMAN

In a best-selling book of the 1970s, *The Total Woman,* Marabel Morgan advised wives on how to keep their husbands happy and their marriages exciting. Her advice can be condensed into her four "A's" for success.

Accept him. "Your husband is what he is. Accept him as that. This principle is as old as life itself . . . . Tolerance is not acceptance. Your tolerance only makes your husband feel incomplete and unworthy. He can sense when he's not being accepted, and is not able to love you fully . . . . Your man needs to feel important, loved, and accepted. If you won't accept his idiosyncrasies, who will? A Total Woman caters to her man's special quirks, whether it be in salads, sex, or sports. She makes his home his haven, a place to which he can run. She allows him that priceless luxury of unqualified acceptance."

Admire him. "Women need to be loved; men need to be admired. We women would do well to remember this one important difference between us and the other half . . . . It is our nature to give. It is your highest privilege to assure him that he is as special as he hoped he was . . . . Give him one good compliment a day and watch him blossom right before your eyes."

Adapt to him. "The biblical remedy for marital conflict is stated 'You wives must submit to your husbands' leadership in the same way you submit to the Lord.' God planned for woman to be under her husband's rule . . . . God ordained man to be the head of the family, its pres-

ident, and his wife to be the executive vice-president. There is no way you can alter or improve this arrangement . . . . Adapting to his activities, his friends, and his food is not always easy, but it's right. And I know when I don't want to adapt, it's my problem, not his. It is only when a woman surrenders her life to her husband, reveres and worships him, and is willing to serve him, that she becomes really beautiful to him. She becomes a priceless jewel, the glory of femininity, his queen! . . ."

Appreciate him. "Stop a moment and check your gratitude meter. Are you guilty of that heinous act of ingratitude? Are you appreciative of the basics your husband knocks himself out to provide? Not just the birthday and Christmas 'specials,' but money for the groceries, doctor bills, and pillow cases? . . . . Appreciate all he does for you. Sincerely tell him 'Thank you' with your attitude, actions, and words. Give him your undivided attention, and try not to make any telephone calls after he comes home, especially after 8:00 P.M. . . ."

What do you think of Morgan's rules for marital happiness? Do you think husbands should be given the same advice about their wives? Why or why not? Do you believe that it is up to the wife to cater to her husband alone, or should husbands and wives cater to each other? Do you think men and women would be happier if more wives took this kind of advice? Why or why not?

Source: Marabel Morgan, *The Total Woman,* New York: Pocket Books, 1975.

men for financial support, for security, and for identity. As evidence you would cite the fact that women are asked, "What does your husband do?"; rarely "What do *you* do?" Furthermore, female dependency on men is symbolized at birth when babies are given the last names of their fathers. It is carried through to marriage when women take the names of their husbands.

The idea of gender roles is so strong in our society that most of us would have no trouble describing the traditional middle-class American stereotype of the ideal woman (left) and the ideal man (right).

You might conclude by saying that society's middle-class stereotype expects that the "real" woman should spend most of her time caring for her home and family. She should get pleasure from keeping her house clean, serving healthy and delicious meals, seeing to it that the laundry is clean and fresh, the dishes are washed, and the family is comfortable. Society expects, in short, that a good woman will put her husband's and her children's needs above her own and will gladly make sacrifices for their happiness.

How about the traditional stereotype for middle-class men? What natural attributes are they supposed to have? According to the stereotype, men should always be strong. They should never allow their emotions to get the better of them. They should not cry when they are unhappy. Men should not have temper tantrums; they should not show fear or self-doubt; they should be ready to protect their families in emergencies.

In addition, husbands and fathers are expected to be good providers. It is thought that something is wrong with a man who is not willing to work hard and get ahead in his occupation in order to give his family all the good things in life. Therefore, all men are expected to be breadwinners. Men are respected if they are ambitious and work hard.

The ideal male is also thought of as competitive, not only in work, but in sports and games. Males are supposed to be interested in sports—at least in watching them, if not in participating. One often hears of the father who is disappointed because his son is not an athlete or sports-minded. So, "real" men should be strong, fearless, independent, protective, ambitious, and athletic.

355

APPLYING SOCIOLOGY

If you were to create an ideal female and an ideal male, what traits would you want each to have? Are the traits you chose typically masculine or feminine? Do you think our society would be different if all men and women lived up to your ideals? If so, in what ways?

The Consequences of Gender-Role Socialization

These, then, are the gender roles our society has valued in the past and that still persist to a great extent. How do they affect our lives? What consequences flow from the persistence of these stereotypes?

INTERPERSONAL RELATIONSHIPS

Most women and men in American society marry and raise children. Because of this pattern, both wife and husband come to live in restricted worlds. The wife is largely confined to the home, the supermarket, the laundry, and the park if there are children. Even when wives work outside their homes, as more than half of them do, homemaking chores usually head their list of priorities. A husband spends most of his working hours in an office or a factory, and his occupation is supposed to be his main interest. Thus, for most women the primary status is homemaker and for most men it is breadwinner. What do these statuses consist of? What do people do when they are engaged in playing these roles?

The Wife and Mother

Homemaking is the major occupation for almost 50 percent of all married women in this country. Here is how journalist Ann Scott described the job of housewife:

Help Wanted

Requirements: Intelligence, good health, energy, patience, sociability. Skills: at least 12 different occupations. Hours: 99.6 per week. Salary: None. Holidays: None (will be required to remain on stand-by 24 hours a day, seven days a week). Opportunities for advancement: None (limited transferability of skills acquired on the job). Job Security: None (trend is toward more layoffs, particularly as employee approaches middle age). Severance pay will depend on the discretion of the employer. Fringe benefits: Food, clothing, and shelter generally provided, but any additional bonuses will depend on financial standing and good nature of the employer. No health, medical, or accident insurance, no Social Security or pension plan.[22]

Jessie Bernard (1903–   )

Jessie Bernard is noted for her pioneering studies on women, black marriage, and remarriage. One of her more tantalizing notions is that there are really two marriages in every marital union—his and hers. And, according to Bernard, his is much better than hers. In her book *The Future of Marriage,* she reanalyzes the data on married men, unmarried men, married women, and unmarried women on several dimensions. She concludes that although we believe that men try to "escape" marriage and women try to "trap" them into it, married men are better off in almost every way than unmarried men and married women.

According to Bernard, married men are superior both socially and psychologically to unmarried men. They are healthier both physically and mentally; they have a much lower suicide rate; they live longer; they have a ready confidante; and they receive all sorts of personal services, such as having their meals cooked and their laundry done.

Married women, on the other hand, suffer much more mental frustration and dissatisfaction than men and unmarried women. More of them report psychological problems, such as nervous breakdowns, depression, and phobias. They claim to cry more readily, feel hurt and miserable, and fear death.

In short, Bernard demonstrates that married women suffer more than any of the other groups. She attributes this fact to the greater "shock" women experience when marriage occurs. That is, women are expected to adjust to their husbands more than men to their wives. Such an adjustment often leads to a loss of personal identity and a sense of "self" on the part of women. Being housewives, says Bernard, makes women sick!

Bernard does not believe, however, that marriage will eventually disappear. In fact, she states, very few other human relationships have such an assured future. But the institution of marriage may take different forms in the years to come. Husbands and wives will have a variety of ways in which to relate to each other, a variety so great, says Bernard, that it will boggle the imagination.

Perhaps, though, Jessie Bernard's greatest contribution has been as a role model for women sociologists. She has given women an incentive to succeed in a field that in the past had been almost totally dominated by men.

Sociologist Theodore Caplow suggests that the status of housewife has a very low value in our society because anyone can do it at least moderately well.[23] Even housewives themselves are often apologetic when they describe their occupation, saying "I'm just a housewife." It is an occupation that has very little dignity or respect attached to it. Furthermore, when a woman does not work outside her home, she usually has a problem of overdependency on her husband. Such dependency takes three major forms.

357

"Well, for goodness sake, Helene—you were right!"

One is social. Many housewives and mothers do not spend much time during the day with other adults. Since human beings need peers to interact with, housewives are therefore dependent for companionship on their husbands after the workday. Husbands, on the other hand, are often tired of interacting all day with others, and they frequently want only peace and quiet in the evening. Because each partner has different needs, couples sometimes experience marital strain, which can be harmful to the marriage.

A second kind of dependency for the housewife is economic. The law does not state precisely what is meant by the notion that men must support their wives, so wives are really dependent on the generosity of their husbands. In addition, it means that adult women, like children, must ask another adult for money to supply even their personal needs. Finally, the economic dependency of wives on husbands increases the myth that men are more important than women. After all, the person who controls the purse strings usually controls everything else. Economic dependency, then, helps to perpetuate the notion that women are childlike and men are adults.

The third kind of dependency is based on the fact that women do not have separate social identities. One sign of this, as mentioned earlier, is that wives take their husbands' names. Then too, they often are referred to as "John Smith's wife" or "the doctor's wife." Wives are not people in their own right. They need their husbands to give them a position in society.

In short, many women suffer from lack of autonomy in their lives. Since their socialization has encouraged them to be dependent, girls and women are generally not risk-takers. They are often passive and show timidity and weakness. Feminine socialization is likely to lead, then, to a lack of self-assertiveness and self-actualization. Much of a woman's life is lived in the reflected achievements of others—her father, her husband, her children.

The Husband and Father

What about the male breadwinner? Isn't he as tied into his status as his wife is into hers? Being a breadwinner typically means working five days a week, eight hours a day. It means constantly worrying about keeping one's job and getting ahead. It means both physical and emotional separation from the family so that men miss out on much of the excitement and joy of family life and close intimacy. Often men may not even realize what they are missing. In a well-known study by sociologists Jack Balswick and Charles W. Peek, "inexpressiveness" was described as a "particular temperament trait that often characterizes the male in American society."[24] These researchers traced the origins of this inability to express feelings to male socialization. They claim that:

> What parents are really teaching their sons is that a real man does not show his emotions and if he is a real man, he will not allow his emotions to be expressed. These outward expressions of emotion are viewed as a sign of femininity, and undesirable for a male.[25]

Balswick and Peek go on to say that as men progress through the stages of dating, going steady, becoming engaged, and getting married, "they may learn to be situationally rather than totally inexpressive,"[26] because total inexpressiveness would be harmful to their early marriages. But not all men are able to show such situational affection and even when they can, a conflict develops between what males have been taught to define as masculinity as children and what is expected of them in a marital relationship.

Who Has the Better Deal?

There are, of course, benefits that accrue to both male and female statuses. Women, for example, usually have a good deal of free time if they plan their household chores correctly. They can visit with friends, shop, read, watch television, go to the movies, do volunteer work, play with their children, and do many other optional things. They have the legal right to be supported by their husbands. They do not have to enter the commercial world if they do not want to or if the family income doesn't demand it. Furthermore, women can express their emotions more freely than men. They can show fear, anxiety, tension, pain, warmth, sympathy, and so forth without penalty. Consequently, women suffer fewer heart attacks than men, they are less likely to develop ulcers or psychosomatic illnesses or to commit suicide, and they live longer than men. On the other hand, women are more likely than men to suffer from mental illnesses.

Men have even greater benefits attached to their male status. Basically, men have the power in America. They are the people who control the top positions in government, industry, the arts, and the professions. Men have more opportunities to reach high levels in these areas for several reasons. First, they have always had more educational opportunity. Second, there are no norms that mitigate against their ambitions. Third, they are encouraged all through childhood to be aggressive, independent, and risk-taking. In short, men control the avenues of institutionalized power in the United States.

THE WORLD OF WORK

The fact that men control the positions of power in Western societies has severe implications for women. Since power is related, although not always directly, to occupations (see Chapter 14), it follows that women are discriminated against in the job market.

Although most married women consider the status of housewife primary in their lives, the proportion of working women has continuously increased. In the period between 1950 and 1974, the number of working women has almost doubled while the number of working men has increased by only 25 percent. In 1940, 14.7 percent of all married women were in the labor force, compared to 46.4 percent in 1977. Of those mothers with children under the age of six, 10.7 percent worked in 1948, compared to 37 percent in 1975. Interestingly, since 1960, the group that is increasing most rapidly in the labor force are mothers of children under the age of three. In 1960, 16 percent were working; in 1975, 33 percent were employed.[27]

The trend of increasing female participation in the work world can be attributed to at least three factors. One, women have become

360

"Gee, Barbara, when you told me you owned your own plant, somehow I was hoping it was a begonia . . ."

more employable because more educational opportunities have opened up for them. The Bureau of the Census reports that the proportion of college-age women (18 to 24) enrolled in school was significantly higher in 1976 than in 1960. In 1960, 30 percent of these women were enrolled in school, compared to 43 percent in 1976.[28] Two, many women are finding that they need not be economically dependent, and the proportion of those who choose to remain single is increasing.[29] Three, inflation has caused a growing number of married women to work either to maintain or to raise their families' standard of living.

All this makes it appear that women's occupational achievements are improving. But if we look closely at where women are in the labor hierarchy (Table 11–1) and how much they are paid relative to men (Figure 11–1), we can see that there is still a great deal of discrimination against women in the world of work.

Stereotyped Occupations

If you think about the image that comes to mind when you try to portray various occupations, chances are that you visualize some as being "masculine" and others as being "feminine." For example, more

361

**TABLE 11–1
Occupation of the
Employed by Sex
(in thousands)**

Occupation	Employed in 1977	
	Male	Female
Total, 16 years & over	53,861	36,685
Professional & technical	7,856	5,835
Managers & administrators	7,510	2,150
Sales workers	3,250	2,478
Clerical	3,391	12,715
Craft	11,282	599
Operatives, except transport	6,258	4,096
Transport equipment operators	3,238	238
Laborers, except farm	4,079	422
Farm workers	2,283	474
Service workers, except private household	4,679	6,555
Private household workers	35	1,123

Source: Adapted from U.S. Bureau of Labor Statistics, *Employment and Earnings*, Vols. 23, 24, 25; and U.S. Bureau of the Census, unpublished Current Population Survey data, 1978.

likely than not, you would think of dentist, carpenter, and engineer as masculine occupations. In contrast, you would probably think of librarian, social worker, and nurse as being feminine. From the images you have formed we can see that occupations are sex-linked. It is thought that one sex *should* be in certain occupations, while the opposite sex *should* be in others. Furthermore, particularly in the professions, occupations are stratified and masculine occupations are ranked higher than feminine ones. Doctors have more prestige than nurses, pilots more than stewardesses, professors (who are predominantly male) more than elementary-school teachers. The American value system, then, places men in the more "important" positions and women in the less important ones.

Part of the reason for this is that society imagines that each sex has specific characteristics. Men are supposed to be more intelligent, more

**FIGURE 11–1
Average Income in
1976 and 1970 for
Males and Females**

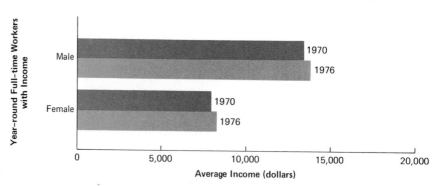

Source: Adapted from U.S. Bureau of the Census, *Current Population Reports*, Series P-60, Nos. 80, 105, and 107, October 1971, June 1977, and September 1977; and unpublished Current Population Survey data.

362

Many occupations are stereotyped as being "masculine" or "feminine." For example, although there are several well-known women jockeys, such as Robyn Smith, most of us, if asked to visualize a jockey, would think of a man.

aggressive, and more committed to work than women. Therefore, men are trusted to handle society's important work. Women are thought of as more nurturing, kinder, and gentler. They work at jobs that are devoted to caring for people, like nursing and teaching small children. But the fact is that we are not born with these characteristics. We learn them as we are being socialized into our gender roles. If we were to train our children to display opposite characteristics—that is, if we taught girls to be aggressive and boys to be gentle—we would probably come to believe females were "naturally" more aggressive and males were "naturally" more gentle.

Income

The fact that men hold the more prestigious jobs creates a differential between the sexes in terms of income (see Figure 11–1). Income, of course, is related to other variables besides sex, such as educational and occupational levels, region of the country, work experience, age, and race. But here we are concerned with the effects of sex on income.

Women are typically employed in occupations that pay lower wages, they more often work part-time than men and they are paid less than men even when they have the same credentials and the same type of job. Furthermore, even with all the agitation for equal pay for equal work in recent years, the differences between male and female incomes for full-time workers has not narrowed. Women earn approximately 60 percent of what men earn in comparable jobs.[30] This differential holds from the top of the work hierarchy (professionals and corporation executives) to the bottom (manual workers).

Money, in and of itself, is important because it allows people to be independent of others and to do and buy things that give them pleasure. But money has other meanings. In their discussion of what they call the "sexual meaning of money," sociologists Jean D. Grambs and Walter Waetjen point out that money also means power and it is men who control the money. These writers contend that one reason for the income differential between men and women is that men cannot tolerate their wives earning more money than they do, even if a wife's job is less prestigious than her husband's.

> In our culture it is psychologically essential to a man that he make more money than his spouse. Through this means, men feel powerful, masculine, in charge of things. . . . This male psychological need may account . . . for the fact that women consistently receive lower pay for doing the same work men do."[31]

These authors point out that fear of competition from women in the job market is so pervasive that women themselves avoid competition, even with other women. Many factors—for example, lack of sup-

Traditional gender roles seem to be becoming less rigid in the United States. For example, in many households husbands and children are taking on more of the household chores so that wives and mothers can devote more time to their education and careers.

port from unions or government agencies—mediate against women fighting for equal income. Among these factors one stands out—women have come to believe they cannot do a job as well as a man.

Changing Gender Roles

Because gender-role socialization in almost all societies throughout history has been both rigid and effective, both men and women have always been less free than they might have been. Yet there are signs that traditional gender roles may be changing in some countries. In the United States, for example, women have been somewhat successful in gaining equal educational, political, and occupational opportunities through legal channels. And the new morality of sexual permissiveness is diminishing the strength of the double standard.

In addition, changes in our social institutions have prompted changes in gender roles. The family, as an institution, is losing or has already lost many of its traditional functions, so that women's home chores are becoming less necessary and less satisfying. The economic institution grows constantly more diversified and our production

APPLYING SOCIOLOGY

"Equality of rights under the law shall not be denied or abridged by the United States or by any state on account of sex."

Section 1. The Equal Rights Amendment

The twenty-four words above have been the subject of bitter controversy throughout our country as states debated the merits of this amendment to the Constitution. How do you think the Equal Rights Amendment will affect traditional gender roles? Do you believe this amendment will really promote equality between the sexes? Why or why not?

methods are becoming increasingly more sophisticated, both of which help to eliminate the need for the ancient division of labor along sex lines. Educational opportunities for women are making them increasingly employable at higher levels in the labor force. In short, there seems to be a growing mood in America of equality for all.

There are, of course, many barriers retarding the equalization of the sexes. Men have still to share their power voluntarily. This is an obstacle that promises to be difficult to overcome since history has shown that those who possess power rarely surrender it willingly. Women themselves present another barrier. Many still cling to traditional roles out of a need to be treated "like a lady," or out of a fear that they will not get husbands, or out of a fear that they cannot successfully compete in the world "out there."

Despite progress in recent years, many people feel that the United States has far to go to achieve equality between the sexes. Supporters of the Equal Rights Amendment (ERA) seek to amend the Constitution to forbid discrimination on the basis of sex.

The main thrust of the current liberation movement is toward an egalitarian ethic so that neither males nor females will continue to be constrained by traditional roles. The effort is to liberate both sexes so people can develop as individuals. Children, too, would benefit. They would receive the companionship of both parents who would interact with them equally and because they want to do so. In our current society mothers are usually forced to overinteract, while fathers are forced to underinteract. Thus, if "men's work" and "women's work" could be eliminated from our society, the society would have greater opportunity to utilize the talents of all its people. Then both males and females would be better able to explore their own abilities.

SUMMARY

Each human being is born into a particular *sex status*, either male or female. Sex status, in turn, determines the *gender role* into which a person will be socialized.

Scientists in different disciplines have questioned whether our gender roles are inborn or learned. Some theories claim that since there are inherent physical differences between the sexes, there must be inherent psychological differences as well. Others argue that there are almost no inherent psychological differences between the sexes at birth. Instead, the differences that develop are learned over time.

Yet some differences do exist between the sexes. Females score higher on tests of verbal ability and on memory tests involving verbal skills. Males score higher on tests of mechanical, mathematical, scientific, and motor ability. They also do better on tests involving spatial orientation, and on memory tests involving numerical skills. However, these differences seem to be related to cultural, and not biological, factors.

Socialization into gender roles occurs just like socialization into any role. Children learn the behaviors considered appropriate to their sex status by direct instruction, observation, and imitation. Finally, these norms are internalized so that they seem to be "natural." Males are traditionally taught to be strong, independent, aggressive, rational, and active. Females are traditionally taught to be passive, dependent, inactive, and gentle. Being born male does not guarantee masculinity, nor does being born female guarantee femininity.

There are consequences flowing from gender-role socialization that can be seen in interpersonal relationships between the sexes and in the world of work. Homemaker is the primary status for most women. This often leads to overdependency on their husbands which can take three major forms—social, economic, and identity. The primary status for men is breadwinner. Like the homemaking status for women, this status also has disadvantages. It provokes anxiety about success and keeps men from participating freely in family life.

There are, however, advantages to both the male and female traditional statuses. Women usually have much more free time, do not have to compete in the labor force, and have the right to be supported by their husbands. They also can express their emotions more freely than can men. On the other hand, men have and control the power in society. They, therefore, can more easily reach out to fulfill their potentials and to enjoy feelings of accomplishment in the outside world.

Male power is most easily seen in the labor market. There women are uniformly discriminated against. They are forced into occupations considered inferior by the society, and when they are able to enter the "male" occupations, they are generally kept in the lower echelons. Furthermore, on all levels, women earn less money than men, even in comparable jobs with comparable skills and credentials.

Yet there are signs that traditional gender roles may be changing. The increase of women in the labor force, the women's movement, the new morality of sexual permissiveness, and changes in social institutions are all contributing to a mood of equality between the sexes. Of course, there are still barriers to such equalization. Men are reluctant to voluntarily surrender the power that they have always possessed. And many women still cling to traditional roles. But if distinctions between "men's work" and "women's work" can be eliminated, each sex will be able to develop to its full potential.

GLOSSARY

biological determinism   the belief that psychosexual differentiation is present at birth.

expressive role   the traditional female role, in which the mother keeps her family united by providing love and affection.

gender role   the patterns of behavior attached to a sex status. During the socialization process one becomes masculine if one is a male and feminine if one is a female.

hermaphrodites   individuals who exhibit a contradiction between their external genital appearance and their chromosomes or their internal reproductive systems.

instrumental role   the traditional male role, in which the father, as breadwinner, serves as a bridge between the family and the rest of society.

neutrality theory   the belief that human beings are psychosexually neutral at birth.

sex status   an ascribed social position based on one's sex at birth.

REFERENCES

1. H. A. Moss, "Sex, Age, and State as Determinants of Mother-Infant Interaction." *Merrill-Palmer Quarterly* 13 (1967): 19–36; and S. M. Garn, "Fat, Body Size, and Growth in the Newborn." *Human Biology* 30 (1958):265–280.

2. Corinne Hutt, *Males and Females*. Harmondsworth, England: Penguin, 1972.

3. J. L. Hampson, "Determinants of Psychosexual Orientation." In F. A. Beach, ed., *Sex and Behavior*. New York: John Wiley & Sons, 1965, p. 125.

4. John Money and Anke Ehrhardt, *Man and Woman: Boy and Girl*. Baltimore: Johns Hopkins University Press, 1972.

5. John Money, "Developmental Differentiation on Femininity and Masculinity Compared." In C. Stoll, ed., *Sexism: Scientific Debates*. Reading, Mass.: Addison-Wesley, 1973.

6. Money, "Developmental Differentiation."

7. R. W. Goy, "Organizing Effects of Androgen on the Behavior of Rhesus Monkeys." Proceedings of the London Conference. *Endocrines and Human Behavior*. R. P. Michaels, ed., 1968.

8. S. N. Levine, "Sex Differences in the Brain." *Scientific American* (April 1966):84–90.

9. N. Weisstein, "Psychology Constructs the Female." In V. Gornick and B. Moran, eds., *Woman in Sexist Society: Studies in Power and Powerlessness*. New York: Signet, 1971.

10. See, for example, Susan Goldberg and Michael Lewis, "Play Behavior in the Year-Old Infant: Early Sex Differences." *Child Development* 40:1 (1969):21–31; Jerome Kagan, "The Emergence of Sex Differences." *School Review* 80:2 (1972):217–227; and Paul H. Mussen, "Early Sex-Role Development." In David A. Goslin, ed., *Handbook of Socialization Theory and Research*. Chicago: Rand McNally, 1971, pp. 707–731.

11. Peggy Bam and Michael Lewis, "Mothers and Fathers, Girls and Boys: Attachment Behavior in the One-Year-Old." Paper presented at Eastern Psychological Association Meetings, New York, 1971.

12. Albert Bandura, "Influence of the Model's Reinforcement Contingencies on the Acquisition of Imitative Responses." *Journal of Personality and Social Psychology* 1 (1965):589–595.

13. L. Kohlberg, "A Cognitive-Developmental Analysis of Children's Sex Role Concepts and Attitudes." In E. Maccoby and Carol N. Jacklin, eds., *The Development of Sex Differences*. Stanford, Calif.: Stanford University Press, 1966.

14. Margaret Mead, *Sex and Temperament in Three Primitive Societies*. New York: William Morrow, 1935.

15. Elizabeth Bing, "Effect of Childrearing Practices on Development of Differential Cognitive Abilities." *Child Development* 34 (1963):631–648.

16. Mabel Blake Cohen, "Personal Identity and Sexual Identity." *Psychiatry* 29:1 (1966):1–14.

17. Beverly I. Fagot and Gerald R. Paterson, "An *in vivo* Analysis of Reinforcing Contingencies for Sex-Role Behaviors in the Preschool Child." *Developmental Psychology* 1:5 (1969):563–568.

18. See, for example, Eva P. Lester, Stephanie Dudek, and Roy C. Muir, "Sex Differences in the Performance of School Children." *Canadian Psychiatric Association Journal* 17:4 (1972):273–278.

19. Talcott Parsons and Robert F. Bales, *Family, Socialization, and Interaction Process.* Glencoe, Ill.: The Free Press, 1953.

20. Cynthia F. Epstein, "Sex Roles." In Robert K. Merton and Robert Nisbet, eds., *Contemporary Social Problems.* New York: Harcourt Brace Jovanovich, 1976.

21. Randall Collins, "A Conflict Theory of Sexual Stratification." *Social Problems* 19 (1971):3–12.

22. Ann C. Scott, "The Value of Housework." *Ms Magazine,* (July 1972), pp. 56–59.

23. Theodore Caplow, *The Sociology of Work.* New York: McGraw-Hill, 1954, Chapter II.

24. Jack Balswick and Charles W. Peek, "The Inexpressive Male: A Tragedy of American Society." *The Family Coordinator* (October 1971):363–368.

25. Balswick and Peek, p. 364.

26. Balswick and Peek, pp. 365–366.

27. These statistics were published by the U.S. Bureau of the Census, "A Statistical Portrait of Women in the United States." *Special Studies,* Series P-23, no. 58, April 1976, p. 26.

28. "A Statistical Portrait of Women in the United States," p. 21; U.S. Bureau of the Census, "School Enrollment—Social and Economic Characteristics of Students: October 1976," *Population Characteristics,* Series P-20, no. 319, February 1978, p. 5.

29. Peter J. Stein, *Single.* Englewood Cliffs, N.J.: Prentice-Hall, 1976.

30. U.S. Department of Labor, *U.S. Working Women: A Chartbook,* Bulletin 1880. Washington, D.C.: U.S. Government Printing Office, 1975, p. 33.

31. Jean D. Grambs and Walter Waetjen, *Sex: Does It Make a Difference?* North Scituate, Mass.: Duxbury Press, 1975, p. 231.

SUGGESTED READINGS

Duberman, Lucile. *Gender and Sex in Society.* New York: Praeger, 1975.

> *A short textbook covering the areas of women's place in society, with chapters by Helen Hacker on class and race differences and on cross cultural differences, and by Warren Farrell on men's liberation.*

Francoeur, Robert and Anna (eds.). *The Future of Sexual Relations.* Englewood Cliffs, N.J.: Prentice-Hall, 1974.

> *A series of pertinent articles that explore the future of our sexual rela-
> tions and their effect on gender roles and intimate relationships.*

Friedan, Betty. *The Feminine Mystique.* New York: Dell, 1963.

> *The pioneering book on the problems of American women in the twen-
> tieth century.*

Katchadourian, Herant, and Donald Lunde. *Fundamentals of Human Sexuality.* New York: Holt, Rinehart & Winston, 1975.

> *A comprehensive discussion of psychosexual development and gender
> differentiation.*

Mead, Margaret. *Sex and Temperament in Three Primitive Societies.* New
York: William Morrow, 1935.

> *Classic report on how three societies define gender roles in different ways
> and socialize their children to obey the cultural prescriptions of what is
> "masculine" and what is "feminine."*

Money, John, and Anke A. Ehrhardt. *Man and Woman, Boy and Girl.* Baltimore: Johns Hopkins University Press, 1972.

> *Using the tools of several disciplines, the authors show how children es-
> tablish gender identity and view themselves as masculine or feminine.*

Montagu, Ashley. *The Natural Superiority of Women.* New York: Collier
Books, revised edition, 1974.

> *A humanistic plea for social equality of both sexes.*

Nichols, Jack. *Men's Liberation: A New Definition of Masculinity.* New York:
Penguin, 1975.

> *An account of how males are in as tight a bind as females and how they
> can escape if they can learn to redefine the masculine stereotype.*

O'Neill, William L. *Everyone Was Brave.* Chicago: Quadrangle, 1969.

> *A history of feminism in the United States from 1830 to the present.*

Wollstonecraft, Mary. *A Vindication of the Rights of Women.* New York: W. W.
Norton, 1967.

> *Originally written in 1792, this is a classical account of female suppres-
> sion.*

12

Racial and
Ethnic Groups

In California during the late 1800s a white man was on trial for murder. Although he did, in fact, commit the crime of which he was accused, he was freed by the court because the only eyewitness to the crime, a man of Chinese descent, was not permitted to testify. At that time, the law in California forbade an Indian from testifying against a white person. But, how could the witness be barred from testifying if he was Chinese? It appears that the defendant's lawyer was aware of a new theory holding that American Indians were descended from the Mongoloid people. Thus, he argued, Indians were really of Chinese origin, and therefore the Chinese witness could not testify. The court accepted the argument.

The Supreme Court of the United States has since declared laws of this kind unconstitutional. But the racial prejudices that produced such laws in the first place have not been destroyed. In fact, people have probably been creating "in-groups" and "out-groups" since the dawn of time and they probably will continue to do so. As a result, human interaction and the life chances of each individual are often directly and immediately affected by such divisions. In this chapter we will examine the role that two classifications—race and ethnicity—play in human social life in general and in our daily lives specifically.

Racial and Ethnic Groups

How, if at all, do racial and ethnic groups differ from each other? Are racial and ethnic classifications scientifically valid? How does membership in a particular ethnic or racial group affect one's life? And, to what extent does being a member of one such group affect an individual's behavior? We will explore these questions in this section.

RACIAL GROUPS

According to biologists, the term *race* refers to a group of human beings who share a set of innate physical characteristics. Since people differ from one another in terms of physical characteristics, some biologists believe we can group people into broad categories on the basis of shared physical traits. The three most common classifications are Caucasoid (white), Mongoloid (yellow), and Negroid (black)—although other scientists have devised as many as thirty-two categories. Such biological classifications for race, however, are not adequate for sociological purposes. Nor, as sociologist Raymond Mack points out, are such classifications of much scientific use.[1]

In the first place, it has been impossible for scientists to arrive at a set of physical traits that can be applied uniformly to all members of a given "race." A great many people do not fit neatly into any "racial" category. Australian aborigines, for example, who have dark skin and blond hair, do not fit either the Caucasoid or Negroid category. Neither do the offspring of an interracial marriage. Another reason that such classifications are of little use is that physical similarities among all people greatly outnumber the differences. To illustrate, within all three major races, we have members with brown hair and brown eyes, members who are short or tall, and members with light or dark skin.

Furthermore, there appears to be no clear relationship between physical characteristics and behavior. Knowing a person's racial classification alone, one cannot predict that person's religion, political beliefs, opinions on the energy crisis, marital status, or criminal disposition. According to Mack, "there are no pure races within the human species. It is impossible to devise a system of classification for behavioral science on the basis of inherited physical traits."[2] Although one may find that patterns of behavior vary in terms of racial categories, it is impossible to explain variation in terms of race alone.

It is not race, then, in the physical sense, that is of sociological significance. Rather, it is the *perception* of racial differences and similarities and the ensuing results that are of interest. Wherever racial differences are perceived by people, social consequences are likely to follow.

ETHNIC GROUPS

Just as people generally perceive themselves and others as belonging to a race, they also perceive individuals as belonging to what sociologists call *ethnic groups*. This term comes from the Greek word *ethnos*, which means "a people"—a related aggregate of persons with a distinct common identity. This sense of common identity is known as *ethnicity*. In a strict sense, such identity is based on nationality. In a broader sense, though, the term *ethnic* is used to refer to groups recognized by themselves and others as distinct by any number of criteria. In Ireland, religion serves to divide the population into ethnic groups. In Yugoslavia, Serbs and Croats identify themselves in terms of differ-

---

APPLYING SOCIOLOGY

If you consider yourself part of an ethnic group, to which group do you belong? What factors make your group socially distinct? How important to you is membership in this group? How important do you believe it is to others in the group?

An ethnic group can be distinguished from the dominant group on the basis of race, nationality, religion, language, or customs and traditions.

ences in national origin and religion. The French in Quebec are distinct from other Canadians in terms of religion, language, and cultural heritage. In some cases, only one of the traits is used to determine this ethnic identification. Thus, black people in the United States are considered as one group although their national origins may differ widely.

In short, sociologists and lay people apply the term *ethnic group* to any group of people who perceives itself or is perceived by others as being socially different from the dominant group. This difference can be based on racial grounds, nationality, religion, customs, traditions, or language. *Ethnic group* will be used this way throughout this chapter.

MINORITY GROUPS

Related to the term *ethnic group* is the term *minority group*. A minority group can be defined as a group that is treated unequally because it is perceived as different from the dominant group in terms of physical characteristics, cultural characteristics, or both. It is important to note that sociologically the term minority group has nothing to do with the number of people who comprise such a group. Rather, it is unequal treatment by the dominant group that is the determining factor. Women, for instance, are a numerical majority in the United States, but are considered a minority group. Similarly, the blacks in South Africa are a numerical majority, but they are dominated almost completely by a small group of whites and thus are also considered a minority group.

It is also important to distinguish between ethnic and minority groups. Women in the United States are considered a minority group, but are not an ethnic group. Conversely, a small enclave of Swedes in

Although women are a numerical majority in the United States, they are considered a minority group because they receive unequal treatment by the dominant group. In recent years, however, many women have formed workshops in an attempt to gain equal treatment in such areas as employment and education.

Chicago, which has retained some of its customs, language, and sense of Swedish identity, might be considered an ethnic group. Swedes, however, would not normally be considered a minority group because they are regarded as part of the mainstream and are not treated unequally.

RACE, ETHNICITY, AND BEHAVIOR

Why are factors of race and ethnicity important to a study of society? When people perceive each other as different from each other, regardless of the criteria they use to do so, this is likely to affect their behavior. It does not matter that the distinctions themselves are arbitrary or irrelevant. What does matter is that people are conscious of racial, religious, national, and cultural differences between themselves and others. Such perceived differences can lead people to establish categories of "we" and "they" (black and white, Catholic and Protestant, Chicano and Gringo, Hindu and Moslem, and so forth) and to interact with others on the basis of such categories.

Often, dividing the world into "we" and "they" categories can lead to conflict, antagonism, or such destructive acts as riots, wars, and even genocide. For this reason sociologists have been concerned with race and ethnicity since the discipline was founded.

Ethnicity and Human Differences

If people perceive others as different from themselves, they are likely to believe that other groups possess abilities, accomplishments, and personality attributes unlike their own. Many people probably consider most other groups inferior to themselves in some or all of these areas. In turn, they tend to create myths about the differences they perceive. Many people believe, for example, that Germans are authoritarian; Italians are hot-tempered; blacks are lazy; and Jews are tight-fisted. They then use these beliefs and myths to justify their behavior toward members of out-groups.

All of these ethnic myths remain prevalent today. But on what are such myths based? Do they have any basis in fact? That is what we will investigate now.

RACE AND INTELLIGENCE

We are all familiar with the many "ethnic jokes" that depict members of some ethnic groups as being stupid, inept, and ignorant. Unfortunately, many people go beyond joking and actually believe that the abilities of other peoples are considerably less (or more) than their own. For example, in American society, black people have been depicted as less intelligent than white people, something that has frequently been used to justify barring blacks from certain occupational and social positions. To support this claim, many people point to the differences in the scores achieved by blacks and whites on IQ tests (see Chapter 7).

From the 1950s to the present, various scientists have reported periodically that black Americans on the average score substantially lower on IQ tests than white Americans. Some of these scientists attribute this difference to innate differences in the level of mental ability between the two groups. Psychologist Arthur Jensen, for example, points out that blacks score on the average ten to fifteen points lower on IQ tests than whites do. He attributes this fact to heredity and genetic differences.[3] Psychologist Hans Eysenck argued that at least 80 percent of the differences in IQ test scores for blacks and whites is the result of heredity.[4]

Indeed, blacks do tend to have lower average scores than whites. But this does not mean that blacks are less intelligent than whites or that blacks score lower because they are genetically inferior to whites.

In the first place, it is not fair to compare black and white test performances because the members of the two groups are not subjected to the same social environments. Since intelligence tests traditionally reflect the white culture or environment, it is not surprising that whites score higher. For example, how can a black child be expected to know that an artichoke is a vegetable and not a fruit if he or she has never seen or eaten one? If the test were designed to reflect the black culture, whites would not do as well. In fact, to prove this point, a black psychologist constructed such a black "Culture-Bound Intelligence Test."[5] Here black students were able to identify such terms as "handkerchief head" and "Bo Diddley" while white students were unable to do so. Therefore, it is not fair to expect identical performances from the members of the two groups, unless the tests are free from cultural biases.

Second, average IQ test score differences are just that—averages. They do not apply to any individual. Both whites and blacks score throughout the entire range of IQ levels. If, therefore, some blacks are more intelligent than some whites (as measured by IQ tests), how can one say that blacks are less intelligent than whites?[6]

Thus, we can say that there is no biological correlation between race and intelligence as measured by IQ tests. Whites as a group tend to score higher because of test biases and their social environment, but at the same time we are talking about averages and not individuals.

Just as intelligence is culture-bound, so are the accomplishments of all peoples. There is no correlation between race and what a group achieves.

CULTURAL AND TECHNICAL ACHIEVEMENTS

Today Americans pride themselves on having built the most technologically advanced and economically affluent society in the world. In the eighteenth and nineteenth centuries, European colonists justified their domination of other peoples on the grounds of their political, economic, technological, and genetic superiority. Thus both modern Americans and the European colonialists have found what they believe to be adequate grounds for thinking themselves superior to other peoples. They argue that, if others were their equal, others too would have accomplished "great things."

However, long before the peoples of Western Europe had moved out of the Stone Age, people in other parts of the world were developing technically, culturally, and politically superior cultures.[7] For example, Marco Polo returned from his trip to the Far East with many items such as spices and silks that had been previously unknown to Europeans. Indeed, had it not been for the accomplishments of the peoples of Africa and Asia, it would have been difficult for European culture to develop. The foundations of European civilization were laid in China, Africa, India, and Asia Minor.

Historically, human achievements can in no way be related to ethnic characteristics. They stem, rather, from accident, cultural emphasis, the diffusion of knowledge, the availability of resources, and the pattern of the times. The Iroquois Indians of the American Northeast developed a republic and a representative form of government while European countries were still being ruled by monarchs. The Romans had the wheel and, thus, could excel in developing systems of transportation and were successful at conquest. But the northern Europeans who inherited Roman culture did not take advantage of its technological expertise and instead allowed the world to plunge into a period of regression known as the Dark Ages. In the fertile areas of Nubia and Ethiopia, the Negroid peoples of Africa created impressive civilizations and invented the nation state some 2,000 years before the Europeans got the idea. But when the Europeans colonized the African continent they called its inhabitants "savages."

As sociologist Raymond Mack notes:

> People of every race have at one time or another achieved a high place, held sway over their neighbors, and advanced in knowledge beyond what was generally known among other races at the time.[8]

In short, accomplishment is not related to ethnic characteristics. Rather it is the result of a variety of factors, including accident. And how we rate accomplishment depends upon what we value. As with all other evaluations, what constitutes accomplishment is culture-bound and influenced by ethnocentrism.

377

Prejudice and Discrimination

Characterizing people as different from ourselves can affect our behavior in numerous ways. Two behavioral consequences with which we will be concerned here are prejudice and discrimination.

PREJUDICE

"The price of hating other human beings is loving oneself less,"[9] said Eldridge Cleaver when he reflected on the prejudices he felt toward white Americans and the discrimination he had experienced from them. This is indeed a very high price to pay.

The term *prejudice* is derived from the Latin word *prejudicum*, which means to prejudge individuals without knowing their personal qualities. Today the word is commonly used to refer to a negative attitude toward persons placed in various categories. But the term actually can refer to a positive or a negative orientation. Thus, one can be prejudiced *toward* some group, as when one aspires to be like the members of some group or even to belong to it. Conversely, one can be prejudiced *against* others and assign a host of negative characteristics to the members of that group regardless of their individual attributes. It is this second kind of prejudice that generates fear, suspicion, and hatred of others. When this attitude is expressed toward some group in terms of racial characteristics, prejudice takes the form of *racism*.

One concept closely related to prejudice is *stereotyping*. Stereotyping is the tendency to generalize about, and categorize, elements in our lives on the basis of limited information. This tendency to generalize is something that all of us do everyday about many different aspects of our lives. Many of us, for instance, have stereotyped attitudes about a make of car, an area of the country, or the efficiency of the telephone company. And these attitudes are based on personal information, which is limited. We also have stereotyped attitudes about certain groups of people. An individual might believe, for example, that all people over sixty-five are feeble and hard of hearing, because his or her grandparents are feeble and hard of hearing. Similarly, one might believe that all blacks are musically inclined, because one has often heard this myth and seen black musicians. Thus, having a stereotyped attitude about some things or groups does not necessarily mean that we are prejudiced for or against such things or groups. It merely means that we have generalized about certain phenomena on the basis of our personal experience. Prejudice enters the picture when individuals are unwilling to change their stereotyped attitudes in the presence of new information.

Prejudice against a group becomes racism when it is based on racial characteristics. An example of racism is the negative view that members of the Ku Klux Klan have of black people.

The belief that "all black people are musical" is a stereotype—a generalization based on limited information.

In general, it appears as if a major shift in prejudicial attitudes has taken place in American society since the end of World War II. This shift is toward a less prejudiced view of various groups, even though prejudices still persist.[10] For example, in 1942 a national public opinion poll indicated that over half of the whites questioned believed blacks were less intelligent than whites, but a similar poll in the late 1960s showed that only about 14 percent of the white population believed this to be true. Sociologist Angus Campbell found that white attitudes toward blacks have apparently moderated since the violence of the 1960s. For example, although whites strongly oppose busing in order to create integrated schools, they generally agree that white people do not have the right to keep minority members out of their neighborhood. Similarly, Campbell found that by 1970 over 30 percent of the whites said they had a black friend as against 17 percent in 1964.

In addition, this research shows that prejudice is found in some groups more than in others, but over time the general level of prejudice among all groups in the United States has declined. In other words, groups or areas of the country that exhibited the greatest amount of prejudice twenty years ago are still more prejudiced than other groups or areas, but they are less prejudiced than they were before.

FOCUS ON: AN EXPERIMENT IN PREJUDICE

How can children be taught the true meaning of prejudice and discrimination? How can they be shown what it *feels* like to be discriminated against? In a startling experiment, third-grade teacher Jane Elliot dramatized the effects discrimination can have on individuals. *A Class Divided* by journalist William Peters recounts her experiment.

After Martin Luther King, Jr. was assassinated, Elliot felt compelled to make her students understand the senselessness, the irrationality, and the brutality of race hatred. In order to accomplish this, she divided her class of seventeen all-white third-graders into two groups by eye color—those with blue eyes and those with brown eyes. During the first day, Elliot told the brown-eyed students repeatedly that they were superior and treated them as such. They were given five extra minutes of recess, an opportunity to choose their lunch-line partners, and numerous other privileges. Conversely, she found fault almost exclusively with the blue-eyed students. For example, when a blue-eyed student curled a page of his book, she displayed the book to the class and asked rhetorically, "Do blue-eyed people take care of the things they are given?"

As the day progressed, the brown-eyed children came to believe they really were superior. They were happy and were doing better work than they had ever done before. On the other hand, the blue-eyed children were miserable and displayed attitudes of defeat. As Elliot said, "Inside of an hour or so, they looked and acted as though they were, in fact, inferior. It was shocking."

What was more shocking, however, was the way brown-eyed students turned on their friends. For example, as one blue-eyed girl walked across the playground during recess she was deliberately slapped by a brown-eyed girl who had been her best friend the day before.

During the next class session the roles were reversed. This time the blue-eyed students were treated as superior. But once again the effects were the same. The only real difference was that the blue-eyed children were less vicious in their treatment of their classmates.

Elliot later repeated the experiment with two different classes and in each case she obtained similar results. The "superior" group believed it was superior and the "inferior" group believed it was inferior. In addition, the superior group derived pleasure from persecuting the other group.

What does this study tell us about prejudice and discrimination? In similar circumstances, do you think you would react as these children did? Why or why not?

Source: William Peters, *A Class Divided*, Garden City, N.Y.: Doubleday, 1971.

DISCRIMINATION

Whereas prejudice is an attitude, *discrimination* is an act. As with prejudice, discrimination can be either negative or positive, but in today's usage, discrimination generally refers to negative behaviors toward the members of some group.

Negative discriminatory acts can take a number of forms, but basically they involve either disqualifying people from participating in various activities or belonging to certain groups, or mistreating them because they belong to some group. Discriminatory practices may rest on political and legal barriers. Such was the case with the "Jim Crow" laws (laws that required racial segregation) that many states enacted after the slaves were emancipated, in order to restrict the freedom of blacks (and other minorities) in public places. When not backed by law, discrimination can also exist. In these cases, it is backed by social custom, by lack of effort to enforce laws that prohibit such practices, or simply by subtle interpersonal actions directed toward members of the deprived group.

Whatever its form and no matter how it is sanctioned, discrimination is the most socially harmful consequence of categorizing people into in- and out-groups. Discrimination can range in severity from simple ethnic slurs to outright attempts at genocide. It causes segregation, reduces the life chances of some while enhancing those of others, generates resentment and hostility and, in general, works against human solidarity.

THE RELATIONSHIP BETWEEN PREJUDICE AND DISCRIMINATION

Although prejudice and discrimination tend to go together, this is not necessarily the case. In fact, prejudice does not inevitably lead to discrimination. Group pressures, perceived needs, legal requirements, fear of reprisals, and similar forces can act to produce discriminatory behavior or to inhibit it, regardless of a person's real attitudes. For example, while some people may feel friendly toward members of another ethnic group, fear of ridicule may stop them from interacting with the "outsiders." Conversely, someone may actually hold prejudicial attitudes toward some other group, but might not want to display this attitude openly, perhaps because of peer group pressure.

Research suggests that people do not display prejudice or discrimination "uniformly."[11] Some people hold negative attitudes about all groups except their own. Archie Bunker of the popular television show "All in the Family" displays such universal prejudice. On the other hand, some people are prejudiced only toward specific groups. For example, many Jews and Arabs are prejudiced against each other merely because of the tense Middle East situation.

People may also be prejudiced or practice discrimination in some situations and not in others. For many years, members of different racial groups would play together on the same sports teams, but would occupy separate rooms while traveling on the road. Similarly, even today, people of different ethnic backgrounds may work together or interact as "equals" in some settings, but have nothing to do with one another in other settings.

381

© Punch–Rothco

"Our token Black—is that really how you think of yourself, Ms Corwin? You're much more than that, I assure you. You're also our token woman."

Finally, although prejudice against one group may decrease, there might still be prejudice and discrimination with regard to other groups. For example, prejudice against Catholics in the United States decreased to the extent that it was possible for a Catholic to be elected president. Yet some people still are prejudiced with regard to native Americans, Hispanic-Americans, blacks, and other minorities.

For those groups who experience discrimination, the situation is difficult. They are typically placed in a position wherein their life chances are impeded if not actually reduced. For example, sociologist John S. Butler found that black enlisted men in the Army are not promoted as rapidly as whites.[12] As Butler states, "blacks who were matched up with whites on key universalistic criteria (e.g., performance on Army exams, prior education, etc.) still suffered discrimination on the basis of race."[13] Similarly, a study of residential segregation between the years 1960 and 1970 found that "residential segregation persists in the seventies and . . . shows little indication of significant decline in response to other racial improvements."[14]

In short, prejudice and discrimination do not necessarily go together. Even though there is likely to be a correspondence, prejudice and discrimination are not always directly related or consistent in direction or intensity. Moreover, there is reason to believe that the two may not originate from the same source.

SOURCES OF PREJUDICE AND DISCRIMINATION

There are few rational reasons for people to be prejudiced or to practice discrimination. Nevertheless, a number of scholars have attempted to explain the origins of these phenomena. In general, these theories can be grouped into three types: psychological, economic, and social.[15]

Psychological Theories

Prejudice is in the eye of the beholder and is in no way related to the actual characteristics of the group against whom the prejudice is held. Therefore, it follows that at least part of an explanation of why people are prejudiced must be found in the psychological characteristics of the prejudiced persons themselves. Three major psychological theories try to explain why people become prejudiced and why they act in discriminatory ways.

First, there is the *scapegoat theory*, which argues that people have a tendency to blame their troubles on anyone but themselves. Minority groups are convenient subjects for *scapegoating*, especially if they are easily recognizable by some physical or behavioral trait, are relatively powerless, are readily available for attack, are not popular, and can easily be seen as symbolizing some hated or despised trait or activity.

Scapegoating behavior is likely to occur under a variety of circumstances, but a second theory suggests that people are most apt to be prejudiced and act in discriminatory ways when they experience frustration. This thesis, known as the *frustration-aggression theory*, argues that persons who are incompetent or are failures or whose goals are blocked, may compensate for their own failure through their prejudices. They blame some other group for their own shortcomings (as when the Nazis blamed the Jews in Germany for the loss of World War I and for the economic depression that followed it).

The third and most popular psychological theory suggests that prejudice tends to be most acute among persons who exhibit a certain personality type. Personality specialist T. W. Adorno found that persons who have what he calls an *authoritarian personality* tend to be prejudiced.[16] He describes an individual of this personality type as one who rigidly adheres to conventional middle-class values, is uncritically submissive to idealized authority figures (such as a national or religious leader), is oriented to and desirous of punishing anyone who violates conventional standards, is opposed to imaginative thinking and instead prefers rigid categories and fatalistic beliefs, and is preoccupied with dominance and submission as basic forms of human interaction. According to Adorno, people who exhibit these personality characteristics also tend to exhibit a high degree of intolerance toward others and an inflexibility in their relationships with them.

383

Some social scientists suggest that prejudice is likely to result when groups compete for such scarce resources as housing, jobs, or, as at this antibusing rally in Boston, educational opportunities.

Economic Theories

Undoubtedly personality factors are important in explaining why some people tend to be more prejudiced than others, but personality alone cannot explain why prejudice exists. Other forces also are probably involved. To many social scientists, the most important of these factors are economic in character.[17] These scientists suggest that prejudice is likely to emerge when two or more groups compete with one another for scarce resources—housing, jobs, and educational opportunities.

If this theory is correct, one would expect to find a correlation between the degree of competition between two groups and their prejudices toward each other. History is full of examples of such a correlation. For example, when black people emigrated to northern cities, riots broke out between blacks and whites as they competed for homes and jobs. Similarly, the immigrants to the North American continent did not despise the native Americans because they were "heathens" and

384

"savages," but because the native Americans had the one thing the new arrivals wanted—land. Hence, the newcomers practiced a systematic program of genocide against the Indians out of a desire for their land.[18]

But prejudice does not exist only when groups compete with one another. It is also often present among groups that are engaged in the exploitation of other groups. In these cases the dominant group finds that prejudice enables it to justify or facilitate its exploitation. In the American South, for instance, envisioning blacks as mentally, morally, and genetically inferior contributed to the continuation of slavery. British colonialists in India benefited from the prejudices Moslems and Hindus there held toward each other. Using the principle of divide and conquer, the British helped to foster that antagonism by creating separate waiting rooms, drinking fountains, and other facilities for the two groups. The internment of thousands of Japanese-Americans during World War II was not simply the result of a fear that they would aid the enemy. It was economically profitable for some groups to promote fear of the Japanese in the United States and to confiscate their homes, businesses, and possessions during and after their internment. In short, prejudice seems to be rooted in economic relations as well as in personality traits. But just as important are the social factors that help stimulate prejudices.

Social Theories

People are not born with prejudices. They acquire such attitudes and the behavior patterns associated with them from others. Indeed, children display no sign of prejudice until they "pick it up" by observing their elders. Therefore, prejudice is a part of the cultural heritage of a people—something that is acquired by the members of the group just as they acquire any other group values. Attitudes of prejudice are typically learned in an informal, largely unconscious manner, and many people who hold various prejudices are truly unaware of them and are often ashamed and embarrassed when these prejudices are pointed out.[19]

Prejudices also serve a variety of social functions. Not the least of these is that prejudices help perpetuate the social, economic, and/or political superiority of the dominant group. At the same time, prejudice allows the members of the dominant group to think of themselves as superior.

Often these attitudes of dominance and superiority can function as a vicious circle producing what sociologist Robert K. Merton calls a *self-fulfilling prophecy*. A self-fulfilling prophecy can be defined as a prediction about a series of events that helps to determine their outcome. An example of a self-fulfilling prophecy can be seen in the case of a high-school athletic team that feels inferior to another school's

---

APPLYING SOCIOLOGY

Think of the way you perceive racial and ethnic groups other than your own. Do you assign any negative characteristics to the entire group regardless of the individual attributes of members? Where do you think your prejudices originated? Do you believe anyone can be completely free from prejudice?

---

team. As a result, it is likely to play badly, thus ensuring its defeat. Consequently, the team may come to think of itself as really being inadequate and incompetent. It may come to maintain itself in a position of inferiority that "proves" to both the dominant group and itself that it is inferior indeed.

REACTIONS TO DISCRIMINATION

Groups that experience prejudice and discrimination, especially if they occupy a subordinate position in the society, can react to that situation on two levels: behaviorally and psychologically.[20] Although related and often interdependent, these two patterns of adjustment can be described separately. (See also Chapter 2 for a discussion of patterns of group interaction.)

Behavioral Adjustment

Behavioral adjustment can take several forms. The 1930s movie image of the stupid, lazy, comical black provides a stereotype of a behavior pattern that essentially takes the form of *submission* to the dominant group and acceptance of a low status in life. Persons who exhibit such signs of submission to the dominant group are typically perceived by members of that group as well-adjusted and proper, and usually they gain the approval of their dominators. However, anyone who accepts this status must pay a high price in self-esteem.

Many white Americans think black Americans are "naturally" musical, have more "rhythm," and are better athletes. And to prove their point they show that many blacks participate in sports and in the entertainment industry. But the beliefs themselves may be nothing more than an offshoot of a second form of adjustment adopted by members of groups experiencing discrimination. This form involves *adaptation*—cultivating occupational and social areas of life left open to them by the dominant group. Jews, for example, became entertainers and business people because the dominant group had not totally closed off these occupations to them.

386

Aggressive action is a possible behavioral reaction to discrimination. Here American Indians stage a protest in front of the headquarters of the Bureau of Indian Affairs.

For those who are unable or unwilling to submit to the dominant group or to adapt in spite of discrimination, there is a third behavioral reaction—*aggressive action.* This behavior may be directed toward reform efforts or movements or it can take the extreme form of physical violence. Aggression may produce social change, or it may simply serve to ventilate pent-up frustrations or anger. But whatever aggression accomplishes, its various forms are likely to be used by people who either think it will in some way alter their situation or who feel that they have nothing to lose from aggressive behavior.

The most common behavior adjustment is *self-segregation* or withdrawal. Almost all the ethnic groups who immigrated to the United States gathered together in ethnic enclaves and attempted, at least for a time, to maintain themselves as isolated mini-communities or so-called ghettos. In any of these communities, there is an abundance of shops with foreign-language signs offering a variety of foods and goods from "back home." And in some of these communities, English is at best a second language. Persons not of the area's ethnic background are usually considered strangers and may be subjected to restricted interaction with the people who live there.

Many of these ethnic ghettos came into existence and persist through no choice of the inhabitants. In many cases, though, even when the major barriers preventing entrance into the mainstream have

387

been lowered, some of these people, out of fear or desire, stay and maintain the "old neighborhood." Thus, in many cities a Chinatown, a Little Italy, or a Greektown continues to exist, to some extent closing its inhabitants off from the slurs and aggression of a world that does or did hold them in disrepute. By such segregation these minority groups find not only protection but also a psychological sense of belonging.

Psychological Adjustment

In Chapter 4 we noted that how a person perceives the world and what image a person has of himself or herself depend in large part on the reactions of other people. Although individuals may try to disregard the negative opinions that others express toward them, the more frequent, general, and persistent these expressions are, the more likely individuals are to believe and internalize them. If these opinions are negative, the receivers may develop a negative image of themselves. Members of those ethnic groups that are especially subject to assaults on their self-esteem and that are relatively powerless to resist these assaults are very likely to accept such a negative self-image. Even if they do not totally accept such a self-image, they still may be greatly affected by how people regard them.

Discrimination can lead to low self-esteem, which, in turn, can result in a sense of alienation, apathy, despair, withdrawal, and self-destructive behavior.

Low self-esteem can have two major psychological consequences. In the first place, being rejected by the larger society may produce a sense of *alienation* among the members of the rejected group. Individuals not only feel that they are not a part of the larger society, but also come to lose interest in being included in it. A sense of apathy, boredom, despair, and frustration may lead to actions that either are self-destructive—such as drug addiction—or take the form of withdrawal—a "rejection of one's rejectors."

Along with instilling a feeling of alienation, discrimination can also lead to group *self-hatred*. When the members of a degraded ethnic group believe the negative images other people have of them, they may also come to believe that their situation is not a result of discrimination, but of their actual inferiority. They then must either adjust to their situation and behave in expected ways, or they must find ways to escape from their situation. For some people such escape can be achieved by "passing," by essentially pretending to be something other than what they are.[21] But most people are unable or unwilling to pass. So they must carry out their lives accepting the negative evaluations or they must seek ways of changing those images and the discriminatory reactions that they provoke. At the present time, many blacks are responding with self-pride in their race and willingness to work and fight for acceptance.

Changing Ethnic Relationships

Relationships among the members of ethnic groups often change. Such alterations may occur in a variety of ways, the primary way being when members of individual groups take on the attitudes and behaviors of the dominant group. This happened when the immigrants to the United States became "Americanized" within one or two generations. Change also may involve modifications in the ways other groups feel about or interact with some ethnic group. This type of change can be negative; as when Americans came to despise and fear the Japanese-Americans during World War II. Or such change can be positive. Although at one time the Irish in America suffered much prejudice and discrimination, as a group they are rarely thought of in negative terms today.

Often, however, people think of their beliefs as the only and "natural" way for things to be. Therefore, patterns of discrimination and the underlying attitudes of prejudice may remain virtually intact for generations. In India, for example, the caste system is so ingrained that it has become part of the culture and structure of the society. As a result, people resist altering such patterns and may actively work to block such change from taking place. Thus, in order for real change in ethnic relationships to occur, direct action programs aimed at either modifying prejudicial attitudes or attacking the causes of discrimination may have to be instituted.

CHANGING ATTITUDES

A number of proposals have been made that may be useful in changing people's attitudes toward others. Some say that education is the answer. But the evidence available so far does not show that this technique has had any real impact, in part because prejudiced people rarely subject themselves to the kind of education that counters their beliefs. Similarly, propaganda efforts may not be as effective as some people would like to believe. Indeed, they may even have a reverse effect. The popular television show "All in the Family," which we referred to earlier, may actually help to ingrain prejudice by showing that it is not all *that* evil. After all, Archie Bunker is a "lovable bigot." Primarily, however, people are selective in what they read or in the television shows they watch. Prejudiced people are not likely to submit voluntarily to media attacks on their attitudes or beliefs. And, even if they do submit, they are not always aware that the message applies to them. Thus, propaganda and education do not seem to be the most effective ways of changing people's attitudes.

Since prejudices are largely based on the belief that some groups are inferior, many people have argued that prejudice can be eliminated by increasing contact among members of ethnic groups. Theoretically this seems plausible, and several programs designed to eliminate prejudice and discrimination in America, such as school busing and integrated housing, are based on this idea. The evidence shows, however, that increasing contact works only under certain conditions. First, the individuals in the subordinate group must not be cast in stereotyped roles. Second, the contact must be for the purpose of bringing people together for such functionally important activities as defending themselves against an aggressor or helping one another secure the neces-

---

APPLYING SOCIOLOGY

Archie Bunker, in *All in the Family*, depicts a very prejudiced person. Do you think such programs increase prejudice among Americans or do you think such television shows help rid us of our prejudices? If you were in charge of television programming, would you allow such programs to be aired? Why?

sities of daily life.[22] Under other conditions contact can have a reverse effect. For example, sociologists George E. Simpson and J. Milton Yinger suggest that contact can increase prejudice when such contact is "incidental, involuntary, and tension-laden."[23]

Clearly, it is not that easy to eliminate prejudice. Perhaps, though, since discrimination can generate prejudicial attitudes, we can improve ethnic relations by trying to reduce discrimination. The civil rights movement provides a case in which such action was taken.

CHANGING BEHAVIOR: THE CIVIL RIGHTS MOVEMENT

The black civil rights movement provides us with a classic example of an attempt to improve ethnic relations through changing behavior. From this struggle we can see the difficulties involved in achieving change in ethnic relationships.[24]

From Emancipation to Segregation

Blacks were freed from slavery in the United States by the Thirteenth Amendment to the Constitution, ratified in 1865. During the brief period of Reconstruction that followed the Civil War, black people were legally equal to whites. But by the time the Reconstruction era was over, many states had enacted legislation designed to restrict the liberties of blacks and suppress them as much as possible. This was done in spite of the Fourteenth Amendment, which specifically prohibited states from passing restrictive laws.

These "Jim Crow" laws not only suppressed blacks socially, but also restricted their political and economic power. Hence, despite the amendments to the federal constitution, black Americans maintained their inferior social and legal position, one that was to persist until action to change it was initiated in the late 1950s and carried on throughout the 1960s.

Although prohibited by the Constitution, discrimination was also supported by the United States Supreme Court in many of its decisions, such as the "separate but equal" doctrine established by the Court in its *Plessy* vs. *Ferguson* decision of 1896. Here the Court ruled that separate public facilities—schools, water fountains, and so on—could be established for blacks as long as such facilities were equal to those of whites. This decision not only gave credence to segregation, but also undermined many of the claims against discrimination. Who, it was argued, could oppose discriminatory practices restricting contact as long as the groups in question had equal facilities? Of course, the facilities could never be equal, although they may be identical in structure. Creating two "identical" structures for the same purpose implies that one group must be better than the other. If not, one facility would

A young member of the Congress of Racial Equality (CORE), one of the first civil rights organizations, at a rally in New York City in 1965.

suffice for all. In 1954 the Supreme Court adopted this position with its famous *Brown* vs. *Board of Education of Topeka, Kansas,* decision. Here the Court decided that separate schools were inherently unequal. This ruling not only signaled that a change was taking place in the relationship between blacks and whites in America, but it also provided one of the first concrete means for blacks to achieve the equality and rights initially granted them in 1865.

Protests, Sit-ins, and Riots

The *Brown* decision in 1954 raised hopes that equality between blacks and whites was a real possibility. It created a renewed sense of purpose and direction for black people, giving them the hope that they could change their situation. All that was needed was a spark. Such a spark flashed in Montgomery, Alabama, on December 1, 1955. Rosa Parks, a black woman, was arrested for sitting in a "whites only" section of a city bus. The black community reacted immediately. It instituted a boycott of the bus company, thus demonstrating the underlying unanimity of feeling among blacks and the potential power behind an organized protest.

As a result of this boycott, new organizations were formed. One group called the Southern Christian Leadership Conference (SCLC) came under the leadership of Rev. Dr. Martin Luther King, Jr. Following the precedent set by Mahatma Gandhi in India, Dr. King defined the issue as a moral struggle, and he urged nonviolent, direct action to convince whites of the rightness of racial equality.

Similar in goals and strategy, a second group called the Congress of Racial Equality (CORE), which was actually founded in 1942, began a series of "freedom rides" in 1961 under the leadership of James Farmer. CORE's tactic was to incite local officials to arrest members and then to bring suit against the arresting agents in federal court. CORE's efforts resulted in a riot in Montgomery, Alabama, and its activities were discontinued. Its tactics were adopted, however, by another group—the Student Nonviolent Coordinating Committee (SNCC). This group had been engaged in a similar series of "sit-ins" in which black (and some white) students refused to move from segregated restaurants or other dining areas until they were served.

As a result of these activities, a number of Supreme Court decisions chipped away at many aspects of discriminatory laws. Finally, Congress decided to take action. It passed the Civil Rights Act in 1957, and three others in 1960, 1964, and 1965. All these acts were aimed at eliminating restrictions on black people and other minorities in public places and to help them gain political power.

Though the legal barriers to discrimination were being eroded, little seemed to have changed for blacks in the social and economic spheres. And white resistance on many fronts promised to retard ad-

392

vancement still further. By the mid-1960s, frustration and antagonism were culminating in violence and riots throughout the country. A phrase coined by Stokely Carmichael, the leader of SNCC—"black power"—gained new adherents. Rallying to the battle cry of black power, many new revolutionary groups sprang up and the old nonviolent strategy of Dr. King was replaced by more militant confrontation, championed by such organizations as the Black Panther Party for Self-Defense, headed by Bobby Seale and Huey P. Newton. Similarly, the goal of integration was rejected by the members of other organizations, such as the Black Muslims, who advocated that blacks develop their own identity and their own separate economic position in American society.

The decade of the 1960s saw the most intense and bitter reactions between ethnic groups in the history of America. About a hundred years had passed since black slaves had been freed, and some changes had occurred in black/white relationships. But by the 1970s, the gap of inequality that separated whites and blacks had not been eliminated (see Table 12–1). Like the other ethnic groups that have occupied a second-class position in American society, black people have learned that attaining equality and destroying discrimination are difficult, if not impossible, tasks. Thus we see that as with attempts to change prejudicial attitudes, attempts at changing discriminatory behavior have not been overly successful.

Racial and Ethnic Minorities

In this chapter, we have thus far taken a long look at the most visible of America's minority groups—the blacks. In Chapter 11, we discussed women, another visible minority. In the remainder of this chapter, we will take a look at other minority groups in American society.

TABLE 12–1
Comparison of Blacks and Whites on Selected Social Characteristics, 1976

Social Characteristic	Black	White
Median family income	$9,264	$15,571
Unemployment rate	13.6	7.9
Percentage of persons 25 and over who completed 4 or more years of college	6.6	15.4
Percentage of children under 18 living with both parents	49.6	85.2

Source: U.S. Bureau of the Census, *Current Population Reports*, series P-60, No. 114; series P-20, Nos. 207, 243, 274, 295, and 306; and U.S. Bureau of Labor Statistics, *Employment and Earnings*, monthly, 1976.

393

NATIVE AMERICANS

Native Americans are one of the most abused minority groups in our country. There are approximately 800,000 people in this group, which includes the poorest and most stereotyped of all minorities.

About two-thirds of all native Americans live on reservations under the protection of the Bureau of Indian Affairs. This "protection" has resulted in the average native-American family living on an income of $1,500 per year. Consequently, almost all live in substandard housing—even in caves, tents, or old automobiles. One child in every four dies before the age of four and of those who survive, the average child acquires only five years of schooling. It is hardly surprising, then, that the unemployment rate is about 45 percent, and the average life expectancy is forty-four years of age.

The civil rights movements in the 1960s and the 1970s inspired native Americans to organize to improve their status. As a result, the American Indian Movement (AIM) was formed. This group has insisted on recognition and respect for self-determination on reservations. It is still too early, however, to evaluate its effectiveness.

HISPANIC-AMERICANS

Another group suffering minority status is Spanish-speaking or Hispanic-Americans. This group is composed of about 5 million Chicanos (the female form of the term is Chicana), who have migrated from Mexico and settled primarily in the southwestern part of the United States; and about 2 million Puerto Ricans, who have settled primarily in New York City's *barrios* or ghettos. Other groups of Cubans, Dominicans, and South Americans are scattered throughout the United States. Most Hispanic-Americans came to this country seeking better jobs, but discrimination has, in most cases, prevented the dream from becoming reality.

Like the native Americans, some Hispanic-Americans have become more militant in recent years. The Chicano migrant farm workers have been unionized by César Chavez and a political party, *Raza Unida* (United People), has elected Chicanos to local political offices. Puerto Ricans, however, have been less successful in their efforts to improve their position. Several reasons may account for their failure. One may be that because Puerto Rico is nearby and under American jurisdiction, it is relatively easy to return to the island if they get discouraged. A second reason is the lack of strong leadership in the Puerto Rican community. There has as yet been no charismatic leader like Chavez to act as a voice of the people. A third reason is that the Puerto Rican community is divided. Some members prefer to retain the old traditions, while others attempt to become "Americanized."

César Chavez, leader and organizer of Chicano migrant farm workers.

Chinese immigrants were the victims of cruel discrimination in nineteenth-century America. Perhaps as a result of this, today many Chinese-Americans socialize very little with other Americans.

ORIENTAL-AMERICANS

Oriental-Americans consist of two major ethnic groups—the Chinese and the Japanese—and each has adjusted to American life differently.

The Chinese originally came to California during the middle of the nineteenth century to work in the mines and to help construct the railroads. Anti-Chinese feelings eventually arose, however, because lower-class whites feared that the Chinese would replace them in the job market. In some places, the Chinese were cruelly discriminated against in housing, jobs, and schools. The antagonism grew so strong, in fact, that the Chinese Exclusion Act was passed in 1882, stopping immigration from China completely. Although the law was repealed in the 1950s, most Chinese today live within their own enclaves in large cities and socialize very little with other Americans.

The Japanese began coming to the United States somewhat later than the Chinese and were also considered a threat. As a result, they were also discriminated against. When the Japanese attacked Pearl Harbor in 1941, fear of the "yellow peril" grew to such proportions that all the Japanese on the West Coast, including those who were American citizens, were interned in "security camps," which were really concentration camps. The racial undertone becomes clear when we realize that no German-Americans or Italian-Americans were similarly treated, although the United States was also at war with Germany and Italy. Today the Japanese in America have, for the most part, become quite wealthy and well-educated and have avoided isolation in ethnic neighborhoods.

JEWS

Jews, in reality, are a religious group. But in the perspective of the majority, they are considered an ethnic group as well. Most American Jews, however, are descended from people who came from Russia, Poland, Germany, and other regions of Europe, and thus really belong to a more specific ethnic group—German Jews, Polish Jews, and so forth. Like the other ethnic groups we have discussed, Jews are a minority group because for a long time they were treated unequally.

The first Jews that arrived in the United States came from Brazil in the middle of the seventeenth century. But the real immigration of Jews began in the middle of the nineteenth century and lasted until World War I. These were the European Jews. The 6 million Jews in this country represent the largest Jewish group in any one country in the world, much larger than in Israel. Approximately half of the Jewish population lives in or around New York City.

Jews have prospered in America. They have income levels well above the national average and their children are more likely to be college educated than those in any other group. This is not to say there are no poor Jews; but as a group they have attained high status, despite prejudice and discrimination.

WHITE ETHNICS

Although Americans like to believe that all groups have been blended together in a "melting pot," not all Americans feel they have been accepted equally into American society. Among those who feel they are outside the mainstream of our society are the "white ethics"—those descended from Irish, Polish, Italian, Slavic, or Greek immigrants.

White ethnics cannot visibly be distinguished from the white, Anglo-Saxon Protestants who compose the dominant group. However, differences in religion, language, and culture have served to set them apart from the dominant group. As a result of these differences, white ethnics have developed a distinct value system characterized by ". . . distrust of most politicians, [a] contempt for white rich and black poor, . . . a bristling defensiveness and a yearning for the recent past when life was simpler and loyalties less complex, when children were reared by the Bible and the beltstrap, when the schools stuck to the three R's, and when patriotism meant 'My country right or wrong.' "[25]

Sociologist Perry Weed contends that white ethnics comprise at least 65 percent of our total population. He states that they constitute a high percentage of the working class, tend to reside in large industrial cities in the Northeast, and are overwhelmingly Catholic.[26] They usually live in tight-knit ethnic communities that maintain much of the flavor of the "old country."

In recent years there has been a growth of pride among white ethnics, stemming in part from reactions to the black civil rights movement. It is not uncommon to see people wearing buttons that say, "Kiss Me, I'm Polish" or "Irish is Beautiful." Similarly, in the late 1960s, there was a movement by Italian-Americans to protest the stereotyping of all Italians as members of organized crime or "Godfather-types." Such television programs as *Roots* and *Holocaust* have further contributed to the resurgence of ethnic consciousness, not only among blacks and Jews, but among other minority groups as well.

Despite prejudice, discrimination, and at the same time pressure to become assimilated, each of America's minority groups has maintained its own identity. And with this identity has come a rich cultural heritage that has contributed to America's ethnic diversity and technological achievements.

SUMMARY

Two ways in which people may be classified are by race and ethnic group. *Race* refers to a group of human beings who share a set of innate physical characteristics. Although classification by race is not of much scientific use, the perception of racial similarities and differences among people is of sociological significance.

In the strict sense of the term, *ethnic group* refers to any group of people with a distinct common identity based on nationality. However, sociologists and lay people use the term to also include distinctions based on race, religion, customs, traditions, or language.

Both racial and ethnic groups are related to the concept of *minority group*. A *minority group* is any group of people that is different from the dominant group in terms of physical characteristics, cultural characteristics, or both. As a result of these differences it is treated unequally by others.

Often, people believe that members of a minority group are inferior in certain characteristics. For example, various people believe that blacks are less intelligent than whites, based on IQ scores. However, there is no evidence that this is the case. Although whites tend to score higher, test biases and the social environment of whites are responsible for differences in scores. In addition, some blacks score higher than some whites.

Two consequences that result from classifying people as different are *prejudice* and *discrimination*. *Prejudice* refers to an attitude by which we prejudge people. When we assign negative characteristics based on racial characteristics, prejudice takes the form of *racism*. *Discrimination* is an act that usually refers to negative behavior toward the members of some group. *Stereotyping*, the process whereby one group imposes on another a set of biased, unfavorable, exaggerated, and oversimplified generalizations without regard to individual differences is related to prejudice.

A number of scholars have attempted to explain the origins of prejudice and discrimination. Their theories can be grouped into three types: psychological, economic, and social. Psychological theories include the *scapegoat theory*, the *frustration-aggression theory*, and the *authoritarian personality theory*. Economic theories include the beliefs that prejudice is likely to occur when groups compete with one another for scarce resources, and when groups are exploiting other groups. Social theories state that people acquire prejudices through their culture and that prejudices serve several social functions.

People who experience prejudice and discrimination can react on two levels—behavioral and psychological. The behavioral can take the form of submission, adaptation, aggression, or self-segregation. The psychological can take the form of low self-esteem which can result in alienation or self-hatred.

Suggestions for eliminating prejudice and discrimination involve either changing attitudes or changing behavior. In order to change attitudes some researchers believe that education is the answer. Others believe that increasing contact among members of ethnic groups will improve ethnic relations. At the present time, though, it has not been easy to change people's attitudes and eliminate prejudice. Similarly, as the black civil rights movement suggests, it has not been easy to destroy discrimination through changing behavior.

GLOSSARY

adaptation a process by which a group being discriminated against adjusts positively to the environment, cultivating occupational and social areas of life left open to them by the dominant group.

aggressive action a form of behavioral adjustment in which a group being discriminated against uses aggression to alter its situation.

alienation a feeling of estrangement and hostility toward others and society in general.

authoritarian personality according to Adorno, a set of personality traits that usually accompany prejudice. Includes submission to authority and intolerance toward others.

discrimination a term that usually refers to negative behavior toward a group that involves disqualifying its members from various activities, or mistreating them.

ethnic group a related group of persons with a distinct common identity; any group of people who perceives itself or is perceived by others as being socially different from the dominant group.

frustration-aggression theory a psychological theory which argues that persons who are incompetent or failures or whose goals are blocked, may compensate for their failure through prejudices.

minority group any group that is different from the dominant group in terms of physical characteristics, cultural characteristics, or both, and is treated unequally because of these differences.

prejudice a term that usually refers to a negative attitude toward members of a group.

race a term referring to a group of human beings who share a set of innate physical characteristics. The three most common classifications are Caucasoid, Mongoloid, and Negroid.

racism a negative attitude expressed toward some group in terms of racial characteristics.

scapegoat theory a psychological theory which argues that people have a tendency to blame their troubles on anyone but themselves. Minority groups are often victims of scapegoating.

self-fulfilling prophecy a prediction about a series of events that helps to determine their outcome.

self-hatred a process by which a group accepts the negative opinions other people have of them.

self-segregation a form of behavioral adjustment in which a group being discriminated against isolates itself from the mainstream of society.

stereotyping the tendency to generalize about and categorize elements in our lives on the basis of limited information.

submission a process by which a group being discriminated against adopts behavior perceived as favorable by the dominant group.

REFERENCES

1. Raymond W. Mack, *Race, Class and Power.* New York: American Book Co., 1963, pp. 33–94.
2. Raymond W. Mack, "Race Relations." In Howard S. Becker, ed., *Social Problems: A Modern Approach.* New York: John Wiley & Sons, 1966, p. 337.
3. Arthur R. Jensen, "The Differences Are Real." *Psychology Today,* December 1973, pp. 80–86.
4. Hans J. Eysenck, *The I.Q. Argument: Race, Intelligence and Education.* New York: The Library Press, 1971.
5. *The New York Times,* July 2, 1968.
6. Ken Richardson and David Spears, eds., *Race and Intelligence.* Baltimore: Penguin Books, 1972.
7. George E. Simpson and J. Milton Yinger, *Racial and Cultural Minorities,* 4th ed. New York: Harper & Row, 1972.
8. Mack, "Race Relations," p. 336.
9. Eldridge Cleaver, *Soul on Ice.* New York: Dell, 1968, p. 17.
10. Angus Campbell and Howard Schunon, "Racial Attitudes in Fifteen American Cities." *Report to the National Advisory Committee on Civil Disorders.* Ann Arbor, Mich.: University of Michigan Press, 1968. See also Andrew M. Greeley and Paul B. Sheatsly, "Attitudes Toward Integration." *Scientific American* 225 (December 1971): 13–19. A variety of polls were taken by George Gallup that concerned this subject. See *The Gallup Opinion Index.* Issues 47 through 77. Princeton, N.J.: American Institute of Public Opinion, 1969–1971.
11. Richard T. LaPiere, "Attitudes vs. Actions." *Social Forces* 13 (December 1943): 230–237. Thomas F. Pettigrew, *Racially Separate or Together?* New York: McGraw-Hill, 1971.

399

12. John Sibley Butler, "Inequality in the Military: An Examination of Promotion Time for Black and White Enlisted Men." *American Sociological Review* 41 (October 1976): 807-818.

13. Butler, p. 817.

14. Thomas L. Van Valey, Wade Clark Roof, and Jerome E. Wilcox, "Trends in Residential Segregation: 1960−1970." *American Journal of Sociology* 82 (January 1977): 843.

15. Paul B. Horton and Gerald R. Leslie, *The Sociology of Social Problems,* 5th ed. Englewood Cliffs, N.J.: Prentice-Hall, 1974, pp. 386−391.

16. T. W. Adorno, et al., *The Authoritarian Personality.* New York: Harper & Row, 1950.

17. Michael Reich, "Economic Theories of Racism." In James M. Henslin and Larry T. Reynolds, eds., *Social Problems in American Society,* 2nd ed. Boston: Holbrook, 1976, pp. 136−143.

18. Alexander Lesser, "The Right Not to Assimilate: The Case of the American Indian." In Morton H. Fried, *Readings in Anthropology,* 2nd ed., vol. II, *Cultural Anthropology.* New York: Thomas Y. Crowell, 1968, pp. 583−593.

19. Eugene L. Horowitz, "Development of Attitudes Toward Negroes." *Archives of Psychology* 194 (1936): 34−35; David Gold, "Is Ethnic Prejudice a Unitary Variable?" *Midwest Sociologist* 17 (Spring 1955): 39−43; W. H. N. Hotopf, "Psychological Studies of Race Prejudice." *Political Quarterly* 32 (October-December 1961): 328−340.

20. Simpson and Yinger.

21. An excellent discussion of "passing" can be found in Erving Goffman, *Stigma: Notes on the Management of Spoiled Identity.* Englewood Cliffs, N.J.: Prentice-Hall, 1963.

22. Gordon W. Allport, *The Nature of Prejudice.* Cambridge, Mass.: Addison-Wesley, 1954, Chapter 16.

23. Simpson and Yinger, p. 682.

24. These events are described in greater detail in Clayton A. Hartjen, *Possible Trouble: An Analysis of Social Problems.* New York: Praeger, 1977, pp. 280−301.

25. Peter Binzen, *Whitetown, U.S.A.* New York: Random House, 1970, p. 9.

26. Perry Weed, "Components of the White Ethnic Movement." In Joseph A. Ryan, ed., *White Ethnics: Life in Working-Class America.* Englewood Cliffs, N.J.: Prentice-Hall, 1973, pp. 17−23.

SUGGESTED READINGS

Brown, Dee. *Bury My Heart at Wounded Knee.* New York: Holt, Rinehart & Winston, 1971.

A documentary detailing the history and treatment of native Americans in the American West.

Cleaver, Eldridge. *Soul on Ice*. New York: Dell, 1968.

> *An autobiography of a black American and his reactions to racism.*

Cottle, Thomas. *Black Children, White Dreams*. Boston: Houghton-Mifflin, 1974.

> *A record of the daily lives of several black children and their families in a northern city.*

Duberman, Martin. *In White America*. Boston: Houghton-Mifflin, 1964.

> *A classic play-documentary of the lives of blacks over two centuries in the United States.*

Frazier, E. Franklin. *Black Bourgeoisie*. New York: The Free Press, 1957.

> *A study of black middle-class Americans describing their frustrations, feelings of inferiority, and behaviors.*

Haley, Alex. *Roots*. New York: Doubleday, 1976.

> *A moving account of one man's search for his ancestral heritage.*

Liebow, Elliot. *Tally's Corner*. Boston: Little, Brown, 1967.

> *An anthropological analysis of a group of lower-class black men and their relationships with one another and their loved ones.*

Long, Elton, James Long, Wilmer Leon, and Paul B. Weston. *American Minorities: The Justice Issue*. Englewood Cliffs, N.J.: Prentice-Hall, 1975.

> *A brief overview of the history of injustice to minority groups in America and what strategies have and can be followed to correct the problem.*

Marden, Charles F., and Gladys Meyer. *Minorities in American Society*. 4th ed. New York: Van Nostrand, 1973.

> *A comprehensive and inclusive text on various minority groups in American society and the situations they face now and have contended with historically.*

Pettigrew, Thomas F. *Racially Separate or Together?* New York: McGraw-Hill, 1971.

> *Written by a renowned expert on race and race problems, this is one of the most reasoned and knowledgeable discussions of what the problem is and how it might be solved.*

Rose, Peter I. *They and We*. New York: Random House, 1973.

> *An historical overview of major American minority groups including current circumstances of each.*

13

Social Stratification

lthough Thomas Jefferson wrote in the Constitution of the United States that "all men are created equal," he did not mean that all of us have an equal share in the wealth, prestige, or power resources of a society. He did not mean that all of us are endowed at birth with equal biological traits and talents. Nor did he mean that we all have the same opportunities to achieve to the best of our abilities. If Jefferson had meant these things and if it were possible to implement them, then no American would be richer or have more prestige or power than any other American. If we look around us we know that such equality does not exist. Clearly, then, Jefferson's dream was not of social equality, but of equality under the law.

It is not just in the United States that inequality is a fact of life. Every society, except perhaps the most primitive, differentiates and ranks its members on some scale, depending on what the society values. In a warlike society, soldiers rank high and are greatly rewarded. In a society that treasures learning, scholars receive the rewards. In preliterate societies, the best hunters are ranked highest. Therefore, it can be said that in no society is everyone considered equal.

In this chapter we will explore social inequality or *social stratification*. We will examine different types of stratification and attempt to discover why stratification exists. We will also focus on stratification in the United States and see whether our country is really the land of opportunity it is often believed to be.

What Is Social Stratification?

Sociologists refer to inequality as *social stratification*. Sometimes, however, people confuse this term with *social differentiation*, although both are actually quite different concepts. Social differentiation refers primarily to a division of labor. We can differentiate, for example, between plumbers and doctors or between electricians and lawyers without evaluating or ranking them. Thus, social differentiation is defined as a universal process in which certain statuses are observable and recognized.

Social stratification takes us one step further. Not only do we categorize people, but we rank and reward each category differently based on money, prestige, and power. (Power and prestige are discussed in detail in Chapter 10.) The building contractor, for example, ranks above the bricklayer. The contractor earns more money, is accorded more prestige, and probably has greater power. The physician, in turn, ranks higher than the building contractor. Thus, stratification includes not only noting differences, but also evaluating, ranking, and rewarding members of the society based on certain criteria. Each of

FIGURE 13–1
Comparing Social Differentiation and Social Stratification

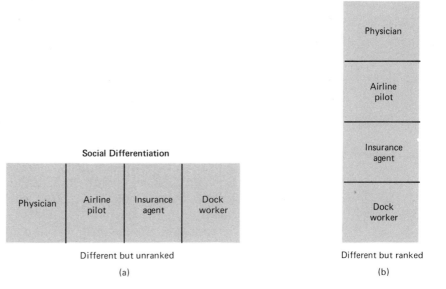

Social Differentiation

| Physician | Airline pilot | Insurance agent | Dock worker |

Different but unranked

(a)

Social Stratification

Physician

Airline pilot

Insurance agent

Dock worker

Different but ranked

(b)

these criteria—money, prestige, and power—is considered important to the survival and well-being of a society.

There are many types of social inequality. The stratification system found in a society depends on that society's degree of technology and its ideology. Let us briefly examine the stratification systems of four types of societies: small-scale, agrarian, industrial, and postindustrial. This will help us to see how our stratification system developed.

SMALL-SCALE SOCIETIES

A small-scale society is one that survives by hunting and gathering food. There is rarely a surplus because whatever is hunted and gathered is eaten the same day. Two types of stratification systems can be found in such societies: egalitarianism and anarchy.

Egalitarian societies display practically no social inequality. There is almost always plenty of food, and it is shared among the members. There is also almost no hierarchy, although especially good hunters and those who are especially generous are accorded higher prestige than others. The Tasaday tribe of the Philippines is an excellent example of a modern-day small-scale society with an egalitarian stratification system.

Anarchy, which is stratification based on sheer physical strength, can be found in small-scale societies that have a scarce food supply. In such societies, each member fends for himself or herself. Distrust and

405

competition form the basis of society. It is important to note, however, that such behavior stems from the environment and not from the people themselves. Such a society is illustrated by the Ik tribe of Uganda. Here no one shows love or kindness to anyone else.

AGRARIAN SOCIETIES

An *agrarian society* is one in which members subsist on what they produce from the land. Such societies first came into existence with the invention of metal tools like the hoe, and with the development of fertilization, irrigation, and terracing methods.

In order to survive, agrarian societies require a large, cheap labor force to work the land. And to produce this labor force, three types of stratification systems have emerged in such societies: slavery, caste, and estate.

Slavery is a system in which there are two strata—masters and slaves. It can be defined as a system in which "a man is in the eyes of the law and of public opinion and with respect to all other parties a possession of another man."[1] Slaves, then, are legal property, and in many agrarian societies the position is ascribed and inherited. The child of a slave is a slave and cannot escape from that status. It is the fact of being owned that makes one a slave, not the kind of work performed. In agricultural societies, where mechanical devices are practically unknown and where a cheap labor force is needed, slavery is usually indispensable to the economic well-being of the society, although peonage or serfdom can also result.

The institution of slavery is ancient and is known to have existed in every agrarian society.[2] American slavery, however, differed from that in ancient societies in several significant ways. For one thing, American slaves were kidnapped and sold, as opposed to being acquired in military conquests. A second difference was that in most ancient societies masters and slaves were of the same race. In contrast, in this country masters were white and slaves were black. This had a profound effect on our emerging stratification system since Americans have traditionally regarded blacks as innately inferior and deserving of a subordinate place in society.

Castes are groups of people whose status in society is considered to be predetermined by their behavior in a previous life. In India, where the caste system of stratification is more institutionalized than in any other known society, caste members usually believe they are descended from a common ancestor. They usually have a common name, they have a hereditary occupation, and they follow strict rules regarding interaction between members of different castes. For example, marriage between members of different castes is forbidden and there are also

406

Although discrimination on the basis of caste was outlawed in India in 1950, the caste system continues to affect the lives of many Indians.

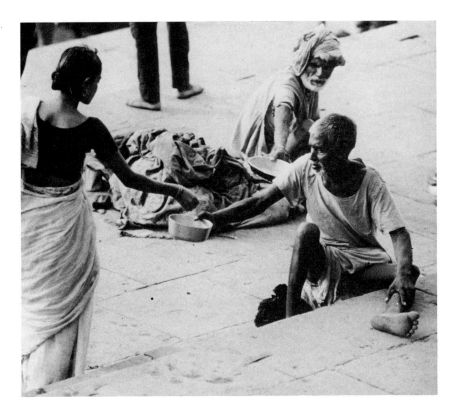

rules concerning food and social contact. Although discrimination on the basis of caste has been forbidden by law in India since 1950, and although urbanization and industrialization have done much to change old avoidance patterns, in the villages of India caste continues to affect the lives of most Indians.

In the *estate system* of stratification people are assigned to an "estate," or stratum, according to birth, land ownership, or military rank. The law defines the obligations, privileges, and rights of each estate. In medieval society, for example, the serf worked for the lord while, at the same time, the lord protected the serf. Unlike the slavery system, where rank is determined by being owned or owning, and unlike the caste system, where position is determined before birth, members of estates are permitted some social mobility through achievement. Estate position is usually not sanctioned by religion and certain kinds of interaction are allowed among members of different groups. In short, it can be said that an estate system relies on contractual arrangements. Each stratum has obligations to the others and each has rights from others. The estate system was prevalent in Europe during the Middle Ages and the late eighteenth century.

407

INDUSTRIAL SOCIETIES

One major technological change distinguishes industrial society from agrarian society. Machines, not animals or human beings, do much of the work of society. Technological advance eventually results in the development of huge corporations that can supply goods and services to the population at relatively low cost. Urbanization invariably results because many workers have to live close to factories. In addition, the standard of living greatly increases for all members of the society.

In industrial societies, members are differentiated by *social class*. A social class can be defined as an aggregate of people in similar occupational statuses, with similar degrees of prestige and privilege, and holding similar amounts of power. We will discuss social classes in greater detail later in this chapter. Here it is only necessary to state that in industrial societies class systems are based on education, one's family of orientation, and one's power in the industrial and political areas of society.

Another thing to note here is that in industrialized societies, the boundaries between social classes are blurred. There are several reasons for this. One is that in industrialized cities, relationships among people are primarily transitory and it is difficult to identify members of classes. Dress, behavior, and habits are at least superficially uniform. Even occupation, which once served as a clear indicator of social position, no longer helps to establish distinctions as readily as before. Finally, class differences are always crosscut by ethnic, racial, and religious lines, which makes placing people in distinct social classes even more difficult.

POSTINDUSTRIAL SOCIETIES

Sociologist Daniel Bell claims that a transition is occurring now in the major nations of the world, especially in the United States, from industrial to postindustrial development.[3] A postindustrial society is one in which the majority of people are engaged in providing services.

In postindustrial societies power is transferred from independent entrepreneurs, family-owned businesses, and landowners to the scientists and technicians with special knowledge and training who work in huge bureaucracies. Such people, according to Bell, comprise the new elite. High-ranking bureaucrats control the country's power, deriving their wealth, status, and influence from their expertise and their ability to control the bureaucracy.

In short, Bell and other social scientists claim that many advanced nations are entering an age in which those who control knowledge will control power. Technocrats and scientists will dominate society. Ac-

408

Some social scientists maintain that the United States is becoming a postindustrial society. In this type of society power will be attained, it is predicted, through education and not inheritance.

cess to power will come from education, not from inheritance. Achievement will become the means of entry, not ascription. Expertise will replace nepotism.

Why Is There Social Inequality?

It is one thing to recognize that social stratification exists, it is another to determine why such inequality exists almost everywhere and at all times. Philosophers and social scientists have argued for centuries about this, centering their attention on three major questions. These are: (1) What are the reasons for social inequality?; (2) Is social inequality inevitable or can societies eliminate it?; (3) If social inequality can be eliminated, how can this be done?

KARL MARX

Karl Marx was one thinker who dealt with these questions. In doing so, he identified two major classes in capitalistic society: the *bourgeoisie* and the *proletariat*.

The bourgeoisie is the class that *owns* the means of production (the land, capital, factories, tools, and so forth) and receives the profits. The proletariat is the class that *works* for those who own the means of production, receiving wages. For Marx, then, one broad definition of a social class is a group of people divided by their relationship to the means of production—one is either a member of the bourgeoisie or one is a member of the proletariat. According to Marx, membership in each class is usually unchangeable and affects all of one's life.

409

Karl Marx (1818–1883)

Karl Marx is one of the most controversial figures of the nineteenth and twentieth centuries. His writings, such as *The Communist Manifesto* (with Engels) and *Das Kapital,* continue to have a major impact on the social sciences. While he covered a vast subject area—philosophy, history, economics—his ideas centered on inequality and social-class stratification.

Marx argued that although inequality had existed throughout history, it would be doomed under industrial capitalism. Under this system, the proletariat—the propertyless people whose labor produced the goods—would rise up against the bourgeoisie—the owners of the means of production. The result, according to Marx, would be a classless society.

Marx was convinced that this conflict would occur when the workers developed class consciousness. That is, when the workers realized that through organization they could better their situation, they would revolt against their oppressors. But what would cause such class consciousness to develop?

Marx believed that *alienation* contributed to the growth of class consciousness among the workers. For example, when the workers recognize that they are an extension of a machine and that they can be replaced, they feel little identification with and derive minimum satisfaction from their work. As a result, they would develop class consciousness. And, according to Marx, such an alienated, class conscious proletariat has the potential for revolution. He believed that they would revolt and overtake the industrial capitalist system.

Although Marx viewed the history of all societies through the perspective of their class struggles, industrial capitalism was a special case. For the first time in history, Marx said, a majority—the workers—would assemble against a minority—the capitalists.

Marx also contended that capitalism itself was responsible for creating the conditions that would lead to the destruction of the bourgeoisie. Factories organized for more efficient production brought more workers together in one place, increasing their ability to assemble and their potential to revolt. The vast difference in life-styles between the proletariat and the bourgeoisie also became easily visible to the workers.

Once the overthrow of the capitalists and the rise of the proletariat had occurred, Marx thought, class antagonism would cease. As a result, inequality and social stratification would be eliminated.

Because the bourgeoisie owns the means of production, Marx asserted that it controls the proletariat. The bourgeoisie, Marx argued, also controls the methods of mass communication, the religious institution, and the government. Thus, the bourgeoisie controls the way the proletariat thinks, providing the proletariat with what Marx called "false consciousness." The values of the bourgeoisie dominate in the society.

410

Marx never clearly defined social class, except in terms of the members' relationship to the means of production. However, he differentiated between what he called a "class-for-itself" and a "class-in-itself." A class-for-itself has *class consciousness*, meaning that the members have a sense of "we-ness," of belonging together, of having common interests, and of recognizing that they are antagonistic toward the other class, who may, potentially at least, threaten their power. According to Marx, the bourgeoisie was a class-for-itself. A class-in-itself, such as the proletariat, is merely an aggregate of people.

In the mid-nineteenth century, Marx argued that the proletariat, even though the members shared a similar economic position all over the industrialized world, was not yet a true social class because it lacked this class consciousness. But he predicted that it would develop such class consciousness eventually, and then become a real social class. Consequently, it would be aware that its members were being exploited and that the bourgeoisie was the enemy.

When this occurred, Marx reasoned, the proletariat would begin a *class struggle*. All the workers of the world would unite to overthrow their masters because they would understand that they have "nothing to lose but their chains." This would produce a worldwide revolution, ending in a classless and stateless society, in which everyone would be equal. The means of production would be owned collectively. In this perfect, socialistic society, everyone would work according to ability and everyone would receive according to need. There would be no masters and no slaves, no rich and no poor, no haves and no have-nots.

Clearly, the worldwide class revolution that Marx predicted has not taken place, and most American social scientists have rejected the theory that it ever will. The workers of the world have not united, and it does not appear likely that they will do so in the near future.

Why has this worldwide revolution not occurred? Sociologists have identified a number of flaws in Marx's argument. First, they feel that he oversimplified the stratification system by recognizing only two classes: the bourgeoisie and the proletariat. In complex, technological societies there are many gradations between these two. Second, he could not foresee the growth of unions, which would improve working conditions. Nor could he predict that feelings of loyalty to one's nation would supersede feelings of loyalty to one's class, preventing the unification of workers from different countries. Third, Marx could not know that the distribution of income would change, giving the worker a larger share of the economic pie. Finally, Marx was naïve in believing that a stateless society could exist in complex cultures. Governments make many decisions in addition to economic ones, such as trade agreements, foreign policy, and domestic policy. According to Marx, if a society had no government, it would have no leaders to decide such issues. But Marx thought only in terms of economics. In short, he was an economic determinist. He believed that the only inequality among people is economic, and he rejected the notion that people can be unequal in many other ways.

Thus, Marx answered the three questions posed at the beginning of this section in the following way. He claimed that social inequality was basically economic in nature and existed because some people owned the means of production and acquired the profits while others worked for wages with no access to profits. He believed that inequality could and would be eliminated when workers all over the industrialized world acquired class consciousness, recognized their inferior position relative to the owners, and united to overthrow the bourgeoisie.

MAX WEBER

Max Weber was another social scientist who attempted to account for social inequality. He felt that it had three dimensions: class, status, and power. The first dimension, class, is economic. Weber agreed with Marx that a class is an economic interest group, with members of a given class having an equal economic opportunity in the society. Unlike Marx, though, Weber thought of classes as merely aggregates of people who are not class conscious and do not share a sense of cohesion. A social class then, to Weber, is a group of people who share the same opportunities in the marketplace, having the same levels of income to purchase goods and services.

Weber's second dimension of social inequality is status. Status groups are stratified according to the amount of prestige or honor bestowed upon them by the society. While classes have different opportunities in the marketplace, status groups have different styles of life. Members of any one status group tend to live in the same kind of house, bring up their children in the same way, and have similar goals, values, beliefs, and attitudes. In addition, status groups possess self-awareness. Members know they belong to the same group and tend to live near each other, interact with each other, and marry each other.

Weber's third dimension of social inequality is power. Although power was covered in detail in Chapter 10, we will redefine it here. Weber defined power as "the chance of a man or of a number of men to realize their own will in a communal action even against the resistance of others who are participating in the action." Power can be acquired in several different ways: among them are influence, exploitation, coercion, or membership in a high class or a high status group.

According to Weber, the three dimensions of inequality usually go together. If people are in a high class (if they are wealthy), they are

APPLYING SOCIOLOGY

Compare the theories of Marx and Weber and note which seems more logical to you. Do you believe that the economic difference between groups is the only really important factor determining social inequality, as Marx would have it? Or do you feel that Weber is correct when he insists that societal honor and social power are just as important as economic position? Do you think a classless society is possible? Or must we always have social inequality because of our different abilities, talents, motivations, and opportunities?

Although Weber's three dimensions of inequality usually go together, this is not necessarily the case. For example, most religious leaders may be high in prestige, although they may not be high in social class or power.

likely to be in a high status group, and they are also likely to have a high degree of power. For example, attorneys are apt to be wealthy, to be given a great deal of social prestige, and to have power over others. At the other end of the scale, migrant farm workers are usually in a low class because they are poorly paid. In addition, society does not show them much respect, and they have little power over others.

On the other hand, people can be high on one or two dimensions and low on a third one. Ministers may be low in terms of social class because they are usually not well paid, and they usually have only moderate power. Still they may be high in prestige. A building contractor without much education could be in a low status group because society does not afford him much prestige, or in a high social class because he earns a great deal of money, and he may have a great deal of power because many people may work for him.

Thus, Weber's answers to the three questions differed from those of Marx. Unlike Marx, Weber did not hold out hope for eliminating social inequality. Because people are inherently unequal in terms of talent and ability to succeed, he felt they would always reach different levels of class, status, and power.

STRUCTURAL-FUNCTIONALISM AND CONFLICT THEORY

The two major sociological theories that address the issue of social stratification are structural-functionalism and conflict theory. Since each holds a different view of society, each also explains stratification differently.

Functionalists claim that stratification is inevitable in any social group. Evaluating others is a natural thing for people to do. In fact, even in a group as small as a dyad, one person will have more power than the other. And such ranking is based on what is collectively considered valuable by the group. Each person knows his or her job, accepts the position and the responsibility of it, and works for the good of the

413

group. According to this point of view, then, the result of stratification is an integrated society.

A famous article on the subject of stratification was written by sociologists Kingsley Davis and Wilbert E. Moore.[4] In their article, which implied that people start life with equal opportunities, they stated that not only is stratification inevitable and integrative, but it is also necessary. It enables societies to ensure that the most important positions will be filled by the most competent people. The functionalists claim that without incentives, we would not be able to get people to enter occupations that require long training periods, hard work, and great expense. If everyone were rewarded equally—if there were no differences in income, prestige, and power between janitors and doctors, for example—why would anyone bother to become a doctor? In short, the functionalists stress position over individuals and argue that there is stratification in all societies because it encourages the most qualified people to enter the most demanding, but most needed, positions in society.

Conflict theorists take the opposite point of view. To them inequality does not guarantee that the most important positions will be filled by the most able people. On the contrary, since groups start out unequally, the victory for the limited goods and services in a society often goes to the group in the higher status. High social position is not necessarily attained through talent or ability; it is just as often attained by force, coercion, exploitation, fraud, dominance, or accident of birth.

Conflict theorists believe that social stratification harms society because it deprives some people (those born into poverty and low social status) of the opportunity to develop and contribute their talents.

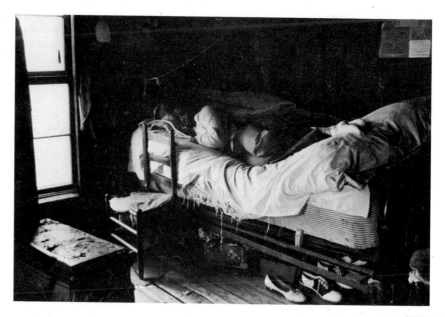

To conflict theorists, then, stratification is not a way of ensuring that the most needed positions will be filled by the most able people. Actually, it can result in the loss of talent because many talented people never get the opportunity to use their abilities. Furthermore, the greatest rewards do not necessarily go to those who are most valuable to society. In fact, there are positions that actually hurt society but are highly rewarded. For example, criminals often are wealthy, sometimes earn the esteem of other criminals, and sometimes achieve a great deal of power.

In short, conflict theorists argue that the present stratification system, instead of being integrative and useful, is harmful to society. It deprives some people of the chance to contribute their abilities and it creates hostility between social groups.

Which theory is correct? Are these theories really contradictory? Sociologist Gerhard Lenski[5] attempts to answer these questions. Lenski acknowledges that resources in a society are always scarce and groups are inevitably in competition for them. At the same time, though, in order to survive, human beings must cooperate. Therefore, says Lenski, both theories have elements of truth. There is both cooperation and conflict in all social groups. The two theories, then, complement, rather than contradict, each other.

The Social Class System in the United States

As we have seen, Karl Marx defined class in economic terms. To him, people were stratified according to their relation to the means of production. One class was made up of the owners of these means; the other class, of those who worked for the owners. Max Weber thought that people were stratified on the basis of three dimensions—class, status, and power. Today, most sociologists also use three criteria when they attempt to determine where people fit into a stratification system—income, level of education, and occupation.

Table 13-1 shows how Americans can be stratified by income. According to this table, the incomes of all Americans range from less than $3,000 to over $25,000. Table 13-2 depicts stratification by education. As in the case of income, the level of education attained by Americans covers a wide spectrum.

It is more difficult to rank people according to occupation than by income and educational level. There are, however, a number of ways sociologists have found useful. Some divide occupations into manual and nonmanual categories, meaning people who work with their hands and people who work with ideas. Others use categories of blue-collar workers, white-collar workers, and professional/managerial workers.

415

**TABLE 13-1
Money Incomes of
Families, 1976**

Income Class	Percentage of Families
Under $3,000	3.9
$3,000–$4,999	6.5
$5,000–$6,999	7.8
$7,000–$8,999	8.0
$9,000–$11,999	11.9
$12,000–$14,999	12.1
$15,000–$19,999	19.1
$20,000–$24,999	12.9
$25,000 and over	17.8
Total number of families: 56,710,000	
Median income: $14,958	

Source: U.S. Bureau of the Census, *Current Population Reports,* series P-60, No. 114.

**TABLE 13-2
Educational Attainment
of Employed Persons,
1974**

Educational Level	Numbers (in thousands)	Percent
Total	89,633	100%
Less than 4 years of high school	27,580	30.8
Less than 8 years of elementary school	11,397	12.7
High school, 1–3 years	16,183	18.1
Four years of high school or more	62,053	69.2
High school, 4 years	35,132	39.2
College: 1–3 years	13,493	15.0
4 years or more	13,402	15.0

Source: Adapted from Special Labor Force Report 175, *Educational Attainment of Workers, March 1974.* Washington, D.C.: United States Department of Labor, Bureau of Labor Statistics, 1975, p. 66.

Some classify people into unskilled, semi-skilled, skilled, and professional/managerial categories.

In 1947, the National Opinion Research Center conducted a well-known study in which approximately 3,000 people, representative of the population of the United States, ranked ninety occupations on the basis of prestige.[6] In 1964, sociologists Robert W. Hodge, Paul M. Siegel, and Peter H. Rossi replicated the original study (see Table 13-3) and concluded that there has been remarkably little change in the way Americans evaluate occupational prestige. Examining some studies that dated back as far as 1925, they were able to see that over a period of thirty-eight years, people still ranked a United States Supreme Court Justice first, physicians second, and college professors eighth. Coal miners still rank seventy-seventh, and garbage collectors eighty-eighth. The lowest rank continues to be held by shoe shiners.[7] Not only have

416

TABLE 13-3 Occupational Prestige Rankings in the United States, 1963

Occupation	Score	Occupation	Score	Occupation	Score
U.S. Supreme Court Justice	94	Public school teacher	81	Traveling salesman for a wholesale concern	66
Physician	93	Building contractor	80	Plumber	65
Nuclear physicist	92	Owner of a factory that employs about 100 people	80	Automobile repairman	64
Scientist	92			Barber	63
Government scientist	91	Artist who paints pictures that are exhibited in galleries	78	Machine operator in a factory	63
State governor	91	Author of novels	78	Owner-operator of a lunch stand	63
Cabinet member in the federal government	90	Economist	78	Playground director	63
College professor	90	Musician in a symphony orchestra	78	Corporal in the regular army	62
U.S. Representative in Congress	90	Official of an international labor union	77	Garage mechanic	62
Chemist	89	County agricultural agent	76	Truck driver	59
Diplomat in the U.S. Foreign Service	89	Electrician	76	Fisherman who owns his own boat	58
Lawyer	89	Railroad engineer	76	Clerk in a store	56
Architect	88	Owner-operator of a printing shop	75	Milk route man	56
County judge	88	Trained machinist	75	Streetcar motorman	56
Dentist	88	Farm owner and operator	74	Lumberjack	55
Mayor of a large city	87	Welfare worker for a city government	74	Restaurant cook	55
Member of the board of directors of a large corporation	87	Undertaker	74	Singer in a nightclub	54
Minister	87	Newspaper columnist	73	Filling station attendant	51
Psychologist	87	Policeman	72	Dock worker	50
Head of a department in a state government	86	Reporter on a daily newspaper	71	Coal miner	50
Airline pilot	86	Bookkeeper	70	Night watchman	50
Civil engineer	86	Radio announcer	70	Railroad section hand	50
Priest	86	Insurance agent	69	Restaurant waiter	49
Banker	85	Tenant farmer who owns livestock and machinery and manages the farm	69	Taxi driver	49
Biologist	85	Carpenter	68	Bartender	48
Sociologist	83	Local official of a labor union	67	Farmhand	48
Captain in the regular army	82	Manager of a small store in a city	67	Janitor	48
Instructor in public schools	82	Mail carrier	66	Clothes presser in a laundry	45
Accountant for a large business	81	Railroad conductor	66	Soda fountain clerk	44
				Sharecropper who owns no livestock or equipment and does not manage farm	42
				Garbage collector	39
				Street sweeper	36
				Shoe shiner	34

Source: Adapted from Robert W. Hodge, Paul M. Siegel, and Peter H. Rossi, "Occupational Prestige in the United States: 1925–1963," *American Journal of Sociology* 70 (November 1964).

Americans remained constant in their opinion of occupational prestige, but cross-national studies reveal a "striking uniformity of occupational prestige from country to country."[8]

As we have mentioned, the ways in which people are ranked determine their social class. We will now examine the number of social classes in America.

NUMBER OF CLASSES

How many classes are there in modern American society? The answer to this question is one few sociologists agree on. Some, like Marx, claim there are only two classes: the owners and the workers. Others use a three-class system, consisting of an upper class, a middle class, and a lower class. Still other social scientists claim there are nine categories: upper-upper, middle-upper, lower-upper, upper-middle, middle-middle, lower-middle, upper-lower, middle-lower, and lower-lower. None of these systems, however, is very useful. The first two methods are too simple, and sociologists use them only when their sample is very small. The third system is useful only when the sample being studied is very large.

Many sociologists use the classical six-class system devised by Lloyd Warner.[9] According to Warner, society can be divided as follows:

1) The upper-upper class, comprising about 2 percent of the population, is composed of families who have been wealthy for two or more generations.

2) The lower-upper class contains about 2 percent of the population, and its members have newly acquired wealth.

3) The upper-middle class, which is comprised of moderately successful business and professional people, consists of about 10 percent of the population.

4) The lower-middle class contains about 28 percent of the population and generally is composed of white-collar workers, teachers, and some foremen.

5) The upper-lower class, representing about 33 percent of the population, consists of blue-collar workers and often semi-skilled or unskilled wage-earners.

6) The lower-lower class, including derelicts and the unemployable often dependent on social welfare, makes up approximately 25 percent of the population.

Sociologist Joseph Kahl used a slightly different approach and divided the population of the United States into five classes: the upper class (1 percent), the upper-middle class (9 percent), the lower-middle

"There goes the neighborhood!"

class (40 percent), the working class (40 percent), and the lower class (10 percent).[10] Many sociologists use this approach.

Kahl claims that the members of each social class develop shared value orientations. A *value orientation* can be defined as the things that a person or a group considers important or proper as expressed by behavior. For example, when Protestant parents object to their son marrying a Catholic, they are implying that they value marriage to people of the same religion. Thus, according to Kahl, there is a tendency for people who work in similar occupations, who earn similar sums of money, and who live in similar dwellings to interact with each other, to spend money in similar ways, to value similar things, to hold common ideals, and so forth. But value orientations are not the only ways in which social classes differ. Following Kahl's class structure, we will now look at these value orientations and at some other differences, bearing in mind that not all members of these classes follow these patterns exactly. There is always a great deal of individual variation.

The Upper Class

Approximately 1 percent of the population can be classified as upper class. These are the people whose names appear in the *Social Register*, which is an acknowledgment that one's family has been wealthy for at least two generations. They are the people who serve on boards of directors of banks, very large corporations, and universities.

419

The stress in this class is on family lineage and tradition. Children are taught very early in life that they are members of an exclusive group and they must never do anything to embarrass the family or harm its reputation. They must also be careful to preserve the family's fortune. There is great stress on the accomplishments of past generations and of the living members.

Upper-class people do not have jobs. If they work at all, they hold a position, such as being president of a bank. Usually, however, they are involved in community activities or they spend their time simply managing the money they possess. Generally, upper-class men or women have more free time than others in classes below them, and so they travel and learn about music, art, the theatre, and the ballet.

Literary critic Paul D. Zimmerman reviewed a book written by Stephen Birmingham, called *The Right People,* which described life in this class. Here is part of that review:

> Free-lance writer Stephen Birmingham turns a jaundiced, sometimes unsteady eye upon "Real Society." "In America," he explains, "there is Society. Then there is Real Society. Real Society is part of Society—the upper part. Everybody who is in Society knows who the people in Real Society are. But the people in Real Society do not necessarily know who the other Society people are."
>
> Nor, Birmingham adds, do they really care. The denizens of Real Society carry impeccable credentials and need only know who is in, not who is out. Perhaps, once upon a time, they were parvenus but their money is "old money" now, their antecedents have been respectable for at least several generations and, most important, their sense of their rightful place in the social stratosphere is secure enough to relieve them of the chore of following the ups and downs of social climbers beneath them.
>
> Members of Real Society, Birmingham contends, have a "look" about them, a simple style of dressing that never falls from fashion, an accent all their own, a particular way of thinking, and even, according to one observer, a special smell of their own.
>
> They are not so much special by birth as by breeding. The "right people" send their children to the "right schools." Boys go to Princeton or Yale—not Harvard. The girls continue their education at one of the Seven Sisters schools of which Barnard is considered the toniest. The girls will come out at private parties given by their parents.
>
> To those who say Society is dead, Birmingham offers proof that it is alive and well. "When a person says . . . Real Society is dead and gone, it is reasonably safe to assume that that person is not a member. People in Real Society know that their world is very much alive. But they don't think it is quite polite to say so."[11]

Upper-class people, then, have a special attitude toward life that is not acquired just by having money. It is based on a full awareness that they are members of established, respected families. They have a sense of position and permanence. Members of their families have been important for a long time and they expect to maintain the pattern. They believe in tradition and they have respect for the past. The significant factor is not their money itself, but the way it is used. The key value orientation is *gracious living*.

The Upper-Middle Class

The class just below the upper class includes about 9 percent of the population and is composed of the businesspeople and professionals in our society. Most upper-middle-class members are American-born and white. Almost all have college degrees, and some have advanced degrees. Like the upper class, members of the upper-middle class do not have jobs; they hold positions. But unlike the upper class, they consider that position to be the most important part of their lives. Therefore, the value orientation for this class is *career*. These are the members of our society who are most likely to be listed in *Who's Who in America* because they are the achievers. These are the people who make the important decisions guiding the work of those in classes below them.

In contrast to the upper class, upper-middle-class people are present- and future-oriented. They wear the latest fashions, drive the newest model cars, and own modern houses. There is a great deal of stress on consumption patterns. These families must demonstrate their success to the world.

Career men of this class learn how to mix well with people. They are outgoing and friendly, cultivating those who are important to their careers. Motivation is kept at a high level by constant, self-generating needs—redecorating the house, giving parties, sending children to private schools—in short, keeping up with the Joneses.

A career is a life-style. It does not stop when the man comes home from the office. Often he brings work home with him. He entertains business acquaintances. He plays golf with business associates. His friends are contacts. He is always in the public eye. He is always competing. The commodity that the corporate upper-middle-class man sells is his personality. All the members of his family are committed to the career and its continuous success. The wife in such a corporate family is an important cog in the husband's aspirations. She too must fit the corporate image—in her personal appearance, her activities, her associational memberships, her friends, and her home.

The following description of an upper-middle-class community called Crestwood Heights reveals how an orientation toward success is perpetuated in the children of this class:

> The career is set before the boy as a central life goal at an early age. He is encouraged jokingly almost as soon as he can talk to speculate upon what he is going to do when he grows up.
>
> Career considerations seem to "come from nowhere" in the environment of the young child. He senses them only at the deepest level and expresses them in those flashes of insight which surprise and amaze parents. Yet from the beginning these considerations shape his orientation toward adulthood.
>
> The child's developing notion of the career derives in large part from his immediate social circumstances. The occupational roles filled by Crestwood adults contribute alike the information and misinformation which become incorporated into his conception of himself and his future. The high incomes and the high-status occupations which are enjoyed by the adults, the reputable houses, the automobiles, and other material manifestations of success, are not mere statistical data to the child. He is constantly apprised of their meaning by parent, teacher, and especially peer.
>
> The Crestwood child is reared in an environment of prosperity and success, comes to feel that life's opportunities are limitless, that he can become anything he wishes to become. This environment, provided by the father as a result of successful prosecution of his career and by the other successful fathers who live in Crestwood Heights, sustains a feeling of well-being in, and is at the same time a source of pride to, the child, who easily learns to enjoy the comparative affluence and power enjoyed by his father and the fathers of his friends. Many advantages will be his: he will be sent to college and his father's "contacts" will be at his disposal when his career is formally launched.
>
> He knows that he will be "given every opportunity" to get started, that his parents will not spare themselves to help him, but that he will also be called on to "exert himself." He knows that he is expected to excel.[12]

The Lower-Middle Class

Kahl divides the classes into the "big" people and the "little" people. The two groups just described make up the "big" people. The lower-middle class, composed of about 40 percent of the population, is the highest ranking class among the "little" people. The members of this social grouping earn their living as white-collar workers and as high-ranking, blue-collar workers, such as electricians, plumbers, foremen in large factories, and highly skilled craftsmen.

Sociologist Herbert L. Gans describes life among the lower-middle class:

The lower-middle class, to which about 40 percent of all Americans belong, includes such high-ranking blue-collar workers as skilled craftspeople.

If "blandness" is the word [to describe lower-middle-class life], it stems from the transition in which the lower-middle class finds itself between the familial life of the working class and the cosmopolitanism of the upper-middle class. The working-class person need conform only within the family circle and the peer group, but these are tolerant of his other activities. Believing that the outside world is unalterably hostile and that little is gained from its approval, he can indulge in boisterousness that provides catharsis from the tensions generated in the family and peer circles.

Lower-middle-class people seem to me to be caught in the middle. Those whose origins were in the working class are no longer tied so strongly to the extended family, but although they have gone out into the larger society, they are by no means at ease in it. They do not share the norms of the cosmopolitans, but, unlike the working class, they cannot ignore them. As a result, they find themselves in a situation in which every neighbor is a potential friend or enemy and every community issue a source of conflict, producing a restraining and even inhibiting influence on them. Others, lower-middle class for generations, have had to move from a rural or small-town social structure. They too are caught in the middle, for now they must cope with a larger and more heterogeneous society, for which their cultural and religious traditions have not equipped them.

If left to themselves, lower-middle-class people do what they have always done: put their energies into home and family, seeking to make life as comfortable as possible, and supporting, broadening, and varying it with friends, neighbors, church, and a voluntary association. Because this way of life is much like that of the small-town society or the urban neighborhood in which they grew up, they are able to maintain their optimistic belief that Judeo-Christian morality is a reliable guide to behavior.

Of course, life is not really [as happy as lower-middle class people like to envision it], for almost everyone must live with some disappointment: an unruly child, a poor student, an unsatisfied husband, a bored wife, a bad job, a chronic illness, or financial worry. These realities are accepted because they cannot be avoided; it is the norms of the larger society which frustrate. Partly desired and partly rejected, they produce an ambivalence which appears to the outsider as the blandness of lower-middle-class life.[13]

As Gans suggests, the lower-middle class is characterized by a value orientation toward *respectability*. Its members exert much time and effort on the activities that proclaim respectability: having attractive homes, going to church, educating their children, conforming to societal rules. There is a moderate amount of occupational success and satisfaction. Family life is close and stable. To some people such a life may appear dull, but for those in the lower-middle class, despite its rigidity, life is peaceful and quietly satisfying.

The Working Class

About 40 percent of our population is in the working class, which is composed mainly of semi-skilled factory operators. Many of these workers are high-school dropouts and therefore have no special skills to offer an employer. Since the pattern is frequent job change as the market dictates, there is some work instability, and the difference in earnings may be very little between those who have worked for one year and those who have worked for twenty years. For these reasons, the value orientation of this class is *getting by*.

The most famous research of this class was conducted in the 1950s by the late sociologist Ely Chinoy,[14] who studied the assembly-line worker in the automotive factory. Chinoy found that the basic factor about such work is that it is flat, in every sense of the word. Jobs, responsibility, and pay hardly vary from year to year or from job to job. Since there is little possibility of promotion to a skilled position, there is little incentive to work hard and get ahead.

Even the work these people do is flat and dull. Tasks are divided into small routine operations. Each worker tightens a bolt or sprays on a little paint as the cars move past on the line. Each operation is performed over and over again for eight hours a day. No one enjoys the work or is particularly interested in it. Unlike the career worker or the white-collar worker, both of whom find work stimulating, the blue-collar worker is alienated from the job.

For most, according to Chinoy, this alienation spills over into their private lives. They rarely talk about their work in their homes and they are usually so tired from the dullness of the work that they become alienated from leisure activities as well.

When a society stresses work as a central life interest, as ours does, Chinoy argues that the person who is estranged from work is also often estranged from life itself. Thus, blue-collar workers pay little attention to public affairs and world events and live in a very narrow world. They consider themselves anonymous, powerless people and therefore they become spectators of life. They do their work unthinkingly because there is no challenge to think about. They spend a great deal of time watching television in the same way.

It seems from more recent research that little has changed for the blue-collar worker. Writing about such workers, sociologist Gus Tyler claims that they are angry, but unsure against whom to direct their fury:

> As a child of toilers [the blue-collar worker] holds the traditional
> view of those who labor about those who don't. He feels that those
> inflated prices, those high taxes, those inadequate wages are all part of
> a schema for fattening up the fat. While he rarely, if ever, uses the
> words "establishment" or "system," he instinctively assumes there's an
> establishment that exploits him through a devilishly devised system.[15]

424

In short, blue-collar workers are often alienated and their only hope is to get by. They tend to retreat from work and outside affairs and turn to their families for what satisfactions they can get. Their aspirations gradually become minimal as they eventually realize that nothing better is going to happen to them. Then they settle down to the dull routine of their jobs simply because working is preferable to idleness and the pay is steady.

The Lower Class

In America, 10 percent of the population is poor. Members of the lower class consist of migrant farm workers, sharecroppers, domestic servants, and the chronically unemployed. These are the families that may have been on welfare for two and three generations. Yet most members of the lower class actually are unable to help themselves, primarily for societal reasons. Most of this class is composed of dependent children and people who are chronically ill, elderly, and illiterate.[16] Many are migrants from the rural south, Mexico, and Puerto Rico, and most lack education, English language skills, and industrial skills. If they can find jobs at all, they receive the lowest wages and have the lowest prestige.

Because of their situation, lower-class people tend to be stereotyped as disinterested in helping themselves and therefore not deserving of help from others. According to this stereotype they have no respect for law; they produce the violent crime, juvenile delinquency, and illegitimate babies. They are characterized as stupid, uneducable, sexually promiscuous, and a threat to the rest of society. To-

Migrant farm workers, along with sharecroppers, domestic servants, and the chronically unemployed are members of the lower class.

FOCUS ON: THE CULTURE OF POVERTY

Why do some people live in poverty? Oscar Lewis deals with this complicated question in his book *La Vida*.

In this book Lewis distinguishes between those experiencing poverty and those living in the culture of poverty. Those experiencing poverty are subject to low or inconsistent income. Lewis argues that the problems created by poverty can be solved by raising income. On the other hand, the culture of poverty is the reaction and long-term adaptation of a group to poverty. Problems created by the culture of poverty are more persistent and difficult to resolve. Lewis reported that the families he studied in Mexico City and San Juan and about 20 percent of the American poor are living in the culture of poverty.

Lewis cites several features of the culture of poverty. First, groups in the culture of poverty have few, if any, positive contacts with much of the larger society. While the reasons for this are complicated, two of the most important are fear and suspicion combined with lack of access to sources of power. Moreover, when poor people have contact with the larger society, the experience is very often negative. For example, their frequent contact with the police, public relief systems, and the Army tend to reinforce their negative opinions of society.

Second, the culture of poverty, at the local level, usually exists in an environment of crowding, poor housing, and minimum social organization. Lewis argues that most primitive groups have more organization than urban slum dwellers.

Third, family life in the culture of poverty is usually structured differently from that in other groups. Often, childhood is not considered a dis-

tinct period in the life cycle. Consequently, children are not as well protected from sexual contacts and other "adult" behavior as are children in middle-class households. In addition, according to Lewis, men and women frequently live together without being married, and men frequently abandon their women and children. This leads to a mother-centered or matrifocal family structure.

Finally, the individual in the culture of poverty may develop feelings of helplessness, dependence, inferiority, and other personality traits consistent with the circumstances of his or her life. Lewis describes these people as fatalistic and present-time oriented. This often prevents them from planning for the future or sacrificing an immediate need or want in order to achieve a long-term goal.

In addition, because they are absorbed in their own struggle to survive, those in the culture of poverty may not see their problems as common to others in the same circumstances. They have no "class consciousness," to use Marx's term. Instead, they tend to be aware of differences rather than similarities between their situation and that of others around them.

As people become increasingly embedded in the culture of poverty they become more and more resistant to change. In other words, they see no way out of their dilemma and often refuse to explore new avenues that might lead them out of their poverty.

Do you think there really is a culture of poverty? Why do you think those living in the culture of poverty do not develop class consciousness? How would you solve the problems created by the culture of poverty? Do you think such problems can be solved?

Source: Oscar Lewis, *La Vida*, New York: Random House, 1968.

tally lacking any social power, they are discriminated against in most areas of social life and can do little to escape or even protest. Kahl claims that because of their helplessness the central value orientation of the lower class is *apathy*. They cease to care. They know there is no way out. They cannot help themselves and there is no one to help them.

The following quote from Kahl portrays the situation of the lower class:

> The central assumption of the lower-class value system is that the situation is hopeless. Because he [the lower-class person] has to struggle merely to stay alive, because he knows that respectable people sneer at him as "no good," because he lacks the technical and social skills necessary for success, the lower-class person gives up.[17]

SOCIAL CLASS LIFE-STYLES

Membership in a social class affects practically all facets of life. As we have seen, different social classes hold different value orientations, and these value orientations are reflected in life-styles and personal satisfactions. Each class has different characteristics, different aspirations and goals, and different means of attaining them. The realities of life, then, vary by social class. Let us examine a few of these differences.

Marriage and Family Life

To the upper-class individual, the family is a very important unit because the person derives his or her social standing from it. Families are often extended, with the oldest member in the position of patriarch or matriarch. Sons are expected to enter their fathers' occupations; daughters have traditionally been expected to marry "well" and become wives. Parents exercise strong influence on mate choices because marriage to a member of one of the "right" families enhances the family's fortune and prestige. Marriage, then, is often as much a "merger" as it is a personal relationship.

Most upper-class families are patriarchal. A wife does not get involved in her husband's business affairs. But her domestic role is often more symbolic than real inasmuch as she does not actually engage in domestic chores or child rearing. Ties between upper-class husbands and wives are not as close as in some other classes because of the family structure and because money permits them to become involved in independent activities. However, generational ties are strong because a great deal of prestige comes from the past.

In the corporate family of the upper-middle class, the wife shares her husband with his corporation. Wives also become team members.

427

They can further their husbands' careers provided they conform to the corporate image and behave in acceptable ways. The corporate wife must wear the "right" clothes, have the "right" friends, join the "right" social organizations. She must entertain her husband's business associates and provide a background that reflects his success.

In the lower-middle-class family, where the insistence on respectability is strong, so is the stress on strong family ties. Wives are "junior partners," expected to provide companionship for their husbands. Lower-middle-class wives are freer than those in the other classes to pursue their own interests. Frequently a lower-middle-class wife will work, but she does not see her job as a career as much as a means of increasing the family's income. Her "real" job, she believes, is always her home and children.

In the working class, the sexes are more segregated than in the classes above them. Women are often quite isolated and have few friends. Much of their social lives revolves around their mothers and sisters, who often live nearby. A working-class husband can be extremely patriarchal. His desires and needs are the wife's first consideration. He may pay little attention to his wife and children, may refuse to share in household chores, and may consider he has done his "part" by providing most of the family's living. Often there is not very much interaction, then, between the wives and husbands in this group.

Among people in the lower class, marriage is viewed in two ways simultaneously. A high premium may be placed on marriage because it is seen as "respectable." But at the same time there is pessimism and disenchantment with it. Both partners contribute to this pessimism. The lower-class male, who is failing in the work sector, also expects to fail as a husband and father. The female, in turn, frequently does not trust her mate and stays close to her female relatives upon whom she can depend. Indeed, lower-class people approach marriage expecting to be emotionally isolated from each other. Although most marry at least once, lower-class men usually feel coerced into marriage. It "just happened" to them. Like in most of life, they believe that fate deals the cards and that they have little power to make decisions.

Language and Speech

Several studies have shown that speech patterns are excellent indicators of social class.[18] In some European countries this is even clearer than in the United States, where regional patterns somewhat obscure or modify social-class patterns. Upper-class English people, for example, speak very differently from their lower-class compatriots.

In the United States, lower-class people are most apt to use double negatives. For example, a lower-class person might say "I ain't got no place to go" as opposed to "I have no place to go." They also frequently

FOCUS ON: CHRISTMAS CARDS

Social status and prestige have become part of our everyday lives. In her article "Sociology of Christmas Cards," Sheila K. Johnson takes a look at how prestige enters into such a commonplace activity as the exchange of Christmas cards. It should be noted, however, that her article is based on a limited telephone survey and therefore we should be cautious in generalizing these findings.

Johnson points out that people ask themselves who is important and by whom they would like to be remembered when deciding to whom they will send cards. These and other considerations reflect the average card sender's status awareness and aspirations for social mobility.

Johnson suggests that there is a pattern to the card-sending behavior of people. Both the style of the card selected and the people to whom cards are sent are significant. Many card senders unconsciously group their friends and acquaintances into three categories: those individuals to whom they send cards each year, but from whom they receive none; those individuals with whom they regularly exchange cards; and those individuals from whom they receive cards each year, but to whom they send none.

This pattern is most representative of upwardly mobile middle-class card senders in the social and business arenas. Because of their careers, middle-class individuals have many business acquaintances with whom they would like to keep in touch. Their card sending is a practical way to maintain contact with individuals considered important or influential to them. In addition, because of geographical mobility stemming from their careers, middle-class individuals often live a distance from family and friends. The exchange of greeting cards serves as a substitute for personal contact.

This pattern contrasts with patterns in other classes. Those in the lower and working classes are less career-oriented and less geographically mobile. As a result, they have fewer business acquaintances and more frequent personal contact with kin. In addition, they have less money to devote to nonessentials. Thus, they are less likely to send Christmas cards than are those in the middle class.

The upper class is also less likely to send Christmas cards, but for different reasons. Members of the upper class are self-assured in their knowledge of intimates and acquaintances, so they do not need to send cards. Illustrating this in a humorous way, Johnson points to the British upper-class tendency to dispense with card sending altogether. In the place of cards, some members of the upper class in Britain place notices in *The London Times* stating that "Lord and Lady So-and-So send warm greetings to all their friends for Christmas and the New Year, as they will not be sending cards."

Besides prestige, other aspects of a person's life-style are conveyed in his or her card-sending behavior. Johnson points out that cards often advertise the political and social views of the sender. For example, UNICEF cards or cards that support the local symphony association are strong indications of a person's convictions.

Also, the size of the card may reflect the mobility and value orientation of the sender. Johnson notes that many businesspeople take the "bigger is better" approach to cards. On the other hand, reverse snobbery may be evident in the selection of a smaller than usual card.

Do you think that card sending includes messages about social status and mobility? Do you think that people are aware of the prestige element in sending cards? Have you ever purchased cards because you thought they would "say" something about you?

Source: Sheila K. Johnson, "Sociology of Christmas Cards," *Transaction*, vol. 8, January 1971, pp. 27–29.

mispronounce words and accent the wrong syllable. Clifton Fadiman[19] listed several characteristics of upper-class speech in contrast to the patterns of other classes. According to Fadiman, the upper class:

1) Avoids jargon and slang, except in upper-class sports and colleges.

2) Uses fewer words to express the same thought. Fadiman estimated that upper-class people use 20 percent fewer words than lower-class people to convey the same idea.

3) Prefers direct, simple words and avoids euphemisms.

4) Avoids dramatic or striking language.

5) Has a tendency to use words derived from French, such as lingerie instead of underwear.

6) Accents the first syllable of many words which are accented on the last syllable by those in classes below them, for example, inquiry, harass, and trespass.

7) Has a neatness of enunciation.

8) Has a speech pattern characterized by a different pitch and tone than the speech of others.

Differing speech patterns are important for two reasons. One, changing one's speech habits is extremely difficult, if not impossible. Two, because lower-class people can be identified by the way they speak, they may be discriminated against in job interviews and other situations. People, such as personnel managers, are less likely to hire someone who uses lower-class speech patterns. And people in the upper classes are likely to avoid social interaction with those using lower-class speech patterns.

Food and Drink

According to sociologist Thomas E. Lasswell, social classes differ in terms of what, how, where, and when they eat and drink.[20] One reason, of course, is cost. A second reason is that members of different social classes acquire different tastes and habits in childhood.

Lasswell shows that upper-class people eat either very elaborate or very simple meals. They rarely use pre-packaged or frozen foods. They dine in dining rooms or on terraces. In contrast, middle-class people eat in dinettes, and lower-class people eat in kitchens. Upper-class people rarely dine before eight o'clock; middle-class people tend to eat about six in the evening; lower-class people eat as early as five o'clock because many work on shifts that end at four in the afternoon and dinner is expected to be on the table when the breadwinner returns home.

The social classes even have different terms for meals. Upper- and middle-class persons have breakfast when they awake in the morning,

Drinking habits differ among the social classes. For example, most drinking by members of the middle class takes place at parties or business gatherings, rather than at home or in bars.

lunch about noon, dinner after work, and supper in the evening. Lower-class people also have breakfast in the morning, but dinner is at noon and supper is the evening meal.

Drinking habits also differ. Upper-class people do not consider drinking a moral issue. They are concerned with the behavior that accompanies drinking and are intolerant of boorish manners while drinking. The middle class is more likely than any other to worry about the morality of drinking. Middle-class women tend to drink less than middle-class men. Most middle-class drinking takes place at private cocktail parties or at business gatherings. Lower-class people are concerned neither with the morality nor their behavior while drinking. They tend to drink in sex-segregated groups, usually in public places like taverns rather than in their homes. Beer and sweet wines are preferred by the lower classes; scotch, bourbon, and medium-priced wines by the middle class; cognac, sherry, vintage wines, and champagne by the upper class.

Sexual Behavior

Popular opinion has it that the upper class is sexually immoral and decadent, the middle class is sexually repressed, and the lower class is animalistic. But studies of sexual behavior show that most of these beliefs are merely stereotypes. Nevertheless, sociologists have identified some distinctions among classes in terms of premarital, marital, and extramarital sexual behavior.

According to sociologists Joann DeLora and Carol Warren, lower-class males are more likely than males in other classes to engage in premarital intercourse with women friends and with prostitutes, to have extramarital sexual relations, and to have homosexual contact. Lower-class males are more likely to exploit females sexually and are more concerned with self-satisfaction than with satisfaction for their partners. It is not surprising, then, that lower-class women report less interest and pleasure in sexual activity than do middle- and upper-class women.

Furthermore, state DeLora and Warren, as social-class position rises, males are more likely to masturbate and to pet to achieve orgasm, to prefer nudity during sexual intercourse, and to engage in oral-genital sexual practices. Females also are more likely to masturbate, to have homosexual relations, to achieve orgasm frequently, and to engage in extramarital sex. For both sexes, the higher the social class, the more elaborate the sexual foreplay and the more creative and innovative the sexual activities.[21]

While sociologists have found it possible to note differences in sexual behavior among social classes, no patterns are completely restricted to any one class and no stereotypes are possible. Homosexual-

431

ity crosses all class lines, upper- and middle-class men are also capable of sexually exploiting women, many lower-class women enjoy sexual activities, and so forth. In short, distinct practices are discernible, but none are exclusive within any class.

Consumption Patterns and Recreation

Consumption patterns among social classes are becoming more alike because of the rise in the general standard of living. For example, the ownership of automobiles, television sets, home appliances, and so forth is found in every layer of the social hierarchy. Nevertheless, each social class retains distinctive consumption patterns. For example, while almost all classes own cars, each class is attracted to different makes of cars, partly, of course, because of price. However, according to sociologists Handel and Rainwater, lower-class people generally maintain and repair their own cars, while middle- and upper-class people pay others to service their cars. The same may be said about such items as washing machines, dryers, or refrigerators.[22]

Handel and Rainwater also found that manual and blue-collar workers seek recreation in their own homes and in the homes of neighborhood friends and relatives. When they do go out, often in sex-segregated groups, they attend spectator sports, bowl, go to bars, or go to the movies. Nonmanual and professional workers more frequently go out in mixed sex groups, usually couples, and attend the theatre, concerts, art galleries, or museums. If they are interested in spectator sports, they prefer to watch them on television. Frequently it is college sporting events that they prefer.

Even vacation choices differ. The lower the social class, the more likely people are to visit distant relatives, camp, fish, hunt, or travel around in the family car. The higher the social class, the greater the probability that the people will go to hotels or summer resorts, travel in foreign countries, or travel long distances by air.

Sociologist Alfred Clarke, in his study of leisure patterns by social class, discovered that the highest and the lowest strata indulged in the greatest number and most diversified activities. Apparently the middle classes are the least adventurous.[23]

APPLYING SOCIOLOGY

To which social class do you think you belong? Why do you place yourself in this category? Are you aware of any ways in which your values, attitudes, or behaviors differ from those in other social classes? What are they?

Members of the lower social classes are more likely to spend vacations camping or visiting relatives or friends *(top)*. Members of the higher social classes tend to go to hotels or resorts *(bottom)*.

SOCIAL MOBILITY

While it is clear that a number of classes exist in American society, they should not be thought of as totally rigid. Social mobility—the movement of an individual or a group from one social stratum to another—is possible. The late sociologist Pitirim Sorokin was the first to write on social mobility.[24] He pointed out that there is social mobility in all societies. However, mobility is easier in some societies than in others. An *open-class society* is one in which people are ranked only according to their ability and accomplishments. A *closed-class society* is one in which status is ranked on the basis of heredity alone. No society is either completely closed or completely open, but the more open a society is, the more likely social mobility will occur.

Vertical and Horizontal Mobility

Sorokin identified two kinds of social mobility: vertical and horizontal. *Vertical mobility* is the movement of an individual or a group up or down the social-class ladder. For example, if a salesclerk were promoted to sales manager, he or she would have moved up in the class structure and would be displaying vertical mobility. But if this person were then demoted back to salesperson, vertical mobility would once again have occurred. *Horizontal mobility* is movement within the same stratum, without a significant change in income, prestige, or power. A salesclerk who leaves one department store to be a salesclerk in another department store exemplifies horizontal mobility.

Although all societies allow some mobility, everyone within a given society is not equally capable of movement. One reason for this is that not everyone is equally intelligent, talented, or motivated. A more important reason, though, is that not everyone starts life at the same point. Upward social mobility is obviously more likely to occur if one is born into a family with a good income than if one is born into a poor family, because the child of well-paid parents is more likely to be educated, to meet people who can help him or her to move upward, and so forth.

Intergenerational and Intragenerational Mobility

When sociologists study social mobility, they use one of two measures: intergenerational mobility or intragenerational mobility. *Intergenerational mobility* refers to vertical mobility from one generation to another. For example, the highest position ever held by the parent is compared to the highest position ever held by the child. If, let us say, the father had been an electrician and the daughter was an accountant, then upward vertical intergenerational mobility had occurred.

Intragenerational mobility is also called *career mobility*. Researchers trace one person's work career from the first to the last job. If someone begins a career as an errand runner in a company and works his or her way up to salesperson, sales manager, and then vice president, upward intragenerational mobility will have occurred.

APPLYING SOCIOLOGY

Trace your family heritage back a few generations. Compare the highest position held by your grandparent with that held by your parent. How much intergenerational mobility has occurred in your family? How much intragenerational mobility has occurred? What effect does being a member of certain groups, for instance being black or being a woman, have on some people's social mobility?

Female Social Mobility

In the past, studies of social mobility have generally concentrated on men. Men were the important job holders and their wives and growing children merely followed them up or down.

Now, though, more and more women are better educated than they were in the past and they are assuming career positions. So they should be able to achieve greater job mobility and thus greater social mobility on their own. But are they? Several sociologists have conducted occupational studies to discover whether or not this is the case.

Most of the research has been done on women professionals. In one such study, sociologist Cynthia Epstein demonstrated how, in recent years, women have moved into some upper-level occupations, which in the past have been the exclusive province of men. However, she also shows that women have not risen to the top of these professions because of the special limitations placed on them.[25]

One of these limitations is the sex-typing of occupations, for example, medicine, architecture, engineering, and the ministry. When women try to enter these "male" occupations, they are still regarded as "deviant" and hence they face many obstacles. Women are not promoted as quickly as men. The receive lower wages. They are not encouraged to compete for high-ranking positions.

Another impediment is the homogeneity of most professions. Members of any given profession tend to share similar values and life-

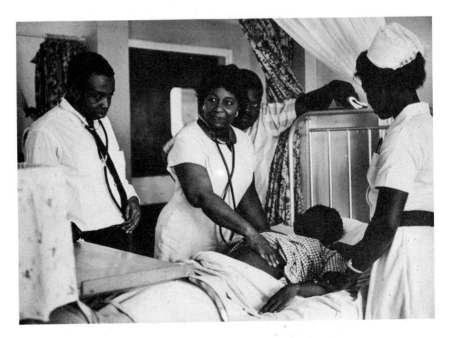

Although increasing numbers of women are moving into upper-level professions that have been almost exclusively male (for example, medicine), they have had difficulty rising to the top of those professions.

styles and interact frequently on an informal level. Because women are "different," they are often excluded from such networks and are thus denied access to informal information that could advance their careers. A part of this informal colleague system is the protégé system, in which establishment professionals initiate and help neophytes. According to Epstein, males do not like to sponsor females because they cannot envision women as their successors. This reluctance helps to exclude the female professional from the "inner circle."

A third problem is that women usually enter the "hidden" parts of each "male" profession. In medicine, for example, they often avoid having a private practice. Instead, they often take full-time positions in public health. In law, they are less likely to be in highly visible positions in corporate or criminal law. Instead they relegate themselves to trust and family law. In universities, they are often research assistants or adjuncts rather than full-time faculty members. In short, women are often less visible in their occupations and this hinders advancement.

In a more general study of female mobility, sociologist Peter DeJong and his associates offer evidence that contradicts Epstein's research. They claim that there is little difference between female and male intergenerational mobility patterns.[26] These investigators believe that female occupational inheritance is similar to that of males, that women are as mobile as men, and that the same barrier (between manual and nonmanual) exists for both sexes. DeJong and his associates argue that other researchers have erroneously stated the barriers to female mobility.

But DeJong stands alone. Other researchers, for example Elizabeth Haven and Judy Corder Tully, criticize DeJong's research and claim that his findings are not valid.[27] At any rate, information on female mobility patterns is limited. Undoubtedly there will be more research in the future. But at this point it must be concluded that since women have less chance for job advancement and thus more income growth, social mobility for men continues to be greater than it is for women.

IS AMERICA REALLY THE LAND OF OPPORTUNITY?

Part of the American ideology states that ours is the land of opportunity. All people can get to the top by pulling up their bootstraps and keeping their noses to the grindstone. Abraham Lincoln, for example, was born in a log cabin and became President of the United States. Poor boys, like John D. Rockefeller and Henry Ford, grew up to become millionaires. But what about the thousands who may have had as much motivation, ability, and talent, only to remain in the bottom echelons of our social hierarchy? The fact is that hard work alone rarely gets any-

436

one to the top of the heap. Most often, children remain in the same social stratum as their parents. Sociologists Elton J. Jackson and Harvey J. Crockett, Jr., point out that of the professional people they studied, 40 percent were the children of professionals, which is almost five times as many as we could expect were our system truly an open one.[28]

The most comprehensive study of social mobility in recent years was conducted by Peter Blau and Otis Dudley Duncan.[29] It would be impossible to mention all the findings from this study, but some of the important ones are listed below:

1) Most social mobility is upward. If a person moves into a different class from that of his or her parents, it is more likely to be a higher class than a lower one.

2) More children of the upper classes remain in their own class than children of lower classes.

3) Rarely does anyone move into the highest class from a class below.

4) Most social movement is short distance. People usually move just one step upward, such as from the lower-middle class to the middle-middle class.

5) Race is the greatest impediment to social mobility, especially in the South.

6) The most difficult line to cross is the one between manual and non-manual work. That is, very few "little" people (to use Kahl's term) move into the "big" people classes.

7) The inheritance of occupational status is not direct. Instead, the parent's occupation influences the child's level of education, which then influences occupation level.

Comparisons with other Western industrialized countries also reveal that our occupational system is not as open as we believe. In fact, we note that there is little difference in intergenerational mobility rates from blue- to white-collar occupations. According to one study, the mobility rate in the United States is 34 percent as compared with 32 percent in Sweden, 31 percent in Great Britain, 25 percent in West Germany, and 29 percent in France.[30] Clearly, there is not much more social mobility here than in similarly industrialized countries.

There is, however, one exception and that is movement from the working to the professional class. According to several sociologists, about 10 percent of the professionals in this country come from working-class origins, compared to 7 percent in Holland, 3 percent in Great Britain, 2 percent in West Germany and France, and less than 1 percent in Italy.[31] But the percentage of working-class Americans who become professionals is still small.

437

In short, our ideology does not square with the facts. People most often do not move out of the stratum of their parents and even when such movement occurs, it is only to the next highest level. America is not the land of opportunity we believe it to be.

SUMMARY

The process by which societies differentiate, evaluate, and rank their members is known as *social stratification*. The type of stratification found in a society depends to a large degree on that society's degree of technology and ideology.

Several social scientists have tried to explain why stratification exists. Karl Marx believed that social inequality existed because those controlling the means of production—the *bourgeoisie*—exploited those working—the *proletariat*. He believed that inequality would be eliminated when the proletariat acquired class consciousness and over-threw the bourgeoisie.

Max Weber also tried to account for social inequality. He believed there were three forms of inequality—inequality based on wealth, inequality based on prestige, and inequality based on power. Weber believed these inequalities would always exist because people are inherently unequal in terms of talent and ability to succeed. Hence, they always would reach different levels of class, status, and power.

Structural-functionalists claim that social inequality is necessary and integrative in society because, by rewarding people differently, society motivates the best qualified members to enter the most valued occupations. Furthermore, all members work together and cooperate to ensure the survival of society. Conflict theorists, on the other hand, claim inequality is neither necessary nor integrative. They state that people attain high social status, not necessarily by possessing talent or ability, but by force, coercion, exploitation, fraud, dominance, or accident of birth. Rather than cooperating, subgroups compete for the scarce goods and services that are available. Gerhard Lenski has demonstrated that since both competition and cooperation exist and are necessary in all societies, the two theories complement each other.

When studying the social class system in the United States, most sociologists rank people according to income, education, and occupation. Although it is relatively easy to rank people based on the first two criteria, the latter presents more of a problem.

Few sociologists agree on the number of classes in modern American society. Many, however, use the five categories suggested by Joseph Kahl: the upper class, the upper-middle class, the lower-middle class, the working class, and the lower class. The members of these classes tend to differ in terms of their *value orientations*. In addition, social classes have different life-styles, speech patterns, food preferences, sexual attitudes and behaviors, consumption patterns, and recreational preferences.

Social mobility occurs in all societies, but the more open the stratification system in a society, the more mobility will be possible. *Vertical mobility* is movement up or down the social ladder; *horizontal mobility* is movement within the same social stratum. *Intergenerational mobility* refers to vertical mobility from one generation to another. *Intragenerational mobility*, or career mobility, refers to a person's work career within his or her own lifetime.

Almost all research on social mobility has concentrated on males. Only recently have career patterns of females been explored. The results of the few available studies are somewhat contradictory, but it seems there are barriers for females that are absent for males. Further research will probably show that male mobility is greater and easier than female mobility.

In answer to the question: Is America the land of opportunity?, we would reply that there is a great deal of social mobility in the United States, but not as much as most people believe. Most social mobility is only one step up the social ladder, and most people remain in the same stratum as that of their parents.

GLOSSARY

agrarian society a society in which members subsist on what they produce from the land, thus requiring a large, cheap labor force.

anarchy a stratification system found in small-scale societies with scarce food supplies in which physical strength alone determines social rank.

bourgeoisie according to Marx, the class that owns the means of production and receives the profits.

caste system a stratification system found in agrarian societies that is based on heredity. All social relationships are severely defined and enforced by law.

class consciousness an identification with others holding the same social-class position.

egalitarian society a stratification system found in small-scale societies with plentiful food supplies in which there is practically no social inequality.

estate system a stratification system in which people are assigned to an "estate" according to birth, land ownership, or military strength. Members of estates are permitted some social mobility through achievement.

horizontal mobility movement within the same stratum without a significant change in income, prestige, or power.

industrial society a society in which machines do most of the work; members are differentiated by social class.

439

intergenerational mobility   vertical mobility from one generation to another.

intragenerational mobility   a person's work career in terms of vertical movement.

proletariat   according to Marx, the class that works for those who own the means of production and receives wages.

slavery   a stratification system in which a person becomes the legal possession of another person.

small-scale society   a society in which there is little technology and in which people survive by hunting and gathering food for daily consumption.

social class   an aggregate of people in similar occupational statuses, with similar degrees of prestige and privilege, and holding similar amounts of power.

social differentiation   the division of labor in which occupational statuses are recognized but not ranked.

social mobility   the movement of an individual or a group from one social stratum to another or within one stratum.

social stratification   the evaluation, ranking, and differential rewarding of positions and roles based on socially accepted criteria.

vertical mobility   movement of an individual or a group up or down the social-class ladder.

REFERENCES

1. M. J. Finley, *Slavery in Classical Antiquity*. Cambridge, England: Heffer, 1960, p. 145.

2. Finley, p. 16.

3. Daniel Bell, *The Coming of Post-Industrial Society*. New York: Basic Books, 1973.

4. Kingsley Davis and Wilbert E. Moore, "Some Principles of Stratification." *American Sociological Review* 10:2 (1945): 242–249.

5. Gerhard Lenski, *Power and Privilege*. New York: McGraw-Hill, 1966.

6. National Opinion Research Center, "Jobs and Occupations: A Population Evaluation." *Opinion News* 9:3–13 (1947).

7. Robert W. Hodge, Paul M. Siegel, and Peter H. Rossi, "Occupational Prestige in the United States: 1925-1963." *American Journal of Sociology* 70 (November 1964): 286–302.

8. James S. Coleman, *Introduction to Mathematical Sociology*. New York: The Free Press, 1964, p. 27.

9. Lloyd Warner and Paul S. Lunt, *The Social Life of a Modern Community*. New Haven, Conn.: Yale University Press, 1941.

10. Joseph A. Kahl, *The American Class Structure*. New York: Holt, Rinehart & Winston, 1957, p. 187.

440

11. Excerpted from Paul D. Zimmerman, "The Upper Crust: Review of Stephen Birmingham's *The Right People." Newsweek*, April 22, 1968.

12. John R. Seeley, R. Alexander Sim, and Elizabeth W. Loosley, *Crestwood Heights*. New York: John Wiley & Sons, 1967, excerpted from pages 123–124.

13. Herbert L. Gans, *The Levittowners*. New York: Vintage Books, 1967, excerpted from pages 201–203.

14. Ely Chinoy, *Automobile Workers and the American Dream*. Boston: Beacon Press, 1955.

15. Gus Tyler, "White Workers: Blue Mood." In Joseph A. Ryan, ed., *White Ethnics*. Englewood Cliffs, N.J.: Prentice-Hall, 1973, p. 131.

16. Judah Matras, *Social Inequality, Stratification, and Mobility*. Englewood Cliffs, N.J.: Prentice-Hall, 1975, p. 163.

17. Joseph A. Kahl, *The American Class Structure*. New York: Holt, Rinehart & Winston, 1967, p. 213.

18. Charles Clifford Crides, "Regional Variations in the Estimation of Social Class from Auditory Stimuli." Unpublished doctoral dissertation, University of Southern California, 1962.

19. Clifton Fadiman, "Is There an Upper-Class American Language?" *Holiday*, October 1956.

20. Thomas E. Lasswell, *Class and Stratum*. Boston: Houghton-Mifflin, 1965.

21. Joann S. DeLora and Carol A. B. Warren, *Understanding Sexual Interaction*. Boston: Houghton-Mifflin, 1977, pp. 115–120.

22. G. Handel and L. Rainwater, "Persistence and Change in Working-Class Life-Style." *Sociology and Social Research* 48 (1964): 281–288.

23. Alfred C. Clarke, "Leisure and Occupational Prestige," *American Sociological Review* 21 (1956): 301–307.

24. Pitirim Sorokin, *Social Mobility*. New York: Harper & Bros., 1927.

25. Cynthia Epstein, "Encountering the Male Establishment: Sex-Status Limits on Women's Careers in the Professions." *American Journal of Sociology* 75:6 (1970): 962–982.

26. Peter Y. DeJong, Milton J. Brawer, and Stanley S. Robin, "Patterns of Female Intergenerational Occupational Mobility." *American Sociological Review* 36:6 (1971): 1033–1042.

27. See, for example, Elizabeth M. Haven and Judy Corder Tully, "Female Intergenerational Occupational Mobility: Comparison of Patterns?" *American Sociological Review* 37:6 (1972): 774–777; see also Andrea Tyree and Judith Treas, "The Occupational and Marital Mobility of Women." *American Sociological Review* 39:3 (1974): 293–302.

28. Elton F. Jackson and Harry J. Crockett, Jr., "Occupational Mobility in the United States: A Point Estimate and a Trend Comparison." *American Sociological Review* 24 (1964): 5–15.

29. Peter M. Blau and Otis Dudley Duncan, *The American Occupational Structure*. New York: John Wiley & Sons, 1967.

441

30. S. M. Lipset and Reinhard Bendix, *Social Mobility in Industrial Society.* Berkeley: University of California Press, 1959.

31. Thomas G. Fox and S. M. Miller, "Economic, Political and Social Determinants of Mobility: An International Cross-Sectional Analysis." *Acta Sociologia* 9:1-2 (1966): 76—93. See Blau and Duncan.

SUGGESTED READINGS

Baltzell, E. Digby. *The Protestant Establishment.* New York: Random House, 1964.

> *A rare view into life among the wealthiest Americans, presented by a member of the upper class.*

Bottomore, T. B. *Classes in Modern Society.* New York: Pantheon, 1966.

> *A brief critical review of the literature on social stratification, with a discussion of socialism and capitalism.*

Duberman, Lucile, *Social Inequality: Class and Caste in America.* Philadelphia: J. B. Lippincott, 1976.

> *A comprehensive overview of the sociological field of social stratification.*

Fitzgerald, F. Scott. *The Great Gatsby.* New York: Charles Scribner's Sons, 1920.

> *A well-known novel describing how the rich are "different" from you and me.*

Harrington, Michael. *The Other America.* New York: Macmillan, 1962.

> *A description of that part of the American population rarely seen—the very poor.*

Lenski, Gerhard. *Power and Privilege: A Theory of Stratification.* New York: McGraw-Hill, 1966.

> *An in-depth analysis of power and privilege in societies at various levels of technological development.*

Lundberg, Ferdinand. *The Rich and the Super Rich.* Secaucus, N.J.: Lyle Stuart, 1968.

> *A look at the very wealthy in America.*

Ryan, William. *Blaming the Victim.* New York: Vintage, 1972.

> *An account of how the lower class is considered by others to be responsible for its own low evaluation in society.*

Sennett, Richard, and Jonathan Cobb. *The Hidden Injuries of Class.* New York: Alfred A. Knopf, 1972.

> *An account of the psychic pain and loss of dignity felt by the working class in status-conscious America.*

14

Work and Leisure

f you think back about your childhood, chances are that most of you will remember being asked, "What are you going to be when you grow up?" And more likely than not, you gave some response to the question. No matter what answer you gave, however, most of you were sure that when you reached adulthood you were going to be *something*. Why? Because, even at an early age, you realized that most human beings spend substantial segments of their lives engaged in the activity of *work*. In fact, work is the central experience of life for most people.

When human beings are not working, they are often involved in some form of *leisure*. Except for such necessary physical activities as eating and sleeping, almost all human activity consists of, and takes place within, the spheres of work and leisure. In this chapter we will analyze several aspects of work and leisure, particularly as they relate to life in modern Western society.

The Meaning of Work

What do we mean when we speak about "work"? Obviously, "work" means different things to different people, and its definition also varies from society to society. Today, for example, in industrialized societies such as ours, work is usually thought of as paid employment. As a result, a large number of "working" people—for example, full-time homemakers and students—who actually do work, often quite hard, are not listed in the "labor force." Thus, when people speak about work (in other than the sense of pure physical or mental "effort"), they usually refer to the realm of employment. A person is thought of as employed when he or she takes part in the society's industrial economy, as either a producer or a distributor of goods or services. To be a worker, then, is to be a person who is engaged in some socially recognized economic activity. Work is not labor so much as it is employment.

Our conception of work corresponds with our reasons for working. A study by Koya Azumi illustrates this point.[1] Azumi reports on a survey that attempted to measure the attitudes of youths in various countries toward work. Their answers varied, depending upon the type of society in which they lived. In heavily industrialized societies only about 11 percent chose the answer "to do his duty as a member of society . . ." while between one-half and three-fourths responded ". . . to earn money." In comparison, more of the respondents in less industrialized countries than in heavily industrialized nations thought people worked as a social duty.

A NECESSARY EVIL

If there is one universal function of work, it is economic. It is the way human beings earn their livelihood. With the creation of money economies, work became the chief way of securing the resources necessary for purchasing the requirements of life. Hence, work has been necessary for economic survival, and today money or something else that can be exchanged (for example, food or trinkets) is the chief reward and gain from working.

Throughout history many societies also have regarded work as a "necessary evil." The ancient Greeks conceived of work as an activity for women and slaves. Work was menial and necessary, but without intrinsic gratification. The Romans felt the same way about work, and the ancient Hebrews believed God forced sinners to work as punishment. These attitudes toward work persisted through the medieval era until the advent of Protestantism in the sixteenth century.

A SIGN OF GRACE

In a classic study Max Weber argued that both the economic foundation of Western society, as well as the *ethic*, or system of beliefs, on which it rests, changed dramatically in Europe with the development of Protestantism.[2] According to Weber, certain specific values inherent in the *Protestant ethic* set the stage for the birth of capitalism. These values essentially transformed the meaning of work from that of a debasing form of drudgery only for slaves, servants, and women into a righteous pursuit that signified one's standing in the eyes of God. Work became the symbol of a relationship with society and God, and justified occupying social space.

Central to Protestant teaching were the ideas that avoiding pleasure, devoting one's life to work, and practicing economic thrift were virtues. Idleness was an evil. This philosophy left people with almost no choice but to reinvest their money in their businesses, hence giving rise to capitalism. The economic success resulting from such a philosophy was "proof" that one was among the "elect" or "chosen" (those who were preordained to enter heaven). Martin Luther, for example, taught that labor was service to God. One's *vocation* was one's calling and the better it was performed, the better one served God. John Calvin expanded on this notion considerably by insisting that success at one's vocation (primarily the accumulation of wealth) was a sign of grace, indicating that one was a member of the elect.

It remains an open question whether the Protestant ethic caused the emergence of capitalism or simply helped to justify the new economic mode. What is quite clear to sociologists, however, is that

445

Max Weber (1864–1920)

Max Weber is considered one of the world's foremost sociologists and is especially well known for his contribution to the sociology of religion. But Weber did not study religion in and of itself; rather he tied religion to economic developments. Consequently, Weber posed the basic question: To what extent have religious conceptions of the world and of life influenced the economic activities of people in different societies at different times in history?

Like Karl Marx, Weber wanted to explain some of the reasons for the emergence of modern capitalism. Unlike Marx, however, he believed that religious values and attitudes played a major role in capitalism's explosive growth. To advance his point, Weber compared the religions of Western and non-Western societies.

In one of his principal works, *The Protestant Ethic and the Spirit of Capitalism,* Weber concluded that a certain Protestant outlook—Calvinism—was especially favorable to the rise or the "spirit" of modern capitalism. Two basic tenets of Calvinism led to this conclusion. First, any self-indulgent expenditures beyond basic necessities were forbidden. According to the Calvinists, extreme self-denial glorified God. The second tenet was a basic anxiety about "pre-destination." Calvinists held that it was decided before birth whether one would go eventually to heaven or hell. Thus, during one's lifetime one could only try to discern one's fate. Worldly success (i.e., making a lot of money through hard work) was a good sign of one's predestined lot.

It is not difficult, then, to see why Weber thought that Calvinism, or the "Protestant ethic," was particularly responsible for the "spirit of capitalism." If one looks anxiously for a sign of salvation by working hard to make profits, and cannot spend such profits on pleasure, what does one do with the extra money? Weber said the capitalist reinvests these profits (capital) into the business, making more profits, which are reinvested, creating even more profits. This combination of elements, Weber argued, created an historically unique situation that gave rise to ever-growing productive facilities and later to the Industrial Revolution. Weber recognized that although people have always sought profits, the religious outlook of Calvinism enabled them, for the first time, to accumulate profits in great amounts due to the high rate of reinvestment. The emergence of modern capitalism was the end result. In comparison, countries that did not have ethics or religious beliefs similar to European Protestantism did not develop the same kind of capitalism that arose in seventeenth-century Europe.

In conclusion, we should note that Weber also argued that such a religious perspective was necessary only in the beginning and early stages of modern capitalism. He felt that once modern capitalism was established, its own internal requirements would ensure its continuation and growth.

work has come to occupy a central place in the lives of almost all people in the industrialized world.

FEELING USEFUL

All societies have rites of passage and ceremonies that indicate one's transformation from child to adult. In the industrialized world, one sign that people are adults is that they are workers; they are engaged in "serious" activity.[3] Working is one of the chief mechanisms whereby people come to be considered worthy members of society. Work, in other words, is more than an economic necessity. It is necessary also for the maintenance and advancement of the individual and society. For the individual, work may give structure to the day and a feeling of personal adequacy. It contributes to a person's self-image, feelings of responsibility and respectability, good mental and physical health, and family relationships. Work also gives a person an identity. By being able to say "I am a lawyer" or "I am a teacher," a person knows who he or she is.

A person's work also helps to determine the income received, and, thus, location in the class structure, style of life, and associates. As a result, we know how to react to a person just by knowing what that person does for a living. For example, chances are that we would act differently toward the president of a corporation than toward a mailroom clerk. In addition, a person's work influences his or her beliefs, values, and patterns of behavior. People in all occupations tend to draw most of their friends and associates from similar occupations or economic realms. Professionals tend to associate almost exclusively with other professionals. Manual laborers are not likely to feel comfortable at a party comprised of physicians. Police officers interact largely with other officers, and secretaries are not likely to live next door to the president of the company.

When people are unemployed for long periods of time, they tend to lose the feelings of usefulness that their jobs had once provided. Even many people who live on inherited wealth or other nonwork income—for example, Nelson Rockefeller—engage in charitable or other activities, in part possibly because such behavior allows them to feel useful and occupied. The unemployed miss the money they earned and the friends they had at work. But even more important, they may come to lose the feeling of self-worth, the sense of being members of the community, deserving of the respect with which their employment provided them. This last aspect, the self-esteem that one gains from working (irrespective of the job), has replaced the Protestant ethic somewhat.

Rather than providing people with a sign of grace, today one's job provides members of industrialized societies with a main source of personal prestige. Not only do people gain a sense of accomplishment, control, and self-confidence from their work, but they also gain an image of self—as respectable, productive members of society. Thus, even though it may be more prestigious to be a doctor, lawyer, or corporation president than it is to be a bricklayer, sanitation worker, or coal miner, each of these occupations provides the worker with a feeling of being a useful and contributing member of society.

It is these economic, social, and psychological factors that give work its prime sociological significance. And because of this significance, much sociological inquiry centers on the world of work. Topics studied include the composition and characteristics of the labor force and the problems and prospects of employment and unemployment both now and in the years to come.

The Labor Force

Each month the federal government gathers statistics to determine the composition, trends, and shifts in the size and make-up of the labor force. As defined by the federal government, the *labor force* consists of all persons, aged sixteen and over, not in institutions (for example, schools, prisons, or hospitals), who worked for pay at least one hour in one week during the time the survey was taken (the employed).[4] The labor force also includes those who did not work during the survey period and did not have a job, but were actively seeking work (the unemployed).[5] Those persons who are employed but who may not have earned an income in the survey period and those persons not seeking work are excluded from the total. As a result, this measure underestimates the actual number of persons employed or unemployed. Nevertheless, the statistics that the government gathers each month provide about the only readily available picture of the labor force.

AGE AND SEX COMPOSITION

The composition of the civilian labor force in the future will probably be affected by the raising of the retirement age and the increasing number of women workers.

In 1977, the total labor force passed the 100 million mark for the first time in history; the average for that year was 99.5 million persons. The civilian labor force consisted of about 97.4 million persons, with the remainder working for the government. Figure 14–1 shows the age and sex composition of the civilian labor force at five-year intervals starting from 1970 and projected to 1990. According to this chart, there will be no change in the age of the vast majority of workers of both sexes between these years. However, the increase in the retirement age

448

FIGURE 14–1
Distribution of Civilian
Labor Force
by Age and Sex

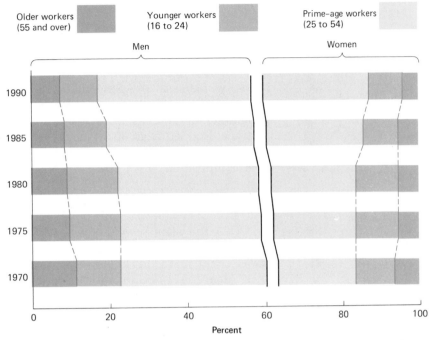

Source: Howard N. Fullerton, Jr. and Paul O. Flain, "New Labor Force Projection to 1990," *Monthly Labor Review*
(U.S. Department of Labor, Bureau of Labor Statistics, December 1976), p. 4.

to seventy will probably change this picture somewhat. In addition, as the figure shows, the "prime-age" group will grow in relative size as the proportion of younger and older workers shrinks. This shrinkage is probably the result of several factors, including an increase in the amount of time young people are spending in school, improved disability and retirement plans, and the increase in the number of women workers.

Another factor is the decline in the birth rate (see Chapter 16) that occurred in the 1960s and is still occurring. By 1990, the ages of people born in the 1960s will be 21–30. More than half of them will be in the "prime-age" group—25–54. Fewer than half will be in the "young" group—16–24. Hence, by 1990 there will be fewer younger workers in the labor force than there are today.

The current ranks of the prime-age workers have been swollen by the post-World War II "baby boom." The large number of births that occurred in the late 1940s and continued throughout the 1950s resulted in a flooded labor market in the 1970s, when most of the people born during that time span entered the labor market. After the 1990s, as they grow older, it is likely that the relative proportion of older workers will increase.

449

The composition of the labor force by sex has undergone significant changes over the past twenty years. The increase of women in the labor force primarily accounts for this transformation. Since 1960, about 16.7 million women have joined the labor force, making their total about 40 million. Whereas in 1960, the labor force participation rate for women was 37.7 percent, in 1977 it was 48.4 percent.

While the participation rate for women has increased, the participation rate for men has declined over the same period. Male participation has dropped from 83.3 percent in 1960 to 77.7 percent in 1977. Thus one of the major trends affecting the labor force has been the shift in its composition by sex.

OCCUPATIONAL GROUPINGS

Over the years, several other significant trends have also operated to change the composition of the labor force. Perhaps the most profound change affecting the occupational structure of our society has been America's transformation from an agricultural to an industrial economy. Whereas in some Third-World countries, as much as 80 percent of the labor force is engaged in agriculture, it takes fewer than 4 percent of the total American work force to grow enough food for the rest, as well as a surplus.

It was only a few generations ago that most workers had to be engaged in the production of food. With the advances in farm technology that occurred in the nineteenth and twentieth centuries, however, it was no longer necessary for the majority of people in industrialized societies to farm. Instead, fewer farmers could feed increasing numbers of people, freeing a larger segment of the labor force to work in other occupations. This, in turn, spurred the growth of cities and further technological advances so that by the middle of the 1950s, most Americans were urban dwellers, and a proportionate decrease in the absolute as well as the relative number of farmers took place. In a fairly short time, America changed from a nation of farmers to a nation of factory and office workers.

At the present time, white-collar workers—persons engaged in professional, managerial, clerical, and sales occupations—comprise the single largest category of workers in the nation. This shift in the labor force occurred over twenty-five years ago. Although the proportion of blue-collar workers has remained relatively stable over the last twenty-five years, the composition of these workers has changed considerably. The proportion of unskilled laborers has decreased, while skilled and semi-skilled workers have become more numerous. Finally, the segment of the labor force classified as service personnel—for example, guards, barbers, and restaurant workers—has grown to about

450

White-collar workers—people in professional, managerial, clerical, and sales occupations—comprise the largest category of workers in the United States.

10 percent of all the employed from the 4 percent it comprised at the turn of the century.

A NATION OF EMPLOYEES

Another major shift in the American occupational structure has been the dramatic decline in the number of self-employed persons, such as shop owners, independent farmers, independent professionals ("solo" lawyers, for example), and free-lance workers. Fewer than 9 percent of the total labor force can be classified as "self-employed" (as contrasted with 90 percent at the turn of the century), which is in contradiction to the ideal of the self-reliant, independent homesteader that characterizes the American value system.

Each year the number of independent businesses decreases and so does the number of people who start their own businesses. So now, like most industrialized countries, the United States has become a nation of employees who work for large, bureaucratic organizations. Even those professionals, like doctors and lawyers who zealously guard their independent standing, are finding it increasingly difficult to survive economically outside of some organization. Hence, professionals are increasingly becoming "employees" of large universities, hospitals or clinics, or law firms. A few "Ma and Pa" stores can still be found, but they and the way of life they symbolize are passing from the scene.

Many factors have contributed to this change. Perhaps the greater security offered by employment in a large bureaucratic organization dissuades people from venturing the risks entailed by self-

451

APPLYING SOCIOLOGY

If you were a guidance counselor and a student asked for advice about opening a small business, what kind of advice would you offer? Would you encourage the student to pursue this idea or would you suggest that he or she look for a job in a large corporation? What are the advantages and disadvantages of each type of employment?

employment. Also, small, independent businesses simply find it almost impossible to compete with the large conglomerates because they cannot provide the variety or the competitive prices that larger organizations can. As a result, they are either forced out of business or purchased by some larger organization. Moreover, to satisfy the growing needs and wants of an expanding population, it is often necessary for the production and distribution sectors to organize on a large scale.

SPECIALIZATION

Along with changes in the composition and organization of the work force, an ever-increasing division of labor (a phenomenon studied by Émile Durkheim in the late 1800s) into occupational specialties has occurred (see Chapters 3 and 9). Over 20,000 different job titles are listed in the *Directory of Occupational Titles* published by the federal government. People are no longer engineers. Now they are aeronautical, hydraulic, civil, or chemical engineers. Similarly, in nearly every other occupation or field of employment, more and more specialized skill is demanded of the worker. Even the authors of this book specialize in different areas of sociology so that neither is equally familiar with the body of knowledge possessed by the other. This specialization has occurred in spite of the fact that both have degrees in sociology, went to school together, and work in the same sociology department.

Specialization should not, however, be confused with *fragmentation* of work. A neurosurgeon may be a highly specialized worker, but the work he or she engages in is not fragmented in the same sense as that of a worker on an automobile assembly line, whose sole activity consists of tightening three bolts. While specialization may be a product of a highly sophisticated technology that requires high levels of skill and training, work fragmentation is a production technique geared to efficiency and mass production. Work fragmentation, in other words, is simply a way of breaking down the various operations and movements into component parts so that one person performs only one, or a small number, of these operations. A specialized person, on the other hand, may engage in a variety of unique, but often interrelated tasks, each of which requires skill and training.

Fragmentation occurs when each worker performs only one or two operations needed to manufacture a product—such as counting and inspecting Monopoly money.

452

Yet even in the realm of specialties demanding high levels of skill, it appears that some fragmentation is developing. For example, many dentists who used to perform all manners of oral medication now hire aides to do many of these tasks, such as cleaning teeth, making dentures, or taking x-rays. As a result of such professional fragmentation, the practitioner may lose concern with the total product.

WAGES AND HOURS

Although by no means the only one, a major motivation for working as far as many people are concerned is money—the wages or salary one receives for his or her labor. Table 14–1 shows what has happened to the economic reward Americans earned from working, and the amount of time it has taken to earn it, from 1959 to 1976.

The table shows that, on the average in 1976, nongovernment employees (total private sector) worked 36.2 hours per week, and earned $176.29 for their week's work. This represents an increase in average weekly salary of $97.51 over 1959—a jump of more than 100 percent. But with the rate of inflation that has existed since that time, the average worker certainly has not experienced such a large gain in expendable income, although our standard of living is constantly rising.

For the most part, these changes pertain to all occupational groups, although as the table indicates the changes have not occurred equally across categories. For example, although persons in the wholesale and retail trades earned more per week in 1964 than service workers, by 1976 service workers outearned them by a substantial amount.

So far we have viewed the American labor force and the working scene and how they have changed over the years. Now let's turn our attention to some of the ways working affects people, some of the things people can expect in the world of work, and what may lie ahead for those of us who are or will be in the labor force (or excluded from it) in the years to come.

Work: Problems and Prospects

As we have noted, most people expect to spend some portion of their lives, usually the bulk of their adult existence, working. Most also hope to achieve a sense of fulfillment and accomplishment from their work. Or they at least hope to receive the economic rewards necessary for a comfortable life and a secure old age. And when the time comes, most people anticipate retiring from work and enjoying some period of well-earned rest and relaxation. In short, since most human beings are

453

TABLE 14–1
Hours and Earnings by Industry Division, 1959–76

Year	Average weekly earnings	Average weekly hours	Average weekly earnings	Average weekly hours	Average weekly earnings	Average weekly hours	Average weekly earnings	Average weekly hours
	Total private		Mining		Contract construction		Manufacturing	
1959	78.78	39.0	103.68	40.5	108.41	37.0	88.26	40.3
1960	80.67	38.6	105.44	40.4	113.04	36.7	89.72	39.7
1961	82.60	38.6	106.92	40.5	118.08	36.9	92.34	39.8
1962	85.91	38.7	110.43	40.9	122.47	37.0	96.56	40.4
1963	88.46	38.8	114.40	41.6	127.19	37.3	99.63	40.5
1964	91.33	38.7	117.74	41.9	132.06	37.2	102.97	40.7
1965	95.06	38.8	123.52	42.3	138.38	37.4	107.53	41.2
1966	98.82	38.6	130.24	42.7	146.26	37.6	112.34	41.3
1967	101.84	38.0	135.89	42.6	154.95	37.7	114.90	40.6
1968	107.73	37.8	142.71	42.6	164.49	37.3	122.51	40.7
1969	114.61	37.7	155.23	43.0	181.54	37.9	129.51	40.6
1970	119.46	37.1	164.40	42.7	195.45	37.3	133.73	39.8
1971	127.28	37.0	172.14	42.4	211.67	37.2	142.44	39.9
1972	136.16	37.1	187.43	42.5	222.51	36.9	154.69	40.6
1973	145.43	37.1	201.03	42.5	235.69	37.0	166.06	40.7
1974	154.45	36.6	220.90	42.4	249.08	36.9	176.40	40.0
1975	163.89	36.1	249.57	42.3	265.35	36.6	189.51	39.4
1976	176.29	36.2	274.78	42.8	284.93	37.1	207.60	40.0

Year	Average weekly earnings	Average weekly hours	Average weekly earnings	Average weekly hours	Average weekly earnings	Average weekly hours	Average weekly earnings	Average weekly hours
	Transportation and public utilities		Wholesale and retail trade		Finance, insurance, and real estate		Services	
1959	....	....	$ 64.41	38.8	$ 72.74	37.3	....	....
1960	....	....	66.01	38.6	75.14	37.2	....	....
1961	....	....	67.41	38.3	77.12	36.9	....	....
1962	....	....	69.91	38.2	80.94	37.3	....	....
1963	....	....	72.01	38.1	84.38	37.5	....	....
1964	$118.37	41.1	74.28	37.9	85.79	37.3	$ 69.84	36.0
1965	125.14	41.3	76.53	37.7	88.91	37.2	73.60	35.9
1966	128.13	41.2	79.02	37.1	92.13	37.3	77.04	35.5
1967	131.22	40.5	81.76	36.5	95.46	37.0	80.38	35.1
1968	138.85	40.6	86.40	36.0	101.75	37.0	83.97	34.7
1969	148.15	40.7	90.78	35.6	108.70	37.1	90.57	34.7
1970	155.93	40.5	95.66	35.3	113.34	36.8	96.66	34.4
1971	169.24	40.2	100.39	35.1	120.66	36.9	103.28	34.2
1972	187.92	40.5	105.65	35.1	126.88	37.1	110.14	34.1
1973	204.62	40.6	111.04	34.7	132.10	36.9	117.64	34.0
1974	218.29	40.2	118.33	34.1	140.19	36.7	127.46	33.9
1975	234.43	39.6	126.75	33.8	150.75	36.5	137.23	33.8
1976	257.75	39.9	133.39	33.6	159.58	36.6	146.06	33.5

Source: *Monthly Labor Review* (U.S. Department of Labor, Bureau of Labor Statistics, April, 1977), p. 101.

obligated to work, they would like it to be as enjoyable and rewarding as possible. The real world, however, has a way of frustrating even the most reasonable of desires. As sociologists have long recognized, the world of work is filled with difficulties. Three major ones are discussed in this section—alienation, unemployment, and retirement.

ALIENATION

According to Karl Marx, constructive labor is the distinctive feature of human beings. People realize themselves as human beings through their work.[6] Yet often work is not constructive and people do not achieve this sense of self-recognition. Instead they may feel separated from their work, themselves, the economic system, and society in general. Marx believed that the basis for this separation stems from the nature of the class system.

Marx claimed that human society has always been divided into two major, and opposing, classes. These consist of the small, powerful, upper class that controls the means of production and the larger, helpless, lower class that works for and is exploited by the owners of the means of production.

Marx felt that the exploitation of the workers by owners, especially under the factory system, was extreme and would dramatically affect future economic development. In the factory system not only did workers not own the means of production, but their jobs became increasingly fragmented and removed from the end product. Marx thought that these developments led to a situation in which work becomes meaningless for the worker, and the worker becomes increas-

When work is routine, fragmented, and removed from the end product—such as sewing buttonholes all day rather than creating an entire garment—workers can become alienated.

FOCUS ON: WORKING

How do most people feel about their jobs, about the time that they spend working? Do they find their jobs boring, humiliating, and impersonal? Or, do they find their work exciting, exhilarating, and all-encompassing? Do they think that what they create will be beneficial to the rest of the society? Or do they believe they are performing some needless task? Radio-broadcaster Studs Terkel sought the answers to these questions in his book *Working,* a series of first-hand accounts of the world of work.

In this book Terkel recounts over one hundred taped conversations on how individuals feel about their jobs. He has found enthusiasm for certain types of jobs, and contentment with the rewards whether they be monetary or self-satisfying. For example, a heavy equipment operator from a Chicago suburb speaks of pride in his work. "You drive down the road and you say, 'I worked on this road.' . . . Maybe it don't mean anything to anybody else, but there's a certain pride knowing you did your bit."

On the other hand, Terkel found many people who were disappointed, unhappy, and careless in their work. For example, a young assembly worker at an automobile plant admits that shoddy work is a fairly frequent occurrence. Anything, even a short conversation with a fellow worker, might result in something being omitted or carelessly put together.

Another interesting point that Terkel makes in his book is that people often approach the same job from different perspectives. What may be humiliating to one person is not considered so by someone else. One waitress in a fashionable restaurant did not think of her work as humiliating. "When I put the plate down, you don't hear a sound. When I pick up a glass, I want it to be just right. When someone says, 'How come you're just a waitress?' I say 'Don't you think you deserve being served by me?' " Another waitress found the job very demeaning. "One guy said, 'You don't have to smile; I'm gonna give you a tip anyway.' I said, 'Keep it, I wasn't smiling for a tip.' Tipping should be done away with. It's like throwing a dog a bone. It makes you feel small." A third waitress found her job gave her an opportunity to be graceful. "I feel like Carmen. It's like a gypsy holding out a tambourine, and they throw the coin."

With people displaying such varying opinions about their jobs, what do you think can be done to achieve a greater overall satisfaction in the world of work? Do you think some jobs automatically will produce dissatisfaction and alienation no matter what attempts to the contrary are made? What effect do you believe our rapidly changing society will have on people's job outlooks?

Source: Studs Terkel, *Working,* New York: Random House, 1974.

ingly powerless to control the course of his or her own activity. In this sense, work becomes simply labor, not the means of self-realization. As Marx stated it, work ". . . is therefore not the satisfaction of a need; it is merely a *means* to satisfy needs external to us."[7]

Marx used the term *alienation* to describe this situation. Alienation is a broad concept generally denoting the idea that in the world of work, as in other spheres of life, workers feel like "aliens" in their own land. They have a feeling of estrangement and hostility toward others and their society in general. It was Marx's prediction that alienation would become so widespread and pervasive that workers would finally develop a true class consciousness and rise up in unified opposition to the owners of the means of production (see Chapter 13). This rebellion, however, would be successful only if it were a worldwide revolution designed to destroy the capitalistic economic system. Such a revolution would restore what Marx considered the "natural" relationships of work and worker wherein the worker could identify with the product of his or her labor. In this way workers would regain pride in themselves and their accomplishments.

Whether or not Marx was correct about worker alienation is highly debatable. But it is well documented that for many people, work produces neither fulfillment nor satisfaction. Indeed, it is often a major source of dissatisfaction and unhappiness.

Measuring Job Dissatisfaction

In studies in which people were asked if they were satisfied with their jobs, between 80 and 90 percent typically answered yes.[8] And, when asked if they would continue working even if they were to inherit enough money to live comfortably, the vast majority of respondents still said they would continue to work. These findings would seem to indicate that people are not only content with working, but they are also reasonably happy with their jobs.

Other findings, however, seem to indicate that the situation is not quite so rosy. Most people who would continue to work even though they did not have to responded that they would do so simply because they wanted to keep busy. Moreover, when asked if they would choose the same job again if given a choice, few said they would. Of course, the responses vary considerably by category of job. Blue-collar workers tend to be the most dissatisfied. Only 24 percent said they would choose the same job. But even among white-collar workers, only 43 percent indicated that they would stay in the same line of work. Only higher-status professional workers seem to show a great degree of job satisfaction. For example, 93 percent of urban university professors and 83 percent of lawyers said that they would choose the same profession if they had to do it over again.

It is clear that the more prestigious, the more economically, socially, and psychologically rewarding, and the more autonomous jobs are the most satisfying, while the reverse is the case for jobs that elicit low prestige and few rewards. But sociologists are still not sure what factors lead to job satisfaction or what can be done to increase it.

Causes of Job Dissatisfaction

According to sociologist Gresham Sykes,[9] work contains four major components: 1) the decision of what to do, 2) the procedures for achieving the goal, 3) the means of implementing these procedures, and 4) the reaction to the procedures and/or the results of the activity.

457

Sykes suggests that "only when all four of these elements are present *in one job* is the worker working in a fully human sense, and anything less is debasing."[10]

The free-lance artist, perhaps, comes closest to this ideal. Aside from the pure economic requirement of producing what sells, the artist can largely determine what he or she will paint, what materials to use (oils or water colors, for example), and what techniques to use. And, even in the face of critics, the artist can evaluate the product in any way he or she desires. The automobile assemblyline worker, on the other hand, possibly comes closest to the opposite situation. Workers in assembly plants have little decision-making power as to what tasks to perform, how to accomplish them, what techniques to employ, and how good or bad the end product of their labor is.

It may very well be that worker dissatisfaction and alienation have been the direct result of the separation of these four components of modern industry, particularly among blue-collar workers. Those jobs that have a greater degree of freedom in terms of deciding what to do, how and when to do it, and what the quality of the finished product will be are considered by people to be relatively satisfying. However, as the work of most people becomes increasingly fragmented, these components are becoming increasingly separated. As Sykes states:

> This dehumanization of work has come to be taken for granted by many people, as far as blue-collar jobs are concerned. Perhaps the repetitive mindlessness is not usually as extreme [as it is in factory work]; perhaps, in many cases, there is more opportunity to horse around, to set your own pace, to feel that you as a person are making something rather than being transformed into a robot. But in general we have come to believe, like good technicians, that industrial production is most efficiently organized by separating the functions of choosing, designing, doing, and reacting; and we have allowed ourselves to move in the direction of fragmentation in the name of efficiency.[11]

458

APPLYING SOCIOLOGY

Many companies are hiring specialists to help eliminate worker alienation. If you were hired for such a position, how would you approach this problem? Do you believe that alienation really can be eliminated or do you think that workers will always find dissatisfaction with their jobs?

Alleviating Alienation

If alienation from work exists in many occupations, then it follows that many companies are affected by such consequences as high rates of absenteeism, high rates of turnover, and low rates of productivity. In an effort to combat these ills, many have taken steps to alleviate alienation. This often involves some drastic and creative alterations in the present structure of work and worker relationships. General Foods, for instance, built a new plant where self-managing work teams had full collective responsibility for significant parts of the production process.[12] All activities relating to that process were also considered a part of the work team's responsibility. Efforts were made to eliminate dull, routine jobs and to make the work challenging. Supervisors were eliminated, decisions were arrived at collectively, and status symbols were eliminated. This experiment resulted in lower rates of absenteeism, increased productivity, better quality control, and lower operating costs.

Obviously any one technique will not work in all industries, and many other techniques are being tried or have already become part of the operations of many businesses. These approaches include profitsharing programs, programs in which workers sign their own work, participatory management programs, and the four-day work week. Many of those programs that appear to have met with success either offer the worker a stake in the product and its outcome or are oriented to stimulating worker pride in work. This latter idea, based on the principle that to be proud of your work is to be proud of yourself, is reminiscent of Marx's early realization that human beings can find fulfillment in their jobs.

UNEMPLOYMENT

While worker alienation may have a long-term and probably corroding impact on workers and industry alike, perhaps the most serious problem faced by modern industry and government—and those individuals who suffer from it—is that of unemployment. During the 1970s more than 6 million people, approximately 7 percent of the labor force, were unemployed at any one time. This figure does not include those who were underemployed (working part-time or at marginal jobs that

TABLE 14-2
Major Unemployment Indicators for 1974, 1975, 1976, and 1977 (seasonally adjusted unemployment rates)

Year	Total	Male, 20 years and over	Female, 20 years and over	Both sexes, 16 to 19 years	White	Black and other races
1974	5.6	3.8	5.5	16.0	5.0	9.9
1975	8.2	6.7	8.0	·19.9	7.8	13.9
1976	7.7	5.9	7.4	19.0	7.0	13.1
1977	7.0	5.2	7.0	17.7	6.2	13.1

Source: Adapted from U.S. Bureau of Labor Statistics, *Handbook of Labor Statistics 1975- Reference Edition, Employment and Earnings,* Vol. 25, No. 4, April 1978, and unpublished Current Population Survey data.

paid subsistence wages), or those who were so poorly paid that they barely subsisted at the poverty level. When these individuals are added to the official unemployment rolls, we are including close to 30 million people.

Unemployment by no means affects everyone equally. If we look at Table 14-2 we will note that unemployment varies greatly by age, sex, and race. According to this table, those sixteen to nineteen years old suffer the highest rate of unemployment. Females also are affected more than males. Similarly, black people and other racial minorities experience unemployment rates approximately twice as high as those for whites of either sex. These rates remain almost constant, regardless of the overall rate of unemployment. There are also regional, seasonal, and occupational variations in the rate of unemployment, so that while some groups or segments of the population prosper, others experience frustration and economic impoverishment.[13]

In part, these inequities in employment are industry-related. For example, white-collar workers usually have lower rates of unemployment than blue-collar workers. In part also, minority and younger workers are more likely to be unemployed because they lack the required skills or are the victims of the "last hired, first fired" syndrome stemming from the seniority system, which keeps older, long-time employees in their jobs.

Whatever the causes for unemployment or its distribution over the labor force, anyone who experiences unemployment first suffers some loss of income. Perhaps even more important, though, is the loss of the psychological support that being employed carries. As mentioned earlier, one's work largely defines one's place and worth in the larger society. In fact, the predominant ethic of Western society defines unemployment (especially for males) as an individual's *moral* failure, even though it may not be the person's fault at all. As a result, unemployment can have serious social, psychological, and economic consequences for both the worker and his or her family.

460

On the average, most unemployed persons today remain without work for approximately fourteen weeks. But even that relatively short period can lead to health problems, family breakups, and depression. A variety of studies has demonstrated that unemployment upsets social and familial relationships and seriously undermines the person's and family's economic security. People differ considerably in their reactions to unemployment and their ability to bounce back when it occurs, but as one study shows, long-term unemployment is a disaster for most people.

In their discussion of the problem of unemployment, sociologists Robert Weiss, Edwin Harwood, and David Riesman note that:

> Despite severance pay (now written into many union contracts) and Unemployment Insurance benefits (first introduced in the late 1930's), a single year of unemployment brought men to financial desperation. Their severance pay was spent early, for the most part on debts already incurred; Unemployment Insurance brought in less than they needed and ended abruptly after twenty-six weeks. The men felt stigmatized by their lack of work and, out of embarrassment as well as lack of money, withdrew from friends and social groups, including their church and union. Since they had already lost the community of men with whom they worked, their lives became increasingly empty. As time went on and their helplessness turned to hostility, they directed their anger toward the system, the company, their families, and themselves.[14]

"I'm sorry, Gilhorn, but J.W. himself has decided you are no longer bright-eyed and bushy-tailed."

Drawing by Geo. Price; © 1978 The New Yorker Magazine, Inc.

Other research shows that besides disrupting people's relationships and altering their self-images and attitudes toward others, unemployment has detrimental effects on health and on one's commitment to society. Thus, although many people may not find great pleasure in their work and instead dream of relaxing in the sun, being employed remains of primary importance to many adult Americans. One would think, therefore, that major efforts would be made by the government to arrive at "full employment." Why this policy has not been pursued with great vigor remains to be explained. Perhaps maintaining some segment of the population in a condition of unemployment serves certain functions for other segments of American society. Economists generally believe, in fact, that full employment would mean a higher level of inflation. Or it may be that some level of unemployment is the price Americans have to pay for a free economic system. If the government regulates unemployment, many might accuse the government of becoming too heavily involved in the operation of the economy. Whatever the reason, it is clear that the problem of unemployment is a task modern society has yet to solve.

RETIREMENT

Being unemployed temporarily is one situation many people face at some point in their lives. Permanent unemployment, in the sense of retirement from work, however, is a relatively new phenomenon. It is one that promises to have dramatic social, economic, and political implications in the future as the number of retired people increases continually between now and the turn of the century. In 1900, approximately two out of every three men aged sixty-five or over in the United States were part of the labor force. Sixty years later, this proportion had dropped to one out of three, and by the mid-1970s it was down to one in four. By that time there were over 20 million men and women aged sixty-five and over in the United States,[15] the vast majority of whom were no longer working because they were unable or prohibited to work or did not desire to continue doing so. For some individuals, retirement offers an opportunity to do many things for which there had been little time while they were employed. For example, for the healthy and financially comfortable retiree, there is now time to enjoy club membership, sports, hobbies, friends, and family to a greater degree than previously.

Unfortunately, however, some negative consequences are also likely to ensue from retirement. First, retirees often experience almost the same loss of status that other unemployed people experience. Second, many retired people frequently spend their time doing little or engaging in activities designed to conceal the fact from themselves and

462

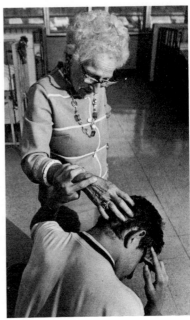

For some people, retirement offers the chance to enjoy their families and to help others.

others that they have little to do.[16] They may become less socially active and their participation in various associations—churches, clubs, and unions—may decline.

One reason for this situation is that advanced age almost always brings disabling physical ailments that impede activity. Since most people can expect to live for ten or more years beyond retirement, it is likely that they will, at some time, suffer one or more of these ailments.

Another equally significant factor contributing to the plight of the aged is that almost 50 percent of the persons aged sixty-five or older in the United States are the victims of severe economic need. As Gresham Sykes points out:

> When most people arrive at the end of their careers, they have acquired insufficient resources to provide an adequate income, let alone meet a serious emergency. The bulk of the population must depend primarily on Social Security benefits, which are insufficient for a decent life. Some 50 percent of the persons aged sixty-five and older receive less than $1,500 [in 1971 dollars] in total cash income.[17]

According to the *Social Security Bulletin*, the average monthly benefits awarded to retired workers at the close of 1976 amounted to $232.75, hardly enough to pay the rent on a moderately priced, urban apartment. Embarrassed by their poverty, unable to share in the affluent society, socially disenfranchised, and often painfully disabled, many

463

Americans find that the "golden years" of retirement bring little more than heartache and disillusionment.

This reality, however, is not experienced equally by all older persons. Blue-collar workers, for example, are more likely to experience greater difficulty during retirement than white-collar workers. The reasons for this are only partially economic. White-collar workers are less likely to suffer the chronic physical ailments of persons who have spent a lifetime doing physical labor. They are also more likely to be able to continue work-related activities after retirement. For instance, some "retired" executives serve on the boards of their companies or act as consultants, often unpaid, so that others can benefit from their experience.

Yet, as we mentioned, for many retirement is not very fulfilling, and in recent years the public and the government have become increasingly aware of the plight of the elderly. As a result, a variety of programs have been proposed not only to aid the elderly economically, but also to provide them with comfortable surroundings and meaningful activities. For example, some hospitals have instituted a practice of having elderly people as "adopted grandparents" visit children who are patients. This, apparently, not only gives reassurance and comfort to the children but has had beneficial implications for the elderly as well. It provides them with a sense of purpose and companionship they would otherwise lack.

As the segment of the population classified as "old" increases steadily during the coming decades, it is likely that these efforts will intensify. Thus, by the time most of us reach retirement, we may be able to partake of the fruits of our life-long labors more fully.

In conclusion, for a variety of reasons, working is a central aspect in the lives of many people despite the problems that may result from it. And more likely than not, working will remain important to many people in the foreseeable future. It is probable, however, that the meaning of work will become redefined as our society changes. One possibility is that the central aspect of life for future generations may shift from a world of work to a world of leisure.

Leisure as Fun and Fulfillment

Just as the ancient Greeks assigned work to women and underlings, they assigned leisure to men, defining it as the proper activity for a man to pursue. That concept of leisure derived from the Greek *scholē* meaning school. It would seem, then, that our modern definition differs substantially from that of the ancient Greeks, since probably few students today think of school as leisure. But do the two ideas really differ that much?

According to the Greeks, school was pleasurable and leisure was a process of contemplation—a time for the cultivation of the mind and the self. Clearly, we also look at leisure as a time for self-expression and self-realization. In fact, although implicit in our modern definition is the notion of choice, it is often considered inappropriate for people to simply waste their leisure time by doing "nothing." Instead, the activities pursued during leisure must be ends in themselves, intrinsically rewarding.

In modern society leisure time is "free time." It should be free of hope, fear, urgent interest, strong passion, and social and economic pressures. Above all, leisure time is spent as a person chooses, not as others might think would be best for his or her well-being.

In our contemporary society, not only has the amount of leisure time available to people increased in recent decades because of a shortened work week, early retirement, and more frequent holidays, but people have more widespread opportunities to spend their money on leisure pursuits than ever before. And although it is doubtful if modern society would ever completely abandon the work ethic or the central role of work in everyday life, it is quite conceivable that the trend toward a "leisure society" will continue. At the very least, "leisure-time" activities probably will have a greater significance for many more people in the future than was true a few generations ago. This is especially likely as the industrial capacity of the world requires fewer and fewer active participants in the labor force, and as facilities and programs designed for the expenditure of leisure time expand.

As a result, the question of "How will I spend my leisure?" may become almost as important as "What am I going to be when I grow up?" This may be particularly true because so many people are failing to find fulfillment and a sense of self-realization in their work. In their leisure time they may come to engage in activities that seem to express their "true self," or, at least, the self they would like to think, and have others believe, they are.[18] Indeed, for the most alienated workers, non-work activities, such as participating on a bowling team or watching television, are considered equally as significant, and often more meaningful, than their work.

SPENDING LEISURE TIME

There is an infinite variety of ways in which people can spend leisure time. In part, what people do with their leisure depends on social class and economic factors. But more important, leisure energies are related to the world of work. Research shows that rather than choosing

FOCUS ON: LEISURE

What types of leisure activities do Americans pursue? A special report in a recent issue of *U.S. News and World Report* deals with this question.

According to this study, almost two out of every five Americans take part in some sort of craft—wood carving, ceramics, quilting, candle-making, weaving—and about 50 percent of American households include an amateur gardener. Another 16 million Americans are stamp collectors, 3 million are photographers, and 1 million collect coins. In 1965, Americans spent $600 million annually on hobbies. That figure is expected to jump to $2 billion by 1980.

Cultural pursuits are also very popular among Americans. Almost 78 million are now involved in some leisure activity of a cultural nature, such as painting, playing music, or handicrafts. According to a Harris Survey for the National Committee for Cultural Resources, 39 percent of this group participate in handicrafts, 22 percent engage in painting and drawing, 18 percent play musical instruments, and 11 percent sing in choirs.

A growing number of Americans are going back to school. Some want to further their educations, but others are interested in changing careers, learning a skill, partaking in arts and crafts, or simply occupying their leisure hours with something they consider beneficial. Courses aimed at satisfying the educational appetites of America's adult population have been established by colleges, universities, churches, libraries, retirement homes, hospitals, and other public facilities. In addition, lifelong learning centers are being organized in many parts of the country. Some, such as the Institute for Retired Professionals at the New School for Social Research, have no paid teaching staff—students learn from each other. Another innova-

tion in education has been the Elder Hostel, which organizes a series of week-long summer sessions in sixty-one colleges throughout twelve states for a small tuition and housing fee.

Spectator sports also seem to be increasing in popularity. Horseracing is the most popular with an attendance of over 50 million in 1976, followed by auto racing, major league baseball, college football, harness racing, and college basketball. Many more people, however, participate in sports than watch them. Over 100 million claim to swim, 75 million bicycle, 63 million fish, 58 million camp, and 44 million bowl.

Which leisure activities do you pursue? Do you think you will continue to pursue your leisure activities after you've finished your education? Or, do you think you might switch to other leisure pursuits later in life? Do you think that certain pursuits, such as swimming, camping, bicycling, or tennis, might be more suited to younger people? What activities might be followed by older people, by poorer people, by the middle classes, by the upper classes?

Source: "How Americans Pursue Happiness," *U.S. News & World Report,* May 23, 1977, pp. 60–73.

leisure activities that are in opposition to work activities, many people spend leisure in routines reminiscent of their jobs.[19] They engage in structured, organized leisure pursuits, such as package tours or resort "deals" that resemble the regimentation of the office and factory. In these activities the fun people have and the things people do are often highly programmed and standardized just as in the work settings they are supposedly escaping.

People also frequently have hobbies related to their field of work—carpenters may spend their nonwork hours making furniture or toys in their "workshops," book editors may fill their hours outside of work writing books, or college professors may think that nothing is nicer than to curl up with a good professional journal.

MASS LEISURE

The growth of mass cultural activities promoted by the mass media for mass audiences or participants further demonstrates our tendency to spend our leisure time in highly structured environments. On almost any Sunday afternoon a large segment of the male population (and now many females as well) in the United States is propped in front of television sets vicariously enjoying professional football, hockey, or baseball games.

Leisure pursuits have also become big business and one of the fastest growing industries in the nation. We spend literally billions of dollars annually on "having fun." Whereas once just having a day off and some money with which to enjoy it was considered enough, now many of us are hockey buffs, stock-car race lovers, connoisseurs of art, or movie-goers. And with the growth of the leisure industry a new hierarchy of status definitions has emerged, influencing how we are viewed by others, the kinds of people we are likely to associate with, and how we view ourselves.

LEISURE AND SELF-IMAGE

The Saturday morning tennis enthusiast may really love the physical exuberance of a close match in the hot sun. Some people cultivate their taste of wine and discuss the latest French films. Others spend their leisure hours snapping photographs, seeking out a new piece of equipment for their stereo set, anxiously waiting in line for hours to purchase theatre tickets, or sipping beer before the television set. Although all are leisure activities, all are differently evaluated by those who participate in them as well as by those who do not. For example, the weekend skier decked out in the latest line of equipment would

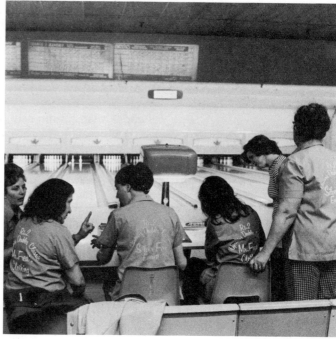

The leisure activities we choose are related to our self-image and the image we project to others.

probably be viewed as high on the social scale by skiers and nonskiers alike. Conversely, the Thursday night poker player would probably be ranked low on the same scale. Thus, regardless of our employment we can gain or lose status in the eyes of others depending on the type of leisure activities we choose to pursue.

Not only are these activities related to the self we seek to present to others, but they are also related to one's own self-image. Thus, the factory worker who spends his or her daily life doing a monotonous job may gain a sense of self-esteem and importance from membership on a bowling league.

In short, as the pursuit of leisure increasingly becomes a central feature of life and self-expression, a greater amount of energy, time, and resources is likely to be channeled into leisure activities. As this happens, a paradox may result. We engage in leisure as an escape from work. Yet to the extent that leisure becomes a standard of self and self-worth, then leisure activities become serious, important activities. As a result, they may become less "fun" and more like the work we are escaping. For example, instead of enjoying the walk and fresh air for their own sake, golfers and tennis players may come to practice their technique in order to perfect their "game" in the same way that they now strive to perfect their skill and standing on the job.

468

APPLYING SOCIOLOGY

Think about your favorite leisure activities. How seriously do you pursue such activities? If, for example, you are interested in sports, do you play to "improve your game" or just for pleasure? How strongly do you care about winning or losing?

Indeed, the pursuit of leisure has already provided work for many people, such as ski slope operators, the persons who service and sell boating equipment, and hunting guides, not to mention those who are laboring in factories manufacturing the equipment increasingly becoming defined as essential for having fun. Similarly, the world of sports has become big business ranging from the major league teams to the Little Leagues. Ironically, in this realm "play" means to work. The command "Play ball" is really a command to go to work. Players in the major leagues of football, baseball, basketball and so forth have become highly paid workers, for when one plays for pay, it becomes work regardless of how similar that activity may be to playing for fun. Thus, it is not always clear what line separates the worlds of work and leisure, and it is not inconceivable that in some distant day the barrier between the two will indeed be breached.

The worlds of work and leisure are not always separate. Some leisure activities, such as spectator sports, have become "big business," and professional "players" have become highly paid workers.

SUMMARY

Work is a central and economically essential aspect of human social life. In modern society, a person's work provides not only the monetary means for physical survival and comfort, but work has also come to serve as an important criterion by which the person's self-worth is determined.

Throughout history many societies regarded work as a "necessary evil." It was only since the advent of Protestantism that work was given a positive image—it was something people did to display their standing with God. Although modified considerably, that image is still the predominant one underlying work today.

When examining the labor force we note certain changes. The number of prime-age workers has increased substantially in recent years as has the relative proportion of women who work. Similarly, the kinds of work people do has changed considerably over the years. Once the labor force largely consisted of independent farmers and small business owners. Now it is made up of factory or white-collar workers employed by large corporations. In addition, work is becoming increasingly specialized so that high levels of skill are demanded of workers who have less and less personal attachment to the end product or work activity. Finally, people work fewer hours, earn more money per hour, and have increased their annual income. However, inflation has absorbed much of the worker's monetary gains.

Because work is so important, it is not surprising that the world of work is filled with difficulties. Among the more important of these is worker alienation, or job dissatisfaction. This phenomenon may have several causes, but it is surely precipitated by the fragmentation of work. Although worker alienation has been recognized as existing for some time, it is only recently that industry began taking steps to alleviate the problem with some apparent success. Much more difficult to deal with are the problems of unemployment and retirement. Both have severe economic as well as social and psychological consequences for those who experience them. And both seem to be experienced unequally by various groups of people. However, little progress has been made to date in attacking these problems or helping those who suffer from them.

Perhaps the idea that the Western world is moving toward a leisure society is true. If so, people will no longer find, or even pursue, fulfillment of psychological and social needs solely in the world of work. However, the way people spend their leisure time is often related to their working environments. They frequently engage in structured pursuits that resemble the regimentation of their jobs or choose hobbies that are work related. The growth of mass cultural activities further demonstrates our desire to spend our leisure time in structured situations.

With the growth of the leisure industry comes a new hierarchy of status definitions. As a result, people will also define their status and acquire their self-images in terms of their leisure activities. Yet as the pursuit of leisure increasingly becomes a central part of our lives, it may become more like the work world we are trying to escape. Thus, in the future it is possible that the boundaries that separate the worlds of work and leisure may eventually be breached.

GLOSSARY

alienation feelings of estrangement and hostility toward others and society in general.

ethic a system of moral beliefs held by the members of some group or society.

ideology a system of ideas and beliefs about the world or some aspect of it.

labor force those persons aged sixteen or over who are able to work, including those who are actually employed, either part-time or full-time, and those who are unemployed but seeking work.

leisure nonwork activities; free-time; those activities engaged in for pleasure that are not oriented to productive labor for which one is paid.

Protestant ethic a system of beliefs which held that avoiding pleasure, devoting one's life to work, and practicing economic thrift were virtues.

work the activity of expending energy to produce goods or services. In our society, work is thought of as paid employment.

work fragmentation the process by which the various operations and movements of a job are broken into component parts so that one person performs only one, or a small number, of these operations.

REFERENCES

1. Koya Azumi, "The Japanese Changing World of Work." *The Wilson Quarterly* 1:4 (July 1977):72–80. For an in-depth discussion of the meanings given to work see Adriano Tilgher, "Work Through the Ages," in Sigmund Nosow and William H. Form, eds., *Man, Work and Society*. New York: Basic Books, 1970, pp. 11–23.

2. Max Weber, *The Protestant Ethic and the Spirit of Capitalism*. Trans. by Talcott Parsons. New York: Scribner & Sons, 1958.

3. See Peter Berger, ed., *The Human Shape of Work*. New York: Macmillan, 1964.

4. Robert S. Weiss, Edward Harwood, and David Riesman, "The World of Work." In Robert K. Merton and Robert Nisbet, eds., *Contemporary Social Problems*. 4th ed. New York: Harcourt Brace Jovanovich, 1976, pp. 616–617. Also see Joseph Julian, *Social Problems*. New York: Appleton-Century-Crofts, 1973, pp. 398–402.

5. This is the definition used by the Department of Labor in gathering information on employment and earnings and which serves as the basis for the statistics reported in this chapter.

6. Karl Marx, *Economic and Philosophical Manuscripts of 1844*. New York: International Publishers, 1964. See also Henri Lefebvre, *The Sociology of Karl Marx*. Trans. by Norbert Guterman. New York: Pantheon, 1968.

7. Marx, p. 111.

8. Nancy C. Morse and Robert S. Weiss, "The Function and Meaning of Work." *American Sociological Review* 20 (April 1955):191–198. See also Michael McKee and Ian Robertson, *Social Problems*. New York: Random House, 1975, pp. 186–193.

9. Gresham M. Sykes, *Social Problems in America*. Glenview, Ill.: Scott, Foresman, 1971, pp. 162–163.

10. Sykes, p. 163.

11. Sykes, pp. 164–165.

12. McKee and Robertson, pp. 193–194.

13. This information is published monthly in various Labor Department publications. See, for example, the current *Employment and Earnings*, U.S. Department of Labor, Bureau of Labor Statistics, for up-to-date information.

14. Quoted from Weiss, et al., p. 620.

15. Sykes, pp. 180–181.

16. Monica Talmon, "Aging: Social Aspects." In *International Encyclopedia of the Social Sciences*, vol. 1, New York: Macmillan, 1968, pp. 191–193.

17. Sykes, pp. 159–160.

18. Nels Anderson, *Work and Leisure*. New York: The Free Press, 1961.

19. Julian, p. 418.

SUGGESTED READINGS

Berger, Peter, ed. *The Human Shape of Work*. New York: Macmillan, 1964.

>   *A collection of essays on the meaning of work for the workers.*

DeGrazia, Sebastian. *Of Time, Work, and Leisure*. Garden City, N.Y.: Doubleday, 1962.

>   *An analysis of work-time and leisure and how we spend it. The book analyzes and attacks the myth that we have achieved more leisure time and that we spend it in a meaningful way.*

Hall, Richard H. *Occupations and the Social Structure.* Englewood Cliffs, N.J.: Prentice-Hall, 1969.

An excellent textbook on the topic of work and occupations.

Huizinga, Johan. *Homo ludens.* Boston: Beacon Press, 1950.

A study of the play element in culture.

Mills, C. Wright. *White-Collar: The American Middle Class.* New York: Oxford University Press, 1951.

A major study and description of the American middle class, white-collar worker at home and in the office.

Rosow, Jerome M., ed. *The Worker and the Job: Coping with Change.* Englewood Cliffs, N.J.: Prentice-Hall, 1976.

A look at the world of work and changes designed to improve work.

Smigel, Erwin O. *Work and Leisure.* New Haven: College and University Press, 1963.

A collection of readings on the meaning of leisure to different occupational groups.

Terkel, Studs. *Working.* New York: Random House, 1974.

A collection of interviews with workers that provides insight into their work and their feelings about it and themselves.

Work in America: A Report of a Special Task Force to the Secretary of Health, Education, and Welfare. Washington, D.C.: U.S. Government Printing Office, 1973.

A major study dealing with alienation among workers, offering a clear and readable appraisal of work as a major social problem.

15

Deviance

About three hundred years ago a wave of mass hysteria swept through several small New England communities in Massachusetts. No one is quite sure how the "witchcraft episode" began, but before it ended hundreds of townspeople had been accused of being witches and several were hanged or crushed to death. Were these people really witches? Had they actually made a pact with the Devil? Upon closer examination, it seems that for the most part these people were ordinary citizens. Similarly, during the McCarthy era in the 1950s many ordinary people were accused of being "communists." As a result, they were blacklisted and persecuted.

What caused these people to be singled out as deviant? And why did the society take such strong actions against them? In this chapter we will examine the concept of deviance. We will focus on explanations of deviance, types of deviance, functions and dysfunctions of deviance, and mechanisms for social control. After reading this chapter, you should be able to answer the questions we have posed.

What Is Deviance?

As the categorization of people as witches and as communists suggests, the definition of deviance seems to be quite flexible. Sociologist J. L. Simmons reached this conclusion in a study he conducted. When Simmons surveyed a number of citizens and asked them whom they considered deviant, he found that they listed more than two hundred fifty different types of persons. Those labeled deviant included drug addicts, criminals, and prostitutes, but also listed were artists, divorcees, "know-it-all" professors, Democrats, and girls who wear make-up.[1] Several other researchers who conducted similar experiments obtained parallel results.[2]

With such a variety of responses, how can we define deviance? How can we define a concept that seems to include at one time or another much of the entire population? In an attempt to answer these questions, many sociologists have adapted an approach called the *labeling perspective.*

Sociologists taking the labeling approach argue that no behavior in and of itself is deviant. Rather, they feel that an act becomes deviant only if the members of a society believe that it violates a group rule, and consequently label it as deviant by applying negative sanctions to some person thought guilty of violating the rule. Sociologist Howard Becker states: "The deviant is one to whom that label has been successfully applied; deviant behavior is behavior that people so label."[3] Similarly, sociologist Kai Erikson argues: "Deviance is not a property *inherent* in any particular kind of behavior; it is a property *conferred*

476

The behaviors that are labeled deviant vary from group to group. Although many would consider the behaviors of this gang member deviant, others would not agree.

upon that behavior by the people who come into direct or indirect contact with it."[4]

According to these sociologists, then, deviance is relative. What may be viewed as deviant in one situation might be viewed as perfectly acceptable in another. For example, if an ordinary citizen speeds through a red light while intoxicated, that person would probably be labeled a deviant for violating a rule. On the other hand, if a plainclothes police officer in an unmarked car ran the light while rushing an injured child to a hospital, the act of running the light would be viewed positively. Although initially both actions appear to be identical, the settings (in part) cause only one to be reacted to as deviant.

Similarly, smoking marijuana is not perceived as deviant in all instances. Among friends who are smoking, one who smokes is not considered a deviant. In fact, if one abstains from smoking, a deviant label might then be applied. However, if one decides to smoke marijuana while in school, the behavior is likely to be perceived as violating the criminal law and probably would be subject to negative sanctions by school and law officials.

Also, consider the example of the man who enthusiastically prepares for a mardi gras parade in a neighboring community. For the evening he gets dressed as a baby girl, wearing a bonnet and carrying a bottle and pocketbook. His behavior and attire are considered to be perfectly normal for the duration of this special event. Yet when he walks down the street to a local restaurant to call home, the costume he is dressed in is no longer considered acceptable. An observer not aware of the earlier event may question the normality of this adult male with a mustache dressed in a baby girl's outfit.

We can also note that what one group defines as deviant might be thought of as acceptable in another group. For example, theft is viewed as deviant in our society. In fact, we have laws specifying that such behavior is unacceptable. Yet members of a youth gang might consider *not* engaging in theft as deviant; the norms of their group might say it is necessary to steal.

The behaviors or individuals that are labeled deviant vary not only from situation to situation and group to group, but also from time to time. For example, driving at sixty-five miles per hour several years ago was viewed as normal behavior whereas at the present time anyone driving over fifty-five miles per hour on an interstate highway is violating a rule. Similarly, whereas women who wore slacks in public about thirty years ago were considered deviant, today such attire for women is perfectly acceptable.

These examples point out that no act is inherently deviant. Rather, deviance exists only when members of a society perceive others as violating a rule and punish them for doing so. The key word in this sen-

477

APPLYING SOCIOLOGY

Some people argue that deviance is not the result of labeling; instead they believe that certain acts are deviant in and of themselves. For example, they would say that such acts as rape, killing, and robbery are deviant under any circumstances. Do you agree? What arguments could you give that would contradict their beliefs? What arguments support the idea of inherent deviance?

---

tence is *perceive.* If individuals are perceived to be violating rules when in fact they are not, they will still be labeled deviant. For example, students falsely accused of cheating on an exam are punished as if they did indeed commit the deviant act. Conversely, individuals who engage in rule-violating behavior and are not caught will not be given the deviant label. Thus, many Americans who cheat on their income taxes without getting caught by Uncle Sam are thought of as respectable citizens. We can define deviance, then, as *a socially created phenomenon resulting from negative societal reaction toward persons who are believed to have violated a group rule.*

Explanations of Deviant Behavior

If violating a group rule often brings forth strong negative sanctions, then it would seem that people would behave within society's guidelines. Yet we know from experience that this is not always the case. Most people break some rules at some time in their lives. Social scientists have attempted to explain such rule-breaking behavior. Three general types of explanations for why deviant conduct arises have been offered: biological explanations, psychological explanations, and sociological explanations.

BIOLOGICAL EXPLANATIONS

Perhaps the most persistent approach to deviant conduct has been to attribute it to an innate biological or physical characteristic or defect in the person. In other words, according to some of those taking this view, deviants are born that way. Italian criminologist Cesare Lombroso,[5] for example, held this opinion.

After measuring the skulls and bodies of dozens of convicted criminals in the early 1900s, Lombroso concluded that criminals could be distinguished from nonoffenders on the basis of such physical characteristics as long arms, excessive hair, and peculiar facial features.

478

According to Lombroso, criminals were a distinct type of subhuman called *atavists* who never quite made it up the chain of evolution.

While this theory gained substantial support, one major flaw existed. Lombroso failed to measure the brains and other physical characteristics of noncriminals. When such experiments were carried out, for example by British physician Charles Goring in 1913,[6] no physical differences were found between criminals and the rest of the population.

Biological explanations for criminal behavior, however, were not put to rest with this refutation of Lombroso's theory. Modern theorists have persisted in similar searches. For example, in the late 1940s, psychologist William Sheldon developed a classification of three body types.[7] Sheldon claimed that *endomorphs* have round, soft bodies; *mesomorphs* have square, hard bodies; and *ectomorphs* are thin and delicate. And, according to Sheldon, people's body types were related to psychological traits. Endomorphs are friendly, happy-go-lucky people; mesomorphs are full of nervous energy, active, and impulsive; and ectomorphs are shy, sensitive, and introverted. Sheldon concluded, after studying two hundred male juvenile delinquents, that mesomorphs were more likely to be offenders.

Using William Sheldon's classifications, Sheldon and Eleanor Glueck[8] conducted a study of five hundred delinquent and five hundred nondelinquent boys. They too concluded that more mesomorphs could be found in the delinquent sample, although they later disavowed a biological explanation of juvenile delinquency.

Most biological theories of deviance, however, have been discarded for lack of evidence clearly showing a direct relationship between physical features and different types of deviance. Yet studies based on biology continue. Some of these have relied on chromosomal defects to explain deviant behavior.

Among the twenty-three pairs of chromosomes found in any human cell, the normal female has one consisting of two X chromosomes and the normal male has one consisting of an X and a Y pair. This difference is thought to determine sexual characteristics. The Y chromosome found in males, however, is also thought to be related to aggressiveness.

With this in mind, researchers began to test the notion that perhaps persons who committed extreme acts of aggression would be found to have an extra Y chromosome in their cells. In testing what came to be called the XYY theory, some of these researchers initially found that more people in prison for committing serious acts of aggression had this chromosomal pattern than the general population. But within a few years, continued research showed that there was little reason to assume that having an extra Y chromosome

479

caused people to act aggressively. Indeed, sociologist Richard Fox, who reviewed all this research, concluded that those males who have an extra Y chromosome do not appear to be any more aggressive than normal XY males. In fact, they seem to be less aggressive.[9]

Biological explanations for deviant behavior are not confined merely to criminal behavior. For example, some research claims that schizophrenia, a mental disorder, is related to differences in the body's chemical make-up. In one study it was found that a substance called taraxein was contained in the bloodstream of schizophrenics.[10] When this substance was injected into nonschizophrenics, they displayed schizophrenic-like behavior. Similarly, research suggests that there is a biological basis for heroin addiction. If a pregnant woman is addicted to the drug, the baby will become addicted while still in the womb.

Undoubtedly, there will continue to be searches for a biological cause of deviant behavior. But it is unlikely that any singular biological trait is the sole cause of all deviant behavior. That is why social scientists have looked for other explanations of these diverse forms of conduct labeled deviant.

PSYCHOLOGICAL EXPLANATIONS

Some psychological explanations, like biological explanations, locate deviance within the individual. These psychological arguments differ from biological explanations, however, in that they seek the causes of deviance in personality rather than in biology. Instead of saying a person is defective physically, the proponents of these arguments say he or she is psychologically sick.

Many psychological arguments center around the theories of Sigmund Freud.[11] According to Freud, the human personality is made up of three parts, the *id* (or the natural impulses), the *ego* (or the conscious aspect of the self), and the *superego* (or the conscience). In order for an individual to function properly, each part must develop thoroughly (see Chapter 4). Hence, it is believed that deviant behavior may arise basically from two sources: 1) inadequate development of the ego or superego, leaving id impulses uncontrolled, or 2) severe conflicts among the three parts. Furthermore, Freud argued that deviant behavior is rooted in early childhood experiences, since the ego and superego are developed from childhood onward. In other words, if a child experiences a trauma such as parental rejection, the superego and ego will not develop properly, and deviant behavior might result at some later age.

Not all psychologists, however, subscribe to Freud's viewpoint. The social learning theorists, for example, place less emphasis on an individual's personality and more emphasis on the environment. Social learning theorists believe that human behavior, both normal and deviant, can best be understood in terms of principles of learning. In other words, these theorists believe that people learn to behave in certain ways from interacting with others in their environment. For example, if a child is often exposed to aggressive role models, the child will imitate those people and adopt their behavior patterns. Similarly, adolescents or adults might learn certain forms of deviant behavior regardless of the personalities they developed as children.

SOCIOLOGICAL EXPLANATIONS

Several sociological theories attempt to explain deviance in terms of the environment. Some of the more important theories are those of Durkheim, Merton, and Sutherland.

Durkheim's Theory

Émile Durkheim observed that deviance (specifically crime) was a universal phenomenon.[12] Consequently, he concluded that it must be a normal condition of human societies and could never be eliminated. Indeed, Durkheim believed that the very rules of a society promote deviance.

According to Durkheim, rules are necessary for a society's existence. Yet because people are not all alike, someone will always depart from or violate the group's rules and be subject to punishment for doing so. Hence, deviance will always exist as long as society exists. And, Durkheim believed, deviance defines the boundaries of a society, thus contributing to social solidarity.

Durkheim further argued that a relatively unchanging rate of deviance in a society was a healthy sign. Deviance, in other words, was not something to become concerned about as long as the amount and kinds of deviance that took place remained constant. But what determined the rate of deviance in a society?

Durkheim said that deviance increased when the norms holding a society together become weak or ineffective. He used the term *anomie* to describe this situation of normlessness. Such a condition often results when a society is undergoing rapid social change. For example, Durkheim argued that suicide rates rise during periods of economic prosperity as well as during periods of economic depression. According to Durkheim, then, the rate of deviance in a society is closely related to its level of anomie.

Whether Durkheim's theory is correct or not has not been demonstrated. By linking the rates of deviance to characteristics in a society, though, Durkheim did open the door for other theories, one of which was offered by Robert K. Merton.

481

Innovation takes place when a person accepts a socially approved goal (such as financial success) but uses improper means to attain it (such as illegal drugs).

Merton's Theory

Sociologist Robert Merton[13] also used the term *anomie* to characterize the social condition he believed was linked to deviance. However, he altered the meaning of this concept considerably. Instead of using anomie to refer to normlessness, Merton used it to refer to a situation that results when there is a conflict between a society's approved goals and acceptable opportunities for achieving them. In American society, for example, financial success is a valued goal. Hard work is an acceptable means of achieving this goal. But sometimes work may not be available and thus some groups or individuals may be denied access to legitimate means to achieve financial success. When this occurs, pressures build up for these individuals or groups to engage in deviant rather than conforming behavior. Thus, during the depression of the 1930s, many people out of work became hoboes, turned to petty crime, or took to begging.

Merton notes four types of deviant alternatives that can occur if people are blocked from achieving success goals. These are *innovation*, *ritualism*, *retreatism*, and *rebellion*. *Conformity*, which is another alternative but a nondeviant one, occurs when an individual has the opportunity to use culturally accepted means to reach culturally approved goals (see Table 15-1).

Innovation takes place when a person accepts the goal, but resorts to deviant behavior because the proper means of attaining it are not available. A thief, for example, believes in the culturally approved goal of acquiring money, but steals instead of earning it through legitimate work.

A second deviant alternative is *ritualism*. The ritualist is more concerned with the means—sticking to the rules—than with the goals. An example of a ritualist would be a bureaucrat who becomes so involved with the rules that he or she loses sight of the goal.

TABLE 15–1
Merton's Typology of Modes of Individual Adaptation

Mode of Adaptation	Cultural Goals	Institutionalized Means	Example
Conformity	+	+	Doctor
Innovation	+	−	Thief
Ritualism	−	+	Bureaucrat
Retreatism	−	−	Drug addict
Rebellion	±	±	Revolutionary

(+ = accepts, − = rejects, and ± = rejects existing goals and/or means and substitutes new ones)

Source: Adapted from Robert K. Merton, *Social Theory and Social Structure*, New York: The Free Press, 1968, p. 104. Reprinted with permission of Macmillan Publishing Company, Inc. Copyright © 1968, 1967, Robert K. Merton.

482

Robert K. Merton (1910–   )

In his classic work, *Social Theory and Social Structure* (1949), Robert K. Merton views most deviance as a "normal" response to conflicting pressures within society. American society, claims Merton, places a high value on success, especially monetary success. The need to succeed reaches all sectors of society by way of such devices as public education and the mass media. The legitimate opportunities available to different social groups to reach such success, however, vary considerably. Therefore, says Merton, one way of resolving this dilemma is through the use of illegitimate means, such as crime. There are, of course, cultural values that tell us how to reach success legitimately (through hard work and perseverance, for example), but the end goal (success) is valued more in our society than are the means to that end.

Merton notes that "the greatest pressures toward deviation are exerted upon the lower strata." He warns us, though, not to simply regard poverty, or lack of opportunity as *the* cause of deviance. Many societies have existed in which the poor have committed relatively few crimes. Rather, says Merton, it is because of the *shared* belief that success is necessary, together with the democratic belief that *everyone* should have the opportunity to realize such success, that intense pressures toward deviant behavior are generated among certain groups.

If an individual turns to crime because of the conflicting societal pressures described above, Merton would call this type of response "innovation." He also considers three other deviant responses to conflicting values, but none of them is as common. Briefly, "ritualism" is the response of an individual who has abandoned the common goals, but nevertheless "goes through the motions" as if he or she is striving toward those goals. The classic illustration of this type of response is the bureaucrat who is obsessed with following petty rules without being interested in their end result. "Retreatism" is the response of a person who has abandoned both the proper means and common ends. A "flower-child" of the 1960s illustrates this type of response. Finally, "rebellion" is characterized by substituting new means *and* new ends. The revolutionary would be an example of this type of response because he or she is interested in replacing the overall structure of society.

Retreatism is the third deviant alternative offered by Merton. A retreatist is a person who accepts neither the goals nor the means and, in effect, drops out of society. Derelicts and youthful runaways could be examples of those who resort to retreatism.

Rebellion is yet another deviant mode of adaptation. Those who use this alternative reject the accepted goals and means and substitute new ones in their place. Frequently such people are concerned with political change, as were the activist groups of the 1960s. But, they also can be involved in social change, as are members of communes.

Other sociologists have applied Merton's theory to their own research. For example, Albert Cohen[14] noted that lower-class boys are often unable to meet the middle-class standards that confront them in school. Because of their backgrounds they tend to find it difficult to be future-oriented, to exert self-control, and to be ambitious. As a result, they constantly experience both internal and external negative evaluations of their abilities. This often causes them to withdraw from school at an early age and to form gangs with others who have also rejected their middle-class evaluators. Here they can achieve status among their peers by establishing standards and patterns of behavior that are in conflict with those of middle-class society.

While some sociologists accept this reason for deviant behavior, others do not believe that it alone accounts for deviance. For example, not all lower-class boys who are frustrated in their attempts to achieve success at school will turn to juvenile gangs. One theory that many sociologists subscribe to is the *theory of differential association*.

Sutherland's Theory

The *theory of differential association* was originated by criminologist Edwin Sutherland in an attempt to explain criminal conduct.[15] In this theory Sutherland suggests that criminal behavior, like any other kind of human social behavior, is learned through interaction with others, particularly within intimate personal groups. In other words, we learn deviant behavior through socialization. For example, Becker has shown that in order to become a marijuana user, one must go through a complicated socialization process.[16] During this procedure, one learns to properly smoke marijuana, to recognize the effects of the drug, and to perceive the effects as favorable. He contends that a person will not become a marijuana user unless he or she meets all three conditions.

As we interact with others we discover which behaviors are admired and which are condemned. Through rewards we are encouraged to repeat those that are regarded favorably. Hence, if people belong to a group that respects conformity, they will learn to conform. Conversely, if people associate with a group that rewards deviant behavior, they will continue their deviant actions.

Since all people come into contact with both deviant and conforming individuals, however, contact alone cannot determine deviance. Sutherland recognized this and noted certain conditions under which deviance is more likely to occur. He noted that the frequency, intensity, duration, and number of contacts all play a role in determining whether or not a person will become deviant. In addition, he believed that a person will be more susceptible to deviance at an early age than as an adult.

While Sutherland's theory has been useful, there are still several unanswered questions. Why people should want to learn deviant conduct or why they would become involved in a situation in which this learning is likely to take place are among the questions that remain. Also, Sutherland's theory fails to account for some deviant behaviors that are not learned, such as impulsive and irrational acts.

Each of the explanations we have discussed—the biological, the psychological, and the sociological—provides us with some insight into the source of deviant conduct. Yet none gives us a definite answer as to why it occurs. Perhaps future theories will shed more light on the subject. Let us now see what types of deviance are considered pressing concerns in our own society, and how people are affected.

Types of Deviant Behavior

We have mentioned that deviance occurs when the members of a society perceive others as violating a group rule and punish them for doing so. The rules people break, however, can vary in scope from committing a murder to wearing clothes inappropriate to an occasion. Noting this variation, we can divide the types of deviance into two categories—criminal deviance and noncriminal deviance. Because of the large number of acts that can be classified under each heading, we will discuss only an important few.

CRIMINAL DEVIANCE

The Federal Bureau of Investigation has been the major source for measuring the amount of criminal behavior in the United States. Based on reports from local police departments, this agency compiles national statistics on various crimes and publishes these statistics annually in the Uniform Crime Reports. Table 15-2 presents an estimated number of major crimes in the United States in 1975 based on these figures.

Although we would like to think that these statistics are accurate, there is reason to believe that they do not present a complete picture of the amount of crime in our country. For one thing, the information obtained from the local police departments may not really reflect the true situation. Not all police departments provide statistics and of those that do, some overreport or underreport crimes and some have inefficient methods of keeping records.

More important, though, the FBI only compiles statistics on crimes that are reported to the police. But often people do not report crimes. They may believe that the police are incapable of doing any-

TABLE 15–2
Estimated Number of Major Crimes in the United States, 1975

Crime Index Classification	Number
Murder	20,510
Forcible rape	56,000
Robbery	464,970
Aggravated Assault	484,710
Burglary	3,252,100
Larceny, $50 and over	5,977,700
Auto theft	1,000,500
Total	11,256,000

Source: Adapted from Federal Bureau of Investigation, Uniform Crime Reports for the United States, Washington, D.C.: U.S. Government Printing Office, 1975, 11.

FOCUS ON: FEMALE CRIMINALITY

It is becoming clear that many women are no longer allowing themselves to be placed in stereotyped categories, even in categories labeled "deviant." In her book *Sisters in Crime,* sociologist Freda Adler discusses how women have entered areas of crime formerly regarded as "male only."

According to Adler, in the past female crimes had primarily been confined to prostitution and shoplifting. Recently, however, women have been committing such "male" crimes as robbery and burglary, as well as crimes of a violent nature.

The rise in female criminality is reflected in the Uniform Crime Reports issued yearly by the FBI. Between 1960 and 1972, the number of female arrests for robbery rose by 277 percent; for embezzlement 280 percent; for larceny 303 percent; and for burglary 168 percent. In every category, the increase for men was much lower.

Adler contends that these facts can be explained in the same way that women's entrance into other male-dominated areas is explained. In crime, as in other work areas, there is a hierarchy, and women have always occupied the lower rungs of the ladder. But women are refusing to be "second rate" criminals any longer, just as they are refusing to be "second-rate" job-holders in other occupational areas. They are attempting, and apparently succeeding, in scaling the barriers erected against women in the world of crime.

Do you think female crime rates will continue to rise? Which types of crimes do you think women will not commit? What effects do you believe the rise in female criminality will have on women's fight for equality?

"*I was raped by a willowy blonde from the women's liberation movement.*"

Source: Freda Adler, *Sisters in Crime: The Rise of the New Female Criminal,* New York: McGraw-Hill, 1975.

486

thing helpful, they may fear reprisal, they may not want to get the offender in trouble, or they may fear that any subsequent investigation would prove damaging. Also, the police do not report crimes committed among themselves. Furthermore, since white-collar crime is often resolved by administrative agencies, even though violations of the criminal law are involved, a large amount of such crime goes unnoticed.

In addition, certain types of crimes are not considered crimes at all and are excluded from the FBI statistics. For example, if slum landlords do not repair their property and people die as a result of their negligence, it is not considered murder. Federal crimes such as treason also are not tabulated by the FBI.

Thus, it has been estimated that the rate of crime is much higher than we are led to believe. A study conducted by the National Opinion Research Center (NORC) supports this finding.[17] This organization conducted a survey in which 10,000 people were asked if they had been victims of crime and if so whether they had reported the crime to the police. In crimes involving personal injury, the statistics obtained by the NORC were twice as high as those in the Uniform Crime Reports. In addition, in other studies that asked people about any crimes they may have committed, many admitted criminal activity although their crimes were never detected.

Judging from these statistics, we can see that the FBI statistics may indeed give us only part of the picture. We will now take a look at certain important types of crimes that commonly occur.

White-Collar Crime

The term *white-collar crime* was first used by Edwin Sutherland. It describes certain types of offenses committed by members of the middle and upper classes in the course of their jobs. Examples of white-collar crime include fraud, bribery, false advertising, and price-fixing.

White-collar crime is less frightening to the American public than many other forms of crime. It often goes unreported and is often not even considered criminal. Yet its effects can be devastating. For example, illegal air and water pollution have caused immeasurable damage to the environment. In the mining industry, violation of federal mine safety laws has contributed to hundreds of deaths from black lung disease.

Financially, it has been estimated that the cost of white-collar crimes to its victims amounts to over $40 billion a year.[18] Sociologist Stuart Hill estimated the financial costs of white-collar crime to be twice as high as the total loss from armed robbery, burglary, automobile theft, and pickpocketing.[19]

Although considered less frightening than other forms of crime, white-collar crime can have long-lasting, devastating effects.

487

FOCUS ON: WHITE-COLLAR CRIME

White-collar crime has no special class of victims—poor and rich, young and elderly, laborer and banker are all potential targets of the criminal's tricks. This type of crime covers a wide range of criminal activities from simple embezzlement to massive bank frauds. It includes the "flim-flam" artist who operates in the local bar as well as the high-placed government official who "rips off" a social welfare program.

According to United States Attorney Robert J. Del Tufo, who has established an "Economic Crime Unit" to ferret out white-collar criminals in New Jersey, "economic crime" bilks about $77 billion annually from government, business, and consumers throughout the nation. Although it is difficult to estimate how much the consuming public loses to white-collar criminals, it is estimated that corporate fraud costs about $50 billion per year, and $14 billion is taken from government programs.

The price of white-collar crime unfortunately is paid by the consumer and taxpayer. If the fraud is committed against a government agency, it is the taxpayer who eventually must replace the loss by paying added taxes. When the crime is committed against a corporation, the consumer eventually pays an increased price for the corporation's product or service.

Another facet of white-collar crime is that frequently the white-collar criminal is not treated in the same manner by the criminal justice system as those who commit more violent types of crime or as other robbers or burglars are. The white-collar criminal is often a first offender and thus may not get as harsh a sentence as other criminals. Often, too, the white-collar criminal is a member of the middle class and therefore may receive more favored treatment than members of lower socioeconomic categories.

Do you think white-collar criminals should be treated differently from other criminals? Should separate correctional facilities be established for incarcerating and rehabilitating such criminals? How do you think you would react if you discovered someone had committed a fraud against you, for example, sold you a piece of worthless real estate? Would you admit your gullibility and report the crime?

Source: "State to Start Drive on White-Collar Fraud," *Newark Star Ledger,* October 22, 1978.

Despite such costs, Americans tend to "coddle" white-collar criminals. Several reasons account for this behavior. First, white-collar crime does not receive much publicity, and it does not seem as personal as other forms of crime. Companies and not people are being "ripped off," and nobody is usually injured in a physical sense. Second, it is often difficult to detect these crimes and to point to specific culprits or victims. Third, Americans may be reluctant to punish white-collar criminals. For example, we may be hesitant to punish a politician accused of bribery after he or she has served the community well for twenty years. In addition, we often believe that these people have suffered enough for their crimes—they have damaged their reputations in the eyes of the public. Finally, the high social and economic positions of white-collar criminals often allow them to escape punishment. Thus, while the effects of white-collar crime are severe, the punishment tends to be lax.

"My client would like to remind the Court that until recently he himself was a member of the bench."

APPLYING SOCIOLOGY

Many people take it for granted that it is perfectly all right to take home from their offices such items as pencils and pads of paper. On the other hand, some criminologists consider this behavior to be white-collar crime, resulting in losses amounting to millions of dollars. Do you think this type of offense should be punished? How severe do you think the punishment should be? Can this behavior be eliminated? Why or why not? How would we have to alter our values to curtail such behavior?

Juvenile Delinquency

Juvenile delinquency is a major concern in our society for two main reasons. As is the case with most crime, we are concerned with the resulting injuries to persons and property. But, perhaps more important, we are concerned that we have failed in the way we have reared our children. Thus, our concern centers around our urge to save the young.

Yet the rate of juvenile delinquency has steadily been increasing. Between 1960 and 1973, the rate of juvenile arrests for all types of offenses increased by 144 percent.[20] In 1975, about 30 percent of all persons arrested were under the age of eighteen.[21] In addition, the types of crimes committed by young people have changed dramatically. Whereas in the past juvenile delinquency was confined primarily to what we would call mischievous behavior, today much of juvenile crime involves such offenses as murder, assault, and robbery. About 43 percent of all serious crimes listed in FBI reports are now committed by persons under eighteen.

With such a large increase in the rate and seriousness of juvenile crime, it would seem that punishment would be quite severe. In recent years several people, alarmed by this upsurge in rates, have called for a crackdown on juvenile "criminals" and the handing out of severe punishment for serious offenses. This demand, however, conflicts with the basic philosophy of the juvenile justice system.

A separate, and seemingly lenient, system of justice for juveniles was originated in the United States in 1899 in reaction to the harsh penalties that were being given out to youthful offenders at that time. The idea was that juveniles were not culpable in the same sense as adults and, therefore, should not be punished for their conduct. Rather, they were to be given the care and treatment necessary to reform them from the path of crime.

In creating this system of justice, all the safeguards found in the adult criminal court were dispensed with for juveniles. Many youngsters were put away for long periods of time for committing trivial offenses. It was the character and not the behavior of the juvenile that was to guide the judge in dealing with the offender.

By the mid-1960s the possible abuses of the juvenile justice system became apparent. In a landmark decision, the United States Supreme Court restored to juveniles many of the rights enjoyed by adults. More recently, some states have begun to toughen up the dispositions received by juveniles, treating them more like adults. It is too early to tell, however, what effects such changes will have on the administration of juvenile justice or the involvement of juveniles in serious offenses.

Prostitution is considered a "crime without victims." Although no one usually suffers from such crimes, they are morally objectionable to most people.

Crimes Without Victims

Other types of criminal offenses are often called "crimes without victims."[22] We can include in this category such crimes as prostitution and gambling. These are crimes from which no one suffers, except perhaps the deviant. Nevertheless, society defines such acts as crimes because they violate mores—they are morally objectionable.

Despite our beliefs that such acts are morally wrong, much controversy surrounds the elimination of these crimes. On the one hand, we do not take such crimes too seriously since, as is the case with white-collar crime, many respectable people commit them and nobody is usually physically injured. Yet, on the other hand, we try to enforce laws forbidding victimless crimes in order to maintain our moral code. As Thurman Arnold noted, "[Laws regarding victimless crimes] are unenforced because we want to continue our conduct, and unrepealed because we want to preserve our morals."[23]

In addition, crimes without victims are almost impossible to eliminate even if we wanted to, primarily because there is no victim to press charges or to testify in court. Also, those involved in such crimes sometimes have little respect for the law they are breaking and do not feel guilty for breaking it. Furthermore, the behavior often occurs in private and is therefore virtually undetectable by law enforcement officials. Thus, although this country has spent an enormous amount of money to control victimless crimes, the effort has not been very successful.

Organized Crime

Laws surrounding crimes without victims have enabled organized crime to flourish. *Organized crime* refers to a network of syndicates that provide such illegal goods and services as drugs, loan sharking, and prostitution to those willing to pay high prices for them. It has been said that organized crime is one of the largest "industries" in this country, grossing about $37 billion in 1973 and presently having a gross income twice that obtained from all other crimes combined.[24]

Organized crime is able to function because of social, cultural, political, economic, and legal conditions historically prevalent in American society. In addition, it is supported and protected by otherwise "respectable" citizens who also profit from its operation and who want the goods and services offered. If the public did not sanction it, organized crime could not exist.

Throughout its history, organized crime has attempted to "go respectable" by investing in such legitimate businesses as restaurants, banking, and hotels. In fact, it is quite possible that organized crime has a financial interest in many legitimate business enterprises.

491

All of these types of activities—white-collar crime, juvenile delinquency, crimes without victims, and organized crime—can be considered deviant because they violate legal norms. We will now take a look at some forms of deviance that violate only social norms.

NONCRIMINAL DEVIANCE

Whereas it is relatively easy to identify criminal deviance because the norms that are violated are written down, it is not so easy to determine what constitutes noncriminal deviance. For the most part, norms surrounding noncriminal deviance are subject to a variety of interpretations. What is considered deviant by one segment of the population may be considered normal by another. For example, while some people thought that long hair on males was a sign of deviance, others found it perfectly acceptable. Thus, the major way by which noncriminal deviance is determined is through labeling. We affix the label of "deviant" to people for a variety of reasons and then treat them as if they really were deviant. We will see how the labeling process operates in the noncriminal deviant behaviors we will examine.

Mental Illness

Mental illness is one form of noncriminal deviance because to be mentally ill is to violate social norms. Yet to be mentally ill is not clearly definable. What is considered sane in one situation is considered abnormal in another. For example, psychiatrist Robert Coles notes:

> What indeed is mental health? Who indeed is normal? . . . If a man tells me he is going to kill himself, I call him "suicidal" and want to hospitalize him. If a man in Vietnam runs into a burst of machine gun fire, urging his comrades to do likewise, I call him a hero. If a man wants to kill someone, he is homicidal and needs confinement. If a man drops a bomb on people he doesn't even see or know, he is doing his duty.[25]

Mental illness, then, is a value judgment imposed on people so as to make their behavior comprehensible and manageable to the society. It is the label given to certain acts that the majority of people find strange, odd, frightening, or undesirable in some way.

Not only do we have difficulty precisely defining mental illness, we also have difficulty measuring it. Sociologist Jack Gibbs suggests that about the only way to measure the actual amount of mental illness is to note the number of people hospitalized for mental illness.[26] Yet even this may not give us an actual count. For example, although in 1974, New York had a higher incidence of hospitalization than Michigan, this does not mean that there were really more mentally ill people in New York. Rather, the availability of facilities for treating the mentally ill and the criteria for admitting patients may account for the differences.

Even when people are confined to mental hospitals, does it really mean that they are mentally ill? Judging from a study conducted by psychiatrist D. L. Rosenhan, one would have to answer "no." In this study, eight sane people gained admission to twelve different psychiatric hospitals by falsely complaining that they had been hearing voices. Once admitted, however, they ceased to display any symptoms of abnormality. Yet all were treated as if they really were mentally ill and when discharged they were diagnosed as being "in remission." None of the doctors recognized that these individuals were "faking it"; only the real patients detected their sanity.[27]

Mental illness, then, is a form of deviant behavior only because people say it is. Any society can label any form of behavior "mental illness." If enough people accept the definition, all of those who fit within its boundaries will be considered mentally ill and will be shunned by other people.

Alcoholism

Alcoholism is also a form of noncriminal deviance and, just as with other forms of deviance, no one is sure how to count the number of alcoholics in our society. Indeed, no one is sure just what constitutes alcoholism, or at what point a person becomes an alcoholic. Is the wino derelict who consumes a fifth of muscatel every day any more of an alcoholic than the suburban housewife who must have three martinis every evening? Can we define an alcoholic in terms of the number of

What constitutes alcoholism? Is a "social drinker" any less of an alcoholic than a wino derelict?

drinks consumed? Is an alcoholic a person who *must* have a drink at least once a day? Alcoholics Anonymous, one of the most successful organizations in treating alcoholics, defines an alcoholic as a person whose drinking makes life unmanageable. That is, drinking interferes with that person's ability to function at work, at home, and in interpersonal relations. On the other hand, someone with very stern notions about liquor might well define an individual who has one beer before dinner as an alcoholic. Whose label do we accept?

These definitions of who is an alcoholic also vary with respect to an individual's social characteristics. We tend, for example, to "allow" men to drink more than women. Drinking is more permissible among the lower classes and the upper classes than the middle classes because middle-class people are more concerned with respectability. In addition, the definition of alcoholism has varied throughout history. At various times and in various places, alcoholism has been defined as a crime and under other circumstances as a sin. All this means, then, that alcoholism, like other forms of deviance, is not clearly definable. If enough people agree that it is deviant, then it will be viewed as deviant; if not, the label will disappear.

Drug Addiction

What has already been said about mental illness and alcoholism can be said about the use of drugs. Drugs have always been used by large segments of our population. Opium and heroin, for instance, were widely dispensed before 1914 as medicine by licensed doctors to bona fide patients. No one labeled people who took these drugs as "addicts." But in 1914 controls were placed on opium and heroin, and in 1937 marijuana was declared illegal. By the 1960s, the use of many other drugs, including amphetamines and barbiturates, was restricted thus making many people taking such substances "drug abusers." Why did the label change? The reasons are very complex and many have to do with economic and political factors, but perhaps the most significant reason was related to social class. As long as the use of drugs was confined to the lower and working classes, no one showed much concern. However, once drugs were used by middle-class youth, it sparked great fear within our society. As one coauthor has written in an earlier work:

> The fear of middle-class parents was not only that their children were becoming addicted but also that they were becoming like "those people"—the criminals and degenerates they had come to associate with drugs. The image of an entire generation doped up and strung out in a hippie pad was a popular one in the journalistic accounts of the time and one that shook the souls of many middle-aged Americans.[28]

In recent years sexual morality has been redefined to accept most behaviors between consenting adults. Homosexuality, however, is still considered deviant by many people.

Homosexuality

Certain sexual practices have also been labeled deviant in our society. In fact, almost any sexual practice that occurs outside of marriage and not for the purpose of reproduction is considered deviant by some portion of American society. In recent years, however, sexual morality has gradually been redefined. Today, sexual acts are less frequently rigidly defined as "right" or "wrong." The tendency presently is to accept many behaviors as long as they are between consenting adults, there is mutual respect, and no one is harmed. One outstanding exception to this is homosexuality.

Although the gay liberation movement has done a great deal to encourage gay people to "come out of the closet" and to make heterosexuals aware of homosexual life-styles, most people do not consider homosexuality as simply another sexual orientation. Homosexuality is still labeled "deviant." Throughout much of history, homosexuality has been labeled as a sin, as a crime, or as a sickness. The question is: Why has this particular sexual orientation antagonized people to such an extent?

One reason can be traced back to the Judeo-Christian tradition, which stresses sexual acts as legitimate only within marriage and for the purpose of producing children. Homosexuality, of course, does not occur within marriage and is definitely not for reproductive purposes. It is, instead, sexual pleasure for its own sake and as such, it is incompatible with our traditional notions of marriage and the family. In addi-

495

tion, many people believe that sexual acts are legitimate only when they occur between two people of opposite sexes. Clearly, homosexuality does not fit this criterion. Thus, homosexuality is labeled immoral, dysfunctional, and downright dangerous to society. Many, for example, fear that homosexual teachers will corrupt their children or that homosexual police officers will not command respect. Of course, given the concern with the world population explosion, one could make the case that homosexuality is actually functional since children do not result from homosexual unions. But many do not accept this view and continue to label homosexuality as deviance.

In summary, all the forms of noncriminal deviance we have discussed—mental illness, alcoholism, drug abuse, and homosexuality—are not in any sense "naturally" deviant. These behaviors are deviant merely because people have labeled them as such. But labels can and do change.

In order for change to occur, it must be caused by some force in society. How do deviant acts affect society? What functions or dysfunctions does deviance have? These questions will be answered in the next section.

The Functions and Dysfunctions of Deviance

When we think of deviance we tend to think of it as disruptive to society. The word itself conjures up images of muggings, drunkenness, prostitution, child abuse, and so on. None of these evokes very pleasant images. However, deviance also serves some positive functions for society. In this section, we will look at the more easily recognized dysfunctions and at the less easily understood positive effects deviance can have.

DYSFUNCTIONS OF DEVIANCE

The disruptive effects of deviance on a society can be seen in relation to the society's size and complexity. If one member in a small community that depends on fishing deliberately destroys a day's catch, the negative effects on the entire group could be disastrous. On the other hand, large complex societies, such as the United States, can tolerate a relatively high rate of deviance with little effect on the society as a whole. However, if deviance rates rise suddenly or if the high rate continues for a long time, deviance becomes dysfunctional in several ways.

APPLYING SOCIOLOGY

We mentioned earlier in this chapter that almost any kind of behavior is defined as deviant by at least one group. Even the following have been defined as deviant: being fat, wearing glasses, being single, going for psychotherapy, driving a motorcycle, and being childless. Do you agree that these are deviant behaviors? What norms are being violated by each?

One way in which deviance is disruptive is that it can cause members of the society to wonder why they should conform to the rules when others are "getting away with it." For example, when students see other students cheating on exams without the teacher noticing, they begin to question their own reasons for being honest. One dysfunction of deviance, then, is that it weakens people's adherence to the societal norms. If others can escape punishment for deviance, what is the point of conforming?

A second dysfunction of widespread, continual deviance is that it interferes with the smooth running of society. In Chapter 3 we noted that Durkheim described complex societies as characterized by organic solidarity. That is, each member has a specialized role in the society and therefore people become dependent on each other for the necessities of life. If members fail to fulfill their obligations or if they do their work poorly, cooperation will be destroyed. If carried to an extreme, society could become chaotic. For example, if there should ever be a general strike involving hundreds of thousands of workers, the effects on business, government, our social relationships, and even international relations would be disastrous. Thus, for society to be efficient, the members must assume responsibility for their part in its operation.

A third dysfunction of deviance is that it can arouse fear and distrust among the members of a society. For example, "crime in the streets" evokes tremendous fear in Americans and destroys the underlying harmony in our society. That is why there is so much pressure on police departments to protect us. Similarly, deviance on an impersonal level as in government, can cause citizens to question the government's honesty and competence. It leads people to believe that their elected and appointed governmental officials will not be responsive to their needs and choices, will not act in good faith on their behalf, and will not spend government money in beneficial ways. Consequently, as in the case of Watergate, it can take some people a long time to reestablish their belief and trust in government.

In short, deviance can have several dysfunctions, all of which can

have serious consequences for the society. At the same time, though, deviance can be beneficial to society in some ways as we will now see.

FUNCTIONS OF DEVIANCE

Durkheim was the first sociologist to point out that deviance serves positive functions for society. Since then other sociologists have expanded on this notion. Kai Erikson,[29] for example, noted that the stability of any group rests on a shared identity, a sense of "we-ness," and belonging together. And he believed that deviance helps promote this sense of belonging.

Erikson recognized that any group must draw moral and behavioral boundaries so that the members can identify who and what "belongs" to the group. One way in which to draw these boundaries is to exclude those persons who commit acts that violate the group's norms. In this manner, those who could harm the integrity of the group are controlled and, at the same time, the unity of the group is enhanced.

Thus, the first function of deviance is to bring nondeviant group members together. By recognizing that they share a common attitude toward the outsider and that they must take communal action to protect themselves against the intruder, they solidify the boundaries of their community. Those who are conforming also realize that conformity is rewarded and, hence, feel virtuous because they are not among the deviant group. In an indirect manner, then, deviance promotes social stability and cohesion when the main group reacts against the deviants.

A second function deviance fulfills is to clarify and highlight a society's norms. Frequently, social norms are poorly defined or vague, and it is not until they are broken that people become aware that they exist and require clarification and/or enforcement. For example, in most of the fifty states there have always been "blue laws," one of which forbids business transactions on Sundays. For decades no one paid much attention to such laws. Then, retail stores began to stay open on Sundays. This aroused attention and the "blue laws" began to be stated explicitly and negative sanctions became stringent. Even today there is controversy in some cities or states over the norm against conducting business on the Sabbath. Thus, deviance helps to make our mores and laws clearer and more concise.

The third function of deviance was also noted by Durkheim. He pointed out that rule-breakers promote change by showing others new ways of doing things and by helping to change the society's norms. To illustrate, during the black civil rights movement many people engaged in civil disobedience in an effort to prove that the "separate but equal" policy was wrong. Partially as a result of their behavior, many laws were changed and segregation by race became illegal.

Thus, deviance has some positive as well as negative consequences. Nevertheless, it is necessary to control deviance to make sure the majority of people conform to group norms, otherwise we would have social chaos. This is usually accomplished through various forms of social control.

Social Control

Social control can be defined as any mechanism used to encourage conformity and discourage deviation from social rules or acceptable patterns of behavior. Wherever deviance is found in society, there are always social control mechanisms. In general, these mechanisms can be classified as informal and formal and may involve either positive or negative sanctions.

INFORMAL AND FORMAL CONTROL

Although all people deviate from norms at some time in their lives, most people conform to most norms most of the time. In large part, they do so because they believe such behavior is proper. Perhaps more important, though, they have internalized the norms of the soci-

The application of positive sanctions—praise, a gesture, or other signs of approval—is a form of informal control.

ety during socialization and do not perceive any alternatives (see Chapters 4 and 5).

The internalization of the group's norms is part of *informal control* and involves the application of both positive and negative sanctions. *Positive sanctions* are essentially rewards whereby the individual is praised for engaging in behaviors considered appropriate or desirable. Informal positive sanctions can consist of such signs of approval as a word of praise, a "loving" look, or acceptance by some group. These actions function to encourage conformity and repetition of the behavior that won the approval.

In contrast, behavior that others consider wrong or harmful may elicit *negative sanctions*—punishments such as ridicule, withdrawal of affection, frowns, or even physical attacks. These informal tactics operate to curb deviations not only by deterring the person from engaging in that conduct again, but also by showing the offender that other types of conduct are more desirable.

Informal control can be carried out by any person, but usually people are controlled informally by family members, friends, or associates. Strangers can convey a sense of disapproval or approval, but intimates seem to have a greater impact on an individual's behavior.

In all human societies, people are subjected to the praise and rebuke of others throughout their lives. Since conformity to, rather than deviation from, group norms is the rule, it would seem that informal mechanisms of control work quite effectively. Yet informal control mechanisms are not always successful and formal control mechanisms must be used when people insist on ignoring the society's norms.

Formal control is appropriate when informal techniques have proved ineffective or inadequate or when society seeks to suppress the

Formal control is needed when informal techniques are ineffective or inadequate. Incarceration is a negative sanction through which formal control is achieved.

behavior of a particular person or group. These mechanisms of control are carried out by authorized agents such as the police, the courts, psychiatrists, or teachers.

As is the case with informal control mechanisms, formal control can occur through either positive or negative sanctions. Positive sanctions can take the form of awards such as the Nobel Prize, the Heisman Trophy, or medals for performance. Negative sanctions, which occur more frequently, can take the form of punishment, arrest, incarceration, hospitalization, or rehabilitative therapy. Presently, there is a general movement toward the use of therapy to treat or cure deviators. At the same time, though, there has been an outcry for more stringent pressures concerning habitual offenders. For example, the push for capital punishment is very strong in several states.

THE PARADOX OF SOCIAL CONTROL

Social control mechanisms supposedly exist to curb deviant forms of behavior and to encourage desired conduct. Children are praised, reasoned with, spanked, or scolded to teach them how to behave in accordance with societal norms. Once in school, they are praised for performing well and thus are encouraged to strive even harder. The members of peer groups are laughed at or teased in order to make them conform to the group's informal codes. Military cadets are subjected to expulsion for cheating, not only to prevent such behavior, but also to instill in them values of honesty and integrity. Criminals are punished not only to inflict harm on those who have harmed others, but also to demonstrate to the public what will happen to those who stray from the "straight and narrow."

Undoubtedly any mechanism of control may have a variety of effects on those who experience it.[30] Punishing a person for deviating from group norms may operate to deter the person from ever committing the offensive act again. Or the punishment may have no impact whatsoever. Some sociologists have even suggested that, at least in some cases, negative societal reaction may actually operate to push individuals further into deviance. For example, it has been reported that in 1971, about 85 percent of the offenders admitted to prisons and reformatories in Massachusetts had served time previously.[31] This leads us to believe that prisons might not be doing the job for which they were designed. Of course this research is by no means conclusive, and many still believe that stricter penalties will help deter crime.[32] But the idea that negative reaction to an offender might produce further deviation has received a good deal of attention in recent years, in part because it is contrary to the whole idea of social control as it has been practiced for centuries.

501

There are a number of reasons why subjecting a person to negative social control, especially by imprisoning the individual and requiring that he or she interact with other offenders, can foster further deviation. Simply associating with other outcasts can increase the possibility that a person will learn to deviate further. But negative reaction may also generate additional deviation in a more indirect and obscure way. As sociologist Frank Tannenbaum[33] has suggested, societal reaction to deviance can "dramatize the evil" of a norm-breaker's conduct. This occurs because the person's behavior is made a public issue and the offender is held up as a public symbol of evil. The problem Tannenbaum noted, however, was that the harder society works to reform the evil, the more it seems to grow.

Thus it seems that deviance is a pervasive part of human society. Perhaps, though, if our society can come up with some real solutions to various problems, there will be less reason to single out people as deviants. For example, if the causes of drug addiction or alcoholism were discerned and dealt with before people harmed themselves and others, there might be less reason to call those afflicted "deviants." Similarly, if people were educated to accept homosexuality they might be less likely to label gays as different. Hence, social change and acceptance of it may eventually result in the relabeling of some deviance as normal.

SUMMARY

Deviance can be defined as a social phenomenon resulting from negative societal reaction toward persons who are believed to have violated a group norm. Many sociologists—those taking the *labeling perspective*—believe that no behavior in and of itself is deviant. Rather, they feel that a behavior is deviant only if the members of a society label it as such.

Throughout history there have been various explanations for deviant behavior. Those taking the biological approach attribute deviance to an innate biological or physical characteristic in the person. In contrast, many adhering to psychological explanations believe that the causes of deviance are rooted in personality. Sociologists tend to suggest that social forces—the social environment and socialization—account for deviant behavior.

The amount of criminal deviance in our country is measured primarily by the Federal Bureau of Investigation (FBI). However, the statistics that are published tend to underestimate the rate of crime. Many people do not report crimes, white-collar crimes are not indexed, and certain types of crimes are not considered crimes at all and are excluded from the FBI statistics. Major types of criminal deviance that plague our society include white-collar crime, juvenile delinquency, crimes without victims, and organized crime.

Whereas criminal deviance can be easily identified because the norms that are violated are written down, noncriminal deviance is determined only through labeling. As a result, what is considered normal in one society is regarded as deviant in another. In our society mental illness, alcoholism, drug addiction, and homosexuality are considered to be major forms of noncriminal deviance.

Deviance is both functional and dysfunctional to a society. The more obvious dysfunctions are that it weakens people's adherence to societal norms, it interferes with the smooth running of a society, and it can arouse fear and distrust among the members of a society. On the positive side, deviance brings nondeviant group members together, it classifies and highlights a society's norms, and it promotes social change.

Social control can be defined as any mechanism used to encourage conformity and discourage deviation from social rules or acceptable patterns of behavior. Mechanisms for social control can be either informal or formal and can involve both positive and negative sanctions. Despite methods of social control, though, deviance is a pervasive part of human society.

GLOSSARY

anomie   a state of normlessness; the absence of group norms.

atavist   according to Lombroso, a distinct type of subhuman who has not progressed up the chain of evolution.

crimes without victims   crimes such as vagrancy, prostitution, and gambling in which no one suffers except perhaps the victim.

deviance   a socially created phenomenon resulting from negative societal reaction toward persons who are believed to have violated a group rule.

ectomorphs   according to Sheldon, those individuals who are thin and delicate.

endomorphs   according to Sheldon, those individuals with round, soft bodies.

formal control   a type of social control carried out by such authorized agents as the police, the courts, psychiatrists, or teachers.

informal control   a type of social control that usually is handled by family members, friends, or associates.

innovation   according to Merton, a deviant alternative that occurs when a person accepts a goal, but for one reason or another is prevented from attaining it.

labeling perspective sociological approach following the belief that no behavior in and of itself is deviant; rather, deviant behavior is labeled as such by others.

mesomorphs according to Sheldon, those individuals with square, hard bodies.

negative sanctions punishments by which an individual is thought to be deterred from engaging in deviant conduct.

organized crime a network of syndicates that provide such illegal goods and services as drugs, loan sharking, and prostitution to those willing to pay high prices for them.

positive sanctions rewards whereby an individual is praised for engaging in behaviors considered appropriate or desirable.

rebellion according to Merton, a deviant alternative that occurs when a person rejects the accepted goals and means and substitutes new ones in their place.

retreatism according to Merton, a deviant alternative that occurs when a person accepts neither the goals nor the means for attaining them, and in effect drops out of society.

ritualism according to Merton, a deviant alternative that occurs when a person is more concerned with the means—sticking to the rules—than the goals.

social control any mechanism used to encourage conformity and discourage deviation from social rules or acceptable patterns of behavior.

theory of differential association a theory proposed by Sutherland suggesting that deviant behavior is learned through interaction with others, particularly within intimate personal groups.

white-collar crime term used to describe certain types of offenses such as fraud, bribery, false advertising, and price-fixing committed by members of the middle and upper classes in the course of their jobs.

REFERENCES

1. J. L. Simmons, *Deviants.* Berkeley, Calif.: The Glendessary Press, 1969, p. 3.

2. A number of these investigations are summarized in Don C. Gibbons and Joseph F. Jones, *The Study of Deviance.* Englewood Cliffs, N.J.: Prentice-Hall, 1975, pp. 67–72.

3. Howard Becker, *Outsiders: Studies in the Sociology of Deviance.* New York: The Free Press, 1963, p. 9.

4. Kai T. Erikson, *Wayward Puritans.* New York: John Wiley & Sons, 1966, p. 6.

5. Cesare Lombroso, *Crime: Its Causes and Remedies.* Boston: Little, Brown, 1911.

6. Charles Goring, *The English Convict.* London: His Majesty's Stationery Office, 1913.

7. William J. Sheldon, S. S. Stevens, and W. B. Tucker, *Varieties of Delinquent Youth*. New York: Harper & Row, 1949.

8. Sheldon and Eleanor Glueck, *Unraveling Juvenile Delinquency*. New York: Commonwealth Fund, 1950.

9. Richard Fox, "The XYY Offender: A Modern Myth?" *Journal of Criminal Law, Criminology, and Police Science* 62(March-April 1971): 59–73. Also see Herman A. Witkin, et al., "Criminality in XYY and XXY Men." *Science* 193 (August 13, 1976): 547–555.

10. See G. G. Heath, et al., "Behavioral Changes in Nonpsychotic Volunteers Following the Administration of Taraxein, the Substance Extracted from the Serum of Schizophrenic Patients." *American Journal of Psychiatry* 114 (1958): 917–920.

11. Sigmund Freud, *Civilization and Its Discontents*. Trans. and ed. By A. A. Brill. New York: The Modern Library, 1938.

12. Émile Durkheim, *The Rules of Sociological Method*. Trans. and ed. by Sarah A. Solovay and John H. Mueller and ed. by George E. Gatlin. New York: The Free Press, 1964.

13. Robert K. Merton, *Social Theory and Social Structure*. New York: The Free Press, 1956.

14. Albert K. Cohen, *Delinquent Boys*. New York: The Free Press, 1955.

15. Edwin H. Sutherland and Donald R. Cressey, *Criminology*. 9th ed. Philadelphia: Lippincott, 1974, pp. 75–76.

16. Becker, pp. 40–58.

17. A. D. Biderman, "Surveys of Population Samples for Estimating Crime." *Annals of the Academy of Political and Social Science* 84 (November 1967); The President's Commission on Law Enforcement and Administration of Justice, *The Challenge of Crime in a Free Society*. Washington, D.C.: U. S. Government Printing Office, 1967.

18. "The Losing Battle Against Crime in America." *U.S. News & World Report*, December 16, 1974, p. 36.

19. Stuart L. Hill, *Crime, Power, and Morality*. Scranton, Pa.: Chandler, 1971.

20. "All Kinds of Crime—Growing, Growing, Growing." *U.S. News & World Report*, December 16, 1974, pp. 33–34.

21. "Total Arrest Trends by Sex—1974–75."*The World Almanac and Book of Facts 1977*. New York: Newspaper Enterprise Association, Inc., 1977, p. 967.

22. Edwin M. Schur, *Crimes Without Victims—Deviant Behavior and Public Policy*. Englewood Cliffs, N. J.: Prentice-Hall, 1965.

23. In S. Kadish, "The Crises of Overcriminalization." *The Annals* (November 1967): 161–162.

24. "The Losing Battle Against Crime in America," p. 39; Donald R. Cressey, *Theft of the Nation*. New York: Harper & Row, 1969.

25. Robert Coles, "A Fashionable Kind of Slander." *Atlantic*, vol. 226, no. 5, November 1970, p. 54.

505

26. Jack P. Gibbs, "Rates of Mental Hospitalization." *American Sociological Review* 27 (December 1962): 782–792.

27. D. L. Rosenhan, "On Being Sane in Insane Places." *Science* 179 (1973): 250–258.

28. Clayton A. Hartjen, *Possible Trouble.* New York: Praeger, 1977, p. 90.

29. Kai T. Erikson, "Notes on the Sociology of Deviance." In Earl Rubington and Martin S. Weinberg, *Deviance: The Interactionist Perspective*, 2nd. ed. New York: Macmillan, 1973, pp. 26–30.

30. Gibbons and Jones, pp. 143–170.

31. Sutherland and Cressey, p. 608.

32. Gordon Tullock, "Does Punishment Deter Crime?" *The Public Interest* (Summer 1974): 109.

33. Frank Tannenbaum, *Crime and the Community.* New York: Columbia University Press, 1938, pp. 19–20.

SUGGESTED READINGS

Akers, Ronald L. *Deviant Behavior: A Social Learning Approach*, 2nd. ed. Belmont, Calif.: Wadsworth, 1977.

An in-depth discussion of the learning approach and its relevance to understanding deviant behavior. It also offers good summaries of the major ideas regarding different kinds of deviance.

Becker, Howard S. *Outsiders: Studies in the Sociology of Deviance.* New York: The Free Press, 1963.

One of the first major statements of the labeling view of deviance, offering both a classic statement of this perspective and stimulating reading on deviant phenomena ranging from a discussion of jazz musicians to the origins of antimarijuana legislation.

Cohen, Albert K. *Deviance and Control.* Englewood Cliffs, N.J.: Prentice-Hall, 1966.

A study of the field of deviance and an attempt to construct a broad theory of deviant behavior that concerns both its occurrence and the different forms it takes.

Gibbons, Don C. and Joseph F. Jones. *The Study of Deviance.* Englewood Cliffs, N.J.: Prentice-Hall, 1975.

A brief but inclusive analysis of the field of deviance and its dimensions and problems. The book offers a brief and easy-to-read discussion of what the sociology of deviance is all about.

Hartjen, Clayton A. *Crime and Criminalization*, 2nd ed. New York: Praeger, 1978.

A presentation of a conflict-labeling perspective of criminal phenomena ranging from the formulation of law, illegal behavior, the administration of justice, and corrections to the understanding of crime rates and the study of criminology.

Steffensmeier, Darrell J. and Robert M. Terry (eds.). *Examining Deviance Experimentally.* Sherman Oaks, Calif.: Alfred Publishers, 1975.

    A variety of readings on numerous kinds of deviant activity and on how they may be understood in a systematic manner.

Traub, Stuart H. and Craig B. Little (eds.). *Theories of Deviance.* Itasca, Illinois: Peacock, 1975.

    A presentation of the major theories of deviance available to sociologists as well as some of the controversies and policy issues involved in the study of deviance.

16

Population.
Urbanization.
and Ecology

In 1970 a leading advocate of the ecological movement, Paul R. Ehrlich, made the following prophecy:

> Millions of people are going to starve to death and soon. There is nothing that can be done to prevent it. They will die because of short-sighted government attitudes. They will die because some religious organizations have blocked attempts over the years to get governmental and United Nations action under way to control human birth rates. They will die because scientists have managed to persuade many influential people that a technological rabbit can always be pulled out of the hat to save mankind at the last moment. They will die because many people . . . who recognized the essential role of overpopulation in the increasing woes of *Homo sapiens,* could not bring themselves to leave the comforts of their daily routine to do something about it. Their blood will be distributed over many hands.[1]

Although the entire world has not yet fallen into the misery of being unable to feed its members, many people do go hungry each day, suffer from malnutrition, or simply are unable to enjoy the comforts that scientific advances and modern technology make available to many others. Clearly, overpopulation is a serious problem we all must face. In this chapter, we will focus on the study of population, examining the determinants of population size, composition, and distribution. We will also examine population growth, urbanization, and ecological problems that have occurred as a result of population growth. We will conclude the chapter with a look at the population situation in our own country.

Despite scientific advances and modern technology, millions of people, especially those in Third-World nations, do not get enough to eat. Here residents of Dacca, Bangladesh, beg for food.

Demography: The Study of Population

Sociologists have always regarded the study of population as an essential topic of the discipline. They have discovered that the size of a group, its standard of living, and its culture and social system are all interrelated. Sociologists who study population are known as *demographers*. Their area of interest and concern is known as *demography*, which is the study of the size, composition, and distribution of human populations.

Before we can fully understand this definition, we must first define each of the component terms. What do we mean by population, size, composition, and distribution?

Demographers define a *population* as an aggregate of people who share at least one specific characteristic. Although just about any characteristic can be used, residence in a given territory, such as a country, is the most commonly used measure among social scientists. Still, a population can also be all the red-haired people in the world, or all those over six feet tall. For most purposes, however, residence is the most important factor.

Size usually refers to the number of people who live in a certain area. Hence, the size of the "American" population can be determined by counting the number of people in the fifty states, the District of Columbia, Puerto Rico, and the nation's territories. The United States Census Bureau does just that every ten years.

The *composition* of a population refers to the social and physical traits of the individuals within it. These traits include age, sex, race, occupation, education, income, and a number of other factors. The *distribution* of a population is the spatial arrangement of its members. Basically, distribution has to do with geographical area, the type of community (for example, farm, city, or suburb), and density of settlement (the number of people per square mile).

Now that we are familiar with the necessary terms, we can study population as a demographer would. Let us now examine in detail each of the three areas of concern—the size, composition, and distribution of human populations.

DETERMINANTS OF POPULATION SIZE

Three factors directly affect population size: births, deaths, and migration. Changes in one or more of these factors will result in an increase or decrease in the size of the population. These factors, in turn, are strongly influenced by cultural, social, economic, and biological variables.

The distribution of a population refers to the spatial arrangement of its members. This section of Queens, a borough of New York City, can be considered densely populated.

Birth Rate

One of the more important determinants of population size is the birth rate or fertility of a people. *Fertility* refers to the *actual* number of children a woman gives birth to during her childbearing years. We must be careful not to confuse this concept with *fecundity*, which refers to the *potential* number of births biologically possible. To illustrate, whereas women are capable of bearing about twenty children during their reproductive lives (fecundity), in no society does fertility approach this figure. Consequently, fertility is not simply a result of biological factors. People have more or fewer children because of the social and economic forces that affect their behavior, not because of their biological capacity.

What are some of these social and economic forces? For one thing, marriage customs can alter the birth rate in either direction. For example, a population can lower its fertility rate by simply encouraging the postponement of marriage. In contrast, societies can encourage fertility by lowering the age requirement for marriage. Societies can also subsidize young couples by such customs as giving large monetary gifts to newlyweds, or by generous college loans or grants, thus allowing unemployed people to marry.

Sexual norms also operate to raise or lower birth rates. In many societies, for example, there are taboos against sexual intercourse if a woman is menstruating or nursing a child. Since women in preliterate societies tend to nurse children for as long as two or three years, this taboo acts as a natural birth control device that helps to keep the population small and helps to ensure the survival of the nursing child. It also contributes to the health of the mother by reducing the frequency of reproduction and the physical strains of excessive childbearing.

In some societies premarital sexual intercourse is permitted or even encouraged, thus raising the birth rate. As anthropologist Bronislaw Malinowski reported, in the Trobriand Islands, marriages were arranged after conception had occurred.[2] Sociologist Harold Christensen noted that in modern Denmark premarital pregnancy is not negatively sanctioned, and Danes are more likely than Americans to bear out-of-wedlock children, thus contributing to a rising birth rate.[3]

The use of contraception and abortion are other means of controlling fertility. When societies want to curb fertility, they may distribute free contraceptive devices and encourage abortion. For example, between 1945 and 1965, Japan reduced its fertility rate by more than 50 percent, largely because it instituted a national policy that legalized abortion and encouraged the use of contraceptive devices. On the other hand, if a society wants to raise the birth rate it may prohibit the use of these birth control methods. For example, in 1974 the government of

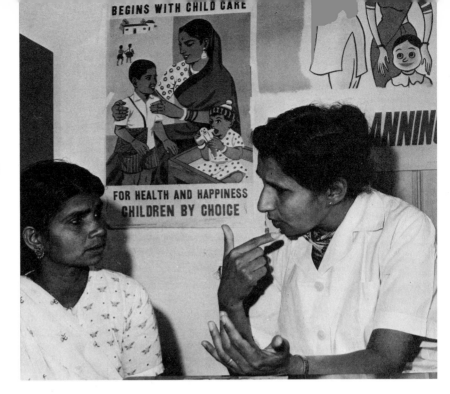

One means of controlling fertility is through the use of contraceptives, which are often dispensed through family planning centers such as this one in India.

Argentina prohibited the use of contraception in order to increase its numbers and consequently gain economic strength.

Nevertheless, contraception and abortion exist even in societies where the norms of the culture strongly condemn them. To illustrate, although abortion was illegal in this country until 1973, when the Supreme Court overruled state laws prohibiting it, abortion was widely practiced throughout the nation. Actually, abortion is thought to have been very common throughout history all over the world.

In general, we can say that cultural attitudes toward sex and children determine the rate of fertility. If societies do not want large families, in most cases they are likely to restrict reproduction in one way or another. If large families are valued, societies will encourage reproduction. We can see that this has been the case throughout the world. In most developing countries, for example, people cannot rely on Social Security or pensions to provide for them in old age. Consequently, they expect to be cared for by their children, and usually are, so they try to have as many children as possible. In addition, in most nonindustrial societies children are considered economic assets, working a dairy farm, assisting in the field, and so on. The attitude in these societies, then, is the more children the better. Also, the fact that many of the children may not survive to adulthood further encourages people to have a high number of offspring.

Even in societies in which children are considered economic liabilities, they may be desired for prestige. Women in ancient China, for example, wanted children because having many children, especially sons, increased the woman's status in the household. A study in Puerto Rico in the 1950s found that while women desired fewer children, their husbands preferred large families because children are viewed as proof of virility. Unfortunately for the Puerto Rican woman, at the time this study was done, the man ruled the house and she had little to say about how many children she might have.[4] This seems, however, to be changing somewhat in recent years, since it appears that Puerto Rico has reduced its rate of fertility.

Throughout this section we have been discussing factors that affect fertility rates. One problem we have yet to consider, though, is how demographers measure such rates.

The *crude birth rate* is the most commonly used measure of fertility. This measure tells us how many children are being born for every thousand people in a country over a certain period of time. It should be noted that this rate varies dramatically from country to country. For example, in 1976, Panama had a crude birth rate of 32.2 and West Germany had a crude birth rate of 9.8. Table 16-1 presents the crude birth rates of selected countries.

TABLE 16-1
Crude Birth Rates for Selected Countries (Per 1,000 population), 1970 and 1976

Country	Birth Rate	
	1976	*1970*
Australia	16.7	20.6
Austria	11.6	15.2
Belgium	12.3	14.7
Czechoslovakia	19.2	15.9
Denmark	12.9	14.4
Finland	14.1	14.0
France	13.6	16.8
Germany, West	9.8	13.4
Greece	15.7	16.5
Ireland	21.6	21.8
Israel	28.1	26.9
Italy	14.0	16.8
Japan	16.4	18.9
Luxembourg	10.9	13.2
Panama	32.2	37.2
Sweden	11.9	13.7
Switzerland	12.0	15.8
United Kingdom	12.1	16.3
United States	14.7	18.3

Source: Statistical Office of the United Nations.

**TABLE 16–2
Crude Birth Rate of the
United States,
1960–1972**

| | Crude Birth Rate | |
Year	White	Nonwhite
1960	22.7	32.1
1962	21.4	30.5
1964	20.0	29.2
1966	17.4	26.1
1968	16.6	24.2
1970	17.4	25.1
1972	14.6	22.9

Source: U.S. Department of Health, Education and Welfare, *Vital Statistics of the United States, 1973, Vol. 1—Nativity* (Washington, D. C.: U.S. Government Printing Office), pp.1–5.

The crude birth rates of certain groups within a country can also be measured. Table 16-2 gives the crude birth rates of the white and nonwhite populations in the United States from 1960 to 1972. As we can see, the nonwhite birth rates are generally higher than white rates. Both, however, show downward trends, with the nonwhite rate declining faster on the average than the white rate (approximately 1.72 per every two years compared to 1.44).

Given the previous discussion, it would seem that a population will increase in size if its birth rate increases and will decline in size as the birth rate declines. Yet, even though the birth rate is declining throughout much of the world, the populations of almost all nations are growing. How does this happen?

Death Rate

A population's size is influenced not only by the number of children added each year through fertility. How large a population is and how fast it grows or shrinks in size are also affected by the number of people who die each year. In general, a population will remain stable in size if it produces the same number of babies each year to replace those individuals who die. When fertility is equal to mortality (assuming there is no migration), a country will have a *zero population growth rate.*

Like fertility, mortality can be greatly affected by a number of factors that determine if people will survive to old age or not. These include nutrition, famine, medical technology, and living and working conditions. Because of variations in these factors, wide differences exist in mortality rates among different countries.

There are a number of ways to measure the rate of mortality in any society. The *crude death rate* is similar to the crude birth rate in that it measures the number of deaths per thousand living persons in a given population over a given period of time. This is the measure most commonly used to compare the mortality of different populations.

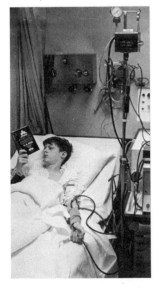

Advances in medical technology are prolonging lives that could not have been saved years ago, contributing to declining mortality rates.

515

TABLE 16–3
Crude Death Rates for Selected Countries (Per 1,000 population), 1970 and 1976

Country	Death Rate	
	1976	1970
Australia	8.3	9.0
Austria	12.6	13.4
Belgium	12.1	12.3
Czechoslovakia	11.4	11.6
Denmark	10.7	9.8
Finland	9.4	9.6
France	10.5	10.7
Germany, West	11.9	12.1
Greece	8.2	8.4
Ireland	10.5	11.4
Israel	6.9	7.1
Italy	9.7	9.7
Japan	6.3	6.9
Luxembourg	12.6	12.3
Sweden	11.0	9.9
Switzerland	8.8	9.1
United Kingdom	14.2	11.8
United States	8.9	9.4

Source: Statistical Office of the United Nations.

Table 16-3 shows the crude death rates for selected countries throughout the world.

Another important measure of mortality is the *infant mortality rate*. This measure is determined by dividing the number of infants under one year of age who die in a given year per thousand live births for that year. The infant mortality rate has many uses, but it is especially important when we want to compare industrialized with nonindustrialized societies. Even though infant mortality has declined throughout the world, babies are still much more likely to die before they are one year of age in less developed countries than they are in more developed ones. In less developed countries, infant mortality ranges from 50 to 250 deaths per thousand live births, whereas in more developed nations it is usually around 25 deaths per thousand live births. In some of these less developed countries, the rate of infant mortality may be so high that, coupled with the death rate of all other people at all ages, it may cause the population to shrink in size.

One concept that is closely related to the death rate of a society is *life expectancy*. This term refers to the average number of years that members of a population can expect to live, given the conditions of a society. We must be careful not to confuse this concept with *life span*, which refers to the maximum number of years that it is biologically possible for people to live. For example, although it may be theoretically possible for people to live to be one hundred years of age (life span), the life expectancy for a given society may only be sixty-five.

516

Common sense tells us that the life span of human beings is not increasing. In other words, people are not living to be two hundred years old. Rather, more people are living *to be* old. For example, at the turn of the century in the United States over one-half of the population died before they were forty-five years old. Today, however, less than one-sixth die by that age. Over one-half of the people presently survive to at least sixty-five years of age. In contrast, in 1900 only one-quarter of the people lived to be sixty-five years old. Thus life expectancy in our society has increased.

Although the life expectancy of a particular society may increase or decrease, it does not necessarily mean that all members will live to the designated age. In some societies, life expectancy may be very low simply because of the high infant mortality rate. But those individuals who survive infancy could very well live to old age. On the other hand, the residents of another country with a high life expectancy may not live any longer than the aged person in the society with a low life expectancy.

Migration Rate

In addition to fertility and mortality, *migration* also influences the size of a society's population. There are basically two types of migration—immigration and emigration. Whereas *immigration* refers to the movement of people into a country, *emigration* refers to the movement of people out of a country. Hence, immigration increases a country's population, while emigration decreases it.

Throughout history, migration has greatly affected the population size of different societies. For example, the mass of European immigrants who came to the United States since the beginning of the nineteenth century added nearly 70 million people to this nation's population. Similarly, the potato famines in Ireland during the 1800s forced people to emigrate to more promising lands, thus reducing Ireland's population.

Migration can also alter the composition of a nation. Present-day Great Britain is an example of a country that has been affected this way. Because of recent inward migrations of 2.5 million people born outside the British Isles and an outward migration of 3.1 million native-born English, 5.4 percent of Britain's population is now composed of foreign-born immigrants.[5]

In general, migration can take place under two conditions: *forced* or *free*. The 10 to 20 million black slaves who were forced to migrate to the New World comprised probably the largest forced migration in the world's history. Likewise, thousands of American Indians were forced to migrate internally in the United States when they were driven from their original homes to reservations. Migration can be forced in other ways, too. Many Europeans "freely" migrated to the New World because of adverse economic and political conditions in their homelands. Had they the choice, they would frequently have preferred to stay home. Many other people such as British convicts were forced to leave home to avoid threats of imprisonment.

Free migration occurs when people move because they feel they can achieve something they want in a new place. Many of the more privileged residents of less developed countries are moving to the more developed ones, not only because they cannot get a good education in their homelands, but also because they are likely to find greater social and economic rewards in the countries to which they migrate.

It is difficult to say precisely what consequences migration has for the receiving and sending populations besides its effect on population size. We can, however, make some observations. Since many of the migrants tend to be males, migration surely influences the sex composition of a country, but this differs greatly from one case to another. Also, migrants often fill the undesirable jobs in the host country and reduce unemployment rates in the countries they leave. In addition, immigrants contribute their ideas, customs, and knowledge to their new country's culture, thus providing for cultural diversity. If we look at our own society, we will note that this indeed has been the case. Conversely, those leaving a country often deprive that nation of valuable contributions. Other than these effects, though, the exact consequences of migration cannot be determined.

DETERMINANTS OF POPULATION COMPOSITION

The second area with which demographers are concerned is the composition of a population. Demographers measure the composition of a population by counting the number of individuals in it who share certain biological or social traits, such as sex, race, ethnic background, age, education, and occupation.

A society's population composition is important for a number of reasons. First, the composition characteristics of a country or community are immediately relevant to government and industry. By knowing the age distribution of a country or state, for example, government can plan for public facilities such as schools and parks, housing, Social Security benefits, employment opportunities, and the like. In a similar way, industry relies on population data to make decisions concerning business expenditures and employment probabilities. If, for example, a large segment of the population is between fifteen and nineteen years of age, industry can allocate a certain proportion of its resources to cater to the needs and desires of that age group.

Second, information about composition gives us clues to the character and health of a society and enables social scientists to predict what may happen to a society in the near future. The income distribution, for example, reveals the economic stratification structure of a country. Countries differ greatly in the way income is distributed, so that in some countries almost everyone gets an equal share while in others income is concentrated in the hands of a few. In the same way, employment statistics tell social scientists something about a country's economic health. And the sex and age structures of a society are closely related to its rate of population growth. These two areas are of particular concern to demographers.

Sex Ratio

The sex composition of a population is measured by its *sex ratio*. This ratio is the proportion of males to females in a society. It is calculated by counting the number of males per every hundred females. A sex ratio of 100 means that there are an equal number of males and females. A figure greater than 100 means there are more males than females and one lower than 100 indicates that there are more females than males.

What implications does the sex ratio have for a country? For one thing, it theoretically tells us the chances of marriage for men and women. For example, in the United States in 1910 the sex ratio was 106 while in 1970 it had dropped to 95. Therefore, in 1910, women theoretically had a greater chance of marrying than they did in 1970, since there were six extra males, on the average, for every one hundred females. In 1970, five out of every hundred females should have been unable to marry because there were fewer men than women.

The sex ratio also tells us that even though more boy babies are born each year than girl babies, by old age there are considerably more females than males. This fact appears to be universal in all societies. Why is this so? It is because the mortality rate for females is less than that for males although the rates for both have decreased in the United States during the twentieth century. In 1970 the mortality rate for males was 10.8 per thousand and for females it was 8.0 per thousand.

The migration pattern also affects the sex ratio. As you have seen, males are more likely to migrate in large numbers. Therefore if a country increases its immigration to the point where more people enter the country than leave, it is likely the number of males per females will increase. This is precisely what happened in the United States during the pioneer days. Women were so scarce on the frontier that men frequently had to advertise for brides and pay for their transportation to the new home.

Age Composition

Can the population of one society be younger or older than the population of another? It surely can. The "age" of a population is mea-

FIGURE 16-1
The Age Structure of
the United States by
Sex: 1900 and 1970*

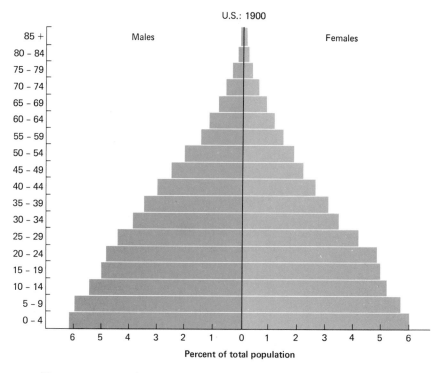

sured by computing the *median age* of all its members. The median age
is that age which divides the population exactly in half so that one-half
of the people are older than the median and one-half are younger. For
example, if there were ten people in a group, aged 2, 4, 6, 8, 10, 12, 14,
16, 18, and 20, the median age of the group would be 11 because one-
half the members are under 11 and one-half are over 11. A *young population* is one that has a low median age and a high proportion of young
people. An *old population* is one that has a high median age and a high
proportion of old people.

Differences and changes in the age and sex composition of various
societies can be seen when we compare their population pyramids. Figure 16-1 shows the population pyramids of the United States in 1900
and 1970. What differences occurred in the age composition of our
country during those seventy years? As we can see, the population
grew older—its median age increased and the proportion of younger
people decreased. Many European countries have populations even
older than that of the United States. Their population structures show
an almost equal number of people in each age bracket. In contrast, most
of the less developed countries today have population pyramids re-
sembling that of the United States before the turn of the century because of their high birth and death rates.

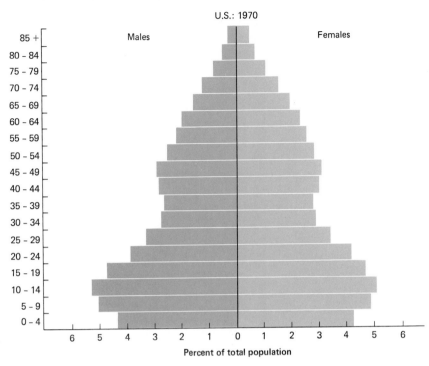

U.S.: 1970

Source: Charles F. Westoff, "The Populations of the Developed Countries," in *The Human Population*. A Scientific American Book, (San Francisco: W.H. Freeman, 1974), p., 74.

What effects might age composition characteristics have on a society? In recent years demographers have increasingly become interested in age composition as an important influence on a society's future growth and economic development. Among the two most important implications of age composition are its impact on *dependency* and *fertility*.

Dependency refers to the act of relying on others for survival. In every country some portion of the population is dependent on other members of the society. But the extent of dependency that exists in a country has consequences for the economic well-being of that nation. If, for example, a country has a large number of dependents, the people who support them must work harder simply to care for the unproductive.

One way to measure a population's dependency is by the *dependency ratio*, which can be calculated in several different ways. One common way is to divide the number of people over age 65 and under age 15 (nonworkers) by the number of people between the ages of 15 and 64 (workers). The higher the ratio, the higher the proportion of dependents.

521

The age composition of a society has a great effect on the degree of dependency (the reliance of a person on others for survival) in that society. Young children and the elderly are especially likely to depend on others for survival.

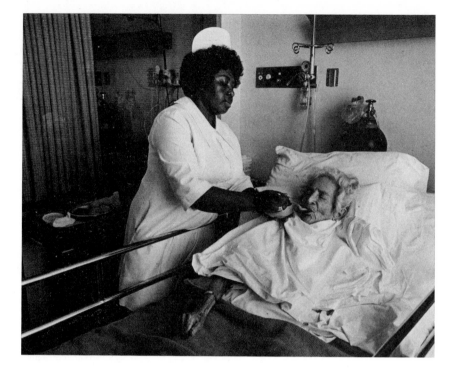

Most developing countries, which tend to have young populations, tend to have high dependency ratios. In 1960, for example, Honduras had a dependency ratio of 1.00, which means that for every person capable of working there was one person who needed support. In that country almost one-half of the population was below the age of 15. West Germany, on the other hand, had a dependency ratio of 0.47; there were approximately two workers to support every dependent. Less than one-fourth of West Germany's population was below age 15 in that year.[6] In the United States, as far as age distribution of the country is concerned, about 40 percent of the population is dependent. In other words, this percentage is under 15 or over 65 years of age. Therefore, the dependency ratio in the United States is about .60.

APPLYING SOCIOLOGY

Do you think this method for measuring the dependency ratio presents a true picture of the dependent population in our own country? Why or why not? What factors other than age might we use to get a more accurate picture of dependency? Do you think actual dependency is higher or lower than the .60 figure suggests?

The other implication of age composition concerns *fertility*. Young populations tend to have high fertility rates whereas old populations have low fertility rates. As a result, young populations tend to grow faster than old populations. Even if young populations actively try to reduce their birth rate, they have a built-in growth tendency. We can easily see why this is so. Since more women are of childbearing age, they are more likely to produce more babies. Their children, in turn, will reach reproductive age themselves and produce even more babies. Thus the population will continue to grow geometrically, even if each generation reduces its fertility considerably.

Countries with an old population, on the other hand, have a small proportion of women of childbearing age. These countries cannot grow very rapidly by natural increases even if fertility is increased. This implies that a population's age is responsible for a major portion of its growth rate. For the less developed countries, this is extremely significant since no matter how hard they try to reduce fertility their populations usually continue to grow because of their age compositions.

DETERMINANTS OF POPULATION DISTRIBUTION

The third area that demographers focus on is the distribution of a population. The major factors that have influenced population distribution are *geography* and *urbanization* and *industrialization*.

Geography

Although human beings can shape to some degree the environment to meet their own needs and desires, the environment still poses limits on individuals. As a result, the world's population has displayed a particular distribution pattern. People have been distributed over only part of the earth's surface area. Let us examine the physical makeup of our planet to see what we mean.

Water covers 71 percent of the earth's surface. Of the remaining 29 percent, more than one-third is desert and slightly less than one-third consists of mountains, marshes, and heavy forests. Thus, more than three-quarters of the earth's surface is basically uninhabitable. Consequently, most of the world's population lives and has lived on a relatively small portion of the earth's surface.

Despite the limited available area, people did not always live close together. Rather, they lived in rural communities that were separated by great distances. In fact, throughout the world today, the majority of people still live in rural areas, in relatively small villages, or on isolated farms. Yet urbanization has had a major impact on population distribution. And it is certain to have an even greater impact in the future.

523

Urbanization and Industrialization

The years between 1900 and 1950 were important for the United States because during that period the country became officially urbanized. That is, one-half of its population were counted as living in cities. Presently, all industrial nations are urbanized, and many less developed countries are rapidly changing from agrarian to urban societies.[7] Some observers estimate that over one-half of the world's population will be living in urban areas by the year 1990.[8] It is highly probable that the entire world will be urbanized by the early part of the twenty-first century.

Urbanization means that societies move from a type of community called *Gemeinschaft* to a type called *Gesellschaft*. These terms were first used in 1887 by German sociologist Ferdinand Tönnies. A *Gemeinschaft* is a small community in which social relationships are based on feelings of sentiment and unity and in which members behave in ways beneficial to the whole group. A *Gesellschaft* is a large community in which social relationships are impersonal, based on practicality and purpose rather than on emotional ties. The goals of the group become subordinate to the goals of the individuals. Many sociologists, in addition to Tönnies, have been concerned with this inevitable shift when societies become urbanized.

Paralleling this trend toward urbanization has been a move toward industrialization. As their technologies have developed, countries have turned to manufacturing for an economic base.

The effects of industrialization and the growth of cities on human life were many and complex and can be treated simultaneously. On the positive side, they increased the amount and variety of goods and services available to people, they increased people's wealth, and they brought many diverse peoples into intimate contact with one another. Consequently, dramatic changes in the composition of many populations occurred. Furthermore, industrialization and urbanization encouraged the development of the arts. Opera houses, theatres, art, music, television, literature, and the whole range of comforts and entertainments we enjoy today became possible only because of urbanization and the bringing together of large numbers of diverse peoples.

On the negative side, though, massive amounts of material resources are necessary to support these large numbers of people. Woods and forests were destroyed to provide housing for these people. Many of the rolling hills of Appalachia have been stripped of their beauty in the search for coal. Fish once filled the Hudson River and other rivers of the world. Today, few rivers can support any but the hardiest forms of life. The list of endangered species grows with each passing day. Industry and the city have brought increased pollution, street crime, traffic jams, hypertension, and other undesirable side-effects.

524

One of the greatest problems facing our world today—and a cause of many of these negative affects—is population growth. In the next section we will deal with this ever-pressing concern.

Population Growth

The fact that there are many more people in the world today (approximately 4 billion) than ever before and that the world's population is growing at a fast rate is undeniable. However, whether or not this is a cause for alarm, or what effects population size might have on human life, depends on how one views population growth. Some "doomsayers" like Rachel Carson and Paul and Anna Ehrlich have argued that the world's population is already so large and growing so fast that we will soon exhaust all the resources necessary for life.[9] Before long, they have argued, if present trends continue, there will be only one square foot of land available for each and every person on the earth. Life would be like living in a sardine can—if, indeed, anyone were still alive at all.

If the world growth rate continues at 2 percent per year, the total population of the world will double in 34.7 years. By the time that younger readers of this book have grandchildren, there will be over 8 billion people living on the earth, and that number will double again before they have great-grandchildren.

Most demographers hypothesize that this rate of growth has never occurred before in the world's history. Rather, before the first century A.D. populations grew at an average rate of .002 percent each year. Even since that time, the growth rate has been only .14 percent. Hence, they suggest that the population explosion is something new. That is, population grew at a slow steady rate until about 1750, when it began a sharp increase.

Other experts suggest that the world has actually experienced not one population explosion but three. The first occurred about 1 million years ago when human beings began to use tools. Tool-making greatly increased human hunting ability and food supply. Thus, societies at that time were able to support larger numbers of people. The second explosion took place with the development of agriculture, and the third was a result of the Industrial Revolution. In each case, the growth rate leveled off to a relatively gradual increase.[10] According to these social scientists, then, populations increase only when, and to the level where, they are able to support additional members.

Although this view is much less pessimistic than that of the "doomsayers," those holding this viewpoint do not deny that the world has experienced profound population growth. They also cannot deny some of the consequences that accompany growth. In the remainder of

525

The least developed nations of the world tend to have the highest rates of population growth and are most prone to suffer from overpopulation.

this section, we will examine the causes of, consequences of, and possible solutions to such growth.

CAUSES OF GROWTH

The rate of population growth throughout the world is the difference between the birth rate and the death rate. Assuming that the birth rate exceeds the death rate, we can say that the larger the difference that exists between the two, the faster the rate of growth will be.

If we look at countries throughout the world, it can be noted that on the average, the more developed countries have a low growth rate, near zero in some cases. On the other hand, the less developed countries have high growth rates, exceeding the average for the world as a whole. Most of the increase in the world's population, then, is the result of the growth in the populations of less developed countries. Since today almost twice as many people live in less developed countries than in more developed ones, if present trends continue, populations of less developed countries will overwhelm the rest of the world.

TABLE 16–4
Theory of Demographic Transition

Types of Countries	Birth Rate	Death Rate	Population Size
Least Developed	High	High	Stable
Developing	High	Low	Increases
Developed	Low	Low	Stable

526

Why do less developed nations have such a high growth rate? What factors are responsible for population growth patterns? One explanation for changes in population size can be found in the *theory of demographic transition* (see Table 16-4). This theory attributes population stability to a balance or imbalance between the birth rate and death rate, which is dependent on technology. Dennis Wrong in his description of this theory states:

> Premodern populations maintain stability of numbers by balancing high, though fluctuating, death rates with high birth rates. As they begin to experience the effects of modernization, improvements in nutritional and health standards reduce mortality while fertility remains high and rapid growth ensues. Later, urbanization and other social changes associated with the more "mature" stages of industrialism create pressure favoring smaller families, and the birth rate falls, once again approaching balance with the death rate, but at low (though fluctuating) rather than high levels.[11]

In other words, there are three stages through which societies pass. During stage one, which occurs in preliterate societies, population stability results from high birth rates and high death rates. As societies modernize and health improves—stage two—the balance is upset because mortality rates decrease and birth rates remain high. Finally, during stage three, which takes place in very modern societies where large families are not economically feasible, the balance is regained because the birth rate is voluntarily decreased to meet the low death rate.

Presently, less developed countries are in the second stage. Thus, although they have made slight reductions in fertility, these are nowhere nearly enough to compensate for the drastic reductions in mortality that occurred in these areas shortly after the turn of the century. It is mortality decline, then, and not fertility increase that primarily has caused the rise of the growth rates in these countries. In fact, a great reduction in the infant mortality rate throughout the world has been the principal factor causing worldwide population growth.

Much of this decline in mortality results from the benefits brought about by industrialization in the West. As industrialized countries expanded and colonized other countries, they brought modern medicine, better living conditions, and food to these nations. But while helping reduce mortality, the benefits of industry have not as yet reduced fertility and thus have contributed to population growth.

SOLUTIONS TO THE GROWTH PROBLEM

Some people suggest that since the less developed countries have the highest growth rates, then a solution to the growth problem must lie with these nations. Of course, in reality, population growth is a

527

FOCUS ON: WORLD POPULATION GROWTH

What does the future hold in store regarding population growth? Some recent studies suggest that the growth rate of the world's population has been declining. This would mean that the forecasts of mass starvation and doom for the near future may have been premature.

In one study on world population growth, demographers Amy Ong Tsui and Donald J. Bogue note that the average rate of childbearing throughout the world declined substantially between 1968 and 1975, contributing to a slower rate of growth. They attribute this decline in fertility to family planning programs in developing countries. They observe that in 1976 almost $1 billion was provided for family planning services in these nations.

In another study conducted by the United States Bureau of the Census, it has been reported that there has been a "perceptible decline" in the rate of world population growth over the past ten years. This study concludes that from the period of 1965–1970 to that of 1975–1977 there has been a decline of about 5 percent in the overall world population growth rate. This drop occurred in both developed and developing countries, with the exception of the African nations.

It must be noted, however, that although the *rate* of growth has been declining, the *number* of people in the world has been increasing. Every day world population increases by more than 200,000 people, totaling about 80 million people a year. Consequently, we are not out of danger yet.

Do you believe that the trend toward a reduction in the rate of world population growth will continue? How might technology influence this trend?

Source: "Experts Find Birth Control Is Slowing World Growth," *The Star Ledger,* October 19, 1978. "World Population Growth Slows," *The New York Times,* November 20, 1978.

worldwide problem because there are presently too many people on our planet using its limited resources. Here, though, let us examine the possibilities for population control in less developed countries, since such control is necessary to curb worldwide population growth.

Studies in a number of less developed nations have found that even though women in these countries want fewer children, they are unable to achieve their desires. One of the reasons for this is the low status of women in many of these areas. Husbands, fathers, and the family in general put pressure on the women to have babies for prestige, as well as for other reasons.

Along with the low status of women, the economic situation of these nations promotes fertility. For the most part, unemployment in these countries is very high. Consequently, the few jobs that are available are taken by men. Women have little choice but to get married, stay home, and have and rear children. If they were able to find employment outside the home, women might be more likely to marry late and to have fewer children than nonworking women.

In addition to these factors, several observers suggest that birth-control programs in these nations are poorly run and ineffective. They

APPLYING SOCIOLOGY

In 1977, the government of Luxembourg expressed concern that the citizens of that small country were not reproducing fast enough to replace themselves. Therefore the population of that country would decline in size if the trend were not reversed. Assuming it were desirable to reverse the trend, how might it be accomplished? What practical measures might the government take to stimulate population growth? From the perspective of world population, what is wrong with the concern shown by the government of Luxembourg?

usually operate as medical programs through clinics. Many people are afraid and suspicious of hospitals and clinics and do not use these facilities even when they are available.

Furthermore, many less developed countries do *not* want to reduce fertility. They believe that larger populations will bring military and international power. Hence, many leaders of these countries think of population control as more of "them" and fewer of "us." They see population control as just another colonial, racist ploy to prevent them from gaining power. As a result, they resist population control efforts and encourage population growth.

It is difficult to say who is correct in this debate. All that is certain is that population growth is occurring at an ever-increasing rate and little seems to be happening to stop it.

ECOLOGICAL CONSEQUENCES OF GROWTH

Along with population growth, the food, energy, and natural environment necessary to sustain life are rapidly being destroyed, depleted, or falling short of needs. *Ecology,* which is the study of the interrelationships of living things to each other and to the environment, is concerned with these problems.

The Problem of Food

One way of enlarging the food supply is to increase the amount of land being cultivated.

In 1798, economist Thomas Robert Malthus published a book in which he argued that human populations tend to increase at a more rapid rate than the food supply necessary to sustain them.[12] According to Malthus, while populations increase geometrically (2, 4, 8, 16, 32) food supply increases arithmetically (2, 3, 4, 5, 6, 7). As a result, he argued, populations will grow in size beyond their capacity to feed themselves unless one of two powerful checks operates to prevent growth. Malthus called these checks the *positive* and the *preventive.* Positive checks are wars, plagues, famine, and the like, all of which

. **529**

Thomas Malthus (1766–1834)

Thomas Malthus was an English country parson who advanced the pessimistic prediction that population growth, if unchecked, would increase geometrically (for example, 10, 20, 40, 80) while food supply could increase only arithmetically (for example, 1, 2, 3, 4). Malthus observed that human populations tend to double approximately every twenty-five years unless checked by war, famine, or disease. Food supplies, though, could never keep pace with this rate of population growth because they are limited, whereas human reproductive capability is unlimited.

Malthus' first book, *An Essay on the Principle of Population*, published anonymously in 1798, was much discussed and highly criticized by the educated public. His critics argued that he was advocating, or at least accepting, slavery, child-murder, and smallpox epidemics. In this book Malthus claimed that by helping the poor, society faced the paradox of allowing its number to increase, consequently causing more poverty and starvation. Therefore he denounced the use of soup kitchens and other forms of relief for the poor. He thought that the best solution to poverty and social inequality was to limit population growth. Ironically, though, contraception—the major technique used to control overpopulation today—was denounced by Malthus and thought of as a form of vice.

Malthus' writings coincided with the beginning of Europe's Industrial Revolution, when poor working conditions and low wages were pervasive. But despite such conditions, Malthus opposed higher wages for workers because he believed that people would have as many children as they could afford to support. This position, of course, supported the inequality of the population and thus was welcomed by many of the wealthy who were benefiting.

Malthus justified his position by contending that poverty was a result of a law of nature and that nature was self-regulative. That is, nature selects those elements that serve it best and, thus, less fit individuals would starve. This is nature's or God's way (he used both terms) of strengthening society as a whole. It is this notion that is perhaps most important in terms of Malthus' influence on later thinkers. It was this idea that helped Charles Darwin to conceive of his revolutionary doctrine of "natural selection" in biology (see Chapter 3). But even more important for social science, it was from Malthus that Herbert Spencer derived his social version of the notion of "survival of the fittest."

---

produce human misery and prevent population growth by raising the death rate. The only preventive check Malthus recognized was *moral restraint in sexual relations*, which lowers the birth rate. Since Malthus had little faith in the ability of human beings to restrain themselves sexually, he believed starvation, disease, war, and so on would be the only checks on population growth.

Not many people accept Malthus' theory in all its aspects today, but a number of people are greatly concerned with his predictions. They claim that in spite of all the advances made in agriculture, most people throughout the world face hunger, malnutrition, and periodic famine every day. As population continues to grow faster than food supplies increase, this situation can only become worse.

At the present time, only about 7 percent of the earth's land area is being cultivated. At best only about one-third of the total land surface of the earth can be cultivated at all. Even then, to turn deserts into gardens would be very expensive. In spite of the expense, though, we could greatly increase the food supply by cultivating some of this land and finding ways of getting a greater yield per acre from those already cultivated. If this is done, it has been estimated that 20 billion people could be fed with no trouble. This is about three times as many people as will inhabit the earth by the year 2,000 if present trends continue.

According to these estimates, then, we should not have a food problem. Technology should enable us to feed the world's population. But will this actually be the case?

Unfortunately, advances in agriculture may not keep up with population growth. Therefore, many people will continue to go hungry even though more and more land is being cultivated and more food is available every year. Even now, most of the world resists changing age-old habits in spite of efforts to teach people new farming methods. And, as populations keep growing, they are rapidly using up good farmland just to find space to live.

It would take more than a breakthrough in technology to reach maximum food production. It would also require a drastic change in the living habits of most of the world's people to ensure that enough land remains free for farming. This would require a total turnabout in the kinds of values and beliefs that have produced the sprawling suburbs now blotting the landscape of most industrialized nations.

Even if it indeed becomes possible to feed the earth's population, some people say that it really does not matter. They believe that long before maximal food production is achieved, all of the earth's other resources necessary for life will have been exhausted. Food is a renewable resource since it is grown. Most other materials are not renewable and will eventually be used up.

The Problem of Energy

Two basic energy sources are necessary to support large numbers of people. These are fossil fuels (for example, coal, petroleum, and natural gas) and electricity (which is usually made by burning fossil fuels). Since these fuels are not renewable, their continued depletion means that they will be used up one day.

FOCUS ON: THE ENVIRONMENTAL CRISIS

What consequences will result from what many scientists and social scientists have termed "the environmental crisis"? Is humankind going to waste the world's resources, so that future generations will be left to scrap over the remains? Will technology be able to overcome increases in the world's population and shortages in the world's resources, so that everyone will be able to have a comfortable standard of living? These are some of the questions that Barry Commoner, biologist, ecologist, and educator, has addressed in his book, *The Closing Circle,* written in 1971.

According to Commoner, scientists are not considering the entire picture when they look at an environmental problem. Instead, they tend to view only a small segment of the picture, thus solving one element without recognizing that the entire ecosystem is affected. This "reductionism," or looking at only one aspect of a problem, has been opposed by such thinkers as René Dubos of Rockefeller University, who espouses the concept of "holism," or looking at the whole problem. For example, when better soaps were needed, technologists developed synthetic detergents, which cleaned better than ordinary soaps, and were less harsh on the hands. But no one considered what would happen when these detergents entered the nation's water systems. The effect of nondegradable detergents on the bacteria in surface waters and sewage systems was devastating, and the new detergents had to be declared unacceptable.

Commoner also feels that scientists tend to isolate themselves and their disciplines from problems that affect the human condition. For example, in order to solve the problem of deteriorating cities, we need to know the principles of economics, architecture, social relations, the physics and chemistry of the air, the ecology of

water systems, and even the habits of the rat and the cockroach. Scientists, however, tend to study each of these principles separately rather than trying to discern how they affect each other.

A third factor that affects the solution of the environmental crisis is the cost of social programs in terms of both money and human lives. Thus, lower costs of energy resulting from the construction of a nuclear plant may also bring higher radiation doses to people in the vicinity of the plant. Or, the use of nitrogen fertilizer may bring a higher crop yield but also prove hazardous to infants in agricultural areas because of higher nitrate levels.

Commoner argues that all of these debates will have to be made public, and he cites some recent strides that have been made when the public and scientists worked together. The redisposal of nerve gas, the halting of the production of biological weapons, the banning of DDT, the defeat of the SST development in the United States, and the defeat of a nuclear reactor plant for Bodega Bay, California, on the San Andréas fault are a few examples of such victories. An ever watchful and informed citizenry is the only way to cope with these menaces, according to Commoner, and he advocates the cooperation of scientists as advisors to the public in such cases. He also regards this effort as only one means of social action and urges us all to search for other ways to respond to the environmental crisis.

Do you know of any ecological problems that are currently being examined in your community? How is the community researching the problem? Are all of the public agencies involved in finding an answer? Are there other forces that you think could be sought out for answers or help? How are you helping?

Source: Barry Commoner, *The Closing Circle,* New York: Alfred A. Knopf, 1971.

The fossil fuels needed to meet the world's energy demands are not renewable—some day they will be depleted. To compound this problem, population increases mean increased energy demands.

As populations keep growing in size, and as they continue to industrialize (which they must do in order to support themselves), the demand for these fuels will increase. We are already using these resources in such great quantities that many of them are expected to run out by the twenty-first century.[13] Figure 16-2 shows the increase in demand and the supply of various energy resources in the United States. As this graph demonstrates, the demand for energy has been increasing at a tremendous rate. The question is how long can we meet the demand?

While most experts agree that there is enough energy to last into the foreseeable future, most contend that alternate resources will have to be discovered in a very short period of time. Some of the alternatives available are nuclear energy through either fission or fusion of materials and solar heating. In the meantime, though, people will have to accept high prices, inconvenience, and government interference, for, unless we change our squandering habits soon, we will not have time enough to develop these alternate resources.

The villain, many people argue, is ourselves. Americans and

APPLYING SOCIOLOGY

Some researchers believe that human beings have always found ways to cope with ecological problems and will continue to do so. They argue that if, for example, our oil reserves are depleted, we will create new sources of energy. How would you react to such arguments? Do you believe we can continue to pull "a technological rabbit out of the hat"? What implications does such an attitude have for our society and for the world?

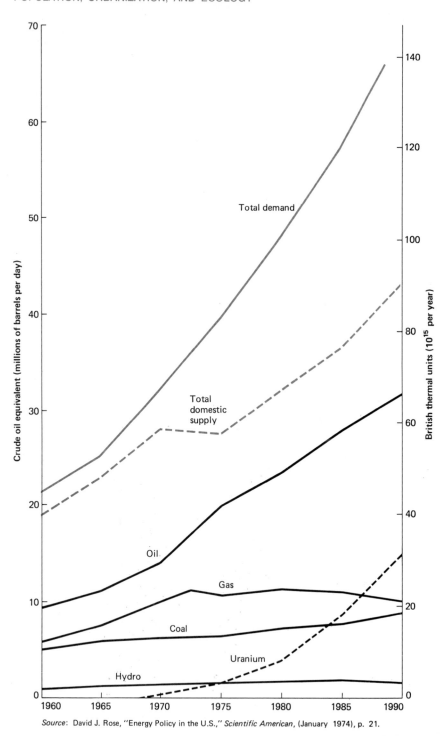

FIGURE 16-2
U.S. Energy Supply and
Demand: Projected
1960-1990

Source: David J. Rose, "Energy Policy in the U.S.," *Scientific American*, (January 1974), p. 21.

others simply want too much: appliances, several cars, overheated and overcooled homes, disposable cans and bottles. The comforts we have come to expect as natural are, in fact, unnecessary and wasteful. It has been predicted that if we do not change our habits soon, we will no longer be able to enjoy many of the comforts we take for granted.

To compound the problem even further, as the other peoples of the world become increasingly modernized, they too will want the things Americans have. If we have barely enough to go around now, what would things be like if two to three times as many people were using up energy as fast as Americans and other Western nations do today? In this regard, the energy crisis is as much a product of cultural values and population as it is a matter of technology.

The Problem of Pollution

As with food and energy, more people also means more pollution. More people generate more smoke, garbage, sewage, plastic containers, scarred land, lost forests, and noise. However, pollution is not simply a function of population size. Rather it is also caused by the living habits of human beings. Early human beings, who were nomadic, could simply move to another locale if their wastes become too offensive. But with the invention of agriculture and permanent settlements, it was the wastes not the wastemaker that had to be removed. As populations grew in size this task became increasingly difficult and costly.

The situation became even more difficult with the advent of industry, urbanization, and rapid population growth. Measures like sewage systems, smoke stacks, and other devices were, of course, adopted to dispose of the wastes. But the developing industrial nations were

Modern living habits, increased population size, industrialization, and urbanization have all contributed to the ever-growing problem of pollution.

more concerned with "progress" than with the cleanliness of the environment. By the middle of the twentieth century, however, pollution was considered a problem. And as cities grew in size and density, getting rid of garbage became a major task. Whereas once people had vast areas where they could dump their wastes, they soon began finding that few places remained to put their garbage. The smoke from one city spilled over to cloud the sky of another. Garbage seemed to be everywhere. Before long it was not only a nuisance, but also a threat to people's health and well-being.

By the 1960s a number of people became greatly concerned about the technological assault on the environment. In fact, some predicted that the world is headed for an eco-catastrophe by the year 2020 A.D.[14]

Population in the United States

In the beginning of this chapter we noted that demographers study the size, composition, and distribution of human populations. Consequently, when studying the population of the United States, they are concerned with these three factors.

Throughout this chapter we have been discussing population and ecological problems primarily from a worldwide perspective. In the remaining pages we will look at the population and ecological situation in our own country.

SIZE

On January 1, 1978, the total population of the United States was estimated to be 217.7 million people, about 1.7 million more than on January 1 of the previous year. This represents an increase of about 0.8 percent.

The birth rate in 1977 was 15.3 per thousand as compared with 14.7 per thousand in 1976 and 1975. In actual numbers this means that about 150,000 more babies were born in 1977 than in the year before. However, this represents a substantial decrease from the rate of 18.3 in 1970.

While the birth rate rose in 1977, the death rate fell to a record low level. It dropped to 8.8 per thousand from 8.9 per thousand in 1976 and 1975. The rate of inward immigration also declined for 1977.

COMPOSITION

When studying the composition of our population over the past few years, demographers note certain interesting trends. For one thing,

APPLYING SOCIOLOGY

Although there is no longer a major flux of immigrants into the United States, migration within our country is quite prevalent. In other words, Americans are a population on the move. What effects might such migration have on our cities, suburbs, and rural areas? How might the migrants and the receiving populations be affected? What trends do you predict for the future?

population in the youngest age groups declined while population in older groups increased. As a result, the median age of our population has risen almost two full years from 1970 to 1977. It was 29.4 in 1977 compared to 27.9 seven years earlier.

In addition, the female population grew at a faster rate than that for males. The female population grew by 6.5 percent over the last seven years whereas the male population increased by only 5.7 percent. As we mentioned earlier in this chapter, the difference between male and female rates can usually be attributed to higher mortality rates for males.

When studying the population situation in our own country, we also must be concerned with race. Blacks, who comprise the largest racial minority in the United States, comprised 11.5 percent of the population in 1977. And since the fertility rate among blacks is higher than that for whites, the black population contains a large percentage of young people. In addition, because blacks experienced a slower decline in fertility between 1970 and 1977 than whites, the black population grew by 11 percent during that period compared to a 4.8 percent growth for whites.

DISTRIBUTION

Several interesting patterns also emerged regarding population distribution in our country. Nonmetropolitan areas as a whole grew more rapidly than metropolitan areas over the past few years. Only in the South are metropolitan areas as a group growing faster than nonmetropolitan regions.

In addition, the Northeast and North Central regions had net outward migration while the "Sunbelt" and Western states continue to grow rapidly. About 40 percent of the growth in the resident population in the United States between 1970 and 1977 occurred in the Sunbelt regions.

What do all these statistics mean? What do they tell us about what the future holds?

537

IMPLICATIONS

Although the United States is a wealthy society with a low population growth rate, the 1972 Commission on Population Growth and the American Future noted that a goal of zero population growth was mandatory for this country as well as the rest of the world.

The Commission pointed out that even if each American couple produced only two children, our population would reach 307 million by the year 2020. This increase in population has multiple meanings. Cities would become more crowded and dirty than they are now. More farm and rural areas would have to be used for housing and industry. All our energy resources would be strained to a breaking point. Pollution would increase. Higher demands for the necessities of life would drive costs skyward. In the United States alone, the Commission predicted, the quality of life would deteriorate and our social problems—crime, pollution, alcoholism, poverty, and mental illness—would increase.

A population increase in this country would also cause worldwide problems. This is because, as the most affluent country on earth, we use more than our share of the world's resources. For example, one-half of the pollution on the globe is generated from the United States and we consume over a third of the world's natural resources. Although at present our surplus food production helps to feed the rest of the world, if our population were to increase and Americans ate that food, the rest of the world would suffer.

In conclusion, the world population problem is not only the concern of developing countries. The United States must assume its share of the responsibility by making provisions to curtail its own population growth.

SUMMARY

Demography is the study of the size, composition, and distribution of human populations. A *population* is a number of people who share at least one specific characteristic.

Three factors that directly affect population size are births, deaths, and migration. These factors, in turn, are influenced by a variety of social factors.

Population composition is measured by counting the number of individuals in a population who share certain biological or social traits, such as sex, race, ethnic background, age, education, and occupation. Two areas of particular concern to demographers are the sex *ratio* and *age composition* of a population.

538

Population distribution is the third area of concern to demographers. Geography, urbanization, and industrialization have had a major influence on population distribution.

One of the greatest problems facing our world today is population growth. There are presently more people in the world than ever before and the current rate of growth has never before occurred. However, whether or not this is cause for alarm is debatable. Some "doomsayers" predict that we will soon exhaust all the resources necessary for life. Other social scientists say that populations increase only when, and to the level where, they are able to support additional members.

When looking for the causes of worldwide population growth, we note that less developed countries have much higher growth rates than more developed nations. Much of this increase in population is because of the drastic reduction in mortality that occurred shortly after the turn of the century.

Some people suggest that since the less developed nations have the highest growth rates, then a solution to the growth problem must lie with these nations. However, curbing population in these areas may not be that easy. For one thing, women occupy a low status in these countries and are often pressured to have babies for prestige, as well as for other reasons. In addition, the high unemployment rates in these nations promote fertility. Also, birth-control programs in these nations are poorly run and ineffective. Finally, many less developed countries do not want to reduce fertility, in the belief that larger populations will bring military and international power.

Accompanying the increase in population growth has been a variety of ecological problems. Among the more significant are the problems of food, energy, and pollution. Even our own country, which has a low growth rate, is affected by these problems. If each American couple produced only two children, it has been predicted that the quality of life would deteriorate in our own country and that worldwide problems would also result.

GLOSSARY

composition the social and physical traits of the individuals within a population, such as age, sex, race, and occupation.

crude birth rate a measure of fertility that tells us how many infants are being born per thousand people in a population over a certain period of time.

crude death rate a measure of mortality that tells us how many people die per thousand living persons in a population over a certain period of time.

demography the study of the size, composition, and distribution of human populations.

dependency ratio a measure of the dependency of a population that is calculated by dividing the number of people over age 65 and under age 15 by the number of people between the ages of 15 and 64.

distribution the spatial arrangement of the members of a population.

ecology the study of the interrelationship of living things to each other and to their environment.

emigration the movement of people out of a country.

fecundity the potential number of births biologically possible.

fertility the actual number of children a woman gives birth to during her childbearing years.

Gemeinschaft according to Tönnies, a small community in which social relationships are based on feelings of sentiment and unity and in which members behave in ways beneficial to the whole group.

Gesellschaft according to Tönnies, a large community in which social relationships are impersonal, based on practicality and purpose rather than emotional ties.

immigration the movement of people into a country.

infant mortality rate a measure that determines the number of infants under one year of age who die in a given year per thousand live births for that year.

life expectancy the average number of years that members of a population can expect to live, given the conditions of a society.

life span the maximum number of years that it is biologically possible for people to live.

median age the age that divides a population exactly in half.

population an aggregate of people who share at least one specific characteristic.

sex ratio a measure of the sex composition of a population that is calculated by counting the number of males per every hundred females.

size the number of people who live in a certain area.

theory of demographic transition theory that attributes population stability to a balance or imbalance between the birth rate and the death rate, which is dependent on technology.

zero population growth a condition in which the fertility of a population is equal to its mortality and hence the size of the population remains stable.

REFERENCES

1. Paul R. Ehrlich, "World Population: A Battle Lost?" In Walt Anderson, ed., *Population and Environment*. Pacific Palisades, Calif.: Goodyear, 1970, pp. 15–16.

2. Bronislaw Malinowski, *The Sexual Life of Savages in North-Western Melanesia*. New York: Harcourt Brace Jovanovich, 1962.

3. Harold Christensen, "Scandinavian and American Sex Norms: Some Comparison with Sociological Explanations." *Journal of Social Issues* 22 (April 1966): 60–76.

4. J. Mayone Stycos, *Family and Fertility in Puerto Rico: A Study of the Lower Income Group*. New York: Columbia University Press, 1955.

5. Kingsley Davis, "The Migration of Human Populations." In *The Human Population*, A Scientific American Book. San Francisco: W. H. Freeman, 1974, pp. 53–65.

6. Nathan Keyfitz and William Fieger, *World Population: An Analysis of Vital Data*. Chicago: University of Chicago Press, 1968, pp. 32–39.

7. Kingsley Davis, "The Urbanization of the Human Population." In *Cities*, A Scientific American Book. New York: Alfred A. Knopf, 1969, pp. 3–25.

8. Davis, "The Urbanization of the Human Population," pp. 3–25.

9. Rachel Carson, *The Silent Spring*. New York: Alfred A. Knopf, 1962. Paul R. Ehrlich and Anna H. Ehrlich, *Population, Resources and Environment*. San Francisco: W. H. Freeman, 1972.

10. Edward S. Darvey, Jr., "The Human Population." In Ian Burton and Robert Kats, eds., *Readings in Resource Management and Conservation*. Chicago: University of Chicago Press, 1960.

11. Dennis H. Wrong, *Population and Society*. New York: Random House, 1967, pp. 18–19.

12. T. R. Malthus, *An Essay on Population*. 2 vols., New York: Dutton, 1914.

13. Gene Marine, "Here Comes the Sun." *Ramparts*, March 1974, pp. 33–37.

14. Paul R. Ehrlich, "Eco-Catastrophe." *Ramparts*, September 1969, pp. 24–28.

SUGGESTED READINGS

Ehrlich, Paul R. *The Population Bomb*. New York: Ballantine, 1968.

> *As its title suggests, Ehrlich argues that population growth is like a bomb ready to explode with a host of negative consequences unless diffused immediately.*

The Human Population. A Scientific American Book. San Francisco: W. H. Freeman, 1974.

> *This stimulating and well-illustrated book provides a combination of readings on population ranging from general discussion to historical analyses, the status of women, and the impact of technology. A valuable resource for anyone interested in the study of population.*

Maddox, John. *The Doomsday Syndrome*. New York: McGraw-Hill, 1972.

> *In contrast to those who warn of problems related to population, Maddox argues that much of the debate is not based on sound information and in some cases is counter-productive. This controversial book provides food*

for additional thought about population and other problems that most people generally take for granted.

Meadows, D. H., et al. *The Limits of Growth.* New York: Universe, 1972.

Based on a computer simulation, this study traces the environmental impact of increased population size and predicts an eco-catastrophe in the twenty-first century if population is not drastically controlled now.

Population Control: For and Against. New York: Hart Publishers, 1973.

This collection of readings by a number of authorities in many fields offers a concise discussion of the various opposing views of the population problem and its solution.

Wrong, Dennis, H. *Population and Society.* 4th ed. New York: Random House, 1977.

The author offers a brief, easy-to-read, and stimulating textbook introducing the significant aspects of the study of demography and ecology, including discussions of population growth, fertility, mortality, migration, and the debates over various issues on population.

Epilogue

We began this book with the following paragraph:

> Imagine being reared in near isolation, with only your very basic needs met. You would not hear people talk, see people walk, or feel the warmth of another's touch. You also would be unable to perform these activities yourself. For although we take walking, talking, and embracing for granted, such actions are learned as we interact with other human beings.

In the pages that followed, we discussed many aspects of human behavior from the viewpoint of sociology. We have seen, for instance, that walking, talking, and embracing are not the only actions that we learn as we interact with other human beings. Through our interaction with many social groups, we learn such things as how to vote, what religion to believe in, and how to behave as a man or woman. In short, we have seen that every aspect of our lives is affected, to some extent, by the groups to which we belong.

We also have noticed that sociologists study many different kinds of social behavior and that they do not always agree with each other about the nature of such behavior or, indeed, about the nature of society. Not surprisingly, they often disagree about the discipline of sociology as well. Let us look at some of the problems sociology faces today and try to shed some light on how these problems might be resolved in the future.

Problems in Sociology

The founders of the discipline tried to provide us with guidelines. For example, Auguste Comte argued that sociology was committed to studying social order (social statics) and social change (social dynamics). Max Weber proposed that sociology should be value-free—the sociologist must never impose personal opinions or beliefs on others. Émile Durkheim laid down rules for sociological research, primarily insisting that sociologists must look at social facts as just that—social reality cannot be reduced to psychological or physical facts.

These prescriptions, and others, have led to disagreements of various sorts among sociologists. A major disagreement has been on the theoretical level. As we have seen throughout this book, social phenomena can be explained in many ways. For example, let us look briefly at social stratification once again. All theorists agree that it is present in all societies in various degrees. But structural-functionalists claim it is necessary, inevitable, and integrative for society. Conflict theorists, on the other hand, claim it is unnecessary, avoidable, and detrimental to social life. Just to complicate the situation further, some modern theorists, such as Randall Collins, are claiming that stratification along racial and sexual lines may be more important than economic stratification.

Sociologists also disagree about research. Some opt for using research methods as close to those used in the physical sciences as possible, such as laboratory experiments. These methods, however, are criticized by other sociologists as being too far removed from "real life." These sociologists might use such methods as participant observation or survey research (see Appendix). But these methods can also be criticized. Opponents say they allow for too much researcher's bias and too much opportunity for respondents' deception or inadequate recall, thus leaving the findings open to question.

A third problem confronting sociologists is that the boundaries of their investigation are unclear. Some say sociology may investigate anything that concerns human beings; others claim sociology must limit itself to large groups of people. In addition, it has been debated whether such topics as interpersonal relations, the arts, and emotions come under the jurisdiction of sociology at all, even though they concern both large and small groups of individuals.

A fourth problem derives partly from Weber's contention that sociology should be "value-free," and that sociologists should not make moral judgments. This problem is whether sociologists should study social phenomena and merely report what they have learned, or instead try to make society better by offering solutions to social problems and actually working personally to change society. For example, sociologists may describe the stratification system of a given society and point out the inequities of that system. But should they, in their role as sociologists, set about the task of changing that system? Sociologists disagree on this point.

The issue, then, concerns a choice between maintaining detachment and thus avoiding social responsibility, or getting involved and thus losing one's objectivity or even credibility. There are those who opt for the first alternative and others who opt for the second. A smaller, but vocal group wants it both ways, insisting that sociologists can be detached and objective, but at the same time informed and responsible citizens.

Most of the above are internal problems, but the last one brings us to one of the more important external problems sociology has had to face. For a long time, until very recently, neither the public nor the government really considered that sociology could be useful in solving social problems. One reason was that sociology, in the public view, was frequently confused with social work and even socialism. But more important, most governmental agencies did not recognize the potential contributions of sociology. It was not seen, as economics and urban planning were seen, as a discipline that could be helpful in a practical sense. For example, there is still no sociological advisor to the President even though there is an economic advisor. The United Nations sends economists and planners all over the world, but rarely does it employ sociologists. This may be especially unfortunate when one thinks of Third-World countries. Economists and planners are sent to such countries to advise on how to industrialize the society; but there has been little or no awareness that when the economic system of a country undergoes radical change, social change and the resulting confusion are bound to follow in such areas as family life and intergroup relations. In recent years, however, sociology has become more and more accepted by the government and by private industry.

Another external threat has been the rise of a new subdiscipline in biology—sociobiology—whose chief proponent has been biologist E. O. Wilson.[1] In his work, *Sociobiology*, Wilson writes that at least some human behavior can be explained in terms of biology or genetics. He argues that sociobiology joins the biological and the social sciences together so as to offer a better explanation of human behavior than each could offer alone. He suggests that biology places boundaries on human capacities to exploit opportunities in society. In other words, biology sets limits within which people are able to take advantage of such opportunities. Moreover, according to Wilson, some human populations have natural abilities and talents over others.

Today most sociologists reject such theories, as they usually have done in the past, claiming that social behavior is learned (see Chapter 4). As sociologist John Kunkel states:

> The examples of *human* social behavior, which is thought to be determined by biological factors, are few, overly general, and, from a sociological point of view, involve a quite unsophisticated analysis.[2]

However, a total resistance to sociobiology on the part of sociologists may be a mistake. In an article written on the subject, sociologist Lee Ellis notes that sociology will virtually disappear if it continues to reject sociobiology. Because it has been slow in recognizing the implications of many biological discoveries made in this century, it will lose funding, stagnate, and completely lose respect as a science.[3]

Gerhard Lenski takes a more moderate view. He writes:

> What is needed is not a life-death struggle between sociology and sociobiology, but two disciplines that can begin to communicate and cooperate with one another and develop more sophisticated models of human societies and individual behavior than either alone can create.[4]

These, then, have been and continue to be the major problems confronting sociology. Most of them are being worked at even though several are not yet resolved. And, as sociologists attempt to solve these problems, many are taking advantage of new opportunities available to them. Let us examine some careers open to sociologists.

Careers in Sociology

Until about twenty years ago, only one career was possible for the sociologist, and that was to be a professor at a college or a university. Teaching is still the major activity of the approximately 15,000 professional sociologists in the United States, but alternative kinds of employment are becoming more and more available. In fact, it is becoming common for undergraduates to major in sociology although they may be planning to go to work or to graduate school in public administration, social work, law, or many other fields.

For those who hold an Associate Degree, or who have obtained a "bachelors" or B.A. in sociology, the chances of professional employment within the actual field of sociology are rather limited. Numerous sociology courses, however, such as those in industrial sociology and formal organizations, help prepare a person for work in business. Or, for those planning to work in the public sector, courses in race and ethnicity, urban sociology, marriage and the family, and social stratification are invaluable. With the growing demand for computer and statistical skills, courses in methodology and statistics are also becoming more and more important.

There are two degrees beyond the B.A. in sociology—the "masters" or the M.A. and "doctorate" or the Ph.D. The M.A. can take anywhere from one to three years to attain and it indicates a sophisticated knowledge of sociology, although not necessarily original research. A sociologist holding a masters' degree is eligible usually to teach at the high-school or community-college levels and, of course, he or she can work in private industry or in public agencies.

The Ph.D. is the highest degree possible in sociology. It usually requires five or six years of education beyond the B.A. In general, the typical Ph.D. candidate takes courses similar to those at the undergraduate level, but they are more sophisticated and specific. For example, in this introductory course, you were asked to read only one chapter in social stratification. If you were to go on to graduate school, you might take an entire course dealing just with theories of stratification. So the graduate student in sociology begins his or her career doing course work, focusing primarily on theory, research methods and statistics, and one or two subareas. Gradually, students zero in on the one area that interests them especially and then most attention is concentrated on that topic alone.

547

The final and most demanding part of attaining a Ph.D. in sociology is the writing of a dissertation. A dissertation is a book-length research study, signifying scholarship and making an original contribution to the existing body of sociological knowledge. The Ph.D. degree is awarded when the dissertation is complete and the student has "defended" his or her work before a dissertation committee. It is at this point that the individual becomes a recognized sociologist and usually makes an important career decision. What possibilities are open to the new Ph.D. sociologist?

As noted earlier, most sociologists still work in universities and colleges. In either setting, the sociologist spends most of the time teaching and doing research.

But what about the sociologist who does not like teaching? What other work is possible? One may do research in any number of settings, such as public health centers, municipal government offices, private industry, federal agencies, or research centers. A sociologist may become an editor for a college textbook publisher. Sociologists can be found in state transportation systems, as personnel managers, as college administrators, in criminal justice departments, on hospital staffs, in libraries, and in agencies dealing with mental illness, drug addiction, or the physically handicapped. In short, because sociologists are always concerned with human behavior in social settings, their occupations cover a very wide range and their skills are useful in many areas beyond the college classroom.

In this book we have introduced you to the field of sociology. We have given you an overview of the traditional interests of sociologists and have described some of the knowledge sociologists have contributed to civilization. We have pointed out that sociology, like all social sciences, is still imperfect, but great advances have been made and will continue to be made. As sociology matures, overcoming its own problems and perfecting its techniques, it will be better equipped to study and help resolve society's problems in the future.

REFERENCES

1. E. O. Wilson, *Sociobiology: The New Synthesis*, Cambridge, Mass.: Harvard University Press, 1975.
2. John Kunkel, "Sociobiology vs. Biosociology," *American Sociologist*, 12:2 (May 1977):70.
3. Lee Ellis, "The Decline and Fall of Sociology, 1975–2000," *American Sociologist*, 12:2 (May 1977):56–66.
4. Gerhard Lenski, "Sociology and Sociobiology: An Alternative View," *American Sociologist*, 12:2 (May 1977):74.

Appendix: Doing Sociology

Lynne R. Davidson, SUNY College at Purchase

It is one thing to read about sociology; it is quite another thing to really do sociology. In this Appendix we will discuss how sociologists go about doing sociological research. We will also look at some of the ethical implications involved.

Research as a Sociological Activity

There are many ways of "knowing" about things, such as faith, common sense, or intuition. For example, common sense tells us that divorce among Americans is increasing since we see more divorced people around us than we did in the past. But common sense is not enough. Sociologists must determine whether or not commonsense notions are really true. To do this, they gather reliable information in order to calculate the *actual* divorce rate. After they show that the divorce rate really is rising, they look at patterns of divorce relative to other social events. In other words, sociologists try to explain why the divorce rate is increasing and what that means in the context of society itself.

One of the major ways in which sociologists accomplish this is through *research*. Research is one method by which sociologists accomplish their three scientific aims: 1) describing social behavior and social events; 2) discovering patterns or regularities in the social world; and 3) explaining and generalizing the meaning of these patterns of behaviors and events. (To generalize means to broaden the relevance of the findings and to apply them to a larger group of people.) What does social research involve?

Social research is really a type of detective work and just as exciting. As in detective work, the researcher is faced with a problem and tries to gather as many clues and as much evidence as possible to solve the "case." Both the detective and the researcher always try to approach problems in a logical and systematic fashion. For the sociologist this involves using different kinds of established research methods and techniques for collecting data. *Data* (the singular is *datum*) are the factual information the researcher collects to answer questions about the social world. Like the detective, the researcher needs solid data—the kind of evidence that will hold up in court. In gathering such data, however, the sociologist encounters problems.

The Problems of Social Research

Because sociologists deal with human beings, they are faced with certain problems that make objective investigation difficult. One problem stems from the fact that human behavior cannot be predicted precisely. For example, although most people consume food every day, it is not possible to always know *exactly* when or what they will eat. As a result, findings in the social sciences may not be as precise as in the physical sciences, where behavior and events are more predictable.

A second problem concerns getting cooperative participants. Some people are hesitant to talk about their personal lives, and hence may not be willing to take part in a study. Even if people do participate, they may distort their responses and behavior in order to appear socially acceptable to the investigator. This is especially true of studies in which people are expected to divulge details about their private lives, such as income, sexual behavior, or mental health. Individuals may hide the truth fearing the interviewer will get a bad impression of them if they give honest responses.

A third problem is that sociologists are themselves human beings. Like all people, they are products of their own culture and thus they may have personal opinions or subjective impressions about the topic they study. For example, suppose your parents were divorced when you were growing up. If you later decide to do research on divorce, you might approach the topic with a bias or value judgment—divorce is either "good" or "bad." While it is perfectly legitimate for researchers to study the values and biases of different groups of people, the researchers themselves must try to avoid making their *own* value judgments about what they study. Many sociologists, however, recognize that it is humanly impossible to completely avoid making value judgments and argue that preconceptions should be stated explicitly so that findings can be understood in terms of them. This means that social scientists must constantly use their critical capacities to ensure that their own values and attitudes do not impinge upon their research.

Despite these problems, sociology has developed a research methodology that has provided a wealth of information about human behavior and all its complexities. Social research has contributed to our understanding of the social world, but it would not have been possible had we not had social theory.

The Relationship Between Theory and Research

In the past, there was a tendency to think of theory and research as two separate ways to gain knowledge about the real world. It was believed that because theory tends to be general and broad in scope, whereas research tends to be specific and narrow in scope, that the two were completely different entities. Nevertheless, the two are closely related.

A *social theory* is a set of logically interrelated assertions and observations that attempt to explain social events. Since theories are general and always connote some uncertainty, a major function of research is to provide concrete evidence to substantiate or "prove" the theory, modify or reformulate the theory, or refute the theory.

An example of theory in the formal sense can be shown by drawing from Durkheim's work on suicide. Durkheim postulated the interrelationship among group cohesion, stress, religion, and the suicide rate. The logic of this theory demonstrates how it is used to generate research questions.

General Assertion #1: High group cohesion leads to a low degree of individual stress within the group.

General Assertion #2: A low degree of stress leads to a low suicide rate.

Factual Observation: Catholics have more group cohesion than Protestants.

Final Assertion: Therefore, Catholics have a lower suicide rate than Protestants.

The final assertion becomes the social scientist's research question: Do Catholics have a lower suicide rate than Protestants? It is then subjected to research.

While the term "theory," as it is used in this example, refers to a formal set of organized ideas and interrelated assertions about social phenomena, sometimes we use "theory" in a less technical sense to mean a general orientation or conceptual framework. For example, in Chapter 15 you learned how some sociologists view deviance as a process of labeling. In this sense, then, we often refer to "labeling theory." Similarly, in Chapter 6 you learned that mate selection is sometimes explained by the "theory of complementary needs."

Regardless of how we use the term "theory," though, social theories are useful to social research for two reasons. First, theories give the researcher a starting point. They provide the general focus and concepts from which the researcher develops specific questions to investigate. For example, there is a classic general theory about how the relationship between two people changes when a third person joins them. Using this theory, researchers can observe what actual changes occur

551

when the additional person becomes a member of the group. In this way, they test the theory for accuracy.

A second use of theory occurs at the end of the research process. Theories allow the researcher to explain sociological findings after the data have been gathered. That is, theories are used to interpret the meaning of the findings. For example, numerous researchers have found that single women experience less emotional and psychological distress than married women.[1] In order to interpret these findings, researchers must review theories in such areas as role and status or social isolation. In these areas, researchers might examine literature that may show that the status of married women is often defined in terms of their husbands and that their roles are confined to family interactions. This, in turn, may lead to lower self-esteem, which may develop into depression. So, theory plays two vital roles in research: 1) it generates research questions; and 2) it provides interpretations. Most sociologists agree that good research begins *and* ends with theory.

The Process of Social Research

Most social research is based on a scientific model. This means that certain logical guidelines are followed throughout a research project—from the first stage to the point of evaluating the results of the research. Social research usually involves four major stages. These are: 1) choosing and formulating the problem; 2) selecting the methods and collecting the data; 3) presenting and analyzing the results; and 4) drawing conclusions, making generalizations, and evaluating the findings. However, this model, which involves step-by-step procedures, is an ideal type.* In other words, once researchers begin their task, they sometimes find it practical to deviate from the ideal model, to be flexible, and to vary the sequence of procedures. Yet, as with cooking, one needs to know the basic recipe before one can creatively change the ingredients.

CHOOSING AND FORMULATING A RESEARCH PROBLEM

The first step involves choosing a topic. This stage requires stating the purpose and clearly defining the problem, reviewing relevant literature, and determining the specific questions to be investigated. In short, at this point the researchers state what they intend to study and why they intend to study it.

---

*It should also be noted that this research model is one of several ways in which sociologists study the social world. Some of the other ways, such as *phenomenology* and *ethnomethodology*, are beyond the scope of this book.

552

There are many different reasons why sociologists choose the research topics they do. Some are concerned with describing and explaining social problems in society, such as alcoholism, discrimination, or white-collar crime. Other sociologists may want to explain and evaluate the special programs set up to alleviate these social problems. These sociologists are concerned with practical application and/or policy decisions. Still other sociologists may choose a topic in order to verify the accuracy of a theory that has never been researched. Or some might choose a topic in order to verify the findings of a previous study on the same topic. When a sociologist duplicates a past study, it is called *replication*. Also, sociologists may note an area of social life that has been totally ignored or neglected in recent sociological research. For example, between 1956 and 1973 no sociologist studied remarriage, even though remarriage rates increased considerably during that time period. Thus, sociologists conduct studies to explain or help alleviate social problems, verify theories, replicate other research, or provide new information to a body of intellectual knowledge.

For whatever reason sociologists choose a topic, they usually do so based on their interests and expertise, always bearing in mind the social significance and relevance of the topic. But practical factors, such as the scope of the project, the availability of equipment, money, and participants, and the length of time needed to complete the study, must also be taken into account. Finally, the sociologist must be certain that the problem is a researchable one. In other words, the topic must be subject to *empirical* investigation—that is, observation and measurement in the real world. No sociologist, for example, would set out to "prove" or "disprove" the existence of the Greek gods.

Hypotheses

Once the topic is chosen the researcher reviews the relevant and empirical literature. Then he or she narrows down the topic by identifying a special problem and formulating a *hypothesis* (or hypotheses). A hypothesis is a tentative assertion about the relationship between two or more factors. (The final assertion in Durkheim's theory is a working hypothesis.)

One should be able to word a hypothesis in one of two forms. A hypothesis can either be stated "If A, then B" or it can take the form "The greater A, the greater (or lesser) B." A hypothesis about remarriage taking the first form might be: If divorced parents have young children, then they are more likely to remarry than divorced parents with teenage children. An example of the second type of hypothesis is: The more religious people are, the more politically conservative they are likely to be.

553

Sociological Variables and Their Operationalization

Each major concept or factor in a sociological hypothesis is called a *variable*. A variable is a social trait, quality, or characteristic that is subject to change in degree or kind. In the previous hypothesis about religion and political conservatism, religion is a variable that is subject to change by degree. That is, a person is *more or less* religious. One can easily see that religion can also vary by kind: In the United States most people are Protestant, Catholic, or Jewish. While most variables differ by degree or kind, some variables vary in a simpler way. They are either present or absent; the variable is either there or not there. For example, one is either a parent or not a parent; one is either pregnant or not pregnant.

Once the researcher proposes a hypothesis, he or she must then *operationalize* each variable. To operationalize a variable, the researcher must state clearly and concisely what each variable refers to in concrete, measurable terms. For example, it is one thing to assert a relationship between divorced parents with young children and remarriage, but how do we operationalize these concepts? "Remarriage" is easy to operationalize. We can say that "remarriage" is any marriage subsequent to the first marriage. But how do we operationalize the second variable, "divorced parents with young children"? Like "remarriage," "divorced parents" can be easily operationalized. But what do we mean by "young children"? Age five? Age ten? Age thirteen? A sociologist might operationally define "young children" as those between newborn and thirteen years old.

Obviously, the more abstract or general the variable, the more difficult it is to operationalize in concrete terms. For example, "political conservatism" is a variable that contains two highly abstract concepts. The researcher must decide what is meant by "political" and what is meant by "conservatism" and then reduce these meanings into specific terms. Ultimately, he or she may choose to measure the political dimension by the number of times a person votes, and the conservative dimension by the party for whom the person votes.

Although operationalization at times may be difficult, it is the crux of good research. Variables must be measured precisely so that hypotheses can be tested accurately.

The Principle of Cause and Effect

A hypothesis always contains at least two variables because the sociologist wants to determine the relationship between two or more factors. Most researchers want to find out if one variable *causes* another. They would like to be able to show that A causes B; or if people do A, the result will be B. For instance, they would like to show that if unemployment rates are low (A), then crime rates (B) will be low.

Hypotheses of this kind assert a *causal*, or cause-and-effect, *relationship*. In such a relationship, the cause is called the *independent variable*; the effect is called the *dependent variable*. In the example given above, a low unemployment rate is the independent variable because it is thought to *cause* low crime rates—the dependent variable.

In order to demonstrate that there is a causal relationship, the researcher must determine three things: 1) that the two variables are correlated; 2) that the cause occurred earlier in time than the effect; and 3) that no alternative variable caused the effect. We will now examine these three conditions more closely.

A simple *correlation* means that two variables are associated with one another in a regular pattern. It means that whenever A occurs, B also occurs; or whenever A increases, B increases (or decreases). But a correlation does not tell us whether A causes B or if B causes A. It only tells us that whenever we have one, we will also have the other. For example, many researchers have found a correlation between level of education and level of income. But does a high educational level cause an increase in income; or does one's income level lead to the opportunity for higher education? We can only tell that a relationship or correlation exists between the two variables. Yet, correlation must exist if the relationship is to be a causal one.

In terms of time, the independent variable must always occur *before* the dependent variable or it could not possibly influence the other. For example, a child must be conceived before it can be born. Clearly, it cannot occur the other way around.

Finally, researchers must demonstrate that no other variable but the independent variable produced the effect. In our low employment rate–low crime rate example, it must be clearly shown that such things as better law enforcement or an improved moral value system were not the influences leading to the low crime rate.

In social science, it is not easy to show a cause-and-effect relationship because in real life human behavior occurs in complex situations. Many things may be happening earlier in time, at the same time, or in between that the investigator may be unaware of or unable to account for. Yet these factors could influence the relationship. One such factor that sociologists try to examine is called the *intervening variable*.

In terms of time, an intervening variable comes *between* the independent and the dependent variables. It is an explanatory link between the two variables that seem to have a causal relationship. The intervening variable explains *why* the independent variable causes change in the dependent variable. Hence, in our remarriage example, divorced parents with younger children (the independent variable) might attend more parent-teacher meetings than parents of older children. As a result, they would get a chance to meet each other, which might lead to

555

remarriage (the dependent variable). "Going to parent-teacher meetings," then, is an intervening variable. The following diagram shows the causal relationship among the three kinds of variables in terms of time.

TIME I	**TIME II**	**TIME III**
Independent variable →	*Intervening variable* →	*Dependent variable*
Divorced parents with younger children	Going to parent-teacher meetings	Remarriage

In sum, the first stage in the research process involves choosing a topic, formulating a hypothesis, identifying and operationalizing each variable, and postulating the relationship between the variables. The researcher is then ready for the next step.

SELECTING THE METHODS AND COLLECTING THE DATA

In general, the method sociologists choose depends on what they want to study. For example, sociologists may conduct an *experiment* if they want to learn how individuals or small groups behave in a controlled setting. They may use *case studies* and *participant observation* in order to observe social interaction in its most natural setting. Or they may use *survey research* when they are examining the patterns of behavior of large numbers of people in society as a whole. It is important to note that there is no right or wrong approach to gathering information. Rather, the researcher chooses the method he or she considers most appropriate for studying the particular subject matter. Often a combination of approaches will yield the best possible evidence or data.

At this stage in the research process the researcher maps out the logic and strategy for gathering data. Once the strategy is decided on, the researcher must actually collect data and systematically record all relevant information. Let us now examine the various research methods.

Experiments

The experimental method is the most effective one for establishing causal relationships between two variables because of the way experiments are carried out. Most experiments take place in a laboratory setting and the researcher can control each step of the study including the way subjects are selected, the kinds of factors that are introduced, and even the physical environment. In addition, because the laboratory experimenter creates and manipulates the situation, he or she can control many factors that might distort the relationship. Also, since subjects in an experiment are a "captive audience," the experimenter can observe what is happening with systematic precision. In the following paragraphs we will describe how an experiment is carried out.

Suppose a researcher wanted to examine the effect of viewing televised violence on a person's attitude toward aggression. How might the researcher proceed? First, the experimenter would choose a number of subjects, let us say sixty. The subjects would then be equally divided into two groups—thirty into an *experimental* group and thirty into a *control* group. The experimental group takes part in the entire experiment and is administered a stimulus—the independent variable. The control group, however, is used for purposes of comparison only. It is not subjected to the independent variable, but is used to show that without the independent variable there would be no effect or dependent variable.

Next, both groups would be tested on their attitudes toward aggression to assure that the two groups are as similar as possible on all relevant factors before the experiment begins. Then the stimulus would be administered to the experimental group. That is, group members would be shown a television program with a great deal of violence in it. Subjects in the control group would not be shown the program. Finally, both groups would again be tested and compared on their attitudes toward aggression.

By taking measurements of each group both before and after the introduction of a stimulus, the experimenter is able to make a confident inference that the independent variable is the "true" cause. Of course, the experimenter must take into account all other factors, such as the subjects' particular mood at the time of the experiment and the demands of the experimenter, that might influence the results. Providing that no other factor interfered and that the two groups were truly the same at the beginning of the experiment, the researcher can conclude that any change in attitude toward aggression that occurs in the experimental group is attributable to the independent variable—viewing violence on television. No change should occur in the control group.

Although the experimental method is the most effective and precise for establishing causal relationships, it also has disadvantages. Since the laboratory experiment occurs in a contrived, artificial situation, there is no guarantee that people will act the same way in their natural, everyday environments. Thus, findings derived from the experimental method are difficult to generalize to the "real world."

A second disadvantage stems from the fact that subjects in both the control group and the experimental group are apt to change their normal behavior patterns simply because they are conscious of being studied or because they are responding to personal attention from the experimenter. For example, in a famous study conducted at Western

Electric's Hawthorne plant, social researchers discovered that the productivity of workers increased even when the environment was manipulated in a way considered negative to productivity. Researchers concluded that the subjects changed their behavior simply because they felt "special" participating in the experiment and being observed. Changes that occur in subjects' behavior as a result of the investigation or observation itself are now known as the *Hawthorne effect*.

Probably the most serious disadvantage of the experimental method, though, is that the subject matter of sociology is often not conducive to experimentation. After all, how can riots, social movements, industrial relations, and family or marital conflict be brought into a laboratory setting? Consequently, sociologists often use other methods to study social phenomena. Nevertheless, when other methods are used, the experiment serves as a valuable model of logic and precision.

Case Studies and Observation

Many sociologists choose a more naturalistic approach by doing field research in a real rather than in a contrived environment. One of the most common types of field research is the *case study*, which is an investigation of an actual group of people, such as a delinquent gang; a specific setting, such as a hospital; or a particular process, such as the women's movement.

Case studies often rely heavily on observation as a technique for data collection. Basically, there are two types of observational case studies—*participant observation* and *nonparticipant observation*. Participant observation is considered most appropriate when sociologists want to study groups or social behaviors about which so little is known that more structured techniques cannot be used. As the name implies, the researcher becomes a member of the group that is being studied. For example, Howard Becker investigated dance band musicians by playing in a band;[2] and Ned Polsky lived among poolroom hustlers to learn the ways they set up their victims.[3] Perhaps the most classic study of participant observation is sociologist William Foote Whyte's study of a street-corner gang. Although Whyte did not actually "join" the gang, he did live in their neighborhood for three and a half years and participated in many of the gang's activities.[4]

In most cases, during participant observation, the subjects are unaware of the researcher's identity. As a result, the researcher's presence is unlikely to affect their behavior. One advantage of participant observation, then, is that it enables the researcher to gain intimate knowledge or inside information that could not usually be obtained by an outsider. Another advantage stems from the extensive contact and involvement that the researcher has with his or her subjects. This involvement and personal experience sensitizes the researcher and provides insight into exactly what is going on.

But many sociologists believe that the advantages of participant observation are outweighed by the disadvantages. If a researcher becomes too involved in the group, he or she may identify with other members of the group to the point of losing objectivity. Also, participation in any group means occupying a particular status within that group. The intrusion of an additional person into a group changes the group's composition and interaction patterns. Furthermore, since the experience of the participant observer is unique, generalizations are limited and other sociologists will find it difficult to replicate the research.

A second type of observational technique is *nonparticipant observation*. Essentially, the difference between the two types is that in nonparticipant observation the researcher's true identity as an investigator and the purpose of the study are disclosed to the people being studied. In addition, researchers who use nonparticipant observation usually have a more clearcut picture of the exact nature of what is to be observed. This means that the researcher can use more structured techniques for gathering data and enter the field with explicitly formulated observational categories.

Like other research methods examined thus far, nonparticipant observation has both advantages and disadvantages. On the positive side, it offers greater precision and control over what is being observed than participant observation. At the same time, however, the natural character of the group is disturbed by the intrusion of the researcher. In addition, nonparticipant observation also has a disadvantage similar to that of the experiment: subjects may react unnaturally since they are aware that they are being studied.

Survey Research

Survey research is the most efficient and least expensive way of collecting information about a large number of people. Since sociologists are interested in society as a whole and large groups within societies, the survey is frequently the sociologist's preferred method for gathering data. In survey research the investigator must make two major decisions after the hypothesis is formulated. These are: 1) Who will be studied?; and 2) How will the data be collected? Each of these decisions will be discussed separately.

In order to make the first decision, the survey researcher must define a population. A *population* consists of all those people whose attitudes, behaviors, or characteristics the sociologist is interested in examining. For instance, in our example of the patterns of remarriage among divorced parents with young children, the population is comprised of *all* divorced parents with young children. If a population is very small, such as the members of the United States Senate, it is possible for the researcher to survey the entire population. But obviously in a population as large as "all divorced parents with young children," it would be impractical, if not impossible, to study all members. In such cases the researcher must survey a sample of people. A *sample* is a smaller number of people (or units) drawn from the population. It is a part of the whole.

Ideally, the researcher wants a sample to be representative of the population—to closely resemble the population on all characteristics. Representativeness is necessary in order to generalize findings from the sample to the population. This principle of representative sampling can be compared to heating soup. All the soup is in one pot. To find out if it is hot enough to eat, we stir the soup and sample one spoonful. If that spoonful is sufficiently hot, we can assume with some confidence that the whole pot of soup is hot. It isn't necessary to eat all the soup to be sure of its temperature because the one spoonful represents the rest of the soup. To ensure representativeness of the population, researchers use random samples. A *random sample* is a sample in which every person in the population has an equal chance of being selected for the study.

To draw a random sample the researcher must first compile a list of all members of the population. Assuming the list is complete, a random sample is obtained by assigning a number to every member. The investigator then selects the numbers to be included in the sample by using standard tables of random numbers or computer-produced random numbers. Another method, called *systematic sampling*, can also be used to ensure an equal chance of representation in the sample. Depending on the desired size of the sample, the researcher selects, say, every fifth, twentieth, or hundredth person from the population list. In either case, though, the researcher must try to eliminate any personal bias or human error that might reduce the equal chance of each person being chosen.

Frequently, of course, we cannot know the entire population nor can we always get a complete list of all the people in the population, as in the case of all alcoholics. In such situations, sociologists can either select a sample from the list of known alcoholics or can resort to using *available samples*. These consist of all the people they can find who have the characteristics they want to study. For reasons of practicality and accessibility many choose this option. However, when this type of sampling is used, it is not possible to make generalizations with as much confidence as sociologists can when using random sampling.

Once the sample has been selected, the researcher is ready to make his or her second major decision: How will the data be collected? The sociologist usually collects data either by conducting an interview or by providing the respondent with a self-administered questionnaire. In both cases, though, the researcher must decide on the kinds of questions *necessary* and *relevant* to the research problem. For example, if a sociologist is concerned with dating patterns among college students, he or she would be unlikely to include questions on political issues, unless such questions were related to the hypothesis.

When an *interview* is conducted, the researcher meets with the respondent and asks the questions in a face-to-face situation. The interviewer may read specific questions from a detailed questionnaire or may adapt questions from an interview schedule—a list of topics to be covered. In either case, the interviewer must establish and maintain a good relationship with the respondent since an interview is itself a social interaction. Also, the interviewer must be careful not to influence the respondent's answers.

When a *self-administered questionnaire* is used, the researcher distributes the questionnaire, usually by mail, to each respondent and the respondents themselves fill in the answers and return the questionnaire to the researcher. While this method of gathering data allows the investigator to reach more people than would be possible in a face-to-face interview, many people simply do not bother to fill in or return mailed questionnaires. Of those who do respond, some misinterpret questions. In addition, people who have a personal interest in a topic are more likely to complete a questionnaire than those who are not directly concerned with the issues involved. Thus, the surveyor cannot be certain that the returned questionnaires include the typical responses of the population.

Many sociologists use a combination of both interview and self-administered questionnaires. But whichever technique is used, the researcher must decide whether the questions asked will be structured or unstructured. A *structured question* is a closed-ended question with fixed choices. For example, the following is a structured question:

Please rate how happy you think your marriage is (circle one):

1. Very happy
2. Happy
3. Unhappy
4. Very unhappy
5. Don't know

On the other hand, an *unstructured question* is open-ended and permits the respondent to answer freely. An unstructured question on the same topic might be stated: Would you please describe how happy you think your marriage is. In the first example, the subject is restricted to one of five specific answers. In the second example, the subject can talk spontaneously about his or her marriage. Obviously, the investigator will gather more information using the second method; however, open-ended answers are more difficult to organize for analysis. For example, how would researchers tabulate the degree of marital happiness if respondents to the above question replied with such statements as, "Sometimes it is and sometimes it isn't," "I'm happier when the kids aren't home," or "My husband earns a great salary"? Because of the shortcomings of each type of question, sociologists frequently find it useful to construct questionnaires using both structured and unstructured questions.

In summary, there are three primary ways in which sociologists gather data. They can use the experimental method which provides more control and precision than any other method. They can use case studies which have the advantage of being more true to life than other methods. Or they can use survey research, which makes investigating large samples possible and makes the findings more readily generalizable. Whichever method is chosen the investigator must obtain the kind of evidence necessary to test the hypothesis.

PRESENTING AND ANALYZING THE RESULTS

After the data have been collected, researchers must detail exactly what has been found and what the findings mean. At this stage in the research process, the investigators must describe, organize and present, and analyze and interpret their findings. We will now examine each of these components.

One way of describing, organizing, and presenting data is through the use of *statistics*. Statistics enable the researcher to quantify and present findings in numerical fashion. There are basically two kinds of statistics: descriptive and inferential. Although we can only give a brief introduction to statistics here, we will try to show their relevance to the research process.

Descriptive statistics provide formulas that allow the researcher to describe numerically the characteristics of the sample. For example, if the sociologist is interested in comparing income levels of working men and working women, he or she could use descriptive statistics to show the average income of both groups. Since there may be a wide distribution or range of incomes for both men and women, computing an average score allows the researcher to simplify the whole range. Other descriptive statistics might be used to show the magnitude or strength of the relationship between the independent and dependent variables.

Inferential statistics provide formulas that allow the researcher to predict the extent to which findings can be generalized to the larger population. They tell the researcher the numerical probability that the relationship found is a real one. For example, if it were determined that a sample of 100 college students out of a total population of 1,600 showed a particular dating pattern, inferential statistics would enable the researcher to predict with confidence the probability that the findings would be applicable to the population. Thus, descriptive statistics are used to describe the sample findings; inferential statistics are used to make inferences from the sample to the population.

Statistics also enable sociologists to classify information into categories so that the trends and relationships among variables can be clearly examined. To illustrate, let us once again return to our original hypothesis about remarriage: Divorced parents with young children are more likely to remarry than divorced parents with teenage children. Let us assume that a survey of 200 people has been conducted using self-administered questionnaires and that all the questionnaires have been returned. Now we want to know the distributional characteristics of the sample. How do we get this information?

In order to learn the distributional characteristics of the sample, we classify responses into age categories by counting all those people who have young children and all those with teenage children. We then can summarize the findings by stating: "Of the 200 people in the sample, 120 or 60 percent have young children." But obviously just knowing this is not enough to test the hypothesis. We also need to know how many parents remarried and how many did not. When these responses are tabulated we discover that 120 are remarried and 80 are not.

So far the information on the two variables (divorced parents with young children and remarriage) has been classified into separate groups. But in order to test the relationship between the two variables we must examine whether those people who have young children *also* remarried. And logically, we also have to know whether those with teenage children did not remarry. When we examine the way a person responds to one question relative to another question, we call it cross tabulating the data. *Cross tabulation* allows us to examine the independent and the dependent variables simultaneously.

One way of organizing and presenting the data, then, is to construct a cross-tabulation table. Table A-1 illustrates cross tabulation of the independent and dependent variables.

The table shows that of those parents with young children 75 per-

TABLE A-1
Percentage of Divorced Parents Remarrying, by Age of Children*

	Young Children	Teenage Children	Total
Parents Who Remarry	75% (90)**	37.5% (30)	120
Parents Who Do Not Remarry	25% (30)	62.5% (50)	80
TOTAL	100% (120)	100% (80)	200

*Data fictitious
*Figures in parentheses show the actual number of people. Often this is shown as n = 90.

cent (90 people) *also* remarried, compared to only 37.5 percent (30 people) of those parents with teenagers. Thus, there is a sufficiently large difference between the two groups. When it has been determined that such a sufficiently large difference exists and is in the direction predicted, we conclude that we have confirmed the hypothesis. In other words, we accept the hypothesis. If there were no difference between the two groups or if those with teenagers had remarried more than those with young children, we would report that the hypothesis was not confirmed. We would reject the hypothesis.

Presenting data in table form is only one of several forms sociologists use to show numerical differences. Some researchers use graphic means of presentation. Figure A-1 shows the same data in different forms.

Thus far we have discussed the organization and presentation of data based on quantitative methodology. *Quantitative methodology* describes data in numerical terms and thus has the advantage of providing simplified and precise measurement. However, many sociologists argue that when data are reduced to mere numbers, some of the richer, more interesting findings are lost. These sociologists opt for a *qualitative* approach. In detailed words they describe the data perceived to be sociologically important. In terms of the three methods of data gathering, those using survey research and experiment usually rely on the quantitative approach, whereas those using case studies and participant observation tend to present their data in a qualitative way.

Regardless of the way researchers present findings, they must also analyze and interpret the meaning of the data. The investigator must explain why the results occurred the way they did. When the hypothesis is confirmed, the researcher must ask: *Why* do parents with

FIGURE A-1
Percentage of
Remarrying Parents, By
Age of Children (N = 120
remarrying parents)

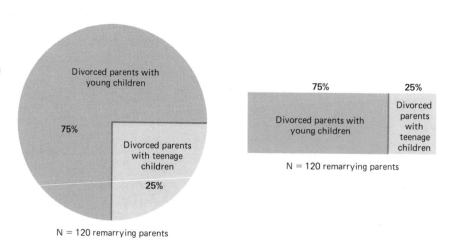

N = 120 remarrying parents

564

younger children tend to remarry more than parents with older children? Here the intervening variables must be examined. Although we suggested earlier one possible intervening variable—parents with young children attend more PTA meetings—there are, of course, numerous other variables that might help to interpret the relationship. Perhaps parents with younger children are themselves younger and thus feel greater social pressures to remarry. Or perhaps they are less financially well-off and seek remarriage for security. Even when the hypothesis is rejected, the sociologist must analyze the data in order to understand why the results turned out the way they did. As we stated earlier, researchers are like detectives: They must analyze all the clues before they offer an explanation.

CONCLUDING, GENERALIZING, AND EVALUATING

The researcher is now ready to enter the final stage of the research process. This includes summarizing the highlights of the research project and drawing conclusions. At this point, sociologists relate their findings back to the original theoretical perspective in order to see if the evidence substantiates the assertions made at the onset. If the hypothesis has been accepted, the researcher may contribute to the credibility of a theory. On the other hand, if the hypothesis has been rejected, the researcher may suggest ways to modify or reformulate the general theory.

The researcher also discusses the significance of the findings that are relevant to other existing research. This usually necessitates discussing the generalizations that can be made to the population from which the sample was drawn. In addition, new and different kinds of questions frequently evolve during the research process and the sociologist offers suggestions for future research.

Finally, the self-reflective and critical sociologist evaluates the contributions, limitations, and possible biases of his or her own study. This provides other researchers, who might want to replicate the study, with a basis on which to strengthen or improve the original research.

In this section we have described the four major steps involved in the research process. It is important to recognize the interdependence of these stages. The quality of the work in the earlier steps determines the quality of the results and the conclusions in the latter stages. For example, if a problem has not been clearly defined, difficulties will arise when one tries to generalize the meaning of the results. But the research is never as neat a step-by-step procedure as the classic model suggests. Once the process begins the researcher must always be willing to modify the strategy and the techniques for collecting data.

565

Nevertheless, the stages we have outlined serve as a useful guide for planning scientific research and for evaluating existing studies. Furthermore, this model is used as the standard format for writing the research report for publication.

Now that we have described the research process, we must critically examine the ethical issues involved in doing research. In the next section we will discuss some of these issues.

Ethics of Social Research

Recently there has been considerable controversy over the ethical implications of sociological research. While some sociologists advocate following a set of formal and rigid guidelines, others believe ethical decisions should be left more to the discretion of the professional researcher. Regardless of which stand one takes, all sociologists agree that researchers must critically evaluate the ethics of their research and approach their study with the utmost integrity and human concern for their subjects.

Each of the three methods we have discussed—experiment, case studies and observations, and survey research—has its own distinct problems in terms of ethics. But the experiment is the most problematic since the control and manipulation used have potentially the greatest chance of harming the subjects. In this section we will discuss some of the major ethical issues involved in all three kinds of social research.

DECEPTION

One ethical concern involves deception or the use of a "cover story" to conceal the real purpose of the study. Yet many researchers argue that deception is necessary in order to obtain valid data. They believe that if the subjects know the exact nature of the research they will adjust their responses to fit the researchers' expectations.

One example of deception can be seen in a series of experiments conducted by social psychologist Stanley Milgram. For the purpose of these experiments, subjects were told that they were participating in a study of learning patterns, when, in fact, the study was about obedience and compliance to authority (See Focus On: Obedience to Authority in Chapter 10). Furthermore, subjects were told that they were administering painful shocks to another person, when the victim was actually a confederate of the experimenter and was not being shocked at all.

Deception can also occur in survey research. In one study respondents were told that they were selected randomly (by chance) when they were really selected because they had been seen performing homosexual acts in public.[5] Obviously, the surveyor believed that if he

566

revealed the true basis on which respondents were selected, they would not consent to being interviewed.

When participant observation is used, frequently the subjects never even learn that they are being studied. The researcher is accepted into the group and his or her ulterior motives are never brought into consideration.

Thus, deception often occurs during the research process. And there is still controversy over the need for it and its ethical acceptability.

HARMING OR DISTRESSING THE PARTICIPANTS

Another ethical concern involves the use of harmful procedures. In the Milgram example just cited, subjects believed that they were administering harmful shocks to a victim. While subjects were actually not hurting anybody, many suffered serious distress themselves— some to the point of nervous collapse. Although a debriefing session followed in which the subjects were told the truth about the experiment, the question still remains whether these subjects suffered irreversible harm.

Ethically, the experimenter has the obligation to create a situation that will not have harmful effects on the subjects. Similarly, in survey research, the sociologist must avoid asking the kind of questions that may seriously and unnecessarily upset a respondent. This is particularly true when the research centers on such topics as sexual practices, death, mental health, or deviance.

INVASION OF PRIVACY

Each of these last two sections raises the issue of the invasion of privacy. Participants in sociological studies may be very sensitive about the kinds of personal information they reveal. Or they might not want to be studied at all. For example, it is more likely than not that those seen performing homosexual acts in public would have preferred not to be part of any research project. At any rate, when people do participate under any circumstances, the researcher must assure them anonymity and guarantee them confidentiality. Even when the results of a study are published, the identity of the participants must never be disclosed without their consent.

SPONSORSHIP AND USE OF RESEARCH

Finally, ethical issues involve two additional questions: 1) Who sponsors or funds the research; and 2) How will the results be used? In one survey, which was actually sponsored by the United States government and used for the purpose of predicting revolution in Latin America, respondents were told that the research was being sponsored by a university-affiliated group for scientific purposes only. While this is an example of deception, it also has other grave implications.[6]

Hence, social scientists must be concerned about how their findings will be used. They must face such questions as: Are the findings going to be used to manipulate people into buying products that they really do not want as is often the case in advertising or market research? Are they going to be used for governmental propaganda or oppression of disadvantaged groups? What will be done with research on the institutionalized—the aged, the mentally impaired, and the imprisoned?

INFORMED CONSENT

As we have seen, social research is plagued by several ethical issues. How do we minimize the ethical problems we have discussed? Obtaining *informed consent* is one way of accomplishing this. This means that subjects are given sufficient information to enable them to make a rational decision as to whether or not they want to participate in the study. They should be warned about any potential harmful effects or stress to themselves or others, the nature of the topics to be discussed, the reason why they were included in the study, the source of sponsorship, and the intended use of the research. Obviously, when deception is an intentional part of research, there is no true informed consent. But, ideally, subjects should be told as much as possible.

Informed consent and other guidelines for doing ethical research have been developed by the Department of Health, Education, and Welfare. In fact, government-sponsored social research now requires that each college and university have an ethics committee to review and approve proposed and ongoing research.

While such committees obviously provide an important check on the kinds of research being done, ultimately it is the moral responsibility of the researcher to protect all the people involved. Although it is important to gather accurate and dependable information about social groups and social behavior, sociologists must use ethical and humanistic means to attain their goals.

GLOSSARY

case study   a method of investigating a single group, organization, or social behavior, often conducted in a naturalistic setting.

causal relationship   a relationship between two variables in which one variable, the cause, precedes and determines the other variable, the effect.

control group   the group in an experiment, used for purposes of comparison to which the stimulus (the independent variable) is not administered.

correlation   an association of two or more variables in a regular pattern.

cross tabulation   a process by which a researcher can examine the independent and dependent variables simultaneously.

data   the factual information researchers collect in order to answer questions about the social world.

dependent variable   a variable, commonly referred to as the effect, that is influenced by another variable.

descriptive statistics   a set of logical procedures and formulas enabling the researcher to describe numerically the characteristics of the sample or population.

empiricism   the doctrine that knowledge can be acquired only through human senses.

ethnomethodology   a subarea of sociology that critically examines assumptions in the traditional scientific approach and investigates how individuals create their external social world.

experiment   a method of investigation, usually in a laboratory setting, in which two groups are used for purposes of control and manipulation of variables.

experimental group   the group in an experiment to which the stimulus (independent variable) is administered.

generalization   the process of broadening the relevance of research findings and applying them to a larger group of people or units.

Hawthorne effect   a change in a subject's performance, behavior, or attitude that occurs as a result of the investigation or observation itself.

hypothesis   a tentative assertion about the relationship between two or more variables.

independent variable   a variable, commonly referred to as the cause, that influences another variable.

inferential statistics   a set of logical procedures and formulas enabling the researcher to evaluate and predict the extent to which findings from the sample can be generalized to the population.

informed consent   the process by which subjects are given sufficient information to enable them to make a rational decision as to whether or not to participate in a study.

nonparticipant observation   a method of observation in which the researcher remains apart from the group. His or her identity as an investigator and the purpose of the study are usually disclosed to the subjects being observed.

operationalization   the process of defining each variable in a hypothesis in specific, concrete, and measurable terms.

participant observation   a method of collecting data in which the researcher actually joins or participates in the unit that he or she is studying.

phenomenology a philosophical orientation that attempts to understand human behavior from the standpoint of how individuals experience their world.

population all the members of a group or unit having the characteristics that a researcher wants to study.

qualitative methodology an approach to research that uses descriptive accounts, presenting data in detailed words rather than in numerical fashion.

quantitative methodology an approach to research that uses numerical measurement, presenting data in numbers rather than words.

random sample a sample of a population that gives every person or unit in the population an equal chance of being selected.

replication the repetition or duplication of past studies conducted to verify other research results.

sample a smaller number of people or units drawn from the population.

self-administered questionnaire a questionnaire in which the respondents themselves fill in the answers.

social theory a set of logically interrelated assertions and observations that attempt to explain social events.

structured question a closed-ended question primarily used in survey research. The subjects have a limited number of fixed responses from which to choose.

survey research a method of investigation of a large group of people in which data are collected using questionnaires and/or interviews.

systematic sampling a method of sampling used to approximate a random sample in which people are chosen at set intervals from the population list.

unstructured question an open-ended question primarily used in survey research. Subjects can respond according to their own frame of reference.

variable a social trait, quality, or characteristic that is subject to change in degree or kind.

REFERENCES

1. Jessie Bernard, *The Future of Marriage*. New York: Bantam Books, 1972, Appendix.
2. Howard S. Becker, *Outsiders: Studies in the Sociology of Deviance*. New York: The Free Press, 1963.
3. Ned Polsky, *Hustlers, Beats, and Others*. Chicago: Aldine, 1964.
4. William Foote Whyte, *Street Corner Society: The Social Structure of an Italian Slum*, rev. ed. Chicago: University of Chicago Press, 1955.
5. L. Humphreys, *Tearoom Trade: Impersonal Sex in Public Places*. Chicago: Aldine-Atherton, 1970.
6. Irving Louis Horowitz, *The Rise and Fall of Project Camelot*. Cambridge, Mass.: MIT Press, 1967.

Glossary

A   **accommodation**   a form of social interaction between two or more opposing individuals or groups who agree to cease hostility and engage in peaceful coexistence.

achieved status   a position in society that one chooses or earns.

adaptation   a process by which a group being discriminated against adjusts positively to the environment, cultivating occupational and social areas of life left open to them by the dominant group.

adolescence   that stage in the life cycle roughly between the onset of puberty and the reaching of maturity, usually beginning at about age twelve and ending at approximately age eighteen.

adult socialization   the process through which postadolescent roles are learned.

aggregate   a gathering of people in close proximity who are unorganized and without a sense of "we-ness."

aggressive action   a form of behavioral adjustment in which a group being discriminated against uses aggression to alter its situation.

agnostic   a person who is undecided about the existence of God.

agrarian society   a society in which members subsist on what they produce from the land, thus requiring a large, cheap labor force.

alienation   feelings of estrangement and hostility toward others and society in general.

anarchy   a stratification system found in small-scale societies with scarce food supplies in which physical strength alone determines social rank.

androgyny   a term describing attitudes and behaviors that are neither strongly masculine nor strongly feminine, but that are *both* masculine and feminine.

anomie   a state of normlessness; the absence of group norms.

anticipatory socialization   a process that involves training for a social status a person will occupy in the future; socialization in advance of attaining a social position.

ascribed status   a position in society into which one is born and which can rarely be altered.

assimilation   a form of social interaction in which different individuals or groups are merged into one entity.

association   a formal group that is organized for some specific purpose, has a name, a location, written rules and regulations, a hierarchy of statuses, and rules for selecting members.

atavist   according to Lombroso, a distinct type of subhuman who has not progressed up the chain of evolution.

atheist   a person who denies the existence of God.

authoritarian personality   according to Adorno, a set of personality traits that usually accompany prejudice. Includes submission to authority and intolerance toward others.

authority   institutionalized or legitimized power.

B   **bilateral descent**   a system in which descent is traced through both parents.

biological determinism   the belief that psychosexual differentiation is present at birth.

bourgeoisie   according to Marx, the class that owns the means of production and receives the profits.

bureaucracy   a highly organized hierarchical group with explicit objectives, rules and regulations, and specifically defined roles with clear rights and obligations.

C   **case study**   a method of investigating a single group, organization, or social behavior, often conducted in a naturalistic setting.

caste system   a stratification system found in agrarian societies that is based on heredity. All social relationships are severely defined and enforced by law.

causal relationship   a relationship between two variables in which one variable, the cause, precedes and determines the other variable, the effect.

cenogamy   a form of marriage in which several men are married to several women at the same time.

charismatic authority   authority based on mystical personal qualities attributed to a popular leader.

civil religion   a type of religion, peculiar to America, which blends a belief in a nondenominational deity and patriotism.

class consciousness   an identification with others holding the same social-class position.

common law   unwritten laws that have developed through custom and precedence.

community   a localized social organization through which members satisfy most of their needs and deal with most of their common problems.

competition   a form of social interaction in which two or more individuals or groups strive toward a goal that only one can attain. The individuals or groups strive to outdo each other without destroying or eliminating each other.

composition   the social and physical traits of the individuals within a population, such as age, sex, race, and occupation.

concomitant statuses   positions in society that are held at the same time.

conflict   a form of social interaction in which two or more individuals or groups strive toward a goal that only one can attain. The individuals or groups strive to destroy, eliminate, or gain control of the opponent.

conflict theory   a sociological perspective based on the premise that the competing interests of individuals and groups in a society cause or result in social change.

conspicuous consumption   a term coined by Thorstein Veblen to describe how wealthy Americans were concerned with impressing others with their wealth.

constitutional laws   norms that are written into the constitutions of the national and local governments.

control group   the group in an experiment, used for purposes of comparison, to which the stimulus (the independent variable) is not administered.

cooperation   a form of social interaction that occurs when individuals band together and pool their resources, talents, and efforts to achieve some common goal.

corporation   a socioeconomic organization that has certain rights such as owning property, signing contracts, and pursuing economic interests for its own benefit.

correlation   an association of two or more variables in a regular pattern.

credentialism   a system of granting official status to an individual by awarding a degree or certificate that attests to expertise in a given area.

crimes without victims   crimes such as vagrancy, prostitution, and gambling in which no one suffers except perhaps the victim.

cross tabulation   a process by which a researcher can examine the independent and dependent variables simultaneously.

crude birth rate   a measure of fertility that tells us how many infants are being born per thousand people in a population over a certain period of time.

crude death rate   a measure of mortality that tells us how many people die per thousand living persons in a population over a certain period of time.

cult   a loosely organized group whose members respond to experience on an emotional rather than on a rational level.

cultural base   the amount of knowledge and techniques available to an inventor.

cultural change   an alteration in the culture of a group.

cultural lag   that period between the time a change is introduced into a group and the time the group adapts to that change.

cultural relativism   an attitude in which one evaluates cultural differences in relation to the culture of the people being studied.

cultural universals   the behavior patterns and other cultural items that are found in every known society.

culture   everything that the members of a society teach one another; the rules, ideas, beliefs, and possessions shared by members of a society; a group's social heritage.

D   **data**   the factual information researchers collect in order to answer questions about the social world.

democracy   a form of government based on rule by the consent of the majority.

demography   the study of the size, composition, and distribution of human populations.

573

denomination   a formal organized religious group within a church.

dependency ratio   a measure of the dependency of a population that is calculated by dividing the number of people over age 65 and under age 15 by the number of people between the ages of 15 and 64.

dependent variable   a variable, commonly referred to as the effect, that is influenced by another variable.

descriptive statistics   a set of logical procedures and formulas enabling the researcher to describe numerically the sample or population.

deviance   a socially created phenomenon resulting from negative societal reaction toward persons who are believed to have violated a group rule.

dictatorship   a form of government in which one person (usually with advisors) controls all the power to make and enforce laws. This form of government is often acquired by usurping the power of the former government.

diffusion   a process of change involving the adoption of cultural items from another society, or from a subculture or group within the society.

discovery   a form of innovation that involves finding something that was already there.

discrimination   a term that usually refers to negative behavior toward a group that involves disqualifying its members from various activities, or mistreating them.

distribution   the spatial arrangement of the members of a population.

division of labor   the distribution of tasks and services in a society by its members.

dyad   a two-person group.

E   **ecology**   the study of the interrelationship of living things to each other and to their environment.

economic institution   the ways people in a society produce, distribute, and consume goods and services.

economic sociology   an area of sociology that deals with the interrelationships between the economic institution and the social world.

ectomorphs   according to Sheldon, those individuals who are thin and delicate.

educational institution   a system of interrelated statuses and roles that ensures the transmission of several kinds of values, attitudes, behaviors, skills, and knowledge from one generation to the next.

effectual goal   a group goal that is vague and not easily definable.

egalitarian family   a type of family in which the husband and wife equally share authority and responsibility.

egalitarian society   a stratification system found in small-scale societies with plentiful food supplies in which there is practically no social inequality.

ego   the term Freud used to describe the aspect of an individual's personality that attempts to satisfy the demands of the id in socially acceptable ways.

elitism   a sociological theory which holds that national power is controlled by the leaders of business, government, and the military.

emigration   the movement of people out of a country.

empiricism   the doctrine that knowledge can be acquired only through human senses.

endogamy   a marriage restriction that requires people to marry within certain groups, usually racial and religious groups and social class.

endomorphs   according to Sheldon, those individuals with round, soft bodies.

estate system   a stratification system in which people are assigned to an "estate" according to birth, land ownership, or military strength. Members of estates are permitted some social mobility through achievement.

ethic   a system of moral beliefs held by the members of some group or society.

ethnic group   a related group of persons with a distinct common identity; any group of people who perceives itself or is perceived by others as being socially different from the dominant group.

ehtnocentrism   the tendency of a group to take for granted the superiority of its own culture, and to see its values, beliefs, and customs as being the only "right" ones.

ethnomethodology   a subarea of sociology that critically examines assumptions in the traditional scientific approach and investigates how individuals create their external social world.

evolution   a pattern of change referring to slow, gradual change that takes place with minimal human intervention.

exchange   a form of social interaction that occurs when one group trades off one service or commodity for another of equal value; according to sociologist Neil Smelser, a form of exchange, not governed by economic factors, in which economic resources are mobilized to achieve public goals.

exogamy   a marriage restriction that requires people to marry outside of certain groups; the forbidden groups vary from one society to another, but the immediate family is excluded in all known present-day societies.

experiment   a method of investigation, usually in a laboratory setting, in which two groups are used for purposes of control and manipulation of variables.

experimental group   the group in an experiment to which the stimulus (independent variable) is administered.

expressive role   the traditional female role, in which the mother keeps her family united by providing love and affection.

extended family   (also called *consanguine family*) a type of family organization, rarely found in Western societies, in which several generations of blood relatives live together.

F   **factory system**   a form of economic organization that revolved around manufacturing.

family a universal institution whose most important functions are socializing and nurturing the younger generation.

family of orientation the family into which one is born and in which one is socialized.

fecundity the potential number of births biologically possible.

fertility the actual number of children a woman gives birth to during her childbearing years.

folkways the customs that the members of a group follow but that do not call forth strong reactions if violated.

formal control a type of social control carried out by such authorized agents as the police, the courts, psychiatrists, or teachers.

formal organization a bureaucracy.

frustration-aggression theory a psychological theory which argues that persons who are incompetent or failures or whose goals are blocked, may compensate for their failure through prejudices.

G **Gemeinschaft** according to Tönnies, a small community in which social relationships are based on feelings of sentiment and unity and in which members behave in ways beneficial to the whole group.

gender role the patterns of behavior attached to a sex status. During the socialization process one becomes masculine if one is a male and feminine if one is a female.

generalization the process of broadening the relevance of research findings and applying them to a larger group of people or units.

generalized other an abstract concept referring to the whole society whose values and expectations individuals observe and follow.

Gesellschaft according to Tönnies, a large community in which social relationships are impersonal, based on practicality and purpose rather than on emotional ties.

guild system a form of economic organization in which persons in the same trade joined together to regulate trade and commerce.

H **Hawthorne effect** a change in a subject's performance, behavior, or attitude that occurs as a result of the investigation or observation itself.

hermaphrodites individuals who exhibit a contradiction between their external genital appearance and their chromosomes or their internal reproductive systems.

horizontal mobility movement within the same stratum without a significant change in income, prestige, or power.

hypergamy the marriage of a woman to a man who is a member of a higher social class.

hypogamy the marriage of a woman to a man who is a member of a lower social class.

hypothesis a tentative assertion about the relationship between two or more variables.

576

I   **id**   the term Freud used to describe the aspect of an individual's personality that contains the innate sexual and aggressive tendencies.

ideas   all the values, myths, superstitions, scientific facts, arts, and religious beliefs shared by members of a society.

ideology   a system of ideas and beliefs about the world or some aspect of it; a system of beliefs held by a group that reflects, rationalizes, and defends the group's own interests, justifying that group's behavior, goals, attitudes, and values.

immigration   the movement of people into a country.

incest taboo   a universal social norm forbidding sexual relations between persons defined by the society as too closely related.

independent variable   a variable, commonly referred to as the cause, that influences another variable.

industrial society   a society in which machines do most of the work; members are differentiated by social class.

infant mortality rate   a measure that determines the number of infants under one year of age who die in a given year per thousand live births for that year.

inferential statistics   a set of logical procedures and formulas enabling the researcher to evaluate and predict the extent to which findings from the sample can be generalized to the population.

informal control   a type of social control that usually is handled by family members, friends, or associates.

informal organization   a social group formed within a bureaucracy which is not officially recognized but which may enhance or detract from the organization's functioning.

informed consent   the process by which subjects are given sufficient information to enable them to make a rational decision as to whether or not to participate in a study.

in-group   that circle of people to which an individual feels he or she belongs.

innovation   a process of change based on the introduction of a new item into a society by that society; according to Merton, a deviant alternative that occurs when a person accepts a goal, but for one reason or another is prevented from attaining it.

installment credit   a form of credit that enables a person to purchase an item by paying for it over a period of time with substantial interest.

institution   an organized, formal, recognized, stabilized way of performing an activity in society.

instrumental role   the traditional male role, in which the father, as breadwinner, serves as a bridge between the family and the rest of society.

intergenerational mobility   vertical mobility from one generation to another.

internalization   the absorption by members of a society of the approved values, skills, attitudes, and norms of their society.

interview   a method of investigation in which the researcher meets with the respondent and asks questions in a face-to-face situation.

577

intragenerational mobility   a person's work career in terms of vertical movement.

invention   a form of innovation in which existing cultural items are recombined into new forms, creating something that did not exist before.

K   **kinship**   a social relationship, defined differently by different societies, based on family ties.

L   **labeling perspective**   sociological approach following the belief that no behavior in and of itself is deviant; rather, deviant behavior is labeled as such by others.

labor force   those persons aged sixteen or over who are able to work, including those who are actually employed, either part-time or full-time, and those who are unemployed but seeking work.

language   a form of communication which provides people with the codes needed to define the world around them.

latent consequence   a consequence of change that is unintended and unrecognized.

laws   deliberately formulated rules of conduct that are enforced by a special authorized agency of the state; folkways and mores that are written down.

legal-rational authority   authority legitimated by a system of formal, written laws, invested in the office rather than in the individual.

leisure   nonwork activities; free-time; those activities engaged in for pleasure that are not oriented to productive labor for which one is paid.

life expectancy   the average number of years that members of a population can expect to live, given the conditions of a society.

life span   the maximum number of years that it is biologically possible for people to live.

looking-glass self   Cooley's theory that the development of the self is the product of interpreting the reactions of others to oneself.

M   **manifest consequence**   a consequence of change that is intended and recognized.

material culture   all the physical objects in our lives.

materiel   our material culture.

matriarchy   a type of family in which power is traced through the female's side of the family to her closest male relative.

matrilineal system   a kind of unilineal descent pattern in which the descent is traced through the mother's family.

matrilocal residence   a type of family residence pattern in which a newly married couple lives with or near the wife's family.

median age   the age that divides a population exactly in half.

mesomorphs   according to Sheldon, those individuals with square, hard bodies.

minority group any group that is different from the dominant group in terms of physical characteristics, cultural characteristics, or both, and is treated unequally because of these differences.

monarchy a form of government in which one person rules by inheritance. The government can either be absolute, in which the monarch is considered to be divine, or constitutional, in which the monarch is the head of state in title only.

monogamy the marriage of one man to one woman at a time.

monotheist a person who believes in one God.

moral community according to Durkheim, a group of people of one faith who share a sense of kinship and integration with each other.

mores the norms that provide the moral standards of the society. Violation of mores often results in severe punishment.

multinational corporation multimillion dollar business establishment that operates and has extensive investment in production and distribution in at least six foreign countries, wielding enough power to affect governmental relationships with these countries.

N **negative sanctions** punishments by which an individual is thought to be deterred from engaging in deviant conduct.

neolocal residence a type of family residence pattern in which a newly married couple lives apart from both the husband's and wife's relatives.

neutrality theory the belief that human beings are psychosexually neutral at birth.

noninstallment credit a form of credit that enables a person to pay for an item in one lump sum without having to pay any interest or carrying charges.

nonmaterial culture the abstract concepts in our lives, consisting of our norms and ideas.

nonparticipant observation a method of observation in which the researcher remains apart from the group. His or her identity as an investigator and the purpose of the study are usually disclosed to the subjects being observed.

norms the standards of behavior that are socially binding, or which people are expected by others to follow.

nuclear family (also called *conjugal family*) a type of family organization, most common in Western societies, in which the family consists of the husband and wife and their dependent children.

O **oligarchy** a form of government in which a few people rule.

operationalization the process of defining each variable in a hypothesis in specific, concrete, and measurable terms.

organized crime a network of syndicates that provide such illegal goods and services as drugs, loan sharking, and prostitution to those willing to pay high prices for them.

out-group that circle of people to which an individual feels no sense of belonging.

579

P **participant observation**   a method of collecting data in which the researcher actually joins or participates in the unit that he or she is studying.

participatory democracy   a type of democracy in which the adult population is directly involved with the decision-making processes of government.

patriarchy   a type of family over which the eldest male has the authority.

patrilineal system   a kind of unilineal descent pattern in which the descent is traced through the father's family.

patrilocal residence   a type of family residence pattern in which a newly married couple lives with or near the husband's family.

peer group   members of a group who are equals, usually in terms of age, education, and social class.

personality   an individual's typical patterns of attitudes and behaviors that are recognized by the individual and by others.

phenomenology   a philosophical orientation that attempts to understand human social behavior from the standpoint of how individuals experience their world.

planned obsolescence   the deliberate attempt by a manufacturer to cause a product to become outmoded.

pluralism   a sociological theory which holds that power is diffused among interest or veto groups.

political institution   the social institution that serves to maintain social order and obedience through the creation and enforcement of rules and laws.

political party   an organization of people who are interested in controlling the political structure of a society.

polyandry   a form of polygamy in which one woman is married to two or more men at the same time.

polygamy   the marriage of one person to two or more people at a time.

polygyny   a form of polygamy in which one man is married to two or more women at the same time.

polytheist   a person who believes in two or more gods.

population   an aggregate of people who share at least one specific characteristic; all the members of a group or unit having the characteristics that a researcher wants to study.

positive sanctions   rewards whereby an individual is praised for engaging in behaviors considered appropriate or desirable.

power   the ability of one person to control the behavior of others; power is based on force and cannot be circumvented.

prejudice   a term that usually refers to a negative attitude toward members of a group.

primary group   a small group in which the members know and interact with each other as individuals in an intimate relationship.

profane things   according to Durkheim, the everyday, ordinary, commonplace items in the world.

proletariat according to Marx, the class that works for those who own the means of production and receives wages.

Protestant ethic a system of beliefs which held that avoiding pleasure, devoting one's life to work, and practicing economic thrift were virtues.

"putting out" system a variation of the guild system in which independent workers manufactured goods for particular merchants who paid the workers a price for each piece produced.

Q **qualitative methodology** an approach to research that uses descriptive accounts, presenting data in detailed words rather than in numerical fashion.

quantitative methodology an approach to research that uses numerical measurement, presenting data in numbers rather than in words.

R **race** a term referring to a group of human beings who share a set of innate physical characteristics. The three most common classifications are Caucasoid, Mongoloid, and Negroid.

racism a negative attitude expressed toward some group in terms of racial characteristics.

random sample a sample of a population that gives every person or unit in the population an equal chance of being selected.

rebellion according to Merton, a deviant alternative that occurs when a person rejects the accepted goals and means and substitutes new ones in their place.

reciprocative exchange according to sociologist Neil Smelser, a form of exchange, not governed by economic factors, in which gifts and services are given and received reciprocally.

redistributive exchange according to sociologist Neil Smelser, a form of exchange, not governed by economic factors, in which wealth is redistributed.

reference group a social group to which individuals want to belong that serves as a model or standard by which they pattern their behavior.

reform a pattern of change that is similar to revolution, but is less drastic and extensive.

reform movement a social movement that is oriented toward modifying some part of society or changing some condition without totally restructuring the culture or organization of the society.

relative deprivation a realization by a group that it is disadvantaged as compared to another group.

religion a social institution characterized by a belief in the sacred quality of the supernatural, a set of rituals, and a moral code.

religiosity interest and participation in religious activities.

religious beliefs the convictions people hold concerning the things they consider sacred.

religious practices the expression people give to their religious beliefs.

581

replication   the repetition or duplication of past studies conducted to verify other research results.

representative democracy   a type of democracy in which adult citizens elect representatives who they feel will best serve their interests.

resistance movement   a social movement that is oriented toward preventing any substantial reforms and revolutions.

resocialization   a process that involves unlearning one set of rules of behavior and replacing it with another.

retreatism   according to Merton, a deviant alternative that occurs when a person accepts neither the goals nor the means for attaining them, and in effect drops out of society.

revolution   a pattern of change referring to rapid, intentional change that can drastically alter a society's existing ways of doing things.

revolutionary movement   a social movement that is oriented toward overthrowing existing systems and replacing them with different forms.

role   the expected behavioral pattern attached to a status, carrying specific rights and obligations.

role conflict   a condition that develops when an individual is expected to perform two roles at the same time that are inconsistent or incompatible.

role model   a person whom one imitates in order to become like that person.

role reciprocity   the mutual acceptance and communication by at least two individuals according to their expected behavioral patterns.

role-taking   a process by which individuals put themselves in the role of another person in order to understand that person's reactions to their selves.

rising expectations   a situation in which people feel they are entitled to more of the society's resources and rewards.

ritualism   according to Merton, a deviant alternative that occurs when a person is more concerned with the means—sticking to the rules—than the goals.

S   **sacred things**   according to Durkheim, those elements that are considered by members of a religious group to be rare and awe-inspiring.

sample   a smaller number of people or units drawn from the population.

scapegoat theory   a psychological theory which argues that people have a tendency to blame their troubles on anyone but themselves. Minority groups are often victims of scapegoating.

secondary group   a group in which relationships and interaction are impersonal and geared toward accomplishing a particular task.

sect   a small group that separates itself from a denomination and which may eventually evolve into a denomination itself.

secularization   the process by which religion becomes less influential in a society.

self-administered questionnaire   a questionnaire in which the respondents themselves fill in the answers.

582

self-fulfilling prophecy   a prediction about a series of events that helps to determine their outcome.

self-hatred   a process by which a group accepts the negative opinions other people have of them.

self-segregation   a form of behavioral adjustment in which a group being discriminated against isolates itself from the mainstream of society.

sequential statuses   positions in society that follow each other.

sex ratio   a measure of the sex composition of a population that is calculated by counting the number of males per every hundred females.

sex status   an ascribed social position based on one's sex at birth.

significant other   a person who has great influence on the development of an individual's self-image.

signs   real objects to which both human beings and animals respond.

size   the number of people who live in a certain area.

slavery   a stratification system in which a person becomes the legal possession of another person.

small-scale society   a society in which there is little technology and in which people survive by hunting and gathering food for daily consumption.

social change   a modification in the social order of a society, such as in its social institutions or its behavioral patterns; an alteration in the structure of a group or in the relationships among its members.

social class   an aggregate of people in similar occupational statuses, with similar degrees of prestige and privilege, and holding similar amounts of power.

social control   the means a society uses to ensure that its members will behave in socially acceptable ways; any mechanism used to encourage conformity and discourage deviation from social rules or acceptable patterns of behavior.

social differentiation   the division of labor in which occupational statuses are recognized but not ranked.

social dynamics   the study of social change.

social group   a set of people who have a common identity, a sense of unity, and at least some common goals and shared norms.

socialization   a process through which a human being learns and internalizes the values, skills, attitudes, and norms of the society into which he or she was born, develops a sense of self, and learns his or her place in society.

socializing agent   a person who teaches the individual the values, skills, attitudes, norms, and morality of the society, his or her place in the society, and a sense of self.

social mobility   the movement of an individual or a group from one social stratum to another or within one stratum.

social movement   a concerted action by a group that is united and has definite aims and a program to change or block change in some aspect of society.

social order   a condition of a society characterized by harmonious social relations and a lack of conflict among individuals and/or subgroups.

social sciences areas of study—such as anthropology or sociology—concerned with the behavior of human beings.

social statics the study of stable social forms.

social stratification the evaluation, ranking, and differential rewarding of positions and roles based on socially accepted criteria.

social structure the social organization of a society consisting of people in various roles and statuses with recognized rights and obligations.

social theory a set of logically interrelated assertions and observations that attempt to explain social events.

society a relatively independent and self-contained group of people that interact with each other within a particular territory and share a distinct culture.

sociology the scientific study of the patterns of human social life in groups.

statistics a set of logical procedures and measurements enabling the researcher to quantify and present findings in numerical fashion.

status a position in society.

status placement the process of putting people into positions in society by using either their innate characteristics or their achievements as criteria.

statutory laws specific norms enacted by a legislative body such as the Senate.

stereotyping the tendency to generalize about and categorize elements in our lives on the basis of limited information.

structural-functionalism a sociological perspective that regards society as a social system dependent upon each part or member for complete and proper functioning.

structured question a closed-ended question primarily used in survey research. The subjects have a limited number of fixed responses from which to choose.

subculture a group of people whose behavior, beliefs, values, and/or life-style is somewhat different from those of the dominant culture; a group who perceives itself and is perceived by others as being distinct from the larger group.

submission a process by which a group being discriminated against adopts behavior perceived as favorable by the dominant group.

superego the term Freud used to describe the aspect of an individual's personality that internalizes the social norms and imposes them on the id. "Conscience" is a suitable synonym.

survey research a method of investigation of a large group of people in which data are collected using questionnaires and/or interviews.

symbolic interaction a sociological perspective that bases its interpretations of social behavior on the verbal and nonverbal symbols shared by members of a society.

symbols socially understood arbitrary words assigned to represent tangible and intangible objects.

systematic sampling a method of sampling used to approximate a random sample in which people are chosen at set intervals from the population list.

T **task goal** a group goal that is highly specific and easily definable.

theory of complementary needs theory holding that "opposites attract" and that most people marry people whose needs and characteristics are the opposite of their own.

theory of demographic transition theory that attributes population stability to a balance or imbalance between the birth rate and the death rate, which is dependent on technology.

theory of differential association a theory proposed by Sutherland suggesting that deviant behavior is learned through interaction with others, particularly within intimate personal groups.

theory of homogamy theory holding that "like attracts like" and that most people marry people who are socially, psychologically, and even physically similar to themselves.

totalitarian state government which is almost completely centralized and controls most aspects of a citizen's life.

totem a plant, animal, or piece of sculptured wood or stone believed to have supernatural powers.

tracking the grouping of school children according to their scores on aptitude, intelligence, and achievement tests.

traditional authority authority derived from custom and accepted by people as being close to sacred.

U **unilateral descent** a system in which descent is traced through either parent, but not both.

unstructured question an open-ended question primarily used in survey research. Subjects are free to respond according to their own frame of reference.

V **values** conceptions of what is desirable, precious, attractive, good, or preferable. Values influence how we evaluate or judge people, thereby shaping our attitudes and behavior.

variable a social trait, quality, or characteristic that is subject to change in degree or kind.

vertical mobility movement of an individual or a group up or down the social-class ladder.

veto groups diversified power groups, each representing special interests and protecting its own rights.

W **white-collar crime** term used to describe certain types of offenses such as fraud, bribery, false advertising, and price-fixing committed by members of the middle and upper classes in the course of their jobs.

work the activity of expending energy to produce goods or services. In our society, work is thought of as paid employment.

work fragmentation the process by which the various operations and movements of a job are broken into component parts so that one person performs only one, or a small number, of these operations.

Z **zero population growth** a condition in which the fertility of a population is equal to its mortality and hence the size of the population remains stable.

Name Index

Abzug, Bella, 75
Aceves Joseph, 103
Adler, Freda, 486
Adorno, T. W., 28, 42, 383, 398, 400
Aiken, Michael, 334
Akers, Ronald L., 506
Aldous, Joan, 160, 167
Allport, Gordon W., 400
Amin, Idi, 306
Anderson, Nels, 472
Anderson, Walt, 540
Ariès, P., 167
Armstrong, Neil A., 74
Arnold, Thurman, 491
Ashe, Arthur, 150n
Assoi, Adiko, 78
Attila the Hun, 325
Azumi, Koya, 102, 281, 298, 444, 471

Bain, Read, 43
Baldick, Robert, 167
Baldwin, James, 140
Bales, Robert F., 71, 352, 369
Ball, Lester, 255
Balswick, Jack, 359, 369
Baltzell, E. Digby, 442
Bam, Peggy, 368
Bandura, Albert, 344, 368
Barber, Kenneth, 208
Barrett, Larry T., 208
Beach, F. A., 368
Beauvoir, Simone de, 168
Becker, Howard S., 167, 240, 399, 476, 504, 506, 558, 570
Becker, Theodore L., 333
Beckwirth, Burnham Putnam, 102
Begin, Menachem, 67
Bell, Daniel, 99, 299, 408–409, 440
Bellah, Robert N., 258, 269
Bendix, Reinhard, 441
Benedict, Ruth, 140
Benne, Kenneth D., 103
Bennis, Warren G., 103
Bensman, Joseph, 330, 334
Benson, Leonard, 197–198, 209
Berelson, Bernard R., 318
Berg, Ivar, 235, 240
Berger, Peter L., 270, 471, 472
Bernard, Jessie, 357, 875
Bernstein, Carl, 320
Biderman, A. D., 505
Bierstedt, Robert, 42, 319, 321–323, 332, 334

Billin, John P., 102
Bing, Elizabeth, 368
Binzen, Peter, 400
Birmingham, Stephen, 420, 441
Bittner, Egon, 71
Blau, Peter M., 437, 441
Block, Jeanne Humphrey, 117, 139
Bogue, Donald J., 528
Bosk, P. G., 298
Bottomore, T. B., 334, 442
Bowles, Samuel, 239
Bralowe, M., 209
Brawer, Milton J., 441
Brian, Miriam, 222–223, 239
Brim, Orville G., Jr., 149–150, 167, 168
Bronfenbrenner, Urie, 114
Brookover, Wilbur B., 239
Brown, Dee, 400
Burnham, Walter Dean, 315, 333
Burton, Ian, 541
Butler, John Sibley, 382, 400

Calvin, John, 445
Campbell, Angus, 399
Campbell, Ernest Q., 143–144, 167
Caplovitz, David, 288, 299
Caplow, Theodore, 357, 369
Carmichael, Stokely, 393
Carroll, John B., 42
Carson, Rachel, 525, 541
Carter, H., 208
Carter, Jimmy, 66
Cartwright, Dorwin, 71
Catlin, George E. G., 71
Chagnon, Napoleon, 139
Chavez, César, 394
Chein, Isador, 42
Chin, Robert, 103
Chinoy, Ely, 424, 441
Christensen, Harold T., 208, 512, 541
Churchill, Winston, 92, 325
Clarke, Alfred C., 432, 441
Cleopatra, 325
Clear, Val, 209
Cleaver, Eldridge, 378, 399, 401
Cobb, Jonathan, 442
Cohen, Albert K., 505, 506
Cohen, Mable Blake, 369
Coleman, James S., 146–147, 167, 168, 227–229, 239, 440
Coles, Robert, 492, 505
Collins, Randall, 233–234, 239, 240, 353, 369, 545

Commoner, Barry, 532
Comte, Auguste, 77, 85–86, 102, 544
Cooley, Charles Horton, 60–62, 71, 122–124, 126, 129, 137, 139
Coser, Lewis A., 71
Cottle, Thomas, 401
Cox, Archibald, 320
Cox, Harvey, 270
Crain, Alan J., 209
Cressey, Donald R., 505, 506
Crides, Charles Clifford, 441
Crockett, Harvey J., Jr., 437, 441
Cuber, John F., 210
Cumming, Elaine, 164, 167
Cummings, Judith, 239

Dahl, Robert A., 330, 334
Dahrendorf, Ralf, 90–91, 102
Darvey, Edward S., Jr., 541
Darwin, Charles, 85, 86, 115, 530
Davis, Kingsley, 112–113, 139, 414, 440, 541
DeGrazia, Sebastian, 472
DeJong, Peter, 436, 441
Della Femina, Jerry, 283, 284, 298
Delora, Jack R., 210
Delora, Joann S., 210, 431, 441
Del Tufo, Robert J., 488
Demerath, N. J., III, 270
Dodic, Isola, 75
Domhoff, G. William, 334
Duberman, Lucile, 102, 209, 210, 369, 442
Duberman, Martin, 401
Dubos, René, 532
Dudek, Stephanie, 369
Duncan, Otis Dudley, 437, 441
Durkheim, Émile, 38, 43, 53, 71, 89, 243–245, 248–250, 267–269, 275, 452, 481, 498, 499, 505, 544, 551, 553

Ehrhardt, Anke, 368, 370
Ehrlich, Anna H., 525, 541
Ehrlich, Paul R., 510, 525, 540, 541
Eisenstadt, S. N., 147–148, 167
Elizabeth II, Queen of England, 305
Elkin, Frederick, 140
Elliot, Jane, 380
Ellis, Lee, 546, 548
Epstein, Cynthia F., 369, 435–436, 441
Erikson, Erik H., 129–133, 137, 139, 140

587

Erikson, Kai T., 476–477, 498, 504, 506
Etzioni, Amitai, 102, 103
Etzioni, Eva, 102, 103
Evans-Pritchard, E. E., 27, 42
Ewald, Robert H., 102
Eysenck, Hans J., 376, 399

Fadiman, Clifton, 430, 441
Fagot, Beverly I., 369
Farmer, James, 392
Farrell, Warren, 369
Fast, Julius, 26
Finley, M. J., 440
Finley, Warren, 222–223, 239
Fishbein, Martin, 42
Fitzgerald, F. Scott, 442
Flain, Paul O., 449
Forbe, C. Daryll, 299
Ford, Gerald R., 66, 314, 320
Ford, Henry, 436
Form, William H., 471
Fox, Richard, 480, 505
Fox, Thomas G., 442
Francoeur, Anna, 370
Francoeur, Robert, 370
Franklin, Benjamin, 97
Frazier, E. Franklin, 401
Freud, Sigmund, 126–129, 137, 139, 480, 505
Fried, Morton H., 400
Friedan, Betty, 370
Fuller, R. Buckminster, 103
Fullerton, Howard N., Jr., 449

Gallup, George, 399
Gandhi, Mahatma, 324–325, 392
Gans, Herbert L., 422–423, 441
Gardner, Allen, 42
Gardner, Beatrice, 42
Garn, S. M., 368
Gaflin, George E., 505
Gebhard, Paul H., 209
Gerth, Hans H., 333
Gibbons, Don C., 504, 506
Gibbs, Jack P., 492, 506
Giddings, Franklin H., 62
Gigliotti, Richard J., 239
Gintis, Herbert, 239
Glick, P., 208
Glock, Charles Y., 245, 269
Glueck, Eleanor, 479, 505
Glueck, Sheldon, 479, 505
Goffman, Erving, 50, 72, 140, 400
Gold, David, 400
Goldberg, Susan, 368
Gordon, C. Wagner, 239
Goring, Charles, 479, 504

Gornick, V., 368
Goslin, David A., 139, 167, 368
Gould, Lois, 348
Goy, R. W., 343, 368
Grambs, Jean D., 363, 369
Greeley, Andrew M., 266, 399
Grasso, Ella, 150n
Green, Robert L., 239
Greenberg, Martin Harry, 209
Greer, Blanche, 240
Greer, Scott, 72
Gusfield, Joseph R., 102, 103
Guterman, Norbert, 472

Hacker, Helen, 369
Haldeman, H. R., 320
Haley, Alex, 401
Hall, Edward T., 26, 43
Hall, Richard H., 473
Hampson, F. A., 368
Handel, Gerald, 140, 432, 441
Hansen, Lee W., 239
Harding, Thomas G., 71
Hare, A. Paul, 55
Harlow, Harry F., 111, 139
Harlow, Margaret K., 139
Harrington, Michael, 442
Harroff, Peggy B., 210
Hartjen, Clayton A., 103, 400, 506
Hartnett, Rodney T., 239
Harwood, Edwin, 461, 472
Haven, Elizabeth M., 436, 441
Havighurst, Robert J., 225
Heath, G. G., 505
Heer, David M., 208
Heilbroner, Robert L., 298
Henderson, A. M., 71
Henderson, Ronald D., 239
Henry, William H., 164, 167
Herslin, James M., 400
Hickson, David J., 298
Hill, Reuben, 160, 167
Hill, Stuart L., 487, 505
Hite, Shere, 193
Hitler, Adolf, 91, 92, 306, 325
Hobbes, Thomas, 302
Hodge, Robert W., 416–417, 440
Hoge, Dean R., 269
Hollingshead, August B., 329, 334
Horowitz, Eugene L., 400
Horowitz, Irving Louis, 279–281, 298, 299, 570
Horowitz, Vladimir, 150n
Horton, Paul B., 400
Horvath, Dezso, 298
Hotopf, W. H. N., 400
Howe, Florence, 224, 239
Hudson, Winthrop S., 269

Hughes, Everett C., 240
Huizinga, Johan, 473
Humphreys, L., 570
Hunter, Floyd, 329, 334, 335
Hutt, Corinne, 341, 368

Ian, Janis, 46

Jacklin, Carol N., 368
Jackson, Elton J., 437, 441
Jackson, Stephen, 216
Jacobs, Jane, 299
Jacobson, Lenore, 238
Jefferson, Thomas, 404
Jencks, Christopher, 236–237, 239, 240
Jensen, Arthur R., 376, 399
Joan of Arc, 324–325
John XXIII, Pope, 325
Johnson, Sheila K., 429
Johnson, Virginia E., 192, 209
Jones, Anne, 240
Jones, Joseph F., 504, 506
Julian, Joseph, 472

Kadish, S., 505
Kagan, Jerome, 368
Kahl, Joseph A., 418–419, 422, 427, 437, 438, 440, 441
Kart, Cary S., 168
Katchadourian, Herant, 370
Katona, George, 298
Kats, Robert, 541
Kaufman, Ira, 104
Keller, Suzanne, 331, 334
Kennedy, John F., 325
Kennedy, Robert F., 325
Kephart, William, 52
Kerr, Clark, 230, 239
Kesey, Ken, 72
King, C. Wendell, 102
King, Martin Luther, Jr., 324–325, 380, 392, 393
Kinsey, Alfred C., 192–193, 209
Kirsch, A. Thomas, 102
Kirshstein, Rita, 231
Kluckhohn, Clyde, 136, 139
Kohlberg, Lawrence, 135–136, 138, 139, 344–345, 368
Kotler, Philip, 104
Kozol, Jonathan, 240
Kroeber, Arthur, 79, 102
Kübler-Ross, Elizabeth, 163, 168
Kunkel, John, 546, 548

LaFarge, Oliver, 43
LaPiere, Richard T., 399
Lasswell, Thomas E., 430, 441

Lauter, Paul, 224, 239
Lazarsfeld, Paul F., 318
Lee, Robert E., 325
Lefebvre, Henri, 472
Lejeune, Robert, 239
Lenin, V. I., 92
Lenski, Gerhard, 72, 258, 269, 270, 415, 438, 440, 442, 546, 548
Leon, Wilmer, 401
Leonard, George B., 240
Lerner, Daniel, 97, 102, 103
Leslie, Gerald R., 400
Lesser, Alexander, 400
Lester, Eva P., 369
Levin, Amy, 193, 209
Levin, Robert J., 193, 209
Levine, S. N., 343, 368
Levinson, Daniel J., 168
Lewis, Michael, 368
Lewis, Oscar, 43, 210, 426
Liebow, Elliot, 401
Lincoln, Abraham, 74, 436
Linton, Ralph, 72
Lipset, S. M., 441
Little, Craig B., 507
Lombroso, Cesare, 478, 479, 504, 505
Long, Elton, 401
Long, James, 401
Loosley, Elizabeth W., 441
Lowie, Robert H., 33, 43
Lundberg, Ferdinand, 442
Lunde, Donald, 370
Lunt, Paul S., 440
Luther, Martin, 445
Lynd, Helen M., 329, 334
Lynd, Robert S., 329, 334

McCarthy, Joseph, 29, 476
McGinnis, Joe, 283, 298
McGovern, George, 320
MacIver, Robert, 335
McKee, Michael, 472
McMillan, Charles J., 298
McPhee, William N., 318
Maccoby, E., 368
Mack, Raymond W., 372–373, 377, 399
Maddox, John, 541–542
Malcolm X, 324–325
Malinowski, Bronislaw, 71, 265, 269, 512, 541
Malthus, Thomas Robert, 529–531, 541
Manard, Barbara B., 168
Manson, Charles, 255
Mao Tse-tung, 28
Marcuse, Herbert, 310, 333

Marden, Charles F., 401
Marine, Gene, 541
Martin, Clyde E., 209
Marx, Karl, 90, 103, 281, 321, 409–413, 415, 438, 439, 440, 446, 455–457, 459, 472
Masters, William H., 192, 209
Matras, Judah, 441
Mattineou, Harriet, 102
Matza; David, 148–149, 167
Mau, James A., 104
Maurer, David, 36, 43
Mead, George Herbert, 123–126, 129, 137, 139
Mead, Margaret, 139, 345–346, 368, 370
Meadows, D. H., 542
Mendell, Lewis, 298
Merton, Robert K., 178, 208, 369, 385, 472, 481–484, 503–505
Meyer, Gladys, 401
Michaels, R. P., 368
Michels, Robert, 304, 333
Milgram, Stanley, 322, 335, 566, 567
Miller, S. M., 442
Mills, C. Wright, 326–330, 332, 333–335, 473
Moberg, David O., 254, 269
Mohammed, 81–83
Monahan, Thomas B., 178, 208
Money, John, 342, 368, 370
Montagu, Ashley, 43, 370
Moon, Sun Myung, 260
Moore, Wilbert E., 151–153, 156–157, 167, 298, 299, 414, 440
Moran, B., 368
Morgan, Marabel, 354
Moriarty, Pia, 239
Morse, Nancy C., 472
Moses, 250
Moss, H. A., 368
Mott, Paul, 334
Mueller, John H., 71, 505
Muhammad, Elijah, 255
Muir, Roy C., 369
Murdock, George Peter, 102, 187–190, 206
Murray, Henry A., 136, 139
Mussen, Paul H., 368

Neill, A. S., 240
Neugarten, Bernice, 225
Newton, Huey P., 393
Nichols, Jack, 370
Niles, Bradley E., 239
Nisbet, Robert, 369, 472

Nixon, Richard M., 283, 320, 325
Nosow, Sigmund, 471
Nye, F. Ivan, 209

Ogburn, William F., 76–77, 102
Olander, Joseph D., 209
Olexa, Carol, 239
Olsen, Marvin E., 46–48, 70–72
O'Neill, George, 204, 209
O'Neill, Nena, 204, 209
O'Neill, William L., 370
Oppenheimer, Martin, 104
Osofsky, Howard J., 209
Osofsky, Joy D., 209

Packard, Vance, 284, 292–294, 298, 299
Pareto, Vilfredo, 334
Parker, Richard, 298
Parks, Rosa, 392
Parry, Joseph B., 209
Parsons, Talcott, 71, 89–90, 189, 231, 352, 369
Paterson, Gerald R., 369
Peacock, James L., 102
Peek, Charles W., 359, 369
Peters, William, 380
Pettigrew, Thomas F., 102, 399, 401
Piaget, Jean, 134–135, 137–140
Pinard, Maurice, 315–316, 333
Pfuhl, Erdwin H., 209
Platt, Gerald M., 231
Plowman, Edward E., 270
Polk, Kenneth, 239
Polo, Marco, 377
Polsky, Ned, 558, 570
Pomeroy, Wardell B., 209
Porter, Sylvia, 298
Porterfield, Ernest, 208

Rainwater, Lee, 239, 333, 432, **441**
Reich, Charles, 104
Reich, Michael, 400
Reiss, Ira, 191–192, 209
Reynolds, Larry T., 400
Richardson, Ken, 399
Riesman, David, 239, 327–329, 332, 334, 461, 472
Rimmer, Robert, 210
Rist, Ray C., 239
Robertson, Don, 240
Robertson, Ian, 472
Robin, Stanley S., 441
Rockefeller, John D., 436
Rockefeller, Nelson, 446
Rogers, Carl, 210
Roof, Wade Clark, 400

Roosevelt, Franklin D., 92
Roosevelt, Theodore, 315
Rose, Arnold M., 335
Rose, Peter I., 401
Rosenhan, D. L., 493, 506
Rosenthal, Robert, 238
Rosow, Jerome M., 473
Rossi, Peter H., 416−417, 440
Rubington, Earl, 506
Ryan, Joseph A., 400, 441
Ryan, William, 442

Sadat, Anwar, 67
Salk, Jonas, 319
Sapir, Edward, 25
Schaffer, Walter E., 239
Schneider, Jeffrey M., 239
Schunon, Howard, 399
Schur, Edwin M., 505
Schwartz, Barton M., 102
Scott, Ann C., 356, 369
Seale, Bobby, 393
Seeley, John R., 441
Sennett, Richard, 442
Shannon, William V., 335
Shapiro, Harry L., 102
Sheatsly, Paul B., 399
Sheehy, Gail, 151
Sheldon, William J., 479, 503−505
Siegel, Paul M., 416−417, 440
Sim, Alexander, 441
Simmel, Georg, 319
Simmons, J. L., 476, 504
Simpson, George E., 391, 399, 400
Singer, Dorothy, 117
Singer, Jerome L., 117
Sjoberg, Gideon, 82
Skinner, B. F., 140
Skolnick, Jerome, 71
Smelser, Neil J., 282, 297, 298
Smigel, Erwin O., 473
Smith, Richard A., 298
Solovay, Sarah A., 71, 505
Sorokin, Pitirim, 88, 434, 441
Spears, David, 399
Spencer, Herbert, 86−87, 530

Spengler, Oswald, 88
Spiro, Audrey G., 140
Spiro, Melford, 140
Stamn, Caroline S., 209
Stark, Rodney, 245, 269
Steel, Marion, 240
Steffensmeier, Darrell J., 507
Stein, Peter, 203−204, 209, 369
Stevens, S. S., 505
Stoll, C., 368
Stouffer, Samuel A., 28, 42
Stycos, J. Mayone, 541
Sumner, William Graham, 18, 42, 62, 71
Sutherland, Edwin H., 20−21, 481, 484−485, 487, 504−506
Swain, Joseph Ward, 269
Sykes, Gresham M., 457−458, 463, 472

Talmon, Monica, 472
Tannenbaum, Frank, 502, 506
Terkel, Studs, 456, 473
Terry, Robert M., 507
Thomas, Dorothy Swaine, 139
Thomas, William I., 122, 139
Tilgher, Adriano, 471
Toffler, Alvin, 210, 292, 294, 299
Toynbee, Arnold, 88
Traub, Stuart H., 507
Treas, Judith, 441
Tretick, Stanley, 335
Tsui, Amy Ong, 528
Tucker, W. B., 505
Tucker, W. T., 285−286, 298, 299
Tullock, Gordon, 506
Tully, Judy Corder, 436, 441
Turnbull, Colin, 43, 104
Tyler, Gus, 424−425, 441
Tyree, Andrea, 441

Van Valey, Thomas L., 400
Veblen, Thorstein, 287, 297, 298
Vernon, Glenn M., 242, 243, 256, 269
Vidich, Arthur J., 330, 334

Waetjen, Walter, 363, 369
Wallace, Anthony, 43−44
Wallace, Ben J., 71
Wallerstein, Immanuel, 102, 104
Walsh, Richard A., 260
Warner, Lloyd, 418, 440
Warren, Carol A. B., 431, 441
Warrick, Patricia, 209
Washington, George, 325
Watson, John B., 115−116
Weber, Max, 71, 250, 269, 323−324, 332−334, 412−413, 415, 445−447, 471, 544, 545
Weed, Perry, 396, 400
Weinberg, Martin S., 506
Weisbrod, Burton A., 239
Weiss, Robert, 461, 472
Weisstein, N., 343, 368
Wernick, Robert, 210
Weston, Paul B., 401
Wheeler, Stanton, 167
Whorf, Benjamin Lee, 25, 42
Whyte, William Foote, 558, 570
Whyte, William H., 44
Wilcox, Jerome E., 400
Wilcox, Kathleen, 239
Willie, Charles V., 210
Wilson, E. O., 546, 548
Wilson, Woodrow, 315
Winch, Robert, 194−195, 209
Witkin, Herman A., 505
Wolff, Kurt H., 334
Wollstonecraft, Mary, 370
Woodward, Bob, 320
Wrong, Dennis H., 527, 541, 542

Yinger, J. Milton, 391, 399, 400
Young, Michael, 223, 240

Zaltman, Gerald, 104
Zander, Alvin, 71
Zimmerman, Paul D., 420, 441

Subject Index

Ability grouping, 222–226
Accommodation, 67
  definition of, 69
Adaptation
  discrimination and, 386, 398
  structural-functional concept of, 189
Addiction, drug, 494
Adolescence, 142–149
  definition of, 166
  Erikson on, 132
  peer groups in, 144–146
  properties of, 143–144
  social systems of, 146–149
Advertising, 283–284
Age composition of populations, 519–523
  dependency and, 521–522
  fertility and, 523
Aggregate, 51
  definition of, 69
Aggressive action, 387
  definition of, 398
Agnostics, 245, 268
Agrarian society, stratification in, 406–407
Alcoholism, 493–494
Alienation
  definition of, 398
  discrimination and, 389
  Marxist conception of, 410
  of work
    alleviation, 459
    Marx on, 455–457
Anarchy, 405
  definition of, 439
Androgyny
  definition of, 207
  marriage and, 202–203
Annulment of marriage, 199
Anomie, 93
  definition of, 101, 503
  deviance and, 481, 482
Anthropology as social science, 3–4
  on gender roles, 345–347
Anticipatory socialization, 153–154, 166
  definition of, 167
  See also Socialization
Assimilation, 67–68
  definition of, 69
Association, definition of, 172, 207

Atavists, 479, 503
Atheists, 245, 268
Authoritarian personality, racism and, 383
Authority
  definition of, 332
  power and, 321–323
  types of, 323–325

Beliefs, religious, 245–249
  definition of, 269
  importance of, in U.S., 263
Bilateral descent, 182, 207
Biological determinism, 341
Biology
  as cultural determinant, 32
  and deviance, 478–480
  and sexual differences, 341–342
Birth rate
  crude, 514–515
    definition of, 539
  population size and, 512–515
  U.S., 536
Blacks, 372–393
  See also Race
Body language, 26
Bourgeoisie
  definition of, 440
  Marx on, 409–412
Bureaucracy, 62–64
  definition of, 69
Bureaucratization, 97

Capitalism
  Marx on, 409–412
  Weber on, 445–446
Case studies, 558
  types of, 558
    nonparticipant observation, 558, 559
    participant observation, 558–559
Caste system, 406–407
  definition of, 439
Castration complex, 127
Causal relationships, 555
  experimental method and, 556
  factors determining, 555
Cenogamy, 177, 207
Change, 74–104
  consequences of, manifest vs. latent, 74

contact vs. isolation and, 81–83
cultural base and, 83
cultural lag and, 76–77
ideology and, 84
patterns of, 84–85
population fluctuations and, 80–81
prediction of, 96–99
processes of, 78–80
  diffusion, 78–79, 100, 101
  innovation, 79–80, 100, 101
rate of, 80–83
religion and, 250–251
social vs. cultural, 75–76, 82
social movements and, 91–95
social structure and, 84
stability vs., 77–78
theories of, 85–90
  conflict, 90–91
  cyclical, 87–89
  evolutionary, 85–87
  functionalist, 89–90
Charismatic authority, 324–325
  definition of, 332
Child rearing, 114
  See also Socialization in childhood
Christmas cards, class and, 429
Church, see Religion
Church attendance, 247
Civil religion, 258–259
  definition of, 268
Civil rights movement, 391–393
Class, 408–413, 415–438
  Christmas cards and, 429
  consumer behavior and, 291–292, 432
  credit and, 287–290
  definition of, 408, 440
  education and
    colleges, 231–233
    income, 226, 236
    intelligence testing, 221–222
    tracking, 224–226
  food and drink and, 430–431
  language and, 428–430
  lower, 425–427
  lower-middle, 422–423
  marriage and family life and, 427–428
  Marx on, 409–412
  mate selection and, 178–179

political party membership and, 315–316
recreation and, 432–433
sexual behavior and, 431–432
socialization and, 108
in U.S., 415–439
  life-styles, 427–432
  number of classes, 418–427
  social mobility, 437–438
  upper, 419–421
  upper-middle, 421–422
  value orientation and, 419
  Weber on, 412–413
  working, 424–425
See also Social stratification
Class consciousness
  definition of, 439
  Marx on, 411
Class struggle, Marx on, 411
Closed-class society, 433
Cohabitation, 203
Common law, 311
  definition of, 332
Community, definition of, 48, 69
Competition, 65–66
  definition of, 69
Complementary needs, theory of, 194–195, 208
Conflict, 65–67
  definition of, 70
Conflict theory
  definition of, 8–11
  and gender roles, 353
  and social change, 90–91
  and social stratification, 414–415
Conjugal family, *see* Nuclear family
Consanguine family, *see* Extended family
Consequences of change, 74, 101
Conspicuous consumption, 287
  definition of, 297
Constitutional laws, 311
  definition of, 332
Consumer behavior, 290–292
  class and, 291–292
  culture and, 290
  group affiliation and, 292
  social class and, 432
Consumer credit, 287–290
Contact and social change, 81–83
Cooperation, 65
  definition of, 70
Corporations, 278–279
  definition of, 297
  multinational, 279–281, 297
Correlation, 555

Credentialism, 233–236
  definition of, 238
Credit, consumer, 287–290
  installment vs. noninstallment, 287–290, 297
Crime, 485–492
  female, 486
  incidence of, in U.S., 485–486
  juvenile, 490
  organized, 491, 504
  victimless, 491, 503
  white-collar, 487–489
  definition of, 504
Cults, 254–256, 260–263
  definition of, 268
Cultural base
  change and, 83
  definition of, 101
Cultural change
  social change vs., 75–76, 82
  See also Change
Cultural lag, 76–77
  definition of, 101
Cultural relativism, 29–30
  definition of, 41
Cultural universals, 39–40
  definition of, 41
Culture, 15–44
  components, of, 16–22
  consumer behavior and, 290
  definition of, 14, 41
  determinants of, 30–33
  ethnocentrism and, 27–29
  individual and, 22–23
  relativism of, 29–30, 40, 41
  subcultures and, 34–39
  transmission of, 23–26
  universals in, 39–41
Custodial function of education, 226, 227

Data
  definition of, 549–550
  presenting, 562–566
    qualitative methods of, 562–564
    quantitative methods of, 562–564
Death, socialization for, 163, 166
Death rate
  crude, 515, 539
  population size and, 515–517
Democracy, 308–310
  definition of, 332
  participatory, 308–310
    definition of, 333
  representative, 309

  definition of, 333
Demographic transition, theory of, 526–527
Demography, 511–542
  definition of, 511, 538, 540
  See also Population
Denominations, religious, 254–256
  definition of, 268
  profiles of, 257
Dependency ratio, 521–522
  definition of, 540
Descent
  bilateral, 182, 207
  family organization and, 181–182
  matrilineal, 182, 207
  patrilineal, 182, 208
  unilateral, 182, 208
Desertion, 199
Development, individual
  Erikson's stages of, 129–133
  Freud on, 126–128
  Kohlberg on, 135–136
  Piaget on, 134–135
  See also Socialization
Deviance, 476–507
  in adolescence, 148–149
  criminal, 485–492
    females, 486
    incidence, in U.S., 485–486
    juvenile deliquency, 490
    organized crime, 491–492
    victimless crimes, 491
    white-collar crime, 487–489
  definition of, 476–478, 503
  dysfunctions of, 496–498
  explanations of, 478–485
    biological, 478–480
    by Durkheim, 481
    by Merton, 483–484
    psychological, 480–481
    by Sutherland, 484–485
  functions of, 498–499
  noncriminal, 492–496
    alcoholism, 493–494
    drug addiction, 494
    homosexuality, 495–496
    mental illness, 492–493
  social control of, 499–502
Dictatorship, 306–308
  definition of, 332
Differential association, theory of, 484–485
  definition of, 504
Differentiation, social, 404
  definition of, 440
Diffusion, 78–79
  definition of, 101

Discovery as form of innovation, 79, 101
Discrimination
    definition of, 380–381, 398
    prejudice and, 380–386
    reactions to, 386–389
        behavioral adjustment, 386–388
        psychological adjustment, 388–389
    theories of, 383–386
Distribution, 273–275
Divison of labor
    definition of, 297
    increase in, 452
    social ranking and, 275
Dominance, power and, 321
Drug addiction, 494
Dyad, 55
    definition of, 70

Ecology
    definition of, 529, 540
    population growth and, 529–536
        energy, 531–535
        food, 529–531
        pollution, 535–536
Economic cooperation, as family function, 183, 188
Economic institution
    definition of, 272, 295–297
    functions of, 272–276
    See also Economy
Economics as social science, 3
Economic sociology, 272
    definition of, 297
Economy, 272–299
    functions of, 272–276
        distribution of power, 276
        production and distribution, 273–275
        social ranking, 275–276
    growth of, 294–295
    social forces and, 281–294
        consumer behavior, 290–292
        consumer credit, 287–290
        forms of exchange, 282
        marketing, 282–287
        waste, 292–294
    types of, 276–281
        corporation, 281
        factory system, 277–278
        guild system, 276–277
        multinational corporation, 279–281
Ectomorphs, 479, 503
Education, 212–240

class and
    colleges, 231–233
    income, 226, 236
    intelligence testing, 221–222
    tracking, 224–226
credentialism and, 233–236
development of, in U.S., 212–214
as family function, 186
functions of, 214–229
    custodial, 226–227
    innovative, 229
    secondary, 226–229
    skills and knowledge transmission, 215–218
    social interaction, 227–229
    status placement, 218–226
    values transmission, 214–215
higher, 230–236
as institution, 212, 237
    definition of, 212, 238
role conflict and, 220
"training" vs. "educating" and, 217–218
Egalitarian society, 405
    definition of, 439
Ego, 127–128, 480
    definition of, 138
Electra complex, 127
Elitism
    definition of, 332
    Mills' conception of, 327–331
Emigration, 517
    definition of, 540
Employees in occupational structure, 451–452
Endogamy, 177–178
    definition of, 207
Endomorphs, 479, 503
Environment, as cultural determinant, 30–32
Estate system, 407
    definition of, 439
Ethic
    definition of, 471
    Protestant, 445–446, 471
Ethnic groups, 372–401
    definition of, 373–374, 398
    nonblack, 393–396
    See also Race
Ethnicity
    cultural achievement and, 377
    intelligence and, 375–376
Ethnic relationships, change in, 389–393
Ethnocentrism
    culture and, 27–29

definition of, 41
Evaluation, educational, 219–220
Evolution and social change, 84–87
    definition of, 101
Exchange, 65
    definition of, 70, 297
    forms of, 282
    reciprocative, 282, 297
    redistributive, 282, 297
Exogamy, 177–178
    definition of, 207
Expectations, rising, 93
    definition of, 101
Experiments, 556–558
    disadvantages of, 557–558
    groups within, 557
Expressive role, 189
    female, 352–353
Extended family, 179–181
    definition of, 207

Factory system, 277–278
    definition of, 297
False consciousness, 410
Family, 174–210
    American, patterns in, 190–205
        marriage, 196–205
        sex, 190–196
    class-specific features of, 427–428
    conjugal, see Nuclear family
    consanguine, see Extended family
    definition of, 174, 207
    descent and, 181–182
    egalitarian, 180, 207
    extended, 179–181
        definition of, 207
    functions of, 182–190
        economic, 183, 188
        educational, 186
        Murdock's theory of, 187–190
        protective, 183–184
        recreational, 184–185
        religious, 184
        reproductive, 187
        sexual regulation, 187–190
        socialization, 188–190
        status placement, 186
    future of, 202–205
    kinship and, 174–175
    marriage and, 175–179
    matriarchal, 181
    nuclear, 179–180
        definition of, 208
        Murdock's theory, 188–190

organization of, 179–182
Parsons on, 189
patriarchal, 181
residence and, 180
Fecundity, 512
definition of, 540
Fertility, 512
age composition of populations
and, 523
definition of, 540
Folkways, 18
definition of, 41
Force, power and, 321–323
Formal control, 500–501
definition of, 503
Formal organizations, 63
definition of, 70
See also Bureaucracy
Fragmentation of work, 452
definition of, 471
Freedoms, individual, 22–23
Frustration-aggression theory, 383
definition of, 398
Functionalism
and social change, 89–90
See also
Structural-functionalism

Gender roles
anthropological view of,
345–346
biological views of, 341–342
changes in, 364–365
definition of, 367
Gould on, 348
interpersonal relationships and,
356–360
husband/father, 359–360
wife/mother, 356–360
psychological views of,
342–345
animal studies, 342–343
cognitive development
theory, 344–345
social learning theory,
343–344
socialization for, 351–364
conflict theory, 353
ideal female and male,
353–355
reasons, 352–353
structural-functionalism,
352–353
"total woman," 354
sociological approach to,
346–347
testing, 347–351

work world and, 360–364
income, 363–364
stereotyped occupations,
361–363
Generalized other, 123–125
definition of, 138
Geography, population distribution
and, 523
Goal attainment, definition of, 189
Goals
effectual, 55–56
definition of, 70
group, 55–56
task, 55–56
definition of, 70
Government, 302–335
development of political units
and, 302–303
forms of, 304–310
democracy, 308–310, 332
dictatorship, 306–308, 332
monarchy, 304–305, 333
oligarchy, 304, 333
functions of, 310–313
coordination, 312–313
maintenance of order,
311–312
protection of citizens, 313
political parties and, 314–318
political power and, 319–331
See also Power
Groups, 51–68
consumer behavior and, 292
formal vs. informal organization
of, 63–64
importance of, 54
in-, 62–63
definition of, 70
influences on, 54–59
cohesion, 58
duration, 57–58
goals, 55–56
internal differentiation, 58
internal interaction, 58–59
membership, 56–57
size, 55
interaction patterns of, 65–68
kinds of, 59–64
out-, 63
definition of, 70
peer, definition of, 70
primary, 60–61
definition of, 70
secondary, 62
definition of, 70
social, definition of, 70
Growth, economic, 294–295
Guild system, 276–277

definition of, 297

Hermaphrodites, 342
definition of, 367
Hispanic-Americans, 394
History as social science, 2–3
Homogamy, theory of, 194–195,
208
Homosexuality, 495–496
Hypergamy, 179, 207
Hypogamy, 179, 207

Id, 126–128, 480
definition of, 138
Ideas
as component of culture, 16–17
definition of, 41
Ideology
change and, 84
definition of, 333
in totalitarian states, 307
Immigration, 517
definition of, 540
Incest taboo, 177, 207
Income
educational level reached by,
226–236
gender roles and, 363–364
Indians, American, 31, 47, 394
Individual
culture and, 22–23
See also Development,
individual
Industrialization, 98, 277–278
population distribution and,
524
Industrial society
definition of, 439
stratification in, 408
Inequality, see Social stratification
Infant mortality rate, 516
definition of, 540
Influence, power and, 320–321
Informal control, 500–501
definition of, 503
Informal organizations, 64
definition of, 70
In-groups, 62
definition of, 70
Innovation, 79
definition of, 101
as deviant alternative, 482
definition of, 503
as function of education, 229
Installment credit, 287–290
definition of, 297
Institution, 172–335

definition of, 172, 207
economic
    definition of, 272, 297
    functions of, 272–276
    See also Economy
educational, 212, 237
    definition of, 212, 238
family, 173–210
political, 302–335
    definition of, 302, 333
    functions of, 310–313
    See also Government
religious, 242, 259–263, 266
    See also Religion
Instrumental role, 189
    male, 352–353
Integration, structural-functional
    concept of, 189
Intelligence, race and, 375–376
Intelligence testing, 220–222
    gender roles and, 347–349
Interaction
    group, 58–59, 65–68
    symbolic, *see* Symbolic
        interaction
Internalization
    definition of, 138
    socialization and, 110
Invention, 79, 101
Isolation and social change, 81–83

Jews, 395–396
Juvenile delinquency, 490

Kinship
    definition of, 207
    family and, 174–175

Labeling perspective, 476
    definition of, 504
Labor force, 448–454
    age of, 448–449
    definition of, 471
    employees in, 451–452
    occupational groupings and,
        450–451
    specialization and, 452–453
    wages and hours and, 453, 454
Labor unions, 276
Language
    class and, 428–430
    definition of, 41
    in transmission of culture,
        25–26
Latency, definition of, 189
Laws, 19–21
    common, 311

definition of, 332
constitutional, 311
    definition of, 332
definition of, 41
statutory, 311
    definition of, 333
Legal-rational authority, 325
    definition of, 333
Leisure, 464–470
    definition of, 464–465, 471
    mass, 467
    self-image and, 467–468
    work and, 465–466, 469
Leisure industry, 469, 471
Life expectancy, 516–517
    definition of, 540
Life span, 516–517
    definition of, 540
Looking-glass self, 60, 122–123
    definition of, 138
Lower class, 425–427
Lower-middle class, 422–423

Marketing, 282–286
    advertising in, 283–284
    sale in, 285–286
Marriage
    American patterns of, 196–205
        alternatives, 202–205
        mate selection, 194–196
        motives, 196–197
        popularity, 196
        remarriage, 201–202
        romantic love, 194
        success and failure, 198–200
    androgynous, 202–203
    class-specific features of,
        427–428
    family and, 175–179
    forms of, 175–177
    open, 204
    restrictions in, 177–179
    socialization for, 157–161, 166
"Marriage work," 197–198
Mate-swapping, 204–205
Material culture, definition of, 41
Materiel
    as component of culture, 21–22
    definition of, 41
Matriarchy
    definition of, 207
    family and, 181
Matrilineal descent, 182, 207
Matrilocal residence, 180, 207
Mental illness, 492–493
Meritocracy, 223
Mesomorphs, 479, 504
Migration rate, 517–518

Minority groups
    definition of, 374–375, 398
    nonblack, 393–396
    See also Race
Mobility, social, 433–439
    definition of, 440
    female, 435–436
    horizontal, 434, 439
    intergenerational, 434, 439, 440
    intragenerational, 434, 439, 440
    vertical, 434, 439, 440
Modernization, 97
Monarchy, 304–305
    definition of, 333
Monogamy, 175
    definition of, 207
Monotheists, 244, 268
Moral community, 249–250
    definition of, 268
Mores, 18–19
    definition of, 41
Multinational corporations,
    279–281
    definition of, 297

Native Americans, 31, 47, 394
Nature and nurture, 114–116
Negative sanctions, 500–501
    definition of, 504
Neolocal residence, 180, 207
Neutrality theory, 341–342,
    346–347
    definition of, 367
Noninstallment credit, 287–290
    definition of, 297
Nonmaterial culture, definition of,
    41
Norms
    as component of culture, 17–21
    definition of, 41
Nuclear family, 179–180
    definition of, 208
    Murdock on, 188–190
Nurture, socialization and,
    114–116

Obsolescence, planned, 292–293
    definition of, 297
Occupational groupings, 450–451
Occupational socialization,
    150–157, 166
Occupational status, gender roles
    and, 361–364
Oedipus complex, 127
Old age, socialization for, 162–166
Oligarchy, 304
    definition of, 333
Open-class society, 433

Open marriages, 204
Organization
    economic, types of, 276–281
    formal, 63–64
        definition of, 70
    informal, 64
        definition of, 70
    religious, types of, 254–256
Oriental-Americans, 395
Other, significant and generalized,
    123–125
    definitions of, 138
Out-groups, 63
    definition of, 70

Parenthood, socialization for,
    161–162, 166
Parties, political, 314–317
    definition of, 314, 333
    in dictatorships, 307
    membership of, 315–316
    voting behavior and, 316–318
Patriarchy
    definition of, 208
    family and, 181
Patrilineal descent, 182, 208
Patrilocal residence, 180, 208
Peer groups, 60
    in adolescence, 144–146
    definition of, 70, 167
    at school, 227–229
Personality
    definition of, 138
    development of, 120–121
Planned obsolescence, 292–293
    definition of, 297
Pluralism
    definition of, 333
    Riesman's theory of, 327–331
Political institution, 302–335
    definition of, 302, 333
    functions of, 310–313
    See also Government
Political parties, see Parties,
    political
Political science as social science,
    3
Political units, development of,
    302–303
Polygamy, 175–177, 208
    definition of, 175–176, 208
Polygyny, 175–177, 208
Polytheists, 244, 268
Population, 510–542
    change and fluctuations of,
        80–81
    composition of, 518–523
        aage, 519–522

definition, 511, 539
    sex ratio, 519
    in U.S., 536–537
definition of, 511, 540
distribution of, 523–525
    definition of, 511, 540
    geographic, 523
    in U.S., 537
    urbanization and
        industrialization,
        524–525
ecological consequences of,
    energy, 531–535
    food supply, 529–531
    pollution, 535–536
growth of, 525–536
    causes of, 526–527
    solutions to problems of,
        527–529
    in U.S., 538
size of, 511–518
    birth rate, 512–515
    death rate, 515–517
    definition of, 511, 540
    migration rate, 517–518
    in U.S., 536
Positive sanctions, 500–501
    definition of, 504
Postindustrial society, 99
    stratification and, 408–409
Power, 318–331
    authority and, 321–324
    definition of, 319–323, 333
    distribution of, 276
    dominance and, 321
    force and, 321–323
    influence and, 320–321
    presidential, 320
    prestige and, 319–320
    rights and, 321
    sources of, 323
    studies on, 329–331
    theories of, 326–331
    Watergate and, 320
    Weber on, 412–413
Power elite, 327–331
Practices, religious, 245–249
    definition of, 269
Prejudice, 378–386
    definition of, 378, 398
    discrimination and, 380–386
    reactions to, 386–389
    theories of, 383–386
        economic factors, 384–385
        psychological, 383
        social function, 385–386
Prestige, power and, 319
Primary groups, 60–61

definition of, 70
Production, 273–275
Profane things, 244–245
    definition of, 268
Proletariat
    definition of, 440
    Marx on, 409–412
Protection as family function,
    183–184
Protestant ethic, 445–446
    definition of, 471
"Putting out" system, 277
    definition of, 297
Psychoanalysis
    by Erikson, 128–133
    by Freud, 126–128
Psychology
    and deviance, 480–481
    and gender roles, 342–345
    and prejudice, 383
    as social science, 3

Race, 372–401
    changing attitudes toward,
        390–391
    civil rights movement and,
        391–393
    cultural achievement and, 377
    definition of, 372–373, 398
    discrimination and, 378–393
        reactions to, 386–389
        theories of, 383–386
    exogamy and, 178
    human differences and,
        375–377
        intelligence, 375–376
Ranking, social, 275–276
Rebellion, 482, 502
Reciprocative exchange, 282
    definition of, 297
Recreation
    as family function, 184–185
    social class and, 432–433
    See also Leisure
Redistributive exchange, 282
    definition of, 297
Reference groups, 123–124
    definition of, 138
Reform
    definition of, 101
    as pattern of change, 84–85
    social movements and, 94, 101
Relative deprivation, 93
    definition of, 101
Relativism, cultural, 29–30
    definition of, 41
Religion, 242–270

characteristics of, 242–250
    beliefs and practices,
        245–249
    moral community, 249–250
    sacred-profane distinction,
        244–245, 268, 269
definition of, 269
Durkheim on, 243–250, 268,
    269
dysfunctions of, 253
exogamy and, 178
as family function, 184
functions of, 250–253
as institution, 242, 266
    changes in, 259–263
organization of, 254–256
science and, 263–266
in U.S.
    changes in, 259–263
    church attendance, 247
    "civil religion," 258–259,
        268
    groups, 256–258
    importance of beliefs, 263
    major faiths, 257
Religiosity, 248
    definition of, 269
Remarriage, 201–202
Replication, definition of, 553
Research, 549
    ethics of social, 566–568
        deception, 566–567
        harming participants, 567
        informed consent, 568
        invasion of privacy,
            567
        sponsorship and use of
            research, 567–568
    methods for conducting,
        556–562
        case studies, 556, 558–559
        experiments, 556–558
        participant observation,
            556, 558–559
        survey research, 556,
            559–562
    problems of social, 837–839
    process of social, 841–867
    relationship between theory
        and, 839–841
Research methodology, 836–871
Residence
    matrilocal, 180, 207
    neolocal, 180, 207
    patrilocal, 180, 208
Resistance movements, 94–95
    definition of, 101
Resocialization

adolescent, 143–144
    adult socialization as, 149
    definition of, 167
Retirement, 462–464
Retreatism, 482, 503
Revolution, 85
    definition of, 101
    social movements and, 94, 101
Rights, power and, 321
Rising expectations, 93
    definition of, 101
Ritualism, 482, 504
Role conflict, 51
    definition of, 70, 238
    in schools, 220
Role models, 123–125
    definition of, 138
Role reciprocity, 50
    definition of, 70
Roles, 50–51
    in adolescence, 144–146
    definition of, 70
    expressive, 352–353
    gender, see Gender roles
    instrumental, 189, 352–353
    socialization and, 119–120
Role-taking, 124–125
    definition of, 138
Romantic love, 194

Sacred things, 244–245
    definition of, 269
Sale in marketing, 285–286
Sanctions, 500–501, 504
Scapegoat theory, 383
    definition of, 399
Science, religion and, 263–266
Secondary groups, 62
    definition of, 70
Sects, 254
    definition of, 269
Secularization, 260–261
    definition of, 269
Self
    looking-glass, 60, 122–123
    Mead on, 123
Self-fulfilling prophecy, 385–386
    definition of, 399
Self-hatred, 389, 399
Self-segregation, 387, 399
Separation, legal, 199
Sex
    adult socialization and, 151
    American family patterns and,
        191
    class and, 431–432
    female attitudes toward, 193
    premarital, in U.S., 191–194

Sex ratio of population, 519
    definition of, 540
Sex roles, see Gender roles
Sex status, 340
    definition of, 367
    See also Gender roles
Sexual regulation, 187–190
Significant other, 123–125
    definition of, 138
Signs
    definition of, 41
    transmission of culture and,
        23–24
Singlehood, 203–204
Slavery, 406
    definition of, 440
Small-scale society
    definition of, 440
    stratification in, 405–406
Social change, 544
    vs. cultural change, 75–76, 82
    definition of, 11, 101
    See also Change
Social class, see Class
Social control
    definition of, 138, 499, 504
    deviance and, 499–502
    informal and formal, 499–501,
        504
    paradox of, 501–502
    religion and, 250
    socialization and, 119
Social differentiation, 404
    definition of, 440
Social dynamics, 77, 86, 544
    definition of, 102
Socialization, 108–168
    adolescent, 132, 142–149
        parents, 146
        social system, 146–149
        status and roles, 146
    adult, 149–166
        death, 163
        definition, 167
        marriage, 157–161
        old age, 162–165
        parenthood, 161–162
        sex, 151
        Sheehy on, 151
        work, 150–157
    anticipatory, 153–154, 166
        definition of, 167
    in childhood, 110–140
        cognitive development
            approach, 133–136
        Cooley's theory, 60,
            122–123
        Davis' theory, 112–113

Erikson's theory, 129–133
functions, 116–121
Harlow's theory, 111
Mead's theory, 123–125
nature and nurture, 114–116
personality development,
120–121
process, 110–114
psychoanalytic approach,
126–133
Singer's theory, 117
social adjustment, 119–120
social control, 119
symbolic interactionists,
121–122
transmission of customs,
116–119
definition of, 108, 138
family and, 188–190
gender-role, 351–364
conflict theory, 353
husband/father, 359–360
ideal females and males,
353–355
income, 363–364
reasons, 352–353
stereotyped occupations,
361–363
structural-functionalism,
352–353
"total woman," 354
wife/mother, 356–360
roles and, 119–120
social structure and, 119–120
statuses and, 119–120
See also Resocialization
Socializing agents, 110–111
definition of, 139
Social learning theory, 343–344,
346–347
Social mobility, see Mobility,
social
Social movements
change and, 91–95
definition of, 102
types of, 94–95
Social order, 544
definition of, 11
Social psychology, 3
Social ranking, 275–276
Social sciences
definition of, 11
sociology and, 2–4
Social statics, 544
Social stratification, 404–442, 544,
545
in agrarian societies, 406–407
conflict theory on, 414–415

definition of, 404–405, 439
in industrial society, 408
Marx's theory and, 409–412
postindustrial societies and,
408–409
in small-scale societies,
405–406
structural-functionalism on,
413–414
in U.S., 415–439
educational level as
criterion, 415–416
income as criterion,
415–416
life-styles, class-specific,
427–432
number of classes, 418–427
occupation as criterion,
415–417
social mobility, 433–439
Weber's theory and, 412–413
See also Class
Social structure, 48–51
change and, 84, 100
definition of, 70
socialization and, 119–120
Social theory
definition of, 551
Durkheim's use of, 551
informal use of, 551
usefulness of, 551–552
Society, 46–72
definition of, 46–48, 70
Sociobiology, 546
Sociograms, 59
Sociology
assumptions of, 5–7
careers in, 547–548
definition of, 11
economic, 272
definition of, 297
perspectives of, 7–10
problems of, 544–547
reasons for study of, 4–5
social sciences and, 2–4
Solidarity, mechanical vs. organic,
248
Specialization, 96
of work 452–453
Sports, 469
Stages, Freudian, 127
Statistics, 562–564
descriptive, 562
inferential, 562–563
Status, 48–49
achieved, 49, 119–120
definition of, 69
in adolescence, 144–146

ascribed, 48–49, 119
definition of, 69
concomitant, 48
definition of, 69
consumer behavior and,
291–292
definition of, 79
leisure and, 468
sequential, 48
definition of, 70
sex, see Sex status
socialization and, 119
Weber on, 412–413
Status placement
definition of, 238
education and, 218–226
evaluation, 219–220
intelligence testing,
220–222
tracking, 222–226
family and, 186
Statutory laws, 311
definition of, 333
Stereotyping
definition of, 399
occupational, by gender,
361–363
prejudice and, 378–379
Stratification, see Social
stratification
Structural-functionalism
definition of, 7–8, 10, 11
on family, 189
on gender roles, 352–353
Parsons' theory of, 189
on social stratification, 413–414
See also Functionalism
Subcultures, 34–39
definition of, 41
language as sign of, 35–37
origins of, 37–39
Submission, 386
definition of, 399
Suicide, 249
Superego, 128, 480
definition of, 139
Supply and demand, 274–275
Survey research, 559–562
interview as part of, 561
questionnaires as part of, 560–
562
sampling during, 560
available sample, 560
random sample, 560
systematic sampling, 560
Symbolic interaction
definition of, 9–11
socialization and, 121–122, 137

Symbols
   definition of, 41
   transmission of culture and,
     23–24

"Throw-away" society, 292–294
Totems, 242
   definition of, 269
Totalitarian states, 306–308
   definition of, 333
"Total woman," 354
Tracking, 222–226
   definition of, 238
Trade unions, 276
Traditional authority, 324
   definition of, 333
"Training" vs. "Educating,"
   217–218

Unemployment, 459–462
Unilateral descent, 182, 208
Unions, 276
Upper class, 419–421
Upper-middle class, 421–422
Urbanization, 524

Value orientation, 419
Values, definition of, 41
Variables, 554–555
   definition of, 554
   operationalization of, 554
   relationships among, 555–556
   types of, 555–556
     dependent, 555, 562
     independent, 555, 556, 557,
      562
     intervening, 555
Veto groups, 328, 330
   definition of, 333
Voting behavior, 316–318

Wages, 453, 454
Waste, 292–294
White-collar crime, 487–489
   definition of, 504
White ethnics, 396
Women's movement, 364–366
Work, 444–464
   alienation of
     alleviation, 459
     Marx on, 455–457
   definition of, 471

dissatisfaction with, 455–459
fragmentation of, 452, 471
gender roles and, 360–364
   income, 363–364
   stereotyped occupations,
     361–363
meaning of, 444–448
Protestant ethic and, 445–446
self-esteem and, 447–448, 453
socialization for, 150–157, 166
Terkel on, 456
in U.S., 448–454
   age of labor force, 448–449
   nation of employees,
     451–452
   occupational groupings,
     450–451
   sex of labor force, 450
   specialization, 452–453
   unemployment, 459–462
   wages and hours, 453, 454
Working class, 424–425

Zero population growth rate, 515
   definition of, 540

Credits

Introduction
1: Leo de Wys, Inc. 4L: Marc & Evelyn Bernheim-Woodfin Camp & Associates. 4R: Tim Eagan-Woodfin Camp & Associates. 6: Jim Green. 7L: Lilo Raymond-Woodfin Camp & Associates. 7R: Gorgoni-Leo de Wys, Inc. 8: Paul Conklin

Part One Opener, 12–13: James H. Karales-Peter Arnold, Inc.

Chapter 1
15: Michal Heron-Woodfin Camp & Associates. 18: E. Johnson-Leo de Wys, Inc. 20: Howard Brainen. 24: Silver Burdett photos. 27: James H. Karales-Peter Arnold, Inc. 29: Robert Phillips- Black Star. 31T: John Running. 31B: John Running-Black Star. 34TL: Sepp Seitz-Woodfin Camp & Associates. 34TR: Ginger Chih-Peter Arnold, Inc. 34BL: Barbara Pfeffer-Peter Arnold, Inc. 34BR: Jane Latta. 37: Museum of the City of New York. 39: Linda Rogers-Woodfin Camp & Associates

Chapter 2
45: Clough/Contact-Leo de Wys, Inc. 47: Marcia Keegan-Peter Arnold, Inc. 49L: Howard Sochurek-Woodfin Camp & Associates. 49R: Jim Green. 52: George A. Tice, Photo Trends 53T: The Bettmann Archive, Inc. 53B: Leo de Wys, Inc. Table 2–1, p. 55: From Hare, *Handbook of Small Group Research.* Copyright © 1962 by The Free Press of Glencoe. 56: Sylvia Johnson-Woodfin Camp & Associates. 57: Christina Thomson. 60: American Sociological Association. 61L: Jim Green. 61R: Dan Brinzac-Peter Arnold, Inc. 65: Jim Green. 66: Jim Anderson-Woodfin Camp & Associates. 67: Leroy Woodson-Woodfin Camp & Associates.

Chapter 3
73: Arthur Levine-Leo de Wys, Inc. 75T: Historical Picture Service. 75B: Sylvia Johnson-Woodfin Camp & Associates. 76L: Culver Pictures. 76R: Marc & Evelyn Bernheim-Woodfin Camp & Associates. 78L: Marc & Evelyn Bernheim-Woodfin Camp & Associates. 78R: J. S. Barry-Nancy Palmer Photo Agency. 81: John Nance-Magnum Photos. 86 & 87: The Bettmann Archive, Inc. 92TL & 92B: Wide World Photos. 92TR: Culver Pictures. 93: Norris McNamara-Nancy Palmer Photo Agency. 94: The Bettmann Archive, Inc. 95: Leif Skoogfors-Woodfin Camp & Associates. 97: Robert Azzi-Magnum Photos.

Part Two Opener, 106–107: Joan Liftin-Woodfin Camp & Associates.

Chapter 4
109: Rae Russell-Monkmeyer Press Photo Service. 110: Jim Green. 111: Harry F. Harlow-University of Wisconsin Primate Laboratory. 112: David R. White-Woodfin Camp & Associates. 115L: Baron Wolman-Woodfin Camp & Associates. 115R: Erika Stone-Peter Arnold, Inc. 118L: Marc & Evelyn Bernheim-Woodfin Camp & Associates. 118R: C. Bonington-Woodfin Camp & Associates. 124: University of Chicago Press. 125: University of Chicago Press. 126: The Bettmann Archive, Inc. 130LR: Jim Green. 131T: Joan Liftin-Woodfin Camp & Associates. 131B: Ginger Chih-Peter Arnold, Inc.

Chapter 5
141: Jim Green. 144: Sepp Seitz-Woodfin Camp & Associates. 145: Alex Webb-Magnum Photos. 148: Charles Gatewood-Magnum Photos. 153: Marc & Evelyn Bernheim-Woodfin Camp & Associates. 156: Michal Heron-Woodfin Camp & Associates. 159: Ellen Pines-Woodfin Camp & Associates. 161: Dan S. Nelken-Photo Trends. 164T: Jim Green. 164B: P. Vannucci-Leo de Wys, Inc.

Part Three Opener, 170–171: Leo de Wys, Inc.

Chapter 6
173: Steve Hansen-Stock, Boston. 175: Photo Trends. 176: Marc & Evelyn Bernheim-Woodfin Camp & Associates. 179: Dorka Raynor-Leo de Wys, Inc. 180: Dorka Raynor-Leo de Wys, Inc. 184: Culver Pictures. 185T: Culver Pictures. 185B: Ray Lanterman for Silver Burdett. 188: Victoria Beller-Smith-Photo Trends. 200: James R. Smith-Photo Trends.

Chapter 7
211: Bill Grimes-Leo de Wys, Inc. 213: Culver Pictures. 215: James R. Smith-Photo Trends. 216: Fred Kaplan-Black Star. Figure 7–1, p. 217: Adapted from The Gallup Opinion Index, American Institute of Public Opinion, September 1972, Report No. 87. 218L: Dan Budnik-Woodfin Camp & Associates. 218R: Jim Anderson-Woodfin Camp & Associates. 224: Ginger Chih-Peter Arnold, Inc. Table 7–1, p. 225: From Robert J. Havighurst and Bernice L. Neugarten, SOCIETY AND EDUCATION, Third Edition. Copyright © 1967 by Allyn and Bacon, Inc., Boston. Reprinted by permission. 228T: Ginger Chih-Peter Arnold, Inc. 228B: Jim Anderson-Woodfin Camp & Associates. 234: James H. Karales-Peter Arnold, Inc.

Chapter 8
241: Thomas Hopker-Woodfin Camp & Associates. 245: Charles May-Black Star. 246L: Horst Schafer-Photo Trends. 246R: Kenneth Murray-Nancy Palmer Photo Agency. Table 8–1, p. 247: Adapted from The Gal-

600

lup Opinion Index, American Institute of Public Opinion, *Religion in America 1976*, Report No. 130, 26.   248: The Bettmann Archive, Inc.   251: Tim Eagan-Woodfin Camp & Associates.   252: Leo de Wys, Inc.   253: Jim Anderson-Woodfin Camp & Associates.   255: Kenneth Murray-Nancy Palmer Photo Agency.   Figure 8–1, p. 256: From Vernon, *Sociology of Religion.* © 1974 by McGraw-Hill, Inc.   Table 8–2, p. 257: Adapted from The Gallup Opinion Index, American Institute of Public Opinion, *Religion in America 1976*, Report No. 130, 39.   Figure 8–2, p. 259: Adapted from The Gallup Opinion Index, American Institute of Public Opinion, *Religion in America 1976*, Report No. 130, 56.   262T: Russell Thompson-Photo Trends.   262B: Jim Anderson-Woodfin Camp & Associates.   Table 8–3, p. 263: Adapted from The Gallup Opinion Index, American Institute of Public Opinion, *Religion in America 1976*, Report No. 130, 9.

Chapter 9
271: Cary Wolinsky-Stock, Boston.   276: Elizabeth Hamlin-Stock, Boston.   280: Barbara Alper-Stock, Boston.   285: Donald C. Dietz-Stock, Boston.   287: D. Krathwohl-Stock, Boston.   289: Freda Leinwand-Monkmeyer Press Photo Service.   291T: Elizabeth Hamlin-Stock, Boston.   291B: Daniel Brody-Stock, Boston.   293: Cary Wolinsky-Stock, Boston.   295L: Sybil Shelton-Monkmeyer Press Photo Service.   295R: Ten Lan-Photo Trends.

Chapter 10
301: J. Berndt-Stock, Boston.   305: Karsch, Ottawa-Woodfin Camp & Associates.   306: Olivier Rebbot-Woodfin Camp & Associates.   309: Mimi Forsyth-Monkmeyer Press Photo Service.   312: Sylvia Johnson-Woodfin Camp & Associates.   314: Peter Southwick-Stock, Boston.   Figure 10–1, p. 318: From Berelson, Lazarsfeld, and McPhee, *Voting.* Copyright © 1954 The University of Chicago Press.   319: Karsch, Ottawa-Woodfin Camp & Associates.   324: Marc & Evelyn Bernheim-Woodfin Camp & Associates.   325: United Press International.   326: Brown Brothers.

Part Four Opener, pp. 336–337 Jim Green.

Chapter 11
339: J. Berndt-Stock, Boston.   344: Michal Heron-Monkmeyer Press Photo Service.   346: Mimi Forsyth-Monkmeyer Press Photo Service.   350: Les Mahon-Monkmeyer Press Photo Service.   355L: Sybil Shelton-Monkmeyer Press Photo Service.   355R: John Running-Stock, Boston.   357: Pennsylvania State University.   363: Russ Reed-Photo Trends.   364: Mimi Forsyth-Monkmeyer Press Photo Service.   365: Christina Thomson.

Chapter 12
371: Dorna Raynor-Leo de Wys, Inc.   374T: Jim Green.   374B: Sybil Shelton-Monkmeyer Press Photo Service.   378: Eric L. Brown-Monkmeyer Press Photo Service.   379: Donald Dietz-Stock, Boston.   384:

Elizabeth Hamlin-Stock, Boston.   387: Paul Conklin-Monkmeyer Press Photo Service.   388: Eric Knoll-Taurus Photos.   392: Frederick de Van-Nancy Palmer Photo Agency.   394: Daniel S. Brody-Stock, Boston.   395: Jim Green.

Chapter 13
403: Thomas Höpker-Woodfin Camp & Associates.   407: Jehangir Gazdar-Woodfin Camp & Associates.   409: Hugh Rogers-Monkmeyer Press Photo Service.   410: The Bettmann Archive, Inc.   413: Sylvia Johnson-Woodfin Camp & Associates.   414: Michal Heron-Woodfin Camp & Associates.   Table 13–3, p. 417: From Hodge, Siegel, and Rossi, "Occupational Prestige in the United States," *American Journal of Sociology.* Copyright © 1964 The University of Chicago Press.   422: Peter Southwick-Stock, Boston.   425: Paul Conklin-Monkmeyer Press Photo Service.   431: Mimi Forsyth-Monkmeyer Press Photo Service.   433T: Baron Wolman-Woodfin Camp & Associates.   433B: Dan Budnik-Woodfin Camp & Associates.   435: Marc & Evelyn Bernheim-Woodfin Camp & Associates.

Chapter 14
443: Tim Carlson-Stock Boston   446: The Bettmann Archive, Inc.   448: Cary Wolinsky-Stock, Boston.   451: Sepp Seitz-Woodfin Camp & Associates.   452: David A. Krathwohl-Stock, Boston.   455: C. Raimond-Dityvon/VIVA-Woodfin Camp & Associates.   463L: James R. Holland-Stock, Boston.   463R: Ellis Herwig-Stock, Boston.   466: Leo de Wys, Inc.   468L: Jean-Claude Lejeune-Stock, Boston.   468R: Elizabeth Hamlin-Stock, Boston.   469: Ira Kirschenbaum-Stock, Boston.

Chapter 15
475: Jim Green.   477: Jim Anderson-Woodfin Camp & Associates.   482: Jim Anderson-Woodfin Camp & Associates.   483: Columbia University.   487: Searchlight-Redding, California.   491: Jim Anderson-Woodfin Camp & Associates.   493L: Jim Green.   493R: Leo de Wys, Inc.   495: Tim Eagan-Woodfin Camp & Associates.   500: Sylvia Johnson-Woodfin Camp & Associates.   501: James H. Karales-Peter Arnold, Inc.

Chapter 16
509: Everett Johnson-Leo de Wys, Inc.   510: Jason Laure-Woodfin Camp & Associates.   513: Sepp Seitz-Woodfin Camp & Associates.   515: Dan Budnik-Woodfin Camp & Associates.   Figure 16–1, pp. 520–521: From "The Populations of the Developed Countries" by Charles F. Westoff. Copyright © 1974 by Scientific American, Inc. All rights reserved.   522: Sepp Seitz-Woodfin Camp & Associates.   526: Thomas Hopker-Woodfin Camp & Associates.   529: Marc & Evelyn Bernheim-Woodfin Camp & Associates.   530: Brown Brothers.   533: Shelly Grossman-Woodfin Camp & Associates.   Figure 16–2, p. 534: From "Energy Policy in the U.S." by David J. Rose. Copyright © 1974 by Scientific American, Inc. All rights reserved.   535: Rick Winsor-Woodfin Camp & Associates.

1 2 3 4 5 6 7 8 9 10—RRD—85 84 83 82 81 80 79